Seeking a Better Future

ALSO BY LUCILLE H. CAMPEY

Planters, Paupers, and Pioneers:
English Settlers in Atlantic Canada (2010)

An Unstoppable Force:
The Scottish Exodus to Canada (2008)

With Axe and Bible:
The Scottish Pioneers of New Brunswick, 1784–1874 (2007)

"A Very Fine Class of Immigrants":
Prince Edward Island's Scottish Pioneers, 1770–1850 (2007)

Les Écossais:
The Scottish Pioneers of Lower Canada, 1763–1855 (2006)

The Scottish Pioneers of Upper Canada, 1784–1855:
Glengarry and Beyond (2005)

After the Hector:
The Scottish Pioneers of Nova Scotia and Cape Breton, 1773–1852 (2004)

The Silver Chief:
Lord Selkirk and the Scottish Pioneers of
Belfast, Baldoon and Red River (2003)

"Fast Sailing and Copper-Bottomed":
Aberdeen Sailing Ships and the Emigrant Scots
They Carried to Canada, 1774–1855 (2002)

Lucille Campey also has two websites:

www.englishtocanada.com
for her books on English emigration to Canada

www.scotstocanada.com
for her books on Scottish emigration to Canada

THE ENGLISH IN CANADA

Seeking a Better Future

The English Pioneers of Ontario and Quebec

Lucille H. Campey

DUNDURN
TORONTO

Editor: Allison Hirst
Design: Jennifer Scott
Printer: Webcom

Library and Archives Canada Cataloguing in Publication

Campey, Lucille H.
    Seeking a better future : the English pioneers of Ontario and Quebec / Lucille H. Campey.

Includes bibliographical references and index.
Issued also in electronic formats.
ISBN 978-1-4597-0351-3

1. British--Ontario--History--19th century. 2. British--Québec (Province)--History--19th century. 3. Ontario--Emigration and immigration--History--19th century. 4. Québec (Province)-- Emigration and immigration--History--19th century. 5. Great Britain--Emigration and immigration--History--19th century. I. Title.

FC3100.B7C46 2012   971.3004'21   C2012-900103-1

1   2   3   4   5   16   15   14   13   12

We acknowledge the support of the Canada Council for the Arts and the Ontario Arts Council for our publishing program. We also acknowledge the financial support of the Government of Canada through the Canada Book Fund and Livres Canada Books, and the Government of Ontario through the Ontario Book Publishing Tax Credit and the Ontario Media Development Corporation.

Care has been taken to trace the ownership of copyright material used in this book. The author and the publisher welcome any information enabling them to rectify any references or credits in subsequent editions.

J. Kirk Howard, President

Printed and bound in Canada.

Visit us at
Dundurn.com
Definingcanada.ca
@dundurnpress
Facebook.com/dundurnpress

Dundurn	Gazelle Book Services Limited	Dundurn
3 Church Street, Suite 500	White Cross Mills	2250 Military Road
Toronto, Ontario, Canada	High Town, Lancaster, England	Tonawanda, NY
M5E 1M2	LA1 4XS	U.S.A. 14150

To Geoff

CONTENTS

List of Maps   9

List of Tables   11

Acknowledgements   13

Preface   15

Abbreviations   17

Chapter 1   Canada's Appeal to the English   19

Chapter 2   The Loyalist Immigrants   36

Chapter 3   South and West of Montreal   53

Chapter 4   The Eastern Townships   72

Chapter 5   The Ottawa Valley   98

Chapter 6   West Along Lake Ontario   121

Chapter 7   The Lake Erie and Thames Valley Settlements   162

Chapter 8   The Rest of the Western Peninsula   199

Chapter 9   Later Emigration from England   224

Chapter 10   The Sea Crossing   261

Chapter 11   The English in Ontario and Quebec   288

Appendix I: Emigrant Ship Crossings from   301
             England to Quebec, 1817–64

Notes   416

Bibliography   467

Index   491

About the Author   525

LIST OF MAPS

1. Reference Map of England   27

2. Reference Map of Upper and Lower Canada   37

3. Loyalist Placements along the Richelieu River, 1775–85   38

4. Loyalists in Upper Canada   40

5. Loyalists in the Gaspé Peninsula   46

6. Yorkshire Origins of the Lacolle Settlers   56

7. English Settlers in the Châteauguay and Richelieu Valleys   58

8. English Settlers in Vaudreuil   69

9. English Concentrations in the Eastern Townships   75

10. Parish-Assisted Emigration from Norfolk and Suffolk to Lower Canada, 1835–37   88

11. English Concentrations in Argenteuil County, Lower Canada   99

12. English Concentrations in the Ottawa Valley   109

13. English Concentrations in Northumberland, Peterborough, Durham, Victoria, Ontario, York, Simcoe, Peel, and Halton Counties   122

14. English Concentrations in Middlesex, Elgin, Oxford, and Brant Counties   164

15. English Concentrations in Essex and Kent Counties   169

16. Principal Township Locations of the Petworth Settlers in Upper Canada, Based on Emigrant Letter Addresses, 1832–37   184

17. English Concentrations in Wellington, Waterloo, Perth, Huron, Bruce, and Grey Counties   201

18. Reference Map of Northern Ontario   232

Note: All maps are © Geoff Campey, 2012

LIST OF TABLES

1. Paupers from Heacham Parish in Norfolk Who Sailed   95
   May 1836 in the *Penelope* from King's Lynn

2. Paupers from Kettlestone Parish in Norfolk Who Sailed   96
   June 1836 in the *Eliza Liddle* from King's Lynn to
   Port St. Francis in the Eastern Townships

3. An Account of the First Settlement of Hull Township, 1820   119

4. Payments Made to Poor People from Alston Parish   153
   (Cumberland) Who Are to Emigrate to Upper Canada in 1832

5. Emigrant Departures from English Ports to Quebec   154
   by Region, 1820–59

6. Paupers Assisted to Emigrate from Stockbury Parish (Kent)   155
   to Upper Canada in 1837

7. Paupers from Heytesbury and Knook Parishes in Wiltshire   156
   Who Sailed March 1831 in the *Euphrosyne* from Bridgwater

8. Paupers from Brinkworth Parish in Wiltshire Who Sailed   157
   from London to Quebec in July 1842 in the *Eliza*

9. Paupers from Brinkworth Parish in Wiltshire Who Sailed   158
    from London to Quebec in May 1843 in the *Toronto*

10. Paupers from Brinkworth Parish in Wiltshire Who Sailed   159
    from London to Quebec in May 1847 in the *Lloyd*

11. Paupers from Brinkworth Parish in Wiltshire Who Sailed   160
    from London to Quebec in June1852 in the *Leonard Dobbin*

12. Destitute Chelsea Pensioners Who Had Settled in Medonte   160
    Township in Simcoe County by 1833

13. Receipts for Downton Emigrant Accommodation and   191
    Food/Drink While Staying at the Quebec Hotel, Portsmouth,
    May 19–24, 1835

14. Passenger List for the Crossing of the *King William* in   192
    April 1836 from London to Quebec with 279 Paupers
    from Wiltshire

15. Emigration Expenses Funded by East Drayton Parish in   198
    Nottinghamshire in 1846 on Behalf of the Hempstall Family

16. Partial Passenger List for the Crossing of the *Caroline* in   222
    May 1832 from London to Quebec

17. Working Men's National Emigration Association: 253
    List of People from London Who Went Mainly to Lennoxville
    in the Eastern Townships, 1870

18. Cotton Workers from Bolton in Lancashire Who Were   254
    Assisted to Emigrate to Ontario and Quebec, 1912–27

19. British Immigrant and Other Arrivals at the Port of Quebec,   281
    1829–55

20. Selected Regular Traders: Passengers Carried and Ship Quality   282

21. Emigrant Ships Which Carried Paupers: Passengers   284
    Carried and Where From

ACKNOWLEDGEMENTS

I AM INDEBTED to a great many people. First, I wish to thank the Foundation for Canadian Studies in the United Kingdom for their grant, which I put toward my research and travel costs.

I am grateful for the many kindnesses of archivists on both sides of the Atlantic. In particular, I wish to thank Jody Robinson at the Eastern Townships Resource Centre in Lennoxville, Mary Bond at Library and Archives Canada in Ottawa, and Marc St-Jacques and Frederic Laniel at Archives Nationales du Québec. I received much help from a great many English record offices. My special thanks goes to Helen Orme of the Centre for Kent Studies, James Collett-White and Trevor Cunnick at the Bedfordshire Record Office, Steve Hardy and Guenever Pachent at the Suffolk Record Office in Ipswich, Steven Hobbs at the Wiltshire History Centre, Heather Dulson at the Shropshire Archives, David Bowcock and Helen Cunningham at the Cumbria Archive Service, Bruce Jackson at the Lancashire Record Office, Crispin Powell at the Northamptonshire Record Office, and Rebecca Jackson at the Staffordshire Record Office.

I am thankful to the many people who helped me to locate and obtain illustrations. In particular, I especially wish to thank Dominic

R. Labbé in McMasterville, Quebec, for providing me with some of his splendid photographs of Anglican and Methodist churches in south-western Quebec and the Eastern Townships. In a similar vein, my thanks go to Marcus Owen, Rector's Warden of St. James' Church in Hudson, Quebec, for supplying me with a photograph of that church. I also thank Lisa Coombes of the Plymouth City Museum and Art Gallery, Dr. John Stedman of the Portsmouth Museum and Records Service, Adrian Green, director of the Salisbury and South Wiltshire Museum, Rob Waddington of Lincolnshire Archives, Peter Collings of the Somerset Heritage Centre in Taunton, and Catherine Wakeling, archivist to the United Society for the Propagation of the Gospel, for their invaluable help locating sources. I am also indebted to Alan Walker of the Special Collections Department at the Toronto Reference Library and Erin Strouth of Archives of Ontario for dealing with my requests for help.

I am greatly indebted to my editor, Allison Hirst, for her meticulous and thorough checking of the manuscript. I also thank my dear friend Jean Lucas who has proofread the text. Her support and sharp eye for detail have kept me on the straight and narrow, and I am extremely grateful to her.

Finally, my greatest thanks go to my husband, Geoff. He is my rock and guiding light and without him none of my books would have seen the light of day. I am grateful for his love and support and for believing in me. We are, of course, a team. He produces the tables, maps, and appendices, locates the illustrations, helps with the research, and deals with all the technical aspects of the book's production. This book is dedicated to him with all my love.

PREFACE

S*EEKING A BETTER FUTURE*, the second of three books in the English in Canada series, tells the story of the English pioneers who settled in Ontario and Quebec. Starting with the early colonizers who began arriving in 1817, it goes on to describe the massive influx that took place after Confederation, when thousands of English immigrants came to live in Canada, particularly in the towns and cities.

Along with the French, the English are regarded as one of Canada's two "founding peoples," but they are not seen as a recognizable ethnic group. They assimilated themselves into a country that had adopted their language and values. Showing a curious disinterest in their national identity, the English were happy to fade into the background. This helps to explain why they have escaped the notice of contemporary observers and later historians. This book aims to redress this past neglect, by concentrating on the important role that they played in the settlement and economic development of Ontario and Quebec.

Emigration was driven partly by major economic changes taking place in England and partly by the lure of distinct opportunities and benefits that people hoped to obtain in their chosen destinations.

Ontario and Quebec each had a different set of advantages, and the emigrant streams from England worked to a different timescale. Why did the English choose to settle where they did? Did they carry a sense of Englishness with them, and how was this revealed? What was their overall impact? These are some of the questions that I have attempted to answer in this book.

The English fall into two categories. The majority came as immigrants directly from England, but there were also Loyalists, having English ancestry, who entered Ontario and Quebec in the late eighteenth century via the United States. They were independent-minded Yankees in every way, and their family links were with the United States rather than England. And yet, they and their descendents regarded themselves as English, even though their ethnic links were very distant. Their presence contributed to the large English concentrations in the southern half of the Eastern Townships of Quebec and along the north shore of Lake Ontario, although both regions also acquired considerable numbers of immigrants directly from England.

Details of over two thousand emigrant ship crossings from English ports to Quebec have been gathered together in Appendix I. Analysis of the data reveals the great geographical spread of the emigrant stream as well as distinct regional patterns that changed over time. Emigration began in the 1820s as a North of England phenomenon, but gradually drew people from north and south more equally. While most English emigrants were able to finance their own travel and other costs, a significant number were very poor. The English scattered to many parts of Ontario and Quebec and left an important legacy behind, which until now has been largely ignored. This book tells their story.

ABBREVIATIONS

ANQ	Archives Nationales du Québec
BRO	Bedfordshire Record Office
CARO	Cambridgeshire Record Office
CKS	Centre for Kentish Studies
CRO	Cornwall Record Office
CAS	Cumbria Archive Service
DCB	*Dictionary of Canadian Biography*
DERO	Derbyshire Record Office
DRO	Devon Record Office
ETRC	Eastern Townships Resource Centre
ERO	Essex Record Office
HRO	Hertfordshire Record Office
HCA	Hull City Archives
LARO	Lancashire Record Office (Preston)
LAC	Library and Archives Canada
LRO	Lincolnshire Record Office
LCA	Liverpool City Archives
NAB	National Archives of Britain, Kew
NAS	National Archives of Scotland

NRO	Norfolk Record Office
NORO	Northamptonshire Record Office
NTRO	Nottinghamshire Record Office
OA	Ontario Archives
RHL	Oxford University, Rhodes House Library
RIC	Royal Institution of Cornwall
SHRO	Shropshire Record Office
SOAS	University of London, School of Oriental and African Studies
SORO	Somerset Record Office
STRO	Staffordshire County Record Office
SROI	Suffolk Record Office (Ipswich)
SROL	Suffolk Record Office (Lowestoft)
UHA	University of Hull Archives
WRO	Warwickshire Record Office
WYAS	West Yorkshire Archive Service
WHC	Wiltshire Record Office

CHAPTER 1

Canada's Appeal to the English

The tide of emigration has set in from various parts of the country, chiefly towards our British American Settlements. During some weeks past the Thames in particular has presented a busy scene from the number of vessels almost daily departing with emigrants, amongst whom were several respectable persons, small tradesmen in London, who have disposed of their business, and farmers from the counties near the metropolis with their families.[1]

THIS ANNOUNCEMENT IN the *Gentleman's Magazine* of the ships that were lining up in London to take emigrants to Quebec in 1832 was one of the very rare occasions when English emigration was actually reported to the outside world. Special prominence was given to "respectable persons," especially tradesmen and farmers, but the labourers, servants, industrial workers, and other people of modest means who formed the majority of those departing were ignored. English emigrants received little attention and they generally slipped away completely unnoticed to many different parts of the world. No one seemed interested to know who they were, why they were leaving, where they were going to settle, or how they fared once they were relocated. Initially, most of these emigrants had chosen the United States, but by the second half of the nineteenth century they increasingly looked to Canada for their future. By the 1830s, their impact on Lower and Upper Canada's development had been huge, and yet their story remains largely untold.

The English influx to the Canadas began shortly after the end of the Napoleonic Wars in 1815, when Britain had been plunged into a deep economic and agricultural depression. By emigrating, people hoped to better their economic prospects. They were especially attracted by the chance of owning land and someday establishing a farm. Although it was not just the poor who emigrated, they were the ones who had the most to gain initially. The shortage of labour in the Canadas worked to their advantage, and they could command much higher wages than in England. And there were other advantages. The New World had no masters and no pecking order. Immigrants could be free-thinking individuals, seeking what was best for their families, rather than being subject to the dictates of landlords, bureaucrats, and factory owners, as was the case in Britain. Thus, by emigrating, people could gain materially, while enjoying the freedom and benefits of a more egalitarian society.

There were other spurs to emigration. Following the Napoleonic Wars and the War of 1812, large numbers of discharged British soldiers faced bleak economic prospects in Britain. Those who had served in North America had seen the land of plenty for themselves and some were tempted to return, as Robert Downes, a British Army officer, observed in 1817:

> The country along the southern shore of the St. Lawrence
> is romantic to the highest pitch of beauty. The land is
> cleared from about a ½ mile from the shore all along
> studded with farm houses all of which being whitewashed
> have a very picturesque effect. The Îsle de Orléans is a
> perfect garden. We saw roses growing in profusion … the

inhabitants provide all their own wants, spin and make their own clothes, grind their own corn with stones, and we ceased to wonder at so many of our discharged soldiers wishing to return and settle in a place where want seemed to be unknown.[2]

In fact, some English ex-soldiers were already forming a settlement in the western stretches of the Eastern Townships in Lower Canada by this time, although their numbers were relatively small.

At the other end of the social spectrum were the sons of the wealthy, whose sense of romantic adventure also prompted an interest in emigration. Lord Talbot,[3] Lord Lieutenant of Staffordshire, was advised by the Colonial Office in 1835 that Canada was a better choice than Australia for his son, since the latter had "a convict taint" that would "never be eradicated for years to come." He was further advised that a "numerous" family had the best chance of success, "for the emigrant's life is one of hardship and banishment and some years must elapse before he can establish himself to tolerable comfort."[4] Hardly the good life, but it was a fair assessment of the hard slog that lay ahead for his lordship's son.

The sudden change in a family's wealth and status, as was the case with the Langton family who emigrated to the Peterborough area of Upper Canada in the 1830s, was another emigration trigger. This desire for a fresh start after a personal tragedy probably explains the relatively high number of men and women who emigrated soon after losing spouses. Typically they were like Dinah Bishop, a Sussex-born widow, who emigrated in 1840 to Belleville (Hastings County) with most of her children and their spouses.[5] Similarly, having lost her husband in 1852, Mary Ford moved from her home in Norfolk to Moore Township (Lambton County), presumably going there because she knew someone in the area. Having remarried by 1859, she was then joined by her brother and sister, who also settled in Moore Township, each having taken local spouses.[6]

Rather than seeking solace in a new life, there were others who simply wanted to leave their troubles behind. Henry Jessopp, a solicitor from Waltham Abbey in Essex, emigrated to Toronto in 1837 to escape financial ruin due to mounting debts. Establishing a new life for himself, he left his brother back home to fob off his many irate creditors who would never see their money again.[7]

Emigration began as a North of England phenomenon. People from Yorkshire were the first to grasp the opportunities to be had from the Richelieu Valley's timber trade in Lower Canada, with the catalyst being an English seigneur's family links with Yorkshire. A steady stream of farmers and tradesmen, who originated mainly from the East Riding, headed for Lacolle between 1817 and 1830, turning it into a major Yorkshire enclave. Similarly, redundant hand-loom weavers from Cumberland piled into Vaudreuil beginning in the 1820s, as a result of intelligence gathered from a local Anglican missionary who knew the area. Unemployed lead miners from Cumberland and County Durham also headed for the north side of Lake Ontario in Upper Canada (Durham and Victoria counties) during this time, as news spread of its good land and farming potential. For northerners, used to living in remote and sparsely populated areas, the prospect of starting a new life in an isolated wilderness was less daunting than it would have been for their more comfortably off southern counterparts. People in the south needed a lot more persuading and only became seriously interested in emigration once the fertile lands in the western peninsula of Upper Canada became more accessible, which happened during the 1830s. However, growing numbers wanted to emigrate but lacked the means to do so.

With the arrival of threshing machines in England by the 1830s, agricultural labourers were increasingly being thrown out of work, creating pockets of high unemployment in many rural areas. In fact, the spread of mechanization in both industry and agriculture destroyed many traditional jobs throughout the entire country. Faced with the prospect of either taking low-paying factory jobs in the burgeoning cities and towns or chancing their luck abroad, many chose the latter option. This route appealed to a group of weavers in Bolton (Lancashire), a major textile centre. Having been made redundant by 1826, they pleaded with the Colonial Office to grant them funds to emigrate to Canada "or any other British settlement," but their petition, like others of this nature, was rejected. The view, expressed in the *Canadian Courant and Montreal Advertiser*, that "the sickly artisan," lacking a farming background, could

The King's Wharf Quebec in the port of Quebec, 1827–41. Trade was booming by this time. All exports such as timber, potash, and wheat passed through this harbour, as did thousands of immigrants. Watercolour by Fanny Amelia Bayfield (1814–91).

expect "to obtain but a bare and miserable existence, even on a farm which has been already brought into cultivation," was part of the explanation.[8] However, irrespective of the outcome, the government was adamant — it would not part with a penny of public money, except in rare circumstances, to fund emigration schemes. They were simply too costly.[9] Yet, all was not lost for the Bolton textile workers, who successfully transferred their skills to the United States, finding employment in the American calico printing trade.[10] In the meantime, as unemployment continued to soar, social tensions increased, causing serious jitters in Whitehall. It soon became obvious that something had to be done.

A crisis point was reached in the 1830s when farm labourers, led by the fictitious Captain Swing, rioted over the high unemployment rates and severe poverty being experienced in agricultural counties, with Kent, Wiltshire, Sussex, and Norfolk being in the forefront of the disturbances.

A debate raged over how public funds might be used to alleviate the situation. This led to the passing of *The Poor Law Amendment Act* of 1834, one of the most significant pieces of social legislation ever enacted. It allowed English parishes to finance the emigration costs of their poor and, in so doing, released their ratepayers from the ongoing burden of having to support them. Important safeguards were also introduced to ensure that parishes did not simply use the legislation to rid themselves of their infirm and work-shy. Poor Law commissioners in London were to keep a watchful eye on the suitability of those selected for emigration schemes. Able-bodied people, preferably families with lots of sturdy teenagers, were to be given priority. Initially, the majority went to Upper Canada, although a significant number of paupers from Norfolk and Suffolk relocated themselves in the Eastern Townships of Lower Canada.[11]

Despite being well-regulated, parish-assisted emigration schemes attracted controversy and concern. In 1831, Alexander Buchanan, the Quebec immigration agent, was said to have complained to British government officials that some of the emigrants being dispatched by the parishes were "indolent and ill-provided," and feared that if they did badly, few would wish to follow them.[12] He thought their previous dependence on parish relief might have sapped their energy, and advised that Poor Law guardians should stress the need for self-reliance when they were approached by people seeking assistance to emigrate.[13] When Mr. Watts, a farm manager acting for a Kent landowner, realized that Lympne Parish would be helping "two or three families, not of the best character" to emigrate, he was delighted, although he "generally disapproved of sending good labourers out of the country."[14] Thus, parishes had a moral dilemma in deciding who should receive help. Should they actively encourage their most suitable people to come forward or did they simply stand back and hope that their troublemakers would apply, as Mr. Watts clearly hoped would happen?

To add to the confusion, the Duke of Somerset's agent considered that the poor were being given an overly optimistic picture of pioneer life. He thought that the time and effort needed to fell trees had been greatly understated, and feared that people, "with their usual suspicions," would think this a "deception held out to entice them from their native

Immigrants in the bush. "This is all yours, 20 good acres of tough trees which must be cleared away before you can even grow a single turnip."

country."[15] The cartoon above, one of a series published at the time in newspapers and magazines pouring scorn on the perceived benefits of emigration, makes the point very nicely.

Against this background, English parishes could hardly coerce their poor and unwanted into moving abroad. However, there was no need for any arm-twisting, since the end-product sold itself. Once letters from early colonizers, extolling the benefits of the Canadas, reached family and friends back in England, fears were allayed, and the rush was on to join them. The perilous sea crossing and the arduous conditions of pioneer life still had to be faced, but people could see the rewards that were within their reach. The prospect of a well-paid job and the opportunity to buy land and own a farm were attainable goals, provided people were willing to work hard.

A year after emigrating in 1832, Edward Bristow, a labourer, and his wife Hannah, wrote to Edward's brother in West Sussex, making these simple points: Upper Canada "is truly a very prosperous country for labouring people, and neither heat nor cold is not anywise disagreeable, but we have a great deal of snow." However, worried that some Sussex people were finding it "hard to believe the good news of this country," they emphasized that "the good news that ever you heard of by letters, are the truth.... For if any of you mean to come, the sooner you come the better, for the [Woolwich] Township [Waterloo County] is good land, and settles so fast that the [ad]joining lots will soon be taken up.... Publish this letter to all that wish to hear."[16]

Although large numbers of agricultural labourers with families were assisted by their parishes to emigrate during the 1830s, the majority of English immigrants who came to the Canadas during this and other decades actually financed their own departures. They came from all walks of life and from many parts of England. Yet, unlike the assisted groups, whose every move was well-documented (owing to their reliance on public funds), little is known about them. They slipped away unreported and unnoticed. Fortunately, the areas in England from which they came can be assessed from seaport passenger statistics, while their places of settlement in the Canadas can be deduced from census data, but beyond this, the data is sketchy and fragmentary. Emigrant letters, diaries, family histories, the reports of Anglican and Methodist missionaries, and descriptions left behind by contemporary observers each reveal various aspects of their story, but the overall picture is incomplete.

Emigrants from Yorkshire, Devon, and Cornwall were especially well-represented in the outflow of people from England (Map 1). Yorkshire people had a special affinity with Lower Canada, dating back to the 1820s, and were also much in evidence along the northwest side of Lake Ontario, as were the Cornish, who joined them in substantial numbers starting in the 1840s. People from Devon created a large community for themselves in the Huron Tract, a vast area within southwestern Upper Canada, while several hundred immigrants from Wiltshire and Somerset made their home along Lake Erie. However, most English left as individuals or in small groups and chose their destinations primarily on economic grounds rather than on any desire to settle with other English. They were not clannish and had no wish to keep themselves apart from other ethnic groups.

Map 1: Reference map of England

Although the Quebec immigration agent had issued grave warnings that England's poor were likely to fall at the first hurdle, he would be proven wrong. Their letters home not only revealed the advantages of the New World, but also disclosed how well-organized and level-headed they were. English labourers came with a strong work ethic, an unshakeable determination to succeed, and much-valued farming skills. Their letters show how they were often snapped up by farmers more or less the

Settler's house in the forest on the Thames River, near London, 1842. Painting by Henry Francis Ainslie (1803–1879).

minute they arrived. Some described being approached with job offers while waiting for their luggage to come ashore at Lake Erie. The high wages they could earn quickly became their passport to land ownership. Far from lacking motivation, as Alexander Buchanan had feared, they grasped their opportunities with both hands and planned land clearance operations with military precision. Groups from the same English village often settled together to enable men to share tools and other resources. They coordinated their actions to best suit the group and, in so doing, made rapid progress. They excelled as pioneers.

Success for any English settler required careful planning and the ability to cope with unending and back-breaking work. This comes across in Joseph Pickering's description of the Northumberland man who had settled in Orford Township (Kent County) sometime before 1830. After six or seven years of hard slog, his dream of owning a farm had finally materialized:

He suffered considerable privations at first, commencing on his lot at the beginning of winter; he had first to build a house and then work out for provisions for his family. He has since built himself another house and barn, dug a well and a cellar, planted an orchard and cleared 40 or 50 acres of land, and is now comfortably situated and thriving, although having only 30s. or 40s. left on his first arrival.[17]

However, this approach did not suit everyone. Edmund Peel, an officer on leave from the British navy with his wife, Lucy, had hoped to establish a farm at Sherbrooke in the Eastern Townships in the 1830s, but they failed and returned home, feeling bitter about their experience. There was nothing wrong with the land they had chosen. They had simply not realized that Lower Canada's wage rates would be so high. The Peels could have employed as many servants and labourers as they wanted in England, where people were paid a pittance, but not so in Lower Canada. The labour costs exceeded their means and, not wishing to do the land clearance work themselves, they had no option but to leave. Thus, there were pitfalls for the unsuspecting and the ill-prepared, but for immigrants with a realistic grasp of what might be achieved, the opportunities were boundless.

Immigrants often experienced great difficulty in acquiring land, mainly because their needs had a low priority. The British government's land policies, such as they were, promoted the interests of the wealthy and did little to assist ordinary colonists. Beginning in the late eighteenth century, the government had granted huge quantities of wilderness land as rewards to favoured individuals.[18] Most recipients sold their land on to speculators, who amassed huge holdings but did little to further colonization. Moreover, people in high office, like Lord Talbot, saw nothing wrong in purchasing land in the Canadas for investment purposes. He was advised in 1835 that "both the Canadas are very desirable — but just now Lower Canada is too much agitated.... Upper Canada is a fine opening for anyone with £400 or £500 — with that capital, excellent land may be bought and all that is required of labour and comforts may be secured."[19] While people like Lord Talbot had first choice of the best land, ordinary colonists had to make do with what was left, and sometimes this meant that their holdings were inferior and scattered over large distances.

Such vestiges of old-world patronage were resented by settlers and were totally inconsistent with the egalitarian society that they were seeking to create.[20] These concerns, together with the dreadful consequences of a severe economic depression in 1837, and general social unrest, led to rioting and a full-scale rebellion. Although the 1837–38 uprisings in Upper and Lower Canada were quelled through military action, they at least challenged the cozy elitism at the heart of government.[21]

In future, more would be done to meet the needs of ordinary people. However, these violent skirmishes brought a sudden halt to the influx from Britain and even prompted some English settlers to return home. Having learned from his brother that he intended leaving Upper Canada, Philip Snape called off his own plans to emigrate. His brother feared that if he stayed there much longer "he will be likely to lose all his money in case Canada should be separated from England, which is very likely from the agitated state which that country is in."[22] Mary Chaplin's account of how the rebels had set fire to parts of Toronto and destroyed a mill and houses at Prescott were hardly going to read well in her native Lincolnshire or in any other parts of Britain receiving news of the disturbances.[23] Yet, the effects were temporary, and by 1842, emigrant numbers were on the rise again.

As the timber trade with Britain soared, and regular and affordable sea crossings became more readily available, the outflow of people from England to the Canadas grew steadily. Emigration was never solely a flight from poverty. In fact, the numbers emigrating rose in parallel with the advance of industrialization throughout Britain. The resulting higher living standards for those in work increased the number of people who could afford the costs of emigrating. While, initially, far more English went to the United States than to the Canadas, arrival numbers at Quebec show that they nonetheless outnumbered the Scots, although they were second to the Irish until the 1860s.[24] After this time, the English influx began to surge ahead, and between 1867 and 1914 they exceeded the combined numbers arriving from both Scotland and Ireland.[25] Yet, Canada did not emerge as the favoured destination of most English people until the 1900s. Before then, Canada had always to fend off competition from the United States to attract them.

Having lost settlers to the United States in substantial numbers from the second half of the eighteenth century, the English had a long-standing affinity with it. In a booklet written in 1826, Henry Boulton emphasized the similarity of Upper Canada's "laws, habits, customs and general state of society to England," but few English people cared.[26] They wanted the better life that only the American economy could bring. Joseph Pickering, who arrived in the United States from Buckinghamshire between 1824 and 1830, was annoyed by the arrogance and conceit he found in Americans, but could not help "admire the energy and enterprise they exhibited, and regretted the apathy of the British government with regard to the improvement of this province [Upper Canada]."[27]

This view was echoed by Lord Durham[28] in his famous report of 1839 on the rebellions, although he ruffled a few feathers for revealing the stark differences between Canada and the United States. As Lord Durham pointed out, the United States had "numerous settlements" with "good houses" and "fine churches … municipal halls of stone or marble, vast array of canals, roads and bridges either completed or under construction," while in British America there was "a widely scattered population, poor and apparently un-enterprising, though hardy and industrious, without towns and markets, almost without roads, living in mean houses, drawing little more than a rude subsistence from ill-cultivated land and seeming incapable of improving their condition."[29] Hardly surprising then that the United States was the first choice of most English immigrants at this time. However, the rapid economic growth that followed on the heels of Confederation in 1867, together with government incentives introduced in the early 1900s, greatly increased Canada's appeal, and after 1905 most English people went to Canada.

Religion is a recurring theme in the story of English emigration. Methodist and Anglican missionaries did their best to save English souls and, in the process, would have brought considerable comfort to countless people struggling to come to terms with pioneer life. The Methodist

The Reverend M. Johnson, one of the Lower Canada Methodist missionaries, circa 1860s. He may have been Moses Johnson, who served at Compton in the Eastern Townships from 1867–69.

preachers, who trudged huge distances speaking of God's love and salvation, had the greatest appeal.[30] They spoke on a personal level to ordinary settlers, avoiding the rigid forms of worship that were the hallmark of Anglicanism.[31] Quaker settlements also formed in Upper Canada, particularly in the Bay of Quinte region at the eastern end of Lake Ontario, in the Niagara District, along Lake Erie, as well as north of Toronto.[32] Despite being the official religion, the Church of England attracted relatively few followers. The Anglican missionaries sent by the London-based Society for the Propagation of the Gospel were remote figures who seemed not to appreciate the hunger among their congregations for uplifting messages and a kindly smile.

Surprisingly, the Anglican Church had some of its greatest successes in the Eastern Townships, particularly in areas that had acquired large numbers of Americans during and after the Loyalist influx of the late eighteenth century. Such places usually had their share of affluent settlers. Seeking the social advantages they believed Anglicanism would bring, they became stalwart supporters of the Church of England. Thus, the Anglican Church essentially became the church of the middle and upper classes, thereby weakening its appeal and influence among the main rural population. Even so, Anglican missionaries took their responsibilities very seriously, especially in Lower Canada. The Reverend E.M.W. Templeman from Derbyshire, who in the early 1900s was based at Bourg Louis about fifty miles to the west of Quebec City, served its "rising settlement of Irish protestants" with great fortitude and determination.[33] "This is a place of magnificent distances with only a few English-speaking people here and there," whom he visited once a month — "12 miles there and back."[34] However, he could not halt the declining numbers. "Soon the Englishman will become as distinct as the dove in the province of Quebec. Everything is French, I even find myself thinking in French — let alone having to speak it at every shop and office ... the poor old English Church is merely an exotic here."[35] The fact was that most of the Reverend Templeman's potential congregation had long since left for either the United States or Ontario.

Meanwhile, growing industrialization throughout Britain helped to stimulate a major movement of people from the countryside to the cities, contributing to the dreadful city slums that came to characterize Victorian England. High unemployment levels raged in urban areas, and once again emigration was invoked as the best way out of the predicament. A great many emigration schemes were launched by philanthropic bodies to assist people from London and other large cities to emigrate to the Canadas. By the 1870s, boatloads of poor and orphaned children were also being sent to work on Canadian farms. While they were being given the chance of a decent livelihood in later life, in the short term they were simply a source of cheap labour. Another scheme, which raised a few eyebrows initially, involved English reformatory school boys. Having been convicted of serious crimes, they had their period of detention reduced on condition that they behaved well in the jobs found for them in the mining districts of Quebec and northern Ontario.

Along with the distress being felt in English cities, people were experiencing extremely difficult times in rural areas by the late nineteenth century because of a growing economic crisis in agriculture. Once again, emigration came to the rescue in mopping up Britain's surplus farm labour. Schemes organized by agricultural trade unions with government support helped to bring thousands of English farm workers to Ontario and, to a lesser extent, the Eastern Townships. These measures were widely welcomed in the Canadas, since they helped to alleviate a continuing shortage of farm labour. However, despite the high visibility of the poor in this later period, the exodus from England continued to be dominated by self-funded emigrants who came from all sections of society and for a variety of reasons. The free land grants being offered by the Ontario government clearly brought some English to the Algoma District of northern Ontario, where, judging from the 1881 Census, they accounted for a substantial proportion of the population in places like Sault Ste. Marie. A significant number of these were Cornish miners and their families, who had been attracted to the area when the Bruce copper mines were first developed.

As Ontario and Quebec became more developed, their cities and towns began to attract a growing number of English immigrants, who by the turn of the nineteenth century were themselves mainly urban dwellers. A rising proportion of these were single men and women from the educated middle classes. Toronto, Montreal, and Ottawa had particular appeal, as did Hamilton, Guelph, and London, located in the rapidly expanding industrial belt in southwestern Ontario. Bowmanville, Whitby, and Oshawa, burgeoning towns along Lake Ontario, also acquired many English.

Ottawa's rapid growth impressed James Moncrieff Wilson, a Liverpool businessman, when he visited it in 1865. "It is now the Capital of Canada ... the timber shops are getting burned and then stone ones are put up in their place.... Twelve years since there were only twenty five stone houses. Now there are hundreds of them."[36]

Visiting Toronto nearly thirty years later, Colonel Francis Fane, a wealthy Lincolnshire farmer, "was amazed at the beauty of the public buildings, the avenues, open spaces ..." and noted that Toronto "had increased from 80,000 inhabitants [in 1880] to 200,000 inhabitants" in 1890, a remarkable growth rate.[37]

A chance collection of letters written by people from the Lancashire town of Clitheroe, who had emigrated to the far corners of the world in the late nineteenth/early twentieth century, reveals just how much the pattern of emigration had changed by this time. The aspiring pioneer farmer was no more, and people now sought the better living conditions that Canadian towns and cities offered. Alice and Jim Parker, then living in Hudson, near Montreal, summed up the general feeling with the simple admission that their "heart was still in Clitheroe."[38] Although emigration had the prospect of bringing people a better future, the human cost of achieving that outcome was daunting, especially for those who had ventured forth in the early nineteenth century.

The English excelled as colonizers and were in the forefront of each new frontier. The 1881 Census shows how they had extended their reach to large swathes of southwestern Quebec and most parts of Ontario. They were primarily concentrated in parts of the Eastern Townships, along the northwest side of Lake Ontario, and in southwestern Ontario. Overall, people having English ancestry represented 28 percent of Upper Canada's population by this stage, second only to the Irish, who accounted for 33 percent.[39] By 1991, just under 40 percent of Ontario's population claimed to have some English ancestry.[40] However, what these censuses do not show is the changing pattern of settlement that had taken place in the past, as families had moved with each new opportunity that presented itself.

The English had been constantly on the move in the Canadas and would later repeat the process in the prairies. Meanwhile, a silent and largely unrecorded success story was about to unfold. The humble labourers, servants, tradesmen, and small farmers who had arrived with little apart from a determination to succeed would suddenly find themselves becoming respectable. This, in itself, was an amazing achievement.

CHAPTER 2

The Loyalist Immigrants

I was always told by my parents that we were United Empire Loyalists. The money inherited by my grandfather, father and then by me, I was told, came from grants to our United Empire Loyalist ancestor. My family showed an intense loyalty to the Crown. No Hallowell child was ever allowed to sing "Yankee Doodle" and it was never heard in this house [Hallowell Cottage] until after the United States came into the Great War.[1]

MILLIE HALLOWELL'S ANCESTORS were among the Loyalist refugees who had fled north following Britain's defeat in the American War of Independence in 1783.[2] Not wishing to live in the new republic being formed out of the old Empire, they and many others like them had sought refuge within what remained of British-held territory in North America. Altogether around forty to fifty thousand Loyalists left their homes for a new life in the future Canada. Their resettlement was carried out at British government expense, both for humanitarian reasons and to bolster British North America's population and defensive capabilities.

The Hallowells were in the relatively small group of six or seven thousand Loyalists sent to the old province of Quebec, while the overwhelming majority were granted land in the Maritime region.[3] Although most of those who went to Quebec eventually settled farther west in the Upper St. Lawrence region, in what would become Upper Canada, some Loyalists, like Millie's ancestors, settled east of Montreal (Map 2).[4] In doing so, they would contribute to the substantial English population that developed in the southern half of the future Eastern Townships.

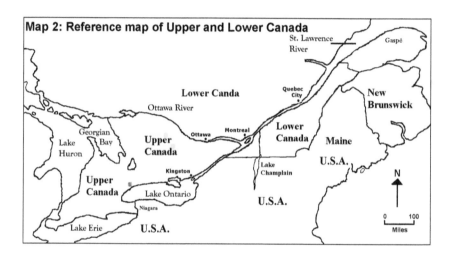

Map 2: Reference map of Upper and Lower Canada

Loyal refugees, many with fighting experience, had travelled from New York, Pennsylvania, and New England to Quebec soon after the outbreak of war in 1775. Particularly well-represented were Scottish Highlanders, German Protestants from the Rhineland in southwestern Germany (the so-called Palatines), and to a lesser extent English Quakers.[5] Initially, most were sent to the military camps and garrisons being established at Sorel and Machiche (now Yamachiche) near Trois Rivières and along the strategically important Richelieu River, notably at Chambly, St. Jean, Noyan, Foucault, and St. Armand (Map 3).[6] American soldiers used the river in 1775 to try to capture Montreal and later travelled down the Chaudière River to lay siege to Quebec, but both assaults were thwarted.[7]

Later, the seigneury of Sorel was purchased by the British government to strengthen and expand the military garrison there.[8] Becoming

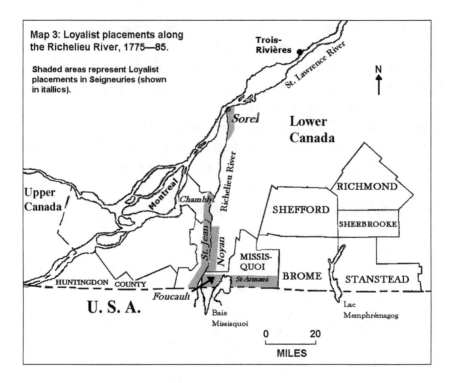

Map 3: Loyalist placements along the Richelieu River, 1775—85.

Shaded areas represent Loyalist placements in Seigneuries (shown in itallics).

the principal Loyalist settlement, Sorel's population grew rapidly.[9] By 1783, nearly two thousand individuals and families were living in the region and in receipt of government provisions, and a year later Sorel became the first Anglican mission in Quebec.[10] But Sorel's unique role was temporary, and when the war ended a year later, most Loyalists left the area. They were granted land far afield in the vacant wilderness along the Upper St. Lawrence River, just to the west of the French seigneuries.[11] When the old province of Quebec was divided into Upper and Lower Canada in 1791, these holdings would lie in Upper Canada. Thus, most of the original Quebec Loyalists ended up in Upper Canada.

Various Loyalist units had been formed at the beginning of the war, including the King's Royal Regiment of New York, the Butler's Rangers, the King's Rangers, the King's Loyal Americans, the Queen's Loyal Rangers, and the Royal Highland Emigrants Regiment. The 1st Battalion of the King's Royal Regiment of New York, the largest of the Loyalist units, was granted land in five of the eight townships set aside between present-day

Cornwall and Kingston (Map 4).[12] Sir Frederick Haldimand, the Quebec governor, took the judicious step of ensuring that the various ethnic groups within this regiment, such as Roman Catholic and Presbyterian Highlanders, Calvinist and Lutheran Germans, and Anglican English, settled together in the various townships. For instance, the German and English Loyalists were assigned to Osnabruck (Stormont County), Williamsburgh, and Matilda townships (both Dundas County) at the eastern end of the block.[13] However, later census data suggests that these English Loyalists failed to attract many followers, although a substantial English presence did develop just to the west in Augusta Township (Grenville County) and nearby Brockville.[14]

In addition to the St. Lawrence River block, five other townships were laid out for Loyalists in the Bay of Quinte region to the west of Kingston (Map 4).[15] Given that people with English ancestry were the most significant ethnic group in the region by the time of the 1881 Census, they were probably particularly well-represented in the early Loyalist influx.[16] This is confirmed by the Anglican minister of Marysburgh Township, who, writing in the mid-nineteenth century, described his parishioners

Courtesy Library and Archives Canada, MIKAN 2833909.

Encampment of Loyalists at Johnston, a new settlement on the banks of the St. Lawrence River, June 6, 1784. The principal Loyalist military leader was Sir John Johnson from the Mohawk Valley of New York, who commanded the two battalions of the King's Royal Regiment of New York, the largest provincial corps in Quebec. Watercolour by James Peachey.

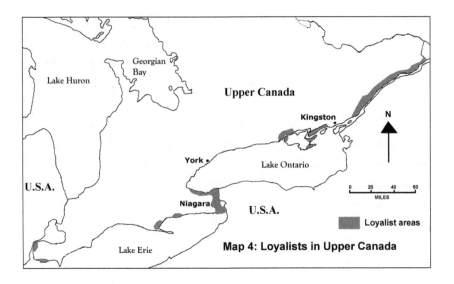

Map 4: Loyalists in Upper Canada

as "mainly descendents of Loyalists," who are a "handsome and intelli-
gent community," having "many farmers who are comparatively wealthy."
And concentrated in nearby Hillier Township were the descendents
of English Quakers who regularly attended the Anglican church.[17]
Meanwhile, a third and smaller group of Loyalists went to the west shore
of the Niagara River, and still others headed for the southwestern tip of
the province (Essex County), across from Detroit, finding homes among
the earlier, French-speaking settlers.[18]

The Loyalists who streamed into Upper Canada had come as refugees and occupied land, the location of which had been determined by
the British government. Their training and experience did not necessarily prepare them for the rigours of pioneer life and, to compound their
difficulties, their sites were chosen more for their military value than the
fertility of the land. Moreover, delays often occurred in administering
land grants. These factors, plus an ongoing desire for a better situation,
caused many to seek more favourable locations. Before long, Loyalists
extended their territory westward along Lake Ontario from the Bay of
Quinte region to York (later Toronto), and later moved farther west from
Niagara to the Long Point area in Norfolk County. This activity attracted
the attention of the Society for the Propagation of the Gospel, which had
established Anglican missionaries at Loyalist strongholds in Kingston,

Ernestown (in the Bay of Quinte), and Niagara by around 1790. But few Loyalists were Anglican, so the response was disappointing.[19] However, the Church of England soon learned that, if it was to achieve its desired aim of influencing communities generally, it had to be fairly accommodating in accepting non-Anglicans.

All the while, Loyalists were being joined by other Americans, who were lured much more by the prospect of free land grants than by any loyalty they might have felt to Britain. By as early as 1799, American colonizers had even penetrated vast swathes of southwestern Upper Canada, being concentrated especially well in York, Wentworth, Lincoln, Welland, Norfolk, and Kent counties.[20] This development was welcomed by the British government, which at the time was loath to see its own people lost to the North American colonies. In any case, the war between Britain and France from 1793 to 1801, and the later Napoleonic Wars that began in 1803 and ended in 1815, made transatlantic travel extremely hazardous and uninviting. As a consequence, much of Upper Canada's population growth before 1815 can be attributed to American immigration. Judging from the fact that the population reached seventy-one thousand in 1806, the influx must have been considerable, involving several thousands of people.[21]

The Loyalists had the advantage of usually being the first to acquire land in townships that fronted on major lakes and rivers. Arriving from New England in 1796, the Bates family settled in Clarke Township (Durham County) fronting onto Lake Ontario.[22] Similarly, the Connecticut-born Timothy Rogers, who arrived in Pickering Township (Ontario County) some years later, in 1807, with a group of English Quakers, was still able to acquire a "front township."[23] Later arrivals could only look on with envy at these early immigrants. Writing to his father in 1834, Lancashire-born John Langton described how the "front townships" on Lake Ontario had long been occupied by "Yankees and the descendents of Yankee United Empire Loyalists," while his land, many miles inland in Fenelon Township (Victoria County), was still being cleared.[24] Sometimes, however, even the descendents of Loyalists had to accept inland sites. For example, Andrew W. Moore, grandson of Jeremiah, a Loyalist who had settled in Pelham (Niagara), was living in Scott Township by 1854 (Ontario County), a site that was well to the north of Lake Ontario.[25]

Roger Conant's settlement in Darlington Township, Durham County. Reproduction by Edward Scrope Shrapnel, 1920. This is yet another example of a Loyalist grant in a "front township." Having acquired a large holding of 1,200 acres near present-day Oshawa, Conant began farming here in 1792.

The initial placement of Loyalists in Upper Canada had, to a large extent, been determined by the British government's defence priorities. The St. Lawrence, Lake Ontario, and Niagara regions were all vitally important boundary locations that were vulnerable to attack from the United States. While the Loyalist influx had strengthened Upper Canada defensively and provided its first immigrant communities, the situation in Lower Canada was totally different. Although Loyalists wished to settle there, the authorities were not disposed to allow them to do so. Lower Canada already had a large and long-established French population with its own religion, language, and land tenure system. Its way of life had continued virtually unchanged following the British Conquest in 1763. This was mainly due to the conciliatory policies of early Quebec governors, the first being General James Murray.

Both Murray and his successor, Sir Guy Carleton, had realized the importance that French Canadians placed on their cultural heritage. In taking this stance they had to withstand the strenuous criticism of newly arrived Anglophone merchants, who wished to have British institutions and customs imposed on the French. The merchants were frustrated by the refusal to call an assembly, since it denied them representative government, and they also disapproved of the French seigneuries, which required people to comply with a near-feudal land system. People could only become tenants, not freeholders. This, the merchants argued, was harmful to the spirit of commercial enterprise that needed to be developed. But the merchants lost the argument and, with the passing of the Quebec Act of 1774, recognizing the right of the French to uphold their culture and seigneurial land tenure, life carried on as usual.[26] Co-operation had been won. When the Americans did attack during the

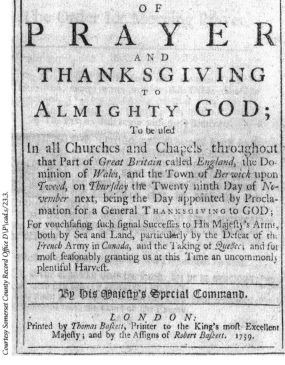

Prayer said in England and Wales commemorating the taking of Quebec on November 29, 1759.

War of Independence, most French Canadians remained neutral. They were staunch supporters of the British side during the War of 1812.[27]

So Haldimand did his best to maintain the status quo, and this meant discouraging Loyalists from settling in Quebec; but he could not stop the inevitable. Having become aware of the rich farmland to the east of the Richelieu River, some Loyalists gravitated toward the American border, seeking land between Baie Missisquoi and Lac Memphrémagog (Map 3).[28] Haldimand argued that the area east of the St. Lawrence, now called the Eastern Townships, should be occupied exclusively by French Canadians, since they regarded it as part of their natural heritage. Moreover, he also saw defensive advantages in having "the frontier settled with people professing a different religion, speaking a different language and accustomed to different laws from those of our enterprising neighbours of New England."[29] So for both political and defensive reasons, all Loyalist petitions for land grants in the Baie Missisquoi region were rejected.

The Swiss-born Sir Frederick Haldimand was governor of Quebec from 1778 to 1786. He was a military officer who served in the British Army during the Seven Years' War and the American Revolutionary War. This painting is a reproduction made circa 1925 by Lemuel-Francis Abbott and Mabel B. Messer.

Nevertheless, despite Haldimand's misgivings, a compromise was reached that enabled Loyalists to settle as tenants in three seigneuries in the region — Foucault,[30] Noyan, and St. Armand (later in Missisquoi County). This was a surprising outcome given the Loyalist aversion to tenancies. Having become accustomed to the egalitarian ideals of the New World, they desired freeholds. Yet, faced with increasing economic hardship, Loyalists were desperate to find land and took up their abode in the seigneuries.[31]

Their future soon brightened, however, with the creation of the Lower Canada Assembly in 1791. Facing increasing pressure to open up the region to colonizers, the government began creating new townships around the existing seigneuries, thus providing freehold tenure to Loyalists and the many New Englanders who flocked across the border, as well as to later immigrants.

This was a major shift in policy.[32] Predictably, Loyalists scattered far and wide. The later concentration of the English in Missisquoi, Brome, Stanstead, and Sherbrooke counties, as revealed in the 1881 Census, might suggest that these were the areas that had attracted English Loyalists (Map 3). Similarly, the dispersal of Loyalists that also took place to the west of the Richelieu River, within Hemmingford and Hinchinbrooke townships (Huntingdon County), might also be linked in part to the arrival of English Loyalists.[33]

Although Loyalists were initially unwelcome in much of Quebec, a concerted effort had been made to establish small numbers of them well to the north in the very remote Gaspé Peninsula. Its strategic location at the entrance to the St. Lawrence made it a prime defensive site. With this in mind, and having received favourable reports about the Gaspé's farming and fishing opportunities, Haldimand had arranged for around four hundred Loyalists to be sent to the north side of Baie-des-Chaleurs, along the border between Lower Canada and New Brunswick (Map 5).[34] Most settled in the area between Pointe au Maquereau (Point Mackerel) and Restigouche, with the largest concentrations developing initially in and around Paspébiac (near New Carlisle).[35] Some Loyalists joined small, already-established communities at New Richmond and Restigouche, while the Paspébiac colonists

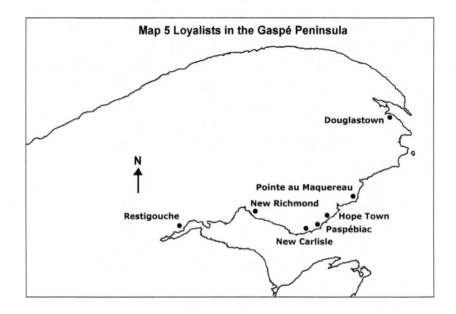

View of New Carlisle circa 1866, from Thomas Pye, *Canadian Scenery: District of Gaspé Montréal, 1866.*

went on to found another community on the east side of the peninsula, which they called Douglastown.

Already present along this same stretch of coastline were Acadian communities at Tracadièche (now Carleton), Bonaventure, and Paspébiac that had been founded some thirty years earlier.[36] Also present were French-speaking Protestants from the Channel Islands of Jersey and Guernsey, who, having arrived shortly after the Acadians in 1764, established fisheries and settlements between New Carlisle and Rivière-au-Renard.[37] Substantial Protestant clusters developed by 1825, especially in New Carlisle, Paspébiac, Hope Town, New Richmond, and Restigouche.[38]

Although the actual number of people by ethnic group is unknown, it would seem from the visit report of Lord Dalhousie, the governor-in-chief of Canada at the time, that Scots predominated among people having British ancestry.[39] However, their numbers were very much in decline. While French Canadians began moving to the Gaspé from the early nineteenth century, few immigrants arrived from Britain.[40] This fact of life was noted by the Reverend George Milne, Anglican minister of New Carlisle and Paspébiac. Writing to church authorities in 1854, he noted ruefully how "the population remains pretty much the same." Nevertheless, there were sufficient Protestants to support his two churches and scattered preaching stations, although probably relatively few would have been of English origin.[41]

Meanwhile, Loyalists and their followers from the United States had continued to stream into Upper Canada during the 1790s. Lieutenant-Colonel John Graves Simcoe, the first lieutenant governor, had actively encouraged them to settle, and had been particularly welcoming to Quakers. As a show of good faith, he exempted Quakers from having to bear arms, in recognition of their pacifist convictions.[42] In the end, a good many of them settled among the Loyalists, and were to be found in significant numbers at the eastern end of Lake Ontario in the Bay of Quinte area.

The policy of encouraging close-knit religious communities such as these to develop made considerable sense, but Simcoe had unrealistic ambitions when it came to his grand design for the province. He fervently believed that all Americans living in Upper Canada could be persuaded to show allegiance to Britain, but this was a vain hope. Americans certainly

Courtesy Library and Archives Canada, C-008111.

Lieutenant-Colonel John Graves Simcoe, lieutenant governor of Upper Canada, 1792–99. After his death in 1806, he was buried in the grounds of the family chapel at Wolford in Devon, England. The chapel is being maintained in perpetuity by the Ontario Heritage Foundation as a place of worship.

did not wish to have the feudal constraints of the Old World imposed upon them. A pioneer society, wedded to egalitarian ideals, had little time for the elitist and class-based ways of the mother country. So, while Simcoe could depend to some extent on people's loyalty to Britain, he could not rely on their willingness to accept British social customs and values.

While Upper Canada wrestled with its land policy and road-building program, problems of a more serious nature were brewing in Lower Canada. Divisions were steadily growing between the Anglophone merchants, who bitterly attacked all that was French, and the French Canadian population, who felt threatened by their attacks. This tension was noticeable when the English auctioneer Samuel Southby Bridge visited Montreal in 1806. He noted with approval that the minister of the "English Church" had referred to the Bishop of Quebec's proclamation in his sermon. It was "amply calculated to quiet the minds of the deluded, ignorant [French] Canadians — who have been led to suppose by some artful villains among them, that the English government wish to oppress them."[43] Given the tone of his remarks, relations between the two ethnic groups were clearly very fragile. Nevertheless, despite having to endure criticisms and insults from some of their Anglophone neighbours, the French remained loyal when Britain went to war with the United States in 1812.

Defended by only a few regular soldiers, and having a mainly American population, whose loyalty to Britain in some cases was doubtful, Upper Canada must have seemed a particularly easy target to the Americans. There was no hope of further troops being sent by Britain while the conflict with Napoleon continued, and so it was a plum ripe for the picking. But Britain had an efficient, though small army on hand and it also controlled the St. Lawrence River, Great Lakes, and coastal waters. Crucially, it also had the support of French Canada. After war was declared, the Lower Canada Assembly voted funds for the British military and raised a six-thousand-strong militia.[44] This practical expression of loyalty was another decisive factor in the defeat of American forces in 1814. The turning point came with the battles fought in 1813 at Châteauguay, in Lower Canada, and at Crysler's Farm, near present-day Morrisburg, in Upper Canada. A small but well-trained army consisting of British, English Canadian, and French Canadian regulars, as well as local militia repelled the advancing American forces and stopped a concerted attempt by them to cut the St. Lawrence River supply lines between Montreal and Upper Canada. In so doing, they changed the course of the war.[45]

The War of 1812–1814 left the people of the Canadas with a clearer sense of their own identity; it also made them more wary of the continuing threat they faced from their republican neighbours. The war had

View of Fort George, Niagara, 1812. The American army captured Fort George at Niagara in May 1813, and went on to occupy the entire Niagara Peninsula. Troops on the British side recaptured the fort later that year. Painting by Alfred Sandham (1830–1910).

demonstrated the importance of holding fast to the British tie for protection and it also identified the folly of relying mainly on American immigration to increase the population. Both lessons had been learned. There was an obvious need to encourage immigration from Britain, but that was no easy matter. Most eighteenth-century emigration had been directed to the Maritime region, which was closer than the Canadas and therefore less costly to reach. But that was due to change. As the much better land and climate that the Canadas had to offer became more widely known, those British immigrants who could afford the longer journey switched their allegiance, and after 1815 they increasingly headed for Quebec. Harsh economic conditions in Britain stimulated the exodus, and with the greater availability of transatlantic shipping made possible by the growing timber trade, it quickly gathered pace.

Initially, England lost fewer people to British North America than did Scotland or Ireland. The English only left in appreciable numbers after 1830, when the economy once again nose-dived. Before then, although there was considerable poverty in parts of England, emigration seemed too risky. The benefits had yet to be proven. Even when the government took the previously unthinkable step of funding emigration schemes in 1815 and the early 1820s, the English did not come forward, leaving the Scots and Irish to take up the offers of free transport to Upper Canada.[46] However, English people did emigrate at their own expense from 1817, although the numbers to begin with were relatively small. Emigration began as a North of England exodus, especially from Yorkshire. People from the thinly populated and remote regions to be found in the north were probably less troubled by the challenges of facing pioneer life than their counterparts in the south would have been. And to help them along, Yorkshire emigrants had the reassurance of knowing what to expect.

The Yorkshire emigrants who left for Quebec starting in 1817 were following on the heels of previous generations who had emigrated to the Maritimes. Some nine hundred of them, having emigrated in the 1770s from the North and East Ridings of Yorkshire, had colonized large swathes of the Chignecto Isthmus connecting Nova Scotia with New Brunswick. Some forty-five years later, people from this same part of England were setting out to repeat the process, this time in the St. Lawrence region. No doubt, they had received reports about the fertile land to be had in south-western Lower Canada. Their chosen site was Lacolle, lying close to the Richelieu River and the boundary with New York.

As was the case with their predecessors who went to the Maritimes, these Yorkshire emigrants left at a time when the English ruling classes were highly critical of emigration, regarding it as harmful to the nation's economic health and military strength. Major William Smelt, a British Army officer from the East Riding of Yorkshire who had served at Quebec in the War of 1812–1814, intended that his disparaging comments to his sisters in Hull would hinder emigration locally:

> I wish I could give you a good description of the country but that is not in my power. It certainly is beautiful but having said that I have said everything as there is not a single thing else to recommend it … every article is immensely dear and there are many things you

cannot get in the country; the women are eminently
ugly…. I recommend to my friends never to think of
coming here.[47]

However, such comments probably had the opposite effect! Lower
Canada's inability to provide luxury items was not a high priority for the
struggling farmers and farm labourers in Yorkshire who were seeking a
better life. In any case, most ordinary people made up their own minds
on whether to emigrate, and usually did so after taking advice only from
friends or family.

Offering good land and being close to markets, Lacolle seemed a particularly good choice for these Yorkshire settlers, but surprisingly it was a
seigneury lying within French-dominated Lower Canada. Why had they
not chosen one of the newly created townships in Upper Canada, where
they could obtain freehold grants and be close to other English-speaking
communities? The answer lies in their understanding of pioneer life.
These were prudent and well-organized people who knew exactly what
they were doing.

CHAPTER 3

South and West of Montreal

A number of houses situated on each side of the road that runs along the ridge from the State of New York about 2 ½ miles towards Lacolle have obtained the name of Odelltown from Captain [Joseph] Odell who was one of the first and most active settlers in this part; he is an American by birth and so are the greatest part of the other inhabitants; but they are now in allegiance to the English government.[1]

WHEN JOSEPH BOUCHETTE visited Odelltown in 1815, he saw a village lying close to the American border in the Lacolle seigneury that impressed him greatly. With its "generally good soil and being very well-timbered," he predicted that it was about to "advance in agricultural improvement and become wealthy and flourishing." Bouchette returned fifteen years later and marvelled at "the immense quantities of timber" being transported along the nearby Richelieu River. Logs were loaded onto "the numerous rafts, that are continually descending, and upon which many hundreds tons of pot and pearl ashes[2] and large cargoes of flour are brought down every summer."[3] Odelltown and the surrounding area were buzzing with activity. By this time, nearly all the people in the area would have been English, most having originated from Yorkshire.

Named after Joseph Odell, who had come from Poughkeepsie, New York, Odelltown had initially attracted Loyalists, but they had not remained. Arriving with his wife and family in 1788, Odell had settled in the southern end of Lacolle seigneury, but the family later moved to Brome County in the Eastern Townships. Other Americans, such as Frederick Scriver, who arrived in 1790, and John Manning and Isaac Wilson, who came in 1802, similarly moved on, in their case to Hemmingford Township in Huntingdon County.[4] As Americans, they had become accustomed to the freedoms of the New World and simply could not submit to the semi-feudal leaseholds being offered by the Lacolle seigneur. Their undoubted preference was to purchase freeholds, and so they moved to the townships, where they were available. However, the Yorkshire families were extremely content with what they found. Having worked on substantial farms in Yorkshire, which had been handed down from father to son, they were accustomed to renting and thus had little aversion to settling in a seigneury. But why had the Lacolle seigneury been their chosen destination?

Yorkshire people had a long history of emigrating to North America, although their colonization efforts had been directed exclusively toward the Atlantic region. Between 1772 and 1775, some nine hundred or so from the North and East Ridings of Yorkshire had relocated to the rich marshlands of the Chignecto Isthmus, linking Nova Scotia and New Brunswick.[5] Their landlords' decision to create large consolidated farms where previously they had been able to rent small holdings, and the continuing rent rises, caused much resentment. And when the immense potential of the fertile land to be had in the Chignecto Isthmus was brought to their attention, they voted with their feet. Their relocation had been encouraged and directed by no less a figure than Michael Franklin, the lieutenant governor of Nova Scotia, who, having fallen into debt, was seeking settlers for his land; but with the outbreak of the American Revolutionary War in 1775, emigration was suddenly halted, only resuming again after 1815 with the end of the Napoleonic Wars.[6] By then, the good land in Franklin's tract and in other parts of the

Maritimes had become occupied, and so it was a case of finding new land and a new patron.

The dire economic depression that followed the Napoleonic Wars made the case for emigrating stronger than ever. News that an English seigneur controlled great tracts of fertile land in the Richelieu Valley was probably conveyed to people in Yorkshire sometime in the 1780s. This was when Napier Christie, the son of the seigneur, married Mary Burton, daughter of an extremely wealthy Yorkshire landowner. The seigneur in question was Gabriel Christie, who, after having served in the Seven Years' War as a general in the British Army, had purchased large quantities of land in Lower Canada twenty years earlier.

His estate included six timber-rich seigneuries that straddled both sides of the Richelieu River.[7] At the southernmost end, on the west side, was Lacolle, and to the north of it was Deléry; on the southeast side was St. Armand, and to the north of it were Noyan, Sabrevois, and Bleury.[8] Mary's father, Ralph Burton, also brought a good deal to the marriage. In addition to being lord of various manors in Yorkshire, he had the added distinction of being the governor of Montreal. Napier even adopted the Burton name on the day he was married. From then on he was to be called Napier Christie Burton — in recognition, no doubt, of the large quantities of capital and prestige that would now come his way. Following Gabriel's death in 1799, Napier inherited the Lower Canada estate.

Unlike most British owners of seigneuries, who simply used them as a base for country pursuits and their business interests, Gabriel and his son were keen to attract colonizers.[9] Given that the Richelieu River was likely to be used by the Americans in launching future attacks, loyal British settlers had an obvious role as a civilian defence line, and hence were to be encouraged. American forces did, in fact, attack Odelltown in 1812–13, but they were beaten back by General De Salaberry and his Canadian militia.[10]

Nevertheless, there was an ongoing need to bolster the region's population. Living in Yorkshire were people seeking a good site on which to settle in the Canadas. The perfect match, of a seigneur seeking colonists and colonists seeking good land, produced a steady stream of people from the East Riding, where Napier's father-in-law's estates were located.

The actual number who came is uncertain. At the very least, some eighty-one families from the North of England, who originated mainly from the East Riding of Yorkshire and to a lesser extent from the North Riding, have been identified as having emigrated to Lacolle between 1817 and the mid 1830s (Map 6).[11]

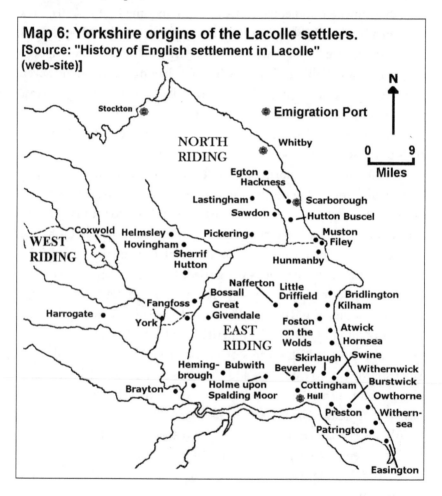

Map 6: Yorkshire origins of the Lacolle settlers.
[Source: "History of English settlement in Lacolle" (web-site)]

The Richelieu Valley's timber trade was the driving force behind the local economy, but exploiting it fully required entrepreneurs with capital who understood the intricacies of the trade. To attract them, Napier Christie had been obliged to increase their share of any profits by relaxing his seigneurial rights over sawmill and other revenues, which he did in 1815. One person who appears to have had a prominent role in his business enterprises was Robert Hoyle. Having originated from Bacup in Lancashire, he had moved in 1806 to Keeseville on Lake Champlain in New York State, where he established himself as a major timber merchant. Then, sometime during the American War of 1812–1814, he moved the short distance north to Lacolle.[12] Settling in the southern end of the Lacolle seigneury, he repeated his success story a second time.

Hoyle had probably been headhunted by Napier Christie, although his loyalties to Britain may also have played some part in his decision to move once war had been declared.[13] Hoyle's economic and social status grew rapidly as his timber-trade operations developed, and he also achieved great success as a farmer. He went on to establish carding and fulling mills for processing wool in nearby Huntingdon County and he also built a store opposite Île aux Noix, farther up the Richelieu River. By 1825, he was operating the ferry service across the Richelieu River to Noyan, and five years later was elected to the House of Assembly.[14]

Hoyle was on hand as the emigrant stream from Yorkshire gathered pace. As the area's principal storekeeper and timber merchant, Hoyle would have played an important role in managing timber cutting and transport operations. Some of the new arrivals may have sought jobs as full-time lumberers, while others would have acquired land with the intention of supplementing their farming income from seasonal employment in the lumber camps. Hoyle would have taken their timber in return for food, clothing, and equipment from his store. Yet this was no ordinary timber operation.

Because of its location at the southern end of the Richelieu River, Lacolle effectively had access to both the English and American markets. For the English market, timber was sent northward on floating rafts via the Richelieu and St. Lawrence rivers to Quebec, and from there was loaded into timber ships for transport across the Atlantic. Following the large increases in tariffs that had been levied on Baltic timber during the Napoleonic Wars, this was a highly profitable trade. Canadian timber had a considerable cost advantage and the trade with Britain soared.[15] For the American market, timber could be sent southward from Lacolle to the southern end of Lake Champlain and then along the Hudson River to New York City.[16]

Little wonder then that Yorkshire people headed for Lacolle. Between 1817 and 1830, Yorkshire lost more people to the Canadas than any other English county. Overall, the exodus was dominated by the North of England. Seventy-five percent of the eighteen thousand or so English people who are known to have sailed for Quebec during this period had left from northern ports and, of these, around a third had sailed from Hull in the East Riding of Yorkshire (Appendix I).[17] Thus, while the zeal to emigrate was particularly strong in the North of England, it was especially pronounced in Yorkshire. In 1819 alone, some nine hundred people sailed from Hull to Quebec.

New communities soon formed in the Lacolle seigneury, where the Yorkshire presence was particularly pronounced. Beaver Meadows and Roxham, situated along the American border, thrived and quickly attracted Methodist preachers, as did Henrysburg and Burtonville on the northern side of the seigneury (Map 7). In time, Yorkshire settlers would extend their territory westward into Bogton and Hallerton in Hemmingford

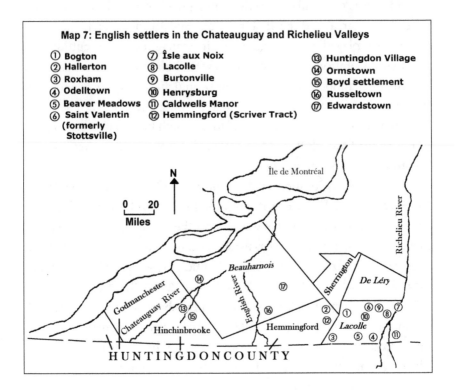

Map 7: English settlers in the Chateauguay and Richelieu Valleys

① Bogton
② Hallerton
③ Roxham
④ Odelltown
⑤ Beaver Meadows
⑥ Saint Valentin (formerly Stottsville)
⑦ Île aux Noix
⑧ Lacolle
⑨ Burtonville
⑩ Henrysburg
⑪ Caldwells Manor
⑫ Hemmingford (Scriver Tract)
⑬ Huntingdon Village
⑭ Ormstown
⑮ Boyd settlement
⑯ Russeltown
⑰ Edwardstown

Township and would later acquire holdings in Ormstown, Russelltown, and Edwardstown in Beauharnois seigneury. This was a major influx.

The Yorkshire settlers who survived the voyage to Quebec in 1817 were lucky to have escaped with their lives. Their ship, the *Trafalgar*, had become grounded on its approach through the Bay of Fundy and, after being rescued, some of its 159 passengers disembarked at Saint John, New Brunswick, while the remainder travelled on to Quebec. That same year, another Yorkshire group had sailed to Charlottetown with the prospect of founding new communities in Prince Edward Island.[18] But this was the last time that Yorkshire immigrants sought destinations in the Maritime provinces. Now that the Canadas were in their sights, there was no contest. Although they were more costly and difficult to

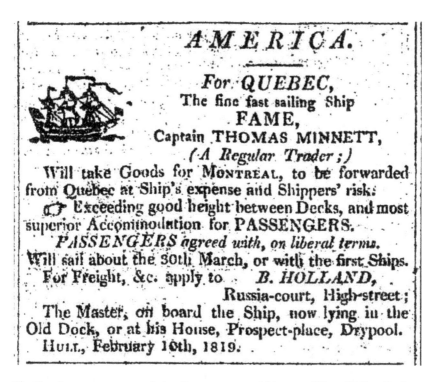

The *Fame*'s roomy accommodation for passengers wishing to sail from Hull to Quebec is highlighted in this advertisement in the *Hull Packet*, February 16, 1819. As the volume of shipping between England and Quebec increased, emigrants could simply purchase places in one of the many timber ships that regularly crossed the Atlantic.

reach, their land and job prospects were far better. This did not mean that the Canadas were an easier prospect for pioneer settlers. Unlike the Maritimes, which had been attracting British settlers since the seventeenth century, the Canadas were just being opened up to them.

Initially, the privations and isolation of pioneer life would be far worse. Andrew Oliver, who had spent time in Montreal, advised would-be immigrants to "be cautious in using the luxuries of the country and in overstretching yourself at your labours; many have suffered materially for overheating themselves and drinking too freely ..." As a tradesmen he had found employment easily on a wage of 5s. a day. "I continued nearly 5 years in the country during which period I succeeded very well."[19] However, for those who were to face the virgin forests, the challenge was much tougher.

Liverpool timber merchants, unhappy at the loss of passengers who had changed allegiance from the Maritimes and were sailing instead to Quebec, also weighed in with negative reports on the perils facing immigrants who sought "the distant and unhealthy regions of Upper Canada and the United States."[20] Even for someone as wealthy and well-connected as William Bowron, a Yorkshire man from Cotherstone in the North Riding who first viewed his four hundred acres in 1821, Lacolle had the appearance of an unbroken wilderness.[21]

Nor was it a simple case of acquiring land in one's preferred location. Mark Elvidge from Kilham in the East Riding only found his land in southern Lacolle after having first settled along the LaTortue River near La Prairie, just to the south of Montreal. He and his three sons came to acquire land in southern Lacolle in 1822, while a member of his family would eventually own a store along the border by the mid-nineteenth century. This slow and complicated process was repeated by others. The English-born Richard Harper only acquired his land at Beaver Meadows after having established himself temporarily near La Prairie at St. Constant. It was the same for William Beswick, who originated from Brompton by Sawdon in the North Riding. After a brief stay at La Prairie, he moved to Stottsville (now St. Valentin). The hand of Henry Edme, Christie Burton's agent, was clearly at work.[22] Being one of the largest landowners in La Prairie by the 1820s, he was well-placed to assist the

Yorkshire arrivals in finding holdings until they had assessed where they would purchase their land in Lacolle.

By 1823, Joseph Keddy, from Pickering in the North Riding, was clearing land on Lacolle's eastern boundary with Hemmingford Township. Having followed his brother George, who had obtained land at Henrysburg two years earlier, Joseph and his family eventually acquired a thousand acres stretching across both Lacolle and Hemmingford.[23] By the second half of the nineteenth century, his oldest son, John, would be running a store in Bogton (Map 7).[24]

While material benefits were beginning to accrue for some, there was an increasing yearning in the early 1820s to have the comforting presence of a religious leader. Their Methodist faith had been a vital support mechanism back in England, drawing people together regularly for worship. Once established in Lacolle, it would do the same. It would also provide an important cultural link with Yorkshire. Answering their pleas for help, the British Methodist Missionary Society sent the Yorkshire-born James Booth to them in 1823.[25]

The Reverend Booth sympathized with the plight of the recently arrived immigrants, who were having to eke out a tough existence in the bush, and deplored the fact that there were "no priests or places of worship." Therefore, he wasted no time in establishing his Lacolle circuit. It encompassed Burtonville to the north, Bogton to the east, and Beaver Meadows and Roxham in the south. And when Edward Braithwaite from Bubwith in the East Riding moved to Henrysburg in 1824, he established a store around which yet another Methodist community would grow.[26] The building of the Odelltown Methodist Church began almost immediately, while the Roxham Methodist Church would be completed in around 1849 and the one at Beavers Meadow by the second half of the nineteenth century.[27]

The Reverend Booth could soon report how "a goodly number of persons ... have been turned from darkness to light," and that he had established ten preaching places. However, a worrying number of people were leaving for Upper Canada and the United States.[28]

The English exodus increased significantly by the late 1820s. The *Montreal Gazette* reported how "emigration is almost daily taking place

Photograph of the Methodist church at Odelltown, built during the 1820s.

from the West Riding of Yorkshire," and calculated that "1,300 emigrants must have quitted the shores of their native country at Liverpool during the last month."[29] English emigrants even outnumbered the Irish at this stage. The *Quebec Gazette* observed that about three hundred immigrants had already arrived in the spring of 1828, "chiefly farmers from Yorkshire." Several had been assisted to emigrate by their parishes, and soon after their arrival most found employment near Quebec "at from £2 to £3.10 a month."

But the majority would be heading for Upper Canada.[30] A year later, a *Montreal Gazette* reporter observed "a more respectable class of farmers than in former years. Most of them possess considerable property. The majority of them proceed to Upper Canada, to join their friends and relations, and particularly to the Newcastle district where arrangements we are informed have been made for their reception."[31] The account given in 1830 gave further details of where the growing number of English immigrants intended to settle:

We are happy to learn that the great majority of these emigrants intend to remain within the British Provinces — the settlements which many have chosen are those in the neighborhood of York [Ontario County] — some are for the shores of the Ottawa [River] — others will "locate" themselves along the Chateauguay [River] — and many are about to take up their residence about Odelltown, and the settlements along the frontier lines.[32]

By the 1830s, the Yorkshire influx to Lacolle had dropped to a trickle. Those who did arrive included men like Charles Collings from Cornwall, who were affluent enough to acquire large, already-cleared lots in the middle stretches of Lacolle. He became one of Hallerton's most prominent residents.[33] William Akester, a Beverley tailor and farmer from the East Riding who came in 1827, was another man of substance. He and his family became the leading lights of the Roxham community.

Eventually Lacolle's appeal waned as the fertile lands in the western peninsula of Upper Canada were becoming more accessible, and it was also adversely affected by the 1837–38 Lower Canada uprising, which tore its communities apart.[34] Widespread discontent over the obvious injustices of colonial rule, coupled with rising economic and political tensions, led many ordinary people to take up arms. Given that much of the organization and leadership of the revolutionary movement was based in Montreal, Lacolle was very much in the firing line. However, the dissent was quickly suppressed. And when the fighting stopped, William Penderlieth Christie, who followed Napier as seigneur in 1835, took his revenge. He expelled those of the French Canadians in his Deléry and Bleury seigneuries who were believed to have joined the rebels, and then sought to attract more British settlers, although he failed to do so.

When normal times resumed, Lacolle attracted the attention of Montreal's Anglican bishop — George Jehoshophat Mountain. Under the auspices of the Society for the Propagation of the Gospel (SPG), the Reverend Charles Morice was duly dispatched to Lacolle in 1841 to form a congregation from its farmers, tradesmen, storekeepers, and merchants. Two years later the Saint Saviours Anglican Church duly appeared, and by

1845 its Anglican congregation was reported to have two hundred members, who included many "settled farmers."[35] By around 1860, Hallerton acquired its Saint John the Baptist Anglican Church. But long before this, as the Lacolle seigneury was filling up with settlers, new arrivals were having to look much farther afield for suitable sites on which to live.

Hemmingford Township (Huntingdon County), lying just to the west of Lacolle, acquired a scattering of English settlers but had surprisingly little appeal despite being in an area in which freeholds could be purchased. Having been appointed in 1843 by the SPG as the Anglican missionary for both Hemmingford and Sherrington townships, the Reverend Henry Hazard reported that the inhabitants were mainly French Canadian and Irish. They were "poor settlers" who survived winters by working in lumber camps and selling firewood.[36] He even had to rely on so-called "dissenters," probably Methodists, to bolster his congregation. English Anglicans were conspicuous by their absence. Oddly enough, they were to be found in much larger numbers in the Beauharnois seigneury, which lay just to the north.

As was the case with the Lacolle seigneury, Beauharnois offered both good farming opportunities and a booming timber trade, although it required people to rent rather than buy land. But there were compensations. As Robert Sellar, author of the History of the County of Huntingdon, pointed out, cut timber or potash produced in the Châteauguay Valley produced sufficient revenue to tide people over "until the clearing yielded enough to maintain the settler's family."[37]

In addition to being able to benefit in this way from the timber trade, English immigrants could expect the Beauharnois seigneury to offer them a fairly secure future. The seigneur, Edward Ellice,[38] a London merchant and land speculator, was obliged to build roads and provide a gristmill. Having considerable capital, he also invested generously in various public buildings, such as schools and churches.[39] As a result, rather than face the prospect of floundering in an empty wilderness, his settlers could rely on reasonable living conditions in well-ordered communities.[40] Although these economic considerations may have lured some immigrants to Beauharnois, most would have preferred to have had the added option of becoming landowners. Ellice realized this and sought to have seigneurial tenure abolished, but despite his connections in the higher echelons of government, he failed to win support and it remained in use until 1856.[41]

Most of the Beauharnois English became concentrated at Ormstown and Edwardstown (Map 7). In 1822, a Methodist missionary found that Lowland Scots and the English were the seigneury's dominant ethnic groups.[42] But ten years later, Joseph Bouchette observed that Scots far outnumbered the English.[43] The English ranked third to Lowland Scots and the Irish in Ormstown and second to the Irish in Edwardstown.[44] Robert Sellars later confirmed that Ormstown's settlers "were, with few exceptions, Lowland Scotch."[45] Nevertheless, Ormstown acquired a large Anglican congregation, which, by the mid-nineteenth century, was erecting its second church, "built of cut stone in the English style" and "lighted with lancet windows."[46] Costing £1,112, local residents found £480, while the rest was raised in other parts of Lower Canada and in New York and Boston.[47] In 1855, Edward Ellice granted the congregation land on which an Anglican parsonage was built.[48]

A winter scene in Châteauguay painted by Philip John Bainbrigge circa 1838–41.

Photograph of St. James Anglican Church, Ormstown.

©Dominc R. Labbé McMasterville, Quebec. Reproduced with permission.

Edwardstown's English settlers were mainly to be found along Norton Creek, a tributary of the English River. One of the earliest known arrivals was John Severs, a butcher from Hull who came in 1820. Obviously succeeding, he used his entrepreneurial skills to open a tavern and store. Several other English families followed, including William Creasor, who appeared with his three sons, "all stout Yorkshire-men," and became a "prominent settler." A school was built in 1818 on land provided by Severs with the stipulation that "the schoolhouse was to be open for the preaching of the gospel by any Protestant minister." This was achieved with services being conducted in turn by Methodist, Presbyterian, and Episcopalian clergymen over many years.[49]

Russeltown, on the Black River, another tributary of the English River, had few English, but, even so, by 1846 it had a substantial Anglican congregation served by a church and ten preaching stations.[50] One of its more prominent inhabitants was Richard Hall, whose family roots were in Northamptonshire. Nancy Hall, a relative, died in 1840 and is buried in the Russeltown cemetery.[51]

Situated much farther to the west in Hinchinbrooke Township (Huntingdon County) were settlers like John Boyd. Having emigrated to Upper Canada from Cumberland in 1818, he appeared in Hinchinbrooke five years later, where he was joined by his brother William and others who had probably also originated from Cumberland. Together they founded the Boyd settlement (Map 7): "For many years the only mode of access was a track that followed the ridges through to the swamp which was crossed by stepping from log to log.... Except in very dry time even an ox-sled could with difficulty reach the settlement and when the swamps were full everything had to be carried on shoulder. Until the land was ditched, potash-making was the main reliance of the settlers, who with a few exceptions were from the north of Ireland."[52]

Evidently, in this part of the Châteauguay Valley the English were very much in the minority.[53] It was a similar situation in Huntingdon village, just a short distance to the north. William Morris, its Anglican minister, grieved over the lamentable number of English who professed to be Anglicans. His congregation was "scarcely represented by Englishmen."[54] The situation was little better for his successor in 1860, who complained that "the roads were frightful ten weeks each year" and disliked being surrounded by so many Irish people — "both Romanist and Protestant."[55]

In addition to supplying the John Boyd contingent, Cumberland had been experiencing a steady loss of people to the Canadas since 1815. The general economic depression following the Napoleonic Wars was bad enough, but in this important textile-processing area, other changes were afoot. With the introduction of power looms, hand-loom weavers were losing their jobs to machines, leading to widespread redundancies and pitiful wages for those who could find work. In these adverse conditions, many emigrated. Some joined communities that were forming in Prince Edward Island[56] and New Brunswick,[57] but one group who hailed from the Penrith area made a beeline for the Vaudreuil seigneury, lying just west of Montreal. At least sixty families are known to have left

Cumberland's Eden Valley to settle there between 1819 and 1837.[58]

Vaudreuil's attractiveness to Cumberland people probably owed much to the Reverend Joseph Abbott, a native of Little Strickland (Westmorland County). His place of birth lies close to the market town of Penrith, in the adjacent county of Cumberland. Significantly, nearly all of the English immigrants who streamed into Vaudreuil came from within a ten-mile radius of Penrith.[59] Having been appointed the Anglican minister of St. Andrews (Saint-André-Est)[60] in the Argenteuil seigneury, the Reverend Abbott made his first appearance in 1818.[61] Being required to tend also to the spiritual needs of the English-speaking inhabitants of Vaudreuil, only a short distance to the east, on the south side of the Ottawa River, he wasted no time in paying them a visit. A keen supporter of emigration, he would have very quickly assessed its potential and probably encouraged people from his homeland to emigrate. The first of the Cumberland immigrants arrived the following year. In some cases, three generations of the same family came, and, according to the Reverend Abbott, many were "excessively poor."[62] His *Memoranda of a Settler in Lower Canada; or the Emigrant in North America*, published some twenty years later, revealed his enthusiastic support for emigration and emphasized his belief that Canada was superior to the United States as a destination for British immigrants.[63]

Cumberland immigrants had a choice of two locations in Vaudreuil. The poorest headed for Côte St. Charles, which, lying some distance from the Ottawa River, offered cheaper rents (Map 8). The more affluent settled along the Ottawa River in Cavagnal (now Hudson), where they would have rented land from John Augustus Mathison, a retired lieutenant in the British Army. Mathison had purchased Cavagnal, a prime portion of the Vaudreuil seigneury, in 1820, and soon after had adopted the airs and graces of a country squire.[64] Despite having only a modest army income, he was able to build himself a stately mansion overlooking the Ottawa River and fund the building of a school.[65]

Arriving in 1819 with his wife and daughter, John Hodgson from Little Salkeld (Cumberland) was the first of the Cumberland settlers to come to Côte St. Charles, a place that would acquire a reputation for being "settled mainly by friends from England."[66] Favourable letters

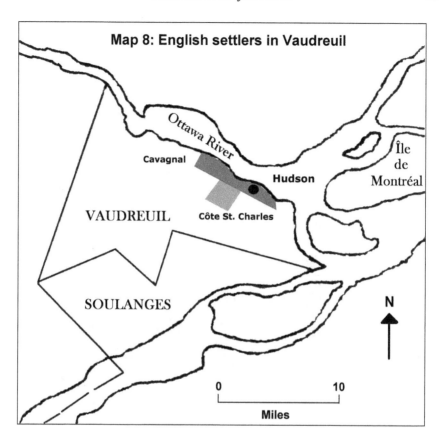

home ensured a steady flow of families who formed a close-knit community. When Thomas Parsons left Renwick (Cumberland) in 1829, he said that it was with "the object of joining friends in Côte St. Charles." That same year, someone in Skirwith (Cumberland) asked Joseph Bleckinship, who had just moved to Côte St. Charles, "how his neighbours the Hodgson and Bird families are getting on."[67] The wives of Robert Hodgson and Joseph Bird were sisters, and they and their husbands and families had arrived within a year of one another. Meanwhile, the more affluent headed for Cavagnal, where they joined American farmers and former employees of the Hudson's Bay Company who had been settling there since 1801.[68]

The Reverend Abbott observed in 1825 how Cumberland people had been "comparatively poor as new settlers ... yet, strange as it may

Photograph of St. James' Anglican Church, at Cavagnal, built circa 1842. The original place of worship was a log schoolhouse in the village of what is now Hudson.

Courtesy of the Anglican Parish of Vaudreuil, Hudson, Quebec.

appear to a dweller in the old country, they are well-off in the [new] world." They had little money with which to buy goods but they had more than acquired the essentials of life. The Côte St. Charles settlers built a schoolhouse in 1825 and employed as a teacher John Benson, who also deputized for the Reverend Abbott by taking on the role of an Anglican pastor. However, most of the settlers were actually Methodists, and would have to wait until 1855 before they had sufficient funds to build their first church.

Given its location close to Montreal, Vaudreuil experienced widespread conflict during the Lower Canada uprising in 1837–38. John Mathison rose to the occasion by organizing a "refuge in the woods for the women and children" and also formed a local militia to help defend the area from attack. The rebels were duly disarmed and the then Major Mathison received a fulsome accolade from Bishop Mountain, who stated that Vaudreuil was fortunate "to have such an officer to head them."[69] Soon after this, an Anglican congregation took shape in Cavagnal that, according to the Reverend George Pyke, its first missionary, consisted of around fifty families, who were "mainly farmers and settled."[70]

Few of the English settled in the French-dominated areas of Lower Canada to the south and west of Montreal, preferring to set themselves apart in the vast expanse of the Eastern Townships. There, a land company was on hand to provide an organizational structure. As the *Montreal Gazette* made clear in 1829, "the townships of Inverness, Leeds, and the adjoining settlements, on Craig's road were being prepared for the purpose of determining emigrants to proper situations."[71] Even the township names had a welcoming ring. The English would come in greater numbers to this part of Lower Canada.

CHAPTER 4

The Eastern Townships

Nothing particular has happened since George left us. Emigrants keep pouring in, and Sherbrooke is full of them; they make provisions very dear, beef has risen from 3d to 6d, and everything else in proportion. I wish the [British American Land] company had taken a fancy to some other country for it is not now the quiet place it was.[1]

LUCY PEEL, WIFE of Edmund, an officer on leave from the British navy, expressed her regret in June 1836 that her newly acquired home in Sherbrooke, in the Eastern Townships, was not the quiet haven it once was. With the recent opening of the British American Land Company, crowds of immigrants, many from England, were everywhere to be seen. While the immigrants would have felt hopeful about the future that awaited them, Lucy and Edmund were already planning their departure back to England.[2]

Having arrived in 1833, the Peels had failed to adapt to pioneer life. "Edmund is, after four years hard labour, convinced that nothing is to be done by farming in Canada; the land here produces too little to pay the labour requisite to cultivate it."[3] However, the issue was not poor land productivity, but rather the high cost of labour. Edmund could have employed all the servants he needed in England, where wage rates were low; however, this was not the case in high-wage North America. His and Lucy's unrealistic pursuit of a pampered life in a re-created English estate was bound to fail:

> This is a country where the active and industrious must prosper, the idle starve; there is on every side endless room for improvement and even our small farm would take thousands to make it look anything like an English estate … the worst is, that one man's life is too transient to receive much benefit from his labour, for after all he can only put things in training for those who follow: we sow what another generation will reap.[4]

While Lucy and Edmund had been defeated by the challenges they faced, plenty of ordinary immigrants held more realistic aspirations of simply owning land and having a better standard of living — although such benefits only came to those willing and able to cope with the rigorous demands of the outback.

Few British colonizers ventured into the Eastern Townships until the British American Company was formed in 1834. Before then, this area of Lower Canada, just to the east of Montreal, had attracted Loyalists who began to arrive in the mid-1780s to settle near the American border. They, in turn, were followed by other Americans, who continued to arrive into the next century. Most were New Englanders, almost certainly of English descent. However, small and scattered American communities having distant British ancestry were an insufficient answer to the region's population needs. There was the further concern that their proximity to the United States made the Eastern Townships particularly vulnerable to attack. The region's good farmland, together with its reasonable access to trade outlets in Quebec City, made it a prime candidate for large-scale colonization.

The Maritime provinces were fast filling up and the longer distance and higher cost involved in reaching Upper Canada did not suit everyone. There was an overwhelming case for attracting settlers directly from Britain, but that was easier said than done. As the Quebec immigration agent made clear to the 1826 Emigration Select Committee, many British people "dislike Lower Canada, on account of the French language and laws; the peasantry all speak French, and the emigrant is quite lost among them."[5]

In making their way into the vast stretches of the Eastern Townships, most British colonizers relied on the organizational structure that only a land company could provide. The highly focussed promotional strategy of the British American Land Company attracted people from particular regions of Britain, with one of the largest contingents coming from Norfolk and Suffolk in East Anglia. Like the others, they were offered land at attractive rates and were provided with an overall infrastructure that included log houses, roads, churches, and schools.[6] However, with the best will in the world such ventures rarely ran smoothly, particularly in the initial stages. Judging from Leonard Stewart Channell's comments in 1896, which would have been based on actual immigrant accounts, conditions must have been grim at the beginning:

> These early English emigrants came out under the auspices of the British American Land Company, but on finding things so different from what they had been accustomed to and so entirely at variance with their preconceived notions, they got disheartened and left their locations in search of more congenial quarters; but others with more pluck and forethought remained and now the comfortable circumstances of their children attest to their wisdom.[7]

Norfolk and Suffolk people came in their hundreds to the Eastern Townships in the 1830s, creating numerous communities across several townships. But because a great many left the region over the following decades, it is impossible to gauge their numerical impact. And yet, irrespective of the influx directly from England, English concentrations continued to build because of the New England advance, which had begun in the late eighteenth century. This had brought a steady flow of Americans with English ancestry to the area, thus creating large English concentrations in the southernmost townships. The 1881 Census would reveal how the English became the dominant ethnic group in eight of the seventeen townships nearest the American border, and became the largest of the British groups, outnumbering both the Scots and Irish, in a further four townships (Map 9).[8]

St. Armand, to the east of Baie Missisquoi, had the region's first Anglican mission, which was established in 1799 by the Society for the Propagation of the Gospel (SPG).[9] A large Loyalist population greeted the Reverend Charles Caleb Cotton on his arrival in 1804 — "everyone speaking the English tongue," although the inhabitants included "German Loyalists" who were joined later by "German emigrants." Most of the population had settled within three miles of Baie Missisquoi:

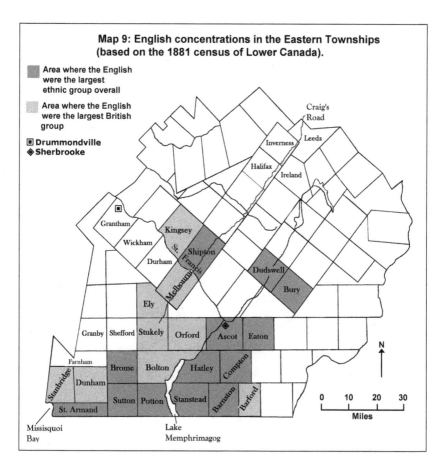

Map 9: English concentrations in the Eastern Townships (based on the 1881 census of Lower Canada).

The people here live very much to themselves and visit but very little. They spin and weave almost all their own clothing, both woollen and linen, besides family articles such as bedding, sheets, stockings … tablecloths; they also tan their own leather, make their own sugar, which I think very inferior, and all this with the daily work of a farm leaves them little or no leisure.… To a person who has resided in England their mode of life appears very parsimonious and uncomfortable.[10]

Moving in 1808 to Dunham, to the north of St. Armand, Cotton boarded at a Dutch farmer's home for short while before acquiring his own log house. Travelling four miles to reach one congregation and ten miles to the other, he conducted services in schoolhouses and private homes. He observed that the people were "very poor" and that conditions seemed so bleak that he wondered how long he could remain; however, he was still the Dunham minister in 1845.[11]

Stanbridge, to the west of Dunham, attracted an SPG missionary by the 1820s who presided over two Anglican churches, one at Bedford,

©Dominic R. Labbé McMasterville, Quebec. Reproduced with permission.

Photograph of Phillipsburg Methodist Church.

the other at Stanford East.[12] Although the Church of England had the largest Protestant congregations, Methodism also had considerable support in the Missisquoi area.[13] The Reverend James Booth, who was based at Philipsburg in St. Armand, had a regular preaching circuit that covered ninety-four miles, taking in St. Armand, Dunham, and Stanbridge townships — the future Missisquoi County. His followers were "mainly American brethren" who endured "extreme poverty."[14]

It was a similar story for the Stanstead area, east of Lac Memphrémagog, and the Brome area to the west of the lake, both regions having attracted American settlers from the 1790s (Map 9). Here, too, there were large English concentrations. By 1881, the English would account for 55 percent of the population in the future Stanstead County (Hatley, Stanstead, and Barnston townships) and 41 percent of the population in the future Brome County (Farnham, Brome, Bolton, Sutton, and Potton townships). However, except for Hatley, which later attracted a substantial number of English immigrants, these were mainly the descendants of Americans.

When the Reverend Thomas Johnson was sent by the SPG to Hatley in 1819,[15] he found that his mainly American congregation shared a large church with other Protestant denominations.[16] The Reverend John Hick, who began building a Methodist circuit at the same time, was sanguine about sharing "with all parties ... a chapel, capable of accommodating 900 to 1,000 people," but bemoaned the insufficiency of lay Methodist preachers.[17]

However, by 1845, Hatley's Anglican minister, the Reverend Christopher Jackson, was witnessing a steady loss of people from the area. Its English immigrants were particularly dissatisfied. They had almost certainly been recruited by the British American Land Company, which had purchased land in Stanstead County a decade earlier. But now they and others in Hatley were "getting disappointed with the severity of the climate and moving to the United States." Also, according to Jackson, the English immigrants had been particularly unwise in "spending their money foolishly and then removing."[18]

Americans continued their northward progression into Shefford and other townships north of Brome; the area would have also attracted

The Reverend Thomas
Johnson circa 1860. Born
in Bampton, Westmorland,
he was sent to the Eastern
Townships in 1819 by the
Society for the Propagation
of the Gospel.

Courtesy Eastern Townships Resource Centre, P009 Thomas Johnson fonds.

British immigrants beginning in the 1830s owing to the British
American Land Company's purchase of holdings in the future Shefford
County. Before then, Methodist Missionary Society clergymen reported
how communities struggled simply to survive. The Reverend Thomas
Catterick preached in 1822 to the "small society" to be found in Granby
Shefford, Farnham, Stukley, Bolton, and Brome — all townships in his
circuit. Some 1,400 families had been without a regular minister until he
had arrived: "The people are very poor and widely scattered from each
other."[19] And Sunday schools were poorly attended, owing "to the bad-
ness of the roads and the inability of parents to provide clothing for their
children to enable them to attend."[20]

Anglican ministers who were installed in the Shefford area, starting
in 1821, faced similar difficulties.[21] When the Reverend David Lindsay

came to Frost village in Stukely Township some thirty years later, his report to the SPG mentioned that, until his arrival, the township had not had a single Protestant church: "Various persuasions have had the rule and passed away."

Insufficient funds to build a church meant that Lindsay had to resort to makeshift arrangements and conduct services in the woods, just a few miles from Frost village: "The roads are so bad, I leave my horse 1½ miles from the place where we assemble and walk as best I can.... A small table serves as a pulpit and desk, planks are placed upon inverted buckets [that] serve as seats and the wooden building in which we meet is as yet unfinished."[22]

It was little better for the Reverend Joseph Scott, who described his parishioners in Brome and Sutton townships as "infidels," having "no respect for the clerical character, the Church or the Sacraments." However, sufficient resources had been raised by 1845 at Sutton to build a stone church, suggesting that some in his congregation, whom he called "backwoodsmen," may have included recent arrivals from England.[23]

The first significant influx to arrive directly from Britain to the Eastern Townships came in 1815 following Britain's near defeat in the close-fought War of 1812–1814. To bolster its North American defence capability, the British government had established a military settlement at Drummondville, on the western end of the St. Francis River, near the St. Lawrence River.[25] Linking the St. Lawrence on the west with Lac Memphrémagog on the east, this river had prime strategic importance (Map 9). While the main settlers would be ex-soldiers, given free land in return for their wartime services, ordinary civilians were also being enticed to live in such areas. A shipping advertisement for the sailing of the *Manique* from Hull in 1817 explained how emigrants could obtain land grants at both the Drummondville military settlement and at a second military settlement being established in the Rideau Valley in Upper Canada,[26] both places having "the great advantage of water carriage for their produce to the capital city of Quebec."[27]

As ever, American colonizers had already moved into the prime sites along the St. Francis River long before this — doing so by the 1790s. Beginning in 1815, the first British arrivals settled along the river in both

Courtesy Eastern Townships Resource Centre, P135 Henrietta K.W. Milne fonds, Bondville Anglican Church, circa 1890.

Anglican Church of the Good Shepherd in what was once the village of Bondville in Brome Township. The church opened in 1887.[24]

Grantham and Wickham townships, but progress was slow. Although former servicemen had the benefit of free land, log cabins, farm implements, and food, they also had to accept the less palatable constraints of living under military rule. Moreover, militarily important sites did not necessarily have good land, and this was certainly the case with Drummondville. Despite these drawbacks, Drummondville had a reasonable stock of houses by 1816, together with a hospital, school, and military barracks.[28] Yet disappointment over the poor quality of the land caused many to leave, and three years later the Drummondville settlement had only 235 residents.[29]

When he arrived at Drummondville in 1845, the Anglican minister, the Reverend George Ross, reported how people in his congregation, who were "ostensibly farmers," had been "drawn off by the tempting wages" they could get for cutting timber for the British market.[30] To make matters worse, British ex-servicemen, in receipt of land grants, had also left the area:

> They were accustomed from long habit to have their wants and comforts provided for without reference to themselves; it is not difficult to imagine that these early military settlers, when thrown suddenly upon their own endeavours in a scene so new to them and within circumstances so disadvantageous, should very soon have discovered a deficiency in the properties necessary for pioneers of the Forest: self-reliance patience, enduring privations and hardships; and that disappointments, dissatisfaction and discontent should have paralyzed their efforts and driven them in numbers to seek out more favourable townships .... Emigrants from the Mother Country ... later take up vacant lots and then again soon become disappointed under the difficulties of first settlements and they leave for more thriving locations in the Eastern Townships.[31]

It is likely that many of the British ex-soldiers who left ended up in Shipton, Melbourne, and Kingsey townships, areas that later acquired a substantial English presence (Map 9). Once again, it was a case of finding suitable locations that had not already been acquired by Americans.[32] A typical example of the latter was Captain Joseph Perkins, a late Loyalist from New Hampshire who could trace his ancestry back to Berkshire. Having loaded his wife and family and "what few things they owned" into an oxen-driven cart, Captain Perkins headed north, following the hardwood ridge through Melbourne Township, where the St. Francis River was crossed. "When he ran out of feed for his oxen he had to use the straw from the mattresses to keep going." Reaching Shipton in 1802, the family "built a log house in the wilderness," and their presumed success probably accounts for the followers from New England who later joined them.[33] It was a similar beginning for Moses Elliott, who arrived two years earlier from New Hampshire with his brother Zekiel, when "there was not a house from Stanstead to Sherbrooke." Settling first near Sherbrooke, Moses later moved north to Melbourne "and became very prosperous," eventually acquiring sawmills, a clothing factory, and a large amount of land.[34] By 1821, American colonizers had been joined by British ex-soldiers.

Thanks to details supplied by the Reverend Richard Pope, the indefatigable Methodist missionary who presided over Shipton and Melbourne, the location of at least one group of ex-servicemen can be identified. Included in his preaching circuit was "a small village, built and inhabited chiefly by the discharged soldiers," which was located twenty-five miles downriver from Shipton.[35] However, the discharged soldiers' "small village" was different in already having attracted the attention of the Reverend Mr. Wood of the Episcopal church (probably Anglican), who had become "established amongst them" by that time.[36] Possibly this small village was the "very promising little congregation at New London" that was mentioned by the Anglican missionary, the Reverend Daniel Falloon, in his report to the SPG in 1858.[37] Two years earlier he had actually visited New London, "celebrating Divine Services in a settler's house ... had a good attendance."[38]

Melbourne was visited in 1840 by the artist Mary Chaplin. Spending the night at Hardy's Inn, she spoke to the landlady, who had come from Yorkshire. "She was delighted when I told her my country [Lincolnshire] ... and said a family of Vasey from Lincolnshire lived six miles off."[39] Reassuring as this was to Mary, she could not help but notice how sparsely populated the region was. Travelling along the St. Francis River through the townships of Grantham, Wickham, and Durham, she had seen "a few houses scattered," but with none "boasting a village." Given that this was one of the vital arteries along which immigrants and others travelled to reach the southern stretches of the Eastern Townships, the region was clearly struggling to build a sizeable population.[40]

A more important route for immigrants was Craig's Road, farther to the north, which linked Quebec City with the northern approach to the townships. The part of the road that traversed Leeds, Ireland, Inverness, and Halifax townships became a conduit for immigrant settlement beginning in the 1820s, the time when land in this region first became available (Map 9). One group of early arrivals along this stretch of Craig's

Road was the thirty or so Methodists from Quebec City who relocated to Ireland Township in 1829.[41]

A year later, Alexander Buchanan,[42] the Quebec immigration agent, congratulated himself on "the great success that has attended the settlements in the townships of Inverness and Leeds, which I began in 1829." He was particularly pleased that there had been "a considerable augmentation, principally the friends of those who came out in 1829 and 1830." To encourage even more followers, Buchanan planned to name new settlements being formed after the places "from whence the majority of emigrants came — names such as Ulster settlement, Yorkshire, Dublin, New Hamilton, and Wiltshire."[43] Perhaps the Leeds and Halifax names were indicative of a substantial influx from Yorkshire — people like Thomas Nutbrown, from Howden (East Riding of Yorkshire) and his wife Ann Cottam from Thormanby (North Riding), who, having emigrated with their eleven children, had settled in Leeds Township by 1831.[44]

Generally speaking, the English came in small numbers to the northern stretches of the Eastern Townships and became widely scattered. The Reverend John Flanagan, Leeds' Anglican minister, noted in his report to the SPG in 1845 that it was already "a settled farming area," his only concern being the loss of "a few families who have moved to the west."[45] By 1855, most of Leeds' inhabitants were Irish and Scottish. Of the relatively few who were English, a striking proportion had originated from Cornwall and Yorkshire.[46] Possibly some of the latter were attracted by the mining jobs that became available when the Harvey Hill copper mines opened in 1858. Advance publicity of the new mining activity being planned may have drawn John Rickard, William Hamley, and John Blake and his wife to the area from Cornwall during the 1850s.[47] The opening in 1854 of a new Anglican mission at the neighbouring townships of Inverness and Nelson may also signify a recent influx of English immigrants to the area.[48]

It was the emergence of the British American Land Company and the financial assistance provided by English parishes that stimulated the really large influx of English settlers during the 1830s. Modelled after the Canada Company, which had been founded eight years earlier to promote the colonization of western Upper Canada, the Lower Canada company actively sought immigrants. Its holdings consisted of 850,000 acres of Crown land stretching across a wide expanse of the Eastern Townships. One section, having 596,000 acres, lay in the St. Francis Tract[49] between Lake Megantic and the St. Francis River, while the second section, containing 251,000 acres, was scattered throughout Shefford, Stanstead, and Sherbrooke counties (Map 9).[50]

Leaflets and posters were produced to attract tradesmen, agricultural labourers, and farmers to the Eastern Townships.[51] Typical of these was the pamphlet written by William Wilson in 1834, which contained correspondence with a friend back home in Ripon (Yorkshire), extolling the benefits of the Sherbrooke area:

> The country between this and the lines [American border] is in general better settled; and consequently more fit for European inhabitants than that towards the north. Innumerable farms are here offered at prices within the reach of small capitalists. The mere wreck or scattered fragments of many an English farmer would supply him with a farm, stock and implements *all his own*, and enable him to look upon his family not with anxious painful doubt but as a certain source of help and comfort.[52]

Although the pamphlet gave the impression of expressing the unbiased observations of a newcomer, it was probably a highly contrived piece of promotional literature that was almost certainly being sponsored by the land company. Facing stiff competition from the Canada Company, the British American Land Company had an uphill struggle to find settlers. With its better climate, job opportunities, and land, most self-funded immigrants understandably preferred Upper Canada. The dominance of French culture was a further deterrent for some English-speaking immigrants. The British American Land Company overcame these hurdles by concentrating its recruiting efforts on those areas of Britain that were experiencing extreme rural poverty. In particular, it targeted those parts of England whose parish councils were willing to assist their poor to emigrate. The company could offer cheaper transport costs because of the shorter distances involved, and it probably provided more generous accommodation and assistance to settlers than did its Canada Company rival. Even so, as was reported in an official investigation undertaken in 1836, many people did not remain, preferring instead to move on to Upper Canada or the United States.[53]

With the severe destitution being experienced in East Anglia, many parishes seized upon emigration as the solution to be adopted in relieving the plight of their poor. Greater mechanization in threshing corn and in land drainage had destroyed countless labouring jobs. With the soaring unemployment that followed, poor relief payments became an increasing burden for parishes. Legislation, passed in 1834, enabled English parishes struggling with this predicament to raise funds for assisted emigration to the British colonies.[54] One-off payments to give the poor a chance of a better life seemed a sensible way forward, and because they were no longer placing an ongoing demand on public resources, ratepayers had a sharp reduction in their poor rates.[55]

However, there were some who argued that emigration was an inhumane solution. The poor were being dispatched to a faraway land simply to lessen the poor rates burden of the rich who wanted rid of them.[56] An 1833 booklet urging "the working and labouring classes of Suffolk and Norfolk" not to emigrate offered "a complete exposure of emigration — showing the hardships and insults the working and labouring classes have to undergo before reaching their destination and of the scandalous tricks practised upon them by certain interested individuals."[57] There was also hostility to the harshness of the new Poor Law regime, which denied wage subsidies to the able-bodied, forcing them to choose between the miseries of a workhouse or the hunt for non-existent jobs.[58] The stark reality was that for those who were unwilling to seek work outside their area — say, in the factories of the industrialized north — emigration was the only viable escape from ongoing poverty.

As emigration fever gripped Norfolk and Suffolk in 1836, protests and riots became more common. The *Norfolk Chronicle* and *Norwich Gazette* lamented the loss of "the bold peasants, who were once England's pride, now driven from her shores by [the] hundreds and thousands to seek their bread in a foreign land."[59] The *Bury and Norwich Post* described the commotion that erupted at the port in Ipswich when poor labourers from Stradbroke, in northeast Suffolk, attempted to board their vessel. A mob tried to stop them from leaving, but most were persuaded by parish officers to return to their ship.[60] Before such expressions of dissent occurred, William Cattermole, agent for the Canada Company, had been seeking to entice local people to emigrate to Upper Canada, but despite his best efforts, he had little success. Only Suffolk people wished to emigrate initially and their first choice was Prince Edward Island.

While the island attracted large numbers from northeast Suffolk between 1830 and 1832, the flow of immigrants was halted in the following year as a result of a letter-writing campaign organized by Cattermole that disparaged its climate, land, and employment opportunities.[61] Through his lecture tours, Cattermole rammed home Upper Canada's many advantages, but the British American Land Company's publicity had also been very effective. In July 1836, the *Quebec Gazette* reported that around 1,400 immigrants had reached Sherbrooke in the Eastern Townships, principally from Norfolk and Suffolk.[62] This can be corroborated by the Poor Law records, which reveal that around 1,025 Norfolk people and 231 Suffolk people were assisted by their parishes to emigrate to Lower Canada between June 1835 and July 1836.[63] The Lower Canada contingent accounted for a third of the total, with the remaining two-thirds having gone mainly to Upper Canada.[64]

The exodus to Lower Canada occurred from north, central, and south Norfolk and from across the border in north Suffolk, all areas with good river access to Great Yarmouth (Map10). The immigrants mostly sailed from the principal port of Great Yarmouth, but smaller numbers also left from King's Lynn, Ipswich, and Lowestoft.[65] The 178 people who sailed in the *Indemnity* from Yarmouth left in September — giving themselves the extra difficulty of coping with an approaching winter on their arrival. In the following year, a further 108 paupers from Norfolk and sixty-three from Suffolk were assisted by their parishes to emigrate to Lower Canada.[66]

The largest group to reach the Eastern Townships in 1836 was the 250 people who had originated from Banham Parish in the Guiltcross Poor Law Union[67] in south Norfolk.[68] Another sizeable group of 158 people had emigrated six years earlier, but their destination is unknown.[69] They had originated from parishes close to Banham on the Norfolk/Suffolk border. Later, the Reverend Scott F. Surtees published the favourable letters he received from some of the Banham people who had left in 1836, in the hope of demonstrating the positive benefits of emigration. He told his parishioners how men who had "worked as labourers alongside of you a few years now have well-stocked farms of their own and write to you about the rates of wages *they* give *their* labourers."[70] One example was William Howse, who was living on a one-hundred-acre rented farm by 1851 and could afford to pay £3 per month plus room and board to a labourer in his employment.

The Docking Poor Law Union in north Norfolk also extolled its emigration successes that same year: "Most gratifying reports have been received," and it was felt that "any number of families may do well by emigration."[71] Ingoldesthorpe, a parish in the Docking Union, had people like the Cross family who were unable to provide for themselves. According to the parish officer, "they will soon become a serious burden to the parish ... [and] will emigrate in view to better their condition."[72] Also, a small group of twenty-three paupers from Heacham Parish, which included one family with fourteen members, were assisted by both their parish and local landowners to go to Upper Canada (Table 1),[73] while ninety paupers from North Creake and forty-seven from Snettisham were assisted by their respective parishes to emigrate to Lower Canada (Map 10).[74]

Many parishes in the Walsingham Poor Law Union, also in north Norfolk, lost substantial numbers to Lower Canada, with the largest numbers leaving from Great Ryburgh and Kettlestone.[75] Apart from a father and son who paid their own expenses, thirty-eight of the forty people who left Kettlestone were assisted. The group comprised seven labourers, together with their wives and children, a "soldier's wife" with her two sons, and two teenage servants.[76] They all might have been inmates of the Walsingham workhouse. Surviving bills suggest that they travelled in reasonable comfort.[77] Seventeen adults and twenty-three children sailed in the *Eliza Liddle* from King's Lynn in June 1836 to the British American Land Company's landing place at Port St. Francis, having received £231 from Kettlestone Parish to fund their emigration expenses (Table 2).

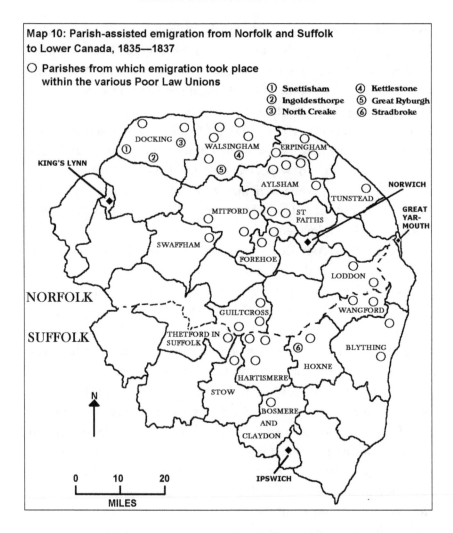

Map 10: Parish-assisted emigration from Norfolk and Suffolk to Lower Canada, 1835—1837

O Parishes from which emigration took place within the various Poor Law Unions

① Snettisham   ④ Kettlestone
② Ingoldesthorpe ⑤ Great Ryburgh
③ North Creake   ⑥ Stradbroke

Fares for their sea crossings cost £149, with an additional £51 of "landing money" being spent on onward travel from the port of Quebec. A total of £11 was spent in transporting the emigrants and their luggage by horse and buggy to King's Lynn. Their food and drink bill came to around £7, the sum including £4.14s. for teas, 16s. for supper at King's Lynn, 2s. 6d. for "wine, Goodwyn's wife," and 14s. 8d. for various beverages drunk at the Crown Tavern. Meanwhile, fewer people left for Lower Canada from north Suffolk, with the only substantial groups being the ninety-one paupers from Stradbroke Parish and the forty-eight from Redgrave Parish.

Arriving in the town of Sherbrooke, some forty miles to the southeast of Port St. Francis, the Norfolk and Suffolk arrivals would have contributed to the hectic scenes that Lucy Peel witnessed in the summer of 1836:

> The roads are now assuming the appearance of those in dear old England, thanks to the Company, which does everything in style, sparing neither labour nor money; they spend a thousand dollars a day in Sherbrooke. The town swarms with emigrants, five hundred more are coming up and buildings are raising their heads in all directions for their accommodation. Mr. Watson has full occupation, he has to visit the sheds twice a day and receives five dollars a day for his trouble; there is I hear to be a Hospital built.[78]

Courtesy Library and Archives Canada, e010858662.

Junction of St. Francis and Magog Rivers (Sherbrooke), from W.H. Bartlett, *Canadian Scenery Illustrated, from Drawings by W.H. Bartlett, the Literary Department by N.P. Willis* London: George Virtue, 1842. When she visited in 1840, Mary Chaplin noted the wooden houses along the side of a hill and the bridge over the Magog River. But she winced at the sight of the "horrid saw mill," which hid "the prettiest river scenery."[79]

Some of the assisted Norfolk and Suffolk immigrants would have acquired nearby company land in Sherbrooke County, but a substantial number made their way to Bury, one of the recently opened townships in the St. Francis Tract, farther to the north (Map 9).[80] Sufficient land would have been available in Bury for them to settle together in distinct communities, and those who settled at what became Brooksbury did particularly well.[81] Josiah Clarke, who arrived in Brooksbury from Suffolk in 1853, was amazed to see the progress that had been made by the early pioneers:

> Here is them that left England seventeen years back and have got cows, oxen and land of their own and a horse to ride on and when in England had not enough to eat and many might be better off than they are if they would work but they are too idle to. A man that will work can live here but a lazy man cannot, as here is no parish to go to.[82]

Several Norfolk-born farmers, including Charles Francis and Dennis Tite, who had both emigrated from Banham in 1836, had success stories to tell later on.[83] But in the 1850s, when the Reverend John Kemp, Bury's Anglican minister, observed his congregation, he found them to be "mostly English pauper emigrants who are as yet comparatively poor." Few were able to meet the interest payments on their land or settle the debts they owed to the local storekeepers, and he observed that "they have hard work to provide for their families."[84] Kemp was also highly critical of those who still had "the souls and minds of poor people" and failed to make sufficient contributions in support of the Anglican Church.[85] Some were clearly reasonably affluent. And as Kemp also observed, the more libertarian attitudes of the New World were blossoming:

> There is more freedom of intercourse less stiffness and formality — The very poorest of the people have a sort of independence about them — not always the most agreeable to a fresh arrival from England. They feel their *own*

importance for it not infrequently happens that a man having a hectare ticket (a sort of promise of sale) has a voice in the elections of all Municipal officers — and even in returning a minister of the provincial Legislature.[86]

Dudswell Township, to the east of Bury, acquired a large number of English inhabitants by the mid-nineteenth century, but they were mainly Americans of English descent. Their Anglican minister, the Reverend Thomas Shaw Chapman, described them as "the Americans by whom Dudswell was colonized 50 years ago."[87] By 1854, Chapman was presiding over a substantial church in Marbleton — "a wooden structure of the early English style of architecture … which can seat 225 people."

The English component of the population was also substantial at Eaton and Compton townships, to the southeast of Bury, but here again their Englishness probably derived mainly from an intake of Americans having English roots.[88] Unlike Dudswell, Eaton had little to offer an Anglican minister. Sending his report to the SPG in 1854, the Reverend John Dalziel complained bitterly: "I cut my own firewood, dig my own garden, for I have no glebe and neither horse nor cow.[89]

Courtesy The Bodleian Library, University of Oxford: USPG E Series.

Drawing made by the Reverend Thomas Shaw Chapman in 1856 of the village of Marbleton, showing the Anglican church.

Colonization of the Eastern Townships relied heavily on the extensive amount of capital that had been advanced by the British American Land Company. But its high spending was unsustainable, and by 1841 the company was close to bankruptcy. To deal with its massive debts, it was forced to hand over 500,000 acres of the St. Francis Tract to the government.[90] Settlers were then able to obtain fifty-acre portions of the land relinquished by the company as free grants from the government. Thus, immigrants could acquire land as before; however, they did not receive the financial support during their first winter that had been given to their predecessors. Despite the ease of obtaining land, the battle to attract, let alone keep, immigrants continued. In 1841, Quebec immigration agent Alexander Buchanan reported that, although "most favourable accounts" had been received from the Eastern Townships extolling job opportunities and good rates of pay, "it is very few who can be induced to go to that section of the province, their prejudices are so strong against our winter."[91]

In 1835–36, when nearly four thousand Norfolk and Suffolk people were assisted to emigrate to the Canadas, just under five thousand people arrived at Quebec from East Anglian ports.[92] This would suggest that 80 percent of the influx that occurred from these two counties during this peak period had been assisted. As stated earlier, around 1,200 of the assisted Norfolk and Suffolk immigrants went initially to Lower Canada, and a high proportion of those who remained almost certainly settled in the Eastern Townships.[93] Because they relied on public funding, their departure was well documented. But little is known about the outflow of people to the Eastern Townships from the rest of England, since they generally paid their way. Self-financed immigrants left virtually unnoticed, with few documents surviving for them. Thus, it is impossible to quantify them. General comments from Anglican and Methodist missionaries suggest that, apart from the large-scale East Anglian influx, relatively few English immigrants settled in the townships and those who did remain were widely scattered in the southern region. In other words, the Norfolk and Suffolk settlers represented a major proportion of the total immigrant stream from England.

Self-financed people arrived on their own or in small groups from many regions of England. Occasional comments from the Quebec immigration agent hint at their presence. In 1842 he mentioned, "passengers per the *Consbrooke* from Liverpool and the *Baltic* from Yarmouth, who are chiefly farmers and labourers; some respectable farmers in the former vessel are proceeding to settle in the Eastern Townships."[94] There would have been many more small groups like this. And odd references to people like the Hampshire-born William Hoste Webb, who emigrated when a child in 1836 and became a successful lawyer in Brompton Township (Richmond County), reveal a tiny snippet of a largely untold story.[95] Another example was the Bristol-born Edward Short, who was living in Sherbrooke by 1839; he, too, was a successful lawyer, and went on to become a judge of the Supreme Court of Lower Canada.

With the industrial expansion that occurred in the Eastern Townships during the second half of the nineteenth century, people had an added incentive to emigrate, although numbers were still relatively low. Arriving in Sherbrooke in 1889, Frank Grundy from Bury (Lancashire) became general manager of the Quebec Railway Company,[96] while Philip Harry Scowen from Ipswich (Suffolk), who arrived in 1909, rose through the ranks of the Brompton Pulp and Paper Company in Richmond County to become its general manager.[97] These success stories happened to find their way into family histories, but most immigrant experiences went unrecorded.

In 1867, people of British descent still predominated in Stanstead and Brome counties as well as in parts of Missisquoi, Richmond, Sherbrooke, and Compton counties. Yet, having previously dominated large areas of the Eastern Townships, people of British ancestry were a mere minority group by the 1940s. Many of their descendents had left and, when they did, French Canadians took their place. Upper Canada's better land and climate, the declining importance of the timber trade, and the rising dominance of French culture made Lower Canada progressively less attractive to later waves of British settlers. Thus the cycle intensified.

Mark James remembered that French and English communities in the Eastern Townships were comfortable with each other in the 1940s:

> I found French-English relations during the war were very good. Everybody said that there was no strain between the two languages, as then the two cultures were considered

very close. One woman spoke with great fondness of her relationship with her French neighbours. It seems that one particularly cold winter her well froze, and she had to collect and melt snow to wash her baby's clothes. One of the French neighbours saw her doing this and the next Saturday he brought his sled with a huge barrel of water on it. He had gone way back in the mountains to an open spring to get the water and continued to do this every Saturday until the well thawed in the Spring.[98]

Thirty years earlier, Robert Sellar, the outspoken Scottish journalist, provided a very different perspective. He was convinced that Protestant farmers had been deliberately squeezed out of the Eastern Townships by the Catholic Church.[99] A change in legislation in 1850 that allowed the Catholic Church to extend its parish system beyond the French seigneuries into the townships was proof, as far as he was concerned, of such a plot.[100] Thus, he blamed the French for the British exodus. However, his hostility toward the French was ill-founded. The simple truth was that the British sought the better economic opportunities that western Canada and the United States had to offer. Once their numbers had declined to the point where they could no longer support their Protestant schools and churches, they left. This pattern was repeated throughout Lower Canada.

Having colonized the southern stretches of Lower Canada, the English also set their sights on the enormous farming and timber trade opportunities to be had in the Ottawa Valley farther to the west. Here different challenges awaited them.

Table 1:

Paupers from Heacham Parish in Norfolk Who Sailed in May 1836 in the *Penelope* from King's Lynn
[NRO PD 699/90/5]

Name	Age	Fare	Landing Money Allowed
Garner, Francis	44	£5.15.0	
Garner, Mary	35	ditto	
Garner, Marian	11	£2.17.6	£8.0.0
Garner, Edward	10	ditto	
Garner, William	5	ditto	
Garner, Susanna	inf	free	
Jickling, Robert	42	£5.15.0	
Jickling, Mary	30	ditto	
Jickling, George	17	ditto	
Jickling, Robert	15	ditto	£10.0.0
Jickling, Sarah	12	£2.17.6	
Jickling, Mary	8	ditto	
Jickling, William	3	ditto	
Jickling, Elizabeth	inf	free	
Jickling, Valentine	29	£5.15.0	
Jickling, Mary	26	ditto	
Jickling, William	6	£2.17.6	£8.0.0
Jickling, Sarah	4	ditto	
Jickling, Robert	2	ditto	
Jickling, Martha	inf	free	
Melton, George	18	£5.15.0	£2.0.0
Williamson, William	31	£5.15.0	£2.0.0
Williamson, Matthew	25	£5.15.0	£2.0.0

Total sum paid £124.6.6. Of this the parish paid £84.7.6 and the landowners paid £40.0.0.

Table 2

Paupers from Kettlestone Parish in Norfolk Who Sailed in June 1836 in the *Eliza Liddle* from King's Lynn to Port St. Francis in the Eastern Townships [LAC MG24-I156–Emigration Records, Norwich]

Males	Age	Females	Age	Occupation of Head of Family
George Moore	40	Mary Moore	42	Labourer
George Moore	7	Mary Anne Moore	11	
Robert Moore	4	Eliza Moore	1	
		Anne Rustmore	15	Servant
Henry Goodwyn	38	Alice Goodwyn	39	Labourer
George Goodwyn	13	Ann Goodwyn	1	
John Goodwyn	11	Marie Green	3	
James Goodwyn	8	Ellen Green	11	
William Goodwyn	5	Eliza Allan	11	
Thomas Jackson	27	Elizabeth Jackson	29	Labourer
John Jackson	5	Phoebe Allan	4	
William Jackson	4			
		Elizabeth Holliday	23	Soldier's Wife
James Green	25	Anne Green	25	Labourer
Robert Allen	31	Bridget Allen	34	Labourer
George Allen	7	Harriett Harrison	1	
William Holiday	6			
Samuel Holliday	3			
Philip Jackson	22	Phoebe Jackson	23	Labourer
Robert Jackson	2			
William Allen	4			

Males	Age	Females	Age	Occupation of Head of Family
Thomas Harrison	25	Lucy Harrison	25	Labourer
William Green	16			

[Total of twenty-one males and seventeen females. Although people are listed in a confusing sequence, family groups are apparent.]

To be landed at Port St. Francis on the St. Lawrence River and located at the Township of Sherbrooke. Besides the above named, who went at the expense of the parish, Thomas Harrison Sen'r and his son James are also gone to Canada at their own expense, making the total forty persons.

June 15, 1836

CHAPTER 5

The Ottawa Valley

Generally the scene is beautifully wooded, opened only
here and there by some poor settlers scattered along ...[1]

L ORD DALHOUSIE'S JOURNEY up the Ottawa River by canoe in August 1820 gave him a bird's-eye view of the clearings being made by settlers in this border region between Upper and Lower Canada. The fifty-year-old governor-in-chief of Canada would have had his endurance tested to the full as he made his way along dangerous rivers and swamps and struggled with rough living and the perils of portage. Yet he was in his element. Although he complained about the heat and the intolerable mosquitoes, he experienced the adventure of a lifetime.

The settlers he noticed were mainly concentrated along the north side of the Ottawa River, in Lower Canada. The village of St. Andrews (Argenteuil seigneury) particularly caught his eye — "a thriving settlement" that already had "a very neat and tasty house" that had been built by a Scottish army officer.[2] Settlements had sprouted in the rest of the Argenteuil seigneury and in Chatham and Grenville townships just to the west of it and also in Hull Township, much farther to the west. Joseph Bouchette's survey of 1832 concluded that the north side of the Ottawa

River had fairly equal proportions of Irish and American settlers, with Scots being present in substantial numbers but less so the English, who were relatively few and far between.[3] However, when Dalhousie came twelve years earlier, there would have been fewer Irish, since they were just beginning to pour into the area at the time he visited. (1820)

By 1881, the English were concentrated mainly in the river frontage townships of Chatham and Grenville and in the villages of Lachute and St. Andrews in the future Argenteuil County (Map 11).[4] The English exceeded

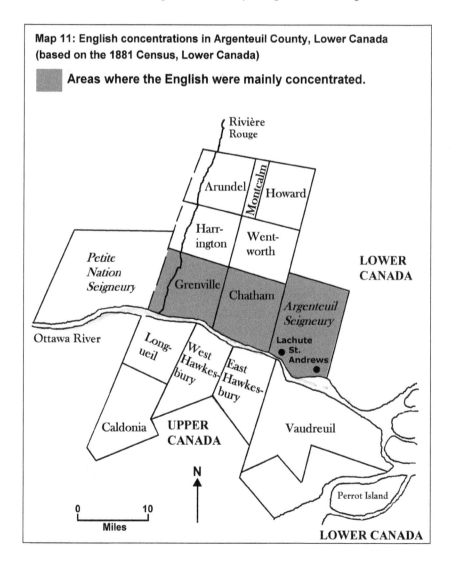

Map 11: English concentrations in Argenteuil County, Lower Canada (based on the 1881 Census, Lower Canada)

Areas where the English were mainly concentrated.

the Irish numerically in St. Andrews, but were second to the Scots. Generally, in the rest of the area, they came a poor third to both the Irish and Scots. The English presence owed a great deal to the stream of New Englanders who had begun to arrive in the 1790s, although a substantial number of immigrants also came directly from England starting in the 1820s. However, this was a trickle when compared with the large influx from Scotland that began in the 1800s and the much larger numbers that began to arrive from Ireland two decades later.[5] Also, because large numbers of Americans and Scots settled in the area during this early period, the Irish never dominated, as was the case in most other parts of the Ottawa Valley.

Anecdotal evidence suggests that a significant proportion of the English in Argenteuil County originated from Yorkshire. They included men such as William Shepherd, who emigrated to St. Andrews around 1825, having worked during his first year for the Reverend Joseph Abbott, the Anglican minister.[6] William's son Thomas clearly prospered, owning a "fine property" in Lachute by the late nineteenth century. John Hodgson, arriving with his father from Yorkshire in 1818 "when quite young," became apprenticed to Samuel Orr of Lachute, "to learn the trade of shoemaker," and with his earnings later purchased a farm in East Hawkesbury, on the south side of the Ottawa River. The barrister Joseph Palliser of Lachute had a Yorkshire grandfather who had emigrated to Lachine in 1832, and Samuel Edmund Smith, "one of the enterprising and leading farmers of Lachute," had a great-grandfather who came from Yorkshire and had been one of the first colonizers of Dunany (Wentworth Township), lying to the north of Lachute.[7]

Yorkshire tailors and cloth manufacturers had also been attracted to the area. Having emigrated from Leeds (Yorkshire) to Chatham around 1830, George Lindley sent for his father back in Leeds. His father "had been a cloth manufacturer, employing many hands," and when he came to Chatham, "he brought quite a quantity of fine broad cloths with him to sell. It is said he was a man of very prepossessing appearance." Also, nine years later, came Peter Webster, a Leeds tailor who settled in St. Andrews and continued his trade there.[8]

And Yorkshire people were in the forefront of the later colonization of Arundel Township, situated many miles inland up the Rivière Rouge

(Map 11).[9] When they first arrived in 1858, "Arundel was a terra incognita" — a district visited only by hunters and trappers. Having emigrated from Yorkshire in 1815, George Staniforth had spotted its potential. He persuaded his sons in Yorkshire to join him in 1858, and together they purchased around one thousand acres that year: "In about 10 years William [one of his sons] had cleared 100 acres of his tract, during which he manufactured many tons of potash, the greater part of which he sent to Montreal…. His first building was a shanty, but this was succeeded two years later by a house. In 1883 he erected a saw mill on his premises and the following year a grist mill."[10]

Then there were men like the Hampshire-born John Wainwright, a captain in the Royal Navy, who came in 1833 with his family to Carillon, near St. Andrews, where he acquired a four-hundred-acre farm: "Possessed as he was, of English ideas with regard to social status, and having been a naval officer, it is not surprising that he should have formed an exclusive circle and been regarded an aristocrat." Dr. Thomas James Howard from Exeter (Devon), who arrived in 1844 with his wife and twelve children, purchased a farm along the Rivière Rouge and later retired to Lachute. Henry, one of his sons, became a notary and leading public figure in St. Andrews. Then there was the opportunistic Nathaniel Burwash, a native of Kent, who used a legacy left to him by his mother to purchase land along the Rivière Rouge for himself and his sons, having first arrived at Carillon from Vermont in 1802.[11] As particularly noteworthy people who made good, these Englishmen were named in later histories, but the experiences of the majority who came to the area went unrecorded.

At the time of Lord Dalhousie's visit in 1820, immigrants were just beginning to arrive from Britain. He witnessed the steps that were being taken to make the region more secure and accessible to them. He noticed "emigrants at work on the [Grenville] Canal," one of a series of canals being built to navigate the Long Sault Rapids on the Ottawa River.[12] Six years later, work would begin on the Rideau Canal, which would link the St. Lawrence and Ottawa rivers. Ongoing fears following the War of 1812–1814 that Americans might attempt to seize control of the St. Lawrence led the British government to finance this major feat of engineering. Dalhousie did not witness the Rideau Canal's construction, but he arrived in time to see the many Scottish and Irish immigrants who were heading for the military settlements being established in the Rideau Valley to further bolster Upper Canada's defensive capability.

While Dalhousie seemed oblivious to the government's defence worries, he greatly approved of the military settlements. He believed that the organization and direction provided by the half-pay military officers who managed the settlements would assist newly arrived immigrants to find their bearings in what was to them a strange environment. Hopefully, it would encourage more of them to remain in Upper Canada rather than drift off to the United States:

> Hitherto we have not retained one third of the emigrants in the country. These people on arrival found so many impediments in their way and such monstrous fees of office before they could get to their land, that they could

Entrance of the Rideau Canal, Bytown, 1839. Watercolour by Henry Francis Ainslie (1803–79). The canal linked Kingston with Bytown (Ottawa) and was completed in 1832.

Courtesy Library and Archives Canada, C-000518.

neither surmount the one nor afford the other. The Americans availed themselves of these circumstances and easily persuaded the distressed wanders to pass over into the United States where all was said to be ready and abundant for them.[13]

Farther down the river, Dalhousie's group headed inland on an arduous twelve-mile journey to view George Hamilton's "extensive saw mills" located near Hawkesbury, on the south side of the Ottawa River.[14] Hamilton was one of the region's up-and-coming timber barons. Having established a major export/import business in Liverpool (England) by the early nineteenth century, he had moved his timber operations to North America when Baltic supplies were interrupted. With the closure of Baltic ports by Napoleon in 1806, and the large increase in tariffs on Baltic timber that followed, Canadian timber had a decisive cost advantage. Three years later, Hamilton announced that he had founded a "New Liverpool" site near Quebec that was ready to receive rafts of timber. In addition to exporting timber to Britain, partly in ships built at New Liverpool, Hamilton also sold timber at Quebec to feed its growing shipbuilding industry.[15] That year, when ninety thousand timber loads crossed the Atlantic, British North America accounted for almost two-thirds of the pine timber imported into Britain.[16] This compared with only twelve thousand loads that had been exported in 1804. As must have been obvious to Dalhousie, timber was being cut in this part of the Ottawa Valley, not as a by-product of land clearance, but as a commodity in its own right.

Proceeding west along the Ottawa River, Lord Dalhousie eventually "passed the little falls of the Rideau on our left and the mouth of the Gatineau on our right," reaching Philemon Wright's home at the Chaudière (or Great) Falls at 8.00 a.m. on Sunday August 20. This was to be a memorable visit for both:

> … on Sunday morning he [Philemon Wright] was in bed, not expecting us and when told that the Governor was arrived at his door, the old man was thrown into such a hurry, bustle and confusion that he was capable of

New Liverpool Cove, near Quebec City (Point Levy side). Watercolour by James Pettison Cockburn (1799–1847). Acquired by the Liverpool-based George Hamilton in 1809, New Liverpool became a shipbuilding site from which vessels loaded with timber were dispatched to Britain.

> nothing…. However, after we had seen him and shook hands and done away all ceremony he became quiet and easy, full of extreme politeness, attentions and anxiety to show himself delighted by the visit."[17]

To Dalhousie, the sixty-year-old Philemon was an "old man." However, the writer, John MacTaggert, who met him nine years later, made no mention of his age, describing him as "about 6 feet high, a tight man with a wonderfully strange, quick, reflective, wild eye."[18] Dalhousie was struck by Philemon's accent — "perfect Yankee from Boston" — and found his use of words strange and at times incomprehensible.[19] But he overcame his difficulties and listened intently as Philemon explained how he had been attracted by Hull's potential when he first saw it in 1798:

> In 1798 he [Philemon Wright] went back to his friends at Boston, told them what he had seen, sold his property,

brought his family and two associates to Montreal ...
and in 1800, having made all arrangements to have a
grant of land, he went directly up [the] Ottawa [River]
to the Gatino [Gatineau] with eight axe-men. There he
first sat down, built his house, cleared a good farm and
then, prospering well, he changed his situation to the
top of the Great Falls, which he thought a fine place for
mills and certainly of being valuable some day, never
expected to see them come to what they are.[20]

Wright had arrived with his family, four other families (three of whom
were related to Wright), and thirty-three single farm labourers, all from
Massachusetts, who together founded Columbia Falls village, the later
Wrightstown, which would evolve into the town of Hull. Wright's initial group was joined by other families, mostly from New England, who
included the fifty-seven-year-old Samuel Benedict and fifty-five-year-old
Nathaniel Chamberlin, both men of substance from Vermont, with an
eye for the future well-being of their children. Other Americans who had
previously settled along the Rideau River also gravitated toward Wright's
settlement. By 1802, Wright had built grist- and sawmills, and two years
after that was building various shops and industrial buildings, including
bake-houses and a tannery. During his first six years in Hull he claimed to
have spent $20,000.[21] By 1808 he had launched his lumber empire, which
would eventually make him one of the region's premier timber exporters.[22]

By 1817–18, Philemon Wright was employing sixty-three men in his
various enterprises and an additional fifty-five in his lumbering business.
Two years later, his firm, P. Wright & Sons, employed 58 percent of the
labouring men in Hull Township, and by 1824 Wrightstown (Hull) was
entirely owned by his firm. When John MacTaggert visited Hull in 1829,
he marvelled at how Wrightstown had become "a fashionable resort; a
splendid hotel was built, livery stables were well installed, a steam-boat
set a-going, flagstaff and bell erected ... and an armoury richly filled
with cannons, muskets and swords.... No one is more the father of his
people than he [Wright] is; when he has been from home any time on
his coming back guns are fired, bells are rung and flags [are] waved."[23]

As was noted by Robert Gourlay, who viewed the future Hull in 1822, Philemon had placed a high priority on establishing a successful agricultural community. The farms were "in a very respectable state of cultivation and progressive improvement…. Mr. Wright, as the head of the township, has been indefatigable in promoting the increase and prosperity of this infant settlement."[24] The timber trade was an important money-maker, but the settlement needed to be self-sufficient in terms of its food production. As if to demonstrate this point, Philemon took Dalhousie by horseback to see his farm, "where he showed us a very fine stock of cows and calves with a Herefordshire Bull from England. It is an establishment that would not disgrace any farmer in England although there is want of that cleanliness and arranged system that is obtained by good servants." They also visited the farm of one of Philemon's sons — Ruggles — "who is just returned from England with two bulls and several cows and calves of the best breed."[25]

Philemon Wright's settlement at Hull showing the sawmill in the centre and a three-storey tavern on the right. Painted by Wright's friend Henry DuVernet, active 1816–42.

Americans continued to trickle into the new settlement after the Napoleonic Wars ended, one of whom was Wright's nephew, Charles Symmes, who, arriving in 1816, acquired land six miles upstream of Hull and founded Symmes Landing — the future town of Aylmer. Some immigrants also began arriving from England, having been "fired by the accounts of the new country" given by Charles's cousin, the aforementioned Ruggles, "who had recently made a journey across the Atlantic."[26]

Some of the Englishmen who are known to have arrived by the 1820s were clearly recruited for their farming skills. They included: Richard Austin, "a good Yorkshire farmer"; Benjamin Simons, "a good farmer from Devonshire"; George Ruthly, "a good farmer from Devonshire"; and William Pitt, a "Devonshire farmer." Also present were Gardner and Girard Church, Thomas Wright, and Isaiah Chamberlin, who were each described as being a "good farmer" (Table 3).[27] They no doubt reflected Philemon's determination to see Hull's farming community flourish. By 1825, Wrightstown had a population of 803 and 108 heads of families, which included far-seeing and benevolent farmers like David Benedict.[28] David would give the farm that he had purchased from Philemon Wright in 1822 to his nephew Moses in 1855 as a wedding gift. Moses would then run it as a successful dairy farm for some forty years.[29]

William Farmer was another larger-than-life character who sought his fortune in Hull as Philemon Wright had done, only he was far less successful. Alexander Buchanan, the immigration agent at Quebec, had been given advance notice of his arrival in August 1834: "By the *Kingston* From Liverpool, a Mr. Farmer, strongly recommended to this Department, and family with some passengers; he proceeds for the present to Sorel. He has with him 50 head of live stock, of the most approved English Breed."[30]

Having sold his considerable estate in Shropshire, Farmer had left his home and proceeded to Liverpool with his family "in a large and roomy coach drawn by four fine grey horses."[31] He had chartered the *Kingston*, with its Yorkshire captain, a ship that offered the benefits of a cabin on deck with "sleeping berths, a sitting room and a dining room." No doubt intending to adopt the ways of a country gentleman in his new home, he brought particularly treasured items from his manor house, including two beds, a sideboard, a clock, and "barrels of china that included six Coalport dinner services, five to six dozen champagne glasses, dozens of wine glasses and various finger bowls and decanters." He also came with considerable livestock, including a grey stallion, a mare, two Durham bulls, two Hereford bulls, six cows, two rams, twenty-six ewes, ten dogs (pointers, bull terriers, and a fox terrier), and cocks and hens. "On stormy days the horses and cattle would be suspended in strong canvas slings from the underside of the deck above them and not a single animal was lost during the long sea journey [of 51 days]."[32]

William Farmer came from Sutton Maddock, in Shropshire, where his family had lived for generations. His prospects improved consider-ably in 1830 when he married his second wife, Eleanor Shelton Devey, daughter of Thomas Devey of Kingslow Hall, a wealthy lawyer who lived in the adjoining parish of Worfield. Soon after his marriage, Farmer decided to emigrate despite the strong misgivings of his mother-in-law and his own ultra-conservative views. This was a man who objected to the attempts being made in England and Wales to improve democratic representation through the parliamentary Reform Act (1832) and to the repeal of the wretched Corn Laws that favoured farmers and made the poor pay inflated prices. How he would cope with a country that believed in egalitarianism and shunned privilege would remain to be seen. Yet it is said that he "had considerable energy, so he decided that the best course would be to emigrate to Canada and start a new life there."[33]

In addition to his family and servants, Farmer brought ten families (forty-six people) with him from Sutton Maddock and nearby Brockton, probably his former tenants and servants. They included a lawyer, a tutor for his children, a housekeeper and nurse, a miller and wheelwright, a blacksmith, a gardener, a sawyer, a mason, a handyman, and various house servants.[34] Upon their arrival in Quebec, Farmer's group travelled on the *Canada* to Sorel, where they lived in temporary accommodation, with Farmer paying everyone's expenses. In November 1834, the group made its way to Hull.

Their ultimate destination was a 2,400-acre site, the future Farmer's Rapids, situated on the Gatineau River, just to the north of Hull and six miles from Bytown (Map 12).[35] The property consisted of both cleared

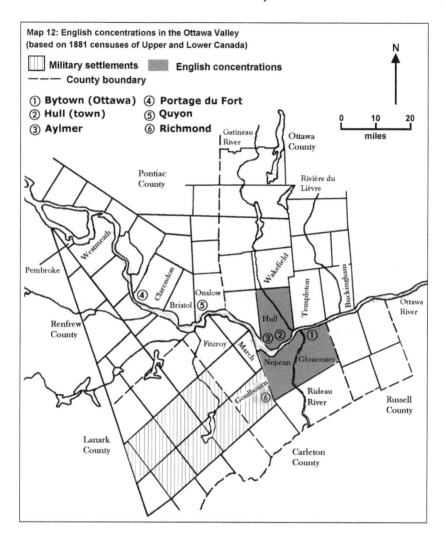

Map 12: English concentrations in the Ottawa Valley (based on 1881 censuses of Upper and Lower Canada)

land and untamed forests, and included "a house of extraordinary size, sufficiently large to hold all the people we brought out of England with us." The house was located directly opposite the rapids, being about a hundred yards from the first drop in the falls. Farmer had apparently chosen this place after taking advice from the agent of Tiberius Wright, one of Philemon's sons. Lying near the confluence of the Gatineau and Ottawa rivers, it would later become the site of an electricity-generating plant owned by the Gatineau Power Company.

During his first year, Farmer built a large sawmill, and two years later constructed a flour and gristmill, employing about one hundred people, who were in addition to the other workforce "who came out with him from England." A major dam was erected on the Gatineau River in 1843 and a new house was in place by 1844. That same year his sister, Mary Alice Farmer, issued a declaration in Shropshire stating that William's children from his first wife, Elizabeth Yates, who had died in 1827, had gone with him to Canada and were living in Hull.[36]

Having resettled all of his family and dealt with the legal aspects of their inheritance, Farmer established what appeared to be a thriving timber business. Initially, his prospects looked very promising. Yet he left, although his reasons for doing so are not clear. His dams suffered damage from spring floods and he had neighbours who objected to his use of the river "for the transport of his logs," but there must have been other factors. In 1848, fourteen years after his arrival, he moved to Upper Canada. Dying in 1880 in his eighty-sixth year, his final resting place was a cemetery in Ancaster, just to the west of Hamilton.

Hull Township, and the area immediately around it, would eventually have the largest English concentration in the Ottawa Valley, a hardly surprising development given Philemon Wright's success in attracting New Englanders since the 1800s and William Farmer's attempts to found an English colony three decades later. The early arrival of Loyalists and Americans of English descent had contributed to the English presence and so had immigration directly from England, although the extent to which either happened is not known. The 1881 Census reveals how the English became clustered in Hull Township, on the Lower Canada side of the Ottawa River, and in Nepean and Gloucester townships, located just opposite, in Upper Canada (Map 12).[37] That said, even in these townships there were four times as many Irish as English, reflecting the explosive growth in the Irish population after the Napoleonic Wars, as labouring jobs in canal building and timber cutting became more widely available.

A newspaper advertisement appearing in June 1829 reported that, in that month alone,[38] one thousand labourers were being sought to help

Courtesy Bibliothèque et Archives Nationales Québec ANQ.P80, S1, D22, P10.

Oxen pulling lumber in the Ottawa Valley. Undated photograph by an anonymous photographer.

in the building of the Rideau Canal, while two years later it was claimed that along one stretch of the Ottawa River some two thousand labourers were employed in the timber trade.[39] Such jobs were being filled largely by the thousands of poor Irish who streamed into the Ottawa Valley. By contrast, the English came in small numbers, often in ones and twos, either to establish themselves as farmers, craftsmen, or tradesmen, or to seek higher status positions in business, the professions, or in public life. Typical examples include the Cumbrian-born James Skead, who emigrated in 1832 and settled in Bytown, where he founded a thriving timber business,[40] and William and Charles Broughton Wilson (brothers) and their sister Jane, all from London, who emigrated to Fitzroy Township (Carleton County) two years later, presumably to establish a farm.[41] They were part of a steady trickle that must have seemed insignificant when compared with the Irish influx.

Oddly enough, the one place where the English did congregate and become the dominant ethnic group had the incongruous name of New

Edinburgh (Gloucester Township).[42] Founded by a Scot in 1829 at the junction of the Ottawa and Rideau rivers, New Edinburgh began life as an industrial centre but became a separate village in 1866. Soon after that, it was incorporated into Ottawa, by which time it had acquired the city's elite, who were primarily of English origin. New Edinburgh would eventually provide the site of the official residences of the governor general and the prime minister.

At the other end of the social spectrum were the Irish lumberjacks, who readily found employment in the region's thriving timber trade. Hiring and managing them were the timber contractors, who organized the felling and transport operations, and financing their operations were the merchants. After being cut, lumber was carried on rafts down the Ottawa River to the St. Lawrence and on to Quebec, where it was loaded onto ocean-going ships to be sold in Britain. Some merchants, like London-born William Price, were actually based in Quebec City, close to the seaport from which the timber would be dispatched.[43] Once the merchant received his money, the various contractors and lumberjacks involved in the complex felling and transport operations received their payments.[44]

James Moncrieff Wilson, general manager of the Queen Insurance Company in Liverpool, visited Ottawa in 1865 to witness for himself how the timber trade functioned:

> I was struck with the number of Inns and found they had sprung up out of the necessities of the timber trade. Most of the Lumberers are *furnished*, that is provided with the means of carrying on operations in the woods by people in Quebec and this furnishing is advanced by instalments, the first being used to buy provisions, clothes and other necessaries, and thus the lumberers are immediately out of money. But they must have men to do the work. At certain seasons thousands of men flock to Ottawa in search of employment in the woods. As a rule they arrive penniless but are hospitably received by the Tavern keepers who follow this line of business.[45]

Thus, at certain times of the year, such was the demand for labour that Ottawa innkeepers were hiring out their lodgers, who were invariably Irish, to work for local lumber contractors as lumberjacks. All this seems relatively peaceful and orderly. Had James Wilson arrived in the 1830s, he would have observed the widespread conflict that was then being engineered by the Liverpool-born Peter Aylen, one of the region's leading timber barons. Determined to dominate the timber trade at any cost, he set Irish and French labourers against each other and then moved the struggle to Bytown (Ottawa) in an attempt to seize control of the town. After much bloodshed, the violence was quelled by government troops in 1837.[46]

Meanwhile, with its substantial English population and rising affluence, Hull led the way in attracting the attention of the Society for the Propagation of the Gospel (SPG).[47] An Anglican missionary was installed in 1830 and the stone-built St. James Anglican Church was founded two years later.[48] The Reverend John B.G. Johnston was installed at Symmes Landing (Aylmer) in 1842 and, judging from his comment that "the lumbering draws away the majority of the male population from their homes for seven or eight months in the year," his congregations varied greatly in size.[49] Aylmer's Christ Church, a fine stone building, was built three years later, and it was from here that Johnston served his widely scattered flock, who were located as far afield as the Chaudière Falls, Farmer's Station [Rapids], and Wakefield.

Johnston's tenacity and endurance were severely tested in what were gruelling excursions through Hull and Aylmer's outback: "There are a great many Church families scattered over a wide extent of country with roads almost impassable over mountains of rocks through rivers without bridges, and swamps without even the assistance of logs laid across to prevent your horse from sinking in the mud."[50] However, judging from the gravestone transcriptions in the St. James (Anglican) cemetery in Hull, Johnston's "Church families" were mainly Irish. Among the minority who were English, there was a scattering of immigrants from Lincolnshire, Staffordshire, Northamptonshire, Kent, and Buckinghamshire, and a slight preponderance of people from northern towns and cities, including Bradford, Wakefield, Stafford, Leicester, and Manchester.[51]

As was the case elsewhere, most of Buckingham's early settlers along the north side of the Ottawa River had been either Loyalists or their descendents: "Lured by the proximity of Quebec province with its untouched forests of virgin pine, many enterprising citizens of the nearby New England states came to Canada and adventured their all in the lumber industry."[52]

Captain Justus Smith, who originated from New Hampshire, heard about the vast forests along the Rivière du Lièvre by picking up gossip in a hotel that he ran in Montreal. Arriving in Buckingham in 1823, he immediately built a sawmill and later returned to Montreal to recruit workmen, one of whom was Baxter Bowman. The cunning Bowman "slipped away to Montreal" unnoticed and returned as the legal owner of Smith's mill site "before the saw mill was in operation, even before it was finished." However, his treachery did not pay the dividends he had hoped, since "his debts caught up with him and the mill and other properties were taken over by the banks." It was a similar story for Levi Bigelow, another New Englander, who arrived in Buckingham in 1824. Having built his sawmill, he lost his business, which was purchased eventually by James MacLaren, who became the area's principal timber baron.

In 1854, when Anglican minister Reverend William Morris wrote his report to the SPG detailing his efforts in promoting the Anglican faith in Buckingham, the area had a mainly Irish and French population. The inhabitants of Buckingham village were chiefly employed as labourers in the timber trade and spent almost no time in farming: "Upwards of 400 men were employed in local [saw] mills and in the shanties and log houses in the woods."[53]

Although the timber trade attracted few English, the area experienced an influx from England in 1878 when the phosphate mines in the mountainous region of Portland Township were opened. Various English businessmen advanced the funds needed to run the phosphate mines and recruited experienced miners from England and Wales to do the work: "The community was a regular village of comfortable homes of which there is now not a trace, save some abandoned machinery and the caves drilled into the mountain…. The [English] gentleman in charge initially was Mr. Pickford…. His home there was the scene of many parties and dances and everything was on a grand scale."[54]

Courtesy Bibliothèque et Archives Nationales Québec ANQ P154, S1, D1.

Aylmer Anglican Church, built in 1845. Undated photograph by an anonymous photographer.

Courtesy Bibliothèque et Archives Nationales Québec ANQ P137, S4, D10, P3.

The Reverend John B.G. Johnston, circa 1860. He was an Anglican missionary who presided over congregations in both Aylmer and Hull from the 1840s.

At about this time, another Englishman, a Mr. I.A. Grant, claimed that he had "a phosphate property in Buckingham." He advised his friend, Colonel E.G.F. Littleton of Staffordshire, who had paid $5,000 for "phosphate lands" in Wakefield Township (north of Hull), to hold on to them. In 1881, mining was "said to be rigorous and the amount shipped this year will be greater than any previous year."[55] But as events would show, the boom years did not last, and following the discovery of abundant phosphate deposits in Florida, production ceased. The Buckingham mines were closed in 1894.

While the Rideau Valley attracted few English, it did acquire a large number of Scots when the government-sponsored military settlements were founded between 1815 and 1820. Concerned that the United States might attempt another invasion, the government had taken the previously unthinkable step of relocating hundreds of Scots at public expense to eight townships in Lanark County to found the Perth and Lanark military settlements (Map 12).[56] In return for having had their expenses paid, these Scots were to protect the Rideau Canal during its construction and be on hand to resist an invasion should one occur. Protestant Irish were also used to found another military settlement at Richmond (Carleton County) in 1818, although they were fewer in number than the Scots.[57] Despite this large intake of Scots, the Irish had exceeded the Scots numerically in Lanark County by the time of the 1881 Census, with the English coming a poor third.[58] And those English who settled in Lanark County were mostly to be found in the towns of Perth and Smiths Falls.

Despite there being relatively few English in the Rideau Valley, the Anglican Church was active in the region, having great success in attracting Protestant Irish to form the congregations for its churches. Predictably, the SPG took a particular interest in the Richmond military settlement. With its many retired, half-pay officers from the 99th and 100th Regiments having substantial army pensions, this was to become a relatively affluent district. Although most of the officers were Irish, they did include some English. The officers and their families, many of whom lived in March Township, enjoyed a high social status, regarding themselves as the region's elite.[59] In his report to the SPG in 1854, Richmond's

Photograph by Geoff Campey.

St. James Anglican Church, Beckwith, near Smiths Falls. The church is one of the oldest surviving Anglican churches in eastern Ontario.

Anglican minister stated that his small, scattered congregation owned very good farmland and he expected that "before many years the people will be wealthy."[60]

It was a similar story in Pontiac County on the Lower Canada side of the Ottawa River, where early arrivals from the New England states and Scotland were followed by waves of Irish settlers who had either migrated from elsewhere in the region or directly from Ireland.[61] However, although the English were only few in number, they had grabbed some of the best locations for themselves, being particularly well-represented in the village of Quyon in Onslow Township, in Bristol Township, and in Portage du Fort and Shawville in Clarendon Township.

The Anglican minister, the Reverend Henry Hazard, tended to the "hardy pioneers from the north of Ireland" from his base at Quyon in Onslow Township from about 1857. A place with ten houses, its chief industry was "the collecting of all logs which were floated down the Ottawa River from the many lumber camps in the vicinity of its banks."[62] Arriving in 1842, Clarendon's first Anglican minister, the Reverend Francis Falloon, witnessed the large influx from the north of Ireland over the following decade.[63] They were later said to have done much better than most other settlers in Lower Canada, thus enabling the Anglican Church to be well-funded. Meanwhile, Methodist ministers had also arrived in Onslow and Clarendon townships starting in the 1830s, although their support was strongest on the Upper Canada side of the Ottawa River, where Methodist preaching circuits had been established in the early 1800s.[64] Pontiac County Methodists clearly struggled to find the funds for their churches. The Ebenezer Church at Radford (near Shawville in Clarendon Township) was built in the second half of the nineteenth century by "old Methodist people," who had previously held their Sunday worship in the bush.[65]

Although Renfrew County on the south side of the Ottawa River attracted few English, there were pockets of English settlers in the northern end of the county, particularly in Westmeath and Pembroke townships. Westmeath had been the choice of James Tate of Bedfordshire, who emigrated with his wife and family in 1857. They were among the 478 people who had sailed from Liverpool in the *Martin Luther* to Quebec in July of that year, joining "the early settlers, who were few in Westmeath, and there were only six homes in the village."[66] The family resided first on the River Road below Westmeath, at a time when James was employed by Captain Findlay. Then, having moved to Ottawa for four years, the family returned to Westmeath "to live in a small log house on the farm of David Chamberlain," with James "being employed by this same gentleman." Finally, James's days as a hired hand came to an end. Having acquired 135 acres of "bush-land" in 1872, he "commenced clearing the ground for a farm," and would eventually become a prominent and respected Westmeath citizen.

Other English almost certainly emigrated to this area during the 1850s and 1860s. By the time of the 1881 Upper Canada Census, Westmeath and the adjoining Pembroke Township both had a particularly high concentration of English inhabitants, although, as ever, they were in a minority when compared with the Irish.

Along with everyone else, the English had benefited from the economic opportunities that had arisen from the thriving Ottawa Valley timber trade. But they shunned the logging camps and regarded timber felling as the means to creating farms, not as an economic end in itself. James Tate was fairly typical. He came with little or no capital, yet had sufficient farming skills and experience to navigate his way through the jobs market to the point where he had saved sufficient money to buy his own land. As they discovered the far better farming land to be had in Upper Canada, the English would transform vast wildernesses into farms and integrate themselves in the agricultural communities being established farther west.

Table 3:

An Account of the First Settlement of Hull Township, 1820
[ANQ P1000, D2, P278 (C141)]

Settlers	Date of Military Location Tickets	Comments
Joseph Badham	Jan. 13, 1820	Settled as a farmer
John Willson	ditto	Nothing done to my knowledge
Francis Morrell	ditto	Nothing done to my knowledge Extended to 25th October by Sec'y General
Charles Thomson	ditto	Not James Thomson as stated in location ticket. Raftsman and farmer.
John Snow	ditto	Wheelwright and farmer
John Hayworth	ditto	Raftsman and farmer
Richard Austin	ditto	A good Yorkshire farmer
Christopher C. Wright	ditto	Settled as a farmer
John Rogers	ditto	Raftsman
John Ball	ditto	Raftsman and farmer
Benjamin Simons	ditto	A good farmer from Devonshire
Colin Redman	ditto	Cabinet maker and farmer
George Ruthly	ditto	A good farmer from Devonshire
John Fromholte	ditto	A good farmer
Col. Duscheney	ditto	

Settlers	Date of Military Location Tickets	Comments
Alex'r Christy	ditto	Nothing done to my knowledge
W'm Smith	ditto	Raftsman
J. S. McConnelley	ditto	Raftsman
Robert Barmer	ditto	Raftsman
Wm Cook	ditto	Raftsman
James Cliton	July 20	Raftsman
Ruggles Wright	ditto	All patented and large Improvements on the same [sic]
Harvey Hardiman	ditto	Shoemaker and farmer
Charles Hardiman	ditto	ditto
John C. Eaton	Settled about the year 1822	Millwright/farmer
Gardner Church	ditto	Good farmer
Rob't Moore	ditto	Farmer and raftsman
Wm. Pitt	ditto	Devonshire farmer
John Chamberlin	ditto	Farmer and carpenter
Joseph Hudson	ditto	Farmer
Thomas Wright	ditto	Good farmer
Nathaniel Shawcross	ditto	Farmer and carpenter
Isaiah Chamberlin	ditto	Good farmer
James Thomson	ditto	ditto
Christopher Alloan	ditto	ditto
Thomas Oatley	ditto	ditto
Samuel Eady	ditto	ditto
Joseph Booth	ditto	Carpenter and farmer
Elisha Sheffield	ditto	Farmer
Charles Walker	ditto	Farmer
T. Brigham	ditto	Farmer
Girard Church	Settled about the year 1824	Good farmer
Wm. Dunlop	ditto	Farmer and saddler
Thos Buck	ditto	Carpenter
John Allen Jnr.	ditto	Farmer and raftsman
Thos. Ames	ditto	Farmer
— Bradley	ditto	Farmer

CHAPTER 6

West Along Lake Ontario

There are people here, who came out as poor as we did,
who have now their cows and oxen, sheep, pigs, etc, in
short everything a heart can wish for …[1]

WILLIAM AND JANE Grant were dumbfounded by the "whole mass of woods" that greeted them on their arrival in Dummer Township (Peterborough County), located as it was many miles inland from Lake Ontario. Nevertheless, they felt optimistic about their future. Having emigrated in 1831 at public expense from Frome in Somerset, they now had the prospect of owning their own farm — the ultimate goal of once-destitute people wishing to better themselves. "Never a township has filled so fast as Dummer — a house on almost every 100 acres." Unlike "a man from [Maiden] Bradley" in Wiltshire, who was returning home, Dummer being "too hard work for him," they were definitely staying. And worried that the unnamed gentleman would give Dummer a bad name, they warned their parents and friends not to believe him.[2]

The Grants' relocation to Dummer Township partly reflected the British government's desire to promote settlement in the more remote stretches of Upper Canada. By the time they arrived, much of the easily

accessible land along and just north of Lake Ontario had long been settled. The Loyalist influx of the mid-1780s, together with later emigration
from the United States, had created an initial nucleus of colonizers. A
typical example was Timothy Rogers, who had led a group of families
from Connecticut to Newmarket (York County) in 1801. Rogers and the
group then moved to Pickering (Ontario County) six years later, where
they finally settled. Particular encouragement had been given to members of the Society of Friends (Quakers), with Rogers donating land that
he owned in Pickering to enable them to build their first Meeting House.[3]
Many more Americans, coming in small groups like this, had found their
way to Northumberland, Durham, and York counties by the early nineteenth century and were even penetrating the Lake Simcoe area (Map
13). The settlers of East Gwillimbury, Vaughan, and Markham townships
in York County were described in a government report of 1830 as being
"affluent farmers," having come from the United States at an early date.[4]
This observation could have applied equally well to the entire stretch
between Kingston and the western end of Lake Ontario.

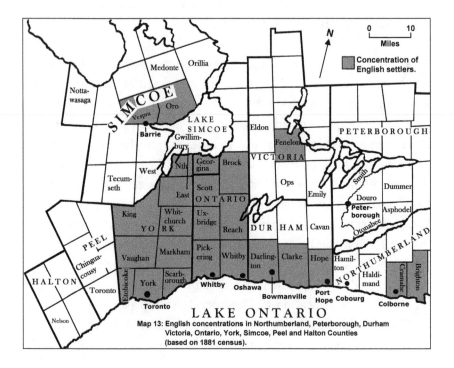

Map 13: English concentrations in Northumberland, Peterborough, Durham
Victoria, Ontario, York, Simcoe, Peel and Halton Counties
(based on 1881 census).

The deep economic recession that followed the Napoleonic Wars stimulated the initial influx from England, which began in 1817 and mainly drew people from the northern counties. As James and Ann (Gardiner) Emerson from Weardale (County Durham) in the northeast of England would soon discover, crossing the Atlantic at this early time certainly had its perils. Setting sail for Quebec with their extended family in 1817, they had to endure two shipwrecks — one at the Orkney Islands and the other near Newfoundland. Then, upon reaching the Gulf of St. Lawrence, they found that no steamer was available to take them up the St. Lawrence — so they had to purchase their own bateau and navigate themselves to Quebec. After living in Kingston for two years, the family finally settled in Cavan Township (Durham County), near present-day Millbrook, where they experienced the gruelling demands of pioneer life:

> The people did not clear their land very fast, about four to five acres each year. As soon as there was any grain to dispose of they had to take it to Port Hope; they drew it with oxen and were two days getting away a small load. Many of them succeeded in securing happy homes for themselves and families, others got discouraged and left for other places; while some got the ague and others fever and a number of them died.[5]

Cavan continued to attract English northerners, especially those from Cumberland County.[6] An example is John Bland from Carlisle (Cumberland), who arrived in the 1850s having failed to find suitable employment in the United States. He had lost his job as a tunneller in Pennsylvania and, after failing to find work in New York State, came to Cavan with just £6 10s. in his pocket. With the help of a Cumberland acquaintance already established in Cavan, he secured a labouring job with John Sutcliffe, a local farmer. Together with the money he expected to acquire at this same time from the sale of a property in Kirkoswald, near Carlisle, he was well-placed to establish himself eventually as a farmer.[7] However, the largest outflow of Cumberland people to Upper

Canada came from nearby Alston, an important lead-mining district, and that stream was directed at Peterborough County.

The first people to leave Alston took advantage of the government's £10 emigration scheme, introduced in 1817, which was intended to encourage colonization by groups of emigrants acting together.[8] Led by Thomas Milburn, an unknown number of Alston people relocated themselves to Smith Township (Peterborough County), and fifteen years later another group left Alston for Upper Canada, having been assisted by their parish (Table 4). They almost certainly settled at Smith.[9] John Langton, an English gentleman farmer who lived near Sturgeon Lake in Victoria County, visited the area in 1835 and described the strong Cumberland presence:

> The junior branches of the Cumberland settlement in Smithtown, near Peterborough, which has been 10 or 15 years in the country and is very thriving, are to have land in the new township on Balsam Lake.... [The] next emigration in 1823 was of Cumberland miners who settled along [the] road from Mud Lake to Peterborough and one of the most thriving settlements in the district; it is of their children that the settlement is forming on Balsam Lake; there are also several Yorkshire and other English in the township and another batch of Peter Robinson's Irish settlers in the northern part ...[10]

People from Newark, in Nottinghamshire, had also been attracted by the government's £10 emigration scheme and came to Peterborough County at around the same time as the Cumberland group. Led by Francis Spilsbury, they chose a site in Otonabee Township. Following them, between 1819 and 1824, was a group from Carlton-on-Trent, near Newark, who were assisted to emigrate by their parish.[11] A chance reference to Hannah Parnham in a letter written in 1832 by W. Mozley, her former teacher, places one other Nottinghamshire immigrant in Pickering Township, farther to the west in Ontario County. Before she had emigrated, Mr. Mozley advised her "to love Jesus Christ and hate

all sin; you know something about religion but you must feel its power
on your heart; you will meet with many unpleasant circumstances in
life — nothing will bear you up through them like heart-felt religion. Be
constant in prayer ... never neglect your Bible, read it in preference to
your books.... Early become a member of a Christian church ... obey
your parents and avoid improper companions."[12] Whether she heeded
this advice is unknown, but she did marry James Parnham, an immigrant like herself, who originated from Sutton-on-Trent.

During the 1820s, some 75 percent of English emigrants departed
for Quebec from northern ports (Table 5). Given that Liverpool departures accounted for surprisingly few, at 16 percent, only a small part of
the exodus came from the Midlands; instead, it was concentrated in the
northern counties. Cumberland and Yorkshire immigrants stand out
as being particularly predominant at this time and were certainly very
much in evidence in the middle stretches of Upper Canada. English
northerners had established footholds at Cavan (Durham County) and
Smith (Peterborough County) by 1820 and had done the same in Simcoe
County. Twenty-five families from the North of England were among
the first to settle in Oro and Vespra townships and northerners also colonized areas of Medonte, Tecumseth, and West Gwillimbury townships
(Simcoe County).[13] A will made in 1861 by Joseph Hodgson of West
Gwillimbury reveals his ongoing links with Cumberland, in that he left
his estate to each of four daughters who were then living in Carlisle.[14]
Thirty years earlier, Alexander Buchanan, the Quebec immigration
agent, reported how the settlements at Lake Simcoe had been proceeding "with great success and rapidity," and he also commented favourably
on "the influx of emigrants and the great extent of improvements" in the
Peterborough and Rice Lake area. These developments, which Buchanan
regarded as "highly cheering," had involved many English northerners,
although very few revealed themselves through any documentation.[15]

A journal kept by George Pashley, a twenty-seven-year-old tailor and
Methodist lay preacher from the West Riding of Yorkshire, reveals something of the traumas and difficulties that immigrants experienced when
they relocated themselves to North America. Setting off from Liverpool
to Quebec in 1833 with his wife Elizabeth (Frith) and family, George

Log house in Orillia Township (Simcoe County). Watercolour and pencil painting produced in 1844 by Titus Ware Hibbert (1810–90).

described how, during the early stages of the crossing, they had to come to terms with the death of their youngest daughter following a sudden illness: "About 9.00 o'clock [in the morning] the shipmate sewed the body up in canvas with some pig iron at the feet to make it sink and about 11.00 it was committed to the Deep with becoming solemnity, while the captain read the service and the sailors and the passengers on deck stood around with hats off." Later, George indicated how pleased he was that many of the fifty-eight passengers on the crossing were northerners like himself, originating from Yorkshire, Lincolnshire, Nottinghamshire, and Scotland, but he took an instant dislike to the Irish, describing them as "filthy." He was equally abusive toward the six French boatmen, whom he had met during the bateau voyage from Montreal to Prescott: "some of them had very bad tempers, and all [were] without religion."[16]

Upon arriving in the town of Cobourg (Northumberland County), the Pashleys went to a boarding house that was run by a fellow Yorkshireman. Although Mr. Dobson, a baker and confectioner from Whitby, had probably been recommended to them, they were very unimpressed with their lodgings: "For this single room we paid $3 a month. Here we lived five weeks during which time we had little of the comforts of life as regards food; we went for several days and had nothing but potatoes and salt and tea without sugar or milk."[17]

George's search for work took the family to a place near Grafton (Haldimand Township), but by 1836 the family returned to Cobourg, where George practised his trades as a tailor and shoemaker and also preached. Among his Methodist preaching companions were R. Jones and T. Bevitt, "the former a Canadian of Yorkshire parents, the latter a real Yorkshireman" from the West Riding who had emigrated to America twelve years earlier."[18] By 1849, the Pashley family was living in Port Hope (Durham County).

Two Yorkshire farmers caught the eye of the Quebec immigration agent in 1839 when they stepped off their ship from Hull. They were not recent immigrants, but instead were "returning to their families in the neighbourhood of Toronto, where they have settled for many years; they have brought out a number of their friends with them who intend to purchase lands and settle in their neighbourhood."[19] A year later he commented on the Yorkshire families living in Markham Township (York County) who had sailed back to England to collect their families and "some very fine sheep and a young Yorkshire colt." Many who sailed with these families from Hull were very affluent, bringing out between £1,200 and £1,500 collectively; but they also included some young men who had lost their jobs in the Yorkshire woollen mills and were "going to Boston for employment in the factories there."[20]

Isaac Bravender was yet another Yorkshireman made good. Originally from Malton in the North Riding, he had adapted easily to pioneer life and by 1846 was singing the praises of Brock Township (Ontario County) to his children still in Yorkshire:

> The sons and daughter that came over with us has bought
> a place about a mile and a half and they had about 200
> bushels of apples and plums in abundance, we have a cow
> and a heifer that we are raising and I bought two ewes
> this Spring ... we have two fat pigs ... I am doing very

well better than I expected for I have very good friends
around me; we had eight ploughs, ploughing some sod
for me belonging to the neighbours in one day. I intend
to have a yoke of oxen in another year if all is well ...[21]

Isaac had purchased eight acres of cleared land and two acres of wilderness land "with a good creek ... and dwelling house on it" for £120.
Declaring that Canada was "a very good country for a labouring man,
for wages are very high; a steady man may get 3s. 9d. per day in summer
and 2s. 6d. per day in winter," Isaac's only complaint was that "whiskey
is too cheap."[22]

Isaac's son wrote home soon after from Vaughan Township (York
County) with an even more upbeat message: "We thank God that we are
in a fine part of the country amongst old neighbours of the Old Country."
He now had a larger farm "and a much more healthy situation with better land ... and more like the Old Country all together," with his neighbours including Robert Hall, James Craven, Thomas Fletcher, and James
Monkman — all Yorkshire people. "If any friends should be wishing to
come to Canada my advice to them is not to go back to the 'Wild Bush'
but to come to the Gore of Toronto or Vaughan where they will be sure
to find some farms to rent or buy."[23]

The Bravenders were well-organized and had planned their land
clearance and farming activities with great care and precision. Isaac's
advice that immigrants had to be able to support themselves for the
first year underscores the scale of the task that was being undertaken.
John Langton's recipe for success was even more daunting. Coming from
an aristocratic Yorkshire family that had lost much of its great wealth,
he was every inch the gentleman farmer.[24] Buying land in Fenelon and
Verulam townships on Sturgeon Lake, he had arrived in 1833 with sufficient capital to buy a farm with cleared land and employ "a good man."
He advised: "In my opinion a man with a family, unless he has boys old
enough to assist him and unless he is determined to work hard for himself — and indeed determined that he and his boys should do the main
part of the work themselves ... he should not attempt to settle on a farm
in Canada with less than £1,000, and even with that he must use great

economy."[25] This advice would have seemed very challenging to those people who could barely scrape together the funds to emigrate. Most pioneer farmers had to do their own heavy labouring work and endured great hardships and privations during their first years.

Anne Langton, John's sister, could barely comprehend her surroundings when she first arrived in 1837 with her parents. She nearly fainted when she viewed Peterborough for the first time. Then a well-established hub with a population of about nine hundred, to her it was shockingly primitive. But Anne had lived in Blythe Hall, a grand house in Lancashire, and so the comparison for her was particularly daunting. Anne and her family had been adjusting to reduced circumstances following the demise of her father's business. Their stately home had to be sold in 1821 and bankruptcy came five years later. It was at this time that Anne helped the family finances by selling her miniature paintings, for which she rightly became famous. The family emigrated in difficult circumstances, although there was clearly sufficient capital for them to buy an already-cleared farm and employ labourers and servants.

Anne's first home on Sturgeon Lake was a small cabin built by her brother John. The family used it as temporary accommodation until John had time to complete their big house, the first double-storey log house in the area. It was called "Blythe" after the Lancashire Blythe Hall.

Soon after arriving, Anne wrote home to her family, disguising her anxieties and trying to be very brave:

> And now you will ask what I think of the spot that has been so much talked of.… What most strikes me is a greater degree of roughness in the farming, buildings, gardens, fences and especially roads.… But when one looks at the wild woods around, and thinks that from such a wilderness the present state of things has been brought about by a few hands … one's surprise vanishes, and one wonders that so much has been done.[26]

In fact, she later admitted how much she had disliked the place: "I shall never forget my feeling of despair at that time." Perhaps the family

Courtesy Archives of Ontario, F 1077-8-1-4-22.

Interior of John Langton's house, 1837. Drawing by Anne Langton.

had been rash "to come out to such a place, but we are very careful in writing home to say as little of our difficulties as possible."[27]

But Anne overcame her woes and became a pillar of her local community. The first schoolteacher in Fenelon Falls and Sturgeon Lake, she gave classes at her home and founded the area's first lending library. Later, she purchased land on which the first public school was to be built. John's political career was on the rise by 1852, and this required the family to move to Peterborough, then quite different from the town Anne had first viewed fifteen years earlier. Now there were "comfortable houses ... that graced tree-lined streets; and an imposing Court House was prominently situated on rising ground."[28]

The Peterborough area was fortunate in having two other talented ladies who, like Anne Langton, left behind heartfelt descriptions of pioneer life. They were two sisters from a gentile Suffolk family — Catherine Parr Traill, who emigrated with her husband Thomas in 1832, and Susannah Moodie, who followed soon after. Both became very

Courtesy Archives of Ontario, F 1077-8-1-2-28

Blythe Mills, Peterborough, 1852. Watercolour by Anne Langton. The mills were purchased by her brother John to supplement his income as the Member of Parliament for Peterborough.

well-known for their evocative tales of everyday life in early Canada.[29]

The emigrant streams from England changed dramatically in direction by the time that the Langtons came to the Peterborough area. By that time emigrants were being drawn more or less equally from the north and south (Table 5). Before then, northerners had dominated, as was noted by the *Montreal Gazette*, which claimed that most emigrants came "almost exclusively" from Yorkshire, Lancashire, "and other northern shires."[30] However, in 1832, as many as ten thousand immigrants left southern ports compared with only seven thousand from northern ports. One factor that helped to drive the growing exodus from the south was the use of public funds by parish councils to finance the emigration expenses of their paupers. This was essentially a South of England phenomenon. Parish-funded schemes brought thousands of paupers to Upper Canada, with most originating from the mainly agricultural counties of Norfolk, Suffolk, Sussex, Kent, Wiltshire, Somerset, and to a lesser extent Surrey.[31] Apart from Yorkshire, these schemes were rarely used in the more industrialized regions of the Midlands and northern counties, which could offer better work alternatives to people who were suffering from the general agricultural depression.

Assisted emigration schemes were intended to provide paupers with an escape from poverty while reducing parish poor rates bills, but their aim was not solely economic. If English parishes had sent their poor to the Maritime provinces instead of Upper Canada, their costs would have been much lower, since they would not have had to pay for the added expense of inland travel. The British government's defence concerns almost certainly explain why parishes paid for the more expensive option of sending their paupers to the Canadas. Ongoing fears of an attack from the United States made the government mindful of the need to bolster their populations with loyal British settlers. This was especially necessary since many self-funded emigrants were rejecting Upper Canada in favour of the Maritimes on cost grounds; but by assisting paupers to go the extra distance, more English settlers could be acquired by the province than would otherwise be the case. The five thousand or so people who were assisted to emigrate in both 1831 and 1832 accounted for 30 percent of the total arrivals from England each year, and assisted emigrants were a similar proportion in 1835–36.[32]

Parish-assisted emigration schemes were generally successful, mainly because parishes made every effort to ensure that their paupers would be able to cope well with the tough conditions to be found in fledgling pioneer communities. They did not use the schemes as an opportunity to get rid of their elderly, infirm, or layabouts, as might have been expected, since it was obvious that such people would fail. Parishes carefully selected families with plenty of teenagers and chose young and healthy single men; they had the best chance of success and their favourable reports home would stimulate the follow-on emigration that parishes hoped to foster.

The policy of directing poor emigrants to Upper Canada was championed by the lieutenant governor, Sir John Colborne, who had become increasingly alarmed by the continuing influx of Americans to the province. Colborne argued that Upper Canada's prosperity and welfare depended on the acquisition of large numbers of British immigrants.[33]

Although he and others had failed to persuade the British government to finance national emigration schemes because of their enormous cost, backing had been given to English parishes to use their poor relief funds to subsidize the emigration of their paupers. Arriving in substantial numbers, they were a useful addition to a colony having many American settlers, whose loyalty to Britain was suspect.

Although the legislation allowing parishes to sponsor emigration did not come into force until 1834, many parishes had assisted paupers since the 1820s, with Kent parishes being some of the earliest to do so. Several Kent parishes, including Tenterden, Headcorn, and Biddenden, began sending emigrants to the United States in the 1820s. Tenterden paupers left in small groups between 1821 and 1827, followed by a larger group of fifty-six in

Sir John Colborne, lieutenant governor, 1828–36. Engraving, made in 1864 of a painting by James Scott in the United Services Club. It was later published in London.

1828,[34] while Biddenden paupers emigrated between 1826 and 1845, with only small numbers, usually one family, leaving in any particular year.[35]

A further group of thirty-nine paupers (eight families) from Stockbury Parish in Kent County were assisted to emigrate in 1837 to Whitby Township (Ontario County), but they had apparently been somewhat reluctant to leave (Table 6). The Reverend Twopenny, who organized their departure, claimed that their connections with already-established Stockbury people living in "New Whitby" made them more receptive to the idea: "Now they really desire to [go] … and more would go next year. Some are respectable and some we shall be glad to be rid of." Perhaps there was an element of truth in Twopenny's final comment.

Three years earlier, some Stockbury paupers had placed conditions on emigrating — possibly sensing the parish's desire to be rid of them. Jesse Stunden said he would emigrate with his wife and eight children "on condition that the parish will pay the expenses of the passage and £50 on his landing in America" — the parish agreed to offer £30 and he is to consider; James Burn said he "would emigrate with his wife and four children if the passage was paid and he was given £30 on landing" — the authorities offered £18, which he declined initially, but later changed his mind; George Kitney, a single man, wanted his passage plus £5, but the parish only offered £3, which he declined.[36] These paupers would only emigrate if sufficient money was offered. Certainly the parish had been very generous in funding the 1837 group, which was given expenses of about £250 — roughly £30 per family — to cover the cost of passages and a clothing allowance.[37] Five years later, the Quebec immigration agent noted the arrival of around 240 paupers, mainly from Kent, many of whom planned to settle with friends who were already ensconced on the northwest side of Lake Ontario or to the west of Hamilton. They also were well-funded, having "received a free passage to Montreal with two day's provisions, and 20s. to each adult on leaving the ship."[38]

As was very much in evidence in Kent, changing work patterns and a growing economic recession were creating particularly distressing conditions for the poor in some English counties. On his travels through Somerset during the 1820s, the anti-emigration campaigner William Cobbett called at the town of Frome, where he noticed "between two and three hundred weavers, men and boys, cracking stones, moving earth and doing other sorts of work, towards making a fine road into the town.... These poor creatures at Frome have pawned all their things, or nearly all. All their best clothes, their blankets and sheets; their looms, any little piece of furniture that they had, and what was good for any thing."[39] Cobbett, who believed that he was championing the cause of the English agricultural labourer, railed against schemes that removed able-bodied workers while leaving behind what he called "the idlers, pensioners, and dead-weights."[40] Like many others, he argued that labourers, no matter how poor, were the life-blood of the country and that under no circumstances should they be assisted to leave. However, believing in a golden age that had never existed, he was somewhat removed from reality. In addition to the continuing demise of traditional agricultural labouring jobs, the decline in local woollen cloth-making was throwing even more people out of work, thus intensifying the already high level of social distress.[41] There was a surfeit of destitute labourers and cloth workers who needed help, and emigration at least offered the hope of a new start and a better life.

The parish of Corsley in Wiltshire, just to the east of Frome, was the first to opt for assisted emigration, doing so in 1830, raising £300 in assisting sixty-six of its paupers, with some of the money being provided by local landowners. The parish of Frome followed suit in 1831, spending £300 on funding the emigration of eighty-five poor people:[42]

> Around 200 people including their families had applied and from these were selected 13 heads of families, 13 married women, 4 young men under 20, 27 daughters and 28 sons going with their parents.... No influence was used ... everyone went entirely of his own free choice, with local people helping them with provisions and clothing; In the night of 21st March, 1831, 85 men, women and children left with their baggage set out in seven carriages, preceded by a band of music. Three proper persons accompanied them to preserve order and attend to their wants.... The women were in tears at the thought of parting forever from their native country.[43]

Apparently, one family went back to Frome, "where they were received as unwelcome visitors, having prevented others from going who would have gladly taken their places."[44] Correspondence from the Frome immigrants, which must have been highly favourable, was widely circulated and had the desired effect of helping to stimulate further emigration. In the following year, 156 paupers emigrated, costing the parish £600, with many being related to people in the earlier group.[45] Their letters home, written in 1831 and 1832, were published by J.O. Lewis, one of several local proponents of Frome emigration.[46]

The 1830 departures from Corsley had been an important catalyst in the sense that a substantial number of people from the neighbouring parishes of Frome in Somerset, and Horningsham and Westbury in Wiltshire emigrated more or less immediately afterward. Between 1830 and 1832, the Corsley/Frome area lost around eight hundred poor people, mainly to Upper Canada, all of whom were assisted by their parishes.[47] While most originated from the parishes closest to Frome and Corsley, smaller numbers of people came also from the nearby Wiltshire parishes of Knook, Heytesbury, Warminster, Longbridge Deverill, Maiden Bradley, and Chapmanslade.[48] Judging from a surviving list of the Heytesbury and Knook people who were assisted, the men in the group were employed mainly as labourers, cloth workers, and shoemakers (Table 7).[49] No doubt, the favourable letters written in 1830 by the first Corsley group, which were published soon after by G. Poulett Scrope, MP for Stroud, helped to attract followers from the surrounding area. This letter, written by William Singer, a former bricklayer, is a typical example:

> If any of my old acquaintances is got tired of being slaves and drudges tell them to come to Upper Canada to William Singer and he will take them by the hand and lead them to hard work and good wages and the best of living. Any of them would do well here.... We have eight English families within about two miles, all from Westbury or Corsley [Wiltshire].[50]

Although most of the Wiltshire and Somerset paupers, including those from Corsley and Frome, went to the Talbot settlements in Elgin County farther to the west,[51] some settled in the newly surveyed areas in Dummer and Douro townships in Peterborough County. And people like Levi Payne did astonishingly well. Having emigrated to Dummer with his wife and extended family, including his brothers from Frome, Levi had acquired a gristmill, sawmills, a general store, and a farm by 1839.[52] Judging from John Langton's observations in 1835, it would seem that the Wiltshire and Somerset paupers went mainly to Dummer. When he saw the area, it was "only lately, but tolerably, well settled — one settlement is of English, another of Scotch, and there are a good many Irish." But Douro had "Peter Robinson's settlers" in its southern part, who, having arrived in 1827–28, "are more prosperous than in other parts."[53] Langton's failure to mention any English in Douro suggests that few went there.

At this time a great many Wiltshire and Somerset paupers were also being sent to equally remote situations in Simcoe County, where they settled alongside people from Yorkshire.[54] In all, a total of three thousand people (430 families) were reported to have been relocated to Oro, Dummer, and Douro townships during 1831–32.[55] Mary Sophia (Gapper) O'Brien, from Charlinch in Somerset, came upon their communities in Oro when she visited in the 1830s:

> Now for the first time I saw quite a new settlement. We passed on for two miles through a road just cut out on each side of which at short intervals were log houses of a very respectable class. Some were finished externally but almost all stood completely in the forest. In some places there was perhaps an acre or two chopped, but generally hardly so many trees seemed to have fallen as were necessary to construct the buildings.... In five or six years every house will be surrounded by a productive farm. Most of these settlers are farmers from England.[56]

Having come to Thornhill in Vaughan Township (York County) in 1825 with the intention of visiting her brothers for a couple of years,

Mary decided to remain in Upper Canada permanently after meeting Edward O'Brien, a half-pay officer who had emigrated in 1829. After their marriage the following year, the O'Briens lived near Thornhill, and three years later built a new place for themselves on Lake Simcoe, in Oro Township, at what came to be called Shanty Bay.

Meanwhile, a steady stream of labourers and servants continued to leave Wiltshire for Upper Canada throughout the 1830s, having been assisted in each case by their parishes.[57] James Whalley and his wife and three children, who came from Longbridge Deverill, emigrated to Peterborough — since he "had children there."[58] Some thirty-six paupers from Durrington, forty-five from Whiteparish, and forty-five from Purton were assisted to emigrate in 1835–36,[59] while another batch of twenty-one left Purton in 1837 — included in their number were a sixty-year-old widower and a couple with nine children.[60]A total of 117 paupers from Brinkworth, a parish adjoining Purton in North Wiltshire, left between 1842 and 1852 on four vessel crossings, although no indication was given of their final destination (see passenger lists in Tables 8–11).[61] However, a letter written in 1844 by James Whale, who had emigrated from Brinkworth at his own expense, provides a clue as to their possible whereabouts. James was desperate to have his wife join him in Brampton (Chinguacousy Township in Peel County), at the west end of Lake Ontario:

> My Dear Wife ... I can tell you that this country is not so well as some people talk about, but it is better than England, for people do get a living and the longer I stop here, the better I like it. I can get a fair living here with perseverance and I think it would be running away from the hand of Providence for me to come to England to live; so my dear Wife and son I hope you will come to this country as soon as you possibly can.... My dear Wife, you said you could not come of your own strength, this I know, but I hope the respectable gentlemen of Brinkworth will be kind to you as they were to those who came out last year ... but if you do not come

after all my exertions, I must come back again but if my
family were here I do not want to come back.[62]

Although James had been able to pay his own way, he could not
afford to bring his wife and son, who had to seek help from their parish. Judging from the inclusion of Jane and Thomas Whale in the list of
people who had sailed for Quebec in the 1843 group, it would seem that
his "dear wife" was already on her way to Brampton Township before
James had written his letter. It was fairly common for men to leave their
wives and families behind in this way, and Brinkworth Parish did what
was expected and agreed to finance Jane and Thomas's expenses in the
belief that this "would be beneficial to its interests as well as promote the
welfare of the emigrants."[63]

Upper Canada acquired another large group of English people during
the early 1830s whose story was particularly sad. The heads of households
were Chelsea pensioners and in a category all of their own.[64] As wounded
British Army war veterans, they had been granted pensions. Foolishly,
many agreed, under encouragement from the British government, to
have their pensions commuted to a lump sum to fund their relocation to
the New World.[65] A cynical and contemptible policy that enabled the War
Office to reduce its pensions bills, the result was misery and chaos for the
hapless thousands who were persuaded to leave England.

Between 1830 and 1839, at least four thousand Chelsea pensioners,
who were mainly English, commuted their pensions for cash. Of these,
some 3,200 emigrated to British America (mainly Upper Canada), with
most aged between forty and fifty.[66] Sir John Colborne made arrangements for the first group of 1,700, who came to Upper Canada in 1832, to
have land in either Middlesex, Simcoe, Victoria, or Peterborough counties.[67] Most ended up in Dummer (Peterborough County) and Medonte
(Simcoe County) townships, with some also settling in Emily, Eldon, and
Ops townships (Victoria County) and Nottawasaga Township (Simcoe
County). However, little care had been taken in selecting people for the
scheme and, except when pensioners had a robust young family to help
them, they floundered. Mrs. Anna Jameson, who travelled from London
to Port Talbot in 1837, was horrified to learn from the Upper Canada

emigration agent that half of the Chelsea pensioners were afflicted in some way: "some with one arm, some with one leg, bent with old age or rheumatism, lame halt and even, will it be believed, blind!"[68] Inevitably, many ended their days in great distress.

In 1833, Colborne received a petition from fifty-five pensioners settled in Medonte (Table 12), and another from sixty-three pensioners who had gone to the Newcastle District (Peterborough, Northumberland, Durham and Victoria counties) requesting aid "to relieve them from their present indescribable destitute situation. The greatest part of your petitioners are, from want of means, wounds, and bad health rendered unfit to provide for their helpless families."[69] Some had immediately taken up work building roads and shanties, having already spent their commutation money before leaving Quebec. When the work was finished, they went to the towns and cities with their families to beg in the streets or receive charity. However, some four or five hundred had successfully established themselves on their lands, and by 1835 it was reported that those who were healthy, industrious, and sober were doing well. They faded from sight, but "the troublesome, improvident men remained to plague the community as public charges."[70] Also to their credit was the staunch support the pensioners gave to the authorities during the 1837 uprising:

> During the late disturbances [Rebellion of 1837], the commuted pensioners capable of bearing arms, without a single exception, came forward in defence of the province ... many of them travelled for miles without shoes, their feet being protected by such old clothing as their circumstances could supply ... in the depth of winter, to offer their services. Whatever vices they may possess, they have always shown they are faithful subjects.[71]

However, irrespective of their patriotic tendencies, the Chelsea pensioners should never have been encouraged to emigrate. Many of them thought that they were giving up their pensions for four years only and would receive them again. Colborne recommended that their commuted pensions be restored, as did the Upper Canada Assembly, but to no avail.

In 1833, Colborne had ordered the cessation of the scheme and decreed that the saddest cases be moved to Penetanguishene, where they were put under the protective wing of an army officer.[72]

Yet the pensioners' plight could not be swept aside so easily. When Lord Durham[73] received Edward Shuel's petition in 1838, he realized that more had to be done. This was a man with a wife and six children who was incapable of work because he was paralyzed on one side of his body from a wound received during twenty-three-years' service in the army. Lord Durham demanded that his and other army pensions be restored immediately. Although this did not happen, at least a system of poor relief was established. When aid was first distributed in 1840 there were 654 Chelsea pensioners still resident in Upper Canada, representing only a quarter of the original group, the rest having already died.[74]

While the Chelsea pensioners could not have been handled more ineptly, the emigration schemes devised for the 1,800 men, women, and children from the West Sussex estate of George O'Brien Wyndham, the third Earl of Egremont, were exemplary. They came to Upper Canada between 1832 and 1838 from over one hundred parishes, having had their departures organized by the Petworth Emigration Committee, under the benevolent leadership of Thomas Sockett, the rector of Petworth. Although most originated from West Sussex, especially the Petworth area, they also included seventy-seven people from Dorking in the neighbouring county of Surrey, as well as people from East Sussex, the Isle of Wight, Cambridgeshire, and a scattering of parishes across southern England.[75]

Once established, the Petworth immigrants wrote a total of 144 letters from Upper Canada, emphasizing its work opportunities and other benefits. Judging from their addresses, most can be placed in the southwest of the province, although an appreciable number also settled in York, Peel, and Halton counties, on the northwest side of Lake Ontario. However, if John Langton's information is correct, another group must have gone to Victoria County: "Thirty two families of old Lord Egremont's people, 250 in number, are to be sent this year [1835] to the land between Balsam Lake and Lake Simcoe and are to open up the road that has been laid out there."[76]

The Petworth immigrants seemed to have been particularly well organized and showed every sign of taking the first opportunity that presented itself, whatever it might have been. Those who went to the long-established townships on the western side of Lake Ontario were able to find farming work very easily, most having considerable agricultural skills. They could thus obtain useful work experience and use the money they earned to buy land and eventually become farmers in their own right. This more enlightened approach replaced Colborne's earlier policy of encouraging assisted immigrants to become instant farmers by locating them on wilderness land and supervising the beginnings of their settlements. This well-intentioned but impractical paternalistic approach failed to recognize that newly arrived immigrants needed time to adjust to their new environment; only then could they fully realize what might be achieved and what their actual options were.

William Wright from Dorking found that "after coming to York [Toronto] I was only three days idle, when I found work about 20 miles from York, where I worked 13 days on the road at the rate of 2s. per day and board." Three days later he was approached by William Dornorman, a farmer from Nelson Township (Halton County), who hired him for a year at an annual wage of £22.[77]

William Spencer from Linchmere in Sussex also had a smooth entry into Nelson: "I have hired with Mr. Truller by the year and I am getting good wages; and if you feels any ways inclined to come I think it would be better for you for I think you will get a better living here than you ever will in England."[78]

But James and Mary (Tilley) Boxall from Petworth warned people with a drink problem not to come:

> A man can get a good living by working hard and enduring a great many hardships for the first year or two till he can get his land cleared and raise his own provisions.... I think it would be folly for persons who are doing comfortably at home to come to Canada.... There is one great evil I am sorry to say in this country. A great many write about the cheapness of whiskey but they say

nothing about the evil of it; so I would not advise any who are given to drink to come to this country for they will do worse here [Nelson] than at home.[79]

Meanwhile, James Helyer from Halsemere in Surrey, who was happily ensconced in Toronto Township (Peel County) by 1833, wrote to a friend with a ringing endorsement of the area:

> Those who emigrated to this country a few years ago, though poor and having to undergo many privations, are now in a state of comfort and independence having fine farms cleared plenty of stock and all the necessaries of life in abundance; but earn it by the sweat of their brow. But there is one comfort enjoyed here, that taxes are a mere trifle: and as to the hateful tithe system and poor rates they are unknown this side of the Atlantic.[80]

Obadiah Wilson, one of a small group from Bassingbourn Parish in Cambridgeshire who travelled with the Petworth Emigration Committee in 1832, went on to acquire a home farm in Whitby Township and numerous other land holdings in Scott and Reach townships, together with a hotel and even more property in the village of Udora, farther to the north. Obadiah, a remarkable example of a poor man who made good, ended his days with an estate valued at $24,000.[81]

Meanwhile, a group of Petworth immigrants from Walburton in West Sussex effectively created a New Walburton for themselves at Thornhill in Vaughan Township (York County). Already having local contacts, new arrivals could all the more easily find work. When Frank Mellish arrived in 1835, "Thomas Messenger came on board the steamer and gave directions where to find George Wells and the two Birchs and I have been at work for George Wells ever since. [William] Cole is working just by and Charles Leggatt is working about three miles from here.... Mr. Birch, Mrs. Norris, G Wells and all the Walburton live close together."[82]

A year later, John Ayling provided a further progress report on the growing Walburton community:

> George Leggatt is at work about one mile from Thornhill, he has $8 a month and his meat; John Norris and George Booker [are] about 10 miles from George Lintot; George has $10 and John $8 a month. George Cole is with George Wells. Charles Richards is about 12 miles from George. John Millyard is 11 miles from here; he has gone apprenticed to a carpenter. Thomas Norris has got a place and has hired for a month. Richard Cooper is at work for Mark Messenger and Cornelius Cook is at work at Toronto as a butcher's boy; he has not been up to Thornhill at all. Ruth Leggatt is with Edmund Birch and I have hired up at Newmarket for $11. I have got a very good place about 18 miles from George Lintot.... I don't work hard but lives very well, that is £2 15s. a month and my board and lodgings, that is better than working in England.... Never be afraid to come to America, don't be afraid to come, you will do better here.[83]

Writing from the city of Toronto, John Barnes from Petworth asked his family to "tell all my old work-mates that enquire after me that if I had known what America had been I would have been there some years ago.... I can earn more money in about 5 or 6 months than at home in a whole year.... Dear brother Henry if you had come out with me it would have been the best thing ... I could have got a place for you with the same gentleman that I am working for; he has got a farm about 10 miles from Toronto which is about 200 acres and about 50 of it cleared."[84]

In a similar vein, Edmund Birch, another Walburton immigrant, had this rather sardonic message for his former employer in Sussex: "I have got a good place farming for an English gentleman, my wages are £4 2s. 6d. per month ... when you write I should like to hear of my old master: tell him this is a good place for farmers, but they must not think to do here as they do at home, telling men if they do not like it they may go, for the master here must humble more to the men, than the men to the master."[85] However, some people, like this anonymous letter-writer from Toronto, clearly disapproved of the Petworth Emigration Scheme:

No-one would come here if they knew how things are; here the labourer has to work a great deal harder than in England and after all cannot get his money. This has happened with several poor fellows who came out in the same ship with me.... If the people knew what poor emigrants have to go through there would not be many come to Canada."[86]

The letter was published in the *Brighton Patriot*, a Sussex newspaper, with the clear intention of casting doubt on the favourable reports being sent from Upper Canada. It went on to allege that the Petworth immigrants "were treated like convicts" during their sea crossing and claimed "that the captain insulted the passengers, got drunk, fought with an Irishmen and kicked a defenceless boy."[87] No doubt, Upper Canada did not have universal appeal, but the success of the emigration scheme was beyond question. Thomas Sockett wasted no time in refuting the writer's wild claims and inaccuracies, but the letter is a reminder that there was still some ongoing resistance throughout England to the policy of assisting poor people to emigrate.

Of course, Sussex emigration was not restricted to paupers. The Hemsley family, who arrived at Belleville in Hastings County around 1840, is but one example of the many Sussex emigrants who would have came to Upper Canada totally unaided. Dinah Bishop, widow of Richard Hemsley, advised her daughter, still in Sussex, that "a man with any kind of trade will do better here than there [England]; or a labouring man or a man that understands farming will do much better here than there. A strong healthy industrious man with almost any trade can live comfortably and save much property. But then I have heard some discontented people that are doing well in this country say they wished they were back home again without any apparent reason whatever."[88] Her son-in-law, William Packham, was adamant that he "does not want to return to England to live but would like to visit.... This is a flourishing country and is improving fast.... They are now building a college [in Belleville] which will cost over £6,000 and an English church which will cost nearly as much."[89] However, ever-present concerns over excessive drinking prompted James Hemsley, Dinah's son, to inform his brothers and sisters in England that "we can live here as cheap as you can there, but lots drink their time away here and some go to a drunkards' grave."[90]

Another exceptionally large group of paupers who were assisted to emigrate in the 1830s originated from rural districts of East Anglia, but unlike the Petworth immigrants, they left little documentation behind.[91] Much of the emigration from this region was being encouraged and directed by William Cattermole, the region's principal Canada Company agent. His fervour in promoting its lands in the southwest of the province was phenomenal. Having spent three years in Upper Canada, he had first-hand experience of its opportunities and used his extensive lecture program to hammer home the merits of emigration. He was instrumental in directing 1,200 people from Norfolk, Suffolk, Kent, and Essex to Upper Canada in 1831, concentrating his efforts in districts with high unemployment.[92]

Parish-assisted farm labourers from Norfolk dominated the exodus that followed, accounting for 58 percent of all pauper emigration in 1835–36. A smaller Suffolk contingent that also relied on public funds left at this time as well, representing 15 percent of the total.[93] Around one-third headed for the Eastern Townships in Lower Canada, leaving 2,043 people from Norfolk and 556 from Suffolk who mainly went to the southwestern peninsula.[94] However, at least one Norfolk group is known to have settled along Lake Ontario. Parish-assisted emigrants from Swaffham went to Port Hope (Durham County) in 1835, joining an already-established Swaffham group who had arrived three years earlier.[95] They were followed in 1837 by people from the neighbouring parish of Beachamwell, who also settled at Port Hope.[96] Meanwhile, small groups of paupers from Haddenham Parish in Cambridgeshire were assisted to emigrate in 1834 and 1836,[97] and similar help was being given at the time to poor people from Widdington, Wimbish, Debden, and Steeple Bumstead parishes in northwest Essex.[98]

The directional flow of emigrants from England had changed once again by the 1840s. Some 57 percent of all departures began in Liverpool, with ports in Yorkshire, Northumberland, Durham, and Cumberland playing little part in the embarkation of emigrants during this and later decades. However, this was also a period when emigration from southwest England surged ahead, with 23 percent of all departures in the 1840s being drawn from this one region. Most of the emigrants originated from Cornwall, and they mainly settled along the western half of Lake Ontario between Port Hope and Toronto (Map 13).

A distinguishing feature of West Country emigration was that it was almost entirely self-financed. A trickle of people arrived during the 1830s, with the Cornish-born Peter Coleman being a typical example. He emigrated with his wife Elizabeth Tamblyn in 1831 when he was twenty-nine. Living in Hope Township (Durham County) initially, he and his family later moved to Bowmanville (Darlington Township) and Peter went on to acquire extensive properties in the town by 1861. His Cornish father, John, a Wesleyan lay preacher, was buried in Bowmanville Cemetery, having emigrated at the age of sixty-three.[99]

Henry Elliott, a native of Cornwall, also emigrated in 1831 at the age of twenty-two, working first at a gristmill in Port Hope. Nine years later he moved to Hampton, a place which would eventually take its name from his birthplace of Kilkhampton. Founding "Elliot's Mill," later known as "Millsville," he became a highly successful entrepreneur and farmer. Having established a sawmill in 1840, then a gristmill in 1851, he opened a general store that same year, which included a post office and tailor's shop. Twenty years later his store would employ three people and produce $2,195 worth of goods annually.[100]

Then there was Peter Davey from St. Neot in Cornwall, who also emigrated in 1831, settling in Cobourg (Northumberland County). His cheerful letter home a year later emphasized both the hard grind and benefits of his new life:

> My dear friend, I should have written to you before, but not having seen sufficient of this country, I thought it better to delay my letter until I had, that I might be more certain of stating the truth…. Soon after my arrival I bought a lot of land (two hundred acres) for which I gave £275; the wood will nearly pay for the land and clearing. We can make 6s. 3d. per cord for wood and 6 dollars per hundred bushels of coals [probably

Bible Christian Church members, Bowmanville, 1865. An offshoot of Wesleyan Methodism, the Bible Christian movement was founded in Upper Canada in the 1830s.

charcoal].... I have burned one pit, and there is a good sale as the smiths all work with them. Everything grows well; the soil is rich and will bear many crops without manure. Cucumbers, pumpkins and water melons grow in the natural soil here, in the season, better than in hotbeds in England, Wheat, Indian corn, pease and potatoes also produce a fine crop.... Land is getting up and the country is improving very fast. I shall have forty acres of wheat next year, and having no rent to pay, no poor rates, no tithes, no church rates, no land tax, and only

about 5s. a year to the government, I may fairly hope to
do well; but it is useless for idlers and drunkards to come
here, as they will be sure to starve. Industrious labourers can support themselves and their families well; wages
are from 3s. 9d. to 5s. a day. Tell Masllett and Keast that
if they could get here their families would soon cease to
be a trouble to them. We live in great harmony, so much
so that we care little about locking our doors by night;
in truth, I would not return to England if I could have
the land of the estate I rented in St. Neot given to me.[101]

William Hore and family, who emigrated around 1830, were near
neighbours of Peter, and living just north of Cobourg at Camborne, a place
named after Camborne in Cornwall. Having acquired 106 acres of wilderness land, William eventually had his own farm and also built a sawmill.[102]

With the deepening economic depression being experienced during
the 1840s in the West Country, especially in its agricultural sector, prospects for ordinary workers were grim.[103] Glowing reports from family and
friends living in Upper Canada offered hope, and emigration numbers
began to soar.[104] In 1840, Alexander Buchanan, the Quebec immigration agent, noted that 146 "very respectable people" had arrived from
the Cornish port of Padstow: "They are all going to settle in the township of Whitby [Ontario County] and near Port Hope [Durham County]
in Upper Canada."[105] In September of that same year, Buchanan noted
fifty-eight more Cornish people, "chiefly mechanics and farmers," who
had sailed from Padstow. Some would seek work in Montreal, but most
were heading for the townships of Asphodel (Peterborough County) and
Darlington (Durham County).[106] By the following year, arrivals from
Padstow tripled to six hundred.[107] They included Henry Pedlar and family, who stayed briefly at a farm in Whitby Township before settling in
the later town of Oshawa. Henry Pedlar prospered, as did his son George,
who founded the Oshawa Sheet Metal Works.[108]

By 1842, some Cornish emigrants were being assisted by their parishes. All together, the parishes of St. Agnes, St. Blazey, St. Columb Major,
Cuby, St. Eval, Mawgan, and St. Merryn assisted thirty-seven people to

reach Upper Canada that year, while in the following year sixty-three people from St. Columb Major, St. Issey, and South Petherwin also received
help.[109] According to Buchanan, the 1843 group arrived at Quebec in a
destitute state:

> Two families received £20, one £15, one £8, three £6
> and one £5 to aid them in preparing for their voyage,

Abbey House in Padstow. Emigrants paid their fares at this building. Between
1831 and 1860 a total of 6,200 people sailed from Padstow for Quebec; in 1841
Padstow was the third most important departure port for Canada, surpassed only by
Liverpool and London.

and towards paying their passage and providing food. One other family was assisted out of charitable funds to the extent of £4. They are going to join their friends in the township of Whitby. These families had expended their means and landed here destitute, not one of them being able to pay their passage even as far as Montreal. The heads of three of the families were stone masons and one a joiner; but no immediate employment for them offering here, and all having large families, I furnished them with a free passage to Montreal.[110]

More poor Cornish people "of the labouring class" arrived at Quebec in 1846 with the intention of settling on the northwest side of Lake Ontario, "where they have friends." Buchanan reported that a large number required assistance to enable them to proceed west, with "36 adults and 47 children forwarded free by this office."[111]

While those requiring help attracted documentation and attention, it should be remembered that the majority — people like John and Mary Clemence from Pelynt Parish — paid their relocation costs themselves. They emigrated in 1849, settling near Port Perry in Reach Township (Ontario County).[112] Another couple, Edmund Allen and his wife Jane from Mevagissey, settled the following year in Smith Township (Peterborough County), where they joined large communities from Cumberland and Ireland.[113] The many Cornish people whose names appear in a Women's Institute survey as having emigrated to Upper Canada during the 1840s and 1850s each paid their own way, and there would have been hundreds more like them. The survey also reveals the extent to which the Lake Ontario region attracted people from Cornwall. The majority of the Upper Canada destinations that are recorded lie between Cobourg and Whitby.[114]

Most of the English who came to the central region of Upper Canada failed to leave much in the way of documents behind. Fragmentary glimpses pinpoint obvious regional trends, such as the strong Yorkshire and Cornish presence in this region. The English were scattered far and wide, but they also formed important settlement clusters along the west side of Lake Ontario. People with English ancestry were predominant in

Durham, Ontario, and York counties, and by 1881 accounted for around 45 percent of the total population in each county. People of English descent were particularly prominent in the townships of Darlington (69 percent) and Clarke (48 percent) in Durham County, and in the townships of Whitby (57 percent) and Pickering (47 percent) in Ontario County. Although some of the English presence can be attributed to the early influx of Loyalists and later Americans having English ancestry, emigration directly from England was clearly the dominant factor.

Since the 1820s, the Lake Ontario region had become a magnet for North of England settlers, especially for people from Cumberland and Yorkshire; but by the 1830s it began to draw its English settlers more or less in equal numbers from the north and south of the country. The major Cornish influx of the 1840s helped to concentrate the English presence even more strongly in York and Ontario counties, while extending the contribution to the population made by the English farther east, as far as Peterborough and Northumberland.[115] Also, with the exception of Norfolk and Suffolk immigrants, who, in some years, were mainly paupers, most of the English who settled in this region had financed their own departures. Somerset, Wiltshire, and Yorkshire paupers contributed significantly to the populations of the more remote areas of Simcoe and Peterborough counties, especially Vespra and Oro townships in the former and Dummer in the latter, while Sussex and Kent paupers were particularly prominent in well-settled areas of Ontario and York counties.

Upper Canada was not colonized in strict chronological sequence from east to west as might have been expected. Loyalist communities on the eastern side of the province were the first to take shape, doing so from the mid-1780s; but the extreme west of the province also had its Loyalists and it also attracted early settlers from Britain, who began colonizing the north shore of Lake Erie beginning in the early nineteenth century. Southwestern Upper Canada had attracted the government's attention because of its vulnerability to attack from the United States. As a consequence, it had granted large tracts of land in the region to proprietors who intended to promote colonization. One of the best known was Colonel Thomas Talbot, an Irishman who ruled his domain with a rod of iron.

Table 4:

**Payments Made to People from Alston Parish (Cumberland)
Who Are to Emigrate to Upper Canada in 1832
[CAS D/WAL/7/D]**

Disbursements	No.	£	s	d
Frances Pearson, Widow, & 4 Children	5	8	0	0
Friend Wallace, Wife, & 4 Children	6	5	0	0
Richard Pattinson, Wife, & 4 Children	6	2	0	0
Robert Carr, Wife, & 8 Children	10	23	0	0
Henry Cowing, Wife, & 4 Children	6	20	0	0
Leonard Bright, Wife, & 2 Children	4	3	0	0
Jane Carr, Widow, & 2 Children	3	14	0	0
Richard Storey, Wife, & 4 Children	6	18	0	0
Jonathan Thompson's Wife, & 7 Children (Husband in Canada)	8	28	0	0
Margaret Cousin, Widow, & 4 Children	5	20	0	0
John Chester, Wife, & 3 Children	5	16	0	0
Jane Elliot, Widow, & 6 Children	7	29	0	0
Robert, Leonard, & William Bright	3	8	0	0
John Lee, Wife, & 4 Children	6	5	0	0
John Barron, Wife, & 4 Children	6	15	0	0
William Hall, Wife, & 4 Children	6	13	0	0
Thomas Armstrong, Wife, & 4 Children	6	15	0	0
Mary Walton	1	3	0	0
Elizabeth Richardson, Widow	1	3	0	0
Mary Featherstonhaugh & 5 Children	6	29	17	6
Robert Walton, Wife, & 3 Children	5	5	0	0
Widow Chester	1	4	0	0
William Armstrong, Wife, & 3 Children	5	6	0	0
Joseph Wallace, Wife, & 5 Children	7	4	0	0
Various expenses in removing the emigrants to The Sea Coast, &c, &c.	-	5	3	6
Balance in the Hands of the Treasurer	-	5	15	0
[Totals]	124	£310	16	0

A Sum of £5, out of the above Balance has been promised to a family of the name of Wharton, who have not yet got off.

Table 5:

Emigrant Departures from English Ports to Quebec by Region, 1820–59
[Source: Newspaper Shipping Reports, British Parliamentary Papers]

	1820–29	1830–39	1840–49	1850–59
North East (Berwick, Newcastle, South Shields, Stockton, Sunderland)				
	534	2,921	1,043	1,015
Yorkshire (Hull, Scarborough, Whitby)				
	2,823	9,642	5,033	4,147
East Anglia (Colchester, Ipswich, Lowestoft, Lynn, Newhaven, Yarmouth)				
	0	6,108	316	0
London	1,366	11,325	6,893	4,471
South (Cowes, Guernsey, Jersey, Portsmouth, Rye, Southampton)				
	74	1,947	1,028	2,151
Southwest (Bideford, Boscastle, Bridgwater, Bristol, Dartmouth, Exmouth, Falmouth, Fowey, Gloucester, Hayle, Helford, Ilfracombe, Milford, Newport, Padstow, Penzance, Plymouth, Poole, Restronguet, St. Ives, St. Michael's Mount, Strangford, Torbay, Torquay, Truro, Weymouth)				
	539	8,057	18,707	14,925
Liverpool	1,258	12,420	45,963	44,261
North West (Carlisle, Fleetwood, Lancaster, Maryport, Poulton, Whitehaven, Workington)				
	1,482	5,180	397	528
Totals	**8,076**	**57,600**	**79,380**	**71,498**

Table 6:

Paupers Assisted to Emigrate from Stockbury Parish (Kent) to Upper Canada in 1837 [CKS P348/8/1]

Name	Age	Name	Age
Thomas Gransden	27	Elizabeth Lambkin	3
Amy Gransden (his wife)	27	George Lambkin	1¾
William Gransden child	6		
Frances Gransden child	7mths	James Burr	35
		Hannah Burr (his wife)	35
William Syflet	35	William Burr	16
Jane Syflet (his wife)	33	Caroline Burr	9
		James Burr	8
William Gibbs	23	Eliza Burr	2½
George Stinden	22	William Beecham	25
Sarah Stinden (his wife)	21	Mary Beecham (his wife)	23
Stephen Lambkin	23	Leonard Lambkin	66
Frances Lambkin (his wife)	25	Elizabeth Lambkin (his wife)	65
Sarah Ann Lambkin	4		
Elizabeth Lambkin	1	Moses Whitehead	17
Richard Lambkin	34	George Mills	33
Rebecca Lambkin (his wife)	36	Ann Mills (his wife)	30
Leonard Lambkin	13	James Mills	9
John Lambkin	12	Jane Elizabeth Mills	6
Mary Lambkin	10	Mary Ann Mills	4
Martha Lambkin	8		
Richard Lambkin	6	George Alfred Mills	1

Table 7:

Paupers from Heytesbury and Knook Parishes in Wiltshire
Who Sailed March 1831 in the *Euphrosyne* from Bridgwater
[CO 384/28 40–1, 48–50]

Name	Age	Occupation	Parish
King, William	50	Quarryman	Tytherington (in Heytesbury Parish)
King, wife	50		Tytherington
Kite, James	19	Labourer	Tytherington
Bevan, William	30	Labourer	Tytherington
Bevan, wife	30		Tytherington
Bevan, daughter	6		Tytherington
Bevan, son	4		Tytherington
Bevan, son	1		Tytherington
Foyle, David	17	Labourer	Tytherington
Parker, Felix	19	Labourer	Tytherington
Miller, George	19	Labourer	Tytherington
Payne, Joel	25	Cloth worker	Tytherington
Noke, Jeffrey	32	Shoemaker & Labourer	Tytherington
Noke, wife	31		Heytesbury
Noke, daughter	11		Heytesbury
Noke, daughter	9		Heytesbury
Noke, son	7		Heytesbury
Noke, daughter	1		Heytesbury
Coleman, William	31	Cloth worker & Labourer	Heytesbury
Coleman, wife	37		Heytesbury
Coleman, daughter	5		Heytesbury
Coleman, daughter	1		Heytesbury
Smith, Thomas	18	Labourer	Heytesbury
Farley, William	17	Labourer	Heytesbury
Young, John	23	Shoemaker	Heytesbury
Young, wife	24		Heytesbury
Young, son	3 mo		Heytesbury
Seyer (Ceyer), Charles	19	Labourer	Heytesbury
Holland, Henry	20	Labourer	Heytesbury
Hinton, Henry	21	Labourer	Heytesbury

Name	Age	Occupation	Parish
Hooker, John	17	Labourer	Heytesbury
Holland, James	25	Labourer	Heytesbury
Hinton, Leonard	25	Shoemaker	Heytesbury
Farley, Joseph	23	Labourer	Heytesbury
Hurdle, William	23	Millwright	Heytesbury
Payne, James*	24	Cloth worker	Knook
Payne, wife	25		Knook
Payne, daughter	4		Knook
Payne, daughter	2½		Knook
Payne, son	6 mo		Knook

*All were assisted except for James Payne who paid his own expenses.

Table 8:

Paupers from Brinkworth Parish in Wiltshire Who Sailed from London to Quebec in July 1842 in the *Eliza*
[WHC 1607/71]

Name	Age	Name	Age
Edward Wait	38	Isaac Matthews	20
Ann	37		
John	18	Matthew Spencer	38
Sarah	16	Margaret	40
Margaret	14	Eliza	16
Thomas	13	Eli	14
Jane	10	Elijah	12
Ann	4	Rhoda	9
Honor	2	Ezra	5
		Gael	5
Thomas Thompson	50	Jabez	1
Jane	41		
Amelia	19	Robert Pinnell	42
Mary Jane	15	Ann	42
Thomas	12	Nathan	20
Edward	9	David	18
Hester	6	Edward	16
Henry	5	Elizabeth	14
Albert	1	George	7

Total 35

Table 9:

Paupers from Brinkworth Parish in Wiltshire Who Sailed from London to Quebec in May 1843 in the *Toronto*
[WHC 1607/71]

Name	Age	Name	Age
		Mary	16
Brinkworth Parish		James	13
Anthony Matthews	37	Elizabeth	7
Ann	36	Louisa	6 months
Jacob	14		
Joseph	12	James Sherwood	20
Sophia	10	Thomas Howell	20
Caroline	7	William H Matthews	19
Sarah	5	Isaac Matthews	21
Henry	1 year 9 months	Henry Iles	21
		Henry Hendin	20
Benjamin Cunand	43	Nathan Webb	31
Winifred	42		
Alfred	16	**Charlton Parish**	
Jeremiah	12	William Golding	35
Adelaide	11	Anne	24
William	8	Sophia	18
Elizabeth	4	Emily	12
Thuza	6 months	Thomas	10
		George	11 months
Edward Pinnell	46	Sophia	11 months
Martha	47		
Dinah	21		**Total of 41**
Aaron	4		
Edward	9 months	Jane Whale	40
		Thomas Whale	18
Isaac Pinnell	32		
Hannah	32		

Table 10:

Paupers from Brinkworth Parish in Wiltshire Who Sailed from London to Quebec in May 1847 in the *Lloyd* [WHC 1607/71]

Name	Age	Name	Age
John Pinnell	38	Joseph Dixon	42
Margaret Pinnell	36	Mary Dixon	38
Phoebe Pinnell	17	Charles Dixon	16
Ellen Pinnell	13	Alice Dixon	13
George Pinnell	10	Edwin Dixon	3
Sarah Pinnell	8	Robert Dixon	3 months
Alice Pinnell	6		
Esther Pinnell	4	Nehemiah Matthews	17
Rebecca Pinnell	6 months	Miriam Matthews	15
		Rhaka Matthews	10
Delilah Fleming	34		
John Fleming	2		Total 20

	£.	s.	d.
Paid for refreshment had at Wootton Bassett Station	4	0	-
Paid turnpike at Bath and Wootton Bassett	2	6	-
Paid for carriage of luggage and party to Wootton Bassett	10	0	-
Paid for luggage and fares from Wootton Bassett to Paddington	5	3	5
Paid for refreshments at Swindon station	2	0	-
Paid for refreshments at Paddington	18	0	-
Paid for the conveyance of luggage and people to the docks	16	0	-
Paid for food put on board on the 27th May	18	0	-
Paid dues at the London Docks	10	9	-
Paid my own fare to Swindon	12	0	-
Paid for making clothing for John Pinnell and family	5	0	-
Paid for tin plates and dishes for the party	4	8	-
My own expenses and time	1	6	2
Total	**£11**	**12s.**	**6d.**

Table 11:

Paupers from Brinkworth Parish in Wiltshire Who Sailed from London to Quebec in June 1852 in the *Leonard Dobbin* [WHC 1607/71]

Name	Age	Name	Age
John Stratton	43	Sarah Jane	6
Mary Ann	43	Ambrose	2
Elizabeth	19	Thomas	3 months
William	17		
John	15	Robert Sherwood	33
Martha	11		
Albert	8	Elizabeth Walker	31
James	6	George	9
Alfred	3	Rhada	7
		Emmy	6
Ambrose Davies	31	Giles	4
Jane	26	Jabez	8 months

Table 12:

Destitute Chelsea Pensioners Who Had Settled in Medonte Township in Simcoe County by 1833* [Aitken, "Searching Chelsea Pensioners in Upper Canada and Great Britain," Part I, 120–21]

Names	Women	Children
Serjeant Thomas Fitzgibbon	1	4
John Hammond	1	4
Thomas Johnson	1	2
Thomas Queale	1	4
John Fullerton	1	5
Samuel Ferguson	1	4
Thomas Kelly	1	2
John Tiernan	1	1
Cornelius Lawler	1	4
Patrick O'Donell	1	2
John Fowler	1	5
Jeremiah Reardon	1	1

Names	Women	Children
John Hine	1	5
Serjeant John Grant	1	4
Joseph Williams	1	1
Serjeant Joseph Butcher	1	1
John Whelan	1	3
William Archey	1	6
George Walker	1	1
Samuel M'Clure	1	5
William Terry	1	2
Patrick M'Gahey	1	4
James Route	1	3
John Seale	1	-
Serjeant J. Rutherford	1	7
Serjeant W. Thompson	1	4
Patrick Hughes	1	2
Patrick Cahehan	1	4
Samuel French	1	6
Serjeant John Bell	1	2
Joseph Evans	1	2
John M'Donnell	1	5
William Smith	1	4
James Fox	1	4
Patrick Carey	-	-
Samuel Cowen	1	6
Serjeant John Byrne	1	5
George Moore	1	6
John Orton	1	3
Thomas Bone	1	2
John Lawler	1	2
Patrick Joyce	1	4
Francis Keane	1	2
Conway Bunten	1	5
Thomas M'Condré	1	2
William Hill	1	3
Andrew Kinghorn	1	3
James Loftus	1	1
Charles Fitzgerald	1	1
John Overs	1	2
John Lucy	1	1

*All were listed as being in "absolute distress."

CHAPTER 7

The Lake Erie and Thames Valley Settlements

*At one time, St. Thomas, which might very well be consid-
ered the capital of the [Talbot] settlement, was the headquarters of a numerous party of English emigrants, who
had been tenant farmers, small landed proprietors, and
tradesmen. There could be no mistaking them, they were
genuine Englishmen; for if their dialect did not convince
you of this, their John bullism was sure to do it. They had
grumbled themselves out of England, and the same spirit
accompanied them to Canada.[1]*

T HESE ENGLISHMEN, LIVING in the town of St. Thomas, impressed fur
trader and author Edward Ermatinger with their "John Bull," no-nonsense
approach to life. It was just as well that these settlers had some backbone,
since much of their world at the time would have been controlled by the
tyrannical Thomas Talbot. This "short and strong-built man, with a ruddy
face and an aquiline nose" managed colonization activities throughout
Elgin County and much of Middlesex, Kent, and Essex.[2] Adopting the
mannerisms of a British lord, and having the air "of a military officer

Thomas Talbot (1771–1853), army officer and colonizer. He died at the age of eighty-one and is buried in the Anglican cemetery at Tyrconnell near Port Talbot in Dunwich Township.

Courtesy Archives of Ontario, S1362.

of distinction," he was clearly a formidable character.[3] To some he was a gentleman with social graces, but most people thought him high-handed, having a "total disregard, or rather total ignorance, of the feelings of others."[4] Unlovable though he was, there was a practical side to his character. Having superb supervisory skills, he eventually became Upper Canada's most successful settlement promoter.

As private secretary to Lieutenant Governor Simcoe from 1792–94, Talbot had been able to travel widely across Upper Canada. His visits to the north shore of Lake Erie opened his eyes to the region's enormous settlement opportunities. By 1803 he had obtained a field officer's grant of five thousand acres in Dunwich and Aldborough townships (Elgin County), but settlers were slow to arrive. Understandably, the ongoing Napoleonic Wars (1803–15) and the War of 1812–14[5] had impeded emigration, but the British exodus grew afterward, and by 1817 Talbot had signed up 840 families.[6] Ignoring the original terms of his grant, he soon extended his superintendence of land settlement to vast areas outside his original holding. The provincial government acquiesced, and even allowed Talbot to privately allocate land without registering transfers through the Surveyor General's Office.[7] So Talbot became a law unto himself, eventually acquiring supervisory control over twenty-nine townships, totalling just over half a million acres, along Lake Erie and in the Thames Valley.[8] His "Princely Domain" extended more than 130 miles, from Long Point in Norfolk County to the Detroit River and north to the boundary of the Huron Tract (Map 14).[9]

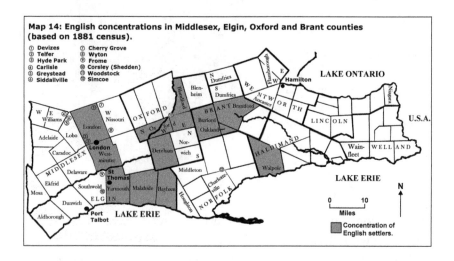

Map 14: English concentrations in Middlesex, Elgin, Oxford and Brant counties (based on 1881 census).

① Devizes   ⑦ Cherry Grove
② Telfer   ⑧ Wyton
③ Hyde Park   ⑨ Frome
④ Carlisle   ⑩ Corsley (Shedden)
⑤ Greystead   ⑪ Woodstock
⑥ Siddallville ⑫ Simcoe

From his command centre — a large log house situated on a cliff above Lake Erie — he masterminded the agricultural and commercial development of the townships entrusted to his care. He made little effort to locate or recruit settlers, but merely accepted or rejected those who came to him. And although he was renowned for his eccentricities and "despotic habits," he got results.[10] He had been fortunate in acquiring good land and wise in anticipating that settlers needed to be set clear land-clearance goals. Lots were granted to "persons of wholesome habits and moral character," who were allowed to select their own locations.[11] He offered each settler a free grant of fifty acres, conditional on the building of a house and the sowing of ten acres within three years.[12] The settler had to clear half of the road in front of his lot as well as one hundred feet adjoining it. Talbot's pencilled notes were the only records kept and only he could understand them. If settlers met his conditions, they could buy additional land; if not, they were forced to vacate. When ousted, he simply erased their names. Thus his terms were clearly stated and ruthlessly monitored.

Realizing the importance of good transport links, he spent considerable sums of his own money on road-building. By the 1820s, his settlers had built a three-hundred-mile stretch of the Talbot Road linking Sandwich (later Windsor) with Aldborough and Dunwich townships.

According to Edward Ermatinger, the people Talbot first attracted as settlers were from the United States or other parts of Upper Canada, "but in the process of time, old countrymen from England, Ireland and Scotland, came in considerable numbers ..."[13] The English settlers apparently "blustered and swore in a manner quite novel to the old settlers," and were initially quite condescending and disapproving of "everything outside of England"; but they became "subdued" once they experienced their first Canadian winter:

> Many of the English settlers, however, are among the best, and most wealthy farmers of this and every other part of Canada. They soon become acclimated, and enjoy a degree of freedom and independence not exceeded, if attained, in any other part of the world. Thousands of them, who might have lived in the old country all their lives, without ever being the owners of horses and cattle, have them here in abundance, besides being the proprietors of valuable freehold estates.[14]

Apparently, Thomas Talbot believed that the "English are the best," preferring them to the Scottish Highlanders, who "make the worst settlers."[15] Talbot's disapproving eye also extended to the many Irish people who were living in his domain — "He disliked them almost as much as he did the Scots."[16]

The "tenant farmers, small landed proprietors, and tradesmen" noted by Edward Ermatinger as having settled in St. Thomas were undoubtedly reasonably affluent people who had funded their own emigration costs; but they were only one strand of the English influx. Throughout the 1830s the Talbot settlements had also attracted a considerable number of poor labourers from Wiltshire and Somerset, who relied on financial assistance from their parishes. Southwold Township (Elgin County) attracted the first group of sixty-six people from Corsley (Wiltshire) in 1830. They appeared to have been influenced by favourable feedback from Joseph Silcox, a Congregational minister and glazier who had emigrated much earlier. Leaving Corsley in 1817, he relocated himself to Southwold at his own expense.[17] "A ragged Christian of the Calvinist type, with an iron frame who made the forest resound with both his axe and his exhortations," the Reverend Silcox soon found the place to his liking.[18] His next move was to persuade his family to join him, although this took some time. Having returned to England in 1821, he emigrated once again to Southwold Township in 1829 with his wife, two sons, and a nephew. Two years later, a second Corsley group of one hundred paupers received funds from their parish to emigrate; they also headed for the Talbot Road in Southwold.[19] No doubt the good reports received from the first Corsley group had helped to reinforce support for Southwold as the favoured destination.[20]

This was a time when the removal of surplus labourers to Upper Canada had won favour, both as a humanitarian measure and to reduce the poor rates bills of English parishes. So, to entice even more potential emigrants, G. Poulett Scrope, MP for Stroud, published the favourable letters that had been written by the first two Corsley groups.[21] Philip Annett's letter was typically upbeat:

> I think you was better sell your house and ... and come to Canada whilst you have a chance If you don't come soon it is likely you will starve and if you don't your children will.... I was agreeably surprised when I came here to see what a fine country it was. It being excellent land bearing crops of wheat and other corn for 20 or 30 years without any dung. You have no rent to pay, no poor-rates and scarcely any taxes. No gamekeepers or Lords over you.... I think no Englishman can do better than come as soon as possible, if it cost them every farthing they have, for I would rather be so here than in England with £100 in my pocket.[22]

W. Clements, formerly "a day labourer of Corsley," wrote that he had acquired a farm of fifty acres, which he bought for £55 (with five years to pay for it) and had a cow and five pigs: "If I had stayed in Corsley I never would have had nothing. I like the country very much…. If the labouring men did but know the value of their strength they would never abide contented in the old country…. No poor-rate, no taxes, no overseers, no beggars." James Treasure, a Corsley shoemaker who emigrated to Yarmouth Township, wrote: "there is not a doubt but all who are willing to work would get a plenty and good pay…. The people here wonder that more do not come…. We are a great deal better and comfortabler [*sic*] than we expected to be in so short a time."[23]

With Corsley people having led the way, emigration fever spread quickly across the county boundary to Frome, in Somerset, and then to the neighbouring parishes of Westbury and Horningsham in Wiltshire. In all, around eight hundred poor people, who had been assisted by their respective parishes, emigrated between 1830 and 1832 from the Corsley/ Frome area. Many headed for the Talbot settlements, although a good number went to more remote districts in Peterborough and Simcoe counties and some settled near Hamilton at the head of Lake Ontario.[24] George Lewis, a day labourer from Corsley, writing from Dundas near Hamilton, stated that "we are very well provided for with regard to a situation. We have a very good house … and George has wages of $100 a year and all his keep, which is much better than ever I should have found in England."[25] Meanwhile, those of the 1832 arrivals who went to live in Elgin County may well have been the "very healthy and well-looking people" who were noted as having come ashore at Port Stanley.[26]

By this time, Joseph Silcox, the man who had spearheaded the Corsley influx to Southwold, was well on his way to becoming an established farmer. Acquiring fifty acres of land for £43 15s., "with 14 acres of improvement on it" as well as livestock, "one yoke of oxen, two cows, one yearling heifer, one mare and colt, four Spring calves, two sows, 11 pigs, 32 geese and a few sheep," he was clearly making very good progress.[27] In addition to satisfying his temporal needs, Joseph had also founded Southwold's first Congregational church, located just to the west of St. Thomas at Frome. As pastor, he preached to a scattered congregation who were based mainly in Dunwich and Southwold townships (Elgin County) and in Westminster Township (Middlesex County).[28] In addition to the Frome that formed just to the west of St. Thomas, a Corsley (later renamed Shedden) also sprouted a short distance away. Both place names were very visible reminders of transferred English origins (Map 14).[29]

As was the case with Corsley, attempts had been made to stimulate emigration from Frome through the publication of letters home, written in 1831 and 1832. Among the Frome letter-writers was William Jeanes, a labourer who had actually emigrated in 1820 and presumably funded his own removal expenses. He had been assigned land by Thomas Talbot in Romney Township, much farther to the west in Kent County (Map 15). Desperate to persuade his wife to join him, he wrote her three letters. His first, written in 1832, mentioned various Frome people who had emigrated to Upper Canada:

> Tell William More that his son came no farther than Prescott with me. He got into work at $8 the month, board and lodgings…. Tell Mrs.Porter on the hill that Mr. and Mrs. Slade send their love to them and tell them that they are in good health and doing well. Likewise tell Samuel White (a shoemaker) and family the same … he might do well if he was to come here as shoes are very dear here.[30]

By the time of his second letter a year later, William had moved to the adjoining township of Tilbury West in Essex County. Advising his wife not to bring "heavy clumsy articles" with her because it would be"expensive carrying them through the country upwards of 800 miles," he explained that he had travelled that far west "for the climate, being somewhat like England, which I know well would suit the mind of an Englishman, and likewise it is the best land calculated to be in Canada."[31] When he wrote his third letter in 1833, he was still working for a "gentlemen," who paid him $13 a month with bed and board. With his earnings, he had been able to buy land:

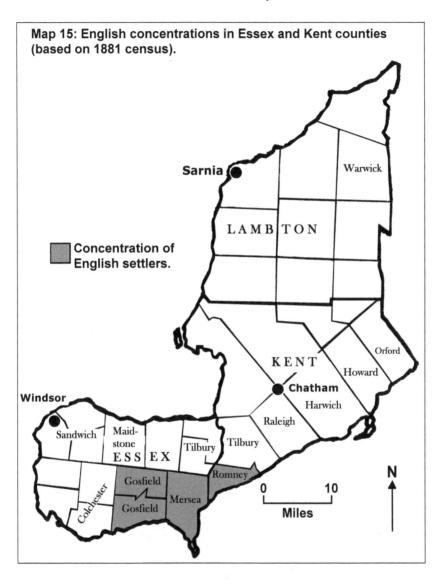

Map 15: English concentrations in Essex and Kent counties (based on 1881 census).

I have 200 acres of land with upwards of six acres of it cleared, a house on it and partly stocked, which has cost me besides my own labour $100.... [But] what is 200 acres to me if you cannot come to me? I would not be cut off from you and the poor children for all America.... O my dear wife and children I wish you all lived as well as I do. I have meat every meal, breakfast, dinner and supper and as much as I like to take, there is nothing wanting.[32]

Whether Frome Parish provided his wife with funds to emigrate is unknown. Apparently, she did want to join him.[33]

The disastrous economic conditions that had afflicted the Corsley area in West Wiltshire were also being experienced in Downton Parish on the southeast side of the county. Poor harvests between 1828 and 1830 added to the gloom, while the growing use of threshing machines on farms threatened the jobs and livelihoods of countless labourers. Predictably, mounting unemployment created extreme social tensions. There were violent disturbances in Downton and the neighbouring parish of Whiteparish during the Swing riots of 1830–31, a time when impoverished labourers agitated for better wages and the removal of the new threshing machines.[34] Failing to win these changes, they were dealt with severely by being deported as convicts to Australia. Although this harsh response restored the peace, it did not resolve Downton's underlying social and economic problems.

Bush Farm near Chatham in Kent County, circa 1838. Painting by Philip John Bainbridge (1817–81).

Matters came to a head in 1835 when unemployment reached unsustainably high levels. Samuel Payne, the assistant overseer of Downton Parish, reported that as many as fifty to one hundred "superfluous labourers of the parish" were being employed routinely on the roads or in digging gravel pits as a makeshift measure to create jobs.[35] And the plight of the poor was made even worse by another catastrophic development. With the introduction of machines for the making of lace, poor households in Downton lost an important supplementary income. For decades, traditional lace-making had been the principal occupation of poor women and girls in Downton, but increasing mechanization from the 1830s made them redundant. By 1834 it was reported that "until some other domestic employment be substituted, industrious wives and children of the labourers are condemned to a material diminution of their scanty comforts."[36]

Emigration to Upper Canada from Downton began very cautiously in 1835. James King, his wife, two other adults, and four children; J. Pressey, his wife, plus another adult and three children; James Chalk, his wife, and five children; and Henry Higgs, E. Brundy, James Perry, and Charles Bundy all headed for Portsmouth. However, this group of twenty-five emigrants had to spend five nights at the Quebec Hotel in Portsmouth Harbour while they waited for their ship to sail. The vagaries of the weather and wind direction had no doubt caused the delay. Judging from the food and drink receipts that were submitted, no expense was spared in looking after their needs.

The Downton group enjoyed sumptuous meals washed down with copious quantities of ale, port, and other alcoholic beverages (Table 13). Breakfasts with lobster, mackerel, or steak were followed in the evening by meals of salmon, steak, and lamb cutlets or chops. The drinks bill for their last night, amounting to 7s. 8d., was roughly the average weekly wage of an agricultural labourer! The total bill came to a staggering £6 3s. 6d., of which the accommodation cost had only been £1. Moreover, this was in addition to other payments these people would have received for their fares in crossing the Atlantic, food and drink while travelling, onward travel in Upper Canada, clothing, spending money, and various other items.[37] The inescapable conclusion is that the Downton Parish

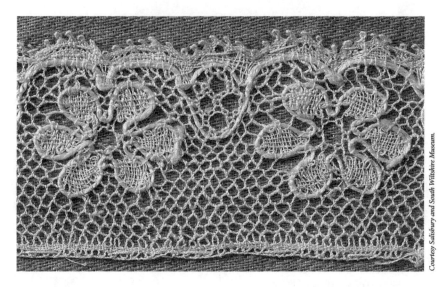

Courtesy Salisbury and South Wiltshire Museum.

"Downton Daisy," a Downton lace sample made in the nineteenth century in Downton, Wiltshire. Girls were trained at lace schools, of which there were two in Downton in 1819.

Courtesy Portsmouth Museums and Records Service Acc. No. 68/1982.

"On the Point, Portsmouth," a watercolour painted in 1857 by William Smyth (later Admiral Smyth). The Quebec Hotel is the white building on the waterfront at the right. It was situated in Bath Square and was famous in its day.

authorities were under orders to give the group anything they wanted to have. Were people celebrating their good fortune in being assisted to emigrate? Possibly, but the more likely explanation is that fine food and drink were being offered to give very apprehensive people some Dutch courage. Nevertheless, however worried they may have been about their prospects, once they arrived in Upper Canada their response was over-whelmingly positive. The vicar of Downton received a number of forth-right letters from Downton people, this being an example:

> You told me that we should repent of coming to Canada, and surely we do, but it is because we did not come before…. This I have to say, that any labouring man can live better by working three days a week than at home by working all of the week…. Here are no poor-rates, for there are no poor here.[38]

So emigration fever also gripped Downton. In April 1836, a much larger group of 220 people from Downton and fifty-nine from Whiteparish sailed from London in the *King William* (Table 14). Downton Parish borrowed £1,000 to finance the scheme, with Lord Radnor, a major landowner, paying the interest on the loan. Most went to the Talbot-controlled townships in Elgin County, although precise informa-tion on where they settled is fragmentary. Some are known to have gone to Bayham Township, while others went to St. Thomas in Yarmouth Township. Given that the 1837 Census reveals a major English cluster in Southwold Township and smaller ones in Malahide and Bayham town-ships, the likelihood is that the Downton paupers became concentrated in these two townships. They may well have added to the English popu-lation in Southwold Township, although it had already acquired a large contingent of settlers from West Wiltshire five years earlier.[39]

Talbot's reign ended in 1838 when the British and Upper Canada governments forced him to wind down his land agency and put it under the jurisdiction of the provincial authorities. Most of the areas under his control had been settled by then. The English communities that had sprouted in Southwold, Malahide, and Bayham townships (Elgin

County) were only a small part of a much wider group of English settlements that extended into Westminster Township in Middlesex County, Blandford, Dereham, and Norwich townships in Oxford County and Brantford Township in Brant County (Map 14).[40]

Although immigrants from England became scattered far and wide in the southwest region of Upper Canada, they continued to maintain a dominance in some or all of these counties. By 1881, they were the largest ethnic group in east Elgin, east Middlesex, much of Oxford County, virtually all of Brant County, and parts of Norfolk County. In addition, the English acquired impressive footholds farther west, representing a staggering 62 percent of the population of Romney Township in Kent County and over 40 percent of the population of Mersea and Gosfield townships in Essex County (Map 15). However, given that the far southwest attracted a considerable population from the United States beginning in the late eighteenth century, a high proportion were probably descended from Americans of English descent, rather than from people who emigrated directly from England.

Looking back over his life, Talbot might have taken pride in having overseen the early agricultural development of this fertile region. Yet, however important he was as a settlement supervisor, success depended on the gallantry, skills, and staying power of the many thousands of individual immigrants who flocked to his and other parts of Upper Canada, usually at their own expense. The American arrivals had a relatively easy time, since they were already familiar with North American conditions. Reuben and Mary Bisbee, both New Englanders, came to London Township in 1828 and immediately founded Devizes, naming it after the market town in Wiltshire from which their ancestors had originated. Reuben built a brickyard and, together with his sons, helped to turn Devizes into an important commercial centre.[41] But the task of creating farms from the wilderness was much more daunting for the British colonizers, who began arriving in greater numbers as the economic depression that followed the end of the Napoleonic Wars in 1815 grew in severity.

John Uren, a native of Cornwall, relocated to Cherry Grove in West Nissouri Township (Middlesex County) in 1820, a place located just to

Courtesy Toronto Reference Library T15406.

Dundas Street in the town of London, 1840. Painting by James Hamilton (1810–96).

the east of the Devizes settlement.[42] Other early English arrivals included London-born Thomas J. Jones and his wife Ann Attfield, who emigrated in 1822, settling the following year in London Township. Describing himself as a "white collar man" who transferred himself to the backwoods of Canada, Thomas applied his organizational skills, acquired while working as a clerk for the Bank of England and later for a shipbuilding firm, to his new environment, eventually establishing a successful general store.[43] However, while most parts of England lost people to Upper Canada, the early exodus, which had gathered steam since 1817, mainly drew people from the northern counties.

Thomas Priestman, a Quaker from near Wigton in Cumberland County, came to Adolphustown (Lennox County), near the Bay of Quinte on Lake Ontario, as early as 1811. Six years later he and his family moved farther west to Wainfleet Township (Welland County) on Lake Erie.[44] By then, his cousin, Thomas Graham, had joined him, while his brother Josiah, a cooper, was thinking of emigrating to Upper Canada, although Thomas warned him that it was "a considerable expense," having spent £32 2s. on his own family's sea crossing.[45] Thomas's letters home reveal a stoic and lonely man who greatly valued his links with Cumberland. In particular, he missed his brother John:

> I have often thought of thee when I have been travelling alone through the wilderness roads and how desirable it would have been to have had a brother to have talked to.... Some of the old English people are a little self-willed and think they could do better but it is necessary to conform to the customs of the country in many respects.... This country is peopled from all nations and everyone has something of their own country plans so this is a mixture of many nations ...[46]

So when Elizabeth Robson, an English Quaker minister from Lancashire, attended a local Quaker gathering, Thomas was over the moon. "She could remember several of you ... you can scarcely think the satisfaction that it gives me to meet with a person that has some personal acquaintance with any of you, my friends and relations ..."[47] His Quaker religion was an extremely important lifeline. In 1830, he was visited by some Quaker friends who still lived at his previous location near the Bay of Quinte area: "It was an opportunity of enquiring after many of my friends and acquaintances in that part of the province."[48] Thomas Priestman's farming activities went from strength to strength, but throughout he was fortified greatly by his family roots and strong religious beliefs. Meanwhile, by 1839, cousin Thomas Graham and his family were planning to leave Wainfleet in order to establish themselves at "their new place" in London.[49]

Cumberland immigrants were some of the earliest to colonize Middlesex County. George Shipley of Carlisle founded Carlisle in East Williams Township, having become the proprietor of a large gristmill,[50] while Thomas Routledge from Bewcastle founded Hyde Park Corner in London Township around 1818, a name presumably chosen because of the family's connections with London, England.[51] Northumberland Shipleys also came to the area. William and Thomas Shipley from Greystead founded a Greystead in Lobo Township (Middlesex County). Lying just to the south of Carlisle, it would seem that Cumberland and Northumberland Shipley families had been acting together in creating these hamlets. Also coming to the area at this time were John and Diana Siddall, from London, England.

They founded Siddallville, located only a short distance from Carlisle and Greystead, in Lobo Township. Their decision to emigrate had been triggered by an inheritance acquired in the 1820s. Having moved initially to New York State, the Siddalls had relocated to Lobo by 1832. Building a gristmill, sawmill, and carding mill, John and his sons helped to transform Siddallville into a thriving business community.[52]

Yorkshire-born John and Thomas Scatcherd founded Wyton in West Nissouri Township (Middlesex County) during the early 1820s, naming it after their home village near Hull in the East Riding.[53] Having founded a woollen mill and tannery, John moved in 1831 to the town of London, where he opened a store.[54] Shortly after this, George Jackson left Berwick-upon-Tweed in Northumberland with his wife and large family. After renting accommodation in Toronto, he ended up in Simcoe in Charlotteville Township (Norfolk County), where he established a hardware store.[55]

As these examples show, English people generally emigrated on their own or in very small family groups. Once they had found their bearings, they usually became assimilated into a community that accommodated many different ethnic groups, including their own; but occasionally people from a particular area of England emigrated as a group in the hope of remaining together in their New World settlement.

An example is the Northumberland group, mainly from Simonburn Parish near Hexham, who moved to London Township in 1821, having emigrated to New York State five years earlier. Moving north, they attracted more followers from Northumberland and founded the "English settlement" in the western part of the township. By 1824, it became known as the "Telfer settlement," in honour of the many Telfer families who lived within the new community.[56] Gravestones in the Telfer cemetery, still visible today, testify to the substantial influx of people from the North of England who laid down roots here and created a once-thriving community.[57]

Cumberland and Durham lead miners were another group who streamed into Upper Canada, but, unlike the Northumberland immigrants, they became more widely dispersed. Led by Thomas Milburn of Alston, in Cumberland, an earlier group had emigrated to Peterborough County in around 1817, having taken advantage of the government's

£10 group emigration scheme.[58] Fifteen years later, when an economic depression gripped this important lead-mining district, more followed from Cumberland and nearby Weardale, in Durham County. Writing from Weardale in 1854, John Graham described how miners from his area, including his brother, had gone to Upper Canada and the United States.[59] Featherston Phillipson, who had emigrated with Thomas Milburn, bought land west of Hamilton near Lake Erie, which he was farming, and a good many other Weardale families were on their way to becoming successful farmers:

> [John] Fleamen and [Joseph] Wearmouth has bought 100 acres of land about the same place and speak highly of the place, they say there is plenty of work to get of all sorts ... and good wages too, it is grandest and flourishing counties they ever saw; We had a man the name of John Featherston who went from this country 20 years ago [to Upper Canada] who is a relation to many a one in Weardale, who is very rich in property now, and when they went first they were a great family of them; they had not a penny left when they landed, and I think that is encouragement, and all the names that I have mentioned over[60] has gone into Upper Canada and a great deal more not mentioned, for their was over a 100 of men, women and children left this Spring, all for America, and John Featherston, who went to America about a year ago, writes that they will very soon have a little Weardale there.[61]

Meanwhile, in 1832, a large group of paupers from the Petworth estate in West Sussex were being assisted to emigrate to the government-supervised settlement in Adelaide Township (Middlesex County), adding significantly to the county's English population.[62] Ample land was available for them to form a compact settlement at the southern end of the township, many of them ending up in the future Napperton.[63] William Cooper's letter home revealed how the Sussex immigrants worked together initially in performing the back-breaking task of clearing the land of its trees:

> I have got 100 acres of land at $2 per acre and 1/4th to be paid at the end of three years and the rest in three years more.... I should like for all my brothers to come here, for here is plenty of work, and no doubt but we shall do very well after next harvest. Edward Boxall and his wife and William Phillips from Merston and we have built us a Shantee and lives and works altogether on our own land. We have got above two acres cleared and shall sow six or seven acres of wheat this autumn and more in the Spring.[64]

In just a few months, William could report that he had built his own log house, measuring sixteen by twenty-two feet, and was planning to build a barn in the summer.[65] No doubt his swift progress encouraged brother James to follow him to Adelaide with his wife Harriet and family, while Harriet's sister Mary, who had married James Budd, also emigrated that same year, but they settled farther to the west in Woodstock (Oxford County).

Shortly after arriving in Adelaide, William Baker boasted about his one hundred acres to his family — as "good land as any in England ... if any of you will come here and live with me you shall have part of my land; or if you choose you can draw another 100 acres and you will get 6 years to pay the money ... at 10s. per acre." As a further sign of coordinated activity, he and William Rapley had "one yoke of oxen between us to do our work, which shall be at your service also."[66]

Stephen Goatcher aimed much higher than being a farmer and decided to launch a dairy completely on his own. However, he learned the hard way that farming methods were very different and that colonization ventures like his required meticulous planning. He had not recruited any workers in advance and was probably unable to attract a workforce in Adelaide because of the high wage rates that labourers expected, which would have been beyond his means. Writing to his wife in Sussex, he asked her to find friends and family who might wish "to come out and live with me ... to manage my dairy.... I shall have plenty of land, I have 14 acres clear now, enough to keep me as long as I shall live.... It is accounted as good land as any in Canada."[67] However good his land was, he failed to attract support and returned to England, possibly as early as 1833, and certainly by 1839.

For Ann (Downer) Mann, who emigrated in 1836, Adelaide was a dream come true, despite its rough and ready state and having to cope with the death of her husband in Montreal. In Adelaide she could, at long last, escape from the poverty that had haunted her all her life. She arrived with four of her youngest sons and her oldest son, together with his wife and children. Despite the loss of her husband, she gave her adult sons back home a glowing account of her new situation. She was elated by the fact that all of her children had found jobs as domestic servants in the nearby towns and that she would never have to face life in the dreaded workhouse ever again:

> I don't want for nothing; my children are all out at service; I could get them places if I had twenty more ... if any of your children wish to come to America do not hinder them; for I shall say this is a good country to come to; I wish I had come when my first son came[68]; but thank God I am here. What would have become of my children if they had been in England and I had been put into some poorhouse; but now if I go out of the [front] door I do see great comfort.... Let my letter be copied off and be stuck up at the Onslow Arms [Inn] to let everyone see that I lives in Adelaide; don't leave no one thing out that I say ...[69]

Assisted emigrants from West Sussex also colonized Delaware Township, to the southeast of Adelaide, adding further to the English component of Middlesex County. George Carver was struck by the different social structure that he encountered and how it gave poor labourers like him an advantage over the "spirited farmers and their wives" who had made his life a misery back in England:

> They would not like to sit down at table after their ser-
> vants have done meals and eat what is left, for here they
> would be obliged to beg and pray to get a man for a few
> days to help them instead of blustering and swearing as
> they do over you in England. Here if a man wants any
> common labour to be done he must do it himself or let
> it go undone, but if he wants to raise a house or a barn
> or any such thing as that his neighbours readily come
> and assist him and he does the same in return.[70]

Thomas Priestman of Wainfleet, mentioned previously, made a similar observation, noting how "labour is done by much fewer hands than
the same would be done in England; wages are high and labour not in
great plenty."[71]

Delaware had good employment prospects for tradesmen, who
could earn considerably higher wages than in England. Alexander Hilton
could hardly believe his luck. Arriving in 1836, he worked as a carpenter,
initially earning $10 per month. This later rose to $16 to $18 per month,
and within a few years he had amassed sufficient funds to purchase a
farm in Adelaide Township.[72] But Delaware was not a home away from
home for Sussex people in the way that Adelaide was. Frances Pullen,
who worked as a domestic servant, found "plenty of English in Delaware,"
but she only knew one person (Amelia Cooper) from her former village
in Sussex. "I often see her; she lives in Delaware."[73]

The pattern of Petworth immigrants sending good reports home
soon after their arrival repeated itself farther east at Woodstock, in
Blandford Township (Oxford County). Henry Heasman apprenticed
himself to a blacksmith for four years and was receiving "3s. 6d. to 4s.
the day, with board," this being a considerable improvement on the 10s.
a week without board that a Sussex labourer could expect.[74] Cornelius
Voice, a carpenter who emigrated to Blandford with his wife and a large
family in 1834, apparently made the transition to pioneer farmer very
speedily and easily. When he and his family reached Blandford they were
given temporary accommodation and were helped to build their first
house: "We were all put up in the squire's barn, while our houses were

building. Our houses were built with round trees laid one on the other, with a few boards for the roof, without any door or window, or fire place; we had to do the rest as we could." The day after their arrival, his two sons "went out ... to get work and got work for all. We get 6s. 3d. a day. We were glad to begin work for we had but three sovereigns. We soon earned some money and then we all went to work at our house and land…. We have now cleared our five acres …"[75]

Petworth immigrants also extended their reach eastward toward Ancaster Township (Wentworth County), located just to the west of Hamilton. George Hills, who arrived from Sussex in 1832, commented on his good pay and employment prospects:

> I like the country here very much but my wife don't seem to be quite so well contented yet. I got work on the first day I was here and have had plenty of work ever since…. Farmers and labourers all sit at one table here. We get 5s. per day, English money, and be boarded. I don't wish to persuade anyone to come over, for they must expect to see a good many hardships; but I know a poor man can do a great deal better here than he can at home.[76]

This area had also attracted people from Dorking, in Surrey, who had been assisted to emigrate to Upper Canada in 1832 under the auspices of the Petworth scheme. Having experienced incendiary attacks during the Swing riots, Dorking's major landowners decided that the time had come to assist its poor to emigrate. In all, seventy-seven paupers, mainly single males and large families, agreed to emigrate, with the necessary funds being paid by subscription as well as by Dorking Parish. Another group was assisted to emigrate in 1833, financed entirely from the poor rates.

While the Dorking immigrants scattered themselves across much of Upper Canada, they were mainly concentrated near the western end of Lake Ontario, especially in the Hamilton area.[77] John Worsfield, a painter and decorator from Dorking, reported: "I am at present at work in the town of Hamilton and there I am treated as a gentleman for the art of graining and flatting [painting terms] is not much known here; I get £1 a week and board and lodging. I have everything that I want. I may have beef steaks or other meat for breakfast and what I like to drink." Joining forces with Mr. (James) Harpur and J. Knight, he used his earnings to purchase land in East Flamborough Township (Wentworth County) and soon had "six acres of it cleared and sowed with wheat."[78]

John Stedman, another of the Dorking immigrants, settled in Malahide Township (Elgin County), where he found work while waiting for his luggage to come ashore at Port Stanley. A local farmer approached him and his travelling companion and offered them jobs:

> We thought we might as well go to work as to wait about after our chests, as [we] should be getting something in pocket ... [the farmer] asked me if I would hire by the year. He said that he would give [me] $100 board, lodging, washing [and] mending for the year, so I thought it wise to hire, as long as I had that chance, as I was a stranger in the country.[79]

Meanwhile, John acquired "100 acres of land, as I may work for myself at times and not work for other people any longer than I am forced."

Surviving immigrant letters reveal that a substantial number of Petworth immigrants settled in Middlesex, Oxford, Brant, and Waterloo counties, although, as previously discussed, they were also to be found in large numbers along the north and west side of Lake Ontario, especially in the counties of York, Halton, and Wentworth (Map 16).[80] Unfortunately, the locations of the two thousand or so Norfolk paupers who emigrated to Upper Canada during 1835–36 remain much of a mystery, since only a tiny amount of documentation relating to their destinations survives. The available evidence suggests that two Norfolk parishes — Briston and Edgefield — assisted their paupers to emigrate and that they mainly went to Oxford and Waterloo counties.[81] One hundred and thirty-three Briston people emigrated to Upper Canada between 1831 and 1834, with the funds having been provided by various landowners and the poor rates.[82] Another eighty-seven people from

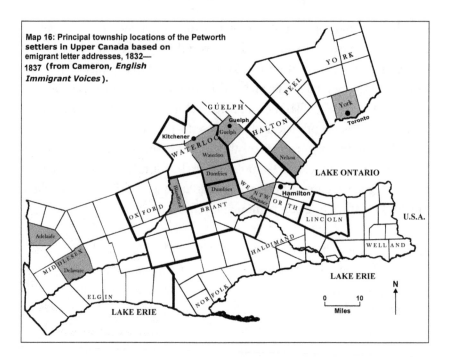

Map 16: Principal township locations of the Petworth settlers in Upper Canada based on emigrant letter addresses, 1832–1837 (from Cameron, *English Immigrant Voices*).

this same parish followed in 1836,[83] and they were joined by 123 people from the neighbouring parish of Edgefield.[84] Two other Edgefield groups followed in later years, with many joining the 1834 Briston group in the southwest region. At one stage, Briston and Edgefield immigrants were living side by side in Bleinhem Township (Oxford County). Perhaps the many Norfolk paupers who left in 1835–36 from the neighbouring parishes of Holt (numbering seventy-two) and Saxthorpe (eighty-one), and the nearby parish of Fulmodeston (eighty-five) also made their way to Oxford County.[85]

Similarly, the destinations of the five hundred or so Suffolk paupers who were assisted by their respective parishes to emigrate in 1835–36 were also unclear. Fifty-two people from Kettleburgh Parish went to Etobicoke Township near Toronto in 1836, where they joined another Kettleburgh group of fifty-two people who had emigrated five years earlier.[86] But apart from this group, which could be traced to its new destination, most of the Suffolk immigrants appear to have vanished without a trace. Forty paupers from Cratfield Parish and twenty-three from Carlton Colville Parish, near Lowestoft, were assisted to emigrate to Upper Canada in 1836, but their locations are unknown.[87]

Meanwhile, a chance survival of the Woolnough family's letters reveals how a handful of Suffolk people, originating from Beccles Parish, came to relocate themselves in the Niagara District at their own expense. Having settled at Queenston in Niagara Township (Lincoln County) sometime before 1832, Susan Woolnough wrote to her father back in Beccles with the news that her brothers "would do better here with two days work in a week than it is possible for them to do in England to work always." As if to anticipate Canada's hard-drinking reputation, she went on to comment that "the people in general are much more moral than in England, and although liquor is so cheap, there is not half the drunkenness that there is in England."[88] However, this is just one tiny glimpse of a major immigrant stream from England to the southwestern region. Statistics were kept of their numbers but few of the immigrants can be given names.

Throughout the 1840s, Alexander Buchanan, the Quebec immigration officer, noted in his reports how many English immigrants, from both north and south, were heading to the western region of Upper Canada. In June 1841, groups of Devon and Yorkshire immigrants were on their way to the Western District and over the following two years a group from Kent, two groups from Yorkshire, and several others from Devon and Cornwall were planning to settle in either the Western or Gore districts.[89] In 1842, some of the North of England immigrants who had arrived from Liverpool and others who had set sail from Falmouth in Cornwall told Buchanan that they intended to settle in either Blenheim Township (Oxford County) or Brantford Township (Brant County).[90] Few paupers were assisted to emigrate by their parishes, although the occasional family received funds. The Hempstall family in the East Drayton parish of Nottinghamshire were given the amazingly generous sum of £38 13s. 11d. to emigrate in 1841, with £18 being allocated for Ann Hempstall's "groceries" — food to be consumed on the sea crossing from Hull (Table 15).[91]

As ever, the majority of immigrants paid their own way and slipped into Upper Canada unnoticed. The jottings of a Cambridgeshire rector, who appeared to know everyone's business in Croydon Parish, hint at the range of people who might have come to the western region during the 1840s:

> Samuel Richardson aged 22 is gone to Canada, given to drinking.… John Hill aged 24 has gone to Canada (can read). John Chapman (28) can read and Thomas Chapman (24), can read, both brothers "are gone to Canada." Charles and Mary Titmus can't read.… They and their children now live at The Limekilns, where Mr. Easy used to live "before he went to Canada." Thomas and Ann Hill, live in the same house (but only married in Autumn, 1843); he can't read; she can read a little; "gone to Canada." John Simpson, widower and a parish clerk, can read; "he went to Canada" before his marriage to Mary Spencer. Isaiah (eldest son of John above) and Sarah Simpson live in same house and can both read, have a child, and are now married. "They went to Canada but returned and now live in London [England]"; Dinah Story, a widow, can read and "goes out washing"; she has 3 children William, Mary and John and she married [Mr.] Easy and "they are all gone to Canada"; Philip Gentle (22) is now in jail for a riot at Caxton Workhouse — is to go to Canada.[92]

But five farm labourers and their families from Tolpuddle in Dorset, who settled in London Township in 1844, did attract attention on both sides of the Atlantic. Having pressed for better wages a decade earlier, the six "Tolpuddle Martyrs" had been convicted of criminal conspiracy in 1834 and deported to Australia in chains as convicts. A statement inscribed by George Loveless, one of the martyrs, outside the Tolpuddle Methodist chapel where he preached, reveals how unjust this conviction was: "My Lord, if we have violated any law, it was not done intentionally, We have injured no person or property. We are uniting to preserve ourselves, our wives, our children from utter degradation and starvation."

The men were meant to remain in exile in Australia for seven years, but such was the outcry in Britain over their harsh treatment that the government was forced to offer them a pardon. They returned to England in 1837. Eventually, their brave stand against Britain's unjust employment laws led to the formation of the trade union movement.

Five of the six Tolpuddle Martyrs moved to Upper Canada in 1844.[93] In doing so, they had rejected their homeland in favour of a new country, within the British Empire, which offered them the freedom of expression that had been denied them earlier. It was also their acceptance of the harsh reality that labourers in England could not easily lift themselves out of poverty, while in Canada they could aspire to far better living conditions and escape from Britain's oppressive class system. George and Elizabeth Loveless settled near Fanshawe, just to the north of the town of London, and both are buried at the Siloam Cemetery, while the other four are buried in or near London.[94]

The yearning to be free of rigid social structures and to seek a better future attracted English immigrants to Upper Canada throughout the nineteenth century. John Wilkinson, from Huxley, near Chester in Cheshire, came with his family to Dereham Township (Oxford County) in 1851, where he joined a friend who had previously settled in the county. A staunch Wesleyan Methodist, John was followed by his sister and brother-in-law the next year. His first house was "a rude shanty 16' by 24' of round logs chinked with moss and plastered with mud." In time the land was cleared: "Having now become lords of the soil we, for the first time, began to feel free: no landlord to annoy us, no anxiety about rent and no Episcopalian dignitary to look down on us because we were [in England] what they pleased to call dissenters."[95] Also emigrating with his wife and nine children from Yarmouth (Suffolk County) in 1852 to Sable in West Williams Township (Middlesex County) was Edward Teeple, who gave his name to the "Teepletown" community that eventually formed.[96]

Yet pioneer life had its perils. In 1868, Joseph Hooper, who had originated from Biggleswade Parish in east Bedfordshire, was badly in debt and risked losing his farm in North Dumfries (Waterloo County). Receiving help from his brother back in England was his only hope:

Photograph by Geoff Campey.

ABOVE: Memorial to the Tolpuddle Martyrs in Tolpuddle, Dorset. Their anguish is depicted in this sombre sculpture of one of the martyrs — probably George Loveless.

LEFT: Tombstones for George and Elizabeth Loveless from Tolpuddle, Dorset, in Siloam Cemetery, near London, Ontario. George died in 1874 aged seventy-seven and Elizabeth in 1868 aged sixty-eight. The inscription reads: "There are they which come out of great tribulation and have washed their robes and wash them white in the blood of the lamb (Revelation 7:14)." George had preached at Siloam Methodist Church.

Photograph by Geoff Campey.

My crops turned out a failure. As I know that you will not want to receive a long letter, I will cut it short. I want to know if you could lend me £100 on my farm and stock, or say stock and furniture. I do not know if I told you that my farm was worn out by cropping before I bought [it], but such was the case and I have only raised enough to keep the house going for the last three years. I now want to put it into crop and I have not the means to buy the seed and that is what I want to raise the money for, so if you could lend it me I should feel obliged if you could let me have it at once.... I was sorry I could not come to see you before I left England but I thought that if I came back to Canada at once I might be able to get along without troubling you, but I find I cannot, so if you can oblige me I will give you the security. You will not be put to too much trouble for if the farm does not pay better I will sell and try something else ...[97]

In that same year, Tingrith Parish in southwest Bedfordshire began losing people to Upper Canada. Emigration had widened its appeal during the second half of the nineteenth century in areas such as this, partly as a result of the greater availability of cheaper and more comfortable Atlantic crossings, made possible by steamships. Another factor was the ongoing agricultural depression being experienced in rural areas, made worse by increasing grain imports from North America. And times were particularly tough for agricultural labourers, whose wages were being held down by the oversupply of labour.

With this in mind, "the Misses Trevor of Tingrith House" paid the emigration costs in 1868 of some of the parish's needy farm labourers and their families. Four years later, the *Bedfordshire Mercury* reported that "upwards of 100 men, women and children" had been assisted to emigrate to Canada "during the past few years" and that "these emigrants are doing well in the land of their adoption."[98] Another report stated that twenty-three people left from Tingrith in 1868, while a second group followed at a later date: "In both cases ... their fare and passage money were paid, and an outfit was provided and a small sum furnished to each emigrant for present need on arrival."[99] The *Bedfordshire Mercury* reported in 1872 that "two young men" who had emigrated in 1860 "came over recently on a visit to Tingrith and we learn that they have given the most favourable account of the prosperity of the 'Tingrith Colony.'"[100]

The fact that Joseph Barnett, a Bedfordshire man from Great Barford who emigrated in 1875, can be traced to Oxford County, may suggest that this was also the location of the Tingrith Colony.[101] Not much of a clue — but this is all that survives! Over the years, Bedfordshire parishes had assisted a small number of their paupers to emigrate, with £101 16s. 10d having been spent in relocating the first seven families in 1831.[102] One or two families continued to emigrate with financial support over the next twenty years from north and mid Bedfordshire, but none came from parishes near Tingrith.[103]

As the spread of settlement pushed northward into the Huron Tract and beyond, English immigrants streamed in ever greater numbers into the western peninsula. Many were attracted by the prospect of settling on the Canada Company's lands. Through its capital investment in roads, bridges, and buildings it attracted emigrants who would otherwise have balked at the prospect of locating themselves in such a remote part of Upper Canada. The English would come in their thousands to help colonize this newly opened frontier.

Table 13:

Receipts for Downton Emigrant Accommodation and Food/Drink While Staying at the Quebec Hotel, Portsmouth, May 19–24, 1835 [WRO 1306/105]

	s.	d.
May 19th		
Salmon & sauce, chicken & ham, vegetables, bread, butter, etc.	10	0
Porter	2	0
Port	5	6
Ale	-	2
Beds	4	0
May 20th		
Breakfast & Lobster	5	0
Paper	-	2
Luncheon	1	0
Porter	1	7
Soles, steaks, vegetables, bread, butter, etc.	6	0
Porter	2	7
Port	5	6
Paper	-	2
Beds	4	0
May 21st		
Breakfast & Mackerel	4	6
Salmon & sauce, lamb cutlets, vegetables, bread & butter, etc.	7	0
Porter	2	0
Port	5	6
Beds	4	0
May 22nd		
Breakfast & Mackerel	4	6
Salmon & sauce, lamb chops, vegetables, bread & butter, etc.	7	0
Porter	2	0
Port	5	6
Beds	4	0

	s.	d.
May 23rd		
Breakfast & steak	4	6
Sherry & Port	4	2
Cider	1	0
Salmon & sauce, steak, vegetables, bread & butter, etc.	7	0
Porter	3	0
Grogs	4	8
Beds	4	0
May 24th		
Breakfast & steak	4	6

Totals £6 3s. 6d.

Table 14:

Passenger List for the Crossing of the *King William* in April 1836 from London to Quebec with 279 Paupers from Wiltshire
[Ken Light, "Wiltshire England Emigrants: The Downton Story 1835–1836" in *Families* Vol. 37, No. 1 (Feb. 1998), 19–26.]

Males	Age	Married	Females	Age
Isaac Barter	42	Married	Ann Barter	32
Frederick Barter	11		Jane Barter	8
Henry Barter	6		Hariet Barter	1½
John Barter	4			
James Prince	47	Married	Ann Prince	45
Abraham Prince	16		Kesia Prince	11
Obiah Prince	9		Rosalinda Prince	3½
John Prince	6			
William Bampton	38	Married	Sarah Bampton	40
John Poore	15	Son in Law	Mary Bampton	4
Charles Poore	13	Son in Law	Sarah Bampton	2
Joseph Poore	10	Son in Law		
James Bampton	6			

Males	Age	Married	Females	Age
Charles King	26	Married	Ann King	30
Charles King	3		Letitia King	1
			Ann King	37
			Charlotte King	18
James Dredge	30	Married	Eliza Dredge	24
George Light	49	Married	Mary Light	42
Charles Light	15		Sarah Light	13
Henry Light	10		Thursa Light	3
George Light	8			
Lazarus Light	5			
Oran Light	3 mths			
William Edmonds	35	Married	Hannah Light	37
John Edmonds	12		Sarah Edmonds	13
Charles Edmonds	10			
George Edmonds	7			
Henry Edmonds	3			
James Biddlecomb	44	Married	Elsay Biddlecomb	41
George Biddlecomb	17		Hannah Biddlecomb	18
Henry Biddlecomb	12		unreadable	6
Charles Biddlecomb	6			
James Champ	36	Married	Eliza Champ	35
William Champ	17		Clarissa Champ	13
Edmund Champ	9			
George Champ	6			
Arthur Champ	1½			
James Jennings	42	Married	Rosanna Jennings	40
Silas Jennings	18		Maria Jennings	7
Robert Jennings	9		Mary Ann Jennings	n/k
Thomas Small	34	Married	Mary Small	34
Charles Small	13			
James Small	10			
William Small	4			

Males	Age	Married	Females	Age
William Webb	50	Married	Martha Webb	38
John Webb	11		Rhoda Webb	11
			Mary Webb	4
			Martha Webb	4
Thomas Pretty	34	Married	Sarah Pretty	37
Henry Pretty	11		Charlotte Pretty	13
			Elizabeth Pretty	7
			Ann Pretty	2
Joseph Dredge	31	Married	Kesia Dredge	31
Henry Dredge	9		Charlotte Dredge	1
William Dredge	4			
George Pressy	38	Married	Mary Pressy	37
Henry Pressy	14		Ann Pressy	4
Phineas Pressy	11			
Frederick Pressy	7			
George Pressy	6 mths			
James Goulding	33	Married	Ann Goulding	40
Henry Goulding	4		Mary Ann Goulding	9
George Goulding	1		Hariet Goulding	6
William Bishop	29	Married	Hariett Bishop	27
			Ann Bishop	7
			Elizabeth Bishop	5
			Clarissa Bishop	2
George Bundy	21	Married	Mary Bundy	25
			Fanny Bundy	5
			Mary Ellen Bundy	3
			Ethelinda Bundy	1
Thomas Chalk	32	Married	Mary Chalk	32
Charles Chalk	8			
Samuel Bundy	60	Married	Ann Bundy	45
Cornelius Bundy	13		Harriet Bundy	19

Males	Age	Married	Females	Age
Mark Bundy	7		Jemima Bundy	10
Daniel Bundy	56	Married	Mary Bundy	53
Mark Bundy	18		Fanny Bundy	22
Jacob Bundy	12		Harriet Bundy	21
			Martha Bundy	16
James Weeks	22	Married	Elizabeth Weeks	23
William Weeks	2			
George Weeks	3 mths			
George Barrow	28	Married	Elizabeth Barrow	30
Henry Barrow	9		Ann Barrow	4
Thomas Barrow	2			
Philip Foe	45	Married	Sarah Foe	40
Edmond Foe	6		Eliza Foe	14
			Harriet Foe	18
Henry Thorn	34	Married	Hannah Thorn	30
George Compton	6			
Joseph Higgs	55	Married	Mary Higgs	43
George Higgs	15		Jane Higgs	7
William Higgs	13		Sarah Higgs	3
Francis Higgs	11			
Charles Higgs	8			
John Light	21	Married	Elizabeth Light	21
Frank Light	1			
Silas Webb	23	Married	Naomi Webb	24
			Emily Webb	8 mths
James Moody	40	Married	Elizabeth Moody	40
Charles Moody	17		Sarah Moody	2
Henry Gilbert	18			

Males	Age	Married	Females	Age
Henry Poore	32	Married	Mary Ann Poore	22
Joseph Gauntlett	35	Married	Ann Gauntlett	35
Joseph Gauntlett	12		Ann Gauntlett	14
James Gauntlett	8		Elizabeth Gauntlett	3
Sidney Webb	21	Married	Elizabeth Webb	22
Joseph Jellyman	50	Married	Frances Jellyman	43
James Jellyman	13		Frances Jellyman	12
Richard Jellyman	10		Mary-Elizabeth Jellyman	5
Joseph Watman Jellyman	9			
George Jellyman	8			
Alfred Jellyman	8 mths			
Thomas Allen	29	Married	(blank) Allen	19
Charles Frampton	20		Jane Moody	69
Stephen Swayne	20		Louisa Moody	17
Richard Latty	17		Hannah Dale	40
Henry Latty	19		Matilda Dale	11
William Bishop	18		Mary Shergold	17
Johnathan Dredge	19			
William Mussel	16			
Stephen Harris	17			
Edmund Forder	21			
George Forder	22			
William Forder	15			
Absalom Jennings	20			
George Alexander	17			
Michael Futcher	17			
Edmund Foe	22			
John Harris	23			
James Westcomb	17			
William Westcomb	19			
William Moody	16			
Charles Friar	19			
Henry Friar	20			
Henry Deere	18			

Males	Age	Married	Females	Age
Charles Light	18			
William Noyse	17			
Silas King	17			
Samuel Eastman	18			
Henry Hudson	19			
Thomas Dredge	22			
George Futcher	18			
John Harrington	33			

Emigrants from Whiteparish (Wiltshire) Who also Travelled On Board the *King William.* (Because of deficiencies in the original document, there is uncertainty about the first names of the males.)

Males	Age	Married	Females	Age
Jonathan Martin	34		Sarah Martin	32
George Martin	8		Elizabeth Martin	6
John Martin	2		Sophia Martin	4
Isaac Deare	28	Married	Lucy Deare	26
Frank Deare	1			
William Harnett	24	Married	Eliza Harnett	26
			Mary Ann Harnett	1
George Wilshire	26	Married	Harriet Wilshire	30
			Mary Wilshire	3
			Fanny Wilshire	2
James Elsbury	31	Married	Ann Elsbury	31
James Elsbury	7		Martha Elsbury	4
Thomas Elsbury	2			
Richard Prince	25	Married	Elizabeth Prince	38
Charles Prince	12			
James Prince	9			
Thomas Prince	1			
Thomas Amor	33	Married	Mary Amor	32
James Amor	6		Maria Amor	3
George Amor	1			

Males	Age	Married	Females	Age
William Gutteridge	21			
Francis Gutteridge	19			
John Gish	15		Elizabeth Penny	19
James Bridle	26			
George Cash	1		Keziah Cash	19

Table 15:

Emigration Expenses Funded by East Drayton Parish in Nottinghamshire in 1846 on Behalf of the Hempstall Family
[NTRO PR1900]

	£	s.	d.
Two journeys to Hull concerning Hempstall family			
Four days at 10s. per day	2	0	0
Blanket rug bedtick	-	9	6
For taking of doctor to Gainsborough	-	10	0
Paid the tinner's bill	-	10	7
Paid the Baker's bill	2	1	7
Paid for meat	6	0	0
Paid their passage to Quebec	8	10	0
Paid their passage to Hull	-	5	6
Paid for luggage	-	5	0
Paid Ann Hempstall for grocers	18	0	0
To Hempstall's money	-	10	7
Postage for 4 letters to Hull	-	-	8

[Total spent by parish £39 3s. 5d.]

	£	s.	d.
Received of Mr. Hempstall	11	0	0

CHAPTER 8

The Rest of the Western Peninsula

*Through all the different townships I passed on my way
up the country, I give the preference to Guelph; the climate
appears to be more like that at home; it is peopled with our
own country people principally, and what few Irish are here,
are selling off their farms and moving farther up the country.*[1]

Robert Fisher liked Guelph, describing it to his parents as "a comfortable little village, nearly as large as Laxfield," this being the name of the Suffolk village from which he had originated. Arriving in 1832, he found Guelph to have "more inhabitants and more public inns" than Laxfield, with two of them being "conducted in quite as fashionable a style as any in Halesworth, and about four times the business."[2] This was high praise indeed given that the market town of Halesworth, near Laxfield, was particularly well-known at that time for its brewing and plentiful pubs. Boasting to his parents that he had already been made the superintendent of the Canada Company's mill in Guelph, he expected his wages to rise to £100 a year, "for the Company's agent is satisfied with my method of conducting business." His future looked bright:

We grind for the settlers from ten to fifteen miles in every direction; many of them have told me when they reached this country they had not a cent to help themselves; for the first year or two they were very much tired — I mean those who took up land for themselves — they endured many hardships, more than many of your paupers ever did, for how should it be otherwise. To maintain their families they had to work for other people, which they did as little as they possibly could, but in two years they had surmounted all their difficulties and by their gradual increase of produce in a few years became totally independent.[3]

Adamant that "in this country you may do well," he advised his parents "to come out next Spring as the prospects here are ten to one above what they are in the old country." However, despite the region's fertile land and good climate, the influx to the western peninsula had been slow in starting. Two key developments had been necessary. The first was the opening up of inland routes beyond the St. Lawrence ports, which only began during the 1820s, while the second was the establishment of the Canada Company, which occurred in 1826.[4] Having acquired vast quantities of wilderness land from the government, the company proceeded to sell it on to settlers. It established Goderich, Guelph, and Galt as company towns and built roads and mills throughout the areas under its control to encourage settlement. A spinoff of the building program were the construction jobs that settlers could take up to supplement their incomes. In addition to supplying land and jobs, the company also offered greatly valued credit facilities to immigrants who arrived with insufficient capital to purchase their own land.[5] It contributed to the support of schools and churches and promoted western Upper Canada in Britain with a new effectiveness. Large numbers of immigrants who would otherwise have been lost to the United States felt its pulling power.[6]

Acquiring two and a half million acres of Crown land in western Upper Canada, its stated aim was "not to encourage or deal with speculators, but to open access to the settlement of lands by a steady, agricultural population."[7] Nearly half of its holdings fell within the Huron Tract, a vast triangular-shaped 1.1 million acreage fronting on Lake Huron (Map 17).[8] The company's remaining holdings, consisting of 1.4 million acres of Crown Reserves, were scattered widely across the province. Settlers could purchase land, either in the reserves or in the Huron Tract, on fairly easy terms, although in later years there were complaints about the company's inflated land prices.[9] To discourage immigrants landing at Quebec from proceeding to the United States, the company offered free

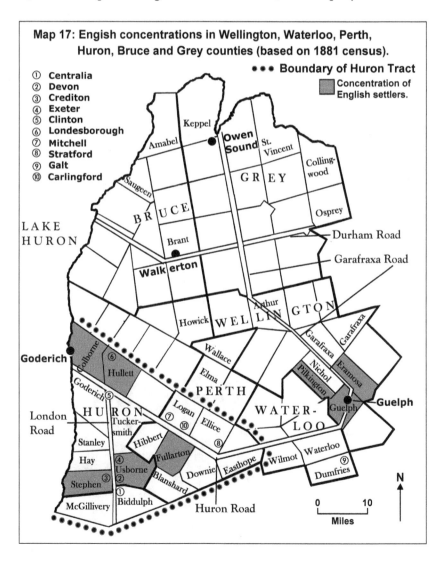

Map 17: English concentrations in Wellington, Waterloo, Perth, Huron, Bruce and Grey counties (based on 1881 census).

transport to the head of Lake Ontario to anyone making a down payment on its land, but such help did not always materialize. Moreover, the company was regularly accused of exaggerating the state of development of its lands, leaving some immigrants with broken promises and little return for the money that they had paid.

John Galt, the well-known Scottish novelist, was the driving force behind the establishment of the company, and became its first commissioner and superintendent.[10] However, his poor management and diplomatic skills let him down and after three years he was sacked from his influential post. Overall, the company earned little credit for its colonizing achievements. Its shareholders expected quick profits that were never realized, while many of the farmers who settled on its lands felt dissatisfied with their treatment.[11]

While the Canada Company's land operations were fraught with intrigue and controversy at board level, it succeeded well in its promotional activities in Britain. Through its smoothly run publicity campaigns, pamphlets were distributed by agents who could slant the company's

John Galt in 1824. He was the Canada Company's first superintendent and he also founded the town of Guelph, its headquarters.

message toward people in their region. William Cattermole, the company's East Anglia agent, knew that farm labourers in his home county of Suffolk faced a particularly bleak future and argued the case for assisted emigration. Having lived in Upper Canada for three years, between 1827 and 1830, he had first-hand knowledge of its benefits and could speak with considerable authority. When he returned, he gave two lectures, one at Colchester in Essex, and the other in Ipswich in Suffolk, which he later published.[12] His comments were directed both to the poor and affluent alike, but he especially sought to attract men with capital and farming experience. Although the 1,200 people who emigrated in 1831 from Suffolk, Norfolk, and Essex under his supervision were mostly poor farm labourers, in the following year Cattermole enticed a select group of moneyed people from Suffolk and Kent to emigrate, whose departure he organized personally. Many settled on the Canada Company lands in Guelph Township.

As he criss-crossed the southeast of England, Cattermole had targeted men with significant capital, such as farmers, professional men, and ex-army officers.[13] In February 1832, he reported to the Colonial Office that he had done particularly well in the village of Laxfield (Suffolk), where he found "a great movement amongst small farmers and capitalists so much so that … on Thursday last 39 persons engaged their passage on board the *Caroline*."[14] Apparently, there was only one pauper family, with the rest being "most respectable citizens." He also found a similarly well-heeled group in Lenham in Kent. Both groups intended to settle on the Canada Company lands near Guelph and Goderich.

By the following month, Cattermole had recruited "a number of most respectable citizens," and had enough emigrants to fill one vessel. Between them, they possessed capital worth £12,000 to £15,000.[15] A week before his departure in March, he wrote again to the Colonial Office, reporting that he was preparing to take six or seven hundred people out in the *Caroline, Marmion,* and *Crown,* "of such a class as have never since the days when Penn emigrated from England." He emphasized that they were leaving "because they can no longer maintain the same standing for themselves and families to which they have hitherto been accustomed but who, nevertheless, have sufficient property remaining to benefit themselves and the country to which they … emigrate."[16]

Sailing in the *Caroline*, Cattermole rubbed shoulders with a mixed group that included a former governor surveyor of Sierra Leone, a builder/architect, a harness-maker, a tailor, a shoemaker, a shopkeeper, various wool merchants, and some farmers. Cattermole announced their arrival at Grosse Île on May 17 in a letter to the editor of the *Courier of Upper Canada*, noting that they had onboard "nearly every variety ... from the Fellow of Oriel College, Oxford [University], to the humble peasant." All came "with a view of bettering their condition."[17] Cattermole's letter also included a partial passenger list, giving details of geographical origins and occupations (Table 16).[18] An additional letter praising "the unwearied and skilful exertions" of Captain James Greig appeared in the *Quebec Mercury* shortly afterward: "Believe it when we say ... that, though we came to the termination of our voyage with joy, we shall see you separate yourself from us with regret. That success and all good fortune may ever hereafter accompany you will be the constant prayer of the undersigned."[19] Gratitude was never more eloquently expressed.

In the end, Cattermole organized the departure of around 750 South of England emigrants in the spring of 1832, slightly more than he had anticipated in his earlier letter to the Colonial Office.[20] On June 26, the *Montreal Gazette* reported the safe arrival of 460 English emigrants, forty of whom left at Kingston, ninety at Cobourg, 156 at York [Toronto], and 174 who "were heading for Hamilton." Many of the latter "were highly respectable families who came out in the *Caroline* with Mr. Cattermole and proceeded to Guelph and Goderich." There were also a number of people from Laxfield in Suffolk. This was just one of the many groups that had been organized by Cattermole. No doubt, the previously mentioned Robert Fisher, employed by the Canada Company as its Guelph miller, had also been in Cattermole's 1832 group, as had Robert Alling, a retired surgeon from Laxfield. Clearly seen as a good catch, the Canada Company made Alling their Guelph emigration agent soon after he arrived. Apart from encouraging his fellow countrymen to write letters home extolling the benefits of the area, he also produced rapturous accounts of the great strides being made by Guelph settlers, which the Canada Company inserted in its promotional literature.

In one of his published letters, written in 1840, Alling was somewhat scathing of the English immigrants in his midst, stating that "if it
were not for the considerable number of good men from Yorkshire and
Nottinghamshire, who are prospering in this part of Canada [Guelph
Township]," he would have regarded his own countrymen as less suitable
than their Scottish or Irish counterparts:

> From pretty close observation over the past eight years,
> I have come to the conclusion that the Scots are the
> best and most successful of all emigrants.... Next to the
> Scotch, I am of opinion the Englishman comes in for
> his need of praise; but it is infinitely more difficult to
> speak of him than that of his Scotch or Irish neighbours,
> as every shade and grade of character, conduct and suc-
> cess is to be found amongst the English in this place
> [Guelph] and its neighbouring townships.[21]

It would seem that Guelph had acquired a good many feisty, work-
ing-class English who were not going to be pushed around. Alling portrayed them as being profligate and foolish: "English families do not
hold together long enough to ensure success; the sons of poor English
emigrants leave their parents and become servants at the usual high
wages and, instead of saving money to purchase land, the same is squan-
dered away in fine clothes and at the numerous country balls."[22] Maybe
so, but that was their choice. Whether Alling approved of them or not,
the English were not necessarily being driven by a desire to own land.
They scattered far and wide, according to where they thought they could
acquire the best jobs or land. In this respect they were very different from
the Scots and Irish, who nearly always remained together in order to
preserve their culture, this being a top priority.

Guelph's appeal to farmers of means is further demonstrated
by the arrival in 1832 of Edward Francis Heming. Originating from
Bognor in West Sussex, he came with sufficient funds to purchase
367 acres of land, paying for it all, "excepting the 100 acres bought
of the Canada Company." He was amazed to see that emigration was

Canada Company coat of arms.

proceeding at such a pace that, before long, "all the land within eight miles of Guelph will be sold." And he could see a profitable future for himself. "The improved land sells for much more than we conceived in England: quite rough land sells for 17s. 6d. per acre, if at all in a desirable situation."[23] Employing Martin Martin, a carpenter by trade who also came from West Sussex, to finish the inside of his log house, Heming would later build a second house, the appropriately named "Bognor Lodge."[24] As he indicated to a friend back in England, Martin could see that it was in his interest to keep tabs on other wealthy arrivals like Heming:

> You would be surprised to see what quantity of respect-
> able people daily are a coming and settling, some buy-
> ing 700, some 1,000 acres of land. Here is a tailor that
> came from Oxfordshire that brought £600. He has 600
> acres of land, 60 cleared, he has a capital-framed barn,
> and a good dwelling house, and out-houses; in short,
> his premises are very complete. There is plenty of work
> for labourers at about a dollar a day ... and no labour-
> ing man need be afraid to come.[25]

Moving later to Elora, in the neighbouring Nichol Township, Martin built and ran its first tavern, but sold it later in order to return to farming.[26] Meanwhile, John and Elizabeth White, also from West Sussex, were far more impressed by their proximity in Guelph to William Penfold, the former superintendent of their local workhouse back in England. Having landed a well-paid job with "John Horning, boot and shoe maker, Guelph," John felt extremely good about his prospects: "I never repent for leaving the old country at present, for I have plenty of good eating and drinking, sometimes beef, and sometimes a young roaster, and I know that any industrious man can do a great deal better here than ever he can in England."[27]

The many English who opted for Guelph Township were in an area that fell under the complete control of the Canada Company. The company's enormous capital investment program was a major factor in its rapid expansion, and soon after its founding in 1827 the town of Guelph possessed "upwards of 200 houses."[28] As a result of this steady influx, centred initially on the Guelph area, the English became a major presence in the southeastern part of Wellington County. By 1881, the English were the largest ethnic group in Guelph, and in Eramosa and Pilkington, its neighbouring townships to the northeast and northwest respectively (Map 17). Most had come entirely unaided, but there were some, like the West Sussex immigrants from the Petworth estate, who had been financed by their landlord. Another group in a similar situation were the sixty farm labourers from Aynho Parish in Northamptonshire who, arriving ten years after the Petworth group, mainly settled in Pilkington and Nichol townships.

Their landlord, William Cartwright, organized the group's departure in 1845 and, judging from the involvement of two church wardens,
funds had probably also been received from Aynho Parish. In all, eight
families, five single men, and two single women were assisted to emigrate.[29] Having accompanied them to Liverpool, William Scott, one of
the church wardens, reported to Cartwright that the people "are full
of gratitude for the kindness you have shown them; there was not an
individual of ours either sick or sorry when I left them this morning ...
John Turner's wife particularly requests me to ask you to inform Mrs.
Cartwright she has received a letter from her son in America which I am
desired to say is a very satisfactory one."[30] Three years earlier, Cartwright
had scribbled "a very good riddance" beside the names of four Aynho
men (Spires, Robbins, Watts, and Anstell) whom he had helped to emigrate; presumably this larger group left under happier circumstances.[31]
Eydon, another Northamptonshire parish to the north of Aynho, assisted
around thirty of its paupers to emigrate to Upper Canada in 1845; the
group included Ann Willoughby who, at the time, was living in the
Brackley workhouse with her seven children.[32] This second group possibly also went to Wellington County.[33]

While a number of well-documented groups from the South of
England revealed themselves in this way, they were just a minority of
the total who settled in Wellington County. Most English immigrants
who came singly or in small family groups left little or no documentary
records behind. Chance examples of individuals mentioned in surviving
records, all arriving in the 1830s, include John Walker,[34] a Derbyshire-
born Methodist lay preacher, who settled in Garafraxa Township, James
Carter and John Iles, both from Wiltshire, and the Northumberland-born
Craster Johnston, who all relocated to Puslinch Township, and James
Cook from Gloucestershire, who settled in Nichol Township.[35] They were
the tip of an enormous iceberg. Most English immigrants slipped into
the western peninsula in this and later decades totally unnoticed.

Meanwhile, even as late as the 1840s, much of the Huron Tract,
encompassing Huron and Perth counties, remained a vast forested wilderness, still waiting to be cleared. Groups of immigrants wishing to
have sufficient land to settle together in one place were attracted to it,

as were poorer individuals who lacked sufficient funds to buy land in more developed areas. Colonization roads built throughout the region by the Canada Company provided access and an ordered basis for settlement. The earliest immigrants were mainly Scottish Highlanders and Pennsylvania Germans, who were better able than most to cope with the extremely harsh conditions.[36] For the English, who arrived later, it was the ultimate endurance test. Reaching Easthope Township (Perth County) in 1834, William Thompson's family, from Preston in Lancashire, felt completely isolated: "We cannot boast much of society, our neighbours consisting of the lowest description of Scotch who can hardly make themselves understood." Not exactly hitting it off with his Gaelic-speaking Highland neighbours, William had to trudge one and a half miles to reach the one English family living in his vicinity. Some six and a half miles away, in Stratford, there were "a few English, Irish and Scotch families of respectability" but that was it. And not only could he and his family not boast of society, "neither can we boast of scenery … for hundreds of miles is a vast forest."[37]

Similarly, nothing could have prepared the Walters family for the shock they had when they first saw Stratford (Perth County) in 1842:

> The new arrivals enquired how far they were from Stratford and were surprised on being informed by their landlady that they had reached their destination. The Frenchman who drove them from Hamilton seeing the bitter disappointment of the couple and pitying them so much, offered to take them back to Hamilton for nothing. But they decided to stay and cast their lot with the half dozen or so families that were already here. Messrs. Linton, Vanstone, McCarthy, Sharman, Colonel Daly and one or two others formed the population.[38]

Petworth immigrants had arrived in Easthope Township two years before William Thompson's family, a time when cholera was raging in the area. John Capling, a labourer from West Sussex, had the sorry and immediate task of burying his wife and four of his eleven children within days of arriving. He had to "wrap them up in the rinds [bark] of trees and dig holes and put them in [himself]."[39] Apparently the Petworth group had been "dumped on the Huron Road" in nearby Wilmot Township (Waterloo County).[40] Of the thirty-two immigrants who travelled with John, twelve succumbed to cholera and died. No doubt the authorities had been anxious to disperse them once they arrived, fearing that they would have caught the disease onboard ship and might still be carrying it. Writing home the following year from Wilmot, William and Elizabeth Daniels advised their family that "if any of you think fit to come … it will be much better for you than it was for us; you will have a place to come to, as we only had the woods to shelter us."[41] Although William Daniels remained a labourer all his life, his sons acquired Canada Company land and became owners of farms.

James Rapson, another Petworth settler, who was a sawyer by trade, bought forty-eight acres of land in the Galt area together with Jesse, Benjamin, and James Wackford, and they "set to cutting and clearing, having just raised a house."

Unfortunately, the cholera death toll continued, claiming adults and children alike. There was no rancour or bitterness, just a simple acceptance that "the Lord hath thinned us out."[42] Thomas Adsett, a labourer from the Petworth estate who had also settled in Galt, commented on "the people where we are," who were "mostly Dutch [i.e. German][43] and a great many English and Scotch" (1833).[44] The Germans referred to may have come from Pennsylvania, since the large influx from Germany did not begin until the 1840s.[45] By 1881, Wilmot Township was primarily German, as was most of Waterloo County. Nevertheless, being a company town, Galt continued to attract a steady trickle of English labourers. Men like William Booty, who arrived from Essex in 1850 together with his wife, Louisa Leatherdale, and settled in the area.[46] Galt gave poor families their first rung on an employment ladder and access to an independent farming life.

The English were far better represented in the Huron Tract farther to the west, which, with its relatively cheap and abundant land, had been attracting settlers since the 1840s. They mainly settled in the southern townships of Huron and Perth counties, with the majority having

A Bush Road, Upper Canada, Winter 1842. Watercolour by Philip John Bainbrigge (1817–81).

originated from Devon and, to a lesser extent, Cornwall. There they created a sprawling settlement that encompassed four townships in two counties. Their communities developed in a north–south direction along both sides of the London Road through Usborne, Stephen, and Biddulph[47] townships in Huron County and eastward along the Thames Road through Fullarton Township in Perth County (Map 17).

The Devon trailblazer had been John Balkwill who, having acquired land in Usborne and Stephen townships by 1831, returned home to Devon to drum up support for his new undertaking.[48] William May, his brother-in-law, arrived a year later, and shortly after that came several brothers, who took up land in Usborne, Stephen, and Hay townships.[49] Other Devon people followed during the 1830s, with some joining

Balkwill; others colonized the future Centralia in the northern tip of Biddulph Township.[50] Two friends, George and John Snell, also settled in the area. While the Balkwills and Snells were well-resourced, many of the others were short of funds, although the plentiful jobs on offer from the Canada Company meant that any hardship was temporary. John Balkwill went on to found the future Devon at the junction of the London and Crediton roads, while John Snell settled a short distance up the London Road at the future Exeter. John Mitchell, another of the early pioneers, acquired land to the west of Devon at the future Crediton.[51] These were all Devon place names, chosen to commemorate the geographical origins of the first wave of settlers.

Despite this steady influx from Devon, the population of south Huron County grew very slowly until the 1840s, but afterward rose sharply as larger-scale immigration brought ever more people to the area. Having only 283 inhabitants in 1845, Usborne Township's population leapt to 1,484 by 1852. Stephen and Hay townships experienced the same increase. In 1841, the total population of Huron County was just over three thousand, but by 1848 it had climbed to nearly 20,500.[52] Although the largest proportion of the immigrants who arrived during the 1840s originated from Scotland, substantial numbers also came from England. The Reverend Archibald Chapman, the Anglican missionary sent to Usborne and Stephen townships by the Society for the Propagation of the Gospel, reported that he had many English parishioners, although they were far more of an overwhelming presence in Usborne than in Stephen. By 1881, Stephen Township had more or less equal proportions of English, Irish, and German inhabitants, with the English having only a slight lead.[53] Meanwhile, Hay Township, having only attracted a few Scots and Irish initially, went on to acquire a sizeable number of English settlers after 1845, but Germans increasingly predominated, becoming the largest ethnic group by 1881.[54]

Exeter (Usborne Township) had received an added boast to its economy during the 1840s when Isaac Carling,[55] a businessman, storekeeper, and politician who had been born in London Township, came to live there. Forming a business partnership with his brother John, they operated a tannery in Exeter, this bringing much-needed employment to the area. Isaac may have acquired some of his work force in Devon, England, since this was a time when he was apparently instrumental in encouraging Devon immigrants to settle in the Exeter area.[56] While Carling's family roots were in Yorkshire, his wife's were in Devon. She was Ann Balkwill, the daughter of John Balkwill, the first Devon man to settle in the area. No doubt, her and her father's continuing contact with family and friends would have enabled Isaac to attract Devon immigrants to Exeter. In addition, it would have also acquired men like Robert Cann, a farm labourer, who, having left Devon in 1849 and settling in Darlington Township (Durham County) for five years, moved to Usborne Township, where he established a three-hundred-acre farm.[57]

The sudden appearance of Wesleyan Methodist congregations in south Huron County in 1844 testified to the strong English presence. This was a most unwelcome development for the Reverend Chapman, the Anglican minister, who lost much of his congregation to the more charismatic Methodist preachers. Speaking of God's love and salvation, while empathizing with the practical day-to-day problems faced by ordinary settlers, they had a much better rapport with pioneer communities and built up their congregations rapidly. The first Methodist preaching circuit extended northward along the London Road, passing through Biddulph, McGillivray, Stephen, Usborne, Hay, and Tuckersmith townships in Huron County (Map 17). Stephen Township had its so-called "Devonshire Chapel" by 1845, and twelve years later a second Wesleyan Methodist chapel appeared at Francistown in Hibbert Township (Perth County), to the northeast of Usborne.

Meanwhile, Bible Christian missions were also being established. Having originated mostly in Devon and Cornwall as a separatist Methodist group, the Bible Christian movement was bound to have widespread appeal in this area. The four Bible Christian preaching circuits that had been formed since 1846 covered much of the Huron Tract. One was based at Clinton (Hullett Township), located at the intersection of the London and Huron roads, a second at Exeter (Usborne Township) to the south along the London Road, a third at Mitchell (Logan Township), situated on the Huron Road, while a fourth one was much farther south in London in Middlesex County. All were positioned on major colonization roads to give Bible Christian preachers the best possible access to their followers. Stephen Township had its first Bible Christian church in 1855 and the following year so did Exeter.[58]

Further corroboration that south Huron County had acquired a great many Devon settlers is revealed in responses to a Devonshire Association survey conducted in 1900. Through a series of newspaper notices that were published across Canada, the association sought details of the descendents of Devon people who had relocated to the British colonies overseas. Replying to this request was John Hurdon, a resident of Exeter in Usborne Township. He reported that his father, a doctor from north Devon, had come to the area along with "a great number of the Devonshire men … who are of the farming class; [they] came out almost penniless and are now fairly well off, by the real estate they owned having increased to twentyfold."

By 1901, the thriving village of Exeter had "about 1,900 inhabitants" and, according to Hurdon, one-quarter were of Devon descent: "Seven miles away is the village of Crediton and to the north 20 miles away is

Courtesy the Plymouth City Museum and Art Gallery.

Emigrant ships leaving Plymouth Harbour in Devon circa 1855. Oil painting by John Callow. Around 18,000 passengers sailed from Plymouth to Quebec between 1840 and 1860, accounting for 150 crossings.

Clinton, all Devonshire names." A great many Devon people were also to be found in the city of London, this being "one of the finest wheat growing parts in Ontario and with a fair climate."[59] W.L. Wickett, a barrister from St. Thomas, to the south of London, who also responded to the survey, went even further, claiming that the town of Exeter and its vicinity was inhabited "almost exclusively by Devonshire people or their descendents."[60] No doubt, the initial influx from Devon had been quite considerable.

While the English were particularly well-represented in south Huron County, they also established major enclaves farther to the north in Colborne and Hullett townships, becoming the dominant ethnic group by 1881 (Map 17). The magnet had been the Canada Company town of Goderich, located in Colborne Township. The town attracted a good many English labourers and tradesmen because of the well-paid and plentiful jobs that it had to offer. A typical example was the Suffolk-born John Freeman who, having arrived in Goderich around 1831, found work as a carpenter more or less immediately and shortly after this acquired 163 acres of land. "If I clear ten acres every year I shall soon have a good large farm.... When I work for the Canada Company I take half cash and the other half I set off towards paying for my land." By November 1832, he hoped to be able to "give up my carpentering trade ... and work wholly on my farm."[61] This was a well-trodden path for people who came with insufficient cash to set up as farmers immediately. A further indication that people of English origin had featured strongly in the early influx is the fact that by 1860 almost half of Goderich Township's population was Church of England, with another 25 percent being Wesleyan Methodists.[62]

As with the rest of the Huron Tract, Hullett Township's population grew very slowly, having only 195 inhabitants in 1844. Most were English. The arrival of Thomas Hagyard, a medical doctor from Londesborough, Yorkshire, was a turning point, in that he had been the first person to appreciate the area's commercial potential. He chose the site for a village and laid it out with great care. Initially known as Hagyard's Corners, its founder felt it deserved a grander name, and so it was changed to Londesborough, after the Yorkshire estate on which Hagyard had been raised. "The village continued to grow and at the height of its prosperity had two general stores, four carriage and wagon shops, four blacksmith shops, a bending factory, two shoe shops, two merchant tailors, a private school as well as a public one, Methodist and Presbyterian churches, and, of course, a tavern."[63]

William Ainley, another Yorkshire man, founded the village of Brussels in Howick Township (Huron County) to the northeast of Hullett. Having settled initially in Fullarton and Logan, he came to the future Brussels in pursuit of cheap land. Satisfied that he had chosen a good site, he moved his family from Logan and founded the village.[64]

Meanwhile, immigrants from Devon and Cornwall were relocating in substantial numbers at the eastern end of the Huron Tract.[65] "Turners, Pridhams, Heals, Moores, Harrises, Beers, Greenwoods, Chaffes and Sharsels" came during the 1840s and mainly settled on the western side of Fullarton Township (Perth County).[66] This placed them alongside the already-established "New Devon" communities in south Huron County. There was now a continuous link between Usborne and Stephen on the west and Fullarton on the east (Map 17).

The eastern townships of the Huron Tract also attracted people from other parts of England, particularly from Northumberland, Kent, Westmorland, and Shropshire. Unlike the Devon and Cornwall arrivals, who settled together, they became widely scattered, although most opted for Fullarton. Carlingford in Fullarton attracted a great many English, and by 1848 it had its first Methodist church. Four years earlier a Bible Christian congregation had been established at the nearby Fullarton Corners.[67]

Hibbert and Blanshard townships, bordering on Fullarton, also acquired many English, who were a close second numerically to the Irish by 1881. Hibbert's first Methodist church was probably the one erected in Staffa in 1856, with others following later.[68] Robert Donkin, who originated from Northumberland, was reputed to have been its first inhabitant. Among the English families who settled in Blanshard during the 1840s were the Harrisons and Marriotts from Yorkshire.[69]

Methodism flourished, and by 1861, Kirkton, situated on the boundary between Usborne and Blanshard, had its first Methodist church. Yet,

Methodism was doing a little too well for some people: "The Presbyterians have no churches in Blanshard, the Church of England only one. The Methodists, it may be said, possess all the church property in this township."[70] This situation irritated James Coleman. Having come from England to St. Marys (Blanshard Township) with his wife, Anne, sometime before 1834, he had found employment as a schoolteacher, physician, and clerk of the Perth Division County Court. Regarding himself as a pillar of the local community, he decried "the strength of the evangelical element in the western part of the Upper Province." In his view, "the true religion in this diocese hitherto has been at a very low ebb in the English church; the clergy have been so few and, of these few, not more than two or three have been of the right stamp."[71] Or, put another way, Anglican ministers had a poorer following than their Methodist counterparts in this part of Perth County.

Downie Township, on the southeastern edge of the Huron Tract, quickly became a Scottish stronghold, but nevertheless, it attracted a small group from Northumberland. John and George Gibb arrived from Rothbury in 1834, and in the following year were joined by George Wood and William Dunn, also from Rothbury.[72] In a letter that he wrote eight years later, George Wood explained that he had come to Downie because his "father-in-law, John Gibb, who was a shepherd at Ryehill," had written home to him "about the state of the country." No doubt it was a favourable report, since George emigrated more or less immediately. Having purchased one hundred acres, he built a log house and log barn and was soon on his way to becoming a substantial farmer: "By adopting this country as the future home of myself and family I am now a master whereas I could never well except otherwise than to see myself and my family as servants [in England]. The facility of acquiring property here is great and any man, single or married, of sober, economical, industrious and persevering habits is sure to do well."[73]

Meanwhile, his brother-in-law William Dunn, who had accompanied him, was enjoying considerable success. Having been a poorly paid farm labourer in Northumberland, he had "not a cent" when he arrived; "but ... was owing George Wood $75.00 for advances made to me, and this sum I have long since paid." Knowing something about milling, William had easily found work at the grist- and sawmill at Stratford, and three years later was able to make his first down payment on one hundred acres of land. In 1842 he wrote: "I am not inclined to over-estimate my property, but I would not accept of $1,500 for my farm and stock; but I feel so comfortably placed, that this sum would not tempt me to sell."[74] However, such endorsements have to be taken with a pinch of salt, since they were deliberately commissioned by the Canada Company to be used in enticing immigrants to their lands.

Other English settlers, like George Pringle, another Northumbrian, came to Downie sometime before 1842, as did Henry Scarth, who came from Shropshire, and William Knott from Derbyshire.[75] It was just a matter of time before Methodism took root. The catalyst was a chance visit by a Methodist missionary named Cleghorn, who lost his way when travelling from Shakespeare to Zorra. He ended up in the village of Harmony, just to the south of Stratford, and held religious services there. "The surrounding backwoodsmen, manifesting an interest in these religious exercises, decided to form a congregation ..."[76]

Elma and Wallace townships, lying just outside of the Huron Tract beyond Logan, acquired their first English settlers in the mid 1850s. While Elma's English population was comparable to the Scots and Irish by 1881, in Wallace they were greatly outnumbered by the Irish and Germans. Elma's earliest English settlers included Thomas Kitchen, Samuel Wherry, Jesse Rowland from Gloucestershire, William Hewitt, Thomas Mann, and Luke Lucas.[77] Meanwhile, Wallace Township was fortunate in attracting migrants from Simcoe County, who came with much-needed skills:

> The pioneers who came from Simcoe had some experience in backwoods life. This was a valuable acquisition to a new country. Their knowledge of the work peculiar to clearing land was of great advantage to the unskilled immigrants from across the sea. Its proximity to Waterloo County and the older sections westward created a large influx of experienced bushmen. In fifteen

years from its rapid settlement Wallace had a population of 3,580 indicating rapid progress.[78]

The even more remote areas between Lake Huron and Georgian
Bay were the last areas in the western peninsula to be colonized. As
Thomas Cholmoneley discovered, the region was still sparsely populated in 1858: "There is nothing more than 10 years old in this lovely
region.... It is a wild place but awful lovely ... from Owen Sound to
Saugeen, I was twelve hours going thirty miles in a cart and such bump-
ing!" He was delighted to meet the "spruce young gamekeeper from
Lincolnshire ... who was running the ... nice little Inn" in Saugeen. And
when he had passed through Goderich, he met "an old Cheshire hunts-
man" who managed the large hotel there. However, although Thomas
enjoyed his reminiscences with fellow Englishmen, he had not reacted
well to local Canadians. He objected to their informality and rough and
ready ways and was horrified by the high crime rate, particularly among
young people. He concluded that the female descendents of his family
would cease to be ladies if they moved to Canada. "There is a great want
of delicacy," he thought.[79]

Writing in 1932, W.M. Brown had a more sympathetic appreciation of the people. He described the first settlers of Grey and Bruce
counties as "men of iron vigour, who underwent labour and hardship and destitution in their battle to overcome the mantle with which
Nature had covered the land."[80] A little excessive perhaps, but he was
right to highlight the enormous challenges that immigrants faced
in venturing this far north into the outback. To encourage settlers
to come to the region, the government had offered fifty-acre lots as
free grants on either side of the new colonization roads that extended
through Bruce and Grey counties. Both the Garafraxa Road, linking
Guelph with Owen Sound (formerly Sydenham), and the Durham
Road, linking Durham with Kincardine, helped to facilitate a growing influx of people (Map 17).[81] The strategy worked, and by as early
as 1843 the government had to announce that "lots on the Garafraxa
and Owen Sound road [were] no longer open for settlement on the
principle of free grants" because most had been occupied. However,

the government would make grants available "on the same conditions in the immediate vicinity of the roads, which will afford the means of advantageous settlement."[82]

The availability of free land grants in a newly opened region was a major lure to already-established settlers as well as to immigrants from Britain. Those contemplating emigration often looked to their relatives and friends to advise them of such opportunities. An example is the Ottewell family from Lincolnshire.[83] Richard Ottewell and his wife, Jane Towle, were the first in their family to emigrate, doing so in 1849. A factor in their decision to leave England was their inability to find employment. Richard's family had produced handmade nails, but with the arrival of manufactured nails made in factories, their job prospects collapsed.[84] Two years after setting sail for Quebec, Richard and Jane were living in Whitby on the northwest side of Lake Ontario, but ten years later were to be found in McGillivray Township (Huron County). Meanwhile, Richard's good reports led his father, Philip, and Richard's two brothers to emigrate in the 1850s, and all three opted for Osprey Township in Grey County. Richard's uncle also emigrated, finding work as a tinsmith in Osprey, thus carrying on the family tradition of metalworking. All of the other members of the family became farmers. By 1861, all six of Philip Ottewell's children were living in various parts of Upper Canada. The next generation of Ottewells would repeat the process and seek new land opportunities in Manitoba and Alberta.

While large Irish and Scottish populations had already developed in Grey and Bruce counties, relatively few English settled in this region. Most of the English were concentrated in Collingwood, Keppel, and St. Vincent townships in Grey County and in Amabel Township in Bruce County (Map 17). Although Owen Sound's population was split three ways between the English, Irish, and Scots, the English were the dominant group in 1881. Writing in a Cornwall newspaper ten years earlier, the Cornish-born Charles Julyan, who lived near Owen Sound, extolled the benefits that Canada offered: "If any of my old neighbours in Kew [Parish] had found their way here last September they would have been surprised to see my vines loaded with fine grapes and apple and pear trees, both dwarfed and standard, covered with fruit. This part of the country is about the extreme northern limit of the vine ..."[85] Nevertheless, Charles's advice to people back in his native Cornwall was to seek land in Manitoba.

The enterprising Joseph Bacon from Essex ventured into Bruce County, having first settled in Arthur Township (Wellington County) in 1840, shortly after the construction of the Garafraxa Road. A labourer from Debden Parish, he and his wife, Susannah Franklin, had arrived in 1835 after almost certainly having received assistance to emigrate.[86] When free grants became available along the Durham Road, the Bacon family moved immediately to Brant Township in Bruce County (Map 17). By 1850 the family was living "in a shanty and clearing." And Joseph's "brave wife" was remembered as "the first woman to become a permanent settler in the township."[87] Initially, Joseph and six of his seven sons owned land near Walkerton, and his four daughters also lived in the area. However, by 1881, only two of his eleven children remained, with the rest having gone to Manitoba or the United States.[88] This pattern of people seeking the newest land opportunities would be repeated over and over again.

As economic conditions continued to deteriorate in England throughout the second half of the nineteenth century, the influx to Upper and Lower Canada intensified. While some sought the advantages that the prairies had to offer, plenty of English people continued to head for Ontario and Quebec. New and attractive emigration schemes brought them to already-established farming areas as well as to the new industrial districts being established farther north. Ontario and Quebec's vast acreages, excellent job opportunities, more liberal social climate, and relatively easy accessibility were strong enticements, contributing to the huge surge of emigration that continued into the twentieth century.

Table 16:

Partial Passenger List for the Crossing of the *Caroline* in
May 1832 from London to Quebec
[Wright, "The *Caroline* and Her Passengers," 35–37.]

Cabin Passengers:
Mesdames Atkinson
Mesdames Palin
Mr. Young and son from London
Messrs J.C. and James Wilson of Bungay, Suffolk
Robert Gough of Somersetshire
Osmond Charles Huntly of Boxwell Court, Tetbury, Gloucestershire
Mr. John Palin, late governor surveyor, Sierra Leone
James Cattermole, surgeon, Camberwell
Mr. & Mrs.George Neeve of Hazlewood, Suffolk
Mr. & Mrs. Mountcastle, builder, London
Henry Fowle
Lieutenant F. Somers
James O'Neil of Demarara, West Indies
Mr. William Hill, wife and niece, a builder and architect from Uxbridge, Middlesex

Steerage Passengers (all heads of households)
From Lenham, Kent
John Huntley
Messrs Strouts, farmers
W. Morris, tailor
George Norris, coach wheelwright, single
Messrs Rugg, Merton, Jull, farmers
Alfred Brown
W. Bottle, harness maker
Mr. Turmston, farmer
David Russel, blacksmith
Mr. Hunt, carpenter

From elsewhere

Mr. Clare, corn merchant

Mr. Stephen Atkinson, wool merchant

Mr. Alchin, wool merchant

Mr. Burgess, farmer

Mr. Drury, brewer

Mr. Jeffries, agent, London

Mr. John Garrod, farmer, Laxfield, Suffolk

Mr. J. Wright, shopkeeper, Laxfield

H. Salmon, mariner, Laxfield

Mr. James Wright, shoemaker, Laxfield

Samuel Tovel, labourer, Laxfield

H. Miles, miller and millwright, Guildford, Surrey

James Cattermole, farmer, Martlesham, Suffolk

W. Mayhew, miller and farmer, Tunstall, Suffolk

Mr. John Neeve and sister, farmer, Kelsale, Suffolk

Mr. Woods, farmer, Earl Soham, Suffolk

Mr. Edmond Miles, upholsterer, Woodbridge, Suffolk

Mr. Martin, shipwright

Mr. Pierson, butcher

Mr. George, wheelwright

Mr. Montcastle, builder

Born en route to British North America

A daughter to Mrs. Somers (wife of Lieut. Somers) on April 8, 1832

A son to Mrs. Norris (of Lenham, Kent) on April 13, 1832

A daughter to Mrs. Atkinson on May 6, 1832

CHAPTER 9

Later Emigration from England

Within the past few weeks numbers of school rooms have been offered to me by the clergymen of the villages through which I was passing, with their influence and assistance, if I would promise not to mention emigration in any way.[1]

As he sought to extol the benefits of Ontario to farm labourers in the South of England, Captain A.J. Whellams, one of the province's immigration agents, encountered serious opposition. During his visit in 1875, some farmers did their best to impede his progress, fearing that emigration would cause such a significant drop in the labour force that wage rates would rise. Thus it was that Captain Whellams sometimes had to contend with small audiences, even to the point of letting poor people attend his lectures free of charge, just to get the numbers up to a reasonable level: "The opposition in the agricultural districts is so strong that I find my advocacy of emigration to Canada is the cause of small receipts.... The employers of labour will not patronize an entertainment that directly or indirectly bears on emigration."[2] However, in other areas agents were far more successful, owing to the support they received from trade union officials.

Despite the steps taken in the 1830s by the Tolpuddle union in Dorset to press for better conditions, English farm labourers had been slower than workers in other industries to form trade unions, not doing so until 1871. Once formed, the agricultural trade union movement more or less immediately advocated emigration. The major selling points were that it would give those members who opted to emigrate a better life and, for those who remained behind, there was the indirect but very welcome outcome of reduced unemployment and hopefully higher wages. Ever anxious to rid itself of its social problems, the British government welcomed the desire for emigration among the English labouring poor, as did Ontario, which had a chronic shortage of farm workers. To entice them to emigrate, both the British and Ontario authorities offered special sea crossing rates starting in 1872. Agricultural trade unionists had only to pay £2 5s. for a crossing to Quebec, and there was an extra bonus for men going to Ontario, who only had to pay £1 8d., with the Ontario government making up the difference.[3] Nevertheless, such was the poverty of most labourers that many had to turn for help to their unions even for these paltry sums.

Trade union–sponsored emigration was most prevalent in central and southern England, the regions where the new trade union organizations had mainly sprouted. As he toured the southwest of England and the Midlands, George T. Denison, the Ontario immigration commissioner to London, England (1872–74), found plenty of enthusiastic gatherings, but he also encountered occasional hostility from local farmers.[4] Choosing the thirteenth-century George Inn at 23 High Street, Salisbury,[5] as his base, he began by holding a lecture in Salisbury in February 1873. From South Wiltshire he hoped to move west to Dorset, but despite a determined effort to hold a lecture at the school room in Milton Abbas, Denison failed to attract any support and so moved north to Wootton Bassett in North Wiltshire, where the reception was a great deal better:

> On Monday, 3rd March I went to Wootton Bassett from there to Broad Hinton, a village about 6 miles south. There was a large number of farm labourers, only as I had obtained the assistance of Mr. Strange, the leader of

the West of England agricultural association and he had
agreed to go with me to four meetings. The Reverend
Thomas Storey, who takes a great interest in emigration,
went out with me and spoke. He spoke at a meeting in
Christian Malford, an agricultural village about 8 miles
to the southwest of Wooton Bassett, where there were
about 400 to 500 present.[6]

Denison and his supporters then attended a large audience at
Hilmarton, a short distance from Broad Hinton. Clearly feeling more
motivated, Denison decided that it was time to tackle Dorset again and
gave his first lecture in the town of Sherborne. However, his failure to
mention the size of his audience suggests that it was poorly attended.

Photograph by Geoff Campey.

The Old Work House, Salisbury. Now the Church House, this building had been
acquired as a workhouse by the city of Salisbury in 1834 and used as such until
1881. Struggling farm labourers and their families were sometimes supported in
workhouses during long periods of unemployment.

Dorset was certainly less welcoming than Wiltshire. Denison reported to the Honorable Archibald McKellar, minister of emigration, that "many of the farmers [in Dorset] are beginning to be afraid of the agitation in favour of emigration and often the clergymen, who have control of the venues, refuse to hire them or let them be used for emigration lectures." Sometimes he had to "speak in the open air to the poor labourers [either] in the street or village green." While "in some places the leading people are very kind and very willing to assist me ... the farmers are very much opposed to our movement." Nevertheless, in one week during mid-March, he managed to canvass north Dorset comprehensively, giving lectures every night for a week (except Sunday) at Weymouth, Bridport, Dorchester, Milton Abbas, Poole, and Wimbourne.[7]

With this success behind him, Denison moved north to Oxfordshire, where a local trade union agent was waiting to help him. His first venue was in Wootton, a village near Woodstock and just to the north of the city of Oxford:

> I had a large audience, the room was crowded to excess, and almost entirely with agricultural labourers. Mr. C. Holloway, a man of influence among them, occupied the chair and made a good speech in favour of emigration. I am told a number are going to emigrate and the want of money alone prevents many more from leaving.[8]

Then it was even farther north to Warwickshire, where Denison spoke "to a good house of agricultural labourers" in Southam, a village about eight miles from Leamington Spa. But here again he met opposition. This was hardly unexpected because of the trouble experienced a year earlier when labourers in the newly formed Warwickshire farm workers' union fought unsuccessfully for higher wages and shorter hours. Two immigration agents quickly appeared on the scene, one Captain Whellams, acting for the Ontario government, and the other representing the Brazilian consul-general. Surprisingly, Brazil was the preferred choice.[9] In all, one thousand people from Warwickshire, with some also from Gloucestershire, Oxfordshire, Dorset, and Wiltshire, emigrated to Brazil in 1872–73, in what proved to be a disastrous venture.[10] So Denison would have found strong anti-emigration feelings in some parts of Warwickshire. In Wellesbourne, close to Leamington Spa, he had to hold his meeting on the village green, where he claimed around 350 to four hundred attended. He spoke to around six hundred people at nearby Fenny Compton, but at Kenilworth, also in the immediate vicinity, he had "only a fair audience."[11]

Learning in April that people in Herefordshire were leaving for Virginia or Minnesota, in the United States, Denison made a beeline for Ledbury, speaking to a large audience at the Town Hall. The next day he travelled north to Shropshire to lecture "at a large meeting" in Ludlow and nearby Leamoon Common, where he "had the chapel crowded to excess." Ending his tour on April 12 at Leintwardine in Herefordshire, a short distance from Ludlow, Denison had the satisfaction of feeling that, through his exertions, "the people were now talking of going to Ontario." He felt that most of the emigrants from Herefordshire, Wiltshire, Dorset, Oxfordshire, and Warwickshire "will have been influenced through me to go to Ontario as I have been almost alone in working up Ontario in Canada among them."[12]

A year after Denison's tour, emigration was given a stimulus in the eastern counties, particularly in Suffolk and Cambridgeshire, when around six thousand agricultural trade unionists were locked out by farmers in an attempt to destroy the union. Many "were in fact escorted by union officials to Ontario, where they were apparently soon able to obtain employment."[13] A further group of 588 farm workers and their families, mainly from Lincolnshire, left in the following year for Ontario. However, by this time trade union involvement in emigration was beginning to wane, and by 1881 it came to an abrupt end. Trade union leaders could see little sense in encouraging the emigration of what were usually their most able members, and doubted the value it had in increasing the bargaining position of those who remained behind, since the numbers leaving at any time were relatively small. So, while the emigration of farm labourers continued after 1881, it did so without any support from the agricultural trade unions. It relied instead on funds provided by parishes, landowners, and the increasing number of philanthropic bodies that were being formed to assist poor people to emigrate.

Although the Industrial Revolution, which began in the late eighteenth century, had made Britain the most powerful and wealthiest nation on earth, it had brought untold grief to workers unable to benefit from the rapid economic expansion that was taking place. People had flocked from the country to the cities to fill the new jobs being created in the factories and related industries. However, while this was happening, traditional forms of employment were being destroyed by the increasing growth of mechanization and factory production. As workers found themselves being replaced by machines, they joined a growing pool of unemployed labourers who, if they managed to find work, had to accept pitifully low wages. Even young children had to take paid employment to supplement their families' meagre income. This situation was creating great misery and squalor in English cities by the late 1860s. It is against this background that Ontario and Quebec came to acquire so many of England's poor. Yet, put in a wider context, they were only a small component of the total who emigrated. Even in these difficult times, most English immigrants were sufficiently affluent to pay their own relocation costs.

When munitions workers at the government factories in Woolwich near the city of London were made redundant in 1857, their first thought was to emigrate.[14] With the end of the Crimean War in 1856, most of the workers who had been taken on earlier for the war effort were no longer needed. Rather than seek alternative employment, they chose to go to Ontario. Money was collected by the Woolwich Emigration Fund Committee and, unusually for the government, it provided a grant of £3,000, while the Duke of Wellington contributed a further £1,000.[15] A total of £6,000 was raised — enough to pay for the relocation costs of around 1,070 people.[16] However, with the closure of the Woolwich naval dockyard in 1869 and the continuing decline in munitions manufacture, the situation deteriorated even further, leading to considerable distress. Once again, Ontario beckoned.

A Relief Committee and an Emigration Society were duly formed to raise funds, but this time the government refused aid, apart from offering the redundant workers free transport in troopships. Contributions from local benefactors enabled just over one thousand former Woolwich dockyard workers to emigrate to Ontario in 1869, while a further 1,500

Courtesy Portsmouth Museums and Art Gallery CR 236/1982/9.

Woolwich emigrants embarking by ship in 1869 for Quebec at the naval dockyard in Portsmouth. Report in the *Illustrated London News* of May 1, 1869.

left the following year. However, the latter group included redundant workers from other naval dockyards along the River Thames, the River Medway, and the south coast.[17]

As these events were unfolding, distressed people living in London were also seeking help to emigrate. Forty single men and women, together with a small number of families — ninety-three individuals in all — were being assisted in June 1870 by the Working Men's Emigration Association to emigrate mainly to Lennoxville in the Eastern Townships of Quebec, "where they hoped to obtain immediate employment" (Table 17).[18] A few had been tradesmen such as bootmakers, carpenters, painters, clerks, bricklayers, and engine drivers, but the majority were labourers.

The domestic servants and agricultural labourers, particularly those who wrote "wants farm work," would have been snapped up straight away, while the tradesmen would have seemed less relevant to local needs. At this stage, Canada was still primarily an agricultural country.

Two months previously, representatives of this same London-based association had written to the Earl of Litchfield, in Staffordshire, asking for a donation to help several other families, about thirty adults, "who have been compelled to sell their homes on account of want of work — and who would be enabled to join a party of our members going to Canada if a sum of £75 could be raised for their assistance."[19] No doubt, other grandees throughout the country were also being pressed to help. In all, just less than four hundred members of the association left St. Pancras railway station in London in May of that year for Liverpool, where they embarked for Quebec in one of five ships.[20]

Meanwhile, Cornwall had been experiencing a downturn in its copper mining as a result of foreign competition, with the industry falling into a steep decline since the 1860s. As conditions deteriorated, the miners looked abroad for new opportunities. They mobilized their own resources, regarding the world's mining centres as mere places from which they could extract success and profit.[21] While most favoured the United States and Australia, the opening up of copper mining in northern Ontario began to attract the interest of Cornish families starting in the mid-1850s. Possibly their contacts in the already-established Cornish communities along Lake Ontario in Durham and Northumberland counties, and farther west in Huron County, had given them advance notice of the new mining developments taking place in the Algoma District. These highly skilled miners took charge of the management of the Bruce copper mines near Sault Ste. Marie, and they were also the key component of its workforce, thus bringing a steady flow of Cornish people to the area. Predictably, when the mines closed in 1876, the Cornish miners moved out, dispersing to other mining centres, especially those in the United States.[22]

By 1870, the Ontario government was running promotional campaigns to attract colonizers to the vast wildernesses of northern Ontario. One-hundred-acre free land grants were offered to settlers in districts like Algoma on condition that a stipulated area was cleared and cultivated within a stated period and a house was built.[23] A farmer from Norfolk who had been living near Sault Ste. Marie for twelve years thought that the district's big advantage was the availability of mining and lumbering jobs in the winter: "The kind of farmers to come here, and the men who would make themselves well-off in a very short time are tenant farmers and others with a little capital and a good practical knowledge of farming …"[24] He may well have been speaking for the Cornish miners, although they were a special case. However, many English must have taken advantage of land offers in southern Algoma, since by 1881 they were the dominant ethnic group in places like Bruce Mines, where they represented 52 percent of the population, and in Sault Ste. Marie, where they accounted for 39 percent of the population (Map 18).

Apart from the Cornish miners, who were able to find mining jobs abroad, there were men like Alfred Jewell, who thought laterally and found work as a lead glazier in Toronto. Having initially moved from Newquay to Cobourg in Northumberland County in 1883 — an area

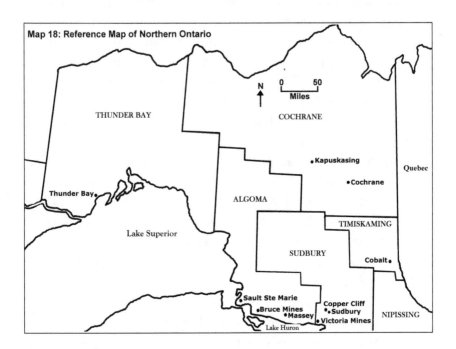

Map 18: Reference Map of Northern Ontario

with many long-established Cornish settlers — he and his wife and six children relocated to Toronto the following year, where he was snapped up by a company that installed stained glass windows.[25]

However, Jane and John Atkinson from Preston in Lancashire learned the hard way that Ontario did not necessarily have the ideal jobs market for tailors. They emigrated to Amherstburg in Essex County in the 1870s, hoping that John would find employment as a machinist, but after three years of working on the railway, they had given up any hope of John finding anything better: "[Although] times are pretty bad here, our folks being in work, we ought not to complain."[26]

Richard Edwards, a skilled ironworker from what is now the Telford area of Shropshire,[27] emigrated to Hamilton in 1886 with his family and fared better. He landed a job as a steam-hammer operator, working for the Steel Company of Canada.[28] Also, when Thomas Hayward, Herbert Barnett, and John Knott, all from Corsham in Wiltshire, an area close to the Somerset coalfields, moved to Cobalt in northern Ontario around the same time, one suspects they had been attracted by the jobs to be had in the silver mines.[29] However, English coal miners seeking to remain working as miners after emigrating generally looked to the United States for employment.[30]

Meanwhile, Ontario immigration agents continued to sing the praises of the province's agricultural opportunities, targeting specific areas of England where they had local contacts. John Bennet, a self-styled agent who said he would not seek payments for his efforts from the government "until I have shown my worth," had a positive story to tell about his own experiences in Stayner in Nottawasaga Township (Simcoe County). It is not clear where in England he was heading in 1876 in his mission to bang the drum for emigration, but it was likely that he went to his former residence, where he would have had friends and family. Once there, he intended to reveal how he had come to Stayner three years earlier with only £3 in his pocket, and how, "through my own industry, I am [now] in possession of 80 acres of first-rate land, and have enough to meet my only payment in May next."[31] Bennet was planning a series of "personal interviews," during which he would "let the public at large know in England what I have done myself and, if that will not be convincing, nothing will."[32]

His sales pitch was intended to appeal to affluent farmers, who were being anxiously courted, to stop them from going to the United States.

The rising number of English farm labourers who wished to emigrate to Ontario were easier to attract, although John A. Donaldson, the Toronto immigration agent, wondered how he was going to cope with the great number who were due to arrive in 1879. According to the warden of Peel County, Donaldson had informed him that "a large number of first-class farm hands are likely to come amongst us ... and will be sent to any part of [Peel] County where required."[33]

With the growing agricultural depression, most of the so-called "first-class farm hands" had needed financial help to emigrate. A particular trouble spot was Bedfordshire, which lost a steady stream of poor farm workers to Ontario during the second half of the nineteenth century. A group of nineteen people from Eversholt Parish were helped to emigrate in 1874 through subscriptions raised by landowners, including the Duke of Bedford, and money provided by the parish.[34] The Haynes Parish emigration fund had been established in 1850 to raise money to assist poor labourers, and it continued to do its philanthropic work until 1907.[35]

At the other end of the social spectrum was James Cross, who had access to the rich and powerful. Having become known in some way to the Duke of Portland in Nottinghamshire, Cross asked his lordship in 1873 for "kind aid towards a fund being raised by the Reverend A.J. Fleming, incumbent of the parish of St. Paul's Church, Clerkenwell [London], to enable myself, mother and wife and 6 children to emigrate to Canada." To bolster his credentials further, he added that the Marquis of Westminster and the Lord Mayor of London had also contributed to his fund.[36]

The free land grants that the Ontario government offered at the time were a great enticement, although the rewards required Herculean effort and stamina. Having qualified for two hundred acres of uncleared land, the Jackson family from Nottinghamshire soon had second thoughts about the wisdom of taking on such a commitment. Mrs. Jackson explained to her cousin in England that she and her husband could no longer cope with the workload. But, being a shoemaker, her husband had been able to find work easily in Toronto; so they had "agreed to stay here and work at shoe making till we can get on a partly cleared farm."[37]

Learning from this experience, Mrs. Jackson advised her cousin to emigrate if he wanted to, but if he did, "that he should take at least £100" in order to buy already cleared land; "you would be a gentleman soon with that.... It is a right place when you have a start, the living is so very cheap." Making a similar point, a government communiqué in 1870 stressed that immigrants who took up free grant lands without first having provided a financial cushion for themselves were likely to fail. They needed to earn sufficient money to enable them to subsist on their land until they could obtain their first crop. And finding basic manual work was remarkably easy given that there was a stated requirement for thirty to forty thousand agricultural labourers in Ontario at the time.[38]

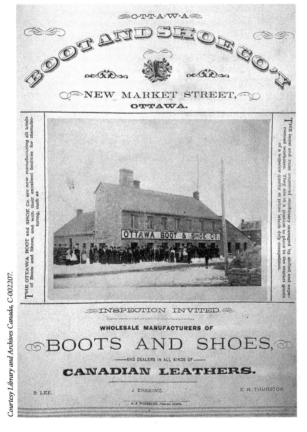

Ottawa Boot and Shoe Factory, New Market Street, Ottawa, 1875. Photograph by William James Topley.

Meanwhile, the Muskoka District, north of Lake Simoce, witnessed the arrival of a new type of immigrant during the 1870s — upper class "remittance men." This term, first coined in Australia, had disparaging connotations, evoking images of the idle and pretentious rich. Primarily an English phenomenon, remittance men received regular payments from a family member or friend, usually on condition that they moved to a stipulated overseas destination. An example was eighteen-year-old Frederick de la Fosse, who, having been orphaned as a child, was sent to Muskoka in 1878 by his uncle, Colonel Montague Ricketts.[39] Acting as his guardian, Ricketts clearly decided that De la Fosse needed to be taught a lesson or two about life, and presumably hoped that three years in the backwoods of Muskoka, learning the basics of farming, would make a man of him. Often, in such cases, there was a hint of scandal and a general desire to be rid of the person in question.

Ricketts enrolled De la Fosse in what was termed an "agricultural school," run by Captain Charles Greville Harston. For the sum of £100 per annum, Harston agreed to take De la Fosse as a pupil for three years, and upon completion of his farming education he was to receive one hundred acres in the Muskoka District. Of course, free land grants were available to all prospective settlers, so the only real benefit of the transaction was Harston's tutelage, which concentrated on the practical skills of land clearance. As might have been expected, Harston was a rogue, disappearing, never to be seen again, once the three-year training period had been completed. All the while, De la Fosse received regular allowances from his uncle, secure in the knowledge that he need never experience the hardships of the ordinary settler:

> Much as we plumed ourselves in being pioneers, the
> reality was that we were only such in the sense of being
> in the district and undergoing many of the discomforts
> of a settler's existence ... and escaped the privations and
> anxieties that were the common lot of those around us....
> It was only when we hade been a considerable time in
> the country that we realized what very ordinary beings

we were and how much the grit and the determination
of those poorer than ourselves were to be admired.[40]

At the age of twenty-one, De la Fosse moved into a log cabin in the
Huntsville area, living near a circle of wealthy friends who also relied on
remittances from England:

> Our dwellings were well furnished, pictures and orna-
> ments sent by kind relatives in England, covered our
> walls, and one or two of us even boasted the possession
> of pianos, banjos and other musical instruments.... All
> of us were imbued with the idea of being gentlemen
> farmers so most of us engaged the services of young
> sons of settlers to perform our chores and help us in our
> housekeeping.[41]

From time to time these aristocratic adventurers enjoyed pastimes
like cricket, presumably having remembered to pack a cricket bat in their
luggage as they were leaving England. Learning about the athletic events
to be held in Huntsville's Gala Day, De la Fosse and his group decided
to join in, challenging the "Huntsville Cricketers" to a match: "The challenge was promptly accepted but we went to our wits' end to find enough
men for the team. This difficulty was finally surmounted by our obtaining the services of sundry baseballers among the younger element, who
were only too anxious to seize the chance of glorification."[42] Before the
match, the cricketers enjoyed dinner together at one of the Huntsville
hotels, "spending a most pleasant hour together." After much bedlam
and hilarity, "the game was a victory for the Huntsvillians.... We found
it hard to find out what the real score was, as the record had been kept by
an individual who had offered his services *gratis* and had been accepted
on the strength of telling us that his grandfather had been a cricketer."[43]

Despite his seemingly frivolous nature, De la Fosse settled down
and made something of himself in the end. After marrying Mary
Bell, he and his wife raised a family in a remote farm located along
Buck Lake, to the east of Huntsville, in Parry Sound District. He later

moved to Peterborough, where he held down a job as a librarian in the Peterborough Public Library for thirty-six years, doing so until his death at the age of eighty-six.

While the Muskoka remittance men were relatively few in number, they had come to a district that had attracted a good many English settlers. No doubt the offer of free land grants and Muskoka's profitable timber trade had been major inducements, although newspaper reports on both sides of the Atlantic continued to cast doubt on the likelihood of success.[44]

A major transition in the nature of English immigration occurred with the arrival during the 1870s of so-called "home children." They were the offspring of the urban poor who were being offered a new life in Canada as indentured farm workers or domestic servants.[45] The intention was that they would help to alleviate Canada's desperate labour shortages and in the process benefit themselves by having the chance of a better life.[46] With the worsening humanitarian crisis building up in cities like London and Liverpool, parents and guardians who were no longer

Log House near Huntsville, 1875. Pencil drawing by George Harlow White (1817–87).

able to provide for their families had placed their children in charitable homes. The escalating costs of caring for these children led to the timely solution of sending them to Canada, and a host of philanthropic people emerged to organize their departures and placements.[47]

Despite grave concerns on both sides of the Atlantic over reports that home children were being neglected, over-worked, and in some cases abused, the emigration schemes grew rapidly.[48] About five hundred home children were sent to Canada annually during the late 1870s, and this number more than tripled between 1879 and 1883.[49] More than eleven thousand children arrived in Canada between 1870 and 1914, and this number mushroomed to eighty thousand by 1925.[50]

The first two removals were launched in 1869–70 by Maria Rye and Annie Macpherson, both deeply religious women, who had been troubled by the suffering they witnessed in the slums of London and Liverpool. Miss Rye's children came from workhouses and industrial schools, while Miss Macpherson's youngsters were mainly street waifs gathered from London's east end.[51]

Upon arriving in Canada, the children were brought to so-called "receiving homes" that sometimes offered training and from which the final placements were determined. Most were located in southern Ontario. Rye's Our Western Home at Niagara-on-the-Lake, and Macpherson's Marchmont Home at Belleville were the first to be established in Ontario, with many others eventually sprouting up as far to the east as Ottawa and to the west as far as London.[52]

Louisa Birt, Annie Macpherson's sister, acquired her home in 1877 at Knowlton, to the southwest of Sherbrooke (Eastern Townships), after previously having sent her children to Nova Scotia.[53] Established in 1872, the Church of England Waifs and Strays Society also joined Birt in the Eastern Townships, establishing homes for both boys and girls at Sherbrooke.[54] Given the substantial English presence in the southern part of the Eastern Townships, Louisa Birt and the Waifs and Strays Society would have easily been able to arrange placements with English-speaking Anglicans (Map 9). John Middlemore, a medical doctor and son of a wealthy businessman from Birmingham, ran his first children's home near London, Ontario, but afterward moved his headquarters to Fairfax, near Halifax, Nova Scotia.[55] Meanwhile, Thomas Barnardo,[56] the doyen of the emigration movement, had his main home for boys in Toronto and for girls in Peterborough.[57]

Through these schemes, children from English city slums were removed from hopeless situations and given the chance of a decent livelihood in later life. After serving their indentures, some followed the promised career of farming, although most opted for the well-paid jobs to be found in towns and cities. But to reach that happy outcome they had to first demonstrate great resilience and courage. They were despised for their poverty and had no one to turn to for help. Well-meaning philanthropists like Mr. Barnardo had torn up family links in a mindless quest for moral correctness. They thought that children had to be rescued from a degenerate home life, seemingly oblivious to the strong family ties and respectability of the labouring poor.[58] That said, most children clearly benefited from going to Canada.

The Girls' Friendly Society,[59] founded in 1875 and run in conjunction with the Church of England, also played its part in furthering juvenile emigration. In addition to offering training and religious instruction, it assisted young girls to work abroad as domestic servants or in factories, becoming particularly active from 1885.[60]

Occasionally, English parishes assisted children in their care to emigrate. The parish of Cambridge, St. Mary the Great, was going to arrange for thirteen-year-old Ellen Black to go with Miss Rye to Canada, but when it discovered that she (Miss Rye) did not "intend having anything to do with the Local Government Board," the £5 payment was refused and the child's emigration was blocked.[61] The parish would not countenance relinquishing full control to Miss Rye, insisting that the child's care needed to be safeguarded through the supervisory role of the local government board. However, the Leeds Board of Poor Law Guardians had no such qualms during the 1880s and 1890s, when they delegated the relocation of some of their poorest children to Maria Rye and Louisa Birt.[62] Their report on the *Emigration of Children from the Leeds Union*, produced in 1891, extolled the merits of "snatching children from pauperism," but because the Guardians had no reliable feedback on what had happened to the children, their ultimate fate was unknown.[63] Nearly all of the children went to Ontario.

Girls with their chaperone on their way to the Marchmont Home in 1922. They would fill the insatiable demand at the time for female domestic servants.

Boys on their way to the Marchmont Home in 1922. Marchmont became a major distribution centre, eventually being used by a number of agencies, including the Barnardo homes.

The English reformatory school boys who began arriving in Ontario and Quebec in 1884 became another source of cheap labour. Having been convicted of serious crimes, initially there was understandable alarm in accepting such children.[64] However, good management and supervision allayed these fears. Through the use of local agents, the behaviour and welfare of each child was carefully monitored, with detailed reports being sent both to the school and parents on a regular basis.[65] One such agent was Mr. Gold, based in Melbourne (Richmond County), who took charge of the many reformatory school boys being sent to the Eastern Townships during the 1880s. Children from the Hertfordshire Reformatory School for Boys normally spent their first year or so under his beady eye in Melbourne.[66]

After working for a milkman in Melbourne, William Forrester moved to Sherbrooke, where, according to his father, "he seems to have quite settled down and is evidently pleased with the country."[67] After working in Melbourne, Anthony Crabb moved to Kingsey, to the north of Melbourne, where he wrote that he "thinks of marrying his master's daughter" and "has changed his name to Smart ... in order to conceal his identity."[68] William Martin was unhappy with Melbourne and wanted to go back to England, but, according to Gold, his mother did not "encourage the thought of his return."[69] After finding him a printing job in Sherbrooke, Gold reported that Martin's mood had improved. James Hoyle and Henry Putt both worked at Windsor Mills, to the east of Melbourne, before landing well-paid jobs in the United States.[70] Having been joined by his father, mother, and sister, Putt was said to be "comfortably situated."[71] After cutting ice in Melbourne, Robert Smitham found lucrative employment in Toronto.[72] And after their time in Melbourne, William Binder joined the Salvation Army in Montreal, while Thomas Ridding joined the army, serving at the Citadel in Quebec.[73]

In addition to these assisted juvenile immigrants, the Eastern Townships also attracted couples like Peter and Ann Cork from Staffordshire, who arrived in 1883 with their eight children in search of good farmland. Before this, Peter had moved from job to job in England, working as a blacksmith, carter, colliery banksman, and grocer, but none provided a decent livelihood. So emigration beckoned. Acquiring land at

Cookshire, just to the east of Sherbrooke, through the British American Land Company, Peter and Ann established a farm and built their first log cabin, which "was soon replaced by a brick-built farmhouse which looks as though it had been transported from late Victorian Staffordshire!"[74]

William Joseph Pitman and his wife, Annie Chin, both Somerset-born, arrived in the late 1880s and tried their hand at farming in Belvedere, near Sherbrooke.[75] The region's mines also attracted Cornish copper miners like William Jenkins. He found work at Albert Mines, to the south of Sherbrooke, and settled at nearby Capelton; but he left just a few years later, when the gold mines in Colorado and Mexico offered him more lucrative employment. He later returned to Sherbrooke to supervise the running of the Suffield copper mine. He worked there until the mine closed in 1919, after which time he retired to a farm in Minton, just to the south of Albert Mines.[76]

Meanwhile, the early 1900s saw the return of the reformatory boys, this time to the mining areas of northern Ontario.[77] One example was Thomas Wells, from the Hertfordshire Reformatory School, who landed his first job as a cook at the Prospect Hotel in Cobalt (Timiskaming District), and later found employment at Copper Cliff (Sudbury District) as a watchman at a silver refinery. By 1906 he was reported to be "in a

View of the bleak industrial landscape in Sudbury, 1888. Image taken by an unknown photographer.

Courtesy Library and Archives Canada, PA-050973.

good position and doing well," having nearly paid off his debt to his brother and sending money to his sister back in England. His situation remained good a year later when he reported from the Larose Mine in Cobalt that he had "plenty of work to do in the silver mines."[78]

Having been released from the Hertfordshire Reformatory School in 1906, John Carrier Eacher found employment initially with a lumbering company in Massey (Algoma District), "at 30s. per week with board." However, lumbering work did not suit him, nor did working as a cook on a steamer based in Toronto, a job from which he was sacked, presumably because of misconduct. His last known address was in North Bay (Nipissing District).

John Ernest Sutton, discharged from the same school in 1909, was recruited by the New Idea Suit Hanger Company in Toronto, being paid $10 a week. His aunt, who lived in Toronto, had apparently "got him" the job, but he hated it; so he moved north, where he found work as a chainman in the Canadian Northern Railway survey party. By 1913 he had moved to Winnipeg and was expecting "to go even further west."

By the latter half of the nineteenth century, immigrants to Ontario and Quebec had a considerably easier time in reaching faraway destinations. They could travel in steamships in a fraction of the time taken by sailing ships, while the burgeoning railway networks on both sides of the Atlantic provided them with an integrated service. Yet, despite these improvements in transport, and the best efforts of Canadian immigration agents, the overwhelming majority of British immigrants were going to the United States. Being more highly developed economically than Canada, the United States had always seemed the better choice. But by the early 1900s, the situation had reversed, and Canada gradually became more successful in attracting immigrants. Meanwhile, the English continued to dominate the British influx to Canada, having done so since 1860.[79]

While the people who received assistance to emigrate generated paperwork and appeared highly visible, it is well to remember that the majority, who went unaided, left no documentation behind. Robert Brewster, the Duke of Bedford's loyal steward for thirty-two years, received funds from the Bedford estate to emigrate in 1884, and was also provided with the services of a local shipping agent, who "promised to see that they [Brewster and his family] have comfortable berths for the long sea voyage."[80]

John Litchfield, an inmate of the Ampthill Union Workhouse in Bedford, had much more basic requirements. Fortunately for him, he had a benefactor in Derby who paid his relocation costs and helped him to make the necessary arrangements. Richard Henson, a baker and provision dealer, began the process in 1885 when he wrote to the workhouse matron, stating that "as you are aware, John Litchfield in your establishment is emigrating to America with his sister Louise, who lives in London." Henson asked the matron to let John come to Derby, "as I shall have to prepare him with an outfit." His sister, travelling from London, was to meet him at the Bedford Railway Station: "If you [the matron] will pay the railway fare for him, I will see that you have it by return of post.... Kindly give him my address; if they miss each other he can travel by himself and I will meet the train which arrives here [Derby] at three o'clock."[81] The matron's willingness to co-operate reveals an unexpectedly humane attitude, which is at odds with the grim imagery normally associated with workhouses.

Ever greater numbers of Bedfordshire people emigrated to Ontario during the 1880s, but, as one local correspondent pointed out, the land of milk and honey was not quite what it seemed. Having received a highly negative letter from his brother, who had emigrated to Toronto some time before, Mr. W. Ball, from Pavenham Parish, forwarded it to the *Bedfordshire Times and Independent*, which duly printed it in its June 22, 1888, edition under the heading, "The Woes of Emigrants." In it, Toronto was described as "a dumping hole for emigrants, who are flocking there daily in shoals of seven or eight hundred. When they get into what is known as the sheds, Mr. Ball says they have no money ... and they have nothing to eat ... no bedding or blankets of any kind are furnished."[82]

These dire conditions attracted the attention of a Canadian newspaper reporter who, upon investigation, found "this long, foul-smelling and disgraceful hole was reeking with scents and crammed with strangers in a strange land. The air was full of the [blank] of angry men, the screams and cries of children and the pitiful wailing of infants."[83]

The immigrant reception centre in Toronto clearly had insufficient buildings and staff in place to cope adequately with the rising influx of immigrants, but was this an ongoing problem or just one isolated incident? Presumably, the local press had been tipped off and duly obliged with vivid imagery, but that probably reflected more on the feelings of local inhabitants, who may have grown uneasy about the rising tide of poor immigrants on their doorstep.

Operating at a much loftier level, the Lincolnshire-born Colonel Francis Fane — one of four wealthy English farmers who visited Canada in 1890 by invitation of the Canadian government to advise on its potential for immigrant farmers and farm labourers — pronounced that the country had a good deal to offer. He noted that an immigrant could buy "a nice farm with a good house and cleared land at about $30 (£6) an acre in the Eastern Townships — in doing this "he would avoid the hardships of Manitoba and the North West and would be in the midst of comparative comforts and society and within easy reach of markets, schools, etc."[84]

Henry Simmons, from Wokingham (Surrey), another member of the group, noted that productive farms could be bought in Ontario at from £10 to £20 an acre "with good houses, buildings and fences, and land all under cultivation, and where every comfort of life can be obtained and enjoyed just as easily [as] and more economically than in England." Simmons also believed that Ontario farmers made excellent prairie settlers, "making openings" in many parts of Ontario for newly arrived immigrants with capital. He travelled to the London area, where he met the Lincolnshire-born J. Gibson, who had a farm in Delaware Township. In driving there he noticed "the original log huts ... standing at the rear of the new, substantial well-built brick residences. All the houses had gardens and trees planted around, giving them a homelike and English appearance."[85]

Colonel Fane's mission and others like it may have helped to turn the immigrant stream away from the United States and toward Canada in the early 1900s. By the end of the previous century there had been an exceptional rise in the number of young and educated single men entering Canada, further signalling its growing appeal over the United States.[86] The English came to Canada in unprecedented numbers starting in 1905, and by 1910 many more went to Canada than went to the United States. Just over 150,000 English immigrants arrived in Canada in

1910 alone, representing 72 percent of the total intake from Britain. That year, roughly half that number had gone to the United States.

This turnaround in Canada's favour, partly driven by the government's economic incentives, stimulated provincial governments to continue sending their agents to Britain. Edward Brewster, the son of an affluent farmer from near Myddle in Shropshire, who had prospered in Compton in the Eastern Townships, was seen as an ideal ambassador. Having emigrated around 1877 when in his early twenties, he had acquired practical knowledge of Canadian farming methods and conditions, and could speak with authority about its prospects. In 1906, Brewster was snapped up by the Ontario government to work alongside the Canadian emigration agent for the West Midlands, who was based in Birmingham.[87]

Brewster's tour of 1906–07 covered the major towns and cities to the north and west of Birmingham, including Wolverhampton, Tamworth, Walsall, Belper, Dudley, Kidderminster, and Stourbridge.[88] He was particularly well received in Shropshire, visiting Shrewsbury, Market Drayton, and Oswestry, where he organized many meetings and held hundreds of interviews.[89] At Rushbury he attracted about one hundred "of the very best class — young men, farmers' sons and farm labourers, also some domestics." At Chetwynd there were "about 80 present, chiefly of the agricultural class, a large number being young men, just the class wanted … at Weston Rhyn: about 100 present, principally young people of the agricultural class [who] showed great interest." And at Pontesbury there was "a splendid audience composed mostly of agriculturalists. Many in the audience had friends and relatives in Canada."[90] The great demand for agricultural labourers and domestic servants was always stressed, while government newspaper advertisements proclaimed that in going to Canada immigrants would "get a piece of the earth in the Empire." They would be "under the Flag, in Britain's nearest overseas dominion."[91]

By the early twentieth century, an increasing proportion of English arrivals were coming from the troubled industrial cities, where unemployment levels were soaring. Owing to the immense increase in agricultural production that had taken place in the United States, Canada, and Argentina, British agriculture was in severe crisis. Poor labourers, unable to find work in the countryside, had gone to the cities, only to find that conditions there were even worse. This movement had concentrated the nation's surplus labour in the city slums. An added problem was the stagnating state of Britain's textile industries. That, too, had its principal cause in foreign competition. A prime trouble spot was the mill town of Bolton, to the northwest of Manchester, which had been a major centre of cotton production. Following the loss of trade, Bolton cotton workers were laid off in great numbers, and emigration was seen as their only hope. Between 1912 and 1926, the Bolton and District Card and Ring Room Operatives' Provincial Association[92] organized the departure of around five hundred of its members to various destinations, including Canada. Since the First World War put an effective stop to emigration between 1915 and 1918, most departures occurred between 1912 and 1914 and 1919 and 1926 (Table 18).[93]

It was a similar story in other English cities. To deal with the growing crisis, the Unemployed Workmen Act was passed in 1905, with one of its measures being the formation of a nationwide network of distress committees to channel funds, raised by city councils, to the unemployed; but the scheme had only limited success. Once again, emigration offered the only viable solution. That year, Leeds City Council assisted six families and two single men to emigrate, nearly all of whom were in their twenties: Arthur Smith was a shoe finisher, Wallis Watson a bricklayer, Charles S. Sidebottom was a rough cutter, while Frank Harvey was a tailor's presser. William and John Dunderdale and William Lister had no stated occupation, while Herbert Barker was a labourer.[94] These young men and their families were clearly being given a chance to make something of their lives.

Judging from the stated destinations of the Leeds families who were assisted to emigrate in 1907, they dispersed widely once they arrived in Canada. Nine out of the fourteen heads of households were heading for eastern Ontario. Thomas Johnstone was going to Perth, Ernest Barlow to Caledonia, Robert Richards to Cornwall, George Thompson to Carleton Junction, Albert Wormald to Lancaster, Patrick McAndrew to Mallorytown, Hiram Holstead and Walter Pattison to Brockville, and John Hughes to Belleville. Harry Clough was heading farther west to Bowmanville on Lake Ontario, as was John Jackson, who was destined for

Dunnville on Lake Erie. Joseph Townend and Henry Hoare were going to Toronto, while Alfred Edward Brown went to Montreal.[95] Presumably, eastern Ontario was the preferred destination for costs reasons.

As was the case in other English cities, by 1905 Norwich had a Distress Committee, which also ran local schemes to help the unemployed, but to little avail. Lying in the heart of an agricultural area, Norwich had suffered badly during the agricultural depression, leaving a great surplus of unwanted labour. Once again, emigration was encouraged, and the first group of eighteen men, two wives, and three children left the following year. They were met at the Toronto train station by an emigration agent "and, miracle of miracles, we all had work offered to us by 9 a.m."[96] With this promising beginning, a second group consisting of eighteen families followed, but they were said to be drunk and unruly. However, despite this setback, many more Norwich people were assisted to emigrate. Between 1905 and the outbreak of the First World War in 1914, a total of 1,501 Norwich people were helped by the city council to emigrate to Canada.[97]

During the last years before the First World War, English emigration peaked, with an increasing proportion being directed to Canada and other parts of the British Empire. Times continued to be extremely tough for the labouring poor. Farm labourers from the Pendley estate in Hertfordshire were desperate to get to Canada in 1913, but only those living in the parish of Tring could receive help, which came in the form of a payment toward an outfit.[98] Declaring that "the fare and outfit" required by his wife and child "is £2 beyond my anticipation," Frank Noyce asked the agent acting for the estate to "help me a little towards this amount," but because Noyce originated from Hampshire, his request was rejected.[99] Similarly Mr. Puddiphatt, a native of Buckland Common who was "out of employment at present," was also turned down. More successful was George Birch, aged eighteen, "who works in Tring Park." He received £1 toward his outfit, while William Iforn, who "has an aunt out there [Canada] getting on well," received the same amount. Mrs. Bessie Brooks from Berkhamsted, east of Tring, asked the estate factor if she could have the "£s you promised when we were going abroad; but owing to not raising enough for all to go we have given up the idea. I am sorry to say we are very hard up and myself and children have no shoes as their feet are on the ground and I should be so very thankful as times are so very bad." But her request for £3 was refused on the grounds that the fund was intended for "emigration purposes" only.[100] Those were desperate times!

Meanwhile, people of moderate affluence continued to arrive in Ontario. William Bilton, an Anglican minister, and his wife Alice, both from Bedfordshire, moved to Sarnia Township (Lambton County) in 1913.[101] They "liked the freeness and liberty of the country," and, given that oil production at nearby Petrolia had already begun, the first in North America, the Biltons could anticipate a prosperous future in an up and coming industrial area.[102] W.H. Barnes, who left Burnley in Lancashire in 1920, waltzed into his first job in the shipping department of a Toronto motor business with a view to landing an even better job: "There is plenty of work here and rather decent money, and better respect for the worker." There were a good many Lancashire people living near his boarding house and, because he knew the family running it, he was being treated like family. Toronto suited him extremely well.[103]

The mass unemployment of the 1920s fuelled ever-rising levels of emigration to the British Dominions — especially to Canada and Australia. A rising proportion of English immigrants came from the towns and cities and consequently lacked the farming skills that were still greatly in demand in Canada. In 1922, the British and Ontario governments launched a scheme for British boys, to teach them Canadian farming methods. Based at Vimy Ridge Farm near Guelph, the boys were to be placed on farms for three years, during which time they would earn wages and also receive food and lodging. Ultimately, it was hoped that they would become self-sufficient.[104]

Meanwhile, philanthropic groups in England continued to help the poor to emigrate. The Nottingham and District Emigration Committee, formed in 1929, raised its funds locally from prominent businessmen and had as its chairman the Duke of Portland.[105] At a public meeting held on March 27, 1929, to promote emigration, music was provided by the Dakeyne Street Lads Band, a local boys' group supported by yet another philanthropic group that had provided assisted passages to Canada.[106]

The Great Depression at the end of the 1920s was a traumatic time for people like Annie and Jack Heathcote, from Nottinghamshire, who had emigrated to Hamilton. Their world began slowly to collapse. Then a major steel-producing centre, Hamilton was particularly badly hit by the economic downturn.[107] In 1931, Annie told Mabel, her sister-in-law in Sutton in Ashfield (Nottinghamshire), "I don't think you would know me now, my hair is nearly white." A few months later she reported that "the work is terrible here [Hamilton] — I think things are getting worse here."[108] A year later, her husband Jack told his father in Sutton that he had been forced to abandon his farm. Having acquired a one-hundred-acre farm, it proved to be too much for them: "We went after the big stuff and got nothing." The "pensions people" told them that if they didn't "get settled, they would either cut the pension or stop it altogether." They had relocated to Hamilton, to "a place where you couldn't keep a rabbit."[109]

By 1934 Jack had became seriously ill. Annie informed Mabel that "when anything does happen, he does not want to be buried in this country, he always wanted to go home … things is very bad here; there is some men been out of work four years. It is terrible. I don't know what some people is going to do." Following Jack's death in December of that year, Annie collapsed with grief. "The doctor says I am not fit to work … I don't know what we are going to live on," she lamented, having had her pension withdrawn when Jack died. "They don't care in this country whether you live or die." Money sent to her by family in England helped her to cope. Yet, she wrote that if she ever acquired enough money to get to England, she would "come home for a while, but not to stay, because of Jack" (who lay buried in a cemetery near Hamilton).[110]

Another more favourable perspective on later emigration can be seen in the happy responses received from former residents of Clitheroe, a Lancashire town that celebrated its eight hundredth anniversary in 1948, three years after the end of the Second World War. Those who had emigrated were asked to give their locations, revealing that most of the respondents were living in the cities and towns of Ontario, Quebec, and British Columbia. Writing from Oshawa, Mrs. L.L. Fowler stated that she had left Clitheroe in 1912 as a child: "I lived in Jubilee Terrace and worked as a weaver after I left school. My name was then Alethea

Langtree, daughter of Thomas and Alice Ann Langtree, my grandparents, who kept the fish and chip shop and tripe business in the market place."

Alice and Jim Parker, living at Hudson, near Montreal, had been Canadian residents for twenty-five years. They were happy, but their "heart is still in Clitheroe," they said. Herbert Chew of Montreal had many happy memories of cycling and walking around various places in Clitheroe and, like some others who responded, he still read the *Clitheroe Advertiser*.[111]

The growing avalanche of English immigrants who flocked to Canada starting in the second half of the nineteenth century came from all parts of the country and had extremely varied social and work backgrounds. By that time, emigration had been well and truly adopted as a solution to England's social problems, although it involved using Canada as a dumping ground for England's surplus population. Nevertheless, England's poor were given a lifeline, while Ontario and Quebec acquired the labouring population they so desperately needed. Despite the high visibility of the very poor in documentary sources, they were, of course, only a minority of the total influx. Most of the people who came in this later period paid their own way and left no records behind. They usually left simply to better themselves. Most did.

Table 17:

Working Men's National Emigration Association: List of People from London Who Went Mainly to Lennoxville in the Eastern Townships, 1870 [LAC RG17 Vol. 39#3609.]

[Note: do = ditto]

Name	Age	Trade	Total in Family	Where Going To
Adam, William	38	Carpenter	6	-
Adams, Henry	24	Labourer	1	-
Bennett, Robert	45	Corn. Traveller	11	-
Brown, George	30	Clerk	1	-
Blake, Eleanor	46	Laundress	6	Hamilton
Batten, John	17	Wants Farm Work	1	Lennoxville
Bareham, George	18	Carpenter	1	-
Curtiss, Edward N.	23	do	1	-
Churchill, William H.	24	do	1	-
Collis, James	23	Grocer	1	-
Coward, H.A.	22	Labourer	1	Lennoxville
Climber, John	36	do	1	do
Chedely, Emily	16	do	1	Toronto
Curtis, George R.	24	Bricklayer	1	-
Cloche, John	32	Gardener	1	Lennoxville
Daves, William C.	28	Labourer	1	do
England, George H.	22	Plasterer	1	-
Franks, James	40	Labourer	2	Lennoxville
Francis, Charles	30	Cabinet maker	1	do
Foster, Frederick	39	Printer	2	-
Giddings, Cornelious	27	Labourer	2	Lennoxville
Gillbank, Ellen	21	Soldier's wife	1	-
Gushing, George	20	Painter	1	-
Hulme, John	20	do	1	-
Holdgate, George	20	Labourer	1	Lennoxville
Harris, Henrietta	36	Domestic servant	1	Toronto
Harding, George H.	19	Carpenter	1	-
Hawkins, George	19	Painter	1	-
Hersee, Alfred T.	22	Carpenter	1	-

Name	Age	Trade	Total in Family	Where Going To
Juniper, Alfred	19	Sawyer	1	Ottawa
Jones, Sophia	25	To join her husband	2	-
Jackson, Henry J.	25	Painter	1	-
Johns, R. Kimber	35	Wants farm work	1	Lennoxville
Lake, John	50	Miller	11	-
Law, Charles	27	Boot maker	4	-
McDonald, Andrew	25	Agricultural Labourer	1	Lennoxville
Moore, William	26	Basket Maker	1	-
Nichol, Christopher	36	Carrier	6	Lennoxville
Smithe, John	29	Labourer	1	-
Shar, Owen	40	Soldier	1	-
Shar, Bridget	35	Domestic Servant	1	-
Smith, Jesse	29	Coachman	2	-
Saunders, J. H.	18	Gardener	1	Lennoxville
Snow, William	17	Labourer	1	do
Trinsey, Ruben	18	Ag. Labourer	1	do
Trigg, Walter	22	Engine Driver	1	-
Thomas, Edward	21	Carpenter	1	-
Turner, John	21	Labourer	1	Lennoxville
Walter Harrison	18	Wants Farm work	1	do
Bargent, Joseph W.	19	Ag. Labourer	1	do
				Total 93

Table 18:

**Cotton Workers from Bolton in Lancashire Who Were Assisted to Emigrate to Ontario and Quebec, 1912–27
[LAC MG40–M10 Bolton and District Card and Ring Room Operatives' Provincial Association]**

Name	Vessel	Destination	Departure Date
Alex'r Allinson	*Empress of Britain*	Quebec	20/06/1912
? Laver	*Virginian*	Quebec	xx/10/1912
James E. Haslam	*Britain*	Quebec	n/k
X Wilson Baker	n/k	Quebec	n/k
Schofield née Redmond	*Empress of Ireland*	Quebec	n/k

Name	Vessel	Destination	Departure Date
? Cooper	*Empress of Ireland*	Quebec	1912
? E. Schofield	*Tunisian*	Quebec	n/k
Peter W. Mather	*Empress of Britain*	Quebec	6/09/1912
Jerome Simpson	do	Quebec	do
Bryan L. Gornall	do	Quebec	14/10/1912
Bruce Grey	*Tunisian*	Quebec	14/10/1912
James Hurdman	*Empress of Ireland*	Quebec	15/10/1912
Charles Williams	*Victorian*	Quebec	n/k
Florence Valentine	*Laurentic*	Quebec	n/k
Ray Leach	*Empress of Britain*	Quebec	14/11/1912
Nestor Higson	*Virginian*	Quebec	05/11/1912
G. Bennett	*Lake Maniotoba*	Quebec	15/11/1912
Sarah A. Seddon	*Laurentic*	Montreal	26/04/1913
Anne Cane Atherton	*Laurentic*	Quebec	18/04/1913
John Barnes	*Tunisian*	Quebec	26/04/1913
Florence Williams	*Victorian*	Montreal	26/04/1913
Ethel Entwistle	do	do	do
Agnes Redwood	*Empress of Ireland*	Quebec	12/05/1913
Annie Harley (née Redmond)	*Empress of Ireland*	Quebec	17/05/1913
Flora A. Owen	*Virginian*	Montreal	12/05/1913
Annie Oates	*Victorian*	Quebec	14/05/1913
James McParrlin & Hannah McParrlin	*Canada*	Montreal	2/06/1913
Ellen Bennett	*Megantic*	Quebec	9/06/1913
Ellen Hare	*Empress of Ireland*	Quebec	9/06/1913
Annie Orrell	*Tunisian*	Montreal	9/06/1913
Hilda Orrell	do	do	do
Eleanor Weston	*Empress of Ireland*	Quebec	9/06/1913
Mary A Chadwick	*Canada*	Quebec	23/06/1913
Annie Hodgson	*Empress of Britain*	Quebec	23/06/1913
Mary McDowell (née Buckthorpe)	*Virginian*	Quebec	23/06/1913
Annie Charlesworth	*Corsican*	Quebec	23/06/1913
Charles Thornley	*Laurentic*	Quebec	23/06/1913
William Fletcher	do	do	do
Thomas Harrison	*Corsican*	Quebec	23/06/1913
Bertha Brown	do	do	do
Isabella Beddows	*Virginian*	Montreal	23/06/1913

Name	Vessel	Destination	Departure Date
Elizabeth A. Beddows	do	do	do
Letitia Kindall	*Laurentic*	Montreal	15/07/1913
Sarah C. Howes	*Empress of Britain*	Quebec	21/07/1913
Peter Allison	*Corsican*	Quebec	do
Alic A. Allison	do	do	do
Hammen Brown	*Corsican*	Quebec	11/08/1913
Lily Southern	*Laurentic*	Canada	18/08/1913
Elizabeth E. Fern	*Corsican*	Montreal	13/09/1913
Edith Fern	do	do	do
Lambert Fatley	*Empress of Britain*	Quebec	19/09/1913
Bertha J. Parker	*Empress of Ireland*	Quebec	3/10/1913
Alice Balshaw	do	Quebec	3/10/1913
Georgina Bolshaw	do	do	do
Sarah A. Napkin	*Tunisian*	Quebec	n/k
Elizabeth Haslam	*Empress of Ireland*	Quebec	n/k
Frances Barton	*Empress of Britain*	Quebec	27/10/1913
Bertha Barton	do	do	do
Mary A. Barton	do	do	do
Louie Hall	*Corsican*	Quebec	10/11/1913
Lily Ryder	*Empress of Ireland*	Quebec	27/11/1913
Louisa Higson	n/k	Montreal	24/11/1913
Florence Greenhalgh	*Canada*	Montreal	27/04/1914
Lucy Greenhalgh	do	do	do
Elizabeth Ince	*Ruthema*	Quebec	16/04/1914
Emily Cook	*Victorian*	Montreal	29/04/1914
Caroline Schofield	*Laurentic*	Quebec	09/05/1915
Annie Sherdon	*Lake Manitoba*	Montreal	06/05/1914
Sarah A. Buckthorpe	*Victorian*	Montreal	27/05/1914
Albert Crook	*Victorian*	Quebec	25/05/1914
Elizabeth Arkinstall	*Orontes*	Quebec	07/05/1914
Lena M. Entwhistle	*Empress of Britain*	Quebec	30/06/1914
Jane Greenwood	*Laurentic*	Montreal	04/07/1914
Mary E. Moore	*Victorian*	Montreal	19/08/1914
Lilian Wright	*Metagama*	Quebec	21/05/1915
Ellen Pendlebury	*Messanabia*	Montreal	04/09/1916
Kathleen M Connolly	*Scandinavian*	Quebec	18/09/1916
Emily Burley#	Secret information	Canada	n/k
Mary Davenport#	Special Regiment	Canada	31/03/1916

British secret agents sent to Canada during First World War

Name	Vessel	Destination	Departure Date
Annie Mitchell	*Melita*	Toronto	23/03/1919
Ada Hughes	*Metagama*	Quebec	25/04/1919
Cath. Kelly	*Tunisian*	Canada	25/04/1919
Annie Roberts	*Melita*	Quebec	03/06/1919
Martha May (Cawley)	*Grampia*	Quebec	14/05/1919
Hannah Taylor	*Melita*	Quebec	03/06/1919
Ethel McQuay (Towns)	*Minnedorsa*	Quebec	13/06/1919
Emma Fern	*Corsican*	Montreal	20/06/1919
Beatrice Fern	do	do	do
Martha McBurne	*Minnedorsa*	Montreal	26/07/1919
Mary Duffy	*Megantic*	Quebec	05/08/1919
Martha A. Fogg	*Adriatis*	Toronto	03/09/1919
Selina Dearden	*Scotian*	Toronto	03/09/1919
Ann Harrison	*Canadian*	Montreal	19/09/1919
Elizabeth A. Porritt (Thompson)	*Melita*	Quebec	19/09/1919
Muriel Leigh	*Empress of France*	Quebec	20/09/1919
Dinah Fearns	do	do	do
Eliza Taylor	*Empress of France*	Montreal	13/10/1919
Elizabeth Cregan	*Metagama*	Toronto	13/10/1919
Elizabeth Thornley	*Victorian*	Canada	23/04/1920
Mary Brook	do	do	do
Dora Asquith	*Melita*	Quebec	30/04/1920
Arthur Asquith	do	do	do
Kate Birtwhistle	*Melita*	Quebec	15/04/1920
Doris Bradshaw	do	do	do
Dorothy Birchall	*Megantic*	Montreal	15/05/1920
Lily Harrison	*Megantic*	Quebec	15/05/1920
Elizabeth Finch	do	do	do
Bertha Hilton	*Corsican*	Quebec	15/05/1920
Sarah T. Whittle	*Empress of France*	Quebec	15/05/1920
Mary A. Bourdman (Parkinson)	*Megantic*	Quebec	12/06/1920
Mary Longworth	*Megantic*	Montreal	12/06/1920
Elizabeth A. Parr	*Minnedorsa*	Hamilton	20/06/1920
Elizabeth Shipperbottom	*Victorian*	Toronto	22/06/1920
M.A. Ashey	do	do	do
Alice A. Lomax	do	Quebec	do
Hilda Lambert	*Corsican*	Quebec	02/07/1920

Name	Vessel	Destination	Departure Date
Mary A. Carney	Minnedosa	Quebec for Vancouver, BC	23/07/1920
Rhoda Ball	Empress of France	Quebec for Hamilton, ON	28/07/1920
Doris Neeves	do	Quebec	do
Maria Cooper	Canada	Quebec for Toronto	05/08/1920
Mary Eva Greenhalgh, 19 Sylvester St.	Corsican	Quebec for Montreal	6/08/1920
M.E. Heaney	Corsican	Quebec	06/08/1920
Alice Cameron	Minnedosa	Quebec	27/08/1920
Hannah Lever	Melita	Quebec	17/09/1920
Alice M. Brooks	Megantic	Quebec	02/10/1920
Charles Platt	Megantic	Quebec	31/10/1920
Nellie Bryant	Haverford	Montreal Quebec	24/11/1920
Maria Alder	Megantic	Halifax Quebec	27/01/1920
Ada Shipperbottom	Metagama	Hamilton	01/03/1921
Alice E. Harrison	Minnedosa	Toronto	09/02/1921
Sarah B. Lee	Minnedosa	Hamilton	19/03/1921
Mary Warwick	Melita	Toronto	12/04/1921
Ethel Barrett	Minnedosa	Quebec	20/05/1921
E.A. Bunford	Empress of Britain	Quebec for Guelph	30/04/1921
Lily Moran	Victorian	Quebec	06/05/1921
Mary Houghton	Megantic	Quebec for Hamilton	07/05/1921
Mary E. Houghton	do	Quebec	do
Elizabeth Derbyshire	Melita	Quebec	12/05/1921
William Marsh	Minnedosa	Quebec for Hamilton	07/05/1921
Hugh Warburton	Empress of France	Quebec	25/08/1921
Ellen Sewell	Melita	Toronto	02/09/1921
Albert Edge	Empress of France	Quebec	15/09/1921
Ellen Wood	Montclare	Quebec	15/08/1922
Alice Jones (née Hough)	Megantic	Quebec	21/10/1922
Alice Schofield	Canada	Montreal	21/04/1923
Joseph Schofield	do	do	do

Name	Vessel	Destination	Departure Date
David E. Fern	*Montcalm*	Quebec	20/04/1923
Norah Byrne	*Canada*	Quebec	21/04/1923
Elizabeth Aitken	*Montcalm*	Quebec	20/04/1923
Sarah A. Naylor	*Canada*	Quebec	21/04/1923
Louisa Smith	*Montcalm*	Quebec for Hamilton	11/05/1923
Catherine Gerrard	do	do	18/05/1923
Maria Gerrard	do	do	do
Florence Jessop	*Montrose*	Montreal	25/05/1923
Jessica Cole	do	do	do
Martha A. Baron	*Montcalm*	Quebec for Vancouver	18/06/1923
Florrie Woods	*Athenia*	Quebec	23/06/1923
Mary Taylor	*Athenia*	Quebec for Hamilton	23/08/1923
Elsie Blackledge Openshaw	*Regina*	Quebec	17/08/1923
Soral E. Eckersley	*Montclare*	Quebec	31/08/1923
Alice Hogan	do	do	do
Emily Hogan	do	do	do
Elizabeth C. Stokes	*Canada*	Montreal	8/09/1923
Sarah E. Heyes	*Montlaurier*	Quebec	21/09/1923
Allan M. Parker	*Montclare*	Quebec	28/09/1923
Mary A. Wilcock	*Montclare*	Quebec	26/10/1923
Sarah J. McCann	*Metagama*	Quebec	22/02/1924
Lucy Alcock	*Montcalm*	Woodstock Ont.	21/03/1924
Felix Sutcliffe	*Montcalm*	Quebec	25/03/1924
May A. Davenport	*Canada*	Montreal	19/04/1924
E. Ada Parkinson	*Montcalm*	Quebec	25/04/1924
Ellen Ryan	*Montclare*	Quebec	09/05/1924
Alice Harvey	do	do	do
Florence Walworth	*Regina*	Quebec	09/05/1924
Arthur Parkinson	*Montrose*	Quebec	30/05/1924
Bessie Dawson	*Canada*	Quebec	13/06/1924
Sarah Ann Moss	*Montcalm*	Quebec	23/06/1924
Elizabeth Rogers	do	do	do
Maggie Sellers	do	do	do
Nellie Hodgkinson	*Montcalm*	Quebec	23/06/1924
Leah Dobbins	*Montclare*	Quebec for Hamilton	04/07/1924

Name	Vessel	Destination	Departure Date
Sarah Ethel Henry	*Montcalm*	Quebec	06/12/1924
Olive Fogg	*Doric*	Quebec	05/05/1925
Ada McDermott	*Athenia*	Quebec	09/05/1925
Eliza Woods	*Montrose*	Quebec	17/04/1926
Agnes Hayes	*Montrose*	Quebec	17/04/1926
H.R. Grundy	*Megantic*	Quebec	17/05/1926
Sarah Alice Lower	*Letitia*	Quebec	12/07/1926
Annie Duffy	*Doric*	Quebec	09/07/1926
Evelyn O'Connor	*Montrose*	Quebec	06/08/1926
Agnes Orwell	*Regina*	Quebec	23/07/1926

CHAPTER 10

The Sea Crossing

One afternoon I went onboard the ship Airthy Castle *from Bristol, immediately after her arrival. The passengers were in number 254, all in the hold or steerage; all English, from about Bristol, Bath, Frome, Warminster, Maiden Bradley, etc. I went below and truly it was a curious sight. About 200 [sic] human beings, male and female, young old and middle-aged, talking, singing, laughing, crying, eating, drinking, shaving, washing, some naked in bed, and others dressing to go on shore; handsome young women (perhaps some) and ugly old men, married and single; religious and irreligious.... These settlers were poor, but in general they were fine-looking people and such as I was glad to see come to America.... It is my opinion that few among them will forget being cooped up below deck for four weeks in a moveable bedroom with 250 fellow-lodgers as I have endeavoured to describe.[1]*

THIS UPBEAT DESCRIPTION of the Wiltshire and Somerset people who were preparing to disembark at the port of Quebec in 1831 is provided by no less a person than William Lyon Mackenzie, the radical reformer and leader of the Upper Canada Rebellion of 1837. Mackenzie clearly marvelled at how 250 people could be cooped up in the hold of a ship for four weeks and still be at peace with themselves and one another when they arrived. Yet, as he rightly commented, few would forget the experience. Travelling as a steerage passenger was fraught with irritation and hardships, but for those who could not afford the greater privacy and comforts of a cabin, it was the only affordable means of crossing the Atlantic.

The fact that there were any ships at all was due entirely to the explosive growth of the timber trade. The higher tariffs imposed on European timber from 1811 effectively priced it out of the British market, making North American timber the cheaper alternative. Ever-increasing numbers of vessels plied between British ports and Quebec to collect timber and, as they did, some carried emigrants on their westward journeys. However, although emigrants were a much-valued source of extra revenue, little attention was paid to their creature comforts. Vessels were selected primarily for their timber-carrying capabilities and robustness in withstanding North Atlantic gales. Passengers were treated as just another commodity to be shipped. They had to endure cramped and crudely built accommodation, foul-tasting water, and, on occasion, harrowing storms that put their lives in real danger.

Accommodation below deck in the steerage was basic, to say the least. Timber, loaded into the ship's hold one way, replaced the passengers who had been accommodated in the same hold going the other way. Wooden planking was hammered over crossbeams and temporary sleeping berths were constructed along each side. George Roberts, travelling in the *Sir Henry Pottinger* from Bristol in 1854, described how "there was no division between the berths, so we put up sheets round to enclose us.... The places to lay in were fixed alongside the ship about three feet wide and 6 feet long, one over the other."[2] The only means of ventilation was through the hatches, and in stormy seas they could be kept battened down for days. It was not that ship owners were being deliberately cruel; this was just how shipping services operated until the advent of steamships.

With the continuing growth of the timber trade, the number of English immigrants who were recorded as having arrived at Quebec rose year by year, although these figures do not signify settler numbers. Because sailing to Quebec was a cheaper way of getting to the United States than going to New York, it attracted many immigrants who were merely in transit, having no intention of settling in the Canadas. To complicate matters further, some immigrants who were bound for the Canadas did the reverse, sailing via New York to gain access to its faster and more comfortable ships, despite having to pay the higher fares. An example of the latter is Derbyshire-born John Walker, who went with his family to New York before proceeding to Guelph in western Upper Canada.[3] During their crossing in the *Queen Adelaide* from Liverpool in 1835, the Walkers and twenty-six other passengers shared a cabin measuring eight yards by twelve, with each family having a space of about two yards by two that "serves for breakfast room, dining room and drawing room, parlour, kitchen, pantry and sleeping room, storeroom wherein are seven boxes, three crates and three barrels."[4] While

Courtesy Toronto Reference Library, J. Ross Robertson Collection, JRR 2014.

An artist's impression of the busy port of Quebec in 1840. Lithograph by Thomas Picken based on a drawing by Captain Benjamin Beaufoy. Most of the elegantly attired people in the foreground appear to be spectators rather than recently disembarked passengers, who would probably have looked considerably more dishevelled.

the space seemed cramped to John Walker, it was palatial compared with accommodation in the steerage!

Standards of service were particularly grim in the early stages of passenger travel. Legislation had been in place since 1803, stipulating minimum space and food requirements for passengers, but it was largely unenforceable. As passenger numbers increased, ship owners began running regular services, doing so by the mid-1820s, with their desire for repeat business being the main factor that maintained standards at a reasonable level. Before then, conditions could be very rough and ready. Robert Downes, a British Army officer travelling to Quebec in 1817 with his regiment, together with some sailors and cabin and steerage passengers, felt alarmed when his vessel's water supply became dangerously low as it reached Île d'Anticosti in the Gulf of St. Lawrence. By the time they got to the village of Trois Pistoles, "there was not a drop of water left and the soldiers and sailors were in a state of mutiny." Having collected water, salmon, eggs, and maple sugar at Trois Pistoles, the vessel continued on its way, but unfavourable winds forced it to return. Four passengers then went ashore determined to walk to Quebec City, "which they accomplished in two days." Meanwhile, men in a Telegraph Boat from Goose Island finally reached the stricken vessel, following which "a government schooner was sent instantly from the port of Quebec with biscuits, pork and rum for the men." However, when it was discovered next morning that there was "nothing at all left for the cabin passengers," the captain and some passengers went to the village of St. Michael, opposite Île d'Orléans, where they were received "with the greatest cordiality." Villagers treated them "with punch and wine and the sailors, who carried our luggage, with grog.... The Curé [curate] spoke English very well, though a [French] Canadian, and we were greatly impressed with the first Catholic priest we saw in Canada."[5] The best of human nature was demonstrated and, despite their ordeal, the passengers seemed to be in very good spirits when they reached Quebec.

While Robert Downes understandably complained about the lack of provisions on his vessel, most passengers had the opposite problem — not being able to face any food at all. They suffered dreadfully from bouts of seasickness that could last for days. Elizabeth Peters managed to keep food down during her crossing in the *Friends* from Plymouth in 1830, but she could not bear the stench and taste of the drinking water: "I am now so well accustomed to the ship that if we could get fresh water, I should not at any time dislike a sea voyage."[6] Because it was stored in crude wooden casks, the water soon became contaminated. Vinegar was added to alleviate the offensive odour and taste, but it was still obnoxious unless it was boiled. Francis Thomas, a cabin passenger travelling in the *Hebe*, was much more scathing about "the very stinking and not drinkable water except when mixed with something else," and claimed that this had caused him and his wife "to give up all thoughts of keeping either ourselves or our children clean or decent."[7] In fact, as far as he was concerned, conditions were completely unbearable:

> The want of bread and fresh provisions is much felt — the very great difficulty to get hot water for breakfast or tea and cook a dinner, twenty or thirty at least all wanting at the same time, added to which we have a low, dirty, brutal fellow for a cook, as complete a blackguard as I ever saw, besides which we have several very low swearing passengers near us, whose language at times is most disgusting; all these things, besides being cooped up in a little damp cabin about eight feet square, take such a complication of misery that is impossible adequately to describe.[8]

A somewhat cheerier perspective of life at sea is provided by George Jackson, who travelled as a steerage passenger in the *Good Czar*: "Our decks are crowded with children playing, women cooking, cocks crowing, geese and hens cackling, swine grunting, sheep bleating, which, if it were not for the movement of the ship, one would think themselves in a barnyard instead of the Atlantic Ocean."[9] No doubt the walking protein helped to supplement their otherwise meagre diet. Jackson greatly approved of Captain Loweryson's kindness in personally visiting seasick passengers in their berths, "offering them brandy, water and oranges to help them recover." He also encouraged William Rawson, a barber, to provide shaves and haircuts after the first week. Because people paid Rawson with their rum rations, "he received a good allowance of grog," which, by the end of the evening, "made him rather troublesome."[10] Meanwhile, Elizabeth Peters, travelling in the *Friends*, appreciated Captain's Butter's diligence in ringing the bell on Sundays for divine service: "The cabin passengers, captain, sailors and steerage passengers all assembled to hear the preachers and they have all been very attentive, more so than some English congregations."[11]

Food provisioning on sea crossings was becoming better-organized by the 1830s and transatlantic fares were costing less. During the 1820s fares had averaged £3. 10s. for steerage passengers who supplied their own food, but in the following two decades they fell to between £2 and £3.[12] Elizabeth Peters was somewhat taken aback by the "extravagantly good" food being offered to the crew of the *Friends* during its 1830 crossing: "It is astonishing to what expense the captain goes to on account of his men.... They have strong tea and coffee with rum in it. Nice potatoes swim in fat and their puddings are generally filled with suet and butter and sugar. They are allowed besides two lbs. of beef a day per man."[13] Even so, Paul Robins, who sailed as a steerage passenger in the *Voluna* of Padstow in 1846 with thirty-nine other passengers, had no complaints about his food. He was almost boastful about the quantity being taken:

> They [the passengers and crew] took with them three Cornish bushels of flour, 140 lbs each; 1½ bush. of potatoes, 10s. worth soft bread, 107 lbs. ham, 13 lbs. beef, three lbs. beef suet, 433 eggs, 14 lbs. butter, 10 lbs. cheese, 10 lbs. rice, 8 lbs. oatmeal, gall. of peas, 6 lbs. treacle, 3 lbs. cocoa, 3 lbs. candles, besides which we had a few turnips, carrots, parsnips and onions, a bottle of pickle, vinegar, ginger, pepper, caraway seeds, nutmeg, carbonate of soda and tartaric acid, some herbs for tea and soap for washing. From the ship we had 1 lb. loaf sugar and 15 lbs. of brown [sugar], 12 lbs. of raisins, 5 lbs. of currants and 12 oz. of tea.[14]

As ever, space was at a premium. The Passenger Act of 1817 specified a space allocation of one and one half tons per person in the steerage, while the 1828 act required a passenger to tonnage ratio of three passengers for every four tons. These regulations were meant to limit overcrowding, but the setting of a minimum height of only 5½ feet between decks reveals that, despite these safeguards, people still had to tolerate very cramped conditions. It would not be until the passing of the 1842 act that six feet would become the minimum height requirement between decks, and it would rise again to seven feet in 1855.[15] Not surprisingly, vessels with a floor to ceiling height in excess of the legal limits were particularly popular with emigrants. For instance, during the 1820s and 1830s, much was made of the *Isabella* of Hull's and the *Triton* of Hull's "good height between decks" in newspaper advertisements,[16] while "the between deck space of six and a half feet" in the *Berwick Castle*, a Berwick-upon-Tweed vessel, gave it extra pulling power.[17] Similarly, Samuel Pedlar and his family were very taken with the *Clio* of Padstow's "roomy space between decks [that] afforded better [steerage] accommodation than other ships calling at Padstow, which were much smaller."[18]

While emigrants sought the most comfortable accommodation they could afford, they had also to cope with ferocious storms. Sailing in the *Good Czar* from Berwick-upon-Tweed, George Jackson described the commotion below deck as high winds and rain swept over the vessel:

> I had scarcely put out my light before the ship began to roll in such a manner that set the tins a tumbling, the ham and fletches of bacon falling, the chain cable on the deck rolling, hen coops tumbling on deck, and the barrels of water rolling about, the kail [kale — cabbage] post upsetting, the loaves of bread hurling about, some laughing, some crying, others tumbling over the front of their beds…. After some little trouble order was restored…. Some got up and dressed themselves, others kept rolling in bed…. Little did I think when I gave out the 107th Psalm in the morning service that we were soon to experience as the Psalmist expresses it."[19]

EMIGRATION TO AMERICA.

THE Fine Fast Sailing SHIP
CLIO,
900 TONS BURDEN,

THOMAS BROWN, Commander,
Is intended to Sail with PASSENGERS, from PADSTOW
for QUEBEC, on or about the 7th of APRIL next. This
ship has superior accommodation for Passengers, being 7
feet high between decks. Early application is recom-
mended, as from the well known good qualities of the
Ship, and long experience of the Master, all berths will
be speedily taken.—Applications to be made to Mr. W.
H. Jenkins, Truro ; Mr. T. Pearse, Mayoralty House,
Bodmin ; Mr. Johns, Cooper, Holsworthy ; Mr. Joseph
Kitto, Mevagissey ; Mr. Chapman, Porthpean, near St.
Austell ; Mr. P. W. Bray, Auctioneer, Stratton ; Mr.
Samuel Cornish, and Mr. Daniel Cornish, Bridgrule ;
Mr. Stoneman, Dolphin Inn, Launceston ; and for fur-
ther particulars, apply to CAPTAIN BROWN, Park Villa,
Endellion ; or at Mr. AVERY'S OFFICES, Boscastle or
Padstow.

The *Clio* of Padstow's ability to offer "seven feet between decks" was a great attraction.
Advertisement in *Cornwall Royal Gazette*, February 14, 1845.

George Roberts and his fellow passengers had an even worse experience in the *Sir Henry Pottinger*. Before the crew could even lower the sails,
high winds had swept away four sails:

> The sea was as high as the top of the mast… It sounded
> as if the ship would go to pieces every minute. It rolled
> and pitched so dreadfully that no-one could stand.
> The captain had to lash himself on deck. The sea car-
> ried away the hatch over our deck and the sea poured
> all over us one foot deep sometimes, in the lower deck.
> Bedding and everything were wet through … the ship
> looked like a log in the water…. The storm drove us
> back 300 miles. A very heavy sea suddenly struck the
> ship and ripped off pieces of timber … knocked the
> captain, cook and carpenter down and disabled them.

They had to be carried to bed.... You cannot in any way conceive what it was [like] below with the passengers, some screaming, some fainting, some praying. It was a dreadful scene.... The captain said he had been to sea for 22 years and to all parts of the world but never was in such a storm as this.[20]

Storms were a constant threat. Samuel Pedlar remembered how Captain Brown, "a short thick-set man with a voice that could clearly be heard above the stormy winds," inspired confidence in "some of the faint-hearted passengers."[21] Thus great relief was felt by him and the others on board the *Clio* of Padstow when the coast of Newfoundland first came into view:

The captain informed the passengers that the coast in sight was near St. John's [Newfoundland].... Language fails to describe the feelings of the travellers. The old, the feeble, the young, all who could get there, found their way to the deck. Great rejoicings and mutual congratulations were the order of the day and several hours after. It dawned upon the wearied people that the long, wished for end of their journey was soon to be reached, and that their eyes were soon to behold the new land.[22]

However, when Francis Thomas, travelling in the *Hebe* from London, reached the southwest coast of Newfoundland, he was "nearly dead with terror." The *Hebe* was being driven onto rocks and the passengers were in imminent danger:[23]

The shock was like that of an earthquake and threw many of the passengers down and bruised several more. After a little time a rope was thrown ashore and two sailors got to land, who were soon followed by several of the passengers and we all now began to hope that our lives would be saved. I now removed Mrs. Thomas and

my family to that part of the ship nearest the land, but
in doing it, we were greatly rolled about from the violent
motion of the ship — after a little time I got the children
up the side of the ship near the shrouds and standing
on the outside myself took them down and threw them
ashore and they were all safely caught by the sailors and
then safely landed. Mrs. Thomas following after.[24]

Similarly, James Tate of Bedfordshire endured a voyage of nearly
three months in the *Martin Luther* when, following a storm in the Bay
of Biscay, the vessel had to be towed by a government mail steamer
to Plymouth for repair, before being able to complete its crossing to
Quebec.[25] While these are all fairly extreme examples, most emigrants
faced harrowing storms when crossing the Atlantic. Their diaries usually record the gratitude felt to the captain for his skill and humanity in
ensuring the safety of the passengers and crew. In addition to this vital
role, the captain was also responsible for the general cleanliness of his
ship. He established daily cleaning tasks for the crew and passengers to
undertake and appointed a committee that inspected the berths every
morning. Good hygiene was paramount, since infectious diseases such
as cholera could flare up at any time.

By 1819, the port of Quebec was having to cope with thousands of
immigrants, some of whom required medical care; to meet this demand,
rudimentary facilities, managed by the Quebec Emigrant Society, were put
in place. Together with charitable donations of "clothing, firewood and
provisions," funds were raised from the general public to cover the running
costs of a hospital, which treated around five hundred sick immigrants in
its first year.[26] Having sent back some of the "deluded and helpless beings"
who arrived in 1819, the Society wrote to the Colonial Office, stating that
it should warn British immigrants of the perils of abandoning their homes
"in a vague expectation of relief" when they reached Quebec.[27] However,
little notice was taken of their warnings and Quebec continued to be inun-
dated with penniless immigrants, many of whom were Irish.

The severe outbreak of cholera in Europe in 1832 was the catalyst
behind the building of a quarantine station at Grosse Île, near the port

of Quebec. Its cost was met through the passing of the Quarantine Act in 1832, which required newly arrived overseas passengers to pay an immigrant tax of 5 shillings.[28] Predictably, the new tax was bitterly opposed by ship owners and agents, who feared that it would deter people from emigrating. As anticipated, emigration numbers fell sharply from the following year and only began to rise again in the early 1840s (Table 19).[29] And although the new quarantine facilities were well-intentioned, they were initially badly managed. Vessels having fifteen or more steerage passengers had only rudimentary inspections, while cabin passengers were usually exempted from the process. These haphazard measures meant that many immigrants unwittingly carried their illnesses to Quebec and Montreal, where thousands died. In fact, 1832 was a particularly disastrous year for cholera deaths. That year there were 2,723 cholera-related deaths in Quebec City, 2,547 deaths in Montreal, and countless more people died elsewhere in the nearby countryside.[30] A contemporary observer captured the growing sense of despair:

> When friends meet they bid each other adieu as though they will never see each other again. Day and night wagons are seen carrying bodies to the cemetery; sorrow and terror reign on every face, and the continuing spectacle of death and the tears and sobbing of those who have lost relatives or friends are enough to sadden the hearts of the most callous.[31]

George Robinson, sailing in a ship that had probably left from London, witnessed the 1832 cholera outbreak first hand. His father had succumbed to the disease soon after the ship sailed and "was resigned to the will of God to live or die." Just before he died he asked George to gather up his extensive family: "He was able to give his last blessing to each one of us separately and commend us to God in a manner which greatly astonished me, considering the state he was in through affliction of the body."[32] Later on, George witnessed other deaths and burials at sea: "The young man … who died this morning was taken in a small boat along with another corpse and buried in the sea. We had a service in the evening, [the captains of] several vessels spoke to us to know how many we had lost."[33] When George and the other passengers finally reached Grosse Île, they "were taken to one of the buildings erected for the quarantine passengers, which was open on one side and nothing but the rocks to lie upon; but there was passengers with them some of which was very kind and lent them what they could spare."[34]

Incredibly, no wharf had been built. George and the other passengers had been put in small boats and simply deposited at the water's edge. They then had to drag their luggage "up the rocks about 200 yards" to reach the quarantine station, where they and their belongings would face inspection.[35] Having left their native land full of hope, they, and others like them, deserved better than this. Conditions improved in the 1840s, but before then the quarantine station at Grosse Île was a place of considerable suffering and turmoil.

Despite the imposition of quarantine regulations and the best efforts of local medical authorities, a second cholera outbreak ran its course in 1834, and was followed by further outbreaks in 1845, 1851, 1854, and 1867. Also, many thousands of mostly Irish immigrants would perish in the dreadful typhus and dysentery epidemic that gripped Grosse Île and Quebec City in 1847. The port had been exceptionally busy that year, with the 1847 arrival numbers being three times greater than normal (Table 19). Around 17,500 Irish emigrants died either onboard ship or shortly after landing. Never before or since had such misery and suffering been witnessed.[36] By this time, Irish immigrants accounted for some 60 percent of the total arrivals at Quebec.[37]

With the continuing growth of the North American timber trade, most English ports were offering regular shipping services to Quebec by the 1830s. Initially, Hull and Liverpool vied with each other as the most popular emigrant ports for North of England passengers, but Liverpool soared ahead after 1836, and by the following decade it dominated the overall trade (Table 5).[38] In fact, a whopping 47 percent of the total number of passengers identified in this study as having sailed for Quebec from English ports between 1817 and 1864 left from Liverpool (Appendix I). Although a major port, London had only 10 percent of the total trade, lying second to Liverpool in the 1830s but losing ground to Plymouth after 1840, a time when Upper Canada experienced a large influx of people from Devon and Cornwall.[39] Although Bristol had a significant passenger trade,[40] Plymouth's passenger numbers were far greater, especially throughout the 1840s and early 1850s, being second only to Liverpool. Meanwhile, smaller ports like Padstow and Bideford attracted only a fraction of the passenger trade.[41] However, after 1858, nearly all emigrants, whether from the South or North of England, left from Liverpool. Before then, Liverpool had become a major embarkation port for poor Irish immigrants, thus making it extremely difficult to assess the number of English people who sailed in Liverpool ships.

Judging from the Quebec immigration agent's descriptions of the dire state of many of the large contingents arriving from Liverpool in the 1840s, they were mostly Irish. A typical example was the *Catherine*'s 286 passengers who came in 1841. The majority were poor labourers, with one hundred originating from the Earl Fitzwilliam's estates in Wicklow (Ireland).[42] The reference to "some few farmers with good means" possibly refers to English passengers, although they could equally well be Irish. However, there were also groups like the 124 people who arrived in the *Chieftain* from Liverpool in 1843, described as "mostly farmers, all landing in good health." Although it is not explicitly stated, the inference is that they had come from the North of England. There are many more examples like this, but because the English might have been interspersed with the Irish, their numbers cannot be quantified. And Liverpool's notorious reputation for cheating emigrants also appears to have affected the Irish and English differently. Yorkshire-born George Pashley, who kept a detailed diary of his crossing in the *Reward* from Liverpool in 1833, failed to mention the many fraudsters who would have been operating in and near the port.[43] Yet, the poor illiterate Irish, being an easy target, suffered terribly at their hands.[44]

Although a considerable number of vessels arrived each year in Quebec from English ports to collect their timber cargoes, only a tiny percentage ever carried emigrants. The Atlantic passenger trade was a specialty service, requiring vessels with capacious holds and convivial captains experienced in people management. Emigrants who sailed from Liverpool or London would have travelled in one of a great many vessels on offer, most making only occasional crossings to Quebec. However, at the medium-sized ports like Hull and Plymouth, the pattern was completely different. Having a more localized trade, these ports offered so-called regular traders — vessels that would leave England with steerage and cabin passengers and, upon reaching Quebec, immediately return to their home ports with timber. They would complete the voyage two, sometimes three times a year, often with the same captain.[45] Regular traders dominated the passenger trade, both in the frequency with which they sailed and the number of passengers carried.

Hull's *Triton* under Captain Keighley, its *Victory* under Captains Simpson and Pecket, its *Meteor* under Captain Brown, and its *Fergus* under Captains Blythe and Martin each attracted a regular passenger trade to Quebec over a period of years, while the *Dahlia,* under Captains Hooper and Tozer, the *Lady Peel* under Captains Johns and Moon, and the *Spermacetti* under Captain Moon did the same from Plymouth. The *Belle* of Padstow, under Captains Brewer and Bisson, and the *Clio* of Padstow, under Captains Brown and Easthope, made regular trips to Quebec, and so it went on. Even smaller ports like Torquay had the *Margaret*, which sailed with passengers to Quebec over a period of ten years, while the *Royal Adelaide* did the same from Fowey over a thirty-year period (Table 20).

In addition to having a well-regarded captain, most regular traders also had another strong selling feature — a good ranking by Lloyd's of London. The *Lloyd's Shipping Register*, a source dating back to the late eighteenth century, gives details of a vessel's age, quality of construction, and state of repair in any given year.[46] It reveals that the Plymouth's *Spermacetti, Daedalus, Dahlia, Lady Peel,* and *Roslin Castle* and Padstow's *Clio* and *Belle* each shared a first-class ranking of A1 or AE1 (Table 20).[47] In fact, apart from vessels sailing out of Hull, most of the twenty-two regular traders that stand out as having done the most consecutive crossings from selected ports during the sailing ship era were top quality vessels.

As major insurers, Lloyd's of London needed reliable shipping intelligence, which it procured through the use of paid agents in the main ports in Britain and abroad. Vessels were inspected by Lloyd's surveyors and assigned a code according to the quality of their construction and maintenance.[48] An honest and open inspection was vital to the insurer's

FOR QUEBEC,
WITH GOODS AND PASSENGERS,
To sail with the first Ships,
The remarkably fast-sailing Copper-bottom Ship
L L A N   R U M N E Y,
(Register 395 Tons,)
Capt. T. SIMPSON, (late of the Victory.)
Has most excellent Accommodation for Cabin and Steerage Passengers.
Apply to the Captain on Board, the South Side of the Old Dock, near Lowgate End.
Hull, Feb. 28, 1837.

Newspaper advertisement for the sailing of the *Llan Rumney* from Hull to Quebec in 1837. A selling point for potential passengers was the experienced Captain Simpson, who had been in charge of the *Victory* on its Quebec crossings from at least 1828. Advertisement in the *Hull Packet*, March 3, 1837.

risk assessment, and the ship owner's ability to attract profitable trade hinged on the classification given to his ships. Ship owners actually complained that the codes were too stringent, particularly in the way a ship's age and place of construction could affect its classification.[49]

Today these codes provide a reliable data indicator of the quality of the construction of ships from that time. They show a predominance of A1 and AE1 (first-class) designations for regular traders, particularly those vessels operating in the southwest region. Shippers had captured the largest share of the passenger trade by offering top quality and, in some cases, new or nearly new vessels. This reveals how competition worked in the emigrants' favour. By contrast, Hull-registered regular traders tended to have a second-class ranking (E1), signifying that, although they were seaworthy, they had minor defects. Hull's less good ships can probably be explained by the smaller margins under which the transatlantic trade operated along the east coast, where far greater distances had to be covered. This added to the owners' costs, which they evidently offset by using second-class ships, although this would have added to their insurance costs.

While there is evidence that top quality shipping was offered to emigrants in certain ports, it seems also to have been a feature of the vessels used to carry the poor. Those people who were assisted to emigrate, either by their parishes or landlords, nearly always sailed in A1 or AE1 vessels (Table 21). In organizing the emigration of Lord Egremont's Petworth tenants in West Sussex, for example, Thomas Sockett insisted that they be sent in A1 ships since he wanted proof of their seaworthiness.[50] This cautious approach was also adopted by English parishes. In 1837, when the parish of Purton in Wiltshire financed the emigration of twenty-one of their paupers in the *Brunswick*, it made clear that the Poor Law Commissioners had approved every detail of their accommodation, including the quality of the ship:

> Mr. Carter was to take charge of them, their bedding and any luggage up to the space of ten cubic feet, exclusive of bedding. Also to arrange for sleeping on board, not less than six feet in length, and eighteen inches in width, for each adult person. The ship, named the *Brunswick* was to sail from the port of London, and be A1 or AE1 in Lloyd's Register: of not less clear height in the between decks than five feet and approved by the Poor Law Commissioners. The destination was to be Quebec, Canada and the emigrants and their luggage were to be landed there free of any charge or deduction.[51]

Lloyd's codes have been located for thirty-three of the forty vessels that were known to have carried paupers. Thirty-one were either A1 or AE ships, while the remaining two had an E, or second-class, ranking. No examples at all were found of unsuitable ships. In other words, a staggering 94 percent of Lloyd's-registered ships that carried paupers had a top ranking. There can be no better endorsement of the high quality of emigrant shipping than this.[52] Landlords and parishes paid the extra cost of sending their poor off to Quebec in good ships to ensure their safety. Emigrants having to pay their own fares might

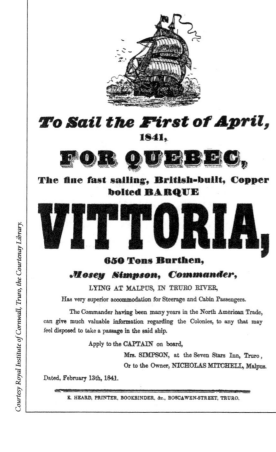

Leaflet advertising the crossing of the *Vittoria* from Truro to Quebec in the spring of 1841. A year later the vessel, registered as AE1, carried 113 passengers, who included a small number of paupers.

have looked upon this with some envy, since many of them travelled in less good vessels, possibly because that was their only choice, or for cost reasons.

Having endured the discomforts of an Atlantic crossing, the arrival at Quebec was a moment to savour. Elizabeth Peters wrote: "[I began] preparing the frills for my children and a cap for myself and hope to be in readiness as soon as the call comes to land." Excited at her first glimpse of "cultivated land," she noted, "the houses look so neat and clean. They are white-washed on the outside."[53] William Thompson from Preston in Lancashire marvelled at "the small houses, some red, buff and yellow," and noticed the "few villages and churches, the roofs of the latter covered with sheets of tar."[54] Meanwhile, Elizabeth's husband, William Peters, was surprised "to discover the trees and shrubs [are] very different to what it is in England, for the trees appear to grow even to the water's edge," but was perturbed that the *Friends'* progress was being delayed as it made its way up the St. Lawrence: "We ran the vessel on a sand bank, and there stuck fast — from which spot I now sit in my berth on the little barrel for a seat and my lap for a writing table and here we must stay until the tide again flows."[55]

Of course, reaching Quebec and continuing on to Montreal was simply the first phase of the journey. People on their way to western Upper Canada would still have to face a gruelling inland journey of several hundred miles. They had a choice of two routes: They could travel on barges, towed by a succession of steamboats along the Ottawa River via Bytown (Ottawa) and then along the Rideau Canal to Kingston, where they could board a steamer taking them across Lake Ontario to Toronto or Hamilton.[56] This was the quickest and most comfortable route.[57] Alternatively, immigrants could travel via the St. Lawrence River but, because of the rapids just beyond Montreal, they needed to transfer to large Durham boats that had to be dragged upriver to Prescott. It was a laborious and very slow means of conveyance:[58] "The boats measuring nearly 100 feet long were powered by sail, pushed by pole, or drawn by horses or oxen part of the way." Sometimes, as George Jackson discovered, "the passengers themselves got out and pulled."[59] Assuming all went well, they would reach Hamilton in about two weeks.

At Prescott, people went by steamer up the St. Lawrence to Lake Ontario, disembarking at either Toronto or Hamilton.[60] The final destination was then usually reached by wagon. This, too, had its perils. Henry Rastall, from Farndon Parish (Nottinghamshire), complained that "the sea voyage was nothing to the journey by land, although I got some very bad gales ... your Boughton back roads are nothing to it; it is very bad indeed, up and down sometimes your head against the top — it broke my hat to pieces, my hat being thick I suppose I did not get bruised."[61]A trip to the western limit of the province, a distance of eight hundred miles, was exhausting and could cost as much as £14 to £15, without provisions or accommodation.[62]

A Durham boat on the St. Lawrence River, 1832. Watercolour by Henry Bryant Martin (1804–33). The Durham boat was flat-bottomed with a large cargo capacity. It could be moved by men with poles in shallow water and oars were used to navigate rapids.

With the coming of the steamship in the 1850s, sea transport entered a completely new phase. Instead of having shipping services that were run solely to meet the stowage and other requirements of the timber trade, much greater priority was given to the accommodation needs of passengers. Steamship crossings were shorter and safer, and because the ships were no longer dependent on the vagaries of the weather and wind direction, they could depart at a predetermined time. Crossing times were greatly reduced and death rates fell rapidly. Thus, with their arrival, sea transport entered the modern era. More and more emigrants opted for their greater speed, safety, reliability, and creature comforts, and by 1870 steam had entirely replaced sail.

Liverpool rose to prominence during the steamship era, becoming England's principal embarkation port for Quebec. Dramatic changes were much in evidence by the late 1850s and early 1860s when steamships like the *Anglo Saxon*, *Bohemian*, *Hibernian*, and *Nova Scotian* carried many thousands of Quebec-bound passengers (Appendix I). With their great size and ability to make up to five crossings per year, they could carry more passengers in a single year than their sailing ship predecessors had achieved over many decades. Of course, with their great size and sophistication, steamships could only operate from major ports like Liverpool. This increasing centralization heralded the introduction of stricter controls and better enforceability of passenger travel regulations. And with the extension of railway networks in Britain and the new railways being constructed in Canada, immigrants really did enter the modern era. They no longer had to endure the four- to six-week sea crossing in a cramped, smelly hold and follow that with an arduous journey west from Montreal by boat, steamer, and wagon. Now there were timetables, booking procedures, enforceable controls, interconnecting shipping and rail services, and few delays.

However, before the arrival of steam, immigrants had to rely on sailing ships. They were helped by the good standards sought by ship owners anxious to attract their fares. With only one or two exceptions the ships always reached Quebec, and there were very few English deaths on sea crossings. Judged by the living conditions of the time, immigrants were well-treated and normally sailed in well-constructed ships. There were many discomforts and anxious moments on crossings, but they were relatively minor when compared with the challenges of adapting to the new way of life that awaited them.

Table 19:

British Immigrant and Other Arrivals at the Port of Quebec, 1829–55
[Annual Reports of the Immigration Agent at Quebec, 1831–55
(note: PP 1837–1838[175] XLVII contains figures for 1829–36)]

Year	England	Ireland	Scotland	Europe	Maritime Provinces	Total
1829	3,565	9,614	2,634	-	123	15,945
1830	6,799	18,300	2,450	-	451	28,000
1831	10,343	34,133	5,354	-	424	50,254
1832	17,481	28,204	5,500	15	546	51,746
1833	5,198	12,013	4,196	-	345	21,752
1834	6,799	19,206	4,591	-	339	30,935
1835	3,067	7,108	2,127	-	225	12,527
1836	12,188	12,590	2,224	485	235	27,722
1837	5,580	14,538	1,509	-	274	21,901
1838	990	1,456	547	-	273	3,266
1839	1,586	5,113	485	-	255	7,439
1840	4,567	16,291	1,144	-	232	22,234
1841	5,970	18,317	3,559	-	240	28,086
1842	12191	25532	6,095	-	556	44374
1843	6,499	9,728	5,006	-	494	21,727
1844	7,698	9,993	2,234	-	217	20,142
1845	8,883	14,208	2,174	-	160	23,375
1846	9,163	21,049	1,645	896	-	32,753
1847	31,505	54,310	3,747	-	-	89,562
1848	6,034	16,582	3,086	1,395	842	27,939
1849	8,980	23,126	4,984	436	968	38,494
1850	9,887	17,979	2,879	849	701	32,292
1851	9,677	22,381	7,042	870	1,106	41,076
1852	9,276	15,983	5,477	7,256	1,184	39,176
1853	9,585	14,417	4,745	7,456	496	36,699
1854	18,175	16,156	6,446	11,537	857	53,183
1855	6,754	4,106	4,859	4,864	691	21,274

Table 20:

Selected Regular Traders: Passengers Carried and Ship Quality

Vessel (tonnage, type)	Captain	Year and Place Built	Lloyd's Code	Departure Years	Departure Port	Number of Crossings/ Passengers
Amazon (442, s)	Broderick/ Pearson	1811 Greenock	E1	1833–46	Hull	9/736
Baltic (252, bg)	Ebbage/ Cawdric	1820 n/k	E1	1831–44	Yarmouth	13/901
Belle of Padstow (346, bk)	Brewer/ Bisson	1840 Shields	AE1	1841–52	Padstow	16/1,580
Clarkson (304, bk)	Cox/ Ward	1806 Selby	E1	1821–32	Hull	11/527
Clio of Padstow (513, bk)	Brown/ Easthope	1838 Nova Scotia	AE1	1840–50	Padstow	22/2,827
Collina (410, bk)	Marshall/ Chadwick	1838 PEI	E1	1841–52	Gloucester	8/620
Daedalus of Padstow (396, s)	Nichols/ Bullman	1835 New Brunswick	AE1	1845–53	Plymouth	11/655
Dahlia (943, bk)	Hooper/Tozer	1840 PEI	AE1	1842–53	Plymouth	17/1,595
Dew Drop of Padstow (203, sw)	Wokes	1810 Hull	AE1	1829–50	Padstow	8/206
Fergus (430, bk)	Blythe/Martin	1833 Glasgow	A1	1842–55	Hull	13/2,064
Lady Peel (567, s)	Johns/Moon	1843 Quebec	AE1	1848–57	Plymouth	9/1,727
Margaret (n/k, s)	Field/ Codner	n/k	n/k	1848–58	Torquay	10/290

Vessel (tonnage, type)	Captain	Year and Place Built	Lloyd's Code	Departure Years	Departure Port	Number of Crossings/ Passengers
Meteor (400, s)	Brown	1825 Hull	AE1	1833–42	Hull	10/1,045
Oriental (713, s)	Tom	1846 New Brunswick	AE1	1849–57	Plymouth	10/2,071
Pearl (361, bk)	Douglas / Chalmers / Davies	1842 Sunderland	A1	1842–58	London	19/375
Rose (550, s)	Moon	1844 Quebec	AE1	1850–55	Plymouth	9/1,811
Roslin Castle (700, bk)	Sadler	1819 Bristol	AE1	1847–57	Plymouth & Falmouth	13/1,103
Royal Adelaide of Fowey (405, bk)	Vivian/Smith	1831 Quebec	A1	1832–62	Fowey	23/circa 900
Spermacetti (412, bk)	Moon	1834 New Brunswick	AE1	1842–53	Plymouth	19/3,217
Spring Flower of Padstow (225, bg)	Brown	1825 Sunderland	n/k	1830–42	Padstow	10/364
Triton (285, bg)	Keighley	1825 Hull	E1	1828–37	Hull	8/800
Victory (420, s)	Simpson/Pecket	1815 Whitby	E1	1828–43	Hull	12/1,397

Table 21:

Emigrant Ships Which Carried Paupers: Ship Quality, Passengers Carried and Where From

Vessel (tonnage, type)	Captain	Year and Place Built	Lloyd's Code	Departure Year	Departure Port*	Number of Passengers (Paupers)
Anglesea (485, bk)	Bull	1850 Nova Scotia	AE1	1851	Liverpool; North of England	241 (50)
Arcturus (228, sw)	Hill	1838 Sunderland	A1	1842	London; South of England	60 (48)
Ava (460, bk)	Suter	1833 New Brunswick	AE1	1851	Southampton; South of England	58 (58)
Brunswick (571, bk)	Atkinson	1833 London	AE1	1837	London;Purton, Wiltshire	258 (21)
Burrell (402, bk)	Metcalf	1825 Newcastle	A1	1835	Portsmouth; Petworth, W. Sussex	250 (250)
Ditto	ditto	ditto	ditto	1843	London; Petworth, W. Sussex	120 (120)
Charles Walton (n/k, bk)	Crawford	n/k	n/k	1851	Southampton; South of England	58 (58)
Charlotte (668, s)	Drewery	1845 Quebec	A1	1846	London; South of England	108 (31)
Diana (321, bg)	Lane	1824 Whitby	AE1	1837	Plymouth; Petworth, W. Sussex	199 (199)

Vessel (tonnage, type)	Captain	Year and Place Built	Lloyd's Code	Departure Year	Departure Port*	Number of Passengers (Paupers)
Eliza (393, bk)	Vandervold	1815 Java	n/k	1842	London; Brinkworth, Wiltshire	81 (35)
Eliza Liddle (261, sw)	Surtees	1834 Sunderland	A1	1836	King's Lynn; Kettlestone, Norfolk	40 (40)
England (320, bg)	Lewis	n/k	A1	1832	Portsmouth	160 (160)
Ditto	ditto	ditto	A1	1833	ditto; Petworth; W. Sussex	205 (205)
Euphrosyne of Whitby (400, bk)	Sampson	n/k	n/k	1831	Bridgwater; Heytesbury and Knook, Wiltshire	200 (40)
Eveline (302, s)	Friend	1826 Quebec	AE1	1832	Portsmouth; Petworth, W. Sussex	230 (230)
George Marsden (277, bk)	Eilley	1834 Sunderland	A1	1841	Rye; Sussex and Kent	213 (213)
Heber (441, s)	Knight	1835 Whitby	A1	1836	Portsmouth; Petworth, W. Sussex	260 (260)
Helen (639, bk)	Foster	1844 Saint John	A1	1851	London; South of England	216 (76)
Hero (409, s)	Trailer	1806 Whitby	E1	1837	Bristol; Wiltshire	67 (45)
John Bull (436, bk)	Duffill	1846 Sunderland	A1	1851	London; South of England	63 (25)
King William (380, s)	Thomas	1831 Whitby	A1	1836	London; Downton and Whiteparish, Wiltshire	279 (279)
Laurel (779, s)	Knarston	1841 New Brunswick	AE1	1851	London; South of England	177 (35)
Leonard Dobbin (611, bk)	Agar	1837 Quebec	AE1	1852	London; Brinkworth, Wiltshire	188 (21)

Vessel (tonnage, type)	Captain	Year and Place Built	Lloyd's Code	Departure Year	Departure Port*	Number of Passengers (Paupers)
Lloyds (536, bk)	Wattes	1830 Hull	AE1	1847	London; Brinkworth, Wiltshire	207 (20)
Lord Canterbury (599, bk)	Tripp	1835 Quebec	AE1	1842	Bristol; South-West of England	273 (54)
Lord Melville (425, bk)	Royal	1825 Quebec	AE1	1832	Portsmouth; Petworth, W. Sussex	333 (333)
Louisa (n/k, bk)	Manning	n/k	n/k	1851	Southampton; South of England	268 (86)
Mentor (n/k, bg)	Barlow	n/k	n/k	1832	London; Kent	75 (75)
Orbit (679, bk)	Robinson	1838 New Brunswick	A1	1842	London; South of England	217 (194)
Orlando (344, bk)	Blair	1836 Sunderland	A1	1841	London; South of England	102 (80)
Ottawa (456, s)	Thrift	1841 Quebec	A1	1848	Bridgwater; South West of England	119 (35)
Penelope (230, sw)	Eddie	1804 Shields	n/k	1838	King's Lynn; Heacham, Norfolk	n/k (23)
Prince George (450, s)	Friend	1808 London	A1	1841	London	190 (190)
Ditto	ditto	ditto	ditto	1842	South of England including Dorset and Kent	262 (219)
Pusey Hall (334, bk)	Ware	1809 Lancaster	AE1	1842	London; South of England	171 (171)
Resource (447, n/k)	n/k	n/k	n/k	1843	London; South of England	n/k (89)

Vessel (tonnage, type)	Captain	Year and Place Built	Lloyd's Code	Departure Year	Departure Port*	Number of Passengers (Paupers)
Secret (372, bk)	Bell	1846 PEI	A1	1851	Bideford; Devon and Cornwall	149 (12)
Severn (479, s)	Smith	1806 Bristol	E1	1835	Bristol; South West England	94 (94)
Sisters (854, bk)	Smith	1841 New Brunswick	A1	1843	London	163 (163)
Ditto	ditto	ditto	ditto	1851	London; South of England	271 (62)
Tay (470, bk)	Adams	1840 Restigouche	AE1	1851	London; South of England	81 (26)
Toronto (350, s)	Morgan	1834 Montreal	A1	1843	London; Brinkworth, Wiltshire	173 (173)
Victory (414, bk)	Pecket	1814 Whitby	E1	1841	Hull; North of England	84 (24)
Vittoria (395, bk)	Simpson	1813 Gainsborough	AE1	1842	Fowey; Devon and Cornwall	113 (14)

* indicates departure port and part of England from which the paupers originated

CHAPTER 11

The English in Ontario and Quebec

The English race proper, when transplanted from their native homes, do not see any especial need for asserting their nationality.[1]

WHEN THE REVEREND Henry Scadding, chaplain to both the St. James Anglican Cathedral in Toronto and the city's St. George's Society, gave his annual address in 1860, he portrayed a great and glorious England that was strangely tight-lipped about its national identity.[2] Then, as now, public displays of what it means to be English were frowned upon. English people did not wrap themselves in St. George's flags, dance around maypoles, or call attention to their ethnic credentials in any other way. Each year, St. George's Day (April 23) passes by almost completely unnoticed. By contrast, the Irish wear their bunches of shamrocks and hold parades on St. Patrick's Day, while Scots wave the St. Andrew's Saltire on their National Day and glory in Burns suppers and pipe bands. Of course, Irish and Scottish symbolism travelled the world, and the Canadas were no exception. After they arrived, the Scots and Irish continued to trumpet the distinguishing features of their culture and heritage, but the English simply faded into the background. They took pride in their Englishness and carried a common sense of their national identity, but they spent little time worrying about who they were.

Although the English lacked the colourful imagery of tartans and pipe bands, they did have John Bull. A fictional cloth trader, invented by a Scot, he, more than anyone else, came to symbolize Englishness.[3] Depicted in cartoons as a pot-bellied, middle-aged man, John Bull epitomized energy and determination and was fiercely independent and practical. However, in North America he could also seem insensitive and irritable. When the 5th Earl of Selkirk visited Quebec and Montreal in 1804, he remarked how "the English cry out in the true John Bull style" over their grievances with French Canadians, which were, in Selkirk's opinion, entirely of their own making. "The string of Oathes ending with Sacré Anglais!"[4] that Selkirk heard reflected French annoyance with the alleged tactlessness of the conquering English. But as Methodist missionary Reverend John de Putron discovered, the French could be pretty intolerant, as well. When he visited Three Rivers in 1821, he "intended preaching in French, but was disappointed nobody came. To be useful is the prevailing desire of my heart, yet how distressing that, through strength of prejudice, they will not hear the Gospel."[5]

Ontario historian Dr. Edwin Guillet gave the English credit for "assimilating themselves more speedily," and for being "less clannish than the Scots and Irishmen," but thought that "some of them arrived with no small amount of self-conceit, bounce and John Bullism, which was quickly taken out of them by their experiences and with the help often of rough-and-ready neighbours."[6] Isabella Lucy Bird, a genteel lady from Cheshire, had an actual encounter with a John Bull type while travelling through the United States in a train:

> The cars were very full, and were not able to seat all the passengers…. "A seat for a lady," said the conductor, when he saw the crowded state of the car. The one gentleman did not stir. "A seat for a lady," repeated the man in a more imperious tone. Still no movement on the part of the gentleman appealed to…. There was

now a regular hubbub in the car; American blood was up, and several gentlemen tried to induce the offender to move…. "I'm an Englishman and I tell you that I won't be browbeaten by you beastly Yankees. I've paid for my seat and I mean to keep it," savagely shouted the offender, thus verifying my worst suspicions.

"I thought so! — I knew it! — a regular John Bull trick! Just like them!" were some of the observations made, and very mild they were considering the aggravated circumstances.[7]

This was the bloody-minded side of John Bull.

Although John Bull was to some extent a figure of fun, he did travel well as a pioneer and came to symbolize the supremely confident English, who proved to be very adaptable and successful settlers. Given that English labourers and tradesmen were much in demand and could thus command far higher pay than was the case in England, they experienced considerable economic benefits in emigrating. They also found that, for the first time in their lives, they were being treated as valued individuals. However, the transition to a pioneering society was often very painful for their wealthier counterparts. It was a culture shock. Having been accustomed to the deference and special privileges that befitted someone of a superior social rank in England, they suddenly found themselves being reduced to the status of an ordinary person in Canada. For obvious reasons, the egalitarian ways of the New World did not suit them. This anonymous English farmer, who visited Upper Canada in 1820, thought he had come to another planet:

An Englishman who expects to find that ready compliance with his wishes and wants, to which he has become accustomed in England, will be greatly disappointed. There are no *bells,* and there are no *servants* at the inns in this country. The traveller finds himself solitary, unnoticed, and left to supply his own wants. If he is loud, peremptory, or remonstrative he is treated in return with insolence or contempt. The chief aim of the host is to get the stranger's money; generosity and benevolence are not ingredients in his composition.[8]

Similarly, Henry Rastall's disapproval of the lack of ceremony in a Canadian hotel dining room shows a man still clinging to his past: "A bell rings, and you all scramble for a place, and devour all as soon as you can, and then you get up from your table and go where you please.... Those who want anything to drink go to the bar and take it [a drink] as they do at a common pub house in England. The people eat terribly fast ..."[9]

When British Army officer Edward Coke was seated at a table with two female servants when dining at the Clifton Hotel in Niagara Falls, it sent him into a frenzy:

I felt my English blood almost boil in my veins when I found myself sitting in company with two servant women at the table d'hôte at the same time that their mistress occupied a place at the other end of the table. I could have very well accustomed myself to such neighbours in the States, but never expected to have found the levelling system introduced into the British provinces to such an extent.[10]

The self-important Edward Coke did not appreciate that Canada's early colonists lacked the time, resources, let alone desire to provide segregated dining, or any other outward show of refinement and gentility. However, there were others, like Lincolnshire-born artist Mary Chaplin, who, while visiting the Eastern Townships in 1840, came to understand the ways of the New World. She had been puzzled when the landlady of the inn in Stanstead where she stayed had not offered to help her put on her shawl when she was about to leave her table, as would have been the case in England. Then, when the lady sat down at her table uninvited and struck up a conversation, Mary realized that the lady "did not mean to be otherwise than civil; these manners arise from considering everybody on an equal footing." Mary was also struck by the large number of Americans living in the area and liked their "casual, easy and familiar manners."[11]

Relatively few wealthy English emigrated during the first half of the nineteenth century, and those who did mainly went to the United States. Some opinion formers in England even considered that such people were failures for seeking to emigrate in the first place. William Harrison from Boughton (Nottinghamshire) was highly disapproving of an acquaintance, Henry Bailey, who wished to emigrate, presumably because he thought such a move was beneath him:

> Henry Bailey is not at home and has been very little at Boughton since you left. No persuasion can alter him in his determination to go to America, and I quite expect that he will leave his native land, but I think he will be back again if he can. Your brothers, Henry and Jonathan have written two excellent letters of advice to him to dissuade him from a step so distressing to his parents ..."[12]

In any case, people like the Devon-born Francis Howell, the under private secretary to Sir Charles Metcalfe, governor general of Canada, felt that the Canadas had little to offer the middle classes. Writing home from Government House in Kingston, he pronounced that "it is utterly useless" for people in England "to indulge any idea of getting employment under government [as he had done] ... the objection to newcomers is an insurmountable barrier."[13] In other words, the special privileges that went hand in hand with social status in England were less likely to materialize in the Canadas.

Meanwhile, William Robinson dreamed of reinstating the English class system on his farm in Delaware Township (Middlesex County) in Upper Canada. He hit upon the idea in 1836 of employing compliant labourers from the Petworth estate in West Sussex, thinking that because they had recently emigrated to Upper Canada, they were ripe for the picking. So he asked the Reverend Thomas Sockett, the man who had organized and raised the finances for their departure, to select a few for his farm:

> My object is to have people about me whose services I
> can rely on, at all seasons; and I am persuaded, the only
> means of obtaining that end, is to get out families direct
> from England, who, by being kept together, are less liable
> to contract wandering habits ... for the more intercourse
> they have with the older inhabitants, the sooner they
> lose their native character, imbibe loose habits, become
> Yankeefied ... insolent, and independent; for which rea-
> son I would avoid giving employment to any person who
> came to this country by way of the United States.[14]

Given that Petworth labourers were practically fighting off job offers the moment they arrived in Upper Canada, it was preposterous for William Robinson to think that he could tempt them with his vision of a feudal England reincarnated. James Parker, one of the Petworth labourers who had settled in Adelaide Township, also in Middlesex County, told a friend that he "could have a dozen masters," but limited his paid employment as much as he could to allow himself more time to clear his own land.[15] This was his route to independence and the way forward for most of the others.

While immigrants experienced pronounced cultural differences when they first arrived in the Canadas, they had far less of an adjustment to make in urban areas, where lifestyles were essentially British, if not English. Military officers, government officials, businessmen, merchants, and professional men, together with their families, enjoyed genteel pursuits while benefiting economically from the rapid growth of cities like Montreal, Toronto, and Quebec. They built elegant houses, dined out regularly, danced at balls, wore stylish clothing, employed servants, and essentially had English lifestyles.

Colonel Francis Fane, a Lincolnshire-born army officer in the 54th Regiment who was stationed at the British garrison in Quebec City in the 1850s, was particularly passionate about horseracing, one of the many sporting pursuits of the English gentleman.[16] First introduced in the late eighteenth century into Quebec by British soldiers serving at the garrison, it had developed into a reasonably popular sport by the time

Pen and ink sketch of people on a skating rink in Quebec City, 1852, by Colonel Francis Fane, a British Army officer who served in Canada during the 1850s.

that Colonel Fane arrived. He boosted its appeal further by raising funds for the Quebec track, helping to organize the actual races and appointing the judges.[17]

Fox hunting with hounds, another English import, was fashionable during the early nineteenth century, although its popularity was very short-lived because of opposition from farmers and the high cost of keeping dogs during long winters. According to Edwin Guillet, the occasional fox hunt caused quite a stir near Woodstock in western Upper Canada:

> There were more aristocrats, "genteel" and cultured people, and other comparatively well-to-do settlers from England than from other parts of the British Isles; and not a few of them came to this country as to a combined fox-hunt and conversazione, accompanied by dogs, rigged out in loud tweeds, patent leather shoes and even monocles.[18]

The English sport of cricket, like horseracing, was introduced to Canada by the military, with the first recorded game being played in

Montreal in 1785. From these small beginnings the sport grew in popularity, particularly in Toronto. The York (Toronto) Cricket Club, founded in around 1829, is the oldest in Canada, while the Upper Canada College Cricket Club, also located in Toronto and formed seven years later, was its main rival. By 1840, Guelph, Kingston, and Woodstock each had their own club, with the Bytown (Ottawa) Cricket Club emerging nine years later.[19] Working as a government official in Kingston, Francis Howell reported with some excitement to his father in Devon that he had actually witnessed a cricket match played in August 1843 between civilians and the military personnel who were based at the garrison.[20] However, despite Sir John A. Macdonald's declaration at the time of Confederation that cricket was to be Canada's national sport, it steadily lost its popularity and succumbed in the end to American baseball.[21]

Rugby, another English passion, struggled for support in Ontario and Quebec, although it had a strong following in British Columbia and

Courtesy Topley Studio / Library and Archives Canada, PA-028030.

Photograph of group of cricketers in Ottawa, July 1898, taken by William James Topley.

Courtesy William James Topley / Library and Archives Canada, PA-009596.

Photograph by William James Topley of an Ottawa versus Montreal rugby game, played in August 1910, at Ottawa.

the Maritimes. Its Canadian roots date back to a match played in 1864 at Montreal, when British artillery men organized themselves into teams. The Montreal Rugby Club was formed four years later and rugby games were played in Toronto soon after. Following the large English influx of the early twentieth century, rugby enjoyed a resurgence, but it was short-lived. Once again the American version of the game won out.[22]

It is hardly surprising that sports such as cricket and rugby, which epitomized the genteel values of the English, would have had such limited support in Canada. However, the influence of the English on Canada's culture went far beyond sport. Being a highly sociable people, they were accustomed to engaging in leisure pursuits and forming clubs and societies that brought people together. Their social networks, love of pastimes, and sense of public service came with them to Canada. Once their communities had developed to the point where people had time to enjoy themselves, the English would have readily formed women's institutes, gardening clubs, amateur dramatic societies, literary clubs, embroidery groups, shooting clubs, arts societies, and other such bodies as they saw fit. Their desire to have organized recreational activities was ingrained in them, and by being proactive in this way they greatly improved the quality of life for themselves and everyone else.

The Mechanics' Institutes were yet another English import. Formed first in England in 1823, their aim was to provide vocational education and training to working men.[23] Montreal had the earliest Mechanics' Institute in Canada, being founded in 1828, while York (Toronto) had its institute two years later and Bytown followed in 1847. The Barrie Mechanics' Institute, established in 1854, proclaimed that one of its primary aims was to provide "useful information to the industrious mechanics." Every skilled worker in Barrie apparently subscribed, since the annual subscription of 5s. "put it in the reach of all." The institute's immediate plan was to purchase books and found a museum.[24]

Although the English made much less of a fuss over their culture than did the Scots or Irish, they nevertheless formed ethnic societies in Canada. The first St. George Society, honouring England's patron saint, emerged in Halifax in 1786 and still remains active today. As with other St. George societies, its original aim was to promote and celebrate English culture and to channel funds to needy English people. Later, the societies changed to becoming immigrant aid organizations that were open to anyone having an interest in promoting English traditions. Toronto and Montreal each had a St. George's Society by 1834, and Quebec followed suit one year later. Clubs formed later in Ottawa (1844), London (1867), and Barrie (1875).[25] There was even a St. George's Club in Sherbrooke, founded in 1890, that had 158 resident members and 101 non-resident members in 1963.[26]

However, the largest and most important English cultural society was the Sons of England, branches of which could be found in most Canadian cities.[27] First established in Toronto in 1874, the society's branches were organized by affluent Englishmen with a military or professional background. Their primary aim was to run social activities, the highlight of which were events modelled on the English Music Hall. At such gatherings people "thrilled to jingoistic songs, they wept at the evocations of England's green and pleasant land, they savoured the unique pleasure of drinking warm, dark ale and they reverted to regional dialects."[28] But there

Photograph by Frank W. Micklethwaite (1849–1925) of those attending the St.
George's Society of Toronto's 75th Annual Dinner at St. George's Hall, April 25, 1910.

was a philanthropic side, as well, in that the Sons of England Benevolent
Society furnished its members with economic support and held out a helping hand to newly arrived English immigrants. By 1913, the society had
forty thousand members across Canada.

The English assimilated readily into Canadian society and, unlike
their Scottish and Irish counterparts, did not seek to highlight the distinguishing features of their culture. They had not done so in their homeland, and therefore there was no reason why they would seek to do so
in the Canadas. They drew little distinction between being English and
being British, regarding the Union Jack, the monarchy, and parliamentary institutions as symbols of their Englishness. Many chose Canada
over the United States because it offered a British version of the New
World, although initially most had gone to the United States. However,
irrespective of this confusion over whether they saw themselves as being
British or English, they each came with a strong sense of their English

identity. Originating from the most powerful nation on earth, having an Empire that dominated the world, they were endowed with a strong sense of self-belief, bordering in some cases on arrogance. This applied to everyone, including the labouring classes. They had "a patriotic identification with the achievements of a great nation at the height of its economic and political power."[29]

Along with other immigrants, the English merged into the cultural melting pot that would eventually identify them as Canadians. However, they did have their problems. Canadian attitudes toward them soured at the turn of the twentieth century when large numbers of poor English immigrants entered the country under various benevolent schemes. There was an understandable outcry that Canada was being used as a receptacle for England's poor and unwanted. Resentment toward them peaked during the depression years of 1907–08, when jobs were in short supply. No ENGLISH NEED APPLY notices proliferated, as the country's anxieties grew.[30] However, this anti-English outburst was short-lived. Canada's expanding economy needed the skills that only English immigrants could offer. This realization may not have endeared them to the general public, but it was a reality that most people recognized.

The English came with deeply embedded and almost unconscious values that contributed greatly to the social fabric of the areas that they inhabited. But first and foremost they were valued for their farming skills, which far surpassed those of their Scottish and Irish counterparts. Some also brought important technical and manual skills. Many had left England in the first place because machines had taken over their jobs. In a pioneering society people who could make tools and household goods were at a premium, and here again the English would have excelled. Their skills were often superfluous to requirements in England but were a vital asset in the Canadas. Later on, with the influx in the late nineteenth and early twentieth centuries of wealthy English males having a business or professional background, they would contribute once again to the growth of the Canadian economy.

Public perceptions of the English changed. At times they were regarded as useless people who had to be removed from their native land, and at other times they were regarded as the indispensable life blood of

England. They came from all parts of England and all walks of life, but many only chose to come to the Canadas once they could match the United States in economic terms. Along with the Irish, the English were the major colonizers of Ontario and Quebec, but they only remained in appreciable numbers in Ontario. They moulded themselves into communities when it suited them, but only rarely sought to settle together. They had no sense of mission other than the desire to better themselves and their families. In this they succeeded beyond their wildest dreams.

The English were a unifying presence in their New World communities. They certainly did not come as empire-builders. This emigration saga is dominated by ordinary people who came with accumulated skills and knowledge and put them to good use for the benefit of all. Their talent, determination, and pioneering successes are plain to see in many parts of Ontario and Quebec. Nobody gave them a second glance when they left England, and few commentators saw fit to record their presence when they reached Canada.

APPENDIX I

Emigrant Ship Crossings from England to Quebec, 1817–64

EXPLANATORY NOTES

Vessel Type

Brig (bg): a two-masted vessel with square rigging on both masts.
Barque(bk): a three-masted vessel, square-rigged on the fore and main masts and for-and-aft rigged on the third aftermost mast.
Ship (s): a three-masted vessel, squared rigged on all three masts.
Schooner (sr): has fore-and-aft sails on two or more masts. They were largely used in the coasting trade and for fishing, their advantage being the smaller crew than that required by square-rigged vessels of a comparable size.
Snow (sw): rigged as a brig with square sails on both masts but with a small triangular sail-mast stepped immediately towards the stern of the main mast.
Steamship (s.s.): steamship

Month

Unless otherwise stated, the month shown is the vessel's arrival month; but where the month is followed by an asterisk it refers to the departure month.

Documentary Sources

The number of passengers carried by ships crossing from England to Quebec has been obtained from a variety of documentary sources, the most important being: Canadian newspaper shipping reports (especially those taken from the *Quebec Mercury*), the Quebec Immigration Agent's Annual Reports, and the Colonial Land and Emigration Commissioners Annual Reports, both taken from the *British Parliamentary Papers*. An important source for Cornish emigration is the Royal Institution of Cornwall's "Records of Emigrant Ships from Cornwall," which is based on newspaper extracts compiled by C.J. Davies. Some passenger figures are approximate. Uncertainties arise as to whether passenger numbers include all adults (not just heads of households) and children and infants.

Passenger Lists

No official passenger lists were kept for ships crossing from Britain to the port of Quebec until 1865. As a consequence, few passenger lists survive from before that time. Where a passenger list has been identified in this study, the documentary reference is given with the crossing information.

Tables 1, 2, 7, 8, 9, 10, 11, 14, and 16 contain partial or full listings of passengers taken on particular crossings. Passenger lists for crossings taking the Petworth settlers to Quebec can be accessed on The Ships List website.

Passenger lists for the period from 1865 to 1935 are held on microfilm by Library and Archives Canada (see the LAC website).

Year	Month	Vessel	Type	Master	Departure Port	Passenger Numbers
1817	05	*Don*	bg	Forest	Newcastle	16
1817	05	*Fame*	s	Minnett, Thomas	Hull	104

Exceeding good height (6'6") between decks (*Hull Advertiser*, February 27, 1817).

Year	Month	Vessel	Type	Master	Departure Port	Passenger Numbers
1817	05	*Sara Ann*	bg	Meldram	Liverpool	22
1817	05	*Trafalgar*	bg	Welburn, John	Hull	113

Passengers disembarked at Saint John (N.B.) and Quebec. For partially reconstructed passenger list, see Campey, *Planters, Paupers and Pioneers*, 131. The *Trafalgar* had been "recently refurbished, height between decks of 6 feet" (*Hull Advertiser*, April 26, 1817).

Year	Month	Vessel	Type	Master	Departure Port	Passenger Numbers
1817	06	*Amphitre*	bg	Dawson	Sunderland	23
1817	06	*Autumn*	bg	Batchelor	London	17
1817	06	*Isis*	bg	Melvin	London	12
1817	06	*Trader*	bg	Hall	London	14
1817	07	*Camden*	s	Johnson	London	240

Travelled via Cork. Passengers were fifty settlers and 190 men of the 37th Regiment (Royal Hampshire).

Year	Month	Vessel	Type	Master	Departure Port	Passenger Numbers
1817	07	*Commerce*	s	Wilson, J.	Liverpool	40
1817	07	*Curlew*	bg	Spence	Sunderland	88
1817	07	*John*	s	Binnington	Hull	44
1817	07	*Manique*	s	Sacker, Robert	Hull	64
1817	07	*Mary*	bg	Wilkinson	Liverpool	11
1817	07	*Renovation*	bg	Stevenson	Newcastle	23
1817	07	*Rosina*	s	Danson, W.	Liverpool	14
1817	07	*Vittoria*	s	Dodd	London	234

Travelled via Cork. Passengers were forty settlers and 194 men of the 37th Regiment (Royal Hampshire).

Year	Month	Vessel	Type	Master	Departure Port	Passenger Numbers
1817	08	*Berwick*	bk	Smith	London	45

Passengers were Lieutenant Hopkins, 76th Regiment, Captain Allison, and forty-three settlers.

Year	Month	Vessel	Type	Master	Departure Port	Passenger Numbers
1817	08	*Clio*	bg	Davidson	Sunderland	50
1817	08	*Daedalus*	bk	Watt	Liverpool	46
1817	08	*Eagle*	s	Henley, Edward	Hull	16
1817	08	*Maria*	s	Williams	London	121
1817	08	*Nancy*	bg	Norman, W.	Hull	43

Year	Month	Vessel	Type	Master	Departure Port	Passenger Numbers
1817	08	*Newbiggin*	bg	Wills	Sunderland	47
1817	08	*Sir George Prevost*	s	Morrison	London	54
1817	08	*Young*	bg	Benson, Thomas	Liverpool	10
1817	09	*Hawker*	s	Price	Liverpool	17
1817	09	*William & Mary*	bg	n/k	Plymouth	73
1818	05	*Harrison*	s	Davies, Henry	Liverpool	117
1818	05	*Maida*	s	Estelle	Hull	29
1818	05	*Monique*	bk	Draper, W.	Hull	129
1818	05	*Penelope*	bg	Doyle, J.	Liverpool	185

Two in the cabin, remainder settlers.

Year	Month	Vessel	Type	Master	Departure Port	Passenger Numbers
1818	05	*Rosehill*	bg	Wilson	Whitehaven	17
1818	05	*William & Matthew*	bg	Evans, William	London	17
1818	06	*Concord*	s	Nessfields	Liverpool	50
1818	06	*Doncaster*	s	Marshall	Newcastle	15
1818	06	*Fame*	bg	Nicholson	Sunderland	40
1818	06	*Fides*	s	Jefferson, Thos	Hull	14
1818	06	*Harriet*	bg	Norway	Guernsey	18
1818	06	*Horsely Hill*	bg	Buck	Sunderland	113

The vessel also called at Charlottetown where an unknown number of passengers disembarked.

Year	Month	Vessel	Type	Master	Departure Port	Passenger Numbers
1818	06	*Hunter*	bg	Grant, A.	London	19

Three cabin passengers, sixteen in steerage.

Year	Month	Vessel	Type	Master	Departure Port	Passenger Numbers
1818	06	*James*	bg	James, William	Liverpool	70
1818	06	*Majestic*	s	Harper	Sunderland	32
1818	06	n/k (?son)	bg	White	Whitehaven	128
1818	06	*Nancy*	bg	Norman, W.	Hull	56

Also called at P.E.I. where an unknown number of passengers left; fifty-six people went on to Quebec. Fares: adults 10 gns. (with provisions), adults to provide themselves 7 gns., children half price (*Hull Advertiser*, April 11, 1818).

Year	Month	Vessel	Type	Master	Departure Port	Passenger Numbers
1818	07	*Brothers*	bg	Moore, W.	Whitehaven	72
1818	07	*Montreal*	s	Hillary, J.	London	120

Passengers part military and part settlers.

Year	Month	Vessel	Type	Master	Departure Port	Passenger Numbers
1818	07	*Nancy*	bg	Norman, W.	Hull	56
1818	07	*Sarah*	bg	Corish, J.	Liverpool	64
1818	08	*Amphitre*	bg	Davidson	Sunderland	69
1818	08	*Bridget*	bg	Walker	Plymouth	29
1818	08	*Lord Exmouth*	bg	Barrett	Plymouth	32
1818	08	*Monarch*	s	Thornhill	Liverpool	50
1818	08	*Reith*	bg	Patterson, G.	Liverpool	34

Two in the cabin, thirty-two settlers.

Year	Month	Vessel	Type	Master	Departure Port	Passenger Numbers
1818	08	*Wilding*	s	n/k	Hull	10
1818	09	*Claremount*	bg	Tolson	Workington	41
1818	09	*Martha*	bg	Bean	Workington	50
1819	05	*Aid*	bg	Lister, John	Whitehaven	27
1819	05	*Blessing*	s	Charter	Shields	10
1819	05	*Canada*	n/k	Davidson, Thos	London	18
1819	05	*Catherine*	bg	Clark, Thomas	Sunderland	90
1819	05	*Eagle*	bg	Henley, Edward	Hull	84
1819	05	*Fame*	s	Minnett, Thomas	Hull	171
1819	05	*Isabella*	s	Brady, Charles	Hull	263

Six feet six inches between decks (*Hull Advertiser*, March 6, 1819).

Year	Month	Vessel	Type	Master	Departure Port	Passenger Numbers
1819	05	*Sir George Prevost*	s	Morrison	Portsmouth	15
1819	06	*Brailsford*	s	Spring, John	London	11

Nine in the cabin, two in steerage.

Year	Month	Vessel	Type	Master	Departure Port	Passenger Numbers
1819	06	*Martha*	bg	Scott	Workington	74
1819	06	*Peggy*	bg	Davis	Bristol	21

Nineteen settlers.

Year	Month	Vessel	Type	Master	Departure Port	Passenger Numbers
1819	06	*Royal Yeoman*	s	Fly	Weymouth	15
1819	06	*Skellton*	s	Dixon, James	London	146
1819	06	*Speculation*	bg	Organ, W.	Portsmouth	104

Departure port might also be Plymouth.

Year	Month	Vessel	Type	Master	Departure Port	Passenger Numbers
1819	06	*Three Brothers*	bg	French, Henry	Sunderland	23
1819	06	*Triton*	s	Marshall	Cowes	135

Officers and men of the 37th, 60th, 68th, 70th, and 76th Regiments.

Year	Month	Vessel	Type	Master	Departure Port	Passenger Numbers
1819	06	*True Briton*	bg	Reid	Liverpool	68

Two in the cabin.

Year	Month	Vessel	Type	Master	Departure Port	Passenger Numbers
1819	06	*Zoma*	bg	Frazer, J.	Sunderland	51
1819	07	*Ann*	bg	Bowman, J.	Whitehaven	43
1819	07	*Elizabeth*	bg	Wickholm, Samuel	Liverpool	56

Four cabin, fifty-two settlers.

Year	Month	Vessel	Type	Master	Departure Port	Passenger Numbers
1819	07	*Harmony*	bg	Taylor, Samuel	Hull	22
1819	07	*Harriet*	bg	Fulford, Robert	Liverpool	46
1819	07	*Harrison*	s	Davies, Henry	Portsmouth	57

Departure port may have been Plymouth.

Year	Month	Vessel	Type	Master	Departure Port	Passenger Numbers
1819	07	*Huddart*	s	Appleton, J.	London	209

One hundred and seventy-two officers and men of the 60th Regiment and staff corps. In addition there were thirty-seven settlers.

Year	Month	Vessel	Type	Master	Departure Port	Passenger Numbers
1819	07	*Kingston*	bg	Stuart, John	Hull	99
1819	07	*Ocean*	bg	Morrison, James	Liverpool	44
1819	07	*St. Helena*	bg	Elliott, James	London	11
1819	07	*Whim*	bg	Barchard, Wm.	Hull	95
1819	07	*William & Matthew*	bg	Evans, William	Sunderland	40
1819	08	*Arethusa*	bk	Wise, William	Hull	123
1819	08	*Hope*	bk	Royal	Plymouth	15
1819	08	*Ben Johnson*	bg	Ostey, George	Portsmouth	125

Officers and men from 60th and 76th regiments plus fifty settlers.

Year	Month	Vessel	Type	Master	Departure Port	Passenger Numbers
1819	08	*Laura*	s	Whitmore, John	Bristol	39

Mr. Ratcliffe and family and thirty-two settlers.

Year	Month	Vessel	Type	Master	Departure Port	Passenger Numbers
1819	08	*Minerva*	s	Dale, Henry	Plymouth	33

Mr. Finton plus thirty-two settlers.

Year	Month	Vessel	Type	Master	Departure Port	Passenger Numbers
1819	08	*Phillis*	bg	Grayson, H.	Workington	154
1819	08	*Streatlam Castle*	bg	Gibson, Robert	Sunderland	85

Crossing of seventy-three days. Vessel name possibly *Sheatlam Castle*.

Year	Month	Vessel	Type	Master	Departure Port	Passenger Numbers
1819	09	*Favourite*	bg	Brisbane	Liverpool	20
1819	09	*Friends*	s	Clarke, George	Hull	10
1819	09	*Kelsick Wood*	bg	Fisher, J.	Liverpool	14
1819	09	*William Pitt*	bk	Stonehouer, Thos	Hull	32
1819	10	*Ceres*	bg	Clementson, Thomas	Liverpool	10
1820	05	*Brothers*	s	Jenkinson	Hull	28

Three cabin, twenty-five settlers.

Year	Month	Vessel	Type	Master	Departure Port	Passenger Numbers
1820	05	*Eagle*	bg	Henley, Edward	Portsmouth	14

An unknown number of passengers disembarked at P.E.I.

Year	Month	Vessel	Type	Master	Departure Port	Passenger Numbers
1820	05	*Harrison*	s	Davis, Henry	Liverpool	36

Two cabin, thirty-four settlers.

Year	Month	Vessel	Type	Master	Departure Port	Passenger Numbers
1820	05	*Integrity*	bg	Wilson, J.	Strangford	46
1820	05	*Lord Exmouth*	bg	Barre, S.	Plymouth	22

Three cabin, nineteen settlers.

Year	Month	Vessel	Type	Master	Departure Port	Passenger Numbers
1820	05	*Maida*	s	Estelle	Hull	87

One cabin, eighty-six settlers.

Year	Month	Vessel	Type	Master	Departure Port	Passenger Numbers
1820	05	*Prince Astutias*	bg	Dorval, A.	Hull	35
1820	05	*Triton*	bk	Hesiltine, W.	Hull	79

Two cabin, seventy-seven settlers. Exceeding good height between decks (*Hull Advertiser*, February 18, 1820).

Year	Month	Vessel	Type	Master	Departure Port	Passenger Numbers
1820	06	*Catherine*	bg	Wake	Sunderland	42
1820	06	*Eagle*	bg	Henly, Edward	Portsmouth	14

Some passengers disembarked at P.E.I.

Year	Month	Vessel	Type	Master	Departure Port	Passenger Numbers
1820	06	*Earl Fitzwilliam*	s	Jackson, Henry	Hull	50
1820	06	*Henry*	bg	Irvine	Liverpool	20
1820	06	*Phillis*	bg	Grayson, H.	Workington	107
1820	06	*Pilgrim*	bg	Kennedy, Robert	Newcastle	14
1820	06	*Speculation*	bg	Richards	Plymouth	10

Year	Month	Vessel	Type	Master	Departure Port	Passenger Numbers
1820	07	*Briton*	bg	Barry, R.	Sunderland	96
1820	07	*Huddart*	s	Appleton, J.	Deptford	61
1820	07	*Kent*	bg	Sterling, John	London	171
1820	07	*Margaret*	bg	McGill	Liverpool	19

Two cabin, seventeen settlers.

Year	Month	Vessel	Type	Master	Departure Port	Passenger Numbers
1820	08	*Alpha*	bg	McCormick	Liverpool	12
1820	08	*Ann*	bk	Clark	Shields	10
1820	08	*Rambler*	bg	Pope	Hull	35
1820	08	*Speculation*	bg	Chapman, Thos.	Liverpool	29
1820	09	*Euphrates*	s	Chanceller, J.	Scarborough	10
1820	09	*Union*	bg	Wallace	London	12

Three settlers.

Year	Month	Vessel	Type	Master	Departure Port	Passenger Numbers
1820	10	*Isabella*	s	Dodd, John	Hull	15

Eight settlers.

Year	Month	Vessel	Type	Master	Departure Port	Passenger Numbers
1820	10	*St. Lawrence*	bk	Douglass	London	22

Seven cabin, fifteen settlers.

Year	Month	Vessel	Type	Master	Departure Port	Passenger Numbers
1821	05	*Earl Fitzwilliam*	s	Jackson, Henry	Hull	80
1821	05	*Isabella*	s	Todd	Hull	33

Four cabin, twenty-nine settlers.

Year	Month	Vessel	Type	Master	Departure Port	Passenger Numbers
1821	06	*Adventure*	bg	Wardle	Liverpool	112
1821	06	*Clarkson*	bk	Cox	Hull	33
1821	06	*Friends*	bg	Foster	Liverpool	19
1821	06	*John Howard*	n/k	Smith	London	100

One hundred settlers from Anticosti, being part of the wreck of the brig *Earl of Dalhousie*.

Year	Month	Vessel	Type	Master	Departure Port	Passenger Numbers
1821	06	*Trafalgar*	bg	n/k	Liverpool	15

One cabin, fourteen settlers.

Year	Month	Vessel	Type	Master	Departure Port	Passenger Numbers
1821	07	*Ferriland*	bk	Stewart	Hull	24

One cabin, twenty-three settlers.

Year	Month	Vessel	Type	Master	Departure Port	Passenger Numbers
1821	07	*Friends*	bg	Renney	Bristol	75
1821	07	*Hope*	bg	Simson, G.	Workington	45

Year	Month	Vessel	Type	Master	Departure Port	Passenger Numbers
1821	07	*Jane*	bg	Fell	Workington	23
1821	07	*Lady Francis*	bg	Barry, Robert	Sunderland	36
1821	07	*Maister*	s	Berriman	Hull	48
1821	07	*Recovery*	s	Fatherguay	London	250
1821	07	*Santon*	bg	Gaitskill, W.	Liverpool	45

Eleven cabin, thirty-four settlers.

Year	Month	Vessel	Type	Master	Departure Port	Passenger Numbers
1821	07	*Sir George Prevost*	s	Morrison	Portsmouth	15
1821	07	*Zodiac*	bg	Hunter	London	11
1821	08	*Albatross*	bg	Emerson, Robert	Sunderland	21
1821	09	*Argo*	bg	Brown, Joseph	Liverpool	17

Eight in cabin, nine settlers.

Year	Month	Vessel	Type	Master	Departure Port	Passenger Numbers
1821	09	*Dryad*	bg	Fell	London	22

Ten settlers.

Year	Month	Vessel	Type	Master	Departure Port	Passenger Numbers
1821	09	*Oxenhop*	bk	Minnett, Thomas	Hull	25

One cabin, twenty-four settlers.

Year	Month	Vessel	Type	Master	Departure Port	Passenger Numbers
1822	05	*Brothers*	s	Jenkinson	Hull	16
1822	05	*Commerce*	s	Chandler	Bristol	17
1822	05	*Lord Exmouth*	bg	Barrett	Plymouth	17
1822	05	*Mars*	bg	Todd, John	Liverpool	13

Nine settlers.

Year	Month	Vessel	Type	Master	Departure Port	Passenger Numbers
1822	06	*Andromeda*	n/k	Swan	London	11
1822	06	*Cumberland*	bg	Smith	Liverpool	10
1822	06	*Henderson*	bg	Steele	Workington	9

Landed nine settlers at Gaspé.

Year	Month	Vessel	Type	Master	Departure Port	Passenger Numbers
1822	06	*Isabella*	s	Todd	Hull	30
1822	06	*Martha*	bg	Moordaff, J.	Liverpool	15

Vessel may be called *Marsea*.

Year	Month	Vessel	Type	Master	Departure Port	Passenger Numbers
1822	06	*Oxenhope*	bk	Minnett, Thomas	Hull	56
1822	06	*Philip*	s	Davis, J. C.	Bristol	29
1822	06	*Sarah and Mary*	bg	Christian	Strangford	170

Year	Month	Vessel	Type	Master	Departure Port	Passenger Numbers
1822	06	*Themis*	bg	Davidson	Shields	15
1822	06	*Three Sisters*	bg	Cord	Liverpool	15
1822	07	*Caldicut Castle*	bg	Charlton	Plymouth	15
1822	07	*Friendship*	bg	Wilkinson	Workington	45
1822	07	*London*	s	Gabbie	London	16

Four cabin, twelve settlers.

Year	Month	Vessel	Type	Master	Departure Port	Passenger Numbers
1822	08	*Ann*	bg	Crosby	Sunderland	31
1822	08	*Barnett*	bg	Scott	Liverpool	18
1822	08	*Unity*	bg	Ward	Bristol	25

One cabin, twenty-four settlers.

Year	Month	Vessel	Type	Master	Departure Port	Passenger Numbers
1823	05	*Ajax*	bg	Watson	Portsmouth	10
1823	05	*Gales*	bg	Dawson	Sunderland	18
1823	05	*Harding*	bg	Bragg	Bristol	11
1823	05	*Henderson*	bg	Steele	Whitehaven	44

One cabin, forty-three settlers.

Year	Month	Vessel	Type	Master	Departure Port	Passenger Numbers
1823	05	*Maria*	bg	Hewitt	Whitehaven	58

Five cabin, fifty-three settlers.

Year	Month	Vessel	Type	Master	Departure Port	Passenger Numbers
1823	05	*Oxenhope*	bk	Minnett, Thomas	Hull	70

Sixty-five settlers plus family in cabin.

Year	Month	Vessel	Type	Master	Departure Port	Passenger Numbers
1823	06	*Columbine*	bk	Arthur	Sunderland	39
1823	06	*Commerce*	bk	Thom	Bristol	11

One cabin, ten settlers.

Year	Month	Vessel	Type	Master	Departure Port	Passenger Numbers
1823	06	*Isabella*	s	Todd	Hull	34

One cabin, thirty-three settlers.

Year	Month	Vessel	Type	Master	Departure Port	Passenger Numbers
1823	07	*Betty*	bg	Wedgewood	Liverpool	13
1823	07	*Blucher*	bg	Thompson	London	95
1823	07	*Dido*	bg	Carns	Liverpool	23
1823	07	*Eleanor*	bg	Wallace	Workington	96
1823	07	*Hannah*	s	Graham	Liverpool	20
1823	07	*Isabella*	bg	Booth	Sunderland	23
1823	07	*Pleiades*	bg	Miller	Liverpool	11

Sailed via Bermuda.

Year	Month	Vessel	Type	Master	Departure Port	Passenger Numbers
1823	08	*Nicholson*	bg	Cairn	Liverpool	20
1823	08	*Thomas Jackson*	bk	Gehl	Hull	14
1824	05	*Brothers*	s	Jenkinson	Hull	18

One cabin, seventeen settlers.

Year	Month	Vessel	Type	Master	Departure Port	Passenger Numbers
1824	06	*Diana*	bk	Braithwaite	Whitby	16
1824	06	*Endeavour*	bk	Collinson	Hull	19
1824	06	*Jean*	bg	Innes	Liverpool	13

Two cabin, eleven settlers.

Year	Month	Vessel	Type	Master	Departure Port	Passenger Numbers
1824	06	*Lady Francis*	bg	Barry, Robert	Sunderland	33

One cabin, thirty-two settlers.

Year	Month	Vessel	Type	Master	Departure Port	Passenger Numbers
1824	06	*William Tell*	bg	Barnes	Workington	14
1824	07	*Active*	bg	Johnson	Whitehaven	85
1824	07	*Bartley*	bg	McDugal	Liverpool	29
1824	07	*Gleadon*	sr	Taylor	Hull	14
1824	07	*Lady Hood*	bg	McKenzie	Liverpool	25
1824	08	*Aurora*	bg	Hodson	Whitehaven	61
1824	08	*Dart*	bg	Gibson	Sunderland	12
1824	08	*John and Mary*	bg	Hall	Liverpool	23

Two in cabin, twenty-one settlers.

Year	Month	Vessel	Type	Master	Departure Port	Passenger Numbers
1824	08	*Latona*	bg	Thompson	Liverpool	32
1824	08	*Susannah*	bg	Birkett	Liverpool	17
1824	09	*Canadian*	bg	Udney, John	Liverpool	12
1824	09	*Love*	bg	Glaves	Liverpool	23

One in cabin, twenty-two settlers.

Year	Month	Vessel	Type	Master	Departure Port	Passenger Numbers
1824	09	*Percy*	bg	Richie	Liverpool	10
1825	05	*Charlotte*	bg	Shearer	Liverpool	30

Two cabin, twenty seamen, eight settlers.

Year	Month	Vessel	Type	Master	Departure Port	Passenger Numbers
1825	05	*Clarkson*	bk	Ward	Hull	18
1825	05	*Emporium*	bg	Croft	London	25

Eleven cabin, fourteen settlers.

Year	Month	Vessel	Type	Master	Departure Port	Passenger Numbers
1825	05	*Lady Gordon*	s	Bell	Liverpool	19

Five cabin, fourteen steerage.

Year	Month	Vessel	Type	Master	Departure Port	Passenger Numbers
1825	05	*Ocean*	bk	Berry	Hull	18
1825	05	*Oxenhope*	bk	Minnett, Thomas	Hull	31

Two cabin, five seamen, twenty-four settlers.

Year	Month	Vessel	Type	Master	Departure Port	Passenger Numbers
1825	06	*Tobago*	bk	Elder	Plymouth	4
1825	06	*Unity*	bg	Ward	London	2
1825	06	*William*	bg	Newell	London	19
1825	07	*Active*	bg	Johnson	Whitehaven	36
1825	07	*Agenoria*	bg	Whiteway	Liverpool	3
1825	07	*Isabella*	bg	Hare	Whitehaven	18
1825	07	*Richard*	bg	Rennison	Scarborough	6
1825	07	*Richard*	bg	Cox	Liverpool	7
1825	08	*Aurora*	bg	Kerr	Whitehaven	13
1825	08	*Britannia*	bg	Hamilton	Liverpool	15
1825	08	*Economy*	bg	Addison	Whitby	3
1825	09	*Betty*	bg	Wedgewood	Liverpool	15

Also three sailors making a total of eighteen passengers.

Year	Month	Vessel	Type	Master	Departure Port	Passenger Numbers
1825	09	*Caledonia*	bg	Lyell	London	3
1825	09	*Hebe*	bg	Taylor	Hull	11
1825	10	*Ontario*	bg .	Willie	Liverpool	4
1825	10	*Rachel*	bg	Adams	Bristol	9
1826	05	*Clarkson*	bk	Ward	Hull	14
1826	05	*Dorcus Savage*	bg	Warnock	Bristol	43
1826	05	*Oxenhope*	bk	Minnett, Thomas	Hull	17
1826	05	*Reward*	s	Terry	Whitby	2
1826	05	*Sir George Prevost*	s	Jackson	London	7
1826	06	*Montreal*	s	Bouch	Hull	8
1826	06	*Sovereign*	bg	Dumble	Sunderland	11
1826	07	*Ann*	bg	Edkin	Workington	14
1826	07	*Eleanor*	bg	Russell	Liverpool	63
1826	07	*Jane*	bg	Thomson	London	9
1826	07	*Traveller*	bg	n/k	London	30
1826	08	*Buenos Ayres Packet*	bg	Cooper	Liverpool	12
1826	08	*Cordelia*	bg	White	Sunderland	5
1826	08	*George Canning*	s	Davie	London	41

Year	Month	Vessel	Type	Master	Departure Port	Passenger Numbers
1826	08	*Monarch*	bg	Hudson	Sunderland	14
1826	08	*Robert James Haynes*	bg	Graham	Liverpool	5
1826	09	*Trident*	bg	Armstrong	London	9
1826	10	*Scipio*	bg	Beadle	London	19
1827	05	*Accatia*	bg	Hetherington	Sunderland	44
1827	05	*Amethyst*	bg	Thomson	London	25

Travelled via Plymouth, fifteen cabin, ten steerage.

Year	Month	Vessel	Type	Master	Departure Port	Passenger Numbers
1827	05	*Attaliah*	bg	Lotherington, William	Sunderland	14
1827	05	*Callisto*	bg	McKenzie	Sunderland	2
1827	05	*Clarkson*	bk	Ward	Hull	44
1827	05	*Donegal*	bg	Heyton	Liverpool	45
1827	05	*Elizabeth*	bg	Murphy	Whitehaven	5
1827	05	*Horatio*	bg	Sparks, John	Liverpool	17

Nine cabin, eight settlers.

Year	Month	Vessel	Type	Master	Departure Port	Passenger Numbers
1827	05	*Priscilla*	s	Mitchell	Plymouth	3
1827	05	*Rolla*	bk	Thursby	Liverpool	11
1827	05	*Teviotdale*	s	Sime	Liverpool	8
1827	06	*Ajax*	s	Robson	Newcastle	9
1827	06	*Bolton*	bg	Biglands	Maryport	2
1827	06	*Countess Morley*	s	Warren	Plymouth	6
1827	06	*Endeavour*	s	Collinson	London	8
1827	06	*Maida*	bk	Pecker	Hull	32
1827	06	*Maria*	bg	Hewitt	Maryport	35
1827	06	*Pons Aelii*	s	Armstrong	Newcastle	19
1827	06	*Unity*	bk	Tor	Hull	28
1827	06	*Urania*	bk	Coltman	Hull	41
1827	06	*Waterhen*	s	Mauleen	London	4
1827	06	*William Pitt*	bk	Weldridge	Hull	27
1827	07	*Ellergill*	s	Knill	Hull	30
1827	07	*Fame*	bg	Udale	Liverpool	23

One cabin, twenty-two settlers.

Year	Month	Vessel	Type	Master	Departure Port	Passenger Numbers
1827	07	*Mars*	bg	Gourlay	Maryport	41
1827	07	*Nelson Wood*	bg	Hall	Liverpool	49

Year	Month	Vessel	Type	Master	Departure Port	Passenger Numbers
1827	09	Clarkson	bk	Ward	Hull	9
1827	09	Elizabeth	bg	Moor	Plymouth	2
1827	09	Erato	bg	Blair	London	18
1827	09	Forster	bk	Bennett	Hull	10
1827	09	John Francis	s	Miller	London	10
1827	10	Margaret	s	Sumpton	Liverpool	9
1828	05	Clarkson	bk	Ward	Hull	42

Two cabin, forty settlers.

Year	Month	Vessel	Type	Master	Departure Port	Passenger Numbers
1828	05	Cybele	bk	Heckler	Scarborough	130
1828	05	Dykes of Maryport	bg	Cockton	Maryport	12
1828	05	John Francis	s	Millar	Liverpool	20

Four cabin, sixteen settlers.

Year	Month	Vessel	Type	Master	Departure Port	Passenger Numbers
1828	05	Kitson	bg	Dixon	Maryport	11
1828	05	Maida	bk	Beckett	Hull	59

Also carried the 2nd mate, and the remainder of the passengers who had sailed in the lost *Aeolus* from Waterford.

Year	Month	Vessel	Type	Master	Departure Port	Passenger Numbers
1828	05	Triton	bk	Keighley	Hull	116
1828	05	Unity	bk	Fox	Hull	35
1828	05	William Pitt	bk	Weldridge	Hull	28
1828	06	Cameron	bg	Hewitt	Liverpool	28

Two cabin, twenty-six settlers.

Year	Month	Vessel	Type	Master	Departure Port	Passenger Numbers
1828	06	Halcyon	s	Berryman	Hull	82

Two cabin, eighty settlers.

Year	Month	Vessel	Type	Master	Departure Port	Passenger Numbers
1828	06	Kamaskda	bk	Dobson	London	30

Four cabin, twenty-six settlers.

Year	Month	Vessel	Type	Master	Departure Port	Passenger Numbers
1828	06	Kirkella	bk	Corhill	Hull	126

One cabin, 125 settlers.

Year	Month	Vessel	Type	Master	Departure Port	Passenger Numbers
1828	06	Resource	bg	Smith	Scarborough	50
1828	07	Aurora	bg	Porteous	Liverpool	11
1828	07	Home	s	Mitchell	Liverpool	17
1828	07	Joseph Hume	bg	Rattray	Liverpool	31
1828	07	Victory	bk	Simpson	Hull	15

Year	Month	Vessel	Type	Master	Departure Port	Passenger Numbers
1828	07	*Westmoreland*	bk	Knill	Hull	62
1828	08	*Ann*	bg	Hallowell	Workington	55
1828	08	*Jane*	bg	Wilkinson	Workington	102
1828	08	*John*	bg	Smith	Scarborough	13
1828	08	*John Barry*	s	Davidson	London	24
1828	08	*Newcastle*	bg	Clay	London	20
1828	09	*Charles Tennyson*	bg	London	London	18

Nine cabin, nine settlers.

Year	Month	Vessel	Type	Master	Departure Port	Passenger Numbers
1828	09	*Indian*	bg	Crosby	Liverpool	17

Three cabin, rest in steerage.

Year	Month	Vessel	Type	Master	Departure Port	Passenger Numbers
1828	09	*Tom*	bg	Pearce, H. G.	Liverpool	14

Nine in steerage.

Year	Month	Vessel	Type	Master	Departure Port	Passenger Numbers
1828	10	*Clarkson*	bk	Ward	Hull	16
1828	10	*Heyden*	bk	Smith	Falmouth	6
1828	10	*Spence*	bk	Morrough	Sunderland	9
1828	95	*Ellergill*	bk	Rorbut	Hull	21
1829	05	*Alexander*	bg	Michison	Maryport	80
1829	05	*British Sovereign*	s	Thompson, Thomas	London	32

Eighteen cabin, fourteen settlers.

Year	Month	Vessel	Type	Master	Departure Port	Passenger Numbers
1829	05	*Charlotte*	bk	Hanson	Liverpool	66

Two officers and sixty-four men of the 68th Regiment.

Year	Month	Vessel	Type	Master	Departure Port	Passenger Numbers
1829	05	*Cicero*	bk	Robinson	London	17
1829	05	*Clarkson*	bk	Ward	Hull	100
1829	05	*Dykes* of Maryport	bg	Cockton	Maryport	107
1829	05	*Horatio*	bg	Sparks, John	Liverpool	20
1829	05	*Minerva*	bk	Carrick	Hull	34
1829	05	*Thomas Wallace*	s	Douglas	Bristol	5
1829	05	*Triton*	bk	Keighley	Hull	157

Many went on to Illinois (U.S.A.).

Year	Month	Vessel	Type	Master	Departure Port	Passenger Numbers
1829	06	*Alicia*	s	Jones	Bristol	5

Year	Month	Vessel	Type	Master	Departure Port	Passenger Numbers
1829	06	*Ann*	bg	Hewson	Shields	39
1829	06	*Graham Moore*	bg	Docker	London	23
1829	06	*Maida*	s	n/k	Hull	151
1829	06	*Margaret Miller*	bg	Kenn	Liverpool	9
1829	06	*Marie Eliza*	sr	Bernier	Jersey	5
1829	06	*Retrieve*	bg	Burton	Milford	22

Probably Milford on Sea, Hampshire.

Year	Month	Vessel	Type	Master	Departure Port	Passenger Numbers
1829	06	*Teviotdale*	s	Dodds	London	60
1829	06	*William Pitt*	bk	Weldridge	Hull	63
1829	07	*Dew Drop* of Padstow	sw	Wokes, Thomas	London	30
1829	07	*Victory*	bk	Simpson	Hull	144
1829	07	*Westmoreland*	bk	Knill	Hull	184
1829	08	*Argus*	bg	Kirkhaugh	Workington	123
1829	08	*Army*	bg	Reynolds	Exmouth	10
1829	08	*Asia*	bk	Parkins	Newcastle	7

Two cabin, five settlers.

Year	Month	Vessel	Type	Master	Departure Port	Passenger Numbers
1829	08	*Brunswick*	bk	Blake, Robert	London	27
1829	08	*Canadian*	bg	Hamilton	Liverpool	11

Two cabin, nine settlers.

Year	Month	Vessel	Type	Master	Departure Port	Passenger Numbers
1829	08	*Itinerant*	bg	Nicholson	Maryport	23
1829	08	*Kingston*	s	Crouch	London	17
1829	08	*Lee*	bk	Cannon, William	Liverpool	17
1829	08	*Pons Aelii*	s	Callender	London	22
1829	08	*Richardson*	bg	Todd	Maryport	104
1829	09	*Carricks*	bg	Stewart, H.	Liverpool	20
1829	10	*Champion*	bk	Chambers	Hull	25
1829	10	*Endeavour*	bk	Collinson	London	14

Four cabin, ten settlers.

Year	Month	Vessel	Type	Master	Departure Port	Passenger Numbers
1829	10	*John Francis*	s	Miller	Liverpool	24

Two cabin, twenty-two settlers.

Year	Month	Vessel	Type	Master	Departure Port	Passenger Numbers
1829	10	*Ottawa*	s	Douglass, G.	Portsmouth	21

Sixteen cabin, five settlers.

Year	Month	Vessel	Type	Master	Departure Port	Passenger Numbers
1829	10	*Sophie*	bg	Neil	London	10

Called also at Plymouth. Four cabin and six settlers.

Year	Month	Vessel	Type	Master	Departure Port	Passenger Numbers
1829	10	*Strathisla*	s	Bonneyman	London	13

Three cabin, ten settlers.

Year	Month	Vessel	Type	Master	Departure Port	Passenger Numbers
1830	04	*Friends*		Butters	Plymouth	n/k

William and Elizabeth Peters of Cornwall sailed in this vessel with their three children and each wrote an account of the crossing (LAC MG24-I131). They settled in Hope Township, Durham County.

Year	Month	Vessel	Type	Master	Departure Port	Passenger Numbers
1830	04	*Janus*	bk	Richards, J.	Falmouth	n/k
1830	05	*Margaret*	s	Sumpton	Liverpool	20

Ten cabin, ten settlers.

Year	Month	Vessel	Type	Master	Departure Port	Passenger Numbers
1830	05	*Susan*	bg	Nicholson	Plymouth	30
1830	06	*Active*	s	Bowie	Newcastle	15
1830	06	*Addison*	bg	Brown	Whitby	85
1830	06	*Almorah*	s	Ward	Hull	149
1830	06	*Argus*	bk	Johnson	Plymouth	16
1830	06	*Baltic*	bg	Miller	Yarmouth	107
1830	06	*British Sovereign*	s	Thompson, Thomas	London	35

Sixteen cabin, nineteen settlers.

Year	Month	Vessel	Type	Master	Departure Port	Passenger Numbers
1830	06	*Brothers*	bk	Jenkinson	Hull	115
1830	06	*Canadian*	bg	Hamilton	Liverpool	18
1830	06	*Concord*	bk	Johns	Bristol	54
1830	06	*Cynthia*	bg	Turner	Sunderland	80
1830	06	*Dew Drop* of Padstow	sw	Wokes, Thomas	London	30
1830	06	*Dykes* of Maryport	bg	Cockton	Maryport	154
1830	06	*Earl of Dalhousie*	bg	Raisbeck	Hull	70
1830	06	*Experiment*	bg	Bruce	Hull	122
1830	06	*Glemora*	bg	Ware	Scarborough	45

Year	Month	Vessel	Type	Master	Departure Port	Passenger Numbers
1830	06	*Harrington*	bg	Halliday	Whitehaven	92
1830	06	*Iphigenia*	bg	Hird	Hull	134
1830	06	*Julius Caesar*	bk	Forster	Plymouth	20
1830	06	*Lord Stanley*	bk	Bains	Hull	54
1830	06	*Maida*	s	Beckett	Hull	186
1830	06	*Mary Ann*	bg	Barnwell	Liverpool	54
1830	06	*Ottawa*	s	Douglass, G.	London	21

Twelve cabin, nine settlers.

Year	Month	Vessel	Type	Master	Departure Port	Passenger Numbers
1830	06	*Pomona*	bg	Brown	Liverpool	15
1830	06	*Preston*	bg	Woodthorp	Yarmouth	137
1830	06	*St. Mary*	s	Gill	Hull	209
1830	06	*Suffolk*	s	Reast	Hull	85
1830	06	*True Briton*	bg	Baldison	Liverpool	47
1830	06	*Urania*	bg	Younger	Hull	14
1830	06	*Westmoreland*	bk	Knill	Hull	181
1830	06	*Wilberforce*	bk	Clark	Hull	200
1830	06	*Winscales*	s	Messenger	Liverpool	10
1830	07	*Chieftain*	s	Blair, H.	Liverpool	19

Two cabin, seventeen settlers.

Year	Month	Vessel	Type	Master	Departure Port	Passenger Numbers
1830	07	*Forster*	bk	Callender	Hull	129
1830	07	*Guimare*	s	Summerson, Wm	Whitby	203
1830	07	*Industry*	bg	Boardman	Liverpool	115
1830	07	*Kelsick Wood*	bg	Glover	Workington	82
1830	07	*Mariner*	bk	Swinton	Liverpool	155
1830	08	*Agenoria*	bg	Hardcastle	Liverpool	14
1830	08	*Briton*	s	Dixon	Bristol	38
1830	08	*Caledonian*	bk	Carrick	Hull	69
1830	08	*Derwent*	bg	Millar	Plymouth	14
1830	08	*Earl Stanhope*	bk	Jamieson	Whitby	60
1830	08	*Jackson*	bk	Jackson	Whitby	22
1830	08	*Julius*	bk	Williams	Hull	74
1830	08	*Lady Ann*	bg	Simpson	Hull	35
1830	08	n/k	bk	n/k	Newcastle	271
1830	08	*Samuel*	bg	McGee	Whitehaven	108
1830	08	*Sir Watkin*	bk	Sanderson	Liverpool	10
1830	08	*Spring Flower* of Padstow	bg	Brown, T.	Padstow	57

Year	Month	Vessel	Type	Master	Departure Port	Passenger Numbers

The passengers included James Pearne, a prominent Methodist, who travelled with his wife and family.

Year	Month	Vessel	Type	Master	Departure Port	Passenger Numbers
1830	09	*Airthy Castle*	bk	Carling	Bristol	50
1830	09	*Danube*	bg	Drummond	Sunderland	11
1830	09	*Waterloo*	s	Rayne	Hull	23
1830	10	*Arabian*	s	Carr, Andrew	London	46

Twelve cabin, thirty-four settlers.

Year	Month	Vessel	Type	Master	Departure Port	Passenger Numbers
1830	10	*Lowland Lass*	bg	Bonifant	Yarmouth	37
1830	n/k	*Rosa*	n/k	n/k	Yarmouth	110

Passengers from Suffolk. A total of 160 passengers had sailed to Quebec in the *Rosa* but fifty settled in P.E.I.

Year	Month	Vessel	Type	Master	Departure Port	Passenger Numbers
1831	03*	*Janus*	bk	Richards, J.	Truro	n/k
1831	04	*Airthy Castle*	bk	Burling	Bristol	254

Two hundred and fifty settlers who included immigrants from Corsley in Wiltshire.

Year	Month	Vessel	Type	Master	Departure Port	Passenger Numbers
1831	04	*Euphrosyne*	bk	Sampson, Joseph	Bridgwater	200

Carried forty paupers from Heytesbury and Knook parishes in Wiltshire. List of names appears as Table 7.

Year	Month	Vessel	Type	Master	Departure Port	Passenger Numbers
1831	04	*Friends*	bg	Hudson	Scarborough	60
1831	04	*Portia*	s	Taylor	Liverpool	14
1831	05	*Almorah*	s	Ward	Hull	186
1831	05	*Amethyst*	bg	Thomas	London	9
1831	05	*Ann*	bg	Steele	Sunderland	15
1831	05	*Briton*	s	Dixon	Bristol	11
1831	05	*Brothers*	bk	Jenkinson	Hull	128
1831	05	*Caledonia*	bk	Carrick	Hull	69
1831	05	*Carouge*	s	Spalding	Liverpool	17
1831	05	*Donegal*	bg	Matches	Maryport	164
1831	05	*Ellergill*	bk	Corbett	Hull	155
1831	05	*Experiment*	bg	Bruce	Hull	140
1831	05	*George*	n/k	Thompson	Maryport	23
1831	05	*Isabella*	bg	Millar	Liverpool	14
1831	05	*James*	bk	Richards	Falmouth	77
1831	05	*James*	bg	Walton	Bristol	23
1831	05	*Jane Vinet*	bk	Gross	Liverpool	97

Year	Month	Vessel	Type	Master	Departure Port	Passenger Numbers
1831	05	John Danford	bk	Hepburn	Yarmouth	250
1831	05	Lord Suffield	s	Castling	Hull	156
1831	05	Margaret	s	Burton	Liverpool	22
1831	05	Montreal	bk	Froste	Hull	94
1831	05	Northumber-land	s	Mitchell	Liverpool	40
1831	05	Priam	bk	Harper	Plymouth	67
1831	05	Procris	bg	Arnold	Poole	66
1831	05	Saint Mary	s	Gill	Hull	193
1831	05	Sarah Marianne	sw	Archibald	Maryport	164
1831	05	Sion Hill	sr	Thomas	Liverpool	20
1831	05	Susan	bg	Nicholson	Plymouth	14
1831	05	Trial	bk	Scott	Plymouth	34
1831	05	Triton	bk	Keighley	Hull	100
831	05	Westmoreland	bk	Knill	Hull	180
1831	05	Wilberforce	bk	Clark	Hull	170
1831	05	William Pitt	bk	Weldridge	Hull	52
1831	06	Ann Mondel	bg	Armstrong	Sunderland	23
1831	06	Argus	bg	Hoff	Workington	69
1831	06	Atalanta	bg	Petrie	Liverpool	36
1831	06	Baltic	bg	Ebbage, Thomas	Yarmouth	114

The *Minerva* sailed with the *Baltic* and together they carried 274 passengers of whom 160 landed at P.E.I. and 114 at Quebec. *Baltic* departure advertised in the *Norwich Mercury* April 9, 1831.

Year	Month	Vessel	Type	Master	Departure Port	Passenger Numbers
1831	06	Bolina	bg	Hardy	Bideford	44
1831	06	Dew Drop of Padstow	sw	Wokes, Thomas	London	50
1831	06	Exmouth	bk	Greig	Plymouth	56
1831	06	Experiment	bg	Collins	Maryport	32
1831	06	Fanny	s	Cosin	Liverpool	180
1831	06	Forster	bk	Callender	Hull	143
1831	06	Hebe	bk	Strangham	London	120
1831	06	Hope	bg	Middleton	Maryport	73
1831	06	Ida	bg	Summerson	Whitby	69
1831	06	Iona	bg	Smith, Hodgson	London	40
1831	06	Jane	bk	Graham	Bristol	180

Year	Month	Vessel	Type	Master	Departure Port	Passenger Numbers
1831	06	*John Bulmer*	s	n/k	Hull	156
1831	06	*Lady Cremorne*	n/k	Hurst	Liverpool	150
1831	06	*Maris*	bg	McLeod	Liverpool	164
1831	06	*Mary*	bk	Driscoll	London	55
1831	06	*Memnon*	s	Mathie	Newcastle	15
1831	06	*Minerva*	bg	Summerville	Yarmouth	114

The *Minerva* sailed with the *Baltic* and together they carried 274 passengers of whom 160 landed at P.E.I. and 114 at Quebec, chiefly farm labourers with their wives and families. They included John Birt, John Cook, William Smith, Charles Gibbs, and Samuel Mayhew.

Year	Month	Vessel	Type	Master	Departure Port	Passenger Numbers
1831	06	*St. David*	bk	Dale, H.	Plymouth	49
1831	06	*Victoria*	s	Simpson	Hull	279
1831	06	*William Dodd*	bg	Chalker	Liverpool	79
1831	06	*Woodthorne*	bg	n/k	Yarmouth	62
1831	07	*Amanthea*	bg	Gamble	Plymouth	11
1831	07	*Catherine McDonald*	bg	Thom	Liverpool	136
1831	07	*Clarkson*	bk	Coltsman	Hull	156
1831	07	*Cossack*	bg	Davenport	Liverpool	266
1831	07	*Kelsick Wood*	bg	Glover	Workington	270
1831	07	*Mint*	bk	Bayle	London	203
1831	07	*Syrian*	bg	Gillam	Yarmouth	62
1831	07	*William Shand*	s	Hunter	Berwick	200
1831	08	*Alarm*	bg	Willis	Poole	10
1831	08	*Archer*	bk	Smith	Liverpool	11
1831	08	*Caroline*	s	Greig, James	London	9
1831	08	*Chieftain*	s	Blair, H.	Liverpool	19
1831	08	*Congress*	bg	Scott	Whitehaven	138
1831	08	*Eliza*	s	Wrangler	Bristol	27
1831	08	*Esk*	s	Gray	Hull	18
1831	08	*Minerva*	bk	Richards	Plymouth	14
1831	08	*Victoria*	bg	Gedds	Whitby	91
1831	09	*Agnes*	bg	McDonald	Liverpool	65
1831	09	*Champlain*	bk	Hughes	Liverpool	12
1831	09	*Concord*	bk	Johns	Bristol	73

Year	Month	Vessel	Type	Master	Departure Port	Passenger Numbers
1831	09	Emperor Alexander	bk	Cleeves	Plymouth	107
1831	09	Euphrosyne of Whitby	bk	Sampson, Joseph	Bridgwater	12
1831	09	Isabella	bg	Donaldson	Liverpool	119
1831	09	Jane	bk	Richards	Penzance	17
1831	09	Manchester	bk	Walker	Hull	78
1831	09	Martin	bg	Martin	London	28
1831	09	Mary	bg	Berry	Sunderland	43
1831	09	Nitherdale	s	Jones	London	95
1831	09	Royal William	bk	Peake	Plymouth	2

Vessel called at Charlottetown. Passengers were Mr. and Mrs. Murray who were on their way to Quebec.

Year	Month	Vessel	Type	Master	Departure Port	Passenger Numbers
1831	09	Sappho	bk	Mullins	London	101
1831	10	Almorah	s	Ward	Hull	44
1831	10	Deveron	bk	Smith	Liverpool	173
1831	10	Peterborough	bg	Magon	Liverpool	49
1832	05	Alert	bg	Bentson	Hull	17
1832	05	Andromeda	bg	Wilkie	Liverpool	30
1832	05	Ariadne	s	Arnold	Bristol	84
1832	05	Asia	bk	Stoveld	Portsmouth	25
1832	05	Baltic	bg	Ebbage, Thomas	Yarmouth	50

Ninety-six passengers in all. Mr. and Mrs. Worthy and son in a cabin plus plus ninety-three people in the steerage. Forty-six went to P.E.I. and fifty went on to Quebec.

Year	Month	Vessel	Type	Master	Departure Port	Passenger Numbers
1832	05	Baltic	bk	Evans	Yarmouth	40
1832	05	Bolivar	bk	Richards	Plymouth	46
1832	05	Branches	s	Atkinson	London	97
1832	05	British Sovereign	s	Thompson, Thomas	London	15

All cabin passengers.

Year	Month	Vessel	Type	Master	Departure Port	Passenger Numbers
1832	05	Brothers	bk	Jenkinson	Whitehaven	110

Departure port may have been Whitby.

Year	Month	Vessel	Type	Master	Departure Port	Passenger Numbers
1832	05	Caroline	s	Greig, James	London	204

One cabin, 203 settlers. William Cattermole's recruits, who were mostly bound for the

Year	Month	Vessel	Type	Master	Departure Port	Passenger Numbers

Canada Company lands in the western peninsula. The partial passenger list appears as Table 16.

Year	Month	Vessel	Type	Master	Departure Port	Passenger Numbers
1832	05	*Cawton*	bg	Lyle	Liverpool	37
1832	05	*Clarkson*	bk	Irwin	Hull	51
1832	05	*Columbus*	s	Bagg	Whitby	240
1832	05	*Concord*	bk	Jones	Bristol	270
1832	05	*Corsair*	bk	Sommerville	Whitby	75
1832	05	*David*	bk	Gilmour	Bristol	38
1832	05	*Donegal*	sw	Matches	Maryport	138
1832	05	*Dykes* of Maryport	n/k	Cockton	Maryport	156
1832	05	*Esther*	s	Clarkson	London	116
1832	05	*Euphrosyne* of Whitby	bk	Sampson, Joseph	Bridgwater	208

Wiltshire settlers.

Year	Month	Vessel	Type	Master	Departure Port	Passenger Numbers
1832	05	*Eveline*	s	Royal	Portsmouth	230

Petworth settlers from West Sussex. A reconstructed passenger list (partial) can be found on The Ships List website.

Year	Month	Vessel	Type	Master	Departure Port	Passenger Numbers
1832	05	*Exmouth*	bk	Greig	Plymouth	92
1832	05	*Fleetwood*	s	Thrift	London	20
1832	05	*Forster*	bk	Callender	Hull	33
1832	05	*General Wolfe*	bk	Redpath	Plymouth	220
1832	05	*Hero*	s	Campion	Bristol	26
1832	05	*Iona*	bg	Smith, Hodgson	London	44
1832	05	*Irton*	bg	n/k	Liverpool	24
1832	05	*James Daughton*	bg	Dawson	Liverpool	14
1832	05	*John & Mary*	bk	Gash	London	220
1832	05	*Justinian*	bk	Reay, T.	London	34
1832	05	*Kingston*	bk	Lewens	Plymouth	114
1832	05	*Marmion*	n/k	Hopper, Robert	Portsmouth	154

William Cattermole's group from East Anglia. Many going to the Canada Company lands.

Year	Month	Vessel	Type	Master	Departure Port	Passenger Numbers
1832	05	*Medusa*	bk	Wilson	Bridgwater	98
1832	05	*Mentor*	bg	Barlow	London	75

Year	Month	Vessel	Type	Master	Departure Port	Passenger Numbers

Paupers from Lenham in Kent whose departure was organized by William Cattermole. Many bound for Canada Company lands.

Year	Month	Vessel	Type	Master	Departure Port	Passenger Numbers
1832	05	*Onondago*	s	Morgan	London	90
1832	05	*Pembroke Castle*	bg	Stanbury	Bristol	50
1832	05	*Preston*	bg	Waters	Yarmouth	74

Vessel called at Charlottetown. A total of 152 passengers sailed: seventy-nine disembarked at Charlottetown and seventy-four went on to Quebec.

Year	Month	Vessel	Type	Master	Departure Port	Passenger Numbers
1832	05	*Procris*	bg	Arnold	Poole	150
1832	05	*Rapid*	bg	Tweedie	Liverpool	10
1832	05	*Regina*	bg	Lang	Whitby	85
1832	05	*Richard Rimmer*	bk	Chambers	Liverpool	224
1832	05	*Sarah*	n/k	Marianne	Maryport	165
1832	05	*Sir William Bensley*	bk	Sellers	Scarborough	12
1832	05	*Six Sisters*	bg	Douthwaite	Lancaster	45
1832	05	*Smales*	bg	Tyers	Whitby	20
1832	05	*Spring Flower of Padstow*	bg	Brown, T.	Padstow	128
1832	05	*St. David*	bk	Dale, H.	Plymouth	80
1832	05	*St. Mary*	s	Gill	Hull	163
1832	05	*Strathisla*	s	Bonneyman	Plymouth	18

Seven cabin, eleven settlers.

Year	Month	Vessel	Type	Master	Departure Port	Passenger Numbers
1832	05	*Superior*	s	Brown	Bristol	22
1832	05	*Tobago*	bk	Stephens	Bristol	129
1832	05	*Triton*	bk	Keighley	Hull	114
1832	05	*Venus*	bg	Simmonds	Yarmouth	119
1832	05	*Vestal*	bg	Taylor	Sunderland	162
1832	05	*Vigilant*	bg	Thorpe	Liverpool	24
1832	05	*William & Mary* of Colchester	n/k		London	120

William Cattermole's group from East Anglia. Many bound for Canada Company lands.

Year	Month	Vessel	Type	Master	Departure Port	Passenger Numbers
1832	06	*Alexander*	s	Jefferson, Thos	Liverpool	203

Year	Month	Vessel	Type	Master	Departure Port	Passenger Numbers
1832	06	*Alice*	bg	Bishop	Liverpool	20
1832	06	*Amanthea*	bg	Gamble	Plymouth	106
1832	06	*Ann*	bg	Moore	Maryport	136
1832	06	*Aurora*	bk	Dearness	Hull	50
1832	06	*Barbara*	bg	Murray	Newcastle	31
1832	06	*Bolina*	bg	Hardy	Bideford	60
1832	06	*Brunswick*	bk	Blake, Robert	London	193

Some of the passengers originated from Dorking in Surrey.

Year	Month	Vessel	Type	Master	Departure Port	Passenger Numbers
1832	06	*Caledonian*	bk	Burnett	Hull	40
1832	06	*Clio*	bk	Terry	London	140
1832	06	*Concord*	bg	Hick	London	35
1832	06	*Courier*	bg	Dodds	Sunderland	17
1832	06	*Crown*	bk	Hopper, Cuthbert	London	240

Letter of commendation to the captain signed by: Meroyn Patterson (surgeon), Edward Moan, Adam Stark, Charles Field, William Jones, Thomas Kelly, John Richardson, Lieutenant R.N. Carthew, Thomas Hodgekin, William Smith, Thomas Dickenson, George Peeknam, John Garner, James Whitican (*Quebec Gazette* June 7, 1832).

Year	Month	Vessel	Type	Master	Departure Port	Passenger Numbers
1832	06	*Dew Drop* of Padstow	sw	Wokes, Thomas	London	30
1832	06	*Donegal*	bg	Matches	Maryport	128
1832	06	*Economist*	bg	Moon	Padstow	179
1832	06	*Edward Colston*	s	Reynolds, R.K.	Bristol	246

Letter of commendation to the captain signed by: J.W. Rose, Chepstow [Wales], A.D. Cook, Dursley [Gloucestershire], Nathaniel Rudder, Dursley, Edward Kenworthy, Bristol, W. Parsons, Chepstow, Rice Williams, Dursley, James Harris, Bristol, John Tummey, Bristol, Robert Watkins, Nailsea (Somerset), William Sweet, Frome [Somerset], Daniel Cotterell, Slimbridge [Gloucestershire], D.G. Martin, Bath, Richard Williams, Durlsey, William Jones, Whitchurch, George Jennings, Huntspill. [Somerset] (*Montreal Gazette*, June 26, 1832).

Year	Month	Vessel	Type	Master	Departure Port	Passenger Numbers
1832	06	*England*	bg	Lewis	Portsmouth	160

Petworth settlers from West Sussex. A reconstructed passenger list (partial) can be found on The Ships List website.

Year	Month	Vessel	Type	Master	Departure Port	Passenger Numbers
1832	06	*Esk*	bk	Hill	Bristol	137

Year	Month	Vessel	Type	Master	Departure Port	Passenger Numbers
1832	06	Fair Isle	bg	Winn	London	146
1832	06	Hebe	bk	Straughan	London	330
1832	06	Lord Melville	bk	Royal	Portsmouth	333

Petworth settlers from West Sussex. A reconstructed passenger list (partial) can be found on The Ships List website.

Year	Month	Vessel	Type	Master	Departure Port	Passenger Numbers
1832	06	Maria	sw	Hewitt	Maryport	136
1832	06	Mary	bk	Hooter	Dartmouth	122
1832	06	Minerva	bg	Catly	Yarmouth	10
1832	06	Miser	bg	Spurgeon	Yarmouth	97
1832	06	Navarino	bk	Craggs	London	223

A letter of commendation to the captain was signed by the following: Benjamin Racey, Henry Hanna, Joseph Coombs, Bryan Thompson, D. McIntosh, John Dunn, J.W. Kempton (surgeon), William Bourne, Samuel Browning, John Stevenson, Thomas Johnson, J.M. Howard (*Quebec Gazette*, June 9, 1832).

Year	Month	Vessel	Type	Master	Departure Port	Passenger Numbers
1832	06	Nelson	bk	Webb	Bristol	300
1832	06	Nicholson	bg	Craig	Maryport	183
1832	06	Preston	bg	Stampwater	Yarmouth	81
1832	06	Regalia	s	Smith	London	311
1832	06	Ruckers	s	Smith	Plymouth	36
1832	06	Saham	bg	Taylor	Sunderland	140
1832	06	Samuel	bg	McGee	Whitehaven	159
1832	06	Sarah Marianne	sw	Archibald	Maryport	165
1832	06	Scarborough Castle	bg	Mosey	London	52
1832	06	Sir George Murray	bg	Beverley	Liverpool	87
1832	06	St. Lawrence	bg	Blair	London	15

Two cabin, thirteen settlers.

Year	Month	Vessel	Type	Master	Departure Port	Passenger Numbers
1832	06	Sylvan	bg	Gillam	Yarmouth	106
1832	06	Syres	bg	Rodgers	Yarmouth	113
1832	06	William Pitt	bk	Mildridge	Hull	79
1832	07	Aimwell	bg	Porder	Liverpool	199
1832	07	Anne	bg	Potts	London	25
1832	07	Cartha	n/k	n/k	Liverpool	239

Year	Month	Vessel	Type	Master	Departure Port	Passenger Numbers

A total of 344 passengers sailed in the *Cartha*: 105 disembarked at Sydney, Cape Breton, and the remaining 239 went on to Quebec.

Year	Month	Vessel	Type	Master	Departure Port	Passenger Numbers
1832	07	*Chapman*	s	Christie	London	124
1832	07	*Dalmarnock*	bg	McFarlane	Berwick	277
1832	07	*Earl Moira*	bg	Lorrens	London	338
1832	07	*Edward*	bg	Dixon	Newcastle	22
1832	07	*Grace*	bg	Little	Workington	85
1832	07	*Grenada*	s	Wright	Liverpool	123
1832	07	*John March*	s	Clucas	Liverpool	247
1832	07	*Lavinia*	bk	Brown	Stockton	128
1832	07	*Lowther*	bg	Pewley	Workington	131
1832	07	*Mint*	bk	Woodward	London	376
1832	07	*Nancy*	bg	n/k	Whitehaven	108
1832	07	*Royal Adelaide* of Fowey	bk	n/k	Plymouth	71
1832	07	*Sir William Wallace*	bg	Hanna	Liverpool	305
1832	07	*Sisters*	bg	Sutton	London	31

Six cabin, twenty-five settlers.

Year	Month	Vessel	Type	Master	Departure Port	Passenger Numbers
1832	07	*Thomas Wallace*	bk	Ford	Hull	53
1832	07	*Ulster*	s	McKie	London	273
1832	07	*Victory*	bk	Simpson	Hull	239
1832	07	*Woodbine*	bg	Honston	London	72
1832	08	*Alchymist* of Falmouth	bk	Mills	Falmouth	42
1832	08	*Ann Wise*	bg	Hoodlap	London	16
1832	08	*Bride*	bk	Moore	London	57
1832	08	*Chieftain*	s	Blair, H.	Liverpool	33
1832	08	*Heath*	bg	Duncan	London	24
1832	08	*Hope*	s	Kent	London	103
1832	08	*Ida*	bg	Seaton, Thomas	London	40
1832	08	*Lady*	bk	Straharn	London	204
1832	08	*Lyra*	bg	n/k	Plymouth	79
1832	08	*Magnet*	sw	Goulder	Whitehaven	146
1832	08	*Manchester*	bk	Harrington	Yarmouth	144

Year	Month	Vessel	Type	Master	Departure Port	Passenger Numbers
1832	08	Merchants Package	bg	Taylor	Bristol	86
1832	08	Minerva	bk	Chark	Plymouth	56
1832	08	Minerva	bk	Barton	Hull	79
1832	08	Nelly	bg	Dale	Whitehaven	73
1832	08	Nightingale	bg	Cruickshanks	Whitby	61
1832	08	Ocean	bk	Baron	London	181
1832	08	Othello	s	Leggett	Bristol	162
1832	08	Phillis	bg	Kipsock	Workington	28
1832	08	Prince of Brazil	bg	Hill	Newcastle	28
1832	08	Warfinger	bg	Carr	London	55
1832	08	Waterloo	s	Smith	Hull	133
1832	08	Woodbridge	s	Ekin	Liverpool	17
1832	09	Breeze	bg	Gorman	Liverpool	39
1832	09	City of Rochester	s	Riches	Liverpool	75
1832	09	Elizabeth	bg	Last	Bristol	24
1832	09	Jackson	bg	Braithwaite, Thos	London	28
1832	09	Jane & Barbara	s	Batten	Bristol	71

Two cabin, sixty-nine settlers.

Year	Month	Vessel	Type	Master	Departure Port	Passenger Numbers
1832	09	Montreal	s	Leitch	Liverpool	84
1832	09	Spring Flower of Padstow	bg	Brown, T.	Padstow	28
1832	10	Artemis	s	Sparks, Joseph	Liverpool	27
1832	10	Caroline	s	Greig, James	London	62
1832	10	Hope	bk	Roan	London	25
1832	10	Intrepid	bk	Robinson	Hull	19
1832	10	Ottawa	s	Douglass, G.	London	55
1833	04*	New Brunswick	n/k	n/k	Falmouth	n/k

Vessel also called at New Brunswick. According to the Royal Institution of Cornwall ships listing there were "a great number of passengers," but the number who sailed is unknown.

Year	Month	Vessel	Type	Master	Departure Port	Passenger Numbers
1833	04*	Spring Flower	bg	Brown, T.	Padstow	25

Year	Month	Vessel	Type	Master	Departure Port	Passenger Numbers
		of Padstow				
1833	04*	*St. David*	bg	Dale, H.	Truro	n/k
1833	05	*Aurora*	bk	Chambers	Hull	18
1833	05	*Caroline*	s	Greig, James	London	86
1833	05	*Earl Ketler*	s	Hindmarsh	London	41
1833	05	*Euphrasia*	bk	Sampson	Bridgwater	16
1833	05	*Margaret*	s	Sampson	Liverpool	53
1833	05	*Meteor*	bg	Weston	Hull	55
1833	05	*Oscar*	bg	Banks	Dartmouth	33
1833	05*	*Royal Adelaide* of Fowey	bk	Taylor, W.	Falmouth	16
1833	05	*Westmoreland*	bk	Knill	Hull	64
1833	05	*Berwick upon Tweed*	bg	Muers	Berwick	n/k
1833	06	*Airthy Castle*	bk	Carling	Bristol	14
1833	06	*Albion*	bg	Ibbs	Southampton	29
1833	06	*Amazon*	s	Broderick	Hull	60
1833	06	*Asturia*	bg	n/k	Dartmouth	33
1833	06	*Baltic*	bk	Freeman, James	Yarmouth	39

In all, the vessel carried sixty-three passengers: twenty-four landed at Charlottetown while thirty-nine went on to Quebec.

Year	Month	Vessel	Type	Master	Departure Port	Passenger Numbers
1833	06	*Bearborough Castle*	bg	Massey	London	84
1833	06	*Dykes* of Maryport	bg	Cockton	Maryport	33
1833	06	*Eleanor*	bg	Ryan	London	149
1833	06	*Endymion*	s	Smith	Gloucester	7
1833	06	*England*	bk	Lewis	Portsmouth	205

Petworth settlers from West Sussex. For a reconstructed passenger list (partial) see The Ships List website.

Year	Month	Vessel	Type	Master	Departure Port	Passenger Numbers
1833	06	*Exmouth*	bk	Comfort	Plymouth	59
1833	06	*Forester*	bg	Callendar	Hull	19
1833	06	*Jane*	bg	Nicholson	Sunderland	5
1833	06	*Minerva*	bg	n/k	Yarmouth	28
1833	06	*New Prospect*	s	Knox	London	133
1833	06	*Pace*	bk	Gill	Chatham	17

Year	Month	Vessel	Type	Master	Departure Port	Passenger Numbers
1833	06	*Queen*	bg	Smith	Plymouth	9
1833	06	*Salem*	bg	East	London	17
1833	06	*Salsian*	bg	Graham	Yarmouth	13
1833	06	*Six Sisters*	bg	Douthwaite	Lancaster	56
1833	06	*St. George*	n/k	Thomson	Maryport	26
1833	06	*Trial*	bk	Wood	Plymouth	104
1833	06	*Woodbine*	bg	Owston	London	7
1833	07	*Addison*	bg	Venill	Stockton	75
1833	07	*Balfour* of Whitehaven	bg	Bee	Whitehaven	272
1833	07	*Grace*	bg	n/k	Whitehaven	132
1833	07	*Hercules*	bg	n/k	Whitehaven	25
1833	07	*Hurlington*	bg	n/k	London	68
1833	07	*Mist*	bk	Fleure	Plymouth	124
1833	07	*St. Mary*	s	Methley	Hull	108
1833	07	*Triton*	bk	Keighley	Hull	69
1833	07	*Victory*	bk	Simpson	Hull	198
1833	08	*Alcyon*	bk	n/k	Liverpool	7
1833	08	*Argus*	bg	n/k	Maryport	115
1833	08	*Berwick upon Tweed*	bg	Muers	Berwick	142
1833	08	*Brixton*	bk	Sparrow	Berwick	22
1833	08	*Celia*	s	Davidson	Liverpool	49
1833	08	*Cheviot*	bg	Bowman	Plymouth	10
1833	08	*Clifton*	bk	n/k	Liverpool	5
1833	08	*George Palmer*	bg	n/k	London	66
1833	08	*Irton*	bg	Little	Liverpool	10
1833	08	*John & Mary*	bg	n/k	Sunderland	16
1833	08	*Jordanson*	bg	n/k	London	44
1833	08	*Lord Sidmouth*	bk	Gales	London	94
1833	08	*Loyalist*	s	n/k	Portsmouth	6
1833	08	*Marmion*	s	n/k	London	7
1833	08	*Notham Castle*	bg	Brown	Berwick	16
1833	08	*Ocean Queen*	bk	James	London	74
1833	08	*Scipio*	s	Shaw	Liverpool	40

Year	Month	Vessel	Type	Master	Departure Port	Passenger Numbers
1833	08	*Waterloo*	s	Frost	Hull	70
1833	09	*Allies*	bg	Hill	Plymouth	19
1833	09	*Amethyst*	bg	Hodgson	London	54
1833	09	*Aminins*	bg	Moore	Plymouth	93
1833	09	*Caroline*	s	Greig, James	London	40
1833	09	*Ipswich*	bk	Clunis	Plymouth	8
1833	09	*Pomona*	bk	Wheatley	London	84

Vessel also carried thirty-three soldiers.

Year	Month	Vessel	Type	Master	Departure Port	Passenger Numbers
1833	09	*Reward*		n/k	Liverpool	n/k

The Yorkshire-born George Pashley, one of the passengers, wrote a journal describing the crossing (see LAC MG24-J12).

Year	Month	Vessel	Type	Master	Departure Port	Passenger Numbers
1833	09	*Rosalind*	bk	Foster	London	34
1833	09	*Spring Flower* of Padstow	bg	Brown, T.	Padstow	45
1833	09	*Success*	bg	Byers	London	17
1833	09	*William Glen Anderson*	bk	Fox	Portsmouth	14
1833	10	*Canadian*	bg	Morgan	London	12
1833	10	*Fairfields*	bk	Black	Hull	8
1833	10	*Iona*	bk	Smith, Hodgson	London	8
1833	10	*Ottawa*	bk	Douglass, G.	London	50
1833	10	*Royal Adelaide* of Fowey	bk	Vivian, J.	Falmouth	13
1833	10	*St. David*	bk	Dale, H.	Plymouth	9
1833	10	*Victoria*	bg	Berry	Liverpool	40
1834	03	*Royal Adelaide* of Fowey	bk	Vivian, J.	Falmouth	n/k
1834	04*	*Berwick upon Tweed*	bg	Loweryson	Berwick	n/k

Carried goods and passengers.

Year	Month	Vessel	Type	Master	Departure Port	Passenger Numbers
1834	04*	*Bragila*	bk	Taylor, W.	Falmouth	n/k
1834	04*	*Caroline* of St. Ives	bg	Daniel, T.	Bristol	n/k
1834	05	*Artemis*	s	Sparks, Joseph	Liverpool	22

Year	Month	Vessel	Type	Master	Departure Port	Passenger Numbers

One cabin, twenty-one settlers.

Year	Month	Vessel	Type	Master	Departure Port	Passenger Numbers
1834	05	*Aurora*	bk	Chambers	Hull	32
1834	05	*Baltic*	bg	Newson	Yarmouth	104
1834	05	*Caledonia*	bk	Luscombe	Liverpool	104
1834	05	*Caroline*	s	Greig, James	London	189

Thirty-two cabin, forty-five intermediate, and 112 settlers. Some passengers signed a testimonial to Captain Greig.

Year	Month	Vessel	Type	Master	Departure Port	Passenger Numbers
1834	05	*Coeur de Lion*	s	Sumpton, Peter	Liverpool	28

Eleven cabin, seventeen settlers.

Year	Month	Vessel	Type	Master	Departure Port	Passenger Numbers
1834	05	*Dove*	bk	Richardson	Stockton	154

Two cabin.

Year	Month	Vessel	Type	Master	Departure Port	Passenger Numbers
1834	05	*Endeavour*	bk	Douglas	London	42

Thirteen cabin, twenty-nine settlers.

Year	Month	Vessel	Type	Master	Departure Port	Passenger Numbers
1834	05	*Endymion*	bg	Plewes	Gloucester	10
1834	05	*Esther*	s	Winby	Liverpool	13
1834	05	*Edward*	bk	McKenzie	Chatham	22
1834	05	*Exmouth*	bk	Grieg	Plymouth	73
1834	05	*Good Czar*	bg	Loweryson	Berwick	109

Carried thirty additional settlers whose ship had been wrecked. Passengers included George Jackson and seventeen members of his extended family.

Year	Month	Vessel	Type	Master	Departure Port	Passenger Numbers
1834	05	*Iona*	bg	Smith, Hodgson	London	18
1834	05	*John*	s	Campbell	Hull	74
1834	05	*Marmion*	s	Hopper	London	51
1834	05	*New Eagle*	bk	Quick	Plymouth	87
1834	05	*Newham*	bg	Robson	Newcastle	25
1834	05	*Oscar*	bg	n/k	Dartmouth	62

Nine cabin, fifty-three settlers.

Year	Month	Vessel	Type	Master	Departure Port	Passenger Numbers
1834	05	*Priam*	bk	Harper	Plymouth	117
1834	05	*Procris*	bg	Arnold	Poole	22
1834	05	*Restitution*	bk	Moon	Plymouth	26
1834	05	*Rokeby*	bg	Davidson	Bristol	16
1834	05	*Royal*	bk	Vivian, J.	Falmouth	59

Year	Month	Vessel	Type	Master	Departure Port	Passenger Numbers
		Adelaide of Fowey				
1834	05	*Sir James Anderson*	s	Reid	Liverpool	102
1834	05	*Six Sisters*	bg	Douthwaite	Poulton-le-Fylde	31
1834	05	*Spring Flower* of Padstow	bg	Brown, T.	Padstow	18
1834	05	*St. David*	bk	Dale, H.	Plymouth	53
1834	05	*St. George*	bg	Poole	Maryport	14
1834	05	*Thomas Ritchie*	bk	Thrift	London	15
1834	05	*Thorntons*	bk	Mitchell	Plymouth	52
1834	05	*Triton*	bk	Keighley	Hull	154
1834	06	*Active*	bg	Hick	London	29
1834	06	*Addison*	bg	Brown	Stockton	41
1834	06	*Arundel*	bg	Barrick	Whitby	145
1834	06	*Astrea*	bg	Park	Maryport	34
1834	06	*Berwick upon Tweed*	bg	n/k	Berwick	214
1834	06	*British Tar*	bg	Crawford	Portsmouth	135
1834	06	*Canada*	bg	Gibb	Newcastle	10
1834	06	*Captain Ross*	bg	Harrison	Whitby	28
1834	06	*Catherine*	bg	Rovely	London	76
1834	06	*Collins*	bg	Moon	Plymouth	49

Nine cabin, forty settlers.

Year	Month	Vessel	Type	Master	Departure Port	Passenger Numbers
1834	06	*Endymion*	bk	Fletcher	Liverpool	213
1834	06	*George Palmer*	bg	Wokes, Thomas	London	46

Twelve cabin, thirty-four settlers.

Year	Month	Vessel	Type	Master	Departure Port	Passenger Numbers
1834	06	*Hampshire*	bk	Temperley	London	42

Twenty-five cabin, seventeen settlers.

Year	Month	Vessel	Type	Master	Departure Port	Passenger Numbers
1834	06	*Heath*	bg	Smith	Liverpool	28

Eleven cabin, seventeen settlers.

Year	Month	Vessel	Type	Master	Departure Port	Passenger Numbers
1834	06	*Hindoo*	bk	Seaton	Whitby	100
1834	06	*Lord*	bk	Todd	London	22

Year	Month	Vessel	Type	Master	Departure Port	Passenger Numbers
		Sidmouth				
1834	06	*Merlin*	bk	Atkinson	London	234
1834	06	*Monica*	bg	Sommerville	Yarmouth	31
1834	06	*St. Mary*	s	n/k	Hull	168
1834	06	*Venus*	bg	Simmonds	Yarmouth	153
1834	06	*Wilkinson*	bg	Pearce	Whitehaven	117
1834	06*	*Parkins*	n/k	Henderson	Berwick	n/k
1834	07	*Abeona*	bk	Chambers	Liverpool	91
1834	07	*Andromache*	s	Hunter	London	36
1834	07	*Chapman*	s	Christie	London	65

Six cabin, fifty-nine settlers.

Year	Month	Vessel	Type	Master	Departure Port	Passenger Numbers
1834	07	*Duke of Clarence*	bg	Brown	Liverpool	51

Nine cabin, forty-two settlers.

Year	Month	Vessel	Type	Master	Departure Port	Passenger Numbers
1834	07	*Mary Cummings*	bg	n/k	London	167

Two cabin, 165 settlers.

Year	Month	Vessel	Type	Master	Departure Port	Passenger Numbers
1834	07	*Princess Charlotte*	s	Roach	Liverpool	87

Two cabin, eighty-five settlers.

Year	Month	Vessel	Type	Master	Departure Port	Passenger Numbers
1834	07	*Victory*	bk	Simpson	Hull	234

Seven cabin, 227 settlers.

Year	Month	Vessel	Type	Master	Departure Port	Passenger Numbers
1834	08	*British Queen*	bg	n/k	Hull	58
1834	08	*Celia*	s	Davidson	Liverpool	56
1834	08	*Dochtour*	s	Johns	Bristol	17
1834	08	*Donegal*	bg	Hodgson	Maryport	173
1834	08	*Eliza*	bg	Purmon	London	44
1834	08	*Hope*	bg	Hick	London	85

Forty-six people left at Quebec and thirty-nine went on to Montreal.

Year	Month	Vessel	Type	Master	Departure Port	Passenger Numbers
1834	08	*Isabella*	bg	Donaldson	Liverpool	61
1834	08	*Nelson*	bg	Waite	Maryport	185
1834	08	*Nelson Wood*	bg	Robinson	Maryport	13
1834	08	*Planter*	bg	Purdy	Liverpool	17
1834	08	*Quinton*	s	Leitch	Liverpool	42

Year	Month	Vessel	Type	Master	Departure Port	Passenger Numbers
1834	08	*Royal William*	s	McNeillage	Liverpool	44
1834	08	*Usk*	bg	n/k	Dartmouth	28
1834	09	*Caroline*	s	Greig, James	London	84
1834	09	*Concord*	bg	Hick	London	55
1834	09	*Dew Drop* of Padstow	sw	Wokes, Thomas	Padstow	11
1834	09	*Ord*	bg	Lang	Portsmouth	22
1835	03*	*Royal Adelaide* of Fowey	bk	Vivian, J.	Falmouth	n/k
1835	05	*Berwick upon Tweed*	bg	Muers	Berwick	20

Berwick Advertiser, March 28, 1835, stated: "Passengers may rely on every attention being paid to their comfort and convenience by Capt. Muers whose conduct hitherto met with the general approbation of those who have gone out with him."

Year	Month	Vessel	Type	Master	Departure Port	Passenger Numbers
1835	05	*Britannia*	bk	Thompson	Bridgwater	2
1835	05	*British King*	bg	Moncrieff	Liverpool	9

All cabin passengers.

Year	Month	Vessel	Type	Master	Departure Port	Passenger Numbers
1835	05	*Calypso*	bk	Graham	Dartmouth	26
1835	05	*Caroline*	n/k	Loweryson	Berwick	50

Berwick Advertiser, March 28, 1835, stated: "A large and elegantly fitted up cabin ... great height between decks ... a second cabin will be fitted up for families who may wish to be by themselves for a small extra charge."

Year	Month	Vessel	Type	Master	Departure Port	Passenger Numbers
1835	05	*Caroline*	s	Greig, James	London	166

Four cabin, 162 steerage.

Year	Month	Vessel	Type	Master	Departure Port	Passenger Numbers
1835	05	*Cybele*	bk	Heckler	Gloucester	6
1835	05	*Dochfour*	s	Johns	Bristol	11

Six cabin, five settlers.

Year	Month	Vessel	Type	Master	Departure Port	Passenger Numbers
1835	05	*Eldon*	bg	Harvey	Plymouth	18
1835	05	*Ellentheria*	n/k	Wheatley	London	47

Two cabin and forty-five steerage. The steerage passengers included thirty-one boys from the Children's Friend Society in London who, according to the Quebec immigration agent, "proceeded to Upper Canada, under the care of Mr. Orrock." Mr. Orrock reported that he found "not the slightest difficulty in placing these boys

Year	Month	Vessel	Type	Master	Departure Port	Passenger Numbers

advantageously at Toronto. A fresh arrival of boys from the same institution may soon be expected, and will be dispatched in a similar manner."[PP 1836(76)XL].

Year	Month	Vessel	Type	Master	Departure Port	Passenger Numbers
1835	05	*Esther*	s	Sumpton	Liverpool	9
1835	05	*Great Britain*	s	Swinburn	London	8
1835	05	*Neptune*	bg	Hutchins	Poole	2
1835	05	*Onondago*	s	Morgan	Liverpool	73
1835	05	*Ottawa*	bk	Hammond	London	18

Nine cabin, nine steerage.

Year	Month	Vessel	Type	Master	Departure Port	Passenger Numbers
1835	05	*Procris*	bg	Arnold	Poole	50
1835	05	*Sarah Marianne*	bg	Archibald	Maryport	33
1835	05	*Severn*	s	Smith	Bristol	94

The ninety-four passengers had been assisted to emigrate by their parishes. According to the Quebec immigration agent, they were "well provided with means to pursue their journey." All went to Upper Canada. Captain Smith improperly withheld some money belonging to the passengers, but the money was returned to them later. [PP 1836(76)XL]

Year	Month	Vessel	Type	Master	Departure Port	Passenger Numbers
1835	05	*Toronto*	s	Collinson	London	26

Twelve cabin, fourteen steerage.

Year	Month	Vessel	Type	Master	Departure Port	Passenger Numbers
1835	05	*Usk*	bk	Prouse	Torquay	10
1835	05	*Victoria*	bk	Mitchell	London	3
1835	05	*Wellington*	bg	Gillam	Yarmouth	86
1835	05*	*Highlander*	n/k	Taylor	Berwick	n/k
1835	05*	*Regatta*	n/k	Fyall	Berwick	n/k
1835	06	*Athelston*	bk	Wilson	Stockton	18

All settlers.

Year	Month	Vessel	Type	Master	Departure Port	Passenger Numbers
1835	06	*Baltic*	bg	Newson	Yarmouth	109

Twelve cabin, ninety-seven settlers.

Year	Month	Vessel	Type	Master	Departure Port	Passenger Numbers
1835	06	*Burrell*	bk	Metcalf, J.	Portsmouth	250

Twelve cabin passengers, 238 steerage. Petworth emigrants from West Sussex. For a reconstructed passenger list (partial) see The Ships List website.

Year	Month	Vessel	Type	Master	Departure Port	Passenger Numbers
1835	06	*Delhi*	s	Deaton	Whitby	57
1835	06	*Dorothys*	bg	Paul	Newcastle	6

Year	Month	Vessel	Type	Master	Departure Port	Passenger Numbers
1835	06	*Forster*	bk	Bibbing	Hull	18
1835	06	*Harmony*	bk	Brown	Hull	73
1835	06	*John Stamp*	bk	Young	London	180

Ten cabin, 170 settlers.

Year	Month	Vessel	Type	Master	Departure Port	Passenger Numbers
1835	06	*Pembroke Castle*	bg	Stanbury	London	13
1835	06	*Robert*	bk	Gardner	Liverpool	6
1835	06	*Sarah & Eliza*	bg	Marshall	Bideford	40

Total of sixty passengers: twenty disembarked at Charlottetown while the remaining forty sailed on to Quebec.

Year	Month	Vessel	Type	Master	Departure Port	Passenger Numbers
1835	06	*St. Mary*	s	Gill	Hull	58
1835	06	*Thomas Ritchie*	bk	Thrift	Bristol	5
1835	06	*Triton*	bk	Keighley	Hull	64
1835	08	*Englishman*	n/k	n/k	London	25

Vessel carried twenty-five boys from the Children's Friend Society in London. They proceeded to Toronto to be apprenticed there. Mr. Orrock accompanied them and reported that they were "in excellent health and spirits." [PP 1836(76)XL]

Year	Month	Vessel	Type	Master	Departure Port	Passenger Numbers
1835	09	*Welsford*	n/k	n/k	Bristol	n/k

Small number of passengers disembarked at P.E.I. Other passengers sailed on to Quebec.

Year	Month	Vessel	Type	Master	Departure Port	Passenger Numbers
1836	04*	*Anne*	n/k	Kemp, John	King's Lynn	n/k

Norwich Mercury (February 8, 1836) stated that the *Anne* "is of the first class, and nearly new, and will be fitted up in a commodious manner for the accommodation of passengers. She will sail from [King's] Lynn for Quebec early April next from which place steam vessels are constantly going to all parts of the country. Many berths are already taken."

Year	Month	Vessel	Type	Master	Departure Port	Passenger Numbers
1836	04*	*Berwick upon Tweed*	bg	Muers	Berwick	n/k
1836	05	*Amazon*	s	Broderick	Hull	11

All settlers.

Year	Month	Vessel	Type	Master	Departure Port	Passenger Numbers
1836	05	*Bragila*	bk	Taylor, W.	Falmouth	11

All settlers.

Year	Month	Vessel	Type	Master	Departure Port	Passenger Numbers
1836	05	*Caroline*	bg	Loweryson	Berwick	18

All settlers. The *Berwick Advertiser* (April 15, 1837) reported that agricultural labourers were very much in demand in Canada.

Year	Month	Vessel	Type	Master	Departure Port	Passenger Numbers
1836	05	*Earl Moira*	bg	Terry	Gloucester	11

All settlers.

Year	Month	Vessel	Type	Master	Departure Port	Passenger Numbers
1836	05	*Eldon*	bg	Harvey	Plymouth	11

All settlers.

Year	Month	Vessel	Type	Master	Departure Port	Passenger Numbers
1836	05	*Eleutheria*	bk	Wheatley	London	7

All settlers.

Year	Month	Vessel	Type	Master	Departure Port	Passenger Numbers
1836	05	*Euphrosyne of Whitby*	bk	Sampson, Joseph	Bridgwater	15

All settlers.

Year	Month	Vessel	Type	Master	Departure Port	Passenger Numbers
1836	05	*James & Ann*	bg	Brown	Portsmouth	91

All settlers.

Year	Month	Vessel	Type	Master	Departure Port	Passenger Numbers
1836	05	*King William*	s	Thomas	London	279

Paupers from Downton and Whiteparish in Wiltshire who were assisted by their parishes to emigrate. The passenger list appears as Table 14.

Year	Month	Vessel	Type	Master	Departure Port	Passenger Numbers
1836	05	*Marmion*	s	Hopper	London	195

All settlers.

Year	Month	Vessel	Type	Master	Departure Port	Passenger Numbers
1836	05	*Mary Bell*	bg	Brown	Newcastle	5

All settlers.

Year	Month	Vessel	Type	Master	Departure Port	Passenger Numbers
1836	05	*Sedulous*	bk	Pearce	Dartmouth	9

All settlers.

Year	Month	Vessel	Type	Master	Departure Port	Passenger Numbers
1836	05	*Westmoreland*	bk	Knill	Hull	34

All settlers.

Year	Month	Vessel	Type	Master	Departure Port	Passenger Numbers
1836	05*	*Ardwell*	n/k	n/k	King's Lynn	n/k
1836	05*	*Penelope*	sw	Eddie, James	King's Lynn	n/k

Twenty-three paupers from Heacham Parish in Norfolk who were assisted to emigrate. The passenger list appears as Table 1.

Year	Month	Vessel	Type	Master	Departure Port	Passenger Numbers
1836	06	*Active*	bg	Hick	London	26

Year	Month	Vessel	Type	Master	Departure Port	Passenger Numbers
1836	06	*Albion*	bk	Thompson	Lowestoft	119
1836	06	*Allendale*	bg	Alcock	Yarmouth	77
1836	06	*Antarnos*	bk	Coulson	Liverpool	174
1836	06	*Asia*	s	White	Liverpool	397
1836	06	*Aurora*	bk	Rods	Liverpool	16
1836	06	*Baltic*	bg	Newson	Yarmouth	182
1836	06	*Bromleys*	bg	Knox	London	49
1836	06	*Carron*	bg	Elliott	Yarmouth	206
1836	06	*Chapman*	s	Christie	Plymouth	13

Vessel due to sail on April 30.

Year	Month	Vessel	Type	Master	Departure Port	Passenger Numbers
1836	06	*Dochfour*	bk	Johns	Bristol	83
1836	06	*Dorothy Gales*	bk	Gain	Sunderland	7
1836	06	*Earl Bathurst*	bg	Stewart	London	30
1836	06	*Earus*	bg	Byers	London	33
1836	06	*Eliza*	bk	Fox	Liverpool	204
1836	06	*Ewretta*	bk	Skinner	Liverpool	247
1836	06	*George*	bg	Cornforth	London	89
1836	06	*Harmony*	s	Brown	Hull	33
1836	06	*Heber*	s	Knight	Portsmouth	260

Petworth settlers from West Sussex. For a reconstructed passenger list (partial) see The Ships List website.

Year	Month	Vessel	Type	Master	Departure Port	Passenger Numbers
1836	06	*Joseph Storey*	bk	Whitfield	London	48
1836	06	*Kelsick Wood*	bg	Collins	Liverpool	23
1836	06	*Lavinia*	bk	Martin	Portsmouth	45
1836	06	*Martha*	bg	Pearson	London	30
1836	06	*Mary*	s	Tucker	Bristol	9
1836	06	*Milo*	bk	Hodgson	Liverpool	197
1836	06	*Preston*	bg	Cordran	Yarmouth	156
1836	06	*Rolla*	bk	Blyth	Hull	105
1836	06	*Runa*	s	Sanderson	London	9
1836	06	*St. Mary*	s	Gill	Hull	47
1836	06	*Tulloch Castle*	s	Roxby	Yarmouth	346
1836	06	*Venus*	bg	Simmonds	Yarmouth	203
1836	06	*Wellington*	bg	Gillam	Yarmouth	153

Year	Month	Vessel	Type	Master	Departure Port	Passenger Numbers
1836	06	*William & John*	bg	Davis	Poole	13
1836	06	*William Ritchie*	s	Kenn	Yarmouth	315
1836	06*	*Eliza Liddle*	sw	Surtees	King's Lynn	40

Paupers from Kettlestone Parish, Norfolk, who disembarked at Port St. Francis in the Eastern Townships (Lower Canada). The passenger list appears as Table 2.

Year	Month	Vessel	Type	Master	Departure Port	Passenger Numbers
1836	07	*Amyntas*	bg	Sloeman	Plymouth	7
1836	07	*Brunswick*	bk	Blake, Robert	Yarmouth	445

Norwich Mercury (May 7, 1836) stated that "this is the most complete passage ship in the trade, with great height and fitted up with every attention to the convenience of passengers."

Year	Month	Vessel	Type	Master	Departure Port	Passenger Numbers
1836	07	*Celia*	s	Black	Liverpool	427
1836	07	*Hartley*	bk	Turnbull	Plymouth	231
1836	07	*Hero*	s	Smallwood	Bristol	275
1836	07	*Hope*	bg	Middleton	London	110
1836	07	*Kingston*	s	McLean	Liverpool	347
1836	07	*Lochiel*	bk	Bewes	Ipswich	231
1836	07	*Morning Star*	bg	Davison	Yarmouth	238
1836	07	*Nospareil*	bg	Williams	London	101
1836	07	*Reward*	s	Tickle	Liverpool	241
1836	07	*Victory*	bk	Heskit	Hull	164
1836	07*	*Dew Drop of Padstow*	sw	Wade, M.B.	Boscastle	n/k
1836	08	*Hampshire*	bk	Temperley	London	127

Sixty-five cabin, sixty-two steerage.

Year	Month	Vessel	Type	Master	Departure Port	Passenger Numbers
1836	08	*Huskisson*	bk	Hill	Liverpool	235
1836	08	*Lady Gordon*	s	Scurr	Maryport	6
1836	08	*Louisa*	bk	Nicholas	Liverpool	47
1836	08	*Mary Stewart*	bg	Morrison	Ipswich	140
1836	08	*Mayflower*	bk	Headley	Portsmouth	142
1836	08	*Portsea*	bk	Woodward	London	105
1836	08	*Vibilia*	bg	Marshall	Liverpool	23
1836	09	*Elizabeth*	bk	Smith	Scarborough	14
1836	09	*Hannibal*	bk	Roche	Liverpool	187

Year	Month	Vessel	Type	Master	Departure Port	Passenger Numbers
1836	09	*Indemnity*	bg	Dodds	Yarmouth	178

Going to Port St. Francis (Eastern Townships) to land her passengers.

Year	Month	Vessel	Type	Master	Departure Port	Passenger Numbers
1836	09	*Industry*	bk	Bartlett	Plymouth	7
1836	09	*Marmion*	s	Hopper	London	66
1836	09	*Mary*	bg	Morton	Liverpool	32
1836	09	*Rajah*	bk	McCoy	Liverpool	185
1836	10	*Bolivar*	bk	Richards	Plymouth	19
1836	10	*Toronto*	s	Collinson	London	29
1837	05	*Brighton*	bk	Sedman	Liverpool	39
1837	05	*Caroline*	bk	Hopper	London	29
1837	05	*Caroline*	bg	Loweryson	Berwick	6
1837	05	*Cybele*	bk	Heckler	Bridgwater	6
1837	05	*Edward*	bk	McKenzie	Plymouth	66
1837	05	*Hero*	s	Trailer	Bristol	67

Forty-five passengers had been assisted by the Earl of Heytesbury to emigrate. All were tenants on his Wiltshire estate.

Year	Month	Vessel	Type	Master	Departure Port	Passenger Numbers
1837	05	*Llan Romney*	s	Simpson	Hull	12
1837	05	*Orlando*	bk	Blair, Thomas	London	7
1837	05	*Posthorn*	bk	Liddle	London	11
1837	05	*Restitution*	bk	Moon	Plymouth	13
1837	06	*Andrew Marvel*	bk	Wright	Hull	94
1837	06	*Atalanta*	bg	Day	Bristol	40
1837	06	*Auxiliary*	bg	Patterson	London	95
1837	06	*Baltic*	bg	Newson	Yarmouth	172
1837	06	*Benjamin*	bg	Pate	London	12
1837	06	*Brothers*	bg	Bell	Liverpool	21
1837	06	*Carron*	bg	Elliott	Yarmouth	193
1837	06	*Centurion*	bg	Hepenstall	Scarborough	21
1837	06	*Charlotte*	bg	Biggs	Liverpool	223
1837	06	*Diana*	bg	Lane, Edward	Plymouth	199

Petworth settlers from West Sussex. For a reconstructed passenger list (partial) see The Ships List website.

Year	Month	Vessel	Type	Master	Departure Port	Passenger Numbers
1837	06	*Dykes* of Maryport	bg	Sharp	Maryport	26

Year	Month	Vessel	Type	Master	Departure Port	Passenger Numbers
1837	06	*Earl of Aberdeen*	bg	Milne	Maryport	12
1837	06	*George*	bk	Day	London	239
1837	06	*Jane*	bg	Collins	Maryport	7
1837	06	*Maida*	s	Willis	Hull	16
1837	06	*Margaret*	s	Chalmers	Liverpool	280
1837	06	*Mary*	bk	Hamilton	Liverpool	168
1837	06	*Medusa*	s.s.	Robinson	Liverpool	222
1837	06	*Nelson Wood*	bg	Robinson	London	68

Also seven in the cabin.

Year	Month	Vessel	Type	Master	Departure Port	Passenger Numbers
1837	06	*New Eagle*	bk	Lovering	Plymouth	43
1837	06	*Preston*	bg	Fish	Yarmouth	112
1837	06	*Prince Leopold*	bg	Richardson	Berwick	13
1837	06	*Symmetry*	bg	Thompson	Sunderland	34
1837	06	*Triton*	bk	Keighley	Hull	25
1837	06	*Usk*	bk	Prouse	Dartmouth	14

Also six cabin passengers.

Year	Month	Vessel	Type	Master	Departure Port	Passenger Numbers
1837	06	*Venus*	bg	Simmonds	Yarmouth	140
1837	06	*Victory*	s	Gowan	Liverpool	26
1837	06*	*Berwick Castle*	n/k	n/k	Berwick	33

Berwick Advertiser, June 25, 1842, described the *Berwick Castle* as "this beautiful barque," which "had been visited by large parties of respectable persons." It had "a between deck space of six and a half feet," and a captain "experienced in the American trade, who has crossed the Atlantic nearly 30 times." The passengers were "agriculturalists and mechanics who plan to go to the Canadas."

Year	Month	Vessel	Type	Master	Departure Port	Passenger Numbers
1837	07	*Brightman*	bk	Nockets	London	162
1837	07	*Brunswick*	bk	Atkinson	London	258

Passengers included twenty-one paupers from Purton in Wiltshire.

Year	Month	Vessel	Type	Master	Departure Port	Passenger Numbers
1837	07	*Caledonia*	bk	Pilcher	Liverpool	214
1837	07	*Cornubia*	bk	Ward	Liverpool	293
1837	07	*Elden*	s	Warren	Plymouth	255
1837	07	*Fairfield*	bk	Slack	Liverpool	87
1837	07	*General Gascoigne*	s	Kendall	Liverpool	27

Year	Month	Vessel	Type	Master	Departure Port	Passenger Numbers
1837	07	*Norfolk*	s	Harrison	Berwick	41
1837	07	*Sceptre*	bg	Anderson	Newcastle	25
1837	07	*Sultana*	s	Sampson	Whitby	71
1837	07	*Venture*	bk	Wilson	Liverpool	58
1837	07	*Victory*	bk	Pecket, Joseph	Hull	127
1837	07	*William Ritchie*	s	Rodgers	Liverpool	265
1837	08	*British Merchant*	bk	Curry	Liverpool	274
1837	08	*Emulous*	bg	Welbank	Liverpool	10
1837	08	*Hope*	bg	Middleton	Maryport	6
1837	09	*Captain Ross*	bk	Morton	Liverpool	25
1837	09	*Hero*	s	Trait	Bristol	7
1837	09	*Robert Thomas*	s	Grandy	Liverpool	11
1837	10	*Thomas Ritchie*	bk	Moorson	Bristol	3
1837	10	*Toronto*	s	Collinson	London	15

Also carried thirten cabin passengers.

Year	Month	Vessel	Type	Master	Departure Port	Passenger Numbers
1838	05	*Andrew Marvel*	bk	Wright	Hull	33
1838	05	*Baltic*	bg	Cordran	Yarmouth	32
1838	05	*Cambrian*	s	Dring	Hull	10
1838	05	*Cato*	bk	Cork	Plymouth	17

Four in cabin.

Year	Month	Vessel	Type	Master	Departure Port	Passenger Numbers
1838	05	*Devereaux*	bg	Eskdale	Liverpool	5
1838	05	*Emmanuel*	s	Dearness	London	9

Five in cabin.

Year	Month	Vessel	Type	Master	Departure Port	Passenger Numbers
1838	05	*Evergreen*	bk	Moran	Liverpool	8
1838	05	*Lian Romney*	s	Simpson	Hull	5
1838	05	*Marchioness of Abercorn*	bk	Webster	London	40

Two in cabin.

Year	Month	Vessel	Type	Master	Departure Port	Passenger Numbers
1838	05	*Norfolk*	s	Krugie	Berwick	7
1838	05	*Procris*	bg	Arnold	Poole	52

Year	Month	Vessel	Type	Master	Departure Port	Passenger Numbers
1838	05	*Royal Adelaide* of Fowey	bk	Vivian, J.	Falmouth	17
1838	05	*Stately*	s	Neagle	London	36

Also two in cabin.

Year	Month	Vessel	Type	Master	Departure Port	Passenger Numbers
1838	05	*Toronto*	s	Douglas	London	17

Also fifteen in cabin.

Year	Month	Vessel	Type	Master	Departure Port	Passenger Numbers
1838	06	*Branken*	bg	Moor	London	7

Three in cabin.

Year	Month	Vessel	Type	Master	Departure Port	Passenger Numbers
1838	06	*Calcutta*	s	McLean	Liverpool	7
1838	06	*Combatant*	bg	Hamilton	Liverpool	140
1838	06	*Venus*	bg	Simmonds	Yarmouth	17

One cabin passenger.

Year	Month	Vessel	Type	Master	Departure Port	Passenger Numbers
1838	06	*Victory*	bk	Pecket, Joseph	Hull	29

Two in cabin.

Year	Month	Vessel	Type	Master	Departure Port	Passenger Numbers
1838	07	*Hibernia*	s	Fowler	London	193

Thirteen in cabin.

Year	Month	Vessel	Type	Master	Departure Port	Passenger Numbers
1838	08	*Banffshire*	s	Pitcairn	Liverpool	134
1838	08	*Cumberland*	bk	Power	Liverpool	34
1838	08	*John & James*	bk	Dale	Plymouth	18
1838	08	*Nereid*	bg	Longford	London	24
1838	09	*Prince George*	s	Forster	London	18
1838	10	*Toronto*	s	Douglas	London	12

Also carried eighteen cabin passengers.

Year	Month	Vessel	Type	Master	Departure Port	Passenger Numbers
1839	05	*Aurelian*	s	Forbes	Liverpool	10
1839	05	*Effort*	bk	Rees	Milford	16
1839	05	*Llan Romney*	s	Simpson	Hull	13
1839	05	*Marchioness of Aberdeen*	bk	Hagarty	Hull	93
1839	05	*Oscar*	bg	Field	Dartmouth	8
1839	05	*Voluna* of Padstow	bg	Seaton	Padstow	9
1839	05	*Wellington*	bg	Forster	Newcastle	7

Year	Month	Vessel	Type	Master	Departure Port	Passenger Numbers
1839	06	*Napoleon*	s	Montgomery	Liverpool	297

Also thirteen cabin passengers.

Year	Month	Vessel	Type	Master	Departure Port	Passenger Numbers
1839	07	*Robert Alexander*	bk	Parke	Liverpool	189
1839	07	*Victory*	bk	Pecket, Joseph	Hull	36
1839	08	*Actress*	s	Thule	Liverpool	29
1839	08	*Calcutta*	bk	Napier	Plymouth	25
1839	08	*Margaret*	s	Chalmers	Liverpool	129
1839	08	*Resolution* of Penzance	bg	Davis	London	22
1839	08	*Urania*	bg	Rohann	London	17
1839	09	*Ludlow*	bk	Thom	London	12
1839	09	*Margaret*	bg	Wakeham	Bristol	11
1839	09	*Mary*	bk	Laing	London	22

Also two in cabin.

Year	Month	Vessel	Type	Master	Departure Port	Passenger Numbers
1840	05	*Amazon*	s	Broderick	Hull	18
1840	05	*Andrew Marvel*	bk	Chambers	Hull	10
1840	05	*Clio* of Padstow	bk	Brown, T.	Padstow	146
1840	05	*Don*	bk	Muir	Liverpool	36
1840	05	*Independent*	bk	Morris	Liverpool	257
1840	05	*John & Jane*	bk	Dale	Plymouth	65
1840	05	*Llan Romney*	s	n/k	Hull	57
1840	05	*Mariner*	bk	Bartlett	Portsmouth	8
1840	05	*Marmion*	bk	Harrison	London	9
1840	05	*Modeley*	bg	Crawford	Newcastle	9
1840	05	*Providence*	s	Wilson	Hull	13
1840	05	*Robert Watson*	bk	Elliott	Bristol	13
1840	05	*Sophia*	bk	Leslie	Liverpool	17

Seamen.

Year	Month	Vessel	Type	Master	Departure Port	Passenger Numbers
1840	05	*Tamarlane*	s	Fisher	Liverpool	72
1840	05	*Thomas*	s	Worthingon	Liverpool	280
1840	05	*Thomas Ritchie*	bk	Thrift	Bridgwater	8

Year	Month	Vessel	Type	Master	Departure Port	Passenger Numbers
1840	05	*Voluna* of Padstow	bg	Seaton	Padstow	15
1840	06	*Aurora*	bk	Hick	Plymouth	10
1840	06	*Baltic*	bg	Cawdrie, W.	Yarmouth	37
1840	06	*Chester*	s	Lawson	Liverpool	90
1840	06	*Dykes* of Maryport	bg	Harrison	Maryport	19
1840	06	*George*	s	Rae	Liverpool	377
1840	06	*George Wilkinson*	bk	Brown	Liverpool	260
1840	06	*Imogene*	bg	Hick	Sunderland	9
1840	06	*Jane & Barbara*	s	Colman	Bristol	9
1840	06	*John & Robert*	s	McKechnie	Liverpool	379
1840	06	*Leander*	s	Phelan	Liverpool	250
1840	06	*Pyrenees*	bg	Warman	Liverpool	134
1840	06	*Urania*	bg	Robson	London	120
1840	07	*Anna Liffey*	bk	Dady	Liverpool	294
1840	07	*Catherine*	s	Mason, George	Liverpool	306
1840	07	*Clyde*	bk	Reid	London	52

Also sixty-seven men of the Royal Artillery.

Year	Month	Vessel	Type	Master	Departure Port	Passenger Numbers
1840	07	*Robert Burns*	bg	Messenger	Liverpool	134
1840	07	*Victory*	bk	Pecket, Joseph	Hull	73
1840	07*	*Clio* of Padstow	bk	Brown, T.	Padstow	n/k
1840	08	*Carlton Packet*	sr	Landry	Carlisle	17
1840	08	*Cumberland*	bk	Power	Liverpool	44

Forty-one steerage, three cabin.

Year	Month	Vessel	Type	Master	Departure Port	Passenger Numbers
1840	08	*Serepta*	bg	Buck	London	19
1840	08	*Sir George Prevost*	bk	Mackay	Liverpool	271
1840	08	*Winscales*	bk	Connolly	Maryport	45

All proceeding to settle near Toronto and Hamilton.

Year	Month	Vessel	Type	Master	Departure Port	Passenger Numbers
1840	09	*Clio* of Padstow	bk	Brown, T.	Padstow	68
1840	09	*Mary Ann Halton*	bk	Vere	Liverpool	57
1840	09	*Ocean Queen*	s	Pitcairn	Liverpool	28
1840	09	*Queen*	bk	Thomson	London	18
1840	09	*Thomas Ritchie*	bk	Thrift	Bridgwater	12
1840	10	*John & Mary*	bg	Harvey, A.	Padstow	23
1840	10	*R. Watson*	bk	Elliott	Bristol	6
1840	10	*Toronto*	s	Morgan, D.	London	6
1841	04*	*Baltic*	n/k	n/k	Yarmouth	32
1841	04*	*Calonia*	n/k	n/k	Gloucester	73

One death on voyage.

Year	Month	Vessel	Type	Master	Departure Port	Passenger Numbers
1841	04*	*Jean Rumney*	n/k	n/k	Hull	99

Two deaths on voyage.

Year	Month	Vessel	Type	Master	Departure Port	Passenger Numbers
1841	04*	*Velania*	n/k	n/k	Padstow	52
1841	04*	*Victoria*	n/k	n/k	Truro	40
1841	05	*Aberdeen*	s	Duggan	Liverpool	46
1841	05	*Ann Jeffery*	n/k	Edwards	Liverpool	253

Nine deaths on voyage.

Year	Month	Vessel	Type	Master	Departure Port	Passenger Numbers
1841	05	*Baltic*	bg	Cawdrie, W.	Yarmouth	32
1841	05	*Clio* of Padstow	bk	Brown, T.	Padstow	251

Departed in April.

Year	Month	Vessel	Type	Master	Departure Port	Passenger Numbers
1841	05	*Collina*	bk	Marshall	Gloucester	73

One death on voyage.

Year	Month	Vessel	Type	Master	Departure Port	Passenger Numbers
1841	05	*Falcon*	n/k	n/k	Bideford	162

Departed in April. Two deaths on voyage.

Year	Month	Vessel	Type	Master	Departure Port	Passenger Numbers
1841	05	*John & Mary*	bg	Harvey, A.	Padstow	108

Departed in April.

Year	Month	Vessel	Type	Master	Departure Port	Passenger Numbers
1841	05	*John & James*	bk	n/k	Plymouth	30

Departed in April.

Year	Month	Vessel	Type	Master	Departure Port	Passenger Numbers
1841	05	*Leander*	s	Phelan	Liverpool	62

Departed in April. One death on voyage.

Year	Month	Vessel	Type	Master	Departure Port	Passenger Numbers
1841	05	*Llan Romney*	s	Simpson	Hull	99

Two deaths on voyage.

Year	Month	Vessel	Type	Master	Departure Port	Passenger Numbers
1841	05	*Minstrel*	n/k	n/k	Liverpool	130

Departed in April. Two deaths on voyage, one in quarantine.

Year	Month	Vessel	Type	Master	Departure Port	Passenger Numbers
1841	05	*Newland*	n/k	Lickis	Hull	52

Departed in April.

Year	Month	Vessel	Type	Master	Departure Port	Passenger Numbers
1841	05	*Prince George*	s	Friend, D.	London	190

Departed in April. Two deaths on voyage. The vessel carried fifteen people who boarded at London and who were assisted by their parishes plus 116 passengers who embarked at Gravesend, "sent out by Lord Portman from his estates in Dorsetshire and Kent"; it also carried fifty-nine people from the House of Industry, Isle of Wight. [PP 1842(301)XXXI]

Year	Month	Vessel	Type	Master	Departure Port	Passenger Numbers
1841	05	*Spring Flower* of Padstow	bg	Simmers	Padstow	33

Departed April.

Year	Month	Vessel	Type	Master	Departure Port	Passenger Numbers
1841	05	*Thomas Ritchie*	bk	n/k	Bridgwater	100

Departed April.

Year	Month	Vessel	Type	Master	Departure Port	Passenger Numbers
1841	05	*Voluna* of Padstow	bg	Easthope, R.	Padstow	52

Departed April. Apply Mr. Seaton (vessel owner) Padstow.

Year	Month	Vessel	Type	Master	Departure Port	Passenger Numbers
1841	05*	*Canadian*	n/k	n/k	London	42
1841	05*	*Harmony*	n/k	n/k	Bristol	83
1841	06	*Horatio*	n/k	n/k	Stockton	33

Departed in April.

Year	Month	Vessel	Type	Master	Departure Port	Passenger Numbers
1841	06*	*Iona*	n/k	n/k	Liverpool	73

One death on voyage.

Year	Month	Vessel	Type	Master	Departure Port	Passenger Numbers
1841	06	*Lady Fitzherbert*	n/k	n/k	Plymouth	135

Departed in May. Principally farmers and going to the Western District.

1841	06	*Oberon*	n/k	n/k	Liverpool	259

Departed in April.

1841	06	*Princess Victoria*	n/k	n/k	Liverpool	292

Departed May. Three deaths on voyage. Possibly 133 passengers embarked at Liverpool and the remainder collected from Ireland.

1841	07	*Albinia*	n/k	n/k	Liverpool	245

Departed in May. One death on voyage.

1841	07	*Centenary*	n/k	n/k	London	158

Departed in May. Four deaths on voyage.

1841	07	*George Marsden*	bk	Eilley, J.	Rye	213

Fourteen deaths, one in quarantine. Mainly labourers and farmers who were assisted to emigrate by their respective parishes in Sussex and Kent.

1841	07	*Grace*	n/k	n/k	Liverpool	303

Departed in May. Seven deaths on voyage.

1841	07	*Huron*	s	Sibbens, A.	Liverpool	334

Departed in June. Four children died on the voyage. A few were going to the United States; about eighteen were leaving at the Lower Ports. Twenty-five are respectable Scotch passengers, who are going to Toronto, and there were also a few English families from Newcastle.

1841	07	*Nelson*	n/k	n/k	Liverpool	74

Departed in April.

1841	07	*Victory*	bk	Pecket, Joseph	Hull	84

Departed May. Twenty-four of the passengers were assisted. Went to Toronto, Hamilton, Whitby and Pickering.

1841	08	*Abercromby*	bk	Louttit, G.	Liverpool	112

Left Liverpool in June. One death from typhus; nine were sent to hospital. Passengers

Year	Month	Vessel	Type	Master	Departure Port	Passenger Numbers

going to Hamilton, in the township of West Flamboro; some to the River Trent, and the remainder to Toronto and Kingston; some of the young men wish to go to Saint John, New Brunswick.

| 1841 | 08 | *Alicia* | n/k | Gaskin, Robert | Plymouth | 6 |

Went to Goderich.

| 1841 | 08 | *Catherine* | s | Mason, George | Liverpool | 286 |

Five deaths, one in quarantine. Some to remain in Quebec, to take up employment on the roads; one family, twelve in number, went to their friends in Waterloo, in Shefford Township, Lower Canada, while the rest are going to different parts of Upper Canada.

| 1841 | 08 | *Clio of Padstow* | bk | Brown, T. | Padstow | 75 |

Departed in July. Included two families, fourteen in number, whose passage was paid by their parish.

| 1841 | 08 | *Dee* | bk | Reid, James | Bristol | 65 |

Departed in June. Eight passengers were assisted by their parishes. Heading for the Western division of the province.

| 1841 | 08 | *Hector* | bg | Patten, David | Liverpool | 80 |

Departed in July. Some went to Montreal, the remainder to the Western District.

| 1841 | 08 | *Independence* | s | McCappin | Liverpool | 242 |

Departed in June. Three deaths, one in quarantine. Several families are going to settle in the Bathurst District at Bytown (Ottawa) and Perth; others are going to to Dumfries and Port Talbot.

| 1841 | 08 | *Marquis of Wellesley* | bk | Laing, James | Liverpool | 54 |

Departed in June. Most passengers going to the Western division of the province; one family going to Guelph.

| 1841 | 08 | *Orlando* | bk | Blair, Thomas | London | 102 |

Departed in June. Eighty passengers were assisted by their parishes. Some are proceeding to Belleville, and the remainder are going to different parts of the Western District.

| 1841 | 08* | *Collina* | bk | n/k | Gloucester | 77 |
| 1841 | 09 | *Agenoria* | s | Giffney | Liverpool | 149 |

Departed in August. Five deaths at sea, one in hospital.

Year	Month	Vessel	Type	Master	Departure Port	Passenger Numbers
1841	09	*Belle* of Padstow	bk	Brewer, G.	Padstow	39

Departed in August. All intend to settle in the Western District.

Year	Month	Vessel	Type	Master	Departure Port	Passenger Numbers
1841	09	*Cate*	bk	Taylor, Joseph	Falmouth	14
1841	09	*Culdee*	bk	Campbell, John	London	31
1841	09	*Cumberland*	bk	Power	Liverpool	15
1841	09	*Nestor*	bk	Smith, Pater	Plymouth	19
1841	09	*Sovereign*	n/k	Marklan	Hull	12

Three of the tradesmen to remain in Quebec for employment and the remainder heading for Upper Canada.

Year	Month	Vessel	Type	Master	Departure Port	Passenger Numbers
1841	09	*Vittoria*	bk	Simpson, Mosey	Plymouth	19
1841	10	*Parmella*	bk	Maxwell, Robert	Liverpool	6
1841	10	*Souter Johnny*	bk	Little, Thomas	Liverpool	29

Departed September with thirty-two passengers. May have been three deaths during the voyage.

Year	Month	Vessel	Type	Master	Departure Port	Passenger Numbers
1842	04*	*Ruby*	bk	Coltman, T.	Fowey	n/k
1842	04*	*Sylvanus* of Truro	bk	Lang, W.	Truro	n/k

Advertised in February for passengers going to Charlottetown and Quebec. Reported in July to have carried 150 passengers to Charlottetown. Number taken to Quebec unknown.

Year	Month	Vessel	Type	Master	Departure Port	Passenger Numbers
1842	05	*Aberdeen*	s	Duffy	Liverpool	371

Farmers, labourers, and mechanics. Some to Gosford Road (Eastern Townships) to work; remainder going to Montreal, Bytown (Ottawa), and Cobourg.

Year	Month	Vessel	Type	Master	Departure Port	Passenger Numbers
1842	05	*Andrew Marvel*	bk	Chambers	Hull	106

Farmers and labourers. To settle in Upper Canada.

Year	Month	Vessel	Type	Master	Departure Port	Passenger Numbers
1842	05	*Andrew White*	n/k	Cawsey, H.	Liverpool	6

Labourers, farmers, and mechanics going to Kingston, Belleville, Port Hope, and Toronto.

Year	Month	Vessel	Type	Master	Departure Port	Passenger Numbers
1842	05	*Belle* of Padstow	bk	Brewwer, G.	Padstow	252

Carried nineteen paupers. Passengers proceeding to Bytown (Ottawa), Kingston, Prescott, and Toronto; a few are going to the United States.

Year	Month	Vessel	Type	Master	Departure Port	Passenger Numbers
1842	05	*Charlotte*	n/k	Ferrie, J.	Lancaster	22

Mainly agricultural labourers; a few farmers and mechanics. Some to remain in Quebec and Montreal; the remainder heading to Kingston, Colborne, Prescott, and Toronto.

Year	Month	Vessel	Type	Master	Departure Port	Passenger Numbers
1842	05	*Clio* of Padstow	bk	Easthope, R.	Padstow	339

Farmers, mechanics, and labourers who are proceeding to the London District, Port Hope, and Peterborough; a few are going to Gosford Road.

Year	Month	Vessel	Type	Master	Departure Port	Passenger Numbers
1842	05	*Delia*	n/k	n/k	Plymouth	102

Farmers and labourers. Proceeding to Canada West; a few to the United States.

Year	Month	Vessel	Type	Master	Departure Port	Passenger Numbers
1842	05	*Edward*	bk	McKenzie	Plymouth	195

Includes nine paupers.

Year	Month	Vessel	Type	Master	Departure Port	Passenger Numbers
1842	05	*Emmanuel*	n/k	Pearson, J.	Bristol	47

Includes nineteen paupers. Mostly agricultural labourers; a few farmers and mechanics. A few to remain in Quebec and Montreal; remainder to Kingston, Colborne, Prescott, and Toronto.

Year	Month	Vessel	Type	Master	Departure Port	Passenger Numbers
1842	05	*Fergus*	bk	Blythe, W.	Liverpool	292

Labourers, farmers, and mechanics going to Kingston, Belleville, Port Hope, and Toronto.

Year	Month	Vessel	Type	Master	Departure Port	Passenger Numbers
1842	05	*Llan Romney*	s	Simpson	Hull	129

Farmers and mechanics. Proceeding to Montreal, Kingston, Bytown (Ottawa), and Toronto.

Year	Month	Vessel	Type	Master	Departure Port	Passenger Numbers
1842	05	*Prince George*	s	Friend, D.	London	262

Includes 219 paupers assisted by their parishes to emigrate. Tradesmen to find work in Quebec; farm labourers going to Kingston, Lanark, Guelph, and Hamilton.

Year	Month	Vessel	Type	Master	Departure Port	Passenger Numbers
1842	05	*Rainbow*	n/k	n/k	London	5

Mechanics seeking employment in Quebec.

Year	Month	Vessel	Type	Master	Departure Port	Passenger Numbers
1842	05	*Rockshire*	n/k	n/k	Liverpool	103

Farmers, labourers, and tradesmen. Proceeding to Montreal, Kingston, Bytown (Ottawa), and Toronto.

Year	Month	Vessel	Type	Master	Departure Port	Passenger Numbers
1842	05	*Royal Adelaide* of Fowey	bk	Leuty, T.	Fowey	100

Includes nine paupers. Mechanics, labourers, farmers, and servants. Some to Montreal, others to Kingston, Port Hope, and Darlington; a few to the United States.

1842	05	*Spermacetti*	bk	Moon, E.	Plymouth	260

Agricultural labourers, mechanics, and farmers; proceeding to Toronto and Lake Simcoe; a few to remain in Quebec and Montreal; remainder going to West Upper Canada.

1842	05	*Vittoria*	bk	Simpson, Mosey	Fowey	113

Includes fourteen paupers. Mechanics, labourers, farmers, and servants. Some to Montreal, others to Kingston, Port Hope, and Darlington; a few to the United States.

1842	05	*Winscales*	n/k	n/k	Liverpool	11

Tradesmen who are proceeding to Bytown (Ottawa), Kingston, Prescott, and Toronto; a few to the United States.

1842	05*	*Spring Flower* of Padstow	bg	n/k	Padstow	30

Vessel was forced to return to Padstow.

1842	06	*Cosmopodite*	n/k	Webber	Plymouth	157

Principally labourers, a few farmers; they went to Bytown (Ottawa), Kingston, Toronto, and Hamilton.

1842	06	*Dahlia*	bk	Robinson	Plymouth	16
1842	06	*Dependent*	bk	Dobson, E.	Bridgwater	98

Fifty-two paupers were sent by the Chard [Poor Law] Union in Somerset. Most of the passengers intend settling in the Western District, while a good many of the paupers intend to go to the United States.

1842	06	*Edmund*	bk	Dobson	London	84
1842	06	*Irvine*		n/k	Bristol	n/k

Included among the passengers were four families (thirty-two in number) who were assisted by their parish to emigrate.

Year	Month	Vessel	Type	Master	Departure Port	Passenger Numbers
1842	06	*Lord Canterbury*	bk	Tripp, J.	Bristol	273

Includes fifty-four paupers who were assisted by their parishes. Mostly farmers, servants, labourers, and mechanics. Going to Kingston, Prescott, Niagara, Toronto, and Hamilton.

1842	06	*Priscilla*	bk	Taylor	Plymouth	106

Chiefly labourers and a few tradesmen. Some to the United States; remainder to Canada West.

1842	06	*Pusey Hall*	bk	Ware	London	171

All paupers assisted by their respective parishes.

1842	07	*Amazon*	s	Picket, J.	Hull	61

Most are going to Ohio in the United States; one family are proceeding to Hamilton and some are going to Toronto.

1842	07	*Ann*	n/k	Cossman, J.	Plymouth	93

Labourers, a few servants, and farmers; all proceeding to Kingston, Bytown (Ottawa), Toronto, and Brockville.

1842	07	*Arcturus*	sw	Hill, David	London	60

Includes forty-eight paupers who were assisted by their parishes to emigrate.

1842	07	*Baltic*	bg	Cawdrie, W.	Yarmouth	24

Labourers; all went to Canada West.

1842	07	*Bragila*	bk	Hale, C.	Falmouth	37

Farmers, mechanics, and labourers; proceeding to Blenheim and Brantford townships, Toronto, and other parts of Upper Canada.

1842	07	*Caledonia*	n/k	Livingford, T.	Liverpool	448

Farmers, mechanics, and labourers; proceeding to Blenheim and Brantford townships, Toronto, and other parts of Upper Canada.

1842	07	*Consbrooke*	n/k	Pollock, J.	Liverpool	103

Mechanics and labourers; all going to Canada West.

1842	07	*Don*	n/k	Muir	Liverpool	248

Farmers, mechanics, and labourers; proceeding to Blenham and Brantford townships, Toronto, and other parts of Upper Canada.

Year	Month	Vessel	Type	Master	Departure Port	Passenger Numbers
1842	07	*George Glen*	n/k	McBride, R.	Liverpool	32

Mostly labourers and some mechanics; proceeding to Kingston, Toronto, and Winchester in eastern Upper Canada.

1842	07	*Imogene*	n/k	Hicks	London	22

Farmers, servants, labourers, and tradesmen; going to Manchester (Durham County), Cornwall (eastern Upper Canada), and other parts of Canada West; some to the United States.

1842	07	*James & Mary Sinnott*	n/k	Connot, P.	London	75

All proceeding to Canada West.

1842	07	*Jessie*	n/k	Horn, J.	Liverpool	104

Farmers, labourers, and mechanics; some going to Kingston and Toronto, some to Caledon and St. Catharines, where they have friends; several going to the Eastern Townships.

1842	07	*Mary*	n/k	Kelso, J.	London	32

Farmers, labourers, and a few tradesmen; one family went to New Ireland in Lower Canada; remainder going to the Upper Province.

1842	07	*Meteor*	bg	Brown, D.	Hull	68

Farmers and labourers; all went to Canada West.

1842	07	*Orbit*	bk	Robinson	London	217

Includes 194 paupers. Farmers, servants, labourers, and tradesmen going to Manchester (Durham County), Cornwall (eastern Upper Canada), and other parts of Canada West; some to the United States.

1842	07	*Port Glasgow*	bk	Blandford, J.	Poole	13

Farmers, labourers, and a few tradesmen; one family went to New Ireland in Canada East; remainder to the Upper Province.

1842	07	*Saphiras*	n/k	Brown, R.	Stockton	94

Mechanics, labourers, and servants; going to Belleville, Kingston, and Toronto; some also going to the United States.

1842	07	*Sherbrooke*	n/k	Gray, A.	Liverpool	202

Labourers, a few servants, and farmers; all proceeding to Kingston, Bytown (Ottawa), Toronto, and Brockville.

Year	Month	Vessel	Type	Master	Departure Port	Passenger Numbers
1842	07	*Silvanus*	n/k	Ocack, J.	Falmouth	133

Agricultural labourers; several went to Illinois (U.S.A.); some went to Gosford Road; many to Eastern Townships and remainder to Upper Canada.

1842	07	*Susannah*	n/k	Hippell, J.	London	15

Farmers.

1842	07	*Victoria*	n/k	McMahon	Liverpool	467

Labourers, a few servants and farmers; all proceeding to Kingston, Bytown (Ottawa), Toronto, and Brockville.

1842	07*	*Alchymist* of Falmouth	bk	Hill	Falmouth	n/k
1842	08	*Berwick Castle*	n/k	Forster, J.	Berwick	33

Labourers, mechanics, a few farmers, and servants who are proceeding to the upper province; some are going to Bytown (Ottawa), Niagara, and Toronto.

1842	08	*Cato*	n/k	Benson, C.	Plymouth	71

Farmers, labourers, and mechanics; who are going to Montreal and Kingston; one family, ten in number, is going to United States.

1842	08	*City of Waterford*	n/k	McGrath	Liverpool	79

Labourers, mechanics, a few farmers, and servants; proceeding to the upper province; some going to Bytown (Ottawa), Niagara, and Toronto; a few are going to join friends and relations in Ohio. (U.S.A.).

1842	08	*Edinburgh*	n/k	Lawson, E.	Liverpool	300

Farmers, labourers, and mechanics; proceeding to Beverly (Wentworth County), Ramsay (Lanark County), Yonge (Leeds County), and Adelaide (Middlesex County); five families went to Prince Edward Island; others to Montreal, Kingston, and Toronto; some to Troy near Hamilton.

1842	08	*Emerald*	n/k	Flegg, W.	London	19

Farmers, mechanics, and labourers.

1842	08	*Huron*	s	Sibbens, A.	Liverpool	154

Farmers, labourers, mechanics and servants. Proceeding to Canada West; a few to find employment at the Gosford Road; three families going to the Eastern Townships.

Year	Month	Vessel	Type	Master	Departure Port	Passenger Numbers
1842	08	*John and Robert*	n/k	McKechnie	Liverpool	152

Tradesmen, farmers, and labourers; proceeding to the London, Gore, Home, and Midland districts; a few of the passengers are going to the Gosford Road.

1842	08	*Mountaineer*	n/k	Stickney	Liverpool	473

Farmers, mechanics, and labourers; a few will remain in Montreal to join relations; the remainder to proceed to Bytown (Ottawa), Kingston, Port Hope, Dundas, and Brockville. Also, some to Buckingham in Lower Canada.

1842	08	*Reward*	n/k	Frost, B.	Hull	22

Labourers, farmers, and mechanics; proceeding to St. Vincent (near Barrie), county of Simcoe, and other parts of Canada West.

1842	08*	*Emmanuel*	n/k	n/k	Bristol	18
1842	08*	*Triton* of Penzance	bk	Wakeham, R. J.	Penzance	n/k
1842	09	*Ann*	n/k	Williamson	London	10
1842	09	*Belle* of Padstow	bk	Brewer, G.	Padstow	71

Seventy-one passengers signed testimonial praising the captain. Farmers, labourers, and tradesmen who are proceeding to Kingston, Whitby, and Lancaster (eastern Upper Canada).

1842	09	*Bows*	n/k	Flemming, A.	London	60

Labourers and mechanics proceeding to Canada West.

1842	09	*Clio* of Padstow	bk	Brown, J.	Padstow	118

Mechanics, farmers, and labourers who are proceeding to Bytown (Ottawa), Whitby, and Darlington; one family is going to Ohio.

1842	09	*Collina*	bk	Marshall	Gloucester	50

Farmers and mechanics, respectable people, in good circumstances, who are going to join relations in Toronto and Hamilton.

1842	09	*Dahlia*	bk	Hooper, J.	Plymouth	20

Labourers and tradesmen who are going to join friends in Upper Canada.

Year	Month	Vessel	Type	Master	Departure Port	Passenger Numbers
1842	09	*Eliza*	n/k	Vandervold	London	81

Farmers, labourers, and mechanics who are proceeding to Canada West. Includes thirty-five paupers from Brinkworth Parish in Wiltshire who were assisted by their parish to emigrate. List of names appears as Table 8.

| 1842 | 09 | *Ellergill* | n/k | Hill, R. | Hull | 12 |

Mechanics, farmers, and labourers who are proceeding to Bytown (Ottawa), Whitby, and Darlington; one family is going to Ohio.

| 1842 | 09 | *Fullentire* | n/k | White | Liverpool | 11 |

Farmers, labourers, and mechanics; some are going to Bytown (Ottawa), Kingston, and Toronto; the remainder are going to Goderich, Gore, and London districts.

| 1842 | 09 | *Ipswich* | n/k | Smith, J. | Plymouth | 81 |

Farmers, mechanics, and labourers; some families are going to Cobourg and Port Hope while others intend to join relations in the United States.

| 1842 | 09 | *Nelson Wood* | bg | Ball, W. | Liverpool | 96 |

Labourers, mechanics, and farmers who are proceeding to Warwick near Lake Huron, Bytown (Ottawa), Kingston, Toronto, and London district; two families to settle in Saint John, New Brunswick.

| 1842 | 09 | *Roseberry* | n/k | Young | London | 13 |

Seven paupers; one family, seven in number, assisted by their parish to emigrate.

| 1842 | 09 | *Sarah* | n/k | McLean | Liverpool | 144 |

Farmers, labourers, and tradesmen; a few will remain in Montreal; one family is going to join relations in Philadelphia; remainder are proceeding to Bytown (Ottawa), Aylmer (near Hull), Toronto, and Hamilton.

| 1842 | 09 | *Souter Johnny* | bk | Little, Thomas | Liverpool | 11 |

Farmers, labourers, and tradesmen; a few will remain in Montreal; one family is going to join relations in Philadelphia; remainder proceeding to Bytown (Ottawa), Aylmer (near Hull), Toronto, and Hamilton.

| 1842 | 09 | *Susan* | n/k | Cant, R. | London | 93 |

Eighty paupers, all labourers who are proceeding to Upper Canada.

| 1842 | 09 | *Watermillock* | n/k | Cower | Bristol | 7 |

Farm labourers; a few will remain in Montreal; remainder going to Upper Canada.

Year	Month	Vessel	Type	Master	Departure Port	Passenger Numbers
1842	09*	*Mary Ann*	n/k	n/k	Bideford	40
1842	09*	*Merchant*	n/k	n/k	Bristol	27
1842	10	*Aberdeen*	s	Duffy	Liverpool	36

Farmers, labourers, and mechanics; who are proceeding to Canada West.

Year	Month	Vessel	Type	Master	Departure Port	Passenger Numbers
1842	10	*Adelaide*	n/k	Gale	Liverpool	35

Farmers and labourers; going to Montreal, Port Hope, Toronto, and Whitby.

Year	Month	Vessel	Type	Master	Departure Port	Passenger Numbers
1842	10	*Brunette*	bk	Thompson	Liverpool	10

Farmers who are proceeding to Canada West.

Year	Month	Vessel	Type	Master	Departure Port	Passenger Numbers
1842	10	*Cornwall*	bk	Richards, J.	Falmouth	23

Farmers going to Canada West.

Year	Month	Vessel	Type	Master	Departure Port	Passenger Numbers
1842	10	*Cosmopodite*	n/k	Webber	Plymouth	7

Labourers who are to remain in Quebec.

Year	Month	Vessel	Type	Master	Departure Port	Passenger Numbers
1842	10	*Crusader*	n/k	Wheatley	London	14

Farmers, all proceeding to Canada West.

Year	Month	Vessel	Type	Master	Departure Port	Passenger Numbers
1842	10	*Douglas*	n/k	Wade	London	33

Farmers, labourers, and mechanics who are to join friends and relations in Canada West.

Year	Month	Vessel	Type	Master	Departure Port	Passenger Numbers
1842	10	*Euclid*	bk	Davidson	Liverpool	20

A few will remain in Montreal; the remainder are going to Toronto and Port Dover on Lake Erie.

Year	Month	Vessel	Type	Master	Departure Port	Passenger Numbers
1842	10	*Jamaica*	n/k	Martin	London	8

Mechanics who are to join friends and relations in Canada West.

Year	Month	Vessel	Type	Master	Departure Port	Passenger Numbers
1842	10	*Mersey*	n/k	Hamilton	Liverpool	17

Labourers going to Upper Canada.

Year	Month	Vessel	Type	Master	Departure Port	Passenger Numbers
1842	10	*Pearl*	bk	Douglas	London	12

Farmers.

Year	Month	Vessel	Type	Master	Departure Port	Passenger Numbers
1842	10	*Royal Adelaide* of Fowey	bk	Leuty, T.	Fowey	27

Labourers and mechanics who are proceeding to Canada West.

Year	Month	Vessel	Type	Master	Departure Port	Passenger Numbers
1842	10*	*Harmonia*	n/k	n/k	Newcastle	43

Year	Month	Vessel	Type	Master	Departure Port	Passenger Numbers
1842	10*	King William	n/k	n/k	Plymouth	36
1842	12*	Mary Ann	n/k	n/k	Newcastle	19
1842	12*	Westminster	n/k	n/k	Plymouth	111
1843	01*	Gloucester	n/k	n/k	Newcastle	14
1843	02*	Lady	n/k	n/k	Newcastle	2
1843	03*	British Lady	n/k	n/k	Bideford	42
1843	03*	British Queen	bg	n/k	Bristol	22
1843	03*	Clipper	n/k	n/k	Newcastle	19
1843	03*	Ireland	n/k	n/k	Gloucester	44
1843	03*	Mohawk	n/k	n/k	Newcastle	8
1843	03*	Rolla	bk	n/k	Sunderland	7
1843	04*	Amazon	s	n/k	Hull	112
1843	04*	Andrew Marvel	bk	n/k	Hull	13
1843	04*	Ann	n/k	n/k	Newcastle	4
1843	04*	Ann	n/k	n/k	Plymouth	27
1843	04*	Ann & Mary	n/k	n/k	Stockton	50
1843	04*	Arab	bk	n/k	Bideford	55
1843	08*	Arab	bk	n/k	Bristol	10
1843	04*	Auxiler	n/k	n/k	Newcastle	1
1843	04*	Belle of Padstow	bk	Brewer, G.	Padstow	147

Passengers included seventy-six paupers. Vessel arrived in Quebec on May 19.

Year	Month	Vessel	Type	Master	Departure Port	Passenger Numbers
1843	04*	Civility	n/k	n/k	Bideford	2
1843	04*	Clio of Padstow	bk	Easthope, R.	Padstow	37
1843	04*	Collina	bk	n/k	Gloucester	40
1843	04*	Cosmo	n/k	n/k	Bristol	82
1843	04*	Cosmopodite	n/k	Webber	Plymouth	94
1843	04*	Dahlia	bk	n/k	Plymouth	169
1843	04*	Delia	n/k	n/k	Poole	29
1843	04*	Druid	n/k	n/k	Bristol	22
1843	04*	Emmanuel	n/k	n/k	Bristol	45
1843	04*	Europe	n/k	n/k	Scarborough	27
1843	04*	Hartland	n/k	n/k	Bideford	80
1843	04*	Industry	n/k	n/k	Penzance	5

Included four paupers.

Year	Month	Vessel	Type	Master	Departure Port	Passenger Numbers
1843	04*	*Jane & Barbara*	n/k	n/k	Bristol	2
1843	04*	*John Clifton*	n/k	n/k	Stockton	10
1843	04*	*Jonothan Bromham*	n/k	n/k	Plymouth	11
1843	04*	*Lady Sale (1)*	n/k	n/k	Newcastle	5
1843	04*	*Lavinia*	bk	n/k	Stockton	49
1843	04*	*Llan Romney*	s	n/k	Hull	115
1843	04*	*Lord Canterbury*	bk	n/k	Bristol	48
1843	04*	*Mary Ann*	n/k	n/k	Bideford	82
1843	04*	*Minstrel*	n/k	n/k	Hull	145
1843	04*	*Phya*	n/k	n/k	King's Lynn	44
1843	04*	*Resource*	n/k	n/k	London	n/k

Vessel called at Portsmouth. Passengers included eighty-nine paupers.

Year	Month	Vessel	Type	Master	Departure Port	Passenger Numbers
1843	04*	*Saint Anne's*	n/k	n/k	Bideford	309

Passengers included eight paupers.

Year	Month	Vessel	Type	Master	Departure Port	Passenger Numbers
1843	04*	*Silvanus*	n/k	n/k	Truro	7
1843	04*	*Sir Edward Hamilton*	s	n/k	Hull	134
1843	04*	*Sisters*	bk	n/k	London	163

All paupers leaving from London. Vessel also called at Plymouth.

Year	Month	Vessel	Type	Master	Departure Port	Passenger Numbers
1843	04*	*Spermacetti*	bk	Moon, E	Plymouth	224
1843	04*	*Sylvanus* of Truro	bk	Smith, J.	Truro	n/k

Lost near Cape Breton. Crew were saved.

Year	Month	Vessel	Type	Master	Departure Port	Passenger Numbers
1843	04*	*Tynemouth Castle*	n/k	n/k	Newcastle	12
1843	05*	*Albion*	n/k	n/k	Newcastle	2
1843	05*	*Comet*	n/k	n/k	Hull	55
1843	05*	*Eliza*	n/k	n/k	Bristol	79
1843	05*	*Ellergill*	n/k	n/k	Hull	26
1843	05*	*Emperor*	n/k	n/k	Stockton	40
1843	05*	*Fergus*	bk	n/k	Hull	204

Passengers included twelve paupers.

Year	Month	Vessel	Type	Master	Departure Port	Passenger Numbers
1843	05*	Forster	bk	n/k	Hull	5
1843	05*	Ocean	n/k	n/k	Newcastle	3
1843	05*	Pomona	n/k	n/k	Newcastle	1
1843	06*	Philomela	n/k	n/k	Whitehaven	24
1843	06*	Reward	n/k	n/k	Hull	10
1843	06*	Victory	bk	n/k	Hull	54
1843	06*	William Peile	n/k	n/k	Whitehaven	35
1843	07	Mary Campbell	n/k	n/k	Liverpool	66

All paupers.

| 1843 | 07 | New Brunswick | n/k | n/k | Hull | 34 |

Included ten paupers.

| 1843 | 07 | Toronto | s | n/k | London | 173 |

All were paupers. Included forty-one people from Brinkworth Parish in Wiltshire. List of names appears as Table 9.

Year	Month	Vessel	Type	Master	Departure Port	Passenger Numbers
1843	07*	Ann	n/k	n/k	Bristol	11
1843	07*	Belle of Padstow	bk	Brewer, G.	Padstow	46
1843	07*	Caroline Alice	n/k	n/k	Bristol	10
1843	07*	Clio of Padstow	bk	Easthope, R.	Padstow	54
1843	07*	Isabella	n/k	n/k	Bideford	12
1843	07*	Milford	n/k	n/k	Bristol	10
1843	07*	Priscilla	bk	n/k	Plymouth	50
1843	08	Baltic	bg	Cawdrie, W.	Yarmouth	72

Included fifty-six paupers.

| 1843 | 08 | Burrell | n/k | bk | London | 120 |

All paupers.

| 1843 | 08 | Clyde | n/k | n/k | Liverpool | 16 |

All paupers.

| 1843 | 08 | Florence | n/k | n/k | Plymouth | 115 |

Included twenty-one paupers.

Year	Month	Vessel	Type	Master	Departure Port	Passenger Numbers
1843	08	*Lady of the Lake*	n/k	n/k	Liverpool	17

All paupers.

Year	Month	Vessel	Type	Master	Departure Port	Passenger Numbers
1843	08	*Royal Adelaide* of Fowey	bk	Leuty, T.	Fowey	70

Included twelve paupers.

Year	Month	Vessel	Type	Master	Departure Port	Passenger Numbers
1843	08*	*Belle* of Padstow	bk	Brewer, G.	Padstow	n/k
1843	08*	*Clio* of Padstow	bk	Symons	Padstow	n/k
1843	08*	*Collina*	bk	n/k	Gloucester	13
1843	08*	*Good Intent (1)*	n/k	n/k	Fowey	44
1843	08*	*John & Mary*	bg	Oliver	Padstow	n/k
1843	08*	*Jonothan Bromham*	n/k	n/k	Plymouth	11
1843	08*	*Orlando*	n/k	n/k	Bristol	111
1843	08*	*Spermacetti*	bk	Moon, E.	Plymouth	49
1843	08*	*Voluna* of Padstow	bg	Easthope, R.	Padstow	n/k
1843	09	*Amazon*	s	n/k	Hull	58

All were paupers.

Year	Month	Vessel	Type	Master	Departure Port	Passenger Numbers
1843	09*	*Cosmo*	n/k	n/k	Bristol	41
1843	09*	*Himalaya*	n/k	n/k	Plymouth	19
1843	09*	*John Hawkes*	n/k	n/k	Bideford	3
1843	10	*Arab*	bk	n/k	Bideford	36

Included six paupers.

Year	Month	Vessel	Type	Master	Departure Port	Passenger Numbers
1843	10	*Pearl*	bk	n/k	London	7

All were paupers.

Year	Month	Vessel	Type	Master	Departure Port	Passenger Numbers
1843	10	*William Wilberforce*	n/k	n/k	Ilfracombe	n/k

Vessel also called at Charlottetown.

Year	Month	Vessel	Type	Master	Departure Port	Passenger Numbers
1843	10*	*Duncan*	n/k	n/k	Bristol	6

Year	Month	Vessel	Type	Master	Departure Port	Passenger Numbers
1843	11*	Theresa	n/k	n/k	Plymouth	17
1843	11*	William Metcalfe	n/k	n/k	Plymouth	54
1843	12*	Sea Queen	n/k	n/k	Plymouth	70
1844	02*	Cumberland	bk	n/k	Whitehaven	4
1844	02*	Ellison	n/k	n/k	Hull	5
1844	03*	Cosmo	n/k	n/k	Bristol	94
1844	03*	Governor Harvey	n/k	n/k	Bristol	28
1844	03*	Jonothan Bromham	n/k	n/k	Plymouth	10
1844	03*	Llan Romney	s	n/k	Hull	158
1844	03*	Madison	n/k	n/k	Newport	37
1844	04*	Adario	n/k	n/k	Plymouth	19
1844	04*	Arab	bk	n/k	Bristol	4
1844	04*	Belle of Padstow	bk	Brewer, G.	Padstow	91
1844	04*	Burrell	n/k	bk	Portsmouth	64
1844	04*	Calcutta	bk	n/k	Falmouth	n/k
1844	04*	Clio of Padstow	bk	Brown, J.	Truro	164
1844	04*	Collina	bk	n/k	Gloucester	7
1844	04*	Conservator	bg	Brown	Stockton	37
1844	04*	Dahlia	bg	n/k	Plymouth	11
1844	04*	Florida	n/k	n/k	Bideford	8
1844	04*	James & Ann	n/k	n/k	Newcastle	4
1844	04*	Lady Sale (2)	n/k	n/k	Bideford	12
1844	04*	Lord William Bentinck	n/k	n/k	Plymouth	31
1844	04*	Lotus	n/k	n/k	Bristol	11
1844	04*	Phya	n/k	n/k	King's Lynn	27
1844	04*	Priscilla	bk	n/k	Plymouth	39
1844	04*	Sir Edward Hamilton	s	n/k	Hull	81
1844	04*	Spermacetti	bk	Moon, E.	Plymouth	207
1844	04*	Tane	n/k	n/k	Newcastle	1
1844	04*	Victoria	n/k	Daniel, T.	St. Michael's Mount	69

St. Michael's Mount is close to Penzance.

Year	Month	Vessel	Type	Master	Departure Port	Passenger Numbers
1844	05	*Haughton le Spring*	bg	Edwards	Sunderland	33
1844	05	*Rainbow*	s	Arnold	Plymouth	19
1844	05	*Souter Johnny*	bk	Little, Thomas	Liverpool	10

Seven cabin, three steerage.

Year	Month	Vessel	Type	Master	Departure Port	Passenger Numbers
1844	05*	*Forster*	bk	n/k	Hull	45
1844	05*	*Medora*	n/k	n/k	Newcastle	4
1844	05*	*Potomac*	n/k	n/k	Hull	4
1844	05*	*St. George*	bg	n/k	Plymouth	42
1844	06	*Abercromby*	bk	Louttit, G.	Liverpool	183
1844	06	*Amazon*	s	Pearson	Hull	152
1844	06	*Astrea*	bk	Lewis	Weymouth	17
1844	06	*Baltic*	bg	Cawdrie, W.	Yarmouth	6
1844	06	*Berwick Castle*	n/k	Forster	Liverpool	12
1844	06	*Bridgetown*	bk	Betty	Liverpool	246
1844	06	*Crowley*	bg	Atkinson	Newcastle	8
1844	06	*Crown*	bg	Laughton	Hull	6
1844	06	*Don*	bk	Muir	Hull	97
1844	06	*Fergus*	bk	Blythe, W.	Hull	130
1844	06	*Henrietta Mary*	s	Brown	Liverpool	338
1844	06	*Huron*	bg	Hedwith	Liverpool	15
1844	06	*Indian*	bg	Mackie	Bristol	34
1844	06	*John Munn*	bk	Watt	Liverpool	254
1844	06	*Lord Ramsay*	bg	England, Richard	Bideford	17
1844	06	*Reliance*	bk	Wilson	Liverpool	109
1844	06	*St. Anne*	bk	Richards	Plymouth	136
1844	06	*Stentor*	bk	Wright	Hull	93
1844	07	*Ellergill*	bk	Hill	Hull	32
1844	07	*Goliath*	s	Slater	Liverpool	11
1844	07	*John & Robert*	s	McKechnie	Liverpool	388
1844	07	*Leander*	s	Phelan	Liverpool	215
1844	07	*Resource*	bk	Buchanan	Liverpool	120
1844	07	*Sarah Richardson*	bg	Elliott	Stockton	14

Year	Month	Vessel	Type	Master	Departure Port	Passenger Numbers
1844	07*	Caution	n/k	n/k	Hull	6
1844	08	Andromache	s	Hunter	Hull	20
1844	08	England	s	Everret	Liverpool	138
1844	08	Marchioness of Abercorn	bk	Hagarty	Liverpool	16

Three cabin, thirteen steerage.

Year	Month	Vessel	Type	Master	Departure Port	Passenger Numbers
1844	09	Astrea	bg	Lewis	Weymouth	20
1844	09	Belle of Padstow	bk	Brewer, G.	Padstow	85
1844	09	Cairo	bg	Treadwell	Plymouth	191
1844	09	Calcutta	bk	Preston	Southampton	58
1844	09	Dahlia	bk	Hooper, J.	Plymouth	15
1844	09	Eleanor	bk	Turney	London	14
1844	09	Great Britain	s	Swinburn	London	7

All cabin passengers.

Year	Month	Vessel	Type	Master	Departure Port	Passenger Numbers
1844	09	Helen Scott	bg	Scotland	Bristol	18
1844	09	Laurel	s	Knarston	Liverpool	169
1844	09	Lune	bg	Andrews	London	40
1844	09	Pearl	bk	Douglas	London	19

Eight in the cabin, eleven steerage.

Year	Month	Vessel	Type	Master	Departure Port	Passenger Numbers
1844	09	Rienza	s	Smith	Liverpool	23
1844	09	Rory O'More	bk	McMaster	Liverpool	7
1844	09	Spermacetti	bk	Moon, E.	Plymouth	8
1844	10	Henry Bliss	s	Cummings	Liverpool	35
1844	n/k	Triton of Penzance	bk	Wakeham, R. J.	Penzance	n/k
1845	05	Amity	bk	Allan	Liverpool	39
1845	05	Andromache	s	Hunter	Hull	26
1845	05	Ann Crossman	s	n/k	Plymouth	8
1845	05	Auckland	bg	Williams	Liverpool	7
1845	05	Blenheim	bk	Jackson	London	134
1845	05	Canning	bg	Hancock	Bristol	54
1845	05	Canton	bk	Tonge	Hull	36
1845	05	Canton	s	Friend, D.	London	101

Four cabin, ninety-seven steerage.

Year	Month	Vessel	Type	Master	Departure Port	Passenger Numbers
1845	05	*Civility*	n/k	n/k	Bideford	n/k

Vessel called at Charlottetown. Thirty-nine passengers in steerage, some left at Quebec.

Year	Month	Vessel	Type	Master	Departure Port	Passenger Numbers
1845	05	*Conservator*	bg	Brown	Stockton	44

One cabin, forty-three steerage.

Year	Month	Vessel	Type	Master	Departure Port	Passenger Numbers
1845	05	*Countess of Durham*	bk	Hogg, J.	Liverpool	28
1845	05	*Dahlia*	bk	Hooper, J.	Plymouth	6
1845	05	*Dependent*	bk	Healy	Bridgwater	14
1845	05	*Great Britain*	s	Swinburn	London	10

All cabin passengers.

Year	Month	Vessel	Type	Master	Departure Port	Passenger Numbers
1845	05	*Ireland*	bk	Matthews	Gloucester	19
1845	05	*John Bell*	bk	Murphy	Liverpool	41
1845	05	*Llan Romney*	s	Willoughby	Hull	39
1845	05	*Margaret*	bk	Quinn	Liverpool	244
1845	05	*Mazeppa*	bg	Webster	Sunderland	249
1845	05	*Messenger*	bk	Wilson	Liverpool	309
1845	05	*Nicaragua*	bk	Marshall	Liverpool	82
1845	05	*Pearl*	bk	Douglas	London	12

All cabin passengers.

Year	Month	Vessel	Type	Master	Departure Port	Passenger Numbers
1845	05	*Priscilla*	bk	Taylor	Plymouth	8
1845	05	*Solway*	bk	McLellan	Gloucester	40
1845	05	*Spermacetti*	bk	Moon, E.	Plymouth	249
1845	06	*Amazon*	s	Pearson	Hull	154
1845	06	*Carthagenian*	s	Jack	Liverpool	144
1845	06	*Coeur de Lion*	s	Kendall	Liverpool	14
1845	06	*Daedalus*	s	Nicholas	Truro	119
1845	06	*Douglas*	bk	Hodson	Hull	32
1845	06	*Eagle* of Padstow	bg	Parnall, M.	Bideford	94
1845	06	*Emmanuel*	s	Bunn	London	21
1845	06	*Empress*	bk	Scott	Southampton	134

Seven cabin, 127 steerage.

Year	Month	Vessel	Type	Master	Departure Port	Passenger Numbers
1845	06	*Fergus*	bk	Martin	Hull	155

Year	Month	Vessel	Type	Master	Departure Port	Passenger Numbers
1845	06	*Governor Jalkett*	bk	Hillman	Liverpool	34

Five cabin, twenty-nine steerage.

Year	Month	Vessel	Type	Master	Departure Port	Passenger Numbers
1845	06	*James & Thomas*	bk	Duncan	Hull	74
1845	06	*John & Robert*	s	McKechnie	Liverpool	334
1845	06	*Lady Sale*	bk	Tilley	London	16

Six cabin, ten steerage.

Year	Month	Vessel	Type	Master	Departure Port	Passenger Numbers
1845	06	*Lord Ramsay*	bg	England, Richard	Bideford	15
1845	06	*Lord Seaton*	s	Harper	Liverpool	353
1845	06	*Ocean*	bg	Quay	Maryport	23
1845	06	*Princess Charlotte*	s	Mickles	Liverpool	247
1845	06	*St. Anne*	s	Richards	Southampton	300
1845	06	*Sunflower*	bg	Reynolds	Padstow	21
1845	06	*Sydney*	bk	White	London	114
1845	06	*Vesper*	bg	Mattrass	London	39
1845	06	*Voluna* of Padstow	bg	Easthope, R.	Padstow	81
1845	07	*Arabian*	s	Hawkins	Liverpool	277
1845	07	*Consbrooke*	s	Finlay	Liverpool	146
1845	07	*England*	s	Thompson	Liverpool	235
1845	07	*Greenock*	s	Fleck	Liverpool	405
1845	07	*John Bentley*	s	Dishrow	Liverpool	437
1845	07	*Lockwoods*	s	Errington	Penzance	70
1845	07	*Mary*	bg	Sullivan	Liverpool	214
1845	07	*Prince Regent*	bk	n/k	Hull	65
1845	07	*Providence*	s	Payn	Liverpool	141
1845	07	*Royal Albert*	bk	Balderson	London	87
1845	07	*Victory*	bk	Hill	London	56
1845	07	*William Gibson*	s	Cookman	Hull	85
1845	08	*British King*	bk	Gortley	Liverpool	176
1845	08	*British Queen*	bg	McLaren	Bristol	16
1845	08	*Columbus*	bk	Mathison	London	80

Fifteen cabin, sixty-five steerage.

Year	Month	Vessel	Type	Master	Departure Port	Passenger Numbers
1845	08	*Jane*	bk	Blain	London	85
1845	08	*Ocean Queen*	s	McBride	Liverpool	225
1845	08	*Spermacetti*	bk	Moon, E.	Plymouth	95
1845	08	*Victoria*	s	Armon	Liverpool	103
1845	09	*Pearl*	bk	Chalmers	London	57
1845	10	*Abigail*	bk	Daly	Liverpool	32
1845	10	*Clio* of Padstow	bk	Easthope, R.	Padstow	119
1845	10	*Lady Seaton*	bk	Duffill, J.	London	22

All cabin passengers.

Year	Month	Vessel	Type	Master	Departure Port	Passenger Numbers
1845	10	*Sir Richard Jackson*	s	Webster	Liverpool	15

One cabin, fourteen steerage.

Year	Month	Vessel	Type	Master	Departure Port	Passenger Numbers
1845	n/k	*Daedalus*	n/k	Nicholas	Truro	n/k
1845	n/k	*Lavinia*	bk	Wilson	Liverpool	210
1845	n/k	*Voluna* of Padstow	bg	Easthope, R.	Padstow	n/k
1846	04*	*Olympus*	bk	Tonkin, H.	Penzance	n/k
1846	04*	*Royal Adelaide* of Fowey	bk	Smith, R.	Fowey	n/k

Adult fare £2 5s.

Year	Month	Vessel	Type	Master	Departure Port	Passenger Numbers
1846	04*	*Voluna* of Padstow	bg	Langford, Robert	Padstow	40

The passengers included Paul Robins, a prominent Bible Christian.

Year	Month	Vessel	Type	Master	Departure Port	Passenger Numbers
1846	04*	*Woodbine*	bk	Skeach, R.	Falmouth	n/k
1846	05	*Aberdeen*	s	McGrath	Liverpool	79
1846	05	*Alchymist* of Falmouth	bk	Wells	Falmouth	8
1846	05	*Amazon*	s	Pearson	Hull	110
1846	05	*Britannia*	s	Hamilton	Liverpool	13

All cabin.

Year	Month	Vessel	Type	Master	Departure Port	Passenger Numbers
1846	05	*Canton*	s	Yonge	Hull	10

Year	Month	Vessel	Type	Master	Departure Port	Passenger Numbers
1846	05	*Charlotte*	s	Drewery	London	108

Five cabin, 103 steerage. Included thirty-one people who were assisted by their parishes to emigrate.

Year	Month	Vessel	Type	Master	Departure Port	Passenger Numbers
1846	05	*Clio* of Padstow	bk	Easthope, R.	Padstow	149
1846	05	*Dahlia*	bk	Tozer	Plymouth	85
1846	05	*Delia*	bk	Adey	Poole	8
1846	05	*Fergus*	bk	Martin	Hull	95
1846	05	*Highland Mary*	bk	Crossley	Liverpool	296
1846	05	*Lavinia*	bk	Brown	Stockton	28
1846	05	*Ocean*	bg	Quay	Maryport	8
1846	05	*Paragon* of Truro	bk	Symons, J.	Truro	16
1846	05	*Pearl*	bk	Chalmers	London	8
1846	05	*Peel's-One*	bk	Askins	Hull	13
1846	05	*Spermacetti*	bk	Moon, E.	Plymouth	246

Three cabin, 243 steerage.

Year	Month	Vessel	Type	Master	Departure Port	Passenger Numbers
1846	05	*Stentor*	bk	Wright	Hull	10
1846	05	*Victoria* of St. Ives	bk	Newton	Hayle	

Sailed from Hayle (Cornwall) on April 9; arrrived with passengers — "all well."

Year	Month	Vessel	Type	Master	Departure Port	Passenger Numbers
1846	06	*Agamemnon*	bk	McKandy	Liverpool	547
1846	06	*Andromache*	bk	Hunter	Liverpool	230

Twelve cabin 218 steerage.

Year	Month	Vessel	Type	Master	Departure Port	Passenger Numbers
1846	06	*Astrea*	bg	Lewis	Weymouth	12
1846	06	*Burnhopeside*	bk	Larby	London	10

All cabin passengers.

Year	Month	Vessel	Type	Master	Departure Port	Passenger Numbers
1846	06	*Defence*	s	Davies	Liverpool	257
1846	06	*Eleutheria*	bk	McDonough	Liverpool	226
1846	06	*Hirundo*	bk	Gray	London	7
1846	06	*Jessie*	s	Oliver	Liverpool	38
1846	06	*Margaret*	bg	Pollock	Liverpool	353
1846	06	*Mundane*	bk	Hutchinson	Liverpool	17

Year	Month	Vessel	Type	Master	Departure Port	Passenger Numbers
1846	06	*Orlando*	bk	Cockerell	London	77
1846	06	*Orwell*	s	Martin	Hull	72
1846	06	*Ottawa*	bk	Spencer	London	52
1846	06	*Pursuit*	s	Spence	Liverpool	430
1846	06	*Rockshire*	bk	Evans	Liverpool	373
1846	06	*Romulus*	bk	Langster	Liverpool	466
1846	06	*Teesdale*	bg	Storey	Stockton	8
1846	06	*Triton* of Penzance	bk	Wakeham, R.J.	Penzance	100

One child died on voyage.

Year	Month	Vessel	Type	Master	Departure Port	Passenger Numbers
1846	07	*Elizabeth*	s	Ducket	Liverpool	265
1846	07	*Graham*	bk	Beart	Plymouth	40

Fourteen cabin, twenty-six steerage.

Year	Month	Vessel	Type	Master	Departure Port	Passenger Numbers
1846	07	*John Bolton*	s	Sampson	Liverpool	437
1846	07	*Mary Bibby*	bk	Archibald	London	43
1846	07	*Queen*	bk	Watson	Hull	96
1846	07	*Sea King*	s	Dunn	Liverpool	139
1846	07	*Sir Edward Hamilton*	s	Lundy	Hull	156
1846	07	*Virginia*	s	Brown	Liverpool	405
1846	07*	*Countess of Durham*	bk	Hogg, J.	Helford	n/k
1846	08	*Arab*	bk	Howe	Bideford	87
1846	08	*Blythwood*	s	Jamieson	Sunderland	4
1846	08	*Carlton*	bk	Bance	Liverpool	241
1846	08	*England*	s	Thompson	Liverpool	30
1846	08	*James Moran*	s	Morrison	Liverpool	329
1846	08	*Leander*	bk	Pringle	London	34
1846	08	*Lord Collingwood*	bk	Renardson	London	51
1846	08	*Spermacetti*	bk	Moon, E.	Plymouth	194
1846	08	*Syria*	bk	Cox	Liverpool	134
1846	08	*Woodbine*	bk	Skeach, R.	Falmouth	6
1846	09	*Great Britain*	s	Swinburn	London	17

All cabin passengers.

Year	Month	Vessel	Type	Master	Departure Port	Passenger Numbers
1846	09	*Intrinsic*	s	Davidson	Liverpool	250

Year	Month	Vessel	Type	Master	Departure Port	Passenger Numbers
1846	09	*Lady Seaton*	bk	Duffill, J.	London	22
Sixteen cabin, six steerage.						
1846	09	*Mary Allen*	bg	Wade	Liverpool	6
All cabin passengers.						
1846	09	*Pearl*	bk	Chalmers	London	20
Nine cabin, eleven steerage.						
1846	09	*Queen Victoria*	bk	Nixon	Plymouth	80
1846	10	*Clio* of	bk	Easthope, R.	Padstow	103
1846	10	*Constance*	bg	Savage	Bristol	19
1846	10	*Douglas*	bk	Douglas	London	6
Five cabin, one steerage.						
1846	10	*Emmanuel*	bg	Burns	Liverpool	58
1846	10	*Resolution* of Penzance	bg	Davis	Penzance	8
1846	10	*Rockshire*	bk	Evans	Liverpool	175
1846	10	*Zealous*	bk	Richards	London	17
Eleven cabin, six steerage.						
1847	04	*Clio* of Padstow	bk	Easthope, R.	Padstow	300
Seven people died on the crossing.						
1847	04*	*Eagle* of Padstow	bg	Parnall, M.	Padstow	n/k
1847	04*	*Roslin Castle*	bk	Sadler, W. S.	Falmouth	211
1847	05	*Aquamarine*	s	n/k	Liverpool	24
1847	05	*Clio* of Padstow	bk	n/k	Padstow	320
1847	05	*Constance*	bg	Savage	Bristol	15
1847	05	*Delia*	n/k	n/k	Poole	4
1847	05	*Douglas*	bk	n/k	London	36
1847	05	*Eagle* of Padstow	bg	n/k	Padstow	115
1847	05	*Fergus*	bk	n/k	Hull	131
1847	05	*Lady Seaton*	bk	n/k	London	20

Year	Month	Vessel	Type	Master	Departure Port	Passenger Numbers
1847	05	*Lord Ramsay*	bg	n/k	Bideford	10
1847	05	*Mersey*	n/k	n/k	Torquay	5
1847	05	*Nestor*	n/k	n/k	Maryport	7
1847	05	*Ocean Queen* of Bristol	n/k	n/k	Bristol	82
1847	05	*Ottawa*	s	n/k	Bridgwater	55
1847	05	*Pearl*	bk	Chalmers	London	11
1847	05	*Resolution* of Penzance	bg	Davis	Penzance	65

Vessel reported as having arrived safely at Quebec with passengers.

Year	Month	Vessel	Type	Master	Departure Port	Passenger Numbers
1847	05	*Roslin Castle*	bk	n/k	Falmouth	212
1847	05	*Spermacetti*	bk	Moon, E.	Plymouth	251
1847	05	*Syria*	bk	n/k	Liverpool	241
1847	05	*Victoria*	bk	n/k	St. Ives	19
1847	05	*Wallace*	n/k	n/k	Liverpool	417
1847	06	*Aberdeen*	s	n/k	Liverpool	392
1847	06	*Achilles*	n/k	n/k	Liverpool	411
1847	06	*Ajax*	n/k	n/k	Liverpool	359
1847	06	*Ann*	n/k	n/k	Liverpool	348
1847	06	*Araminta*	n/k	n/k	Liverpool	412
1847	06	*Argo*	n/k	n/k	Liverpool	590
1847	06	*Astrea*	bg	n/k	Weymouth	4
1847	06	*Birman*	n/k	n/k	London	172
1847	06	*Blonde*	n/k	n/k	Liverpool	424
1847	06	*Clarendon*	n/k	n/k	Liverpool	281
1847	06	*Eliza Caroline*	n/k	n/k	Liverpool	540
1847	06	*Elizabeth*	n/k	n/k	Liverpool	434
1847	06	*George*	n/k	n/k	Liverpool	397
1847	06	*Llan Rumney*	n/k	n/k	Hull	108
1847	06	*Hope*	n/k	n/k	Maryport	24
1847	06	*John Bolton*	n/k	n/k	Liverpool	578
1847	06	*Lady Milton*	n/k	n/k	Liverpool	432
1847	06	*Lotus*	n/k	n/k	Liverpool	546
1847	06	*Maria &* *Elizabeth*	n/k	n/k	Liverpool	81
1847	06	*Mary*	n/k	n/k	Liverpool	37

Year	Month	Vessel	Type	Master	Departure Port	Passenger Numbers
1847	06	*Mountaineer*	n/k	n/k	Hull	28
1847	06	*New York Packet*	n/k	n/k	Liverpool	470
1847	06	*Norna*	n/k	n/k	Sunderland	4
1847	06	*Paragon* of Truro	bk	Dunstone, T.	Truro	96
1847	06	*Phoenix*	n/k	n/k	Liverpool	279
1847	06	*Princess Royal*	n/k	n/k	Liverpool	599
1847	06	*Pursuit*	s	n/k	Liverpool	472
1847	06	*Rankin*	n/k	n/k	Liverpool	573
1847	06	*Royalist*	n/k	n/k	Liverpool	437
1847	06	*Sisters*	n/k	n/k	Liverpool	507
1847	06	*Sobraon*	n/k	n/k	Liverpool	602
1847	06	*Tay*	n/k	n/k	Liverpool	371
1847	06	*Victory*	n/k	n/k	Bristol	5
1847	06	*Wellington*	n/k	n/k	Bideford	9
1847	06	*Wyke Regis*	bg	n/k	Poole	6
1847	07	*Abbey Lands*	n/k	n/k	Liverpool	398
1847	07	*Agamemnon*	bk	n/k	Liverpool	646

There were forty-five deaths on the crossing.

Year	Month	Vessel	Type	Master	Departure Port	Passenger Numbers
1847	07	*Charlotte*	n/k	n/k	Plymouth	330
1847	07	*City of Derry*	n/k	n/k	London	292
1847	07	*Durham*	n/k	n/k	Liverpool	269
1847	07	*Erin's Queen*	n/k	n/k	Liverpool	493

There were 136 deaths on the crossing.

Year	Month	Vessel	Type	Master	Departure Port	Passenger Numbers
1847	07	*Golden Spring*	n/k	n/k	London	149
1847	07	*Goliath*	n/k	n/k	Liverpool	600

There were eighty-nine deaths on the crossing.

Year	Month	Vessel	Type	Master	Departure Port	Passenger Numbers
1847	07	*Graham*	n/k	n/k	Southampton	221
1847	07	*Greenock*	s	n/k	Liverpool	816

There were eighty deaths on the crossing.

Year	Month	Vessel	Type	Master	Departure Port	Passenger Numbers
1847	07	*James Moran*	n/k	n/k	Liverpool	353
1847	07	*John Jardine*	n/k	n/k	Liverpool	389

Year	Month	Vessel	Type	Master	Departure Port	Passenger Numbers
1847	07	*Junior*	n/k	n/k	Liverpool	356
1847	07	*Kilblain*	n/k	n/k	London	253
1847	07	*Leo*	n/k	n/k	Liverpool	8
1847	07	*Lloyd*	bk	Wattes	London	207

Included twenty paupers from Brinkworth Parish in Wiltshire. List of names appears as Table 10.

1847	07	*Manchester*	n/k	n/k	Liverpool	512
1847	07	*Rose*	n/k	n/k	Liverpool	384

There were 139 deaths on the crossing.

1847	07	*Royal Albert*	bk	n/k	London	171
1847	07	*Sarah*	n/k	n/k	Liverpool	249

There were seventy deaths on the crossing.

1847	07	*Tamarac*	n/k	n/k	Liverpool	497
1847	07	*Thistle*	n/k	n/k	Liverpool	381
1847	07	*Triton*	n/k	n/k	Liverpool	462

There were 186 deaths on the crossing.

1848	04*	*Woodbine*	bk	Skeach, R.	Falmouth	n/k
1848	05	*Andus*	bg	Barker	Bristol	37
1848	05	*Ann & Mary*	bg	Cunningham	Newcastle	71
1848	05	*Anne*	s	McGarry	London	1
1848	05	*Charles Jones*	n/k	Cothay	Liverpool	2
1848	05	*Charlotte*	bk	Dennis	Lancaster	87
1848	05	*Clio* of Padstow	bk	Easthope, R.	Padstow	264

Included miners and farmers.

1848	05	*Columbine*	bk	Taylor	Hull	19
1848	05	*Constance*	bg	Savage	Bristol	44
1848	05	*Dahlia*	bk	Tozer	Plymouth	129
1848	05	*Fergus*	bk	Martin	Hull	132
1848	05	*Florence*	n/k	Brumage	Plymouth	25
1848	05	*Great Britain*	s	Swinburh	London	10
1848	05	*Helen*	bk	Foster	London	238
1848	05	*John Bull*	bk	Duffill, J.	London	33

Ten cabin, twenty-three steerage.

Year	Month	Vessel	Type	Master	Departure Port	Passenger Numbers
1848	05	*Lady Elgin*	bk	Jones	London	1
1848	05	*Lady Peel*	s	Johns	Penzance	264

Sailed from Penzance on April 6. There were 258 steerage passengers. One hundred and thirty-four people embarked at Penzance.

Year	Month	Vessel	Type	Master	Departure Port	Passenger Numbers
1848	05	*Margaret*	s	Field	Torquay	8
1848	05	*Montezuma*	bk	Kendall	Liverpool	4
1848	05	*Ocean Queen* of Bristol	s	Williams	Bristol	45
1848	05	*Ottawa*	s	Thrift	Bridgwater	119

Included thirty-five paupers.

Year	Month	Vessel	Type	Master	Departure Port	Passenger Numbers
1848	05	*Pallas*	bg	Perris	Newcastle	8
1848	05	*Pearl*	bk	Chalmers	London	23

Seven cabin, sixteen steerage.

Year	Month	Vessel	Type	Master	Departure Port	Passenger Numbers
1848	05	*Prince George*	s	Chambers	Hull	105
1848	05	*Rhine*	bg	Perry	Stockton	9
1848	05	*Roslin Castle*	bk	Sadler, W. S.	Falmouth	200

Also called at Plymouth.

Year	Month	Vessel	Type	Master	Departure Port	Passenger Numbers
1848	05	*Sir Richard Jackson*	s	Doran	Liverpool	7

Two cabin, five steerage. There were four paupers.

Year	Month	Vessel	Type	Master	Departure Port	Passenger Numbers
1848	05	*Spermacetti*	bk	Moon, E.	Plymouth	240
1848	05	*St. Andrew*	s	Larby	London	9
1848	05	*Syria*	bk	Davis	Liverpool	1
1848	06	*Camoens*	bg	Ritchie	London	99

Eleven cabin, eighty-eight steerage.

Year	Month	Vessel	Type	Master	Departure Port	Passenger Numbers
1848	06	*Conying*	bg	Halbro	Penzance	36
1848	06	*Don*	bk	Stephenson	Plymouth	185
1848	06	*Douglas*	bk	Douglas	London	19

Ten cabin, nine steerage.

Year	Month	Vessel	Type	Master	Departure Port	Passenger Numbers
1848	06	*Elizabeth*	s	Roca	Liverpool	13
1848	06	*Meteor*	bg	Brown, D.	Hull	53
1848	06	*Olympus*	bk	Penyack, R.	Penzance	95
1848	06	*Retriever*	bk	James	Liverpool	162

Year	Month	Vessel	Type	Master	Departure Port	Passenger Numbers
1848	06	*Strong*	bg	Harrison	Liverpool	284
1848	06	*Vivid*	bg	Morrison	London	17
1848	06	*Voluna* of Padstow	bg	Bulman, T.	Padstow	10
1848	07	*Bess Grant*	bk	Cartney	Plymouth	118

Two cabin, 116 steerage.

Year	Month	Vessel	Type	Master	Departure Port	Passenger Numbers
1848	07	*Conquering Hero*	bg	Cockburn	London	70
1848	07	*Lord Elgin*	s	Herron	Liverpool	300
1848	07	*Priscilla*	bk	Taylor	Plymouth	204
1848	08	*Brandon*	s	Rainey	Liverpool	249
1848	08	*Naomi*	bk	Wright	Liverpool	171

Seven cabin, 164 steerage.

Year	Month	Vessel	Type	Master	Departure Port	Passenger Numbers
1848	08	*Oregon*	sr	Carey	Penzance	102
1848	08*	*Eagle* of Padstow	bg	Parnall, M.	Padstow	n/k
1848	08*	*Marchioness of Aberdeen* of Padstow	n/k	Key	Padstow	n/k
1848	09	*Anne*	s	McGarry	Liverpool	12

Six cabin, six steerage.

Year	Month	Vessel	Type	Master	Departure Port	Passenger Numbers
1848	09	*Belle* of Padstow	bk	Bisson	Padstow	8
1848	09	*Britannia*	s	Hamilton	Liverpool	15
1848	09	*Daedalus*	s	Nicholas	Plymouth	107

Three cabin, 104 steerage.

Year	Month	Vessel	Type	Master	Departure Port	Passenger Numbers
1848	09	*Dahlia*	bk	Tozer	Plymouth	20
1848	09	*Durham*	bk	Fesbian	London	127
1848	09	*Great Britain*	s	Swinburn	London	16
1848	09	*John Bull*	bk	Duffill, J.	London	83

Eight cabin, seventy-five steerage.

Year	Month	Vessel	Type	Master	Departure Port	Passenger Numbers
1848	09	*Maid of Erin*	bg	n/k	Falmouth	120
1848	09	*Montezuma*	bk	Kendall	Liverpool	33

Nineteen cabin, fourteen steerage.

Year	Month	Vessel	Type	Master	Departure Port	Passenger Numbers
1848	09	*New Liverpool*	s	Richardson	London	327
1848	09	*Spermacetti*	bk	Moon, E.	Plymouth	60
1848	09	*St. Andrew*	s	Larby	London	39

Eleven cabin, twenty-eight steerage.

Year	Month	Vessel	Type	Master	Departure Port	Passenger Numbers
1848	09	*Victoria*	bk	Martin, J.	St. Ives	58
1848	09	*Woodbine*	bk	Skeach, R.	Falmouth	7
1848	10	*Baron* of Renfrew	s	Robinson	Liverpool	8
1848	10	*Clio* of Padstow	bk	Easthope, R.	Padstow	132
1848	10	*Constance*	bg	Savage	Bristol	24
1848	10	*Marchioness of Abercorn*	bk	Key	Falmouth	121
1848	10	*Pearl*	bk	Chalmers	London	79
1848	10	*Roslin Castle*	bk	Sadler, W. S.	Falmouth	21
1848	10	*William*	s	Stewart	Portsmouth	9
1849	04*	*Priscilla*	bk	Jago, W.	Restronguet (Cornwall)	n/k
1849	05	*Alchymist* of Falmouth	bk	Richards, J.	Falmouth	7
1849	05	*Ava*	bg	Webster	Plymouth	224
1849	05	*Belle* of Padstow	bk	Bisson	Padstow	138
1849	05	*Clio* of Padstow	bk	Easthope, R.	Padstow	68
1849	05	*Daedalus*	s	Nicholas	Plymouth	107
1849	05	*Delia*	s	Adey	Poole	12
1849	05	*Douglas*	bk	Douglas	London	12
1849	05	*Eglington*	bg	Lorby	London	15

Four cabin, eleven steerage.

Year	Month	Vessel	Type	Master	Departure Port	Passenger Numbers
1849	05	*Emperor*	s	Beswick	Plymouth	70
1849	05	*Fergus*	bk	Martin	Hull	156
1849	05	*Lady Elgin*	bk	Irons	Liverpool	39

Five cabin, thirty-four steerage.

Year	Month	Vessel	Type	Master	Departure Port	Passenger Numbers
1849	05	*Lady Peel*	s	Johns	Liverpool	270

Year	Month	Vessel	Type	Master	Departure Port	Passenger Numbers
1849	05	*Laurel*	s	Knarston	London	232

Fifteen cabin, 217 steerage.

Year	Month	Vessel	Type	Master	Departure Port	Passenger Numbers
1849	05	*Margaret*	s	Field	Torquay	67
1849	05	*Neptune*	bk	Turnbull	Whitby	91
1849	05	*Pearl*	bk	Chalmers	London	13
1849	05	*Port Glasgow*	bk	Blandford, J.	Southampton	21
1849	05	*Roslin Castle*	bk	Sadler, W. S.	Falmouth	131

Nine cabin, 122 steerage.

Year	Month	Vessel	Type	Master	Departure Port	Passenger Numbers
1849	05	*Royal Adelaide* of Fowey	bk	Smith, R.	Fowey	114
1849	05	*Secret*	bk	Farthing	Bideford	95
1849	05	*Spermacetti*	bk	Moon, E.	Plymouth	240

Three cabin, 237 steerage.

Year	Month	Vessel	Type	Master	Departure Port	Passenger Numbers
1849	05	*Voluna* of Padstow	bg	Bulman, T.	Padstow	60
1849	05	*William & Mary*	bk	Allen	Colchester	22
1849	06	*Alcyon*	bk	Farrie	Liverpool	185
1849	06	*Aquamarine*	s	Connolly	Liverpool	41
1849	06	*British Merchant*	s	Anderson	Liverpool	323
1849	06	*Brothers*	bg	Burden	London	23
1849	06	*Choice* of Scarborough	bk	Robertson	London	47
1849	06	*Commodore*	bg	Low	Stockton	50
1849	06	*Dahlia*	bk	Tozer	Plymouth	306
1849	06	*Dew Drop* of Padstow	sw	Burke, J.	Padstow	55
1849	06	*Ellen*	bg	Fittman	Newhaven	20
1849	06	*Helen*	s	Jackson	Liverpool	392
1849	06	*Isabella*	s	Faremouth	Torquay	59
1849	06	*Meteor*	bg	Brown, D.	Hull	139

Five cabin, 134 steerage.

Year	Month	Vessel	Type	Master	Departure Port	Passenger Numbers
1849	06	*Ono* of St. Ives	n/k	Williams	St. Ives	95
1849	06	*Oriental*	s	McEacham	London	107

Two cabin, 105 steerage.

Year	Month	Vessel	Type	Master	Departure Port	Passenger Numbers
1849	06	*Portly*	bk	Jackson	London	12
1849	06	*Priscilla*	bk	Pile	Falmouth	82
1849	06	*Triton* of Penzance	bk	Wakeham, R. J.	Penzance	13
1849	06	*William Bromham*	bk	Nance	Plymouth	168
1849	06	*Wilson*	bg	Stoup	London	7
1849	06	*Wyke Regis*	bg	Meadus	Poole	6
1849	07	*Forfarshire*	s	Plott	Liverpool	588
1849	07	*Lord Wellington*	s	Winsted	Liverpool	49
1849	07	*Minstrel*	bk	Jenkinson	Hull	107
1849	08	*Argo*	s	Smith	Liverpool	371
1849	08	*Elphinstone*	bk	Richardson	Plymouth	92

Thirteen cabin, seventy-nine steerage.

Year	Month	Vessel	Type	Master	Departure Port	Passenger Numbers
1849	08	*Jessie Stevens*	bk	Wilson	Liverpool	14
1849	08	*Kalmia*	bk	Gilpin	Liverpool	306
1849	08	*Lord Ashburton*	s	Forrest	Liverpool	462
1849	08	*Mayflower*	bk	Joll	Plymouth	128
1849	08	*Prince Albert*	s	Freeman	London	6
1849	08	*Sarah*	bk	Wilson	Liverpool	332
1849	08	*Souter Johnny*	bk	Ellis	Liverpool	11
1849	08	*Spermacetti*	bk	Moon, E.	Plymouth	170
1849	08	*Toronto*	s	Wilburn	London	66
1849	08	*Victoria*	bk	Mitchell	Bideford	57
1849	08*	*Quebec* of Penzance	n/k	Pearson	Penzance	n/k

Master received letter of appreciation from passengers who arrived safely in Quebec.

Year	Month	Vessel	Type	Master	Departure Port	Passenger Numbers
1849	09	*Albion*	bk	Robertson	Plymouth	7
1849	09	*Alchymist* of Falmouth	bk	Richards, J.	Falmouth	10

Year	Month	Vessel	Type	Master	Departure Port	Passenger Numbers
1849	09	*Belle* of Padstow	bk	Bisson	Padstow	157
1849	09	*Clio* of Padstow	bk	Easthope, R.	Padstow	65
1849	09	*Daedalus*	s	Nicholas	Plymouth	31

Ten cabin, twenty-one steerage.

Year	Month	Vessel	Type	Master	Departure Port	Passenger Numbers
1849	09	*Dahlia*	bk	Tozer	Plymouth	41

Eight cabin, thirty-three steerage.

Year	Month	Vessel	Type	Master	Departure Port	Passenger Numbers
1849	09	*Elizabeth*	s	Grieves	Liverpool	39
1849	09	*John*	bk	Hutchins	Plymouth	13
1849	09	*John Bull*	bk	Duffett	London	90

Eight cabin, eighty-two steerage.

Year	Month	Vessel	Type	Master	Departure Port	Passenger Numbers
1849	09	*Lady Peel*	s	Johns	Plymouth	42
1849	09	*Margaret*	s	Field	Torquay	32
1849	09	*Royal Adelaide* of Fowey	bk	Smith, R.	Falmouth	n/k
1849	09	*Royalist*	bg	Campbell	Fleetwood	82
1849	09	*Victoria*	bk	Marshead	St. Ives	11
1849	09	*Wave*	bk	Halpin	Liverpool	28
1849	10	*Lady Elgin*	bk	Irons	Liverpool	112
1850	04*	*Countess of Mulgrave*	bk	Constance, T.W.	Falmouth	n/k
1850	04*	*Woodbine*	bk	Skeach, R.	Falmouth	n/k
1850	05	*Abigail*	bk	Wells	Liverpool	34
1850	05	*Aurora*	bg	Carmish	Scarborough	11
1850	05	*Ava*	bk	Webster	Southampton	248
1850	05	*Calypso*	bk	Anderson	Dartmouth	5
1850	05	*Charlotte*	bk	Davidson	Berwick	156
1850	05	*Clara Symes*	s	Duncan	Liverpool	401
1850	05	*Clio* of Padstow	bk	Easthope, R.	Truro	55
1850	05	*Collins*	bk	Perry	Gloucester	10
1850	05	*Cornwall*	bk	Charles	Plymouth	184
1850	05	*Corsair*	s	Nance	Gloucester	246
1850	05	*Dahlia*	bk	Tozer	Plymouth	78

Year	Month	Vessel	Type	Master	Departure Port	Passenger Numbers
1850	05	Davenport	bg	Long	Cowes	7
1850	05	Dibdie	s	Kier	Liverpool	32
1850	05	Fergus	bk	Wharton	Hull	168
1850	05	Gift	bk	Grey	Shields	26
1850	05*	Good Intent	bk	Warburton, J.	Fowey	56

To sail from Fowey with emigrants for Quebec about April 6. Reported to have arrived in June after a pleasant voyage.

Year	Month	Vessel	Type	Master	Departure Port	Passenger Numbers
1850	05	Greenock	s	McCutcheon	Liverpool	13
1850	05	Jane Lowden of Padstow	n/k	Langford, Robert	Padstow	23

Short crossing of twenty-three days. Vessel also called at Falmouth.

Year	Month	Vessel	Type	Master	Departure Port	Passenger Numbers
1850	05	Josepha	bk	England, Richard	Bristol	25
1850	05	Lady Falkland	s	Smith	Liverpool	39
1850	05	Laurel	s	Knarston	London	233
1850	05	Margaret	s	Dodge	Liverpool	10

All cabin passengers.

Year	Month	Vessel	Type	Master	Departure Port	Passenger Numbers
1850	05	Margaret	s	Field	Torquay	74
1850	05	Olive Branch	bk	n/k	Stockton	27
1850	05	Pearl	bk	Christie	Plymouth	15
1850	05	Prince Regent	bk	Martin	Hull	173
1850	05	Robert McWilliam	bk	Webster	Sunderland	10
1850	05	Rose	bk	Moon	Plymouth	112
1850	05	Roslin Castle	bk	Sadler, W. S.	Falmouth	46

Vessel due to leave in the first week of April.

Year	Month	Vessel	Type	Master	Departure Port	Passenger Numbers
1850	05	Royal Adelaide of Fowey	bk	Smith, R.	Fowey	102

Due to sail from Fowey about April 3.

Year	Month	Vessel	Type	Master	Departure Port	Passenger Numbers
1850	05	Secret	bk	Farthing	Bideford	72
1850	05	Spermacetti	bk	Moon, E.	Plymouth	225

Year	Month	Vessel	Type	Master	Departure Port	Passenger Numbers
1850	05	*Toronto*	s	Ballatine	Liverpool	9
1850	05	*Victoria*	bk	Moorshead, W.H.	Hayle	8

Due to leave Hayle for Quebec about April 5.

Year	Month	Vessel	Type	Master	Departure Port	Passenger Numbers
1850	06	*Bisson*	bk	n/k	Padstow	97
1850	06	*Charlotte*	bk	Rea	Liverpool	339
1850	06	*Cyprus*	bg	Orchard	London	5
1850	06	*Daedalus*	s	Nicholas	Plymouth	121
1850	06	*Ethelred*	bk	McLeod	London	155
1850	06	*Polly*	bk	Watson	Liverpool	352
1850	06	*Sydney*	bk	Duncan	London	8
1850	07	*Adept*	s	Burns	Liverpool	515
1850	07	*Douglas*	bk	Hubert	Liverpool	28
1850	07	*Gentoo*	bk	Nattrass	London	159
1850	07	*Hampshire*	s	Watts	Southampton	163
1850	07	*Intrinsic*	bk	McFarlane	Liverpool	282
1850	07	*Meteor*	bg	Brown, D	Hull	140
1850	07	*Milicete*	s	Jones	Liverpool	433
1850	07	*Videroy*	s	McMahon	Liverpool	502
1850	07	*Woodman*	bg	Fullerton	Liverpool	147
1850	07*	*Clio* of Padstow	bk	Easthope, R.	Truro	n/k

Due to sail about July 18. *Clio* described as being very spacious between decks.

Year	Month	Vessel	Type	Master	Departure Port	Passenger Numbers
1850	07*	*Dew Drop* of Padstow	sw	Burke, J.	Boscastle	n/k

To sail about July 15.

Year	Month	Vessel	Type	Master	Departure Port	Passenger Numbers
1850	08	*Achilles*	bk	Lewis	Sunderland	20
1850	08	*Alfred*	bk	Paverley	Southampton	213
1850	08	*Bengal*	bk	Ross	Liverpool	14
1850	08	*Calypso*	bk	Anderson	Dartmouth	5
1850	08	*Durham*	bk	Child	London	143
1850	08	*Jane*	s	Brown	Liverpool	32
1850	08	*Lady Fitzherbert*	n/k	Loulitt	Bristol	5
1850	08	*Orbit*	bk	Larkin	London	31
1850	08	*Queen Victoria*	bk	Nixon	Plymouth	18

Year	Month	Vessel	Type	Master	Departure Port	Passenger Numbers
1850	08	*Woodbine*	bk	Skeach, R.	Falmouth	n/k

To sail from Falmouth about August 1.

Year	Month	Vessel	Type	Master	Departure Port	Passenger Numbers
1850	09	*Belle* of Padstow	bk	Bisson	Padstow	46
1850	09	*Colonial*	s	Signoti	Liverpool	215
1850	09	*Daedalus*	s	Nicholas	Padstow	57
1850	09	*Dahlia*	bk	Tozer	Plymouth	8
1850	09	*Elspeth*	bk	Penn	London	91
1850	09	*Good Intent*	bk	Warburton, J.	Fowey	36

Left Fowey in early August. Arrived in Quebec in thirty-five days.

Year	Month	Vessel	Type	Master	Departure Port	Passenger Numbers
1850	09	*Juno*	bg	Tickle	Maryport	8
1850	09	*Larne*	s	Nickie	Liverpool	195
1850	09	*Margaret*	s	Field	Torquay	30
1850	09	*Marquis of Hastings* of London	bk	Anderson	Falmouth	11
1850	09	*Robert Burns*	bg	Stewart	Carlisle	8
1850	09	*Rose*	bk	Moon	Plymouth	98
1850	09	*Royal Adelaide* of Fowey	bk	Smith, R.	Fowey	100
1850	09	*Sarah Fleming*	bg	Crampon	Torquay	14
1850	09	*Secret*	bk	Farthing	Bideford	21
1850	09	*Spermacetti*	bk	Moon, E.	Plymouth	147
1850	09	*St. Andrew*	s	Paton	Liverpool	11

All cabin passengers.

Year	Month	Vessel	Type	Master	Departure Port	Passenger Numbers
1850	09	*Temperance*	sr	Lear	Carlisle	20
1850	09	*Victoria*	bk	Moorshead, W.H.	St. Ives	11
1850	10	*Ava*	bk	Webster	Southampton	68
1850	10	*Essex*	s	Norton	Liverpool	434
1850	10	*James Hutchinson*	bk	Sterling	Liverpool	138
1850	10	*John*	bk	Symond	Plymouth	11
1850	10	*Mary Sharp*	s	Martin	Liverpool	19

Year	Month	Vessel	Type	Master	Departure Port	Passenger Numbers
1850	10	*Mountaineer*	s	Harrison	Liverpool	39
1850	10	*Pearl*	bk	Langford	London	9
1850	10	*Solway*	bk	Shadwick	Gloucester	37
1850	10	*Wolfe's Cove*	bk	Cummings	Hull	6
1851	05	*Ailsa*	bk	Poole	Liverpool	301
1851	05	*Asia*	bk	Webster	Southampton	207
1851	05	*Ava*	bk	Suter, R. E.	Southampton	58

Paupers who were assisted by their parishes.

Year	Month	Vessel	Type	Master	Departure Port	Passenger Numbers
1851	05	*Belle* of Padstow	bk	Bisson	Padstow	124
1851	05	*Charles Saunders*	s	Spencer	Liverpool	198
1851	05	*Collina*	bk	Penny	Gloucester	224
1851	05	*Daedalus*	s	Bullman, T.	Padstow	50

Eleven cabin, thirty-nine steerage. Due to sail from Padstow about April 10, arrived Quebec in late May. Letters of appreciation to the captain signed by Messrs Knight, Beswetherick, Blamey, and Varcoe.

Year	Month	Vessel	Type	Master	Departure Port	Passenger Numbers
1851	05	*Dahlia*	bk	Tozer	Plymouth	139

Twenty-one cabin, 118 steerage. Eight passengers were paupers who were being assisted by their parish.

Year	Month	Vessel	Type	Master	Departure Port	Passenger Numbers
1851	05	*Eliza Ann*	bk	Dugald	Liverpool	41
1851	05	*Fergus*	bk	Lamplough	Hull	165
1851	05	*Glenssilly*	s	Hescroft	Liverpool	10
1851	05	*Good Intent*	bk	Warburton, J.	Fowey	20

Due to leave Fowey in first week of April.

Year	Month	Vessel	Type	Master	Departure Port	Passenger Numbers
1851	05	*Henry Tanner*	bk	Carter	London	102

Five cabin, ninety-seven steerage.

Year	Month	Vessel	Type	Master	Departure Port	Passenger Numbers
1851	05	*Isabella*	s	Martin	Hull	222

Five cabin, 217 steerage.

Year	Month	Vessel	Type	Master	Departure Port	Passenger Numbers
1851	05	*Isabella*	s	Haywood	Torbay	14
1851	05	*Jane*	s	Griffiths	Bristol	27
1851	05	*Lady Peel*	s	Johns	Plymouth	271
1851	05	*Laurel*	s	Knarston	London	177

Thirty-five of the passengers were paupers.

Year	Month	Vessel	Type	Master	Departure Port	Passenger Numbers
1851	05	Ocean Queen of Bristol	bk	Hawes	Bristol	26
1851	05	Pearl	bk	Langford	London	8

All cabin passengers.

Year	Month	Vessel	Type	Master	Departure Port	Passenger Numbers
1851	05	Perseverence	bg	White	Stockton	43

Four of the passengers were paupers.

Year	Month	Vessel	Type	Master	Departure Port	Passenger Numbers
1851	05	Prince Regent	s	Wharton	Hull	171
1851	05	Robert Burns	bg	Stewart	Carlisle	26
1851	05	Rose	bk	Moon	Plymouth	298
1851	05	Roslin Castle	bk	Sadler, W. S.	Plymouth	25

Six cabin, nineteen steerage. Due to sail around April 5.

Year	Month	Vessel	Type	Master	Departure Port	Passenger Numbers
1851	05	Samson	bk	Murdock	Truro	24
1851	05	Wellington	bg	Lawson	London	13
1851	06	Anglesea	bk	Bull	Liverpool	241

Fifty of the passengers were paupers whose expenses were being paid by Mr. Cavanagh.

Year	Month	Vessel	Type	Master	Departure Port	Passenger Numbers
1851	06	British Empire	bk	Allen	London	32

Eight steerage, twenty-four cabin.

Year	Month	Vessel	Type	Master	Departure Port	Passenger Numbers
1851	06	Caroline	bk	Reid	Bideford	51
1851	06	Diana	bk	Toogood	Hull	106

Two cabin, 104 steerage.

Year	Month	Vessel	Type	Master	Departure Port	Passenger Numbers
1851	06	Elizabeth	s	Barclay	Liverpool	33
1851	06	Gartcraig	bk	Strickland	Liverpool	145
1851	06	Helen	bk	Foster	London	216

Seventy-six of the passengers were paupers who were being assisted by their parishes.

Year	Month	Vessel	Type	Master	Departure Port	Passenger Numbers
1851	06	Meteor	bg	Brown, D.	Hull	133
1851	06	Regent	bk	Pickiss	Bristol	11
1851	06	Resolution	bk	Fox	Liverpool	24
1851	06	Sarah Fleming	bg	Crossman	Torquay	49
1851	06	Secret	bk	Bell	Bideford	149

Thirteen cabin, 136 steerage. Twelve of the passengers were paupers.

Year	Month	Vessel	Type	Master	Departure Port	Passenger Numbers
1851	07	*Barlow*	bg	Farquharson	Sunderland	237
1851	07	*Brockett*	bk	Stephenson	Newcastle	9
1851	07	*Clara Symes*	s	Duncan	Liverpool	414
1851	07	*Conqueror*	s	Leitch	Liverpool	280
1851	07	*Louisa*	bk	Manning	Southampton	268

Twelve cabin, 256 steerage. Eighty-six of the passengers were paupers.

Year	Month	Vessel	Type	Master	Departure Port	Passenger Numbers
1851	07	*Mangerton*	n/k	n/k	Liverpool	60

Irish paupers.

Year	Month	Vessel	Type	Master	Departure Port	Passenger Numbers
1851	07	*Margertos*	s	Stevens	Liverpool	518
1851	07	*Rolla*	bk	Taylor	Hull	152

Ten cabin, 142 steerage.

Year	Month	Vessel	Type	Master	Departure Port	Passenger Numbers
1851	07	*Sisters*	bk	Smith	London	271

Sixteen cabin 255 steerage. Sixty-two of the passengers were paupers.

Year	Month	Vessel	Type	Master	Departure Port	Passenger Numbers
1851	07	*The Duke*	s	Welch	Liverpool	50
1851	07	*United Kingdom*	s	Cotter	Liverpool	21

Fourteen cabin, seven steerage.

Year	Month	Vessel	Type	Master	Departure Port	Passenger Numbers
1851	08	*Abbey Lands*	bk	Barclay	Liverpool	319
1851	08	*Charles Walton*	bk	Crawford	Southampton	58

Paupers assisted by their parishes.

Year	Month	Vessel	Type	Master	Departure Port	Passenger Numbers
1851	08	*Ellen*	s	Philips	Liverpool	539

Three cabin, 536 steerage.

Year	Month	Vessel	Type	Master	Departure Port	Passenger Numbers
1851	08	*Montezuma*	s	Lenvitt	Liverpool	442
1851	08	*Snowden*	bk	Walker	Liverpool	25

Two cabin, twenty-three steerage.

Year	Month	Vessel	Type	Master	Departure Port	Passenger Numbers
1851	08	*Spermacetti*	bk	Moon, E.	Plymouth	108

Two cabin, 106 steerage.

Year	Month	Vessel	Type	Master	Departure Port	Passenger Numbers
1851	08	*Tay*	bk	Adams, J.	London	81

Included twenty-six paupers who were being assisted by their parish.

Year	Month	Vessel	Type	Master	Departure Port	Passenger Numbers
1851	08	*William Perrie*	s	Agnew	Liverpool	273

Year	Month	Vessel	Type	Master	Departure Port	Passenger Numbers
1851	08*	*Belle* of Padstow	bk	Bisson	Padstow	140
1851	09	*Anne*	s	McGarry	Liverpool	8
1851	09	*City of Hamilton*	s	Graham	London	12
1851	09	*Dahlia*	bk	Tozer	Plymouth	77
1851	09	*Euclid*	bk	Bainbridge	Liverpool	34
1851	09	*John Bull*	bk	Duffill, J.	London	63

Eleven cabin, fifty-two steerage. Twenty-five of the passengers were paupers who were being assisted by their landlord.

Year	Month	Vessel	Type	Master	Departure Port	Passenger Numbers
1851	09	*Lady Milton*	s	Firt	Liverpool	34
1851	09	*Margaret*	s	Oldrive	Dartmouth	8
1851	09	*Oregon*	s	Herron	Liverpool	452
1851	09	*Oriental*	s	Nicholas	Plymouth	86
1851	09	*Roslin Castle*	bk	Sadler, W. S.	Plymouth	32
1851	09	*Secret*	bk	Bell	Bideford	13
1851	09	*Sir Henry Pottinger*	bk	Crowel	Bristol	11
1851	09	*Sovereign*	bk	Martin	Hull	53

Five cabin, forty-eight steerage.

Year	Month	Vessel	Type	Master	Departure Port	Passenger Numbers
1851	10	*Aberdeen*	s	Dunn	Liverpool	31
1851	10	*Ben Nevis*	s	McKay	Liverpool	52
1851	10	*Effort*	bk	Brown	London	7
1851	10	*Good Intent*	bk	Warburton, J.	Fowey	n/k

Left Fowey on August 18 with passengers.

Year	Month	Vessel	Type	Master	Departure Port	Passenger Numbers
1851	10	*Jane*	s	Philips	Bristol	41
1851	10	*Lord George Bentinck*	s	Farley	Liverpool	15
1851	10	*Pearl*	bk	Langford	London	8
1851	10	*Resolution*	sr	Fox	Liverpool	17
1851	10	*Sir Richard Jackson*	s	Bell	Liverpool	8
1851	10	*Zephyr*	bg	Walker	Southampton	292
1852	05	*Ava*	bk	Gillard	Southampton	200
1852	05	*Belle* of Padstow	bk	Bisson	Padstow	113

Year	Month	Vessel	Type	Master	Departure Port	Passenger Numbers
1852	05	*Clara Symes*	s	Duncan	Liverpool	360

Eight cabin, 352 steerage.

Year	Month	Vessel	Type	Master	Departure Port	Passenger Numbers
1852	05	*Clio*	bk	Robson	Cowes	39
1852	05	*Daedalus*	s	Bullman, T.	Falmouth	17
1852	05	*Dahlia*	bk	Tozer	Plymouth	183
1852	05	*Eliza*	s	Ducket	Liverpool	47
1852	05	*Fergus*	bk	Sykes	Hull	56
1852	05	*Fingal*	s	Black	Hull	327
1852	05	*Good Intent (2)*	n/k	Gill, J.	Fowey	n/k

Sailed on April 8 from Fowey and reached land at Cape Breton seventeen days later. Arrived at Quebec ten days later.

Year	Month	Vessel	Type	Master	Departure Port	Passenger Numbers
1852	05	*Isabella*	s	Martin	Hull	227

Ten cabin, 217 steerage.

Year	Month	Vessel	Type	Master	Departure Port	Passenger Numbers
1852	05	*Jane*	s	Philips	Bristol	62

Nineteen cabin, forty-three steerage.

Year	Month	Vessel	Type	Master	Departure Port	Passenger Numbers
1852	05	*Lady Peel*	s	Moon	Plymouth	235
1852	05	*Laurel*	s	Knarston	London	160

One cabin, 159 steerage.

Year	Month	Vessel	Type	Master	Departure Port	Passenger Numbers
1852	05	*Lord George Bentinck*	s	Kendall	Liverpool	10
1852	05	*Margaret*	s	Codner	Torquay	21
1852	05	*Nelson*	bg	Hinson	Maryport	10
1852	05	*Ocean Queen of Bristol*	s	Hawes	Bristol	37

Seven cabin, thirty steerage.

Year	Month	Vessel	Type	Master	Departure Port	Passenger Numbers
1852	05	*Oriental*	s	Richards	Plymouth	223

Ten cabin, 213 steerage.

Year	Month	Vessel	Type	Master	Departure Port	Passenger Numbers
1852	05	*Pearl*	bk	Davies	London	23
1852	05	*Planter*	bg	Borrowdale	Whitehaven	8

All cabin passengers.

Year	Month	Vessel	Type	Master	Departure Port	Passenger Numbers
1852	05	*Prince Royal*	s	Gilpin	Liverpool	44

Year	Month	Vessel	Type	Master	Departure Port	Passenger Numbers
1852	05	*Queen Victoria*	bk	Nixon	Plymouth	50
1852	05	*Reward*	bg	Smith	Sunderland	6
1852	05	*Robert Burns*	bg	Stewart	Carlisle	81
1852	05	*Rose*	bk	Moon	Plymouth	161
1852	05	*Roslin Castle*	bk	Sadler, W. S.	Plymouth	17
1852	05	*Secret*	bk	Bell	Bideford	82
1852	06	*Andromanche*	bk	Tate	Liverpool	18
1852	06	*Broom*	s	Drysdale	Liverpool	57
1852	06	*Canton*	s	Anderson	Liverpool	23
1852	06	*Carshalton Park*	bk	Hitchins	Plymouth	107

Two cabin, 105 steerage.

Year	Month	Vessel	Type	Master	Departure Port	Passenger Numbers
1852	06	*Collina*	bk	Jenkins	Gloucester	136
1852	06	*Duke of Manchester*	bk	Madge	Dartmouth	8
1852	06	*Eagle* of Padstow	bg	Mabbey	Padstow	69
1852	06	*Favorite*	s	Garrick	Liverpool	13
1852	06	*Jane*	s	Hunter	Liverpool	470
1852	06	*Margaret Ann*	s	Symonds	Liverpool	378

Four cabin, 374 steerage.

Year	Month	Vessel	Type	Master	Departure Port	Passenger Numbers
1852	06	*Mentor*	bk	Brown	Hull	61
1852	06	*Nestor*	bg	Brough	Maryport	17
1852	06	*Niagara*	bk	Parkin	Liverpool	34
1852	06	*Rambler*	bk	Sinclair	Sunderland	214
1852	06	*Rolla*	bk	Taylor	Hull	67
1852	06	*Sisters*	bk	Thomas	London	204
1852	06	*Thomas James*	bk	McLellan	Liverpool	320
1852	06	*Worthy of Devon*	bk	Wilkinson	Bideford	124
1852	07	*Chieftain*	s	Scott	Liverpool	31
1852	07	*Glide*	bk	Harrison	Liverpool	147
1852	07	*Indian*	bk	Davidson	Hull	232
1852	07	*Intrepid*	bk	Philips	Liverpool	363

Year	Month	Vessel	Type	Master	Departure Port	Passenger Numbers
1852	07	*Ottawa*	bg	Cockburn	London	32
1852	07	*Scotland*	s	Hawkins	Liverpool	52
1852	07*	*Good Intent (2)*	n/k	Gill, J.	Fowey	n/k
1852	08	*Arabian*	bk	Christiansen	Dartmouth	230
1852	08	*Chatham*	s	Vinnis	Liverpool	370
1852	08	*Columbine*	s	Sybern	Bristol	14

Five cabin, nine steerage.

Year	Month	Vessel	Type	Master	Departure Port	Passenger Numbers
1852	08	*Infanta*	s	Hyland	Liverpool	30
1852	08	*Leonard Dobbin*	bk	Agar	London	188

Seven cabin, 181 steerage. Included twenty-one paupers from Brinkworth Parish in Wiltshire. The list of names appears as Table 11.

Year	Month	Vessel	Type	Master	Departure Port	Passenger Numbers
1852	08	*Montezuma*	s	Leavitt	Liverpool	99
1852	08	*Secret*	bk	Bell	Bideford	11
1852	08	*Sir Charles Napier*	s	Pettingell	Liverpool	42

Five cabin, thirty-seven steerage.

Year	Month	Vessel	Type	Master	Departure Port	Passenger Numbers
1852	08	*Spermacetti*	bk	Moon, E.	Plymouth	42
1852	08	*Victoria*	n/k	Simmonds	Southampton	100
1852	09	*Affiance*	bk	Barrick	London	75
1852	09	*Annandale*	s	Pearce	Liverpool	353
1852	09	*Belle* of Padstow	bk	Bisson	Padstow	123
1852	09	*City of Hamilton*	s	Graham	London	12
1852	09	*Clio*	s	Richards	Falmouth	7

All cabin passengers. Vessel also called at Padstow.

Year	Month	Vessel	Type	Master	Departure Port	Passenger Numbers
1852	09	*Clyde*	bk	Mills	Liverpool	40
1852	09	*Great Britain*	s	Wade	London	21

All cabin passengers.

Year	Month	Vessel	Type	Master	Departure Port	Passenger Numbers
1852	09	*John Bull*	bk	Duffill, J.	London	15
1852	09	*Lady Hobart*	s	McLeavy	Liverpool	316
1852	09	*Lady Peel*	s	Johns	Plymouth	105

Year	Month	Vessel	Type	Master	Departure Port	Passenger Numbers
1852	09	*Margaret*	s	Codner	Torquay	17
1852	09	*Niagara*	s	Munro	Liverpool	8
1852	09	*Oriental*	s	Nicholas	Plymouth	56
1852	09	*Prince of Wales*	bk	Brown	Liverpool	39
1852	09	*Rose*	bk	Moon	Plymouth	150
1852	09	*Roslin Castle*	bk	Sadler, W. S.	Plymouth	8
1852	09	*Sir Harry Smith*	s	Hawes	Liverpool	12
1852	09	*Sir Howard Douglas*	s	Crawford	Liverpool	29
1852	10	*Acadia*	s	Gallilee	Liverpool	41
1852	10	*Canada*	s	Wylie	Liverpool	8
1852	10	*Fingal*	s	Black	Liverpool	274
1852	10	*Jabe*	s	Smith	Bristol	5
1852	10	*Pearl*	bk	Davidson	London	19
1853	04*	*Daedalus*	s	Bullman, T.	Falmouth	n/k
1853	04*	*Royal Adelaide of Fowey*	bk	Richards	Fowey	98
1853	05	*Genova*	s.s.	Paton	Liverpool	17
1853	05	*Lady Seymour*	s	England, Richard	Bristol	52
1853	05	*Ocean Queen of Bristol*	s	Hawes	Bristol	39
1853	05	*Osward*	s	Welsh	Liverpool	488
1853	05	*Prince Regent*	s	Martin	Hull	156
1853	05	*Queen Victoria*	bk	Nixon	Plymouth	106
1853	05	*Robert Burns*	bk	Stewart	Carlisle	90
1853	05	*Spermacetti*	bk	Moon, E.	Plymouth	202
1853	05	*The Duke*	s	Gould	Liverpool	356
1853	05	*Three Bells*	s	Campbell	London	15

Three cabin, twelve steerage.

Year	Month	Vessel	Type	Master	Departure Port	Passenger Numbers
1853	05	*Yorkshire Lass*	bk	Philips	Falmouth	7

Year	Month	Vessel	Type	Master	Departure Port	Passenger Numbers
1853	06	*Alexander*	bk	Thwaits	Newcastle	32

Seventeen cabin, fifteen steerage.

Year	Month	Vessel	Type	Master	Departure Port	Passenger Numbers
1853	06	*Arran*	s	Myles	Liverpool	498
1853	06	*Ava*	bk	Farthing	Southampton	201
1853	06	*Blanche*	s	Rudolf	Liverpool	588

Eleven cabin, 577 steerage.

Year	Month	Vessel	Type	Master	Departure Port	Passenger Numbers
1853	06	*Crescent City*	s	Balliston	Liverpool	382
1853	06	*Dahlia*	bk	Tozer	Plymouth	292

Six cabin, 286 steerage.

Year	Month	Vessel	Type	Master	Departure Port	Passenger Numbers
1853	06	*Eagle* of Padstow	bg	Mabbey	Padstow	25
1853	06	*Electric*	bk	Molton	Bideford	122
1853	06	*Jane Glassin*	sr	Simpson	Liverpool	36
1853	06	*Lady Eglington*	s.s.	Paton	Liverpool	52
1853	06	*Margaret*	s	Codner	Torquay	21
1853	06	*Nelson*	bg	Hutchinson	Maryport	12

One cabin, eleven steerage.

Year	Month	Vessel	Type	Master	Departure Port	Passenger Numbers
1853	06	*Ross*	bk	Moon	Plymouth	295
1853	06	*Royal Adelaide* of Fowey	bk	Richards	Fowey	95
1853	06	*Thomas*	bg	Hobbs	Hull	12
1853	07	*Ash*	bk	Kenney	Liverpool	272
1853	07	*Charles*	bk	Tottie	Hull	14
1853	07	*Congress*	bg	Grave	Maryport	35
1853	07	*Eurise*	bk	Watson	Liverpool	42
1853	07	*James*	s	Moran	Plymouth	165
1853	07	*James Moran* of St. Ives	n/k	Moorhead	Plymouth	170

A quick passage.

Year	Month	Vessel	Type	Master	Departure Port	Passenger Numbers
1853	07	*Margaret Pollock*	s	Cruickshanks	Liverpool	36
1853	07	*Salem*	bg	McGraith	Liverpool	455

Year	Month	Vessel	Type	Master	Departure Port	Passenger Numbers
1853	07	Zetland	s	n/k	Bristol	64
1853	08	Chatham	s	Vinnis	Liverpool	308
1853	08	Conqueror	s	McAuley	Liverpool	295
1853	08	Edinburgh	s	Blair	Liverpool	52
1853	08	Gratitude	bk	Reynolds	London	18

Ten cabin, eight steerage.

Year	Month	Vessel	Type	Master	Departure Port	Passenger Numbers
1853	08	Lady Hobart	s	Clark	Liverpool	471
1853	08	New Zealand	s	Montgomery	Liverpool	34
1853	08	Sarah Bands	s.s.	Pinkersell	Liverpool	170

Thirty-three cabin, 137 steerage.

Year	Month	Vessel	Type	Master	Departure Port	Passenger Numbers
1853	08	William Perrie	s	Thompson	Liverpool	35
1853	08	Woodstock	bk	Wood	Liverpool	20
1853	09	Charles Chaloner	s	Thompson	Liverpool	315
1853	09	China	s	Simpson	Liverpool	88
1853	09	Countess of London	s	Laurie	Liverpool	32
1853	09	Ellen Oliver	bk	Hyland	Liverpool	72
1853	09	Hope	bk	Rowell	Plymouth	71
1853	09	John	bg	Rowell	Plymouth	74
1853	09	John Bull	bk	Duffill, J.	London	12

All cabin passengers.

Year	Month	Vessel	Type	Master	Departure Port	Passenger Numbers
1853	09	Louise	bk	Howe	Bideford	9
1853	09	Milicete	s	Jones	Liverpool	325
1853	09	Rose	bk	Lester	Plymouth	84
1853	09	Spermacetti	bk	Moon, E.	Plymouth	42
1853	09	Thomas	s	Calhoun	Liverpool	40
1853	09	Yorkshire Lass	bk	Rickard	Falmouth	5
1853	10	Fingal	s	Black	Liverpool	200
1853	10	Sarah Sands	s.s.	n/k	Liverpool	309

One hundred and thirty-four cabin, 175 steerage.

Year	Month	Vessel	Type	Master	Departure Port	Passenger Numbers
1854	05	Abigail	bk	Harris	Plymouth	264
1854	05	Anglo Saxon	s	Sinnoti	Liverpool	627

Year	Month	Vessel	Type	Master	Departure Port	Passenger Numbers
1854	05	*Consul*	s	Smith	Liverpool	30
1854	05	*Equator*	s	Simpson	Newcastle	15

All cabin passengers.

Year	Month	Vessel	Type	Master	Departure Port	Passenger Numbers
1854	05	*Fereda*	bk	Ashlea	Falmouth	33
1854	05	*Fergus*	bk	Edwards	Hull	171
1854	05	*George Smith*	bk	Plant	Sunderland	6
1854	05	*Harlequin*	s	Logan	Liverpool	37
1854	05	*Lady Hobart*	s	Gilmore	Liverpool	438
1854	05	*Lady Peel*	s	Moon	Plymouth	311
1854	05	*Margaret*	s	Codner	Torquay	14
1854	05	*Ocean Queen of Bristol*	s	Hawes	Bristol	27
1854	05	*Oregon*	s	McDonald	Liverpool	488
1854	05	*Oriental*	s	Hunt	Plymouth	358
1854	05	*Osiris*	bk	Scott	London	27
1854	05	*Ottawa*	s	Crawford	London	8

Four cabin, four steerage.

Year	Month	Vessel	Type	Master	Departure Port	Passenger Numbers
1854	05	*Panama*	bk	Reynolds	Liverpool	27
1854	05	*Paragos*	s	Payus	Liverpool	26
1854	05	*Prince Regent*	s	Martin	Hull	176
1854	05	*Robert Burns*	bg	Stewart	Carlisle	148
1854	05	*Sir Henry Pottinger*	bk	Stubbs	Bristol	23

A difficult crossing. George Roberts, one of the passengers, described the terrible storm endured by the passengers and crew in a letter that was later published by the *Montreal Gazette* (see LCA MD 289).

Year	Month	Vessel	Type	Master	Departure Port	Passenger Numbers
1854	05	*Triton*	s	Bond	London	32
1854	05	*Valleyfield*	bk	Pitt	Liverpool	24
1854	05	*Vesper*	bg	Bennett	Newcastle	152
1854	06	*Arran*	s	Miles	Liverpool	21
1854	06	*Charles Chaloner*	s	Hawes	Liverpool	421
1854	06	*Eliza*	bk	Warwick	Bristol	7
1854	06	*Evening Star*	bg	Byers	Sunderland	35

Four cabin, thirty-one steerage.

Year	Month	Vessel	Type	Master	Departure Port	Passenger Numbers
1854	06	*Glenlyon*	s	Oliver	Liverpool	452
1854	06	*Glenmannia*	s	Rogers	Liverpool	574
1854	06	*Good Intent (2)*	n/k	Gill, J.	Fowey	183

Left Fowey on April 11.

Year	Month	Vessel	Type	Master	Departure Port	Passenger Numbers
1854	06	*Infanta*	s	Calhoun	Liverpool	47

Four cabin, forty-three steerage.

Year	Month	Vessel	Type	Master	Departure Port	Passenger Numbers
1854	06	*John Howell*	bk	Johnston	Liverpool	434
1854	06	*Leonard Dobbin*	bk	Wilson	London	108
1854	06	*Lotus*	bg	Dawson	Shields	10
1854	06	*Meteor*	bg	Brown, D.	Hull	112
1854	06	*Onward*	s	Welch	Liverpool	523
1854	06	*Sarah Sands*	s.s.	Roley	Liverpool	416
1854	06	*Storm King*	bk	Ray	London	8
1854	06	*Thompson*	bg	Burton	Workington	11
1854	07	*Blanche*	bk	Whuite	Hull	295
1854	07	*Coriolanus*	s	Rhiad	Liverpool	526
1854	07	*Harmony*	s	Jamieson	Liverpool	471
1854	07	*Jeanet Kidstone*	s	Henrys	Liverpool	48
1854	07	*John Moore*	s	Ellis	Liverpool	29
1854	07	*Northen Light*	s	Slater	Liverpool	110

Seven cabin, 103 steerage.

Year	Month	Vessel	Type	Master	Departure Port	Passenger Numbers
1854	07	*Pilgrim*	s	Richardson	Liverpool	45
1854	07	*Richard & Harriet*	s	Sykes	Hull	33

Six cabin, twenty-sevensteerage.

Year	Month	Vessel	Type	Master	Departure Port	Passenger Numbers
1854	07	*Sir Harry Smith*	s	Hawes	Liverpool	48
1854	07	*Speed*	s	Baxter	Liverpool	51
1854	07	*Sunbeam*	s	Dos	London	39

Five cabin, thirty-four steerage.

Year	Month	Vessel	Type	Master	Departure Port	Passenger Numbers
1854	07	*Symonds*	s	Leavitt	Liverpool	56
1854	08	*Cauntless*	bk	McLaughlin	Liverpool	33
1854	08	*Charity*	s.s.	Paton	Liverpool	254
1854	08	*Congress*	bg	Grand	Liverpool	18
1854	08	*H C Kideton*	s	Patterson	Liverpool	639
1854	08	*John Davies*	s	Hughes	Liverpool	555
1854	08	*Mary Carson*	s	Mills	Liverpool	367
1854	08	*Satellite*	s	Gould	Liverpool	318
1854	09	*Feronia*	bk	Atkin	Falmouth	23
1854	09	*Hotspur*	s	Ray	Liverpool	499
1854	09	*John*	bk	Rowell	Plymouth	250

Five cabin, 245 steerage.

Year	Month	Vessel	Type	Master	Departure Port	Passenger Numbers
1854	09	*Oriental*	s	Tom, H.	Plymouth	348

Nine cabin, 339 steerage.

Year	Month	Vessel	Type	Master	Departure Port	Passenger Numbers
1854	09	*Ottawa*	s.s.	Atkins	Liverpool	200
1854	09	*Vixen*	bk	Ower	Liverpool	9
1854	09	*Zealous*	bk	Thomas	London	25
1854	10	*Admittance*	s	Graham	Liverpool	26
1854	10	*Canadian*	s.s.	McMaster	Liverpool	29

Seven cabin, twenty-two steerage.

Year	Month	Vessel	Type	Master	Departure Port	Passenger Numbers
1854	10	*Charity*	s.s.	Paton	Liverpool	234
1854	10	*Everthorpe*	bk	Harrison	Hull	25
1854	10	*Good Intent*	bk	Gill	Fowey	37
1854	10	*Robert Burns*	bg	Stewart	Carlisle	46
1854	10	*Rose*	bk	Laxton	Plymouth	323

Three cabin, 320 steerage.

Year	Month	Vessel	Type	Master	Departure Port	Passenger Numbers
1855	05	*Belmont*	s	Gilpin	Falmouth	23

Two cabin, twenty-one steerage.

Year	Month	Vessel	Type	Master	Departure Port	Passenger Numbers
1855	05	*Bowes*	bg	Eilwood	Workington	8
1855	05	*Davenport*	bk	McKenzie	Plymouth	282

Three cabin, 279 steerage.

Year	Month	Vessel	Type	Master	Departure Port	Passenger Numbers
1855	05	*Fergus*	bk	Edwards	Hull	209

Year	Month	Vessel	Type	Master	Departure Port	Passenger Numbers
1855	05	*Ocean Queen* of Bristol	s	Dart, Richard	Bideford	22

A letter of commendation to the captain signed by G. Gribble, W. Gliddon, W. Kerswell, F. Gilbert, G. Fleming, R. Moore and others (*North Devon Journal*, June 14, 1855).

Year	Month	Vessel	Type	Master	Departure Port	Passenger Numbers
1855	05	*Oriental*	s	Tom, H.	Plymouth	312

Eleven cabin, 301 steerage.

Year	Month	Vessel	Type	Master	Departure Port	Passenger Numbers
1855	05	*Platina*	bk	Richards	Bristol	10

Three cabin, seven steerage.

Year	Month	Vessel	Type	Master	Departure Port	Passenger Numbers
1855	05	*Royal Adelaide* of Fowey	bk	Mein	Fowey	n/k

Sailed with passengers from Fowey on April 16.

Year	Month	Vessel	Type	Master	Departure Port	Passenger Numbers
1855	05	*Siam*	s	Chapman	Plymouth	311

Three cabin, 308 steerage.

Year	Month	Vessel	Type	Master	Departure Port	Passenger Numbers
1855	05	*Steadfast*	bk	Spencer	London	16

Eight cabin, eight steerage.

Year	Month	Vessel	Type	Master	Departure Port	Passenger Numbers
1855	05	*William Hutt*	bg	Armitage	Liverpool	4

All cabin passengers.

Year	Month	Vessel	Type	Master	Departure Port	Passenger Numbers
1855	06	*Delia*	s	Adey	Portsmouth	8
1855	06	*Dykes* of Maryport	bg	Peters	Liverpool	30

Three cabin, twenty-seven steerage.

Year	Month	Vessel	Type	Master	Departure Port	Passenger Numbers
1855	06	*Matilda*	s	Lee	Shields	17
1855	06	*Meteor*	bg	Brown, D.	Hull	67
1855	06	*Prince Regent*	s	Martin	Hull	71

Highly respectable farmers and mechanics who intend to settle in the Western District.

Year	Month	Vessel	Type	Master	Departure Port	Passenger Numbers
1855	06	*Roslin Castle*	bk	Monday	Plymouth	43
1855	07	*Ann Thompson*	bk	Christie	London	93

Thirteen cabin, eighty steerage.

Year	Month	Vessel	Type	Master	Departure Port	Passenger Numbers
1855	07	*Canopus*	bk	Crosby	London	20

Seven cabin, thirteen steerage.

Year	Month	Vessel	Type	Master	Departure Port	Passenger Numbers
1855	07	*Chance*	n/k		Hull	n/k

Agricultural labourers and farmers.

Year	Month	Vessel	Type	Master	Departure Port	Passenger Numbers
1855	07	*John Howell*	bk	Appleby	Liverpool	440

One cabin, 439 steerage.

Year	Month	Vessel	Type	Master	Departure Port	Passenger Numbers
1855	07	*Queen of the Lakes*	s	Patching	Liverpool	30
1855	08*	*Royal Adelaide of Fowey*	bk	Facey	Fowey	n/k
1855	09	*Agnes Anderson*	s	Keating	Liverpool	52
1855	09	*Crown*	s	Izatt	Liverpool	612

Thirteen cabin, 599 steerage.

Year	Month	Vessel	Type	Master	Departure Port	Passenger Numbers
1855	09	*Kate*	s	Culliton	Liverpool	39
1855	09	*Montezuma*	s	Soles	Liverpool	33
1855	09	*Osprey*	s	Tomlinson	Bristol	10
1855	09	*St. Patrick*	s	Kinney	Liverpool	49

Nine cabin, forty steerage.

Year	Month	Vessel	Type	Master	Departure Port	Passenger Numbers
1855	09	*Venerable*	bk	Allen	Hull	8
1855	10	*Eagle*	bk	Quence	Liverpool	225
1855	10	*Great Britain*	s	Wilson	London	41
1855	10	*Pearl*	bk	Davies	London	24
1855	10	*Pied-Nez*	s	Fitzgerald	Liverpool	23
1855	10	*Rose*	bk	Sexton	Plymouth	201
1855	10	*St. Lawrence*	s	Wylie	Liverpool	9
1855	10	*Stadacona*	s	Willis	Portsmouth	5
1856	03*	*Roslin Castle*	bk	n/k	Plymouth	n/k
1856	04*	*Sarah Louise*	n/k	n/k	Penzance	n/k
1856	05	*Belmont*	s	Gilpin	Plymouth	24
1856	05	*Charles Chaloner*	s	Fox	Truro	128
1856	05	*Sladacona*	n/k	Willis	Poole	19

Year	Month	Vessel	Type	Master	Departure Port	Passenger Numbers
1856	06	*Alice and Anne*	n/k	Cockerill	London	8
1856	06	*Arabian*	n/k	Balmans	Liverpool	398

Twelve cabin, 386 steerage.

Year	Month	Vessel	Type	Master	Departure Port	Passenger Numbers
1856	06	*Clio*	n/k	Huyens	Plymouth	200
1856	06	*Emma*	n/k	Underwood	Liverpool	375
1856	06	*Indian*	s.s	Jones	Liverpool	174

Seventy-three cabin, 101 steerage.

Year	Month	Vessel	Type	Master	Departure Port	Passenger Numbers
1856	06	*Java*	n/k	Reed	Bristol	6
1856	06	*Jeronia*	n/k	Pearce	Falmouth	6
1856	06	*John Howell*	bk	Appleby	Liverpool	342
1856	06	*Meteor*	bg	Brown, D.	Hull	154
1856	07	*Canadian*	s.s	Ballantine	Liverpool	230

Fifty-three cabin, 177 steerage.

Year	Month	Vessel	Type	Master	Departure Port	Passenger Numbers
1856	07	*Shepherdess*	n/k	Rogers	Liverpool	528
1856	08	*Admiral Boxer*	n/k	Jones	Liverpool	415
1856	08	*Anglo Saxon*	s.s.	McMaster	Liverpool	179

Ninety-nine cabin, eighty steerage.

Year	Month	Vessel	Type	Master	Departure Port	Passenger Numbers
1856	08	*Ann Falcon*	n/k	Bowness	Liverpool	5
1856	08	*Douglas*	n/k	MacDonnell	Liverpool	19
1856	08	*Martin Luther*	n/k	Henderson	Liverpool	183
1856	08	*North American*	s.s	Grange	Liverpool	253

One hundred and three cabin, 150 steerage. A Canadian mail steamer.

Year	Month	Vessel	Type	Master	Departure Port	Passenger Numbers
1856	09	*Canadian*	s.s	Ballantine	Liverpool	116
1856	09	*Tom*	n/k	n/k	Plymouth	253
1857	05	*Arran*	s	Cummings	Liverpool	361
1857	05	*Eliza*	n/k	Chandler	Plymouth	255
1857	05	*Great Britain*	s	Wilson	London	7
1857	05	*John Howell*	bk	Appleby	Liverpool	16
1857	05	*Lady Seymour*	s	England, Richard	Bristol	22
1857	05	*Meteor*	bg	Brown, D.	Hull	124

Year	Month	Vessel	Type	Master	Departure Port	Passenger Numbers
1857	05	*Ocean Pride*	n/k	Atkins	Liverpool	395
1857	05	*Oriental*	s	Thomas	Plymouth	251
1857	05	*Petuel*	n/k	Lord	Bristol	94
1857	06	*Alexander Edwards*	n/k	Smith	Bristol	14
1857	06	*Effort*	n/k	Brown	London	12
1857	06	*Florence*	n/k	Shearer	Liverpool	300
1857	06	*Gipsy Queen*	bk	Johns	Plymouth	315
1857	06	*Indian*	s.s.	Jones	Liverpool	360
1857	06	*Inspector*	n/k	Bale	Bideford	7
1857	06	*Lady Peel*	s	Moon	Plymouth	221
1857	06	*Lord Mulgrave*	n/k	Ward	Hull	50
1857	06	*North American*	s.s.	Grange	Liverpool	418
1857	06	*Oregon*	s	O'Flaherty	Liverpool	421
1857	06	*Priscilla*	bk	Chapman	Plymouth	170
1857	06	*Roslin Castle*	bk	Monday	Plymouth	157
1857	06	*Stadacona*	s	Willis	Poole	16
1857	06	*Tomagonaps*	n/k	Pow	Liverpool	16
1857	07	*Anglo Saxon*	s.s.	McMaster	Liverpool	345
1857	07	*Eliza Morrison*	n/k	McBurnie	Liverpool	16
1857	07	*Envelope*	n/k	Power	London	174
1857	07	*Henry Cooke*	n/k	Flaherty	Liverpool	313

Carried assisted munitions workers from Woolwich.

Year	Month	Vessel	Type	Master	Departure Port	Passenger Numbers
1857	07	*Martin Luther*	n/k	n/k	Liverpool	478

Passengers had been upwards of three months onboard the vessel because of damage to the ship's masts in the English Channel shortly after leaving Liverpool. The ship had to return to Plymouth for repair, causing many of the passengers to run out of funds. Some 105 people needed assistance upon arrival in Quebec to reach their destinations. Most joining their relations. [See PP 1857–58(165)XLI]

Year	Month	Vessel	Type	Master	Departure Port	Passenger Numbers
1857	07	*North American*	s.s.	Grange	Liverpool	171
1857	07	*St. Patrick*	s	Kinney	Liverpool	541
1857	08	*Agamemnon*	n/k	Darley	Liverpool	117

Year	Month	Vessel	Type	Master	Departure Port	Passenger Numbers
1857	08	*Indian*	s.s.	Jones	Liverpool	205

One hundred and three cabin, 102 steerage.

| 1857 | 08 | *John Owens* | n/k | Brown | London | 491 |

Carried assisted munitions workers from Woolwich.

1857	08	*United Service*	n/k	Creigh	London	73
1857	09	*Anglesea*	n/k	Crawford	Liverpool	22
1857	09	*Bangalore*	n/k	Gill	Fowey	72

Two cabin, seventy steerage.

1857	09	*Cap Rouge*	n/k	Simmonds	Plymouth	115
1857	09	*Elizabeth Ann Bright*	n/k	Olive	Liverpool	511
1857	09	*Indian*	s.s.	Jones	Liverpool	283

One hundred and thirty cabin, 153 steerage.

| 1857 | 09 | *Ion* | n/k | Hudson | London | 326 |

Carried assisted munitions workers from Woolwich.

1857	09	*Juno*	n/k	Honey	Bristol	48
1857	09	*Melbourne*	n/k	Playter	Liverpool	30
1857	09	*Midlothian*		n/k	n/k	78

Carried assisted munitions workers from Woolwich.

| 1857 | 09 | *North American* | s.s. | Grange | Liverpool | 268 |

One hundred and twenty cabin, 148 steerage.

| 1857 | 09 | *Oriental* | s | Tom, H. | Plymouth | 223 |

Five cabin, 218 steerage.

| 1857 | 09 | *Stadacona* | s | Willis | Portsmouth | 10 |
| 1857 | 10 | *Anglo Saxon* | s.s. | McMaster | Liverpool | 272 |

One hundred and twenty-four cabin, 148 steerage.

1857	10	*Countess of Loudon*	n/k	Richards	Plymouth	16
1857	10	*Eagle*	n/k	Blight	Penzance	5
1857	10	*Hibernian*	s.s	Donken	London	17

Year	Month	Vessel	Type	Master	Departure Port	Passenger Numbers
1857	10	*Lady Peel*	s	Moon	Plymouth	8
1857	10	*Lady Seymour*	s	England, Richard	Bristol	28
1857	10	*M'Dannell*	n/k	Comer	London	128
1858	05	*Anglo Saxon*	s.s.	Borland	Liverpool	344

Eighty-nine cabin, 255 steerage.

1858	05	*Balmoral*	s	Gilpin	Plymouth	6

Sailed with three cows, five sheep, and a cart.

1858	05	*Birmingham*	bg	Johns	London	89

Four cabin, eighty-five steerage.

1858	05	*Culloden*	s	Harley	Liverpool	281

Three cabin, 278 steerage.

1858	05	*Duchess of Northumberland*	bk	Wadle	Portsmouth	6
1858	05	*General Havelock*	bk	Pollyblank	Dartmouth	9
1858	05	*North American*	s.s.	Grange	Liverpool	330

One hundred and twenty cabin, 210 steerage.

1858	05	*Ocean Bride*	s	Akitt	Liverpool	155
1858	06	*Anglo Saxon*	s.s.	Borland	Liverpool	236

Ninety-nine cabin, 137 steerage.

1858	06	*Indian*	s.s.	Jones	Liverpool	264

One hundred cabin, 164 steerage.

1858	06	*James Jardine*	s	Aichison	Liverpool	275
1858	06	*Margaret*	s	Goldsworthy	Torquay	6

Three women and three children.

1858	06	*Minnesota*	s	Flinn	Liverpool	8
1858	06	*Nova Scotian*	s.s.	McMaster	Liverpool	294
1858	06	*Thailata*	s	Stinson	Liverpool	28
1858	07	*Argonaid*	s	White	Liverpool	769

Eight cabin, 761 steerage.

Year	Month	Vessel	Type	Master	Departure Port	Passenger Numbers
1858	07	*Gipsy Queen*	bk	Chapman	Plymouth	170

Nine cabin, 161 steerage.

Year	Month	Vessel	Type	Master	Departure Port	Passenger Numbers
1858	07	*Indian*	s.s.	Jones	Liverpool	216
1858	07	*Mountaineer*	bk	Wilson	LIverpool	15
1858	07	*North American*	s.s.	Grange	Liverpool	168

Eighty-two cabin, eighty-six steerage.

Year	Month	Vessel	Type	Master	Departure Port	Passenger Numbers
1858	07	*Pearl*	bk	Davies	London	8
1858	07	*Windsor Forest*	s	Graffin	Liverpool	379
1858	08	*Culloden*	s	Harley	Liverpool	118
1858	08	*Doreen Prince*	s	Lyons	Liverpool	81

One cabin, eighty steerage.

Year	Month	Vessel	Type	Master	Departure Port	Passenger Numbers
1858	08	*Nova Scotian*	s.s.	McMaster	Liverpool	276

One hundred and ten cabin, 166 steerage.

Year	Month	Vessel	Type	Master	Departure Port	Passenger Numbers
1858	08	*Persia*	bk	Meritt	London	72

Six cabin, sixty-six steerage.

Year	Month	Vessel	Type	Master	Departure Port	Passenger Numbers
1858	08	*St. James*	s	Calley	Liverpool	335
1858	09	*Highland Light*	s	Tripp	Liverpool	185
1858	09	*Louisa*	s	Hawes	Bristol	11
1858	09	*North American*	s.s.	Grange	Liverpool	169

One hundred and fourteen cabin, fifty-five steerage.

Year	Month	Vessel	Type	Master	Departure Port	Passenger Numbers
1858	09	*North Briton*	s.s.	Jones	Liverpool	250

One hundred and thirty cabin, 120 steerage.

Year	Month	Vessel	Type	Master	Departure Port	Passenger Numbers
1858	10	*Anglo Saxon*	s.s.	Borland	Liverpool	201

Ninety-five cabin, 106 steerage.

Year	Month	Vessel	Type	Master	Departure Port	Passenger Numbers
1858	10	*Charlotte A. Stamler*	s	Rogers	Liverpool	144
1858	10	*John Bull*	bk	James	London	7

Year	Month	Vessel	Type	Master	Departure Port	Passenger Numbers
1858	10	*Nova Scotian*	s.s.	McMaster	Liverpool	134

Eighty-five cabin, forty-nine steerage.

1861	04	*Jura*	s.s.	Langlands	Liverpool	325

Twenty-five cabin, three hundred steerage.

1861	05	*Bohemian*	s.s.	McMaster	Liverpool	400

Fifty-four cabin, 346 steerage. Vessel called at Londonderry.

1861	05	*Canadian*	s.s.	Graham	Liverpool	361

Thirty-nine cabin, 322 steerage.

1861	05	*Margaret Ann*	s	Mortley, W.	Plymouth	101

All steerage.

1861	05	*Minnesota*	s	Flinn	Liverpool	21

All cabin passengers.

1861	05	*North American*	s.s.	Borland	Liverpool	312

Forty cabin, 272 steerage. Vessel called at Londonderry.

1861	05	*Nova Scotian*	s.s.	Ballantine	Liverpool	296

Forty-two cabin, 254 steerage.

1861	05	*Ocean Queen* of Bristol	bk	Hawes	Bristol	10

All steerage.

1861	05	*Royal Adelaide* of Fowey	bk	Labb	Fowey	10

All steerage.

1861	06	*Anglo Saxon*	s.s.	Ballantine	Liverpool	294

Seventy-one cabin, 223 steerage.

1861	06	*Bohemian*	s.s.	McMaster	Liverpool	208

Thirty-two cabin, 176 steerage.

Year	Month	Vessel	Type	Master	Departure Port	Passenger Numbers
1861	06	E. Wilder [Farley]	s	Nichols	Liverpool	31
1861	06	Jura	s.s.	Langlands	Liverpool	211

Forty-two cabin, 169 steerage.

| 1861 | 06 | North Briton | s.s. | Borland | Liverpool | 257 |

Thirty-nine cabin, 218 steerage.

| 1861 | 06 | Senator | s | n/k | Liverpool | 290 |

Twenty-three cabin, 257 steerage.

| 1861 | 07 | Hibernian | s.s. | Grange | Liverpool | 168 |

Forty-six cabin, 122 steerage.

| 1861 | 07 | John Bull | bk | Fox | Liverpool | 12 |

All cabin.

| 1861 | 07 | North American | s.s. | Burgess | Liverpool | 174 |

Thirty-one cabin, 143 steerage.

| 1861 | 07 | North Briton | s.s. | Borland | Liverpool | 148 |

Thirty-one cabin, 117 steerage.

| 1861 | 07 | Nova Scotian | s.s. | Aiton | Liverpool | 199 |

Forty-four cabin, 155 steerage.

| 1861 | 09 | Anglo Saxon | s.s. | Graham | Liverpool | 167 |

Fifty-six cabin, 111 steerage.

| 1861 | 09 | Jura | s.s. | Aiton | Liverpool | 188 |

Forty-seven cabin, 141 steerage.

| 1861 | 09 | Minnesota | s | Flinn | Liverpool | 40 |

All steerage.

| 1861 | 10 | Bohemian | s.s. | McMaster | Liverpool | 175 |

Twenty-four cabin, 151 steerage.

| 1861 | 10 | North American | s.s. | Borland | Liverpool | 183 |

Seventy-five cabin, 108 steerage.

Year	Month	Vessel	Type	Master	Departure Port	Passenger Numbers
1861	10	*North Briton*	s.s.	Grange	Liverpool	200

Seventy-eight cabin, 122 steerage. Vessel was wrecked off Labrador on return journey. No loss of life.

1861	10	*Norwegian*	s.s.	McMaster	Liverpool	248

Sixty cabin, 188 steerage.

1861	10	*Oswego*	s	Card	Liverpool	10

All cabin.

1861	11	*Anglo Saxon*	s.s.	Graham	Liverpool	154

Thirty-six cabin, 118 steerage.

1861	11	*Jura*	s.s.	Aiton	Liverpool	92

Seventeen cabin, seventy-five steerage.

1861	11	*Nova Scotian*	s.s.	Ballantine	Liverpool	149

Twenty-eight cabin, 121 steerage. Ship carried a piano and a bell.

1862	04	*North American*	s.s.	Burgess	Liverpool	278

Forty-four cabin, 234 steerage.

1862	05	*Anglo Saxon*	s.s.	Graham	Liverpool	380

Thirty-six cabin, 344 steerage.

1862	05	*Culloden*	s	Harley	Liverpool	130

Three cabin, 127 steerage.

1862	05	*Gipsy Queen*	bk	n/k	Plymouth	130

All steerage.

1862	05	*Hibernian*	s.s.	Grange	Liverpool	439

Forty-six cabin, 393 steerage.

1862	05	*Nova Scotian*	s.s.	Ballantine	Liverpool	361

Forty cabin, 321 steerage.

1862	06	*Bohemian*	s.s.	Burgess	Liverpool	356

Thirty-eight cabin, 318 steerage.

Year	Month	Vessel	Type	Master	Departure Port	Passenger Numbers
1862	06	*Jura*	s.s.	Aiton	Liverpool	290
Sixty cabin, 230 steerage.						
1862	06	*Marion*	s	Bernier	Liverpool	14
All cabin.						
1862	06	*North American*	s.s.	Borland	Liverpool	345
Thirty-five cabin, 310 steerage. Called at Londonderry.						
1862	06	*Nova Scotian*	s.s.	Ballantine	Liverpool	357
Thirty-eight cabin, 319 steerage.						
1862	06	*Royal Adelaide* of Fowey	bk	Lobb	Fowey	6
1862	07	*Anglo Saxon*	s.s.	Graham	Liverpool	238
Twenty-seven cabin, 211 steerage.						
1862	07	*Hibernian*	s.s.	Grange	Liverpool	203
Forty-one cabin, 162 steerage.						
1862	07	*North American*	s.s.	Burgess	Liverpool	248
Thirty-three cabin, 215 steerage.						
1862	07	*Norwegian*	s.s.	McMaster	Liverpool	316
Forty cabin, 276 steerage.						
1862	07	*Nova Scotian*	s.s.	Ballantine	Liverpool	236
Fifty-five cabin, 181 steerage.						
1862	07	*William Rathbone*	s	Pratt	Liverpool	502
All steerage.						
1862	08	*Anglo Saxon*	s.s.	Aiton	Liverpool	288
Seventy-six cabin, 212 steerage.						
1862	08	*Bohemian*	s.s.	Borland	Liverpool	215
Seventy-six cabin, 239 steerage.						

Year	Month	Vessel	Type	Master	Departure Port	Passenger Numbers
1862	08	*Hibernian*	s.s.	Grange	Liverpool	218

One hundred and six cabin, 112 steerage.

Year	Month	Vessel	Type	Master	Departure Port	Passenger Numbers
1862	08	*Jura*	s.s.	Graham	Liverpool	240

Seventy cabin, 170 steerage.

Year	Month	Vessel	Type	Master	Departure Port	Passenger Numbers
1862	08	*Powerful*	s	Nixon	Liverpool	30

All steerage.

Year	Month	Vessel	Type	Master	Departure Port	Passenger Numbers
1862	09	*Bohemian*	s.s.	Borland	Liverpool	427

One hundred and twenty cabin, 307 steerage.

Year	Month	Vessel	Type	Master	Departure Port	Passenger Numbers
1862	09	*Copernicus*	s.s.	Booth	Liverpool	6

All cabin.

Year	Month	Vessel	Type	Master	Departure Port	Passenger Numbers
1862	09	*Gipsy Queen*	bk	Symonds	Plymouth	14
1862	09	*Jessie Boyle*	s	Rawle	Portsmouth	9

All cabin.

Year	Month	Vessel	Type	Master	Departure Port	Passenger Numbers
1862	09	*Mavrocord-atos*	s.s.	n/k	London	7

Five cabin, two steerage. Called at Halifax, Nova Scotia.

Year	Month	Vessel	Type	Master	Departure Port	Passenger Numbers
1862	09	*North American*	s.s.	Burgess	Liverpool	227

One hundred and five cabin, 122 steerage.

Year	Month	Vessel	Type	Master	Departure Port	Passenger Numbers
1862	09	*Norwegian*	s.s.	McMaster	Liverpool	418

One hundred and twenty-one cabin, 297 steerage.

Year	Month	Vessel	Type	Master	Departure Port	Passenger Numbers
1862	09	*Nova Scotian*	s.s.	Ballantine	Liverpool	309

One hundred and two cabin, 207 steerage.

Year	Month	Vessel	Type	Master	Departure Port	Passenger Numbers
1862	09	*Pactolus*	s.s.	Johnson	Liverpool	4

All cabin.

Year	Month	Vessel	Type	Master	Departure Port	Passenger Numbers
1862	10	*Hibernian*	s.s.	Grange	Liverpool	302

Fifty-five cabin, 247 steerage.

Year	Month	Vessel	Type	Master	Departure Port	Passenger Numbers
1862	10	*Jura*	s.s.	Aiton	Liverpool	162

Forty-two cabin, 120 steerage. Vessel called at Londonderry.

Year	Month	Vessel	Type	Master	Departure Port	Passenger Numbers
1862	10	*North American*	s.s.	Burgess	Liverpool	267

Fifty-eight cabin, 209 steerage.

| 1862 | 11 | *Anglo Saxon* | s.s. | Graham | Liverpool | 130 |

Twenty-three cabin, eighty-seven steerage.

| 1862 | 11 | *Bohemian* | s.s. | Borland | Liverpool | 238 |

Forty-one cabin, 197 steerage.

| 1862 | 11 | *Norwegian* | s.s. | McMaster | Liverpool | 147 |

Forty-seven cabin, one hundred steerage.

| 1862 | 11 | *Nova Scotian* | s.s. | Ballantine | Liverpool | 158 |

Forty-three cabin, 115 steerage.

| 1862 | 12 | *Bohemian* | s.s. | Borland | Liverpool | 121 |

Twenty-five cabin, ninety-six steerage.

| 1862 | 12 | *Norwegian* | s.s. | McMaster | Liverpool | 107 |

Eighteen cabin, eighty-nine steerage.

| 1863 | 05 | *Anglesea* | s | n/k | Liverpool | 323 |

All steerage.

| 1863 | 05 | *Bloodhound* | s.s. | n/k | Liverpool | 108 |

Eight cabin, one hundred steerage. These were passengers rescued from the *Anglo Saxon*, Captain Burgess, which hit rocks at Newfoundland. Two hundred and thirty-seven people died.

| 1863 | 05 | *Bohemian* | s.s. | Borland | Liverpool | 506 |

Fifty cabin, 456 steerage.

| 1863 | 05 | *Hibernian* | s.s. | Ballantine | Liverpool | 453 |

Sixty-two cabin, 391 steerage.

| 1863 | 05 | *North American* | s.s. | Dutton | Liverpool | 408 |

Fifty cabin, 358 steerage.

| 1863 | 05 | *Norwegian* | s.s. | McMaster | Liverpool | 501 |

Seventy-four cabin, 427 steerage.

Year	Month	Vessel	Type	Master	Departure Port	Passenger Numbers
1863	05	*Oriental*	s	Tom, H.	Plymouth	107

Two cabin, 105 steerage.

| 1863 | 05 | *Waverley* | bk | n/k | Liverpool | 297 |

All steerage.

| 1863 | 06 | *Bohemian* | s.s. | Borland | Liverpool | 278 |

All steerage. The vessel also carried 104 passengers and forty crew from the wrecked *Norwegian*. Two hundred other passengers arrived on the *St. Andrew*.

| 1863 | 06 | *Jura* | s.s. | Aiton | Liverpool | 510 |

Forty cabin, 470 steerage.

| 1863 | 06 | *Lotus* | s | n/k | Bristol | 8 |

All steerage.

| 1863 | 06 | *Nova Scotian* | s.s. | Graham | Liverpool | 547 |

Forty cabin, 507 steerage.

| 1863 | 06 | *Queen* | bk | Hughes | Liverpool | 29 |

All steerage.

| 1863 | 06 | *St. Andrew* | s.s. | n/k | Liverpool | 427 |

All steerage. Also carried two hundred passengers from the wrecked *Norwegian* (*Bohemian* carried other survivors).

| 1863 | 06 | *St. Patrick* | s.s. | n/k | Liverpool | 331 |

All steerage.

| 1863 | 07 | *Damascus* | s.s. | n/k | Liverpool | 274 |

Eight cabin, 266 steerage.

| 1863 | 07 | *Hibernian* | s.s. | Ballantine | Liverpool | 359 |

All steerage.

| 1863 | 07 | *Jura* | s.s. | Aiton | Liverpool | 301 |

All steerage.

| 1863 | 07 | *North American* | s.s. | Dutton | Liverpool | 220 |

Forty-six cabin, 174 steerage.

Year	Month	Vessel	Type	Master	Departure Port	Passenger Numbers
1863	07	*Nova Scotian*	s.s.	Graham	Liverpool	293
All steerage.						
1863	08	*America*	s.s.	Cook	Liverpool	214
Forty-nine cabin, 165 steerage.						
1863	08	*Bohemian*	s.s.	Borland	Liverpool	180
All steerage.						
1863	08	*Falkenburg*	s	n/k	Liverpool	28
All steerage.						
1863	08	*Hibernian*	s.s.	Ballantine	Liverpool	303
1863	08	*Jura*	s.s.	Aiton	Liverpool	161
Fifty cabin, 111 steerage.						
1863	09	*America*	s.s.	Hockley	Liverpool	188
All steerage.						
1863	09	*Damascus*	s.s.	Brown	Liverpool	275
Twenty-five cabin, 250 steerage.						
1863	09	*Nova Scotian*	s.s.	Graham	Liverpool	293
All steerage.						
1863	10	*Bohemian*	s.s.	Borland	Liverpool	209
All steerage.						
1863	10	*Damascus*	s.s.	Brown	Liverpool	226
All steerage.						
1863	10	*Hibernian*	s.s.	Ballantine	Liverpool	327
Thirty-three cabin, 294 steerage.						
1863	10	*Jura*	s.s.	Aiton	Liverpool	213
All steerage.						
1863	10	*North American*	s.s.	Dutton	Liverpool	170
All steerage.						

Year	Month	Vessel	Type	Master	Departure Port	Passenger Numbers
1863	10	*St. Andrew*	s.s.	n/k	Liverpool	150

All steerage.

1863	11	*Bohemian*	s.s.	Borland	Liverpool	111

All steerage.

1863	11	*Nova Scotian*	s.s.	Graham	Liverpool	241

Fifteen cabin, 226 steerage.

1864	05	*Belgian*	s.s.	Aiton	Liverpool	513

Twenty-nine cabin, 484 steerage.

1864	05	*Gipsy Queen*	bk	n/k	Plymouth	28

All steerage.

1864	05	*Hibernian*	s.s.	n/k	Liverpool	494

All steerage.

1864	05	*North American*	s.s.	Wylie	Liverpool	375

All steerage.

1864	05	*Peruvian*	s.s.	Ballantine	Liverpool	577

Thirty-one cabin, 546 steerage.

1864	06	*Belgian*	s.s.	Aiton	Liverpool	513

Twenty-one cabin, 492 steerage.

1864	06	*Damascus*	s.s.	Brown	Liverpool	284

Twenty-three cabin, 261 steerage.

1864	06	*Hibernian*	s.s.	Dutton	Liverpool	366

Thirty-three cabin, 333 steerage.

1864	06	*North American*	s.s.	Wylie	Liverpool	340

Thirty-one cabin, 309 steerage.

1864	06	*Nova Scotian*	s.s.	Ballantine	Liverpool	457

All steerage.

Year	Month	Vessel	Type	Master	Departure Port	Passenger Numbers
1864	07	*Belgian*	s.s.	Aiton	Liverpool	349

Forty-nine cabin, three hundred steerage.

Year	Month	Vessel	Type	Master	Departure Port	Passenger Numbers
1864	07	*Damascus*	s.s.	Brown	Liverpool	162

All steerage.

| 1864 | 07 | *Nova Scotian* | s.s. | Graham | Liverpool | 402 |

All steerage.

| 1864 | 07 | *Peruvian* | s.s. | Ballantine | Liverpool | 255 |

Sixteen cabin, 239 steerage.

| 1864 | 07 | *Salem* | s | n/k | Liverpool | 14 |

All steerage.

| 1864 | 08 | *Hibernian* | s.s. | Dutton | Liverpool | 196 |

All steerage.

| 1864 | 08 | *North American* | s.s. | Kerr | Liverpool | 164 |

All steerage.

| 1864 | 08 | *Peruvian* | s.s. | Ballantine | Liverpool | 163 |

All steerage.

| 1864 | 08 | *St. David* | s.s. | Wyle | Liverpool | 189 |

All steerage.

| 1864 | 09 | *Belgian* | s.s. | Brown | Liverpool | 225 |

All steerage.

| 1864 | 09 | *Hibernian* | s.s. | Dutton | Liverpool | 225 |

All steerage.

| 1864 | 09 | *Jura* | s.s. | Graham | Liverpool | 189 |

All steerage.

| 1864 | 09 | *North American* | s.s. | Kerr | Liverpool | 78 |

All steerage.

Year	Month	Vessel	Type	Master	Departure Port	Passenger Numbers
1864	09	*Nova Scotian*	s.s.	Wylie	Liverpool	121
All steerage.						
1864	10	*Belgian*	s.s.	Brown	Liverpool	163
All steerage.						
1864	10	*Damascus*	s.s.	Watts	Liverpool	195
All steerage.						
1864	10	*Peruvian*	s.s.	Ballantine	Liverpool	179
All steerage.						
1864	11	*Hibernian*	s.s.	Dutton	Liverpool	135
All steerage.						
1864	11	*North American*	s.s.	Kerr	Liverpool	151
All steerage.						

ERO = Essex Record Office

NAB = Nat.'l Archives of Britain

NOTES

CHAPTER 1: CANADA'S APPEAL TO THE ENGLISH

1. SROI: Education File #26 (*Gentleman's Magazine*, May 1832).
2. ERO D/DVv/87: Robert Downes to his mother in Witham, Essex, 1817.
3. Charles Chetwynd-Talbot, 2nd Earl Talbot.
4. STRO D240/J/4/7: Shrewsbury papers, R.W. Hay, undersecretary in the Colonial Office to Lord Talbot, September 28, 1835.
5. LAC MG24 I19: Richard Hemsley and family fonds.
6. Private communication with David Ford, September 2010. His permission to use this information is gratefully acknowledged.
7. ERO D/DJg/F9: Joseph Jessopp correspondence.
8. *Canadian Courant and Montreal Advertiser*, August 16, 1826, reprinted in the *Liverpool Albion*.
9. The British government's experiments with state-aided emigration are discussed in H.J.M. Johnston, *British Emigration Policy 1815–1830: Shovelling Out Paupers* (Oxford: Clarendon Press, 1972).
10. Stanley C. Johnson, *A History of Emigration from the United Kingdom to North America 1763–1912* (London: 1913), 57–58.
11. By 1840, Australia and New Zealand were the preferred destinations of most parish-assisted immigrants, although their overall numbers were far lower than in the previous decade.
12. DERO D3155/WH 2867: Buchanan's concerns were mentioned in John

Richards's letter to the Right Honourable Wilmot Horton, undersecretary for war and the colonies, April 4, 1831.

13. Buchanan's letter to Daniel Gurney, King's Lynn, Norfolk, July 10, 1835 in PP 1836 (76) XL.

14. CKS U47/18 E5: Walter H. Shadwell papers, Mr. Watts to R.S. Harvey in London, August 23, 1834.

15. DERO D3155/WH3393: Remarks on outline of a plan for emigration by the Duke of Somerset's agent.

16. Wendy Cameron, Sheila Haines, and M. McDougall Maude (eds.) *English Immigrant Voices: Labourers' Letters from Upper Canada in the 1830s* (Montreal: McGill-Queen's University Press, 2000), 138–40 (Edward and Hannah Bristow's letter, July 20, 1833).

17. Joseph Pickering, *Enquiries of an Emigrant Being the Narrative of an English Farmer from the Year 1824 to 1830 During Which Period He Traversed the USA and the British Province of Canada with a View to Settle as an Emigrant* (London: Effingham Wilson, 1831), 44.

18. The Crown and Clergy Reserves provided even further acreages to the British Establishment.

19. STRO D240: Shrewsbury papers: estate memoranda and correspondence. D240/J/4/6: Lord Glenelg's advice to Lord Talbot, September 12, 1835.

20. The government continued to operate its "grace and favour" land policies well into the 1850s. Lillian Francis Gates, *Land Policies in Upper Canada* (Toronto: University of Toronto Press, 1968.), 303–07.

21. J.M. Bumsted, *The Peoples of Canada: A Pre-Confederation History*, vol. 1 (Toronto: Oxford University Press, 1992), 236–57.

22. SHRO 448: Marrington Hall collection, 448/632: Philip Snape to his uncle (n.d.). Some rebels wished to see Upper Canada break free from Britain and this outcome would have been welcomed by many Americans.

23. LRO FANE 6/12/2: Journal of Mary Chaplin, August 30, 1838; August 1, 1839.

24. Many of the passengers arriving at Quebec did not settle in the Canadas. As a consequence, the Quebec arrival statistics do not accurately reflect the number of people who actually came to reside in the Canadas. Also, the ease with which immigrants could cross the American-Canadian border created a steady flow of immigrants in both directions, thus adding to the confusion.

25. N.H. Carrier, and J. R. Jeffery, *External Migration: A Study of the Available Statistics 1815–1950* (London: HMSO, 1953), 95–96.

26. Henry John Boulton, *A Short Sketch of the Province of Upper Canada, for the Information of the Labouring Poor Throughout England* (London, John Murray, 1826), 53–54, 58.

27. Pickering, *Enquiries of an Emigrant*, 36–37.

28. John George Lambton, Earl of Durham, headed an investigation of the disturbances and demands being made for fuller self-government.

29. Lord Durham's Report, vol. 2, 212, quoted in Johnson, *A History of Emigration*, 177–78.

30. Methodism's appeal to pioneer settlers in the Canadas is discussed in S.D. Clark, *Church and Sect in Canada* (Toronto: University of Toronto Press, 1949), 90–100.

31. Some commentators believed that in rejecting a hierarchical structure Methodist preachers were undermining British values and for that reason questioned whether they could remain loyal to the British Crown. David Mills, *The Idea of Loyalty in Upper Canada, 1784–1850* (Kingston, ON: McGill-Queen's University Press, 1988), 55–57.

32. Clark, *Church and Sect in Canada*, 143–44. For example, a Quaker family from Lancashire settled in Reach Township (Ontario County) in 1835. For further details of Agnes and David Cragg's request to join the Yonge Street Monthly Meeting of Friends in Upper Canada, see LARO FRL 2/1/33/164.

33. SPG AR, 1851, lxiii–lxiv.

34. DERO D3349/3: Metcalfe family of Killarch correspondence. Letters to the Reverend J. Metcalfe, in Kilnmarsh, 3/1, July 10, 1908, 3/2, September 27, 1909.

35. *Ibid.*, 3/4, August 9, 1911.

36. LAC 920 MD 154: Journal of James Moncrieff Wilson, 44–45.

37. LRO FANE 6/8/3: Fane Collection. "Report of Col. Francis Fane on His Visit to the Dominion in 1890," 14.

38. LARO DDX 1357 2/1/10: Clitheroe.

39. The Scots represented 20 percent of the population. Many parts of Upper Canada also had sizeable German populations by 1881. Other ethnic groups recorded in the 1881 Census were: Native Peoples, Dutch, African, Swiss, and Welsh, although their numbers were relatively small.

40. Bruce Elliott, "The English," in Paul Robert Magocsi (ed.), *The Encyclopaedia of Canada's Peoples* (Toronto: Published for the Multicultural History Society of Ontario by the University of Toronto Press, circa 1999), 462–65.

CHAPTER 2: THE LOYALIST IMMIGRANTS

1. ETRC P006/009: Millie Hallowell fonds. Millie Hallowell was born in Sherbrooke in 1861.

2. They were known later as United Empire Loyalists in recognition of their loyalty to the Crown after the British defeat.

3.   The actual numbers are uncertain. It is thought that around 35,000 Loyalists arrived initially in Nova Scotia and settled along both sides of the Bay of Fundy, swelling the population of the Nova Scotia peninsula and giving the newly created province of New Brunswick an instant population. Cape Breton and the Island of St. John (later Prince Edward Island) received about one thousand each. Phillip Buckner and John G. Reid (eds.), *The Atlantic Region to Confederation: A History* (Toronto: University of Toronto Press, 1993), 184–209; J.M. Bumsted, "The Consolidation of British North America, 1783–1860," in Philip Buckner (ed.), *Canada and the British Empire* (Oxford: Oxford University Press, 2008), 43–47.

4.   Wilbur Henry Siebert, "American Loyalists in the Eastern Seigneuries and Townships of the Province of Quebec," *Transactions of the Royal Society of Canada*, 3rd series (1913) vol. VII: 3–41.

5.   Robert S. Allen, *The Loyal Americans: The Military Role of the Loyalist Provincial Corps and Their Settlement in British North America 1775–1784* (Ottawa: National Museum of Canada, circa 1983), 92–95. The German Palatines and English Quakers were victims of religious persecution.

6.   Fernand Ouellet, *Le Bas Canada 1791–1840; Changements structuraux et crise* (Ottawa: Ottawa University, 1976) [Translated and adapted: Patricia Claxton, *Lower Canada, 1791–1840: Social Change and Nationalism* (Toronto: McClelland & Stewart, 1980)], 22–36.

7.   Robert Harvey, *A Few Bloody Noses: The American War of Independence* (London: John Murray, 2001), 179–82.

8.   Siebert, "American Loyalists in the Eastern Seigneuries and Townships," 27–30.

9.   By 1820 Sorel was reported to be the only town between Montreal and Quebec "wherein English is the dominant language." William Kingdom, *America and the British Colonies* (London: G. and W.B. Whittaker, 1820), 99.

10. LAC MG 21: Haldiman Collection, "Return of Loyalists in Canada, 1778–87," March 1783. LAC M68-G46: Christ Church Parish fonds (Sorel).

11. For servicemen, land was granted according to rank, ranging generally from one thousand acres for officers to one hundred acres for privates. Civilians usually got one hundred acres for each head of family and fifty additional acres for every person belonging to the family. Helen Cowan, *British Emigration to British North America; The First Hundred Years* (Toronto: University of Toronto Press, 1961), 3–12.

12. Approximately 80 percent of the Loyalists settled in what were known as the Royal Townships: Charlottenburg, Cornwall, Osnabruck, Williamsburgh, Matilda, Edwardsburgh, Augusta, and Elizabethtown. Angela E.M. Files, "Loyalist Settlement along the St. Lawrence in Upper Canada," *Grand River*

Branch (U.E.L. Association of Canada) Newsletter 8, no. 1 (February 1996): 9–12.

13. Many of Major Jessup's corps went to Edwardsburgh, Augusta, and Elizabethtown townships.

14. While the 1881 Census reveals a relatively strong German presence in Dundas County (34 percent), it shows few people of English origin (11 percent).

15. They were known as the Cataraqui Townships and consisted of: Kingston (Frontenac County), Ernestown (Addington County), Fredericksburg and Adolphustown (Lennox County), and Marysburgh (Prince Edward County).

16. For example, in Prince Edward County, people with English ancestry outnumbered each of the other ethnic groups, although they only represented around 30 percent of the population. People with German and Irish ancestry were close seconds to the English, and there was also a substantial Dutch and Scottish element.

17. RHL USPG Series E: Reports from Missionaries (LAC m/f A-223). J. Reynolds Tooke and Robert Gregory Cox, both writing in 1855.

18. The Loyalists also included the Iroquois and other Native Americans who, wishing to maintain their loyalty to the King, fled from New York to Fort Niagara during the Revolutionary War. Numbering almost two thousand, most were granted land to the west of Lake Ontario, but a smaller number went to the Bay of Quinte region.

19. Clark, *Church and Sect*, 90–93. Fahey Curtis, "A Troubled Zion: The Anglican Experience in Upper Canada" (unpublished Ph.D. thesis, Carleton University, 1981), 24–32.

20. John Clarke, "A Geographical Analysis of Colonial Settlement in the Western District of Upper Canada, 1788–1850" (unpublished Ph.D. thesis, University of Western Ontario, 1970), 37.

21. Few immigrants arrived in Upper Canada from Britain until 1815. Joseph Bouchette, *The British Dominions in North America: A Topographical and Statistical Description of the Provinces of Lower and Upper Canada, New Brunswick, Nova Scotia, the Islands of Newfoundland, Prince Edward Island and Cape Breton* (London: Longman, Rees, Orme, Brown, Green and Longman, 1832) vol. II, 235.

22. Raymond Whaley, "The Bates and Lovekin Families: First Settlers of Clarke Township," *Families* 44, no. 1 (February 2005): 3–26.

23. Leslie M. Morley, C.E. Morley, W.C. Murkar *The Village of Pickering* (Pickering, ON: Corporation of the village of Pickering, 1970), 2–3.

24. LAC MG24 I59: John Langton and family fonds.

25. Andrew's grandfather had acquired land in Scott Township in 1809. Allan

McGillivray, *Decades of Harvest: A History of the Township of Scott, 1807–1973* (Uxbridge, ON: Scott History Committee, 1986), 7–27.

26. Hilda Marion Neatby, *Quebec, The Revolutionary Age, 1760–1791* (Toronto: McClelland & Stewart, 1966), 133–41; John A. Dickinson and Brian Young, *A Short History of Quebec*, 2nd edition (Toronto: Longman, 1993), 54–59.

27. The French militia took up arms to defend Quebec from the Americans in 1775, although none volunteered to join the British Army in attacking the American colonies.

28. Gates, *Land Policies in Upper Canada*, 12–23.

29. Haldimand to Lord North, quoted in Ouellet, *Le Bas Canada*, 24.

30. Following later boundary changes, Foucault (renamed Caldwell Manor) is now in the State of Vermont.

31. Siebert, "American Loyalists in the Eastern Seigneuries and Townships," 32–37.

32. Two systems of land tenure were now in place. The original French seigneuries stretched along the St. Lawrence River as far as the Gaspé, and along the Ottawa, Chaudière, and Richelieu rivers.

33. By 1881, most of the English in Huntingdon County were to be found in Hemmingford and Hinchinbrook townships. Siebert, "American Loyalists in the Eastern Seigneuries and Townships," 38–41; Joseph Bouchette, *A Topographical Dictionary of the Province of Lower Canada* (London: H. Colburn and R. Bentley, 1831).

34. There were 129 men, fifty-two women, and 132 children in the first group, followed by fifty-six people in a second group. Wilbur Henry Siebert, "Loyalist Settlements in the Gaspé Peninsula," *Transactions of the Royal Society of Canada*, 3rd Series (1914) vol. VIII: 399–405.

35. Bouchette, *The British Dominions in North America*, vol. I, 323–33; Siebert, "Loyalist Settlements in the Gaspé Peninsula," 403.

36. Having been forcibly expelled from Nova Scotia in 1755, along with many thousands of other Acadians, they were some of the very few who had escaped deportation. Finding a safe haven in the Baie-des-Chaleurs, these Acadians then attracted further followers.

37. Raoul Blanchard, *L'Est du Canada Français, "Province de Québec"* (Montreal: Publications de l'Institut Scientifique Franco-Canadien, 1935) vol. I, 56–65.

38. NAS GD 45/3/153: Population in Baie-des-Chaleurs, circa 1825. For a description of the Gaspé Scots, see Lucille H. Campey, *Les Écossais: The Pioneer Scots of Lower Canada, 1763–1855* (Toronto: Natural Heritage, 2006), 111–22.

39. Marjorie Whitelaw, ed., *The Dalhousie Journals*, vol. 3 (Ottawa: Oberon, 1978–82), 64.

40. Before 1800, the Gaspé Peninsula was predominately British, since few French Canadians had arrived by this time. However, by 1861, French Canadians were the dominant group. People of either English or Scottish origin accounted for only 17 percent of the population, and forty years later they were only 7 percent of the total.

41. RHL USPG Series E: Reports from Missionaries (LAC m/f A-223).

42. Gerald M. Craig, *Upper Canada: The Formative Years, 1784–1841* (Toronto: McClelland & Stewart, 1993), 40–65.

43. LAC MG24 I20: Samuel Southby Bridge collection.

44. John A. Dickinson and Brian Young, *Short History of Quebec*, 2nd edition (Toronto: Longman, 1993), 60–62.

45. The Voltigeurs Canadiens, the first French Canadian regiment of regular soldiers raised under the leadership of Charles-Michel de Salaberry, a Canadian lieutenant colonel in the British Army, helped defend Lower Canada at the Battle of Châteauguay.

46. For details of the Scottish schemes, see Lucille H. Campey, *Scottish Pioneers of Upper Canada, 1784–1855 — Glengarry and Beyond* (Toronto: Natural Heritage, 2005), 35–68. For details of the Irish schemes, see Bruce S. Elliott, *Irish Migrants in the Canadas: A New Approach* (Kingston, ON: McGill-Queens University Press, 1988), 61–81.

47. UHA DDX 60/50: Courtney family papers.

CHAPTER 3: SOUTH AND WEST OF MONTREAL

1. Joseph Bouchette, *A Topographical Description of the Province of Lower Canada, with Remarks upon Upper Canada* (London: W. Faden, 1815), 1789.

2. Potash was the main product of the virgin forest, being the ashes left behind after trees were burned. A simple process turned the ashes into potash.

3. Joseph Bouchette, *A Topographical Dictionary of the Province of Lower Canada* (London: Longman & Co, 1832). See entry for Richelieu River.

4. Robert Sellar, *The History of the County of Huntingdon & of the Seigneuries of Chateauguay and Beauharnois from Their First Settlement to the Year 1838* (Huntingdon, QC: Canadian Gleaner, 1888), 19–20; G.A. Rogers, "The Settlement of the Chateauguay Valley," *Connections* 14, no. 3 (1992): 2–6.

5. Lucille H. Campey, *Planters, Paupers, and Pioneers, English Settlers in Atlantic Canada* (Toronto: Natural Heritage, 2010), 37–59.

6. Britain and France were at war between 1793 and 1801, and again in the Napoleonic Wars between 1803 and 1815.

7. Some of this land had probably belonged to French seigneurs who returned to France after the British conquest of Quebec. Lacolle seigneury

had previously belonged to David Lienard de Beaujeu, after whom it had been named. Following Beaujeu's death in the Seven Years' War, his heirs sold the seigneury to Gabriel Christie.

8. Serge Courville [translated by Richard Howard], *Quebec: A Historical Geography* (Vancouver: UBC Press, 2008), 105–06.

9. By 1791, some 32 percent of the Lower Canada seigneuries were totally or partially owned by English-speaking people. John A. Dickinson and Brian Young, *Short History of Quebec*, 2nd edition (Toronto: Longman, 1993), 31–34, 81, 170–73.

10. Carl Benn, *The War of 1812* (Oxford, UK: Osprey, 2002), 8–9, 48–49.

11. The geographical origins of the English families who settled in Lacolle have been taken from the "History of English Settlement in Lacolle" website: *www.angelfire.com/home/lake/lacolle/hist.html*.

12. During the War of 1812–1814, Hoyle and a business associate, William Bowron, were said to have made large profits from selling American cattle to troops at the British garrison at Île aux Noix.

13. While men like Hoyle went to the Canadas during the war, many Americans living in the Canadas did the reverse and moved south to the United States.

14. *DCB* Vol. VIII (Robert Hoyle). Hoyle played an active role in the Townships Militia. His brother Henry arrived from New York in 1824 and later acquired the Lacolle seigneurial manor house and estate.

15. In spite of widespread and repeated complaints within Britain over the high cost of timber, the protective tariffs remained in place until 1860. Ralph Davis, *The Industrial Revolution and British Overseas Trade* (Leicester, UK: Leicester University Press, 1979), 48–49. Duties increased from 25s. per load in 1804 to 54s. 6d. per load in 1811.

16. The Hudson River could be reached from Lake Champlain by 1819 with the completion of the Champlain Canal.

17. Between 1817 and 1830 just under six thousand people sailed to Quebec from Hull, around 2,700 did the same from Liverpool, as did a similar number who sailed from the combined Cumberland ports of Maryport, Whitehaven, and Workington.

18. Campey, *Planters, Paupers, and Pioneers*, 129–35, 166–68.

19. Andrew Oliver [late of Montreal], *A View of Lower Canada Interspersed with Canadian Tales and Anecdotes and Interesting Information to Intending Emigrants* (Edinburgh: Menzies, 1821), 122–24.

20. *Hull Packet*, March 17, 1823.

21. Sellar, *History of the County of Huntingdon*, 321–22. Bowron was a Quaker who had originally emigrated to New York. When war was declared in 1812, he moved to Montreal, where he founded a linen manufacturing business

that later collapsed. Returning to New York he received word about Lacolle from Robert Hoyle, an acquaintance of his, and decided to join him. He later became the Crown Lands' agent for the area.

22. *DCB* Vol. VII (Henry Edme).

23. John Cockerline, from Easington in the East Riding, settled in Henrysburg in 1833; his father-in-law, Marmaduke Jackson (also from Easington), settled in the Lacolle seigneury.

24. Francis Cookman from Owthorne in the East Riding, who moved to Bogton in 1825, was particularly well-regarded and became known as the father of Bogton.

25. The Wesleyan Methodist Missionary Society was founded in Britain in 1786 to support missionary activities overseas.

26. Hewson and John Paine, both brothers from Maltby le Marsh in Lincolnshire, moved to Henrysburg in 1827.

27. SOAS MMS/North America/Correspondence/FBN2, Box 94/File 4E#1: J. Booth, August 4, 1823. The Reverend Booth also made occasional visits to East Hemmingford (Scrivers settlement), Sherrington (Douglas settlement), Îsle aux Noix, and Caldwell's Manor, the latter being on the east side of the Richelieu River.

28. *Report of the Wesleyan Methodist Society*, 1825, 86; 1826, 100–01; 1827, 93–94.

29. *Montreal Gazette*, July 9, 1827.

30. *Quebec Gazette*, May 19, 1828.

31. *Montreal Gazette*, June 11, 1829. Included among the 150 people from Yorkshire who arrived in one vessel were two families who moved on to Illinois and Ohio to join their friends.

32. *Montreal Gazette*, June 14, 1830.

33. Hallerton is believed to have been named after Charles Ellerton, a native of Cottingham in the East Riding who arrived in 1827.

34. Ouellet, *Le Bas Canada*, 480–81.

35. RHL USPG Series E, 1845–46 (LAC m/f A-221).

36. RHL USPG Series E, 1845–46 (LAC m/f A-221).

37. Sellar, *History of the County of Huntingdon*, 252.

38. *DCB* Vol. IX (Edward Ellice). A fur baron, merchant banker, and major land owner, Ellice had considerable financial interests in North America.

39. G.A. Rogers, "Pioneer Mill Sites in the Chateauguay Valley," *Connections* 15, no. 1 (September 1992): 7–15.

40. The obligations and rights of tenants and seigneurs are outlined in Courville, *Quebec: A Historical Geography*, 49–68, 132–38.

41. DERO D3155/WH2787: Edward Ellice letters (1823–1824). Legislation

was being considered to commute feudal fees and rents to special payments but legal and financial complications blocked progress.

42. SOAS MMS/North America/Correspondence/FBN2 (1821–1824) J. de Putron, April 1, 1822, Box 93/File 3c#54.

43. Bouchette, *A Topographical Dictionary of the Province of Lower Canada* (1832). Of the forty-four English families listed in Beauharnois seigneury, nineteen lived in Ormstown, fourteen in Edwardstown, while the remaining eleven were scattered widely.

44. An 1838 map of Lower Canada reveals four places in Beauharnois seigneury and Huntingdon County having English settlers; however, the people referred to were probably English-speaking Scottish Lowlanders (see NAS RHP 35156).

45. Sellar, *History of the County of Huntingdon*, 253–61.

46. *Montreal Gazette*, March 19, 1855. Ormstown's first Anglican church had been built in 1835.

47. RHL USPG Series E, 1845–46 (LAC m/f A-221).

48. SPG *Annual Report* (1855), l–liii.

49. Sellar, *History of the County of Huntingdon*, 464–65. Severs had initially settled along the La Tortue River near La Prairie.

50. RHL USPG Series E, 1845–46 (LAC m/f A-221).

51. NORO YZ 3305 declaration of Richard Hall (December 10, 1855) re: death certificate of Henry Long Hall who died September 19, 1828.

52. Sellar, *History of the County of Huntingdon*, 422–23.

53. Bouchette, *A Topographical Dictionary of the Province of Lower Canada* (1832). By 1832 most of the Hinchinbrooke inhabitants were Scottish or Irish.

54. RHL USPG Series E, 1845–46 (LAC m/f A-221).

55. RHL USPG Series E, 1860 (LAC m/f A-228).

56. Between 1820 and 1822, just over one hundred people arrived at Charlottetown from the Cumberland port of Whitehaven, but they probably included former weavers from Dumfriesshire and other parts of the southwest Scottish Borders, who were leaving in large numbers at that time.

57. In 1819, the *Dumfries and Galloway Courier* (April 13) fretted over the continuing loss of people to New Brunswick from Cumberland and the Scottish Borders.

58. John Thompson, *Hudson: The Early Years, Up to 1867* (Hudson, QC: Hudson Historical Society, 1999), 78–97. The book includes an updated list of settlers provided by Shirley Lancaster.

59. The families mainly originated from parishes to the east of Penrith: Renwick, Kirkoswald, Great Salkeld, Addingham, Culgaith, and Edenhall.

Fewer numbers came from the area to the west of Penrith and from the northern stretches of Westmorland County.

60. The Reverend Abbott did not have his own church, but instead had to share the use of the local schoolhouse with the St. Andrews' Presbyterian minister, who presided over a large Scottish congregation. C. Thomas, *History of the Counties of Argenteuil and Prescott* (Montreal: John Lovell, 1896), 106.

61. Abbott's eldest son, John Joseph Caldwell, became prime minister of Canada.

62. Abbott's comments as quoted by Thompson in *Hudson: The Early Years*, 8.

63. Abbott's booklet was written under the pseudonym of "an immigrant farmer," *Memoranda of a Settler in Lower Canada; or the Emigrant in North America, Being a Useful Compendium of Useful Practical Hints to Emigrants … Together with an Account of Every Day Doings upon a Farm for a Year* (Montreal, 1842). His booklet was first published in January 1842 by the *Quebec Mercury* as a series of articles.

64. *DCB* Vol. IX (John Mathison).

65. Mathison's house was demolished in the 1960s.

66. A Methodist missionary quoted by Thompson in *Hudson: The Early Years*, 8.

67. Letter to Joseph Blenkinship quoted by Thompson in *Hudson: The Early Years*, 8.

68. Thompson, *Hudson: The Early Years*, 78–80.

69. *DCB* Vol. IX (John Mathison).

70. RHL USPG Series E, 1845–46 (LAC m/f A-221).

71. *Montreal Gazette*, June 11, 1829.

CHAPTER 4: THE EASTERN TOWNSHIPS

1. John Irving Little (ed.), *Love Strong as Death: Lucy Peel's Canadian Journal, 1833–1836* (Waterloo, ON: Wilfred Laurier University Press, 2001), 196–97.

2. Given that Lucy's journal was discovered in a descendant's house in Norwich, the Peels probably originated from Norfolk.

3. Little, *Lucy Peel's Canadian Journal*, 8.

4. *Ibid.*, 4–5.

5. *Report from the Select Committee Appointed to Inquire into the Expediency of Encouraging Emigration from the United Kingdom*, 1826, A1861.

6. Cleared land was offered at from $10 to $12 per acre, but uncleared land, laid out in lots of fifty to two hundred acres, could be purchased from as little as $1.50 to $2.50 per acre. [The dollar was worth about four shillings.] Robert Montgomery Martin, *History, Statistics and Geography of Upper and Lower Canada* (London: Whittaker, 1838), 344–52.

7. Leonard Stewart Channell, *History of Compton County and Sketches of the Eastern Townships of St. Francis and Sherbrooke County* (Belleville, ON: Mika Publishing, 1975) [first published 1896], 242.

8. The English came second numerically to French Canadians in this latter group of townships.

9. For details of the early settlements of the Eastern Townships and the Protestant missionaries who organized religious worship, see Françoise Noël, *Competing for Souls: Missionary Activity and Settlement in the Eastern Townships, 1784–1851* (Sherbrooke, QC: University of Sherbrooke, 1988), 7–41, 56–62.

10. LAC MG24 J47: Charles Caleb Cotton and family fonds, 118, 130: letter to his sister Louise, December 31, 1804, and to his sister Mary in July 1807.

11. *Ibid.*, 152 (sister Anna in August 1810).

12. RHL USPG Series E, 1845–46 (LAC m/f A-221).

13. Anglicans outnumbered Methodists by two to one in 1831, but the numbers were much more even by 1851 (see Noël, *Competing for Souls*, 236–39).

14. SOAS MMS /North America/Correspondence/FBN2, Box 93/File 3c#56: J. Booth, April 16, 1822.

15. Noël, *Competing for Souls*, 104–12.

16. ETRC P009: Reverend Thomas Johnson fonds (1789–1881). In 1830, Jackson was sent to Yamaska mountain (Abbotsford), to the east of Saint Hyacinthe, where he remained until at least 1846.

17. SOAS MMS /North America/Correspondence/FBN2, Box 93/File 3c#24: J. Hick, June 5, 1821. For a description of the Wesleyan Methodist Church in Stanstead during the early nineteenth century, see J.I. Little, "The Methodistical Way: Revivalism and Popular Resistance to the Wesleyan Church Discipline in the Stanstead Circuit, 1821–52," *Studies in Religion* 31, no. 2 (2002): 171–94.

18. RHL USPG Series E, 1845–46 (LAC m/f A-221).

19. SOAS MMS, Box 93/File 3c#52: T Catterick, March 25, 1822.

20. *Report of the Wesleyan Methodist Missionary Society* (1824), 135.

21. The distribution of the different religious congregations established between 1799 and 1820 and from 1821 to 1840 is summarized in Noël, *Competing for Souls*, 23, 24.

22. SPG *Annual Report*, 1854, xlvi–xlviii. By 1881 the English were the largest of the British ethnic groups in Stukely and Ely townships in the future Shefford County.

23. RHL USPG Series E, 1845–46 (LAC m/f A-221).

24. Phyllis Hamilton, *With Heart and Hands and Voices: Histories of Protestant*

Churches of the Brome, Missisquoi, Shefford and Surrounding Area (Montreal: Price-Patterson, 1996), 64.

25. Drummondville was named after General Sir Gordon Drummond, the lieutenant governor of Upper Canada.

26. For details of the Rideau Valley military settlements, see Campey, *Scottish Pioneers of Upper Canada*, 35–68, 80–90.

27. *Hull Advertiser*, April 26, 1817. In July of that year, sixty-four people sailed in the *Manique* to Quebec from Hull.

28. *DCB* Vol. VII (Frederick George Heriot). Heriot was in charge of the Drummondville settlement from 1815.

29. Arthur R.M. Lower, "Immigration and Settlement in Canada, 1812–1820," *Canadian Historical Review* vol. III, 1922: 37–47.

30. RHL USPG Series E, 1845–46 (LAC m/f A-221).

31. RHL USPG Series E, 1854–55 (LAC m/f A-223).

32. The Americans had colonized the St. Francis River area from 1794. Noël, *Competing for Souls*, 21, 39.

33. ETRC P997/001.04/007: Captain Joseph Perkins. The Perkins family were joined later by Alvie and Rayner Leet; a few years later came the Olneys, Nuttings, and Doynes; circa 1820, the Armstrongs, Cassidys, and Sproles arrived.

34. ETRC P997/001.06/005: Moses Elliott fonds.

35. SOAS MMS /North America/Correspondence/FBN2, Box 93/, File 3c#68, R. Pope, August 12, 1822. The Reverend Pope covered an area measuring forty-nine miles in length and twenty miles in breadth, which accommodated less than one thousand inhabitants.

36. *Ibid.*, 3c#38., R Pope, October 28, 1821.

37. RHL USPG Series E, 1854–55 (LAC m/f A-223).

38. SPG *Annual Report*, 1856, l–li.

39. LRO FANE/ 6/12/3: Journal of Mary Chaplin, 1840. Millicent Mary (Reeve) Chaplin (1790–1858) was born in Leadenham, Lincolnshire. She accompanied her husband, Colonel Thomas Chaplin of the Coldstream Guards, to his Quebec posting in 1838. The couple remained in Quebec until September 1842. She travelled extensively during this period, describing her visits in writing and capturing various scenes through her watercolours and drawings.

40. Noël, *Competing for Souls*, 27.

41. *Report of the Wesleyan Methodist Missionary Society* (1829), 76.

42. There were two Alexander Buchanans, who both served as Quebec immigration agents. Alexander, the elder, served as agent from 1828 to 1838. Alexander, the younger, his nephew, was agent from 1833 to 1862. From

as least as early as 1833, Alexander, the younger, looked after the immigration office during the winter, when his uncle took a leave of absence for health reasons.

43. About twenty Wiltshire families settled in Inverness Township at this time. PP 1831–32(724)XXXII.

44. Leslie Stuart Nutbrown, *The Descendants of Thomas Nutbrown* (Lennoxville, QC: The Author, 2001).

45. RHL USPG Series E, 1845–46 (LAC m/f A-221).

46. Gwen Rawlings Barry, *History of Megantic County: Downhomers of Quebec's Eastern Townships* (Lower Sackville, NS: Evans Books, 1999), 128–30.

47. RIC Cornish Memorial Scheme: Women's Institute survey of Cornish people who have emigrated.

48. SPG *Annual Report*, 1854, xli–xlii.

49. The St. Francis Tract consisted of the following townships: Garthby, Stratford, Whitton, Weedon, Lingwick, Adstock, Bury, Hampden, Marston, Ditton, Chesham, Emberton, and Hereford.

50. For an analysis of the British American Land Company's role as a settlement promoter, see John Irvine Little, *Nationalism, Capitalism and Colonization in Nineteenth-Century Quebec, the Upper St. Francis District* (Kingston, Ontario: McGill-Queen's University Press, 1989), 36–63.

51. Cowan, *British Emigration*, 136–37. Many pamphlets were published at the time. See, for example, British American Land Company, *Information Respecting the Eastern Townships of Lower Canada* (London: W.J. Ruffy, 1833).

52. Letter to Mrs. George Coates of Ripon, January 27, 1834, in Dr. William Wilson, *Letters from the Eastern Townships of Lower Canada Containing Information Respecting the Country Which Will Be Useful to Emigrants* (London: 1834), 2.

53. PP 1839 (536-1) XXXIX (Evidence taken by the Canada commissioners at Sherbrooke, September 10, 1836).

54. However, poor people had been assisted to emigrate to British North America by parishes, local organizations, and private individuals long before 1834 without approval from Parliament. *The Poor Law Act of 1834* was merely legitimizing a practice that was already widespread.

55. Parishes drew the necessary emigration funds by borrowing from local sponsors against the security of the poor rates. The payments were organized and administered at a local level by elected boards of guardians and overseen by Poor Law commissioners.

56. Gary Howells, "Emigration and the New Poor Law: Norfolk Emigration Fever of 1836," *Rural History* 11, no. 2 (October 2000): 145–64.

57. *Suffolk Chronicle*, March 9, 1833 (unnamed author, Edgeware Road, London).

58. Workhouses were made as unpleasant as possible in the hope that inmates would wish to leave and find work.

59. *Norfolk Chronicle* and *Norwich Gazette*, April 6, 1836, quoted in Gary Howells, "'On Account of their Disreputable Characters': Parish-Assisted Emigration from Rural England, 1834–860." *History* 88 (4), no. 292 (October 2003): 591.

60. *Bury and Norwich Post*, September 21, 1836, quoted in Bruce Elliott, "Regional Patterns of English Immigration and Settlement in Upper Canada," in Barbara J. Messamore (ed.), *Canadian Migration Patterns from Britain and North America* (Ottawa: University of Ottawa Press, 2004), 72.

61. Most of Prince Edward Island's intake from Suffolk was drawn from the Poor Law Unions of Blything, Plomesgate, Hoxne, and Wangford, all situated in the northeast of the county. See Campey, *Planters, Paupers, and Pioneers*, 180–84.

62. *Quebec Gazette*, July 8, 1836.

63. Poor Law data states that 220 people from Downton in Wiltshire were assisted to emigrate to Lower Canada in 1835–36, but other evidence indicates that their actual destination was Upper Canada. See Chapter 7.

64. Poor Law Commissioners, *The Second Annual Report of the Poor Law Commissioners for England and Wales* (London: HMSO, 1836), 571–74. A total of 3,068 Norfolk and 787 Suffolk paupers had received assistance to emigrate between June 1835 and July 1836, accounting for 73 percent of those assisted from England and Wales. The funds raised for the Norfolk group amounted to £15,198.10s, while £4,198 was raised for the Suffolk group.

65. Between May 1835 and June 1837 a total of 3,171 passengers left from Great Yarmouth: *Wellington* (86) *Baltic* (109) *Allendale* (77) *Baltic* (182) *Carron* (206) *Preston* (156) *Tulloch Castle* (346) *Venus* (203) *Wellington* (153) *William Ritchie* (315) *Brunswick* (445) *Morning Star* (238) *Indemnity* (178) *Baltic* (172) *Carron* (193) *Preston* (112). In 1836, some 555 immigrants left from Ipswich, 810 from Kings Lynn, and 119 from Lowestoft.

66. Poor Law Commissioners, *The Third Annual Report of the Poor Law Commissioners for England and Wales* (London: HMSO, 1837), 126–27. A total of 286 were assisted to emigrate from Norfolk and 296 from Suffolk.

67. A Poor Law Union included several parishes. Unions were created to enable parishes to share the costs of building and supporting a workhouse within the union area.

68. Poor Law Commissioners, *The Second Annual Report*, 571–74.

69. In 1830, a total of seventy-eight men, women, and children from Diss (Depwade Poor Law Union) in South Norfolk, Palgrave, and Wortham

(Hartismere Union), in North Suffolk, and fifty-eight from Winfarthing and Shelfanger parishes (both in Guiltcross Union) in South Norfolk were assisted by their parishes to emigrate to North America. See Eric Pursehouse, "The 1830 Wagon Train for Diss, Emigrants," *Waveney Valley Studies: Gleanings from Local History* (Diss, Norfolk: Diss Publishing Co., 1966), 233–36.

70. Scott Frederick Surtees, *Emigrant Letters from Settlers in Canada and South Australia Collected in the Parish of Banham, Norfolk* (London: Jarrold and Sons, 1852), 3, 10.

71. *Report from the Chairman of the Docking Union*, quoted in Howells, "On Account of Their Disreputable Characters," 600.

72. NAB MH 12/8249, quoted in Howells, *ibid.*, 599.

73. NRO PD 699/90/5: Heacham Parish. The Heacham group sailed in the *Penelope* in May 1836.

74. Poor Law Commissioners, *The Second Annual Report*, 571–74.

75. Great Ryburgh lost sixty-eight people to Lower Canada.

76. LAC MG24 I156: list of people emigrating from Kettlestone to Sherbrooke. Microfilm copy of original documents held by the Reverend H.G.B. Folland of Norwich.

77. NRO DN/BBD/13 Folland. The average cost of the fares was £3 a head.

78. Little, *Lucy Peel's Canadian Journal*, 201.

79. LRO FANE/6/12/3: Journal of Mary Chaplin, 1840.

80. By 1881 the English predominated in Sherbrooke County. They were the largest ethnic group in Ascot Township and the largest British group in Orford Township.

81. Channell, *History of Compton County*, 242.

82. *Sherbrooke Daily Record,* March 16, 1957, quoted in Little, *Nationalism, Capitalism and Colonization*, 57.

83. Channell, *History of Compton County*, 248–55.

84. RHL USPG Series E, 1854–55 (LAC m/f A-223); SPG *Annual Report*, 1855, xlvii–l.

85. RHL USPG Series E, 1854–55 (LAC m/f A-223).

86. RHL USPG E6 Missionary Reports, 1859.

87. RHL USPG Series E, 1854–55 (LAC m/f A-223).

88. By 1881 the English accounted for 60 percent of the population of Eaton and Compton townships.

89. SPG *Annual Report*, 1855, xlvii–l.

90. The company was left with 85,000 acres in Bury, Lingwick, and Weedon townships. With its other holdings in Lower Canada it still controlled over half a million acres.

91. PP w/e August 7, 1841.

92. PP 1841 Session I (298) XV.

93. Patrick Bailey, "Pioneer Settlers: East Anglia and Quebec," *The Amateur Historian* 4, no. 1 (1958): 9–11. Bailey identifies the many Eastern Township place names that are East Anglian in origin.

94. PP, w/e July 23, 1842.

95. ETRC P092: William Hoste Webb fonds.

96. ETRC P074: Frank Grundy fonds.

97. ETRC P129: Philip Harry Scowen fonds.

98. ETRC P059: Tom Martin Fonds.

99. Robert Sellar, *The Tragedy of Quebec: The Expulsion of its Protestant Farmers* (Toronto: University of Toronto Press, 1907), 13–20, 123–28, 196–205. [This title was reprinted by University of Toronto Press in 1974 with an introduction by Robert Hill.] Robert Sellar was editor of the *Huntingdon Gleaner*.

100. "An important letter of a resident of Quebec as to the disabilities of protestants in the province of Quebec: the parish system" (Toronto: Equal Rights Association for the province of Ontario, 1890) typified the grievances being raised by Protestant farmers over the growing powers of the Catholic Church. Colonization societies were formed at this time to encourage French Canadians back from the United States to the Eastern Townships.

CHAPTER 5: THE OTTAWA VALLEY

1.   Whitelaw, *The Dalhousie Journals* vol. 2, 35.

2.   *Ibid.*, 34.

3.   Bouchette, *The British Dominions in North America,* vol. I, 202; Bouchette, *A Topographical Dictionary of the Province of Lower Canada* (1832).

4.   By 1881, 88 percent of the English who lived in Argenteuil County were concentrated in Lachute, St. Andrews, Grenville, and Chatham.

5.   Raoul Blanchard, "Les Pays de l'Ottawa" *Étude Canadienne troisième série,* vol. 3 (Grenoble, France: Allier, 1949): 50–52, 58–64.

6.   The Reverend Abbott was in charge of St. Andrews from 1818, and in 1830 presided over the new Anglican mission at Grenville Township.

7.   Thomas, *History of the Counties of Argenteuil, Quebec and Prescott,* 221–22, 229, 268.

8.   *Ibid.*, 129, 311, 594–95.

9.   Blanchard, "Les Pays de l'Ottawa," 61.

10. Thomas, *History of the Counties of Argenteuil, Quebec and Prescott,* 447–49.

11. *Ibid.*, 100–01, 135, 145–46.

12. Whitelaw, *Dalhousie Journals*, vol. 2, 34. Work began on the Grenville Canal in 1818. Hundreds of Irish immigrants and French Canadians were employed.

13. Whitelaw, *Dalhousie Journals*, vol. 2, 52.

14. *Ibid.,* 34.

15. *DCB* (George Hamilton) Vol. VII.

16. Robert Greenhalgh Albion, *Forests and Seapower, the Timber Problems of the Royal Navy 1652–1862* (Cambridge, Mass: Harvard Economic Studies, 1926), 422. Of the 90,000 timber loads, 17,000 had been sent from Quebec with the remainder being sent from Maritime ports.

17. Whitelaw, *Dalhousie Journals*, vol. 2, 36.

18. John MacTaggert, *Three Years in Canada, An Account of the Actual State of the Country in 1826–7–8 Comprehending Its Resources, Productions, Improvements and Capabilities and Including Sketches of the State of Society, Advice to Emigrants, etc.* Two Volumes (London: 1829), 268.

19. Whitelaw, *Dalhousie Journals*, vol. 2, 36.

20. *Ibid.,* 41.

21. B.S. Elliott, "'The Famous Township of Hull': Image and Aspirations of a Pioneer Quebec C Community," *Social History* 12 (1969): 339–67.

22. By 1812, Wright was in conflict with Archibald McMillan, the region's other major timber contractor. Richard Reid (ed.), *The Upper Ottawa Valley to 1855: A Collection of Documents Edited with an Introduction by Richard Reid* (Toronto: Champlain Society, 1990), xix–xxi, xlvii–l.

23. MacTaggert, *Three Years in Canada*, 268.

24. Robert F. Gourlay, *Statistical Account of Upper Canada Compiled with a View to a Grand System of Emigration* (London: Simpkin & Marshall, 1822) vol. I, 607.

25. Whitelaw, *Dalhousie Journals*, vol. 2, 37.

26. ANQ FC2949AYLM1939 Aylmer Then & Now, 1816–1939.

27. ANQ P1000, D2, P278 (C141): An account of the first settlement of the Township of Hull in 1820.

28. LAC RG313 C-718: Population return of the Township of Hull, 1825.

29. ANQ P98: Moses Benedict papers.

30. 1835(87) XXXIX, Buchanan's Report, 1834 w/e August 9.

31. SHRO N.W. Tildesley, "William Farmer's Emigration to Canada," *Shropshire Newsletter*, no. 40 (June 1971), published by the Shropshire Archaeological Society. The document appears to be based on records held by the Farmer family.

32. *Ibid.*

33. *Ibid.*

34. Names in Farmer's group have been extracted from the *GENUKI* and *Ancestry.com* websites. All are common to both websites except for the names marked by an asterisk which appear only in the *Ancestry.com* website. The names are: Jemima Rudkins, housekeeper and nurse; William Dukes, a lawyer; Arthur Vickers, tutor, a Cambridge student; Thomas Barnfield, miller and wheelwright; Mr. Williams, groom and waiter; Mrs. Williams, his wife; George, Joseph, and James Williams, sons and three daughters; Amos Bonnell, wheelwright; Mrs. Bonnell, Catherine, George, William, Fanny, and Thomas Bonnell and one child born at sea; William Furnivall, blacksmith (Mrs. Bonnell's brother); Samuel Langford, gardener; Mrs. Langford; Mary, Samuel, William, Richard, Annie, and Bessie Langford; Thomas Child, a general purpose man, his wife and seven children; Child's children were: Thomas, Richard, and James Parton (stepchildren), and Peter, Fanny, Mary, Annie Child (his own children); James Green, a mason; Mrs. Green; plus *Ellen Smith, a general house servant (Green's sister-in-law); *William Adderley, a sawyer, along with his wife and three young children.

35. Bytown was renamed Ottawa in 1855.

36. SHRO 1781/2/133: Shackerley estate, declaration of Mary Alice Farmer late of Sutton Maddock, March 21, 1844. William Farmer had a total of twelve children — five by his first wife and seven by his second wife.

37. Nepean's early hamlets and villages included Rochesterville, Mount Sherwood, Stewarton, Billings Bridge, Archville, Bayswater, Hintonburgh, Birchton (later Skead's Mill, which became Westboro), and Stottsvale. See ANQ P11, S2: William H. Johnston and Reby Dodds fonds: *The Clarion*, 1867–1967 (Nepean Centennial Edition), 4, 17.

38. *Montreal Gazette*, June 11, 1829.

39. DERO D3155/WH 2867: John Richards to the Right Honourable Wilmot Horton, March 4, 1831.

40. *DCB* (James Skead) Vol. XI. Skead's Mill in Nepean Township is named after him.

41. LAC MG25 G325: Wilson family collection.

42. The 1881 Census reveals that the English outnumbered all other ethnic groups in New Edinburgh, including the Irish.

43. *DCB* (William Price) Vol. IX. Price also established himself as a major timber contractor in the Saguenay region by 1842.

44. Donald MacKay, *The Lumberjacks* (Toronto: Natural Heritage, 1998), 13–16, 22–27, 40–45.

45. LAC 920 MD 154: Journal of James Moncrieff Wilson, 44–45.

46. *DCB* (Peter Aylen) Vol. IX. Aylen's followers were known as the "Shiners." See Michael S. Cross, "The Shiners' War: Social Violence in the Ottawa

Valley in the 1830s," *Canadian Historical Review* 54, no. 1 (March 1973): 1–26.

47. There had been no regular Anglican services in Hull until 1820 when the Reverend Joseph Abbott, who was based at St. Andrews, came periodically to preside over baptisms and marriages.

48. Elliott, "The Famous Township of Hull," 356–62.

49. RHL USPG Series E, 1845–46 (LAC m/f A-221).

50. SPG *Annual Report*, 1849, xliii–v.

51. The St. James gravestone transcriptions include mention of: Thomas Heath Birks from Stafford, born 1832, and his wife Sabina Broadhead, of Bradford (Yorkshire), born 1847; Charles H. Broadhead from Bradford, born 1852; John Broadhead from Leicester, born in 1820, and his wife Maria Holt, born in Wakefield (Yorkshire) in 1828; Joseph Dey, native of Manchester, born 1830; George Franklin, born 1813 in Northamptonshire; Benjamin Huckell of Lincolnshire, born 1822, and his wife Ann Reading from Buckinghamshire, born 1819; Walter H. Prowse, native of Staffordshire, born 1870; Charles Skipworth, born in Lincolnshire in 1856, and his wife Hannah J Pearson, born Yorkshire 1860; Reuben Traveller, native of London, born 1788.

52. The account that follows is taken from ANQ P80, S1 Ruth Higginson collection. *Buckingham Post*, January 5, 1899; January 26, 1934.

53. RHL USPG Series E, 1845–46, 1854–55 (LAC m/f A-221, A224).

54. ANQ P80, S1 Ruth Higginson collection: *Buckingham Post*, July 2, 1965.

55. STRO D260/M/E/430/38: Hatherton Collection, I.A. Grant to Colonel Littleton, February 10, 1881.

56. The Perth military settlement covered Bathurst, Drummond, Beckwith, and Goulbourn townships; the Lanark settlement covered Ramsay, Lanark, Dalhousie, and North Sherbrooke townships. For further details see Campey, *Scottish Pioneers of Upper Canada*, 35–68.

57. Elliott, *Irish Migrants in the Canadas*, 61–81; Cowan, *British Emigration*, 65–84.

58. For details of the Irish domination of the Rideau Valley, see Elliott, *ibid.*, 116–46.

59. Michael S. Cross, "The Age of Gentility: The Formation of the Aristocracy in the Ottawa Valley," Canadian Historical Association: *Historical Paper* 2, no. 1 (1967): 105–17.

60. RHL USPG Series E, 1854–55 (LAC m/f A-223).

61. LAC MG8 G49: Rev. Mary A. Dougherty, "Quyon Parish History," 1959, 1–5. Many of the communities were formed by the internal migration of people who had previously settled in the Rideau Valley communities on

the south side of the Ottawa River. For the later movement of Irish settlers from Upper Canada into Pontiac County, see Elliott, *Irish Migrants in the Canadas*, 161–70.

62.   LAC MG25 G271 Vol. 17/27: Rev. James Brown, "History of the Parish of Onslow," 1908, 1, 2, 5.

63.   LAC MG25 G271 Vol. 17/15, Vol. 17/17. Before Falloon's arrival, Protestant settlers had to rely on the Methodist ministry in the area.

64.   Michel Pourbaix, *The History of a Christian Community: Eardley, Luskville, Pontiac* (Pontiac, QC: 1999), 12, 28, 32. Daniel Pickett was the first Methodist pastor to visit Hull from the Upper Canada side of the river, and from 1823 Methodist preachers made regular visits. Hull's Methodist circuit founded in 1826 was the first to be established on the north side of the river. For details of the Perth Methodist circuit, founded in 1821, see James M. Neelin and Michael R. Neelin, *The Old Methodist Burying Ground in the Town of Perth, Lanark County, Ontario* (Ottawa: Ottawa Branch, Ontario Genealogical Society, 1978).

65.   LAC MG25 G271: religious notes.

66.   BRO CRT 190/413: "History of the Valley," which gives details of James Tate based on information supplied by two of his granddaughters in 1957. The Tates joined the already-established early settlers who were: John and Rex Tucker, Nelson Fraser, Captain Findlay, the Goddards, the Achesons, and Samuel Adams.

CHAPTER 6: WEST ALONG LAKE ONTARIO

1.   SORO T/PH/SAS/8/925/1: J.O. Lewis, *Letters from Poor Persons Who Emigrated to Canada from the Parish of Frome in the County of Somerset* (Frome, Somerset, UK: Frome Newspaper Co. Ltd., 1945), 5–6 (William and Jane Grant to their parents, September 6, 1831).

2.   *Ibid.*

3.   Morley, *The Village of Pickering*, 2.

4.   Gilbert Patterson, *Land Settlement in Upper Canada, 1783–1840* (Toronto: Ontario Archives, 1921), 157–58. Markham had a particularly large German population.

5.   James Emerson, "Emerson Family History — From Durham Co., England to Durham Co., U.C.," *Families* 29, no. 4 (1983): 229–39. This account of the Emerson family's relocation to Upper Canada, compiled in 1926, is based on information supplied by James Emerson's son.

6.   Patterson, *Land Settlement in Upper Canada*, 127.

7.   CAS D/WAL/3/8: Joseph Bland to his cousin, October 31, 1858.

8. The group leader paid a £10 deposit for each emigrant (repayable once they were settled) for which the group received its land grants free of charge.

9. CAS D/WAL/7/D: payments to people of Alston who are to emigrate to Upper Canada (1832). The group included twenty families with children and a total of £311 was spent by the parish.

10. LAC MG24 I59: John Langton and family fonds, letters to his father June 16, June 28, and August 12, 1835. Langton noted that one of the settlers on the east side of Mud Lake was a Cornishman who had resided there for seventeen years. Peter Robinson's Irish settlers were mostly Roman Catholics, mainly from County Cork, who had arrived in the Peterborough area in 1825.

11. NTRO PR7347: Carlton-on-Trent Parish records. The emigrants included Mary Weightman and her four children (John, Thomas, Hugh, and Ann) and three grandchildren (John's children); Jonathan Selby and his wife and six children; Thomas Marrot and family; and John Batterby and family.

12. NTRO DD592/1, /3: Hannah Barclay letters, April 1, 1832, July 18, 1839.

13. Andrew F. Hunter, *A History of Simcoe County* (Barrie, ON: Historical Committee of Simcoe County, 1948), 63–65.

14. CAS DHod/15/26/7: Estate papers of Joseph Hodgson. He left each daughter £576 — a considerable sum at this time.

15. PP 1833(141) XXVII.

16. LAC MG24 J12: George Pashley fonds: Journal 1: 2, 5, 10. The Pashley family sailed in the *Reward* (Captain Laidley) in August 1833.

17. *Ibid.,* 12.

18. *Ibid.,* 16.

19. Quebec Immigration Agent's Report w/e June 1, 1839.

20. Quebec Immigration Agent's Report w/e May 30, 1840. Twenty in the group were going to settle in Ohio and Indiana.

21. HCA DMJ/415/37-40: Bravender letters, November 30, 1846, December 11, 1846.

22. *Ibid.*

23. HCA DMJ/415/37-40: Bravender letters, May 15, 1847.

24. John Langton, a Cambridge graduate, had exceptional ability. He quickly rose through the ranks as a local politician, becoming the MP for Peterborough County in 1851.

25. Barbara Williams (ed.), *A Gentlewoman in Upper Canada: The Journals, Letters and Art of Anne Langton* (Toronto: University of Toronto Press, 2008), 109–10.

26. Barbara Williams (ed.), *Ann Langton: Pioneer Woman* (Peterborough, ON: Peterborough Historical Society, 1986), 5–6. Anne kept a journal from 1837 to 1846 and wrote many letters detailing her family's experiences. These

have been published in Hugh Hornby Langton (ed.), *A Gentlewoman in Upper Canada: The Journal of Anne Langton* (Toronto: Clark, Irwin, 1950).

27. *Ibid.*

28. *Ibid.*, 12–15.

29. Catherine's *The Backwoods of Canada* and Susanna's *Roughing It in the Bush* and *Life in the Clearings Versus the Bush* are still in print.[Catherine Parr Traill, *The Backwoods of Canada* (Ottawa: Carlton University Press, 1997) and Susannah Moodie, *Roughing it in the Bush or Life in Canada* (London: Virago Press, 1986).] Charlotte Gray, *Sisters in the Wilderness: The Lives of Susannah Moodie and Catherine Parr Traill* (Toronto: Penguin Books, 1999) provides a biography of both sisters. In 1847, the Traill family moved to Rice Lake in Hamilton Township (Northumberland County).

30. *Montreal Gazette*, June 1, 1833.

31. See Appendix 1 for individual sea crossings.

32. PP 1833(141) XXVII. The Quebec immigration agent reported that the paupers arriving in 1832 mostly came from Yorkshire, Norfolk, Suffolk, Bedfordshire, Northamptonshire, Kent, Sussex, Hampshire, Somerset, and Gloucestershire.

33. Rainer Baehre, "Pauper Emigration to Upper Canada in the 1830s," *Social History* 14, no. 28 (1981): 339–67.

34. Helen Allinson, *Farewell to Kent: Assisted Emigration in the Nineteenth Century* (Sittingbourne, Kent: Synjon Books, 2008), 23–25. CKS P364/19/4/18 provides a list of the Tenterden paupers who emigrated between 1821 and 1827. CKS P364/18/8 provides details of the 1828 assisted emigration from Tenterden.

35. CKS P26/8/1: Biddenden Parish records.

36. CKS P348/8/1: Stockbury Parish records.

37. Allinson, *Farewell to Kent*, 72–73. Poor people from the parishes of Lenham and Ulcomb to the south of Stockbury in Kent were also assisted to emigrate to Upper Canada in 1836–37, while another parish-assisted group from Ulcomb went to Upper Canada in 1841–42. See Poor Law Commissioners, *3rd* and *7th Annual Reports*. On June 26, 1832, the *Montreal Gazette* had reported the arrival of seventy-five immigrants in the *Niagara* ("more than half English") who included paupers from Lenham. Most were due to settle in the Newcastle District (Northumberland, Peterborough, Durham, and Victoria counties).

38. PP 1843(109) XXXIV. The agent reported that they planned to settle in Newcastle, Home, and Gore districts.

39. William Cobbett, *Rural Rides in the Counties of Kent, Sussex, Hampshire, Wiltshire, Gloucestershire, Herefordshire, Worcestershire, Somerset, Oxfordshire,*

Berkshire, Essex, Suffolk, Norfolk, and Hertfordshire, published originally in 1830 by William Cobbett (reprinted London: Penguin, 2001), 313–15.

40. Cobbett, *Rural Rides*, 287–88.

41. The local economy depended strongly on woollen cloth-making. Thus, the rise of cotton factories in northern England and the growing preference for cotton over wool had devastating consequences for the area. J.L. and B. Hammond, *The Village Labourer, 1760–1832: A Study in the Government of England Before the Reform Bill* (London: Longmans, 1919), 97–98, 225–29.

42. SRO DD/LW/49: Frome Vestry Book, 1815–78. The Marquis of Bath also helped to finance the emigration of his tenants in Frome.

43. SRO DD/SF/4546: Sanford family papers, Anonymous letter published in *Bath & Cheltenham Gazette*, March 28, 1831, entitled "Emigration from Frome to Canada."

44. *Ibid.*

45. SRO DD/LW/49: Frome Vestry Book, 1815–1878.

46. SRO T/PH/SAS/8/925/1: J.O. Lewis, *Letters from Poor Persons Who Emigrated to Canada from the Parish of Frome*.

47. Alan G. Brunger, "The Geographical Context of English Assisted Emigration to Upper Canada in the Early Nineteenth Century," *British Journal of Canadian Studies* 16, no. 1 (2003): 7–31.

48. Terry McDonald, "Southern England and the Mania for Emigration," *British Journal of Canadian Studies* 16, no. 1 (2003): 32–43.

49. NAB CO 384/28, 40–41, 48–50. Forty paupers from Heyetesbury and Knook sailed in the *Euphrosyne* in March 1831.

50. George Poullett Scrope, *Extracts of Letters from Poor Persons Who Emigrated Last Year to Canada and the United States for the Information of the Labouring Poor in This Country* (London: J. Ridgeway, 1831), 28–29.

51. For details of the Talbot settlements see Chapter 7.

52. Dummer Assessment Roll of 1839 quoted in Terry McDonald, "A Door of Escape: Letters Home from Wiltshire and Somerset Emigrants to Upper Canada, 1830–832," in Barbara J. Messamore, *Canadian Migration Patterns* (Toronto: University of Toronto Press, 2004), 101–19.

53. LAC MG24 I59: John Langton and family fonds, letter to his father, August 12, 1835.

54. However, many of the emigrants were widely scattered. For example, Joseph and Joan Jones and family from Frome, who had emigrated in 1832, were living in Pickering Township (Ontario County) in 1842. LAC MG25-G339: Jones family collection.

55. Cowan, *British Emigration*, 204–05.

56. Audrey Saunders Miller (ed.), *The Journals of Mary O'Brien* (Toronto: Macmillan of Canada, 1968), 152–53.

57. Quebec Immigration Agent's Report w/e May 23, 1835, w/e May 27, 1837.

58. WHC 1020/55: Longbridge Deverill Vestry Minute Book. Paupers were assisted to emigrate between 1832 and 1841 (also see WHC 1020/110).

59. Poor Law Commissioners, *The Second Annual Report*, 571–74.

60. WHC 306/66, 212B/5644: Purton emigration. The group consisted of: William Maule, widower (60), with two sons and daughter; four single men; Charles and Elizabeth Avenill plus nine children; and a widow with two daughters. A further group of fourteen from Purton were assisted to emigrate to Upper Canada in 1844 (Poor Law Commissioners. *The Eleventh Annual Report of the Poor Law Commissioners for England and Wales*. London: Charles Knight & Co., 1845).

61. WHC 1607/64, 1607/71: Brinkworth Vestry Book. The thirty-five people who emigrated in 1842 sailed in the *Eliza* (Table 8); the 41 people who emigrated in 1843 sailed in the *Toronto* (Table 9); the twenty people who emigrated in 1847 sailed in the *Lloyd* (Table 10); the twenty-one people who emigrated in 1852 sailed in the *Leonard Dobbin* (Table 11).

62. WHC 1607/64: Brinkworth Vestry Book, letters concerning James Whale.

63. *Ibid.,* letters from D. Hardy, on behalf of Brinkworth Parish, dated June 25 and June 27, 1844.

64. The Chelsea Pensioners name derives from their association with the Royal Hospital in Chelsea.

65. Chelsea pensioners received one hundred to two hundred acres of free land in Upper Canada.

66. J.K. Johnson, "The Chelsea Pensioners in Upper Canada," *Ontario History* 53, no. 4 (1961): 273–89.

67. PP 1833(141) XXVII. A relatively small number of Chelsea pensioners were given land in Cranbourn Township in Lower Canada.

68. A.B. Jameson, *Winter Studies and Summer Rambles in Canada* (London: Saunders & Otley, 1838), quoted in Johnson, "Chelsea Pensioners in Upper Canada," 279–80. Anna, wife of Attorney General Jameson, was one of the most celebrated female writers of her time.

69. Johnson, "Chelsea Pensioners in Upper Canada," 280.

70. *Ibid.,* 281.

71. Testimony given by A.B. Hawke, the chief Upper Canada emigration agent, quoted in Johnson, "Chelsea Pensioners in Upper Canada," 281.

72. Initially 17 families (68 people) went to Penetanguishene; the number increased to 101 by 1837.

73. John George Lambton, Earl of Durham, headed an investigation that

looked at the causes of the 1837 rebellions and suggested reforms.

74. Johnson, "Chelsea Pensioners in Upper Canada," 282–88. A table of the 654 names has been compiled. See Barbara B. Aitken, "Searching Chelsea Pensioners in Upper Canada and Great Britain," in *Families* 23, no. 3 (1984) [Part I]: 114–27 and no. 4 (1984) [Part II]: 178–97.

75. Wendy Cameron, "English Immigrants in 1830s Upper Canada: The Petworth Emigration Scheme," in Barbara J. Messamore, *Canadian Migration Patterns* (Toronto: University of Toronto Press, 2004), 91–100.

76. LAC MG24 I59: John Langton and family fonds, letters to his father, June 16 and 28, 1835.

77. Cameron, *English Immigrant Voices*, 30–31 (Wright's letter to his father, 1832).

78. *Ibid.,* 49–50 (Spencer's letter to his parents, 1832).

79. *Ibid.,* 141–43 (Tilley's letter to friends and neighbours, 1833).

80. *Ibid.,* 152–53 (Helyer's letter to Peter Scovell, 1833).

81. *Ibid.,* 305, 319, 333.

82. *Ibid.,* 187–88 (Mellish's letter to his parents, 1835.

83. *Ibid.,* 208–09 (Ayling's letter to his parents, 1836).

84. *Ibid.,* 217–20 (Barnes's letter to his family, 1836).

85. *Ibid.,* 204–05. (Birch's letter to his aunt and uncle, 1836).

86. *Brighton Patriot,* November 28, 1837, quoted in Cameron, *English Immigrant Voices,* 258–60.

87. *Ibid.*

88. LAC MG24 I19: Richard Hemsley and family fonds, Dinah to daughter, January 7, 1857.

89. *Ibid.,* William Packham to his uncle, September 22, 1854.

90. *Ibid.,* James Hemsley, March 5, 1857.

91. The number emigrating peaked in 1835–36, a year after the introduction of a new Poor Law, which effectively required paupers to enter a workhouse before being eligible for poor relief.

92. Cowan, *British Emigration,* 180–81.

93. Poor Law Commissioners, *The Second Annual Report,* 571–74.

94. See Chapters 7 and 8.

95. Quebec Immigration Agent's Report w/e June 27, 1835.

96. Quebec Immigration Agent's Report w/e June 10, 1837.

97. CARO Charles F. Bester, *Haddenham, a Parish History,* 128 [typed manuscript (1981)]. In 1833–34, Joseph Howlett, John Hide, Jarvis Porter, and the Wells's, Mustills, and other families were assisted by Haddenham Parish to emigrate. In 1836, assistance to emigrate was also given to Thomas Read's daughter and granddaughter and to John Bridgeman.

98. ERO D/P12/12 (Widdington Parish records), D/P21/18/29 (Steeple Bumstead Parish records). In 1835, fifteen people emigrated from Widdington Parish (John Franklin, wife and family, and nine single men). That same year William Baynes and his wife and family were assisted to emigrate from Wimbish Parish; Also, Debden Parish was planning to spend £70 assisting its poor to emigrate and Steeple Bumstead was also intending to assist an unknown number.

99. LAC MG29 C63: Peter Coleman and family fonds. His brother Francis emigrated in 1834 and settled to the north of Bowmanville in Darlington Township but returned to England for religious training. He and his brother William later went to Upper Canada as ministers of the Wesleyan Methodist Church and preached widely across Upper Canada (see Merrium Clancy et al., *Cornish Emigrants to Ontario* (Toronto: Toronto Cornish Association, 1998), 7–11).

100. LAC MG28 III41: Henry Elliott and son fonds.

101. *West Devon and Cornish Advertiser*, February 10, 1832. Letter to John Davey in St. Neot.

102. Philip Payton, *The Cornish Overseas* (Fowey: Alexander Associates, 1999), 84.

103. By the 1840s, Cornwall's important copper mines declined as a result of foreign competition.

104. Rev. Barry Kinsmen, *Fragments of Padstow's History* (Padstow Parochial Church Council, 2003), 26–27.

105. PP w/e May 23, 1840.

106. Quebec Immigration Agent's Report w/e September 19, 1840.

107. The *Clio* carried 251 passengers who arrived in May and seventy-five who arrived in August; *John and Mary* carried 108; *Spring Flower* thirty-three; *Volunia* fifty-two; and *Belle* thirty-nine.

108. Samuel Pedlar and Charles Wethey, "From Cornwall to Canada in 1841," *Families* 22, no. 4 (1983): 244–53.

109. Poor Law Commissioners, *9th* and *10th Annual Reports*. The parishes of St. Merryn, St. Eval, St. Issey, Mawgan, and St. Columb Major lying to the south of Padstow form a distinct cluster, suggesting that emigration from one parish stimulated interest in its neighbours.

110. Quebec Immigration Agent's Report w/e May 20, 1843.

111. Quebec Immigration Agent's Report w/e May 23, 1846.

112. Clancy et al., *Cornish Emigrants to Ontario*, 21–22.

113. *Ibid.*, 23–30.

114. RIC Cornish Memorial Scheme: Women's Institute survey of Cornish people who have emigrated.

115. The concentrations of Yorkshire and West Country settlers along the western half of Lake Ontario is discussed in Elliott "Regional Patterns of English Immigration and Settlement in Upper Canada," 51–90.

CHAPTER 7: THE LAKE ERIE AND THAMES VALLEY SETTLEMENTS

1. Edward Ermatinger, *Life of Col. Talbot and the Talbot Settlement* (St. Thomas, ON: A. McLachin's Home Journal Office, 1859), 194–96.
2. Edwin Guillet, *Early Life in Upper Canada* (Toronto: University of Toronto, 1963) [reprint, original written in 1933], 133.
3. Fred Coyne Hamil, *Lake Erie Baron, The Story of Colonel Thomas Talbot* (Toronto: Macmillan, 1955), 177.
4. Anna Jameson, quoted in Guillet, *Early Life in Upper Canada*, 135. Having visited Colonel Talbot in 1837, Anna wrote a graphic account of her tour in A.B. Jameson, *Winter Studies and Summer Rambles in Canada* (London: Saunders and Otley, 1838).
5. During the War of 1812–1814, Talbot commanded the 1st Middlesex Militia and supervised the militia regiments in the London District. However, when a force of five hundred men came to be mustered at Long Point on Lake Erie to march to the relief of Fort Amherstburg, there was a mutiny. The men simply refused to march under Lieutenant-Colonel Thomas Talbot.
6. Hamil, *Lake Erie Baron*, 100–13.
7. Talbot supervised the allocation and settlement of vacant Crown lands far removed from his holdings. He kept control over his settlers until they had completed their settlement duties, and withheld their fees to government. Guillet, *Early Life in Upper Canada*, 129.
8. OA MU2928: Talbot Settlement Lease Book, 1825–1845. Talbot had a supervisory role within these townships: Aldborough, Bayham, Dunwich, Malahide, Southwold, Yarmouth (Elgin County); Caradoc, Delaware, Ekfird, London, Mosa, Westminster (Middlesex County); Charlotteville, Houghton, Middleton (Norfolk County); North and South Colchester, Gosfield, Maidstone, Mersea, Sandwich, West Tilbury (Essex County); Harwich, Howard, Orford, Raleigh, Romney, East Tilbury (Kent County); Blandford (Oxford County).
9. *DCB* Vol. XI, Thomas Talbot. Talbot's territory extended from Sandwich and Colchester (Essex County) in the west to Middleton and Charlotteville (Norfolk County) in the east. He never controlled land settlement in an entire township, but in some townships, like Dunwich and Aldborough, there were large areas under his supervision.

10.   Anna Jameson quoted in Guillet, *ibid.*, 135.

11.   *Ibid.* Contrary to Upper Canada regulations, which were supposed to prohibit Americans from acquiring land, Talbot accepted large numbers of them.

12.   By his arrangement with the government he obtained two hundred acres of land for every settler, each of whom he placed on fifty acres of his own land.

13.   Ermatinger, *Life of Colonel Talbot*, 192–93.

14.   *Ibid.*, 194–96.

15.   Charles Oakes Ermatinger, *The Talbot Regime or the First Half Century of the Talbot Settlement* (St. Thomas, ON: The Municipal World Ltd., 1904), 106.

16.   Edwin C. Guillet, *The Pioneer Farmer and Backwoodsman* (Toronto: University of Toronto press, 1963) vol. I, 229.

17.   Joseph's brother Daniel Silcox had emigrated to Southwold in 1816 but Joseph became the Corsley leader.

18.   Ermatinger, *The Talbot Regime*, 280.

19.   A total of £300 was raised to fund the Corsley group, partly by the parish and partly from local landowners.

20.   Brunger, "The Geographical Context of English Assisted Emigration," 7–31.

21.   McDonald, "'A Door of Escape,'" 101–20.

22.   Scrope, *Extracts of Letters from Poor Persons*, 11–12, 14–15.

23.   *Ibid.*, 12–14.

24.   Between 1830 and 1832, 166 people emigrated from Corsley, 370 from Westbury, thirty-one from Horningsham, and 241 from Frome. For details of the Wiltshire/Frome settlements in Peterborough and Simcoe counties, see Chapter 6.

25.   Scrope, *Extracts of Letters from Poor Persons*, 26–27.

26.   Ermatinger, *The Talbot Regime*, 156.

27.   Scrope, *Extracts of Letters from Poor Persons*, 16–17.

28.   Ermatinger, *The Talbot Regime*, 257, 280–81.

29.   Brunger, "The Geographical Context of English Assisted Emigration," 10, 15–18, 22.

30.   SORO T/PH/SAS/8/925/1: J.O. Lewis, *Letters from Poor Persons Who Emigrated to Canada from the Parish of Frome*, 16–18; William Jeanes, September 5, 1832.

31.   *Ibid.*, 19–21, William Jeanes, January 21, 1833.

32.   *Ibid.*, 25–26, William Jeanes, August 20, 1833.

33.   *Ibid.*, editor's note, 26.

34.   Captain Swing, the alleged leader of the riots, has never been identified.

35.   David Waymouth, *Downton: 7,000 Years of an English Village* (Downton, Wiltshire: Cromwell Press, 1999), 129–30.

36. Susan Hartley and Pompi Parry, *Downton Lace: A History of Lace Making in Salisbury and the Surrounding Area* (Salisbury: Salisbury and South Wiltshire Museum, 1991), 6.

37. WHC 1306/105: Downton Parish, receipts for money paid on behalf of the 1835 group of emigrants.

38. The letter-writer was anonymous. Waymouth, *Downton: 7,000 Years of an English Village*, 133; also see *Salisbury Journal*, April 6, 2006.

39. The ethnic composition in 1837 of townships in Elgin, Norfolk, Middlesex, Oxford, and Brant counties is provided by Colin Read in *The Rising in Western Upper Canada: The Duncombe Revolt and After* (Toronto: University of Toronto Press, 1982), 22.

40. *Ibid.*

41. Jennifer Grainger, *Vanished Villages of Middlesex* (Toronto: Natural Heritage, 2002), 111–20.

42. *Ibid.*, 248–49.

43. LAC MG24 D27: Thomas J. Jones and family fonds. Thomas's son Charles married Mary Carter, daughter of George and Deziah Carter, both English-born, and became a successful farmer in London Township.

44. CAS DX 1065/60/1–6: Thomas Priestman wrote six letters from Upper Canada to his brother in Cumberland (1811–39).

45. *Ibid.*, 2, October 5, 1817.

46. *Ibid.*, 3, September 7, 1823.

47. *Ibid.*, 4, March 27, 1825.

48. *Ibid.*, 5 October 25, 1830.

49. *Ibid.*, March 28, 1839.

50. Grainger, *Vanished Villages of Middlesex*, 67–71.

51. *Ibid.*, 300–01.

52. *Ibid.*, 105–08.

53. Ermatinger, *The Talbot Regime*, 96.

54. Grainger, *Vanished Villages of Middlesex*, 265–67.

55. Cheryl MacDonald, *Norfolk Folk: Immigration and Migration in Norfolk County* (Delhi, ON: Norfolk Folk Book Committee, 2005), 34–40.

56. Other prominent surnames included Batie, Charlton, Scott, and Robson. See J.E. McAndless, "Telfer Cemetery (English Settlement) London Township," in *Families* 14, no. 3 (1975): 71–78; Grainger, *Vanished Villages of Middlesex*, 143–46.

57. The Telfer community founded a Secessionist Presbyterian Church, served by a Scottish minister. In more recent times it was renamed Vanneck United.

58. See Chapter 6.

59. Arthur Raistrick and Bernard Jenning, *A History of Lead Mining in the Pennines* (London: Longmans, Green & Co. Ltd., 1965), 324–25.

60. John listed the following people who had previously emigrated from Weardale to Upper Canada: Jonathan Emmerison from Burnhope, Walton and Samuel Elliot from Seadlon, Joseph Thompson from Burnhope, John Featherston from Burnhope, Watson Lowe from Copthill, John Fleamen from Blackdean, Featherston Phillipson from Irsupburn.

61. Letter written by John Graham in Weardale to his brother Joseph in North America, dated August 1, 1854, published in Anon., "Nineteenth Century Emigration from Weardale," in *Northumberland and Durham Family History Society* 21, no. 3 (Autumn 1996): 94. John may have been referring to the sailing of the *Vesper* from Newcastle to Quebec in 1854 — it left with 152 passengers.

62. Those assisted to emigrate under the Petworth Emigration Scheme mainly originated from West Sussex but some also came from East Sussex, Surrey, and Cambridgeshire. The scheme involved 1,800 people who emigrated between 1832 and 1838. Their letters home were collected and published by the Reverend Thomas Sockett, who organized the scheme.

63. Wendy Cameron and Mary McDougall Maude, *Assisting Emigration to Upper Canada: The Petworth Project, 1832–37* (Montreal: McGill-Queens University Press, 2000), 15–24. A smaller number were sent to another government settlement in the adjoining township of Warwick (Lambton County).

64. Cameron, *English Immigrant Voices*, 21–22, 97–100 (Cooper's letters to his family, July 28, 1832, and February 5, 1833).

65. The government provided a log house to married couples but single men were expected to build their own house.

66. Cameron, *English Immigrant Voices*, 110–12. Baker's letter to his parents, March 13, 1833.

67. *Ibid.*, 95–97. Goatcher's letter to his wife, January 17, 1833.

68. Another son had emigrated to Upper Canada in 1832.

69. Cameron, *English Immigrant Voices*, 251–55. Mann's letter to her sons, January 2, 1837.

70. *Ibid.*, 165–66 (Carver's letter to his parents, June 30, 1834).

71. CAS DX 1065/60/3: letter from Thomas Priestman September 7, 1823.

72. Cameron, *English Immigrant Voices*, 233–34 (Hilton's letter to his uncle, October 16, 1836).

73. *Ibid.*, 281–83 (Pullen's letter to sister and brother, December 31, 1838).

74. *Ibid.*, 166–68 (Heasman's letter to his family, October 19, 1834).

75. *Ibid.*, 184–87 (Voice's letter to his brother and sister, September 20, 1835).

76. *Ibid.*, 32–33 (Hill's letter to his parents August 5, 1832).

77. Judy Hill, "The Dorking Emigration Scheme of 1832," *Family and Community History*, vol. 7/2 (November 2004): 115–28.

78. Cameron, *English Immigrant Voices*, 83–86 (Worsfold's letter to his father, December 15, 1832).

79. *Ibid.*, 35–36 (Stedman's letter to his family, August 7, 1832).

80. The Petworth immigrants who settled north of Woodstock, in the valley of the Grand River, are discussed in Chapter 8.

81. Elliott, "Regional Patterns of English Immigration and Settlement in Upper Canada," 72–73.

82. They went in two groups, the first, having seventy-nine people, left between 1831 and 1834, while the second group left in 1834.

83. Poor Law Commissioners, *The Second Annual Report*, 571–74.

84. *Ibid.*

85. *Ibid.*

86. Elliott, "Regional Patterns of English Immigration and Settlement in Upper Canada," 89.

87. SROI Education File 1617: "The Carlton Colville Emigrants," in *The East Anglian*, vol. 10 (1903–04): 278–81. The Carlton Colville group sailed in the *Carron*, which left Yarmouth with 206 passengers.

88. SROL 455/4, /7: Woolnough family correspondence, November 9, 1830; January 16, 1832.

89. PP 1842(373) XXXI; PP 1843(109) XXXIV; PP 1844(181) XXXV. The Gore District contained Halton and Wentworth counties.

90. *Ibid.*

91. NTRO PR1900: East Drayton Parish.

92. CARO P53/1/11: "An Account of the Inhabitants of the Parish of Croydon," by Francis Fulford, rector, January 1, 1843, 5, 24, 34, 43, 49, 50 (1), 54, 67.

93. Grainger, *Vanished Villages of Middlesex*, 123–24.

94. Allen G. Talbot, "In Memory of the Tolpuddle Martyrs," *Ontario History* 62, no. 1 (1970): 63–69. George Loveless and Thomas Stanfield are buried in Siloam Cemetery near London; James Loveless (George's brother) and John Stanfield are buried in Mount Pleasant Cemetery, London.

95. Everett Wilson, "John Wilkinson: Devout Methodist and Dereham Pioneer," *Families* 35, no. 3 (August 1996): 147–51.

96. Grainger, *Vanished Villages of Middlesex*, 272–74.

97. BRO HF89/5/1: Hallowell Papers. Joseph Hooper to his brother Tom, April 18, 1868.

98. *Bedfordshire Mercury*, November 23, 1872.

99. BRO CRT 150/166: *Bedfordshire Mercury*, May 1, 1869.

100. Nigel E. Agar, *Bedfordshire Farm Worker in the 19th Century* (Bedford, UK: Publications of the Bedfordshire Historical Record Society vol. 60, 1981), 172–73.

101. "Condensed History of the Barnett Family," by Brian Jones (*brianjones@cableinet.co.uk*).

102. BRO 40/18/70, /71: Oakley Parish receipts. May 1831. The group included Charles Morris and family, George Jones and family, Samuel Craddock and family, each getting £22.15.0; Joel Webster received £6.10, three families received £4 each; Joel Webster got £1. Another list indicated that the group also included Robert Hewlett and family.

103. BRO PUBV 33/1 Vol. 3. The following people were assisted to emigrate from Bedfordshire during the 1850s: James Lawford and William Mayes, his wife and child from Knotting Parish, n/d; Stephen Croft, Great Barford Parish, 1851; Jonas Darrington, in a workhouse, 1851; Isaac Thomas, wife, and five children, Saint Mary Parish, 1851; John Flanders, widower, and three children, Keysoe Parish, 1851; Andrew Shepherd and wife, Knotting Parish, 1852; people in the parish of Pavenham, 1852; William Lunn with his wife and child, Thomas Prentice, with his wife and five children, and William Pratt with his wife and two children, parish of Sharnbrook, 1852; George Bird with his wife and six children, Sharnbrook Parish, 1852; Thomas Davies Bletsoe Parish, 1853.

CHAPTER 8: THE REST OF THE WESTERN PENINSULA

1. Robert Fisher's letter in 1832 to his parents, quoted in Patterson, *Land Settlement in Upper Canada*, xii–xiii.

2. *Ibid.*

3. *Ibid.*

4. For the background to the setting up of the company, its operations, and the key people who promoted and directed it, see Robert C. Lee, *The Canada Company and the Huron Tract, 1826–1853* (Toronto, Natural Heritage, 2004).

5. ERO D/DU 161/394: "Lands in Upper Canada To Be Disposed of by the Canada Company," 1826.

6. The Canada Company had begun its operations eight years before its main rival, the British American Land Company, whose land holdings were concentrated in the Eastern Townships of Lower Canada. For details of the latter company see Chapter 4.

7. PP 1827, V (550), 461–63: "Prospectus of Terms upon Which the Canada Company Proposes to Dispose of Their Lands."

8. It was originally intended that the company would be offered 829,430 acres of Clergy Reserves, but after opposition from the Church of England they were withdrawn and the Huron Tract was substituted in their place. It had been purchased by the government from the Chippewa First Nation.

9. Gates, *Land Policies of Upper Canada*, 168–70. In 1829, the average price per acre in the Huron Tract was 7s. 6d. It rose steadily and by 1840 the average price was 13s. 3d.

10. Lee, *The Canada Company*, 45–84. The town of Galt, later becoming part of Cambridge, was named after John Galt.

11. *Ibid.*, 205–12.

12. William Cattermole, *Emigration: The Advantages of Emigration to Canada: Being the Substance of Two Lectures Delivered at the Town-Hall, Colchester, and the Mechanics' Institution, Ipswich* (London: Simpkin and Marshall, 1831).

13. Glen T. Wright, *The Caroline and Her Passengers, March–May 1832* (Guelph, ON: Wellington Branch, Ontario Genealogical Society, 2002), 3–38.

14. Cattermole's letter to the Colonial Office, February 6, 1832, quoted in Wright, *The Caroline and Her Passengers*, 7.

15. *Ibid.*

16. Cattermole's letter to the Colonial Office, March 19, 1832, quoted in Wright, *The Caroline and Her Passengers*, 8.

17. Cattermole's letter to the *Courier of Upper Canada* written from Grosse Île, May 17, 1832, and reprinted in the *Ipswich Journal*, September 1, 1832.

18. *Ibid.* Cattermole only listed male heads of households for steerage passengers but included male and female cabin passengers.

19. ERO D/P21/18/29: Steeple Bumpstead Parish. The *Quebec Mercury*, letter dated May 29, 1832, appeared among the papers of John Allan, shipping agent.

20. According to the *Quebec Mercury*, the *Caroline* arrived in May from London with 204 passengers; the *Marmion* came in May from Portsmouth with 154 passengers; while the *Crown* came in June with 240 passengers. This would mean that Cattermole's group consisted of just under six hundred passengers. However, Cattermole's figures, reported in his letter to the *Courier of Upper Canada*, provide different passenger totals. He claimed that the *Caroline* carried 204 passengers, the *Marmion* carried 205 passengers, the *Mentor* carried 75 passengers, the *William and Mary* was expected to have 120 to 130 passengers and the *Crown* was expected to have 150 passengers. This places the total at around 750 passengers.

21. Anon., *A Statement of the Satisfactory Results Which Have Attended Emigration to Upper Canada from the Establishment of the Canada Company until the Present Period* (London: Smith, Elder & Co.,1841),

14–15. Extracts of Dr. Alling's letter to the commissioners of the Canada Company, dated December 16, 1840, were quoted in this pamphlet that was published by the Canada Company in 1841.

22. *Ibid.*

23. Cameron, *English Immigrant Voices*, 59–60, Heming's letter to his mother, September 25, 1832.

24. *Ibid.*, 18–19, extract of a letter written by Heming's aunt, July 1832.

25. *Ibid.*, 55–59, Martin's letter to Mr. Sparks, September 24, 1832.

26. Martin had been landlord of the Fox at Felpham in West Sussex.

27. Cameron, *English Immigrant Voices*, 154–55, White's letter to John's father and mother, October 27, 1833.

28. "Canada Company's Prospectus," in Bouchette, *The British Dominions in North America*, 478–82.

29. The Aynho group consisted of: William Libby, wife and four children; John Turner, wife and four children; Francis Ansty, wife and two children; Andrew Homes, wife and four children; Benjamin Howes, wife, mother, brother, and four children; Joseph Goodwin, wife and five children; George Bye, wife and five children; Fanny French, Alfred Borton, William Giles, Rd Bygrave, David Peckova, John Watts, and Charlotte Ansty. James French, wife and seven children.

30. NORO C/A/85: Cartwright papers, letter from William Scott, April 1, 1845.

31. Nicholas Cooper, *Aynho: A Northamptonshire Village* (Banbury, Oxfordshire: Leopard's Head Press, 1984), 209–11.

32. NORO EY/82–88: Eydon Parish; S.J. Tyrell, *A Countryman's Tale* (London: Constable and Co. Ltd., 1973), 77–79. About twenty-three people sailed in the *Canton*. They included George Dodd and family, John Robinson and family, and Thomas Coy and family. Ann Willoughby and her children sailed in the *William Bromham*.

33. In 1827–28, Geddington Parish had assisted four families to emigrate to Upper Canada (NORO 133 p/14), while Long Buckby Parish did the same in 1830 (NORO 197 p/88).

34. DERO D1559Z/F1. Walker Family of Borrowash (Derbyshire). Transcript of a diary written by John Walker (n.d.), 7, 16 (also see LAC MG24 I181).

35. Jean F. Hutchinson, *The History of Wellington County* (Grand Valley, ON: Landsborough, 1997), 137, 144. James Carter and John Iles went to Puslinch Township in 1831 and 1836 respectively, and each acquired around four hundred acres of land.

36. James Scott, *The Settlement of Huron County* (Toronto: Ryerson Press, 1966), 53, 61.

37. LARO DDX 207/57. Letter to Cuthbert Relph, November 25, 1835.

38. W.S. Johnston and H.J.M. Johnston, *History of Perth County to 1967* (Stratford, ON: Corporation of the County of Perth, 1967), 28.

39. Cameron, *English Immigrant Voices*, 43–45, Capling's letter to his brother, August 28, 1832.

40. Robine Lizars and Kathleen Macfarlane Lizars, *In the Days of the Canada Company: The Story of the Settlement of the Huron Tract and a View of the Social Life of the Period 1825–1850* (Toronto: W. Briggs, 1896), 400–17.

41. Cameron, *English Immigrant Voices*, 135–37, Daniels' letter to his brothers and sisters, July 14, 1833.

42. *Ibid.*, 26–28, 69–71, Rapson's letter to his father, August 1832, October 1832.

43. The so-called Dutch were the Deutch–Germans.

44. Cameron, *English Immigrant Voices*, 87–88, 107, Adsett's letter to the Reverend Robert Ridsdale, December 21, 1832; his letter to friends, March 4, 1833.

45. Very large numbers of Germans and some Scandinavians sailed from Liverpool to Quebec from the 1840s. They were mostly on their way to the United States but some remained in Canada. People were fleeing from the agricultural and economic depression being experienced along the Rhine. Cowan, *British Emigration*, 186–87.

46. ERO T/G44 129: The Bootys of Canada.

47. Biddulph and McGillivray townships were in Huron County until 1865, after which time they became part of Middlesex County.

48. Susan Muriel Mack, *The History of Stephen Township* (Crediton, ON: Corporation of the Township of Stephen, 1992), 17–19, 201. Scott, *The Settlement of Huron County*, 166–67.

49. Scott, *The Settlement of Huron County*, 62; Elliott, *Irish Migrants in the Canadas*, 131, 133–34.

50. Alan E. Richards, "Devonians in Canada," *Devon Family Historian*, no. 40 (October 1986): 24–28. Among the Devon people who came to Centralia were: James Willis, Thomas Trivett, John Oliver, John Snell, and John Essery, the latter establishing the first sawmill in the district.

51. Scott, *The Settlement of Huron County*, 62. Other Devon people who settled in the area included George Webber, Lewis Holman, Richard Bissett, Thomas Friend, William Greenway, Thomas Rowcliffe, and Richard Stanlake.

52. Scott, The Settlement of Huron County, 98–99.

53. RHL USPG Series E, 1854–55 (LAC m/f A-223).

54. However, Germans became the dominant ethnic group by 1881. Scott, *The Settlement of Huron County*, 166, 170–71, 178–79.

55. Isaac Carling was the son of Thomas Carling from Yorkshire, founder of the Carling brewing company. Thomas opened a brewery in London, producing a beer that was based on a recipe from his native Yorkshire.

56. *DCB* (Sir John Carling) Vol. XIV.

57. Anon., *Emigration: The British Farmers and Farm Labourer's Guide to Ontario* (Toronto: Blackett Robinson, 1880), 64.

58. Mack, *The History of Stephen Township*, 254–56.

59. DRO 219/29/22, #137: Roper-Lethbridge letters: Devonshire families resident abroad. Hurdon, N. Dyer writing from Exeter, Ontario.

60. *Ibid.*, #265: W.L. Wickett writing from St. Thomas (Elgin County). His father, Richard, had emigrated to Upper Canada from Devon with his wife and family in 1872.

61. Anon., *Emigration: Extracts from Various Writers on Emigration, with Authentic Copies of Letters from Emigrants from Norfolk, Suffolk, and Sussex, Now Settled in Upper Canada, Containing Useful Information Respecting That Country* (Norfolk, UK: Bacon and Kinnebrook, 1834), 11–15.

62. Scott, *The Settlement of Huron County*, 142.

63. *Ibid.*, 176–78.

64. *Ibid.*, 284–87.

65. H.J.M. Johnston, "Immigration to the Five Eastern Townships of the Huron Tract," *Ontario History*, vol. LIV (1962): 207–24.

66. *Ibid.*, 222.

67. William Johnston, *History of the County of Perth from 1825 to 1902* (Stratford, ON: Beacon Herald, 1976), 199, 202, 204. The Methodist church at Carlingford was founded by George Leversage Senior, William Dickey, Thomas Reid, and William Cole. The Reverand Mr. Dunnett was its first minister.

68. The Bethel Methodist Church was built in 1863 and that same year another Methodist church was built at Salem. The Zion Methodist Church was built on the Huron Road in 1889. Johnston, *History of the County of Perth*, 242, 248.

69. Johnston and Johnston, *History of Perth County to 1967*, 144–45, 150.

70. Johnston, *History of the County of Perth*, 234.

71. LAC MG24 I198: James Coleman fonds, 11–13.

72. Johnston and Johnston, *History of Perth County to 1967*, 144–45.

73. Letters collected by the Canada Company to encourage emigration, 1842.

74. *Ibid.*

75. Johnston and Johnston, *History of Perth County to 1967*, 144–45.

76. Johnston, *History of the County of Perth*, 183–84. The Harmony Methodist Church was founded by J.H. Dunsmore, John Libbins, Charles Lupton Senior, Robert Timmins, and James Dunsmore.

77. Johnston and Johnston, *History of Perth County to 1967*, 172.

78. Johnston, *History of the County of Perth*, 392.

79. SHRO1536/5/5/8: Thomas Cholmoneley to his brother, November 9, 1858.

80. W.M. Brown, *The Queen's Bush: A Tale of the Early Days of Bruce County* (London: John Bale sons and Danielson Ltd., 1932), 2–6.

81. For the building of the Garafraxa Road, see Paul White, *Owen Sound: The Port City* (Toronto: Natural Heritage, 2000), 15–16; for the Durham Road, see Elliott, *Irish Migrants in the Canadas*, 172.

82. NAB CO 384/74: Letter dated March 24, 1843, from the governor general.

83. Private communication with Valerie (Ottewell) Bowden, November 2010. Her work in compiling the information that follows, and her permission to use it, are gratefully acknowledged.

84. Richard's parents had originated from Derbyshire, where they worked as nail-makers, a poorly paid, home-based activity involving both adults and children. By 1816 they had moved to Lincolnshire.

85. John Rowe, "A Cornish Farmer in Ontario," in *Agricultural History Review*, vol. 1 (1953): 44–47. The letter was initially published in *West Briton* (Truro) June 27, 1872.

86. In 1835 the adjoining parish of Widdington St. Mary the Virgin assisted fifteen people to emigrate, including John Franklin — Susannah's brother. That year Debden Parish was reported to be in the process of assisting its paupers to emigrate. ERO DP 12/12 Widdington St. Mary the Virgin.

87. Norman Robertson, *History of the County of Bruce* (Toronto: William Briggs, 1906), 281.

88. Dean Wheaton, *Letters from Bruce County Written by Pioneer Joseph Bacon, 1705–1882* (Bloomington, IN: Author House, 2006), 1–2, 28–33. Two letters written by Joseph Bacon in 1881–1882 reveal his loneliness over the loss of his family to Manitoba and the United States.

CHAPTER 9: LATER EMIGRATION FROM ENGLAND

1. OA RG 11-8-1: A.J. Whellams' letter of August 1, 1875, to the commissioners of immigration in Toronto.

2. *Ibid.*

3. Pamela Horn, "Agricultural Trade Unionism and Emigration," *The Historical Journal* 15, no. 1 (March 1972): 87–102. Incentives offered by the Australia and New Zealand governments were even greater since they provided free passages.

4. OA F1009 MU1724, 35–65: George T. Denison fonds (letter book).

5. The old George Inn has since been demolished. Some of the timbers in the original building can still be seen on the frontage of the present-day George Mall shopping centre.

6. OA F1009 MU1724, 53, 56–59.

7. *Ibid.*, 60–64. Letter to McKellar, March 17, 1873.

8. *Ibid.*, 97–100. Letter to McKellar, April 19, 1873.

9. Some Warwickshire people had already emigrated to Canada. For example, unemployed ribbon weavers from Bulkington Parish in Warwickshire had relocated to Canada and Queensland, Australia, in 1863 (see WRO DR 684/1).

10. Horn, "Agricultural Trade Unionism and Emigration," 89–92.

11. OA F1009 MU1724, 97–100. Letter to McKellar, April 19, 1873.

12 *Ibid.,* 97–100, 104.

13. Horn, "Agricultural Trade Unionism and Emigration," 95. One large group who arrived in London, Ontario, in 1874 were almost all provided with employment "within twenty four hours of their arrival."

14. Peter Baigent and Robert Ruegg, "Pauperism or Emigration? Case Studies of Publicly-backed Emigration Schemes in Woolwich, Kent, 1857 and 1869–70," *Family and Community History*, vol. 10/1 (May 2007), 19–33. Woolwich is situated on the south bank of the River Thames, ten miles downstream of London Bridge. Until 1889 it was in Kent County.

15. *Ibid.*, 25–26. The funds were used to pay for outfits, passages, and onward journeys. A small number were assisted to go to Australia.

16. The *Kentish Independent* reported that the Woolwich emigrants sailed to Ontario in one of four vessels in June/July 1857: *Midlothian* (78 people) *Henry Cooke* (278) *John Owen* (392) and *Ion* (346). The total of those sailing was 1,094 — slightly more than the 1,020 total reported in the newspaper *Kentish Independent* (June 27, July 18, August 8, 1857).

17. The other naval dockyards were at Deptford (Greater London), Chatham, and Sheerness in Kent, Portsmouth in Hampshire, and Plymouth in Devon.

18. LAC RG17 Vol. 39 (#3609): Letter from William F. Lynn to the Canadian minister for agriculture and emigration on behalf of the Working Men's Emigration Association, June 23, 1870.

19. STRO D615/P(L)/6/9. The Working Men's National Association had five hundred members in 1870, who each paid a small subscription and were prepared to raise £2 before emigrating by selling their property.

20. In 1870 a total of just under four hundred emigrants supported by the Working Men's National Association sailed in the *Lake Erie* (44 people), *Lake Superior* (7), *Nestorian* (9), *Strathblanc* (162), and *St. Leonards* (154). *Sessional Papers* of the Government of Canada, 34 Victoria (64) 1871, 24–25.

21. The faltering of the Cornish tin industry in the 1870s made a bad situation worse and contributed to the increasing numbers of miners and their families who decided to emigrate. About 250,000 people left Cornwall for

overseas destinations between 1815 and 1914. This is an extraordinarily large number given that the population of Cornwall at no time reached half a million during this period. For further details see Philip Payton (ed.), "Reforming Thirties and Hungry Forties: The Genesis of Cornwall's Emigration Trade," *Cornish Studies Four* (Exeter, 1996): 107–27; also see Philip Payton (ed.), "Cornish Emigration in Response to Changes in the International Copper Market in the 1860s," *Cornish Studies Three* (Exeter, 1995): 60–82.

22. Clancy Merrium et al., *Cornish Emigrants to Ontario* (Toronto: Toronto Cornish Association, 1998), 13–20.

23. Anon., *Emigration to Canada: The Province of Ontario, Its Soil, Resources, Institutions, Free Grant Lands ... For the Information of Intending Emigrants* (Toronto: Hunter, Rose, 1871), 21–25.

24. Anon., *Handbook of Information Relating to the District of Algoma in the Province of Ontario, Letters from Settlers & Others & Information also Land Regulations* (Minister of the Interior, Government of Canada (London: McCorquodale & Co., 1894?).

25. Clancy et al., *Cornish Emigrants to Ontario*, 53–57.

26. LARO DDX 374/8.

27. The Telford new town was only established in the 1960s, taking its name from Thomas Telford the engineer. Richard Edwards may well have lived in Ironbridge, now a World Heritage site having nine museums and celebrating the birthplace of the Industrial Revolution.

28. Donald F. Harris, "Emigration from the Telford area of Shropshire to the USA and Canada before the First World War," a talk given to the Telford Historical & Archaeological Society, March 2, 2000. With the decline of the Shropshire iron industry, many workers took their skills to the United States, where they were very much in demand.

29. M.J. Lansdown, *Formerly of ... Family Announcements in the Trowbridge Newspapers by Emigrants from West Wiltshire and Others Living Overseas, 1858–1915* (Devizes, Wiltshire: Wiltshire Family History Society, 1996), 72, 74, 76.

30. Coal miners could readily find work in other British coalfields and usually only emigrated to obtain higher wages. Frank Machin, *The Yorkshire Miners: A History*, vol. 1 (Barnsley, Yorkshire: National Union of Mineworkers, 1958), 243, 260, 447, 467.

31. OA RG-11-8-1: letter from John Bennet to David Spence, September 6, 1876.

32. OA RG-11-8-1: newspaper cutting — letter by Richard Hewson, Warden, Peel County, March 10, 1879.

33.   OA RG 11-8-1: letter from John A. Donaldson, emigration agent to David Spence, March 25, 1879.

34.   BRO P42/28/3/35, /36 Eversholt Parish. The 1874 group consisted of William Odell and family, Abel Chew and family, and Thomas Valentine and family.

35.   BRO P6/24: Haynes Parish, emigration fund papers. For example, in 1906, £20 was given to Charles Adams, his wife and three children, while £10 was given to William Brunt (of which £5 had to be repaid by him). The Adams family and Brunt emigrated to Canada "under the auspices of the Church Army." In the following year, £8 was given to John Woodcroft (of which £3 was to be repaid) and £8 to Percy Wood (of which £3 was to be repaid). Woodcroft and Wood were emigrating to Canada.

36.   NTRO DD4p/62/107/11: Portland papers. Letter dated June 9, 1873.

37.   NTRO D744/1: letter from Mrs. E. Jackson in Toronto to unnamed cousin in Hucknall Tockard Parish, Nottinghamshire, May 18, 1876.

38.   It was claimed that "an industrious man may expect to make about one dollar a day throughout the year." STRO D615/P(L)/6/9: Open letter from Sir John Young, governor general of Canada, printed in the *Pall Mall Gazette*, May 28, 1870.

39.   Frederick de la Fosse's memoir of his experiences has been published in Scott D. Shipman (ed.), *English Bloods in the Backwoods of Muskoka, 1878* (Toronto: Natural Heritage, 2004).

40.   *Ibid.*, 113.

41.   *Ibid.*, 134–35.

42.   *Ibid.*, 58–60. To play a cricket match would have required twenty-two men for the teams and two umpires.

43.   *Ibid.*

44.   Anon., *Emigration to Canada: The Province of Ontario*, 29–30.

45.   Joy Parr, *Labouring Children* (London, Croom Helm, 1980), 11–14.

46.   The philanthropists who organized the emigration of the children were swept along by strong moral convictions. Glowing reports of happily-settled children issued by them and the immigration authorities in Canada spoke only of success. The world had to wait until 1979 to learn the truth. When the social worker, Phyllis Harrison, published her book [Phyllis Harrison (ed.), *The Home Children — Their Personal Stories* (Winnipeg: Watson & Dwyer Publishing Ltd., 1979)] containing extracts of letters that she had solicited from former home children and their descendants, she provided firsthand evidence of the scale of physical and sexual abuse and exploitation that had been experienced. Joy Parr's doctoral thesis, completed a year later, examined the case papers of every

tenth Barnardo's child, and she, too, reached similar conclusions.

47. Some workhouse children were assisted by parishes. *The Poor Law Act* had been amended in 1850 to allow Poor Law Guardians to send orphaned and deserted children abroad. Parr, *Labouring Children*, 27–44.

48. Parr, *Labouring Children*, 45–61. Andrew Doyle, a senior inspector for the Local Government Board in Britain, first alerted the British and Canadian authorities to the scandalous treatment of children he observed during a visit to Ontario and Quebec in 1875. Despite his recommendation that reforms were needed to ensure that child placements were properly regulated and supervised, little action was taken to remedy the situation until the early twentieth century.

49. Parr, *Labouring Children*, 32–34.

50. Thomas Bernardo was the principal promoter of child emigration. Between 1882 and 1905 the Barnardo homes sent 27,000 children to Canada, nearly all to Ontario and the Prairie provinces (see Marjorie Kohli, *The Golden Bridge — Young Immigrants to Canada, 1833–1939* (Toronto: Natural Heritage, 2003), 143–68).

51. Kohli, *The Golden Bridge*, 71–104. In 1870, Miss Rye organized the relocation of 253 children who went mainly to Ontario. Annie Macpherson brought over 2,500 children to Ontario and Quebec between 1870 and 1875, establishing three reception homes in Canada that offered training in farming.

52. See Parr, *Labouring Children*, page 49, for the location of the distributing homes that were established in Canada from 1869–1924.

53. For details of Louisa Birt's Knowlton home, see Kohli, *Golden Bridge*, 123–26.

54. Kohli, *Golden Bridge*, 158–62.

55. It is estimated that between 1873 and 1932 a total of five thousand children were brought to various parts of Canada by John Middlemore (see Kohli, *The Golden Bridge*, 131–37). For details of the home children who were sent to the Maritime provinces, see Campey, *Planters, Paupers and Pioneers*, 224–52.

56. Thomas Barnardo described his work as "philanthropic abduction."

57. Between 1882 and 1905 the Barnardo homes sent 27,000 children to Canada, nearly all to Ontario and the Prairie provinces (see Kohli, *The Golden Bridge*, 143–68).

58. Parr, *Labouring Children*, 62–81. Later on some of the children reconnected with their families back in England and a few returned to England permanently.

59. For background information on the Girls' Friendly Society, see Kohli, *The Golden Bridge*, 333–38.

60. DRO D3287/68/1/3: Ellen Joyce (ed.), *Girls' Friendly Society: Report of the Department for Members Emigrating 1883–1897* (Winchester: Girls' Friendly Society, 1897), 12–13, 24–27, 32–41.

61. CARO G/C/AZ 35 A.

62. The Catholic Protection Society in Liverpool dealt with small number of Leeds children who were Catholics, while Protestants were placed in the care of Rye or Birt.

63. WYAS PL 3/7/4: *Emigration of Children from the Leeds Union, Report upon the Scheme* (Leeds: Joseph Rider, 1891), 8–10.

64. The reformatory schools gave children a basic education and taught them a trade and practical skills. See Kohli, *Golden Bridge*, 291–300.

65. Although the reformatory schools housed both boys and girls, it was mainly the boys who were allowed to emigrate. All costs associated with relocating the children abroad were borne by the schools.

66. Kohli gives examples, such as the Bedfordshire Reformatory School, the Boys' Home, Frome (Somerset), and St. Swithin's Industrial School, which sent their children to the Eastern Townships at this time. See Kohli, *Golden Bridge*, 297.

67. HRO D/EHts/Q39: Hertfordshire Reformatory School for Boys, register of boys discharged or released on licence, 1883–87, #282.

68. *Ibid.*, #328.

69. *Ibid.*, #308.

70. *Ibid.*, #303.

71. *Ibid.*, #276.

72. *Ibid.*, #254.

73. *Ibid.*, #300, #271.

74. Private communication, David M. Bowcock, assistant county archivist, Carlisle. I gratefully acknowledge receiving Mr. Bowcock's account of his family and his permission to use it in this book.

75. ETRC P046 Reginald Conner fonds.

76. ETRC P046 Reginald Conner fonds. The fonds contain the manuscript of his work "The Vine and the Branches, History of Minton, Quebec." William Jenkins married Ann Corlett, from the Isle of Man, who came as an infant when her parents emigrated to Sherbrooke.

77. By this time the regulations had been tightened, with boys being admitted only at the discretion of the Canadian High Commissioner in London.

78. HRO D/EHts/Q39: Hertfordshire Reformatory School for Boys, register of boys discharged or released on licence, 1904–10. After leaving Copper Cliff in 1906, Thomas Wells had two other jobs before settling down in 1907 at the Larose Mine in Cobalt. He had worked briefly at Bruce Mines

as a labourer then had moved to Victoria Mines hoping to find work in the gold mines there.

79. Carrier and Jeffery, *External Migration*, 95–96.
80. BRO R4/932: Russell collection.
81. BRO P54/19/1: Ampthill Poor Law Union papers.
82. BRO CRT 150/166.
83. *Ibid.*
84. STRO D593/V/10/474: "The Visit of the Tenant-Farmer Delegates to Canada in 1890," 53–54. Colonel Francis Fane was an officer in the British Army who served in Canada during the 1850s with the 54th Regiment; he returned to Canada in 1864 with the 25th Regiment.
85. *Ibid.*, 101–02.
86. It is estimated that in the last quarter of the nineteenth century, middle/upper class males accounted for 27 percent of all British male emigrants, thus making them second in number to general labourers. Carter F. Hanson, *Emigration, Nation, Vocation: The Literature of English Emigration to Canada 1825–1900* (East Lansing, MI: Michigan State University Press, 2009), 119–20.
87. Donald F. Harris, "The Promotion in Shropshire of Emigration to Canada in 1914 with Particular Reference to the Period from 1890," Ph.D. thesis, University of Birmingham, 1998, 170–92 in ETRC P997/001.04/009: Edward William Brewster papers.
88. Donald F. Harris, "The Role of Shropshire Local Shipping Agents in Encouraging Emigration to Canada, 1890–1914," in *Local Historian* 30, no. 4 (November 2000): 239–89. Many Church of England clergy in Shropshire encouraged emigration. Donald F. Harris, "The Church of England and Emigration to Canada: Rural Clergy in the County of Shropshire," in *Journal of the Canadian Church Historical Society*, vol. XLI (1999): 5–26. From the early 1880s, emigration booklets, giving details of foreign destinations, were produced jointly by the Society for the Propagation of the Gospel in Foreign Parts and the Society for the Propagation of Christian Knowledge. Anglican clergy in England were also encouraged to offer emigrants letters of recommendation to give to the clergy in their chosen destination.
90. Harris, "The Promotion in Shropshire of Emigration to Canada in 1914," 184.
91. Donald F. Harris, "The Canadian Government's Use of Newspapers to Encourage Immigration in the Twenty Years Before the First World War, as Demonstrated in the Newspapers of Shropshire" (The fifth annual lecture of the Friends of Shropshire Records and Research, Shrewsbury, November 3, 1999). For example, see the advertisement in the *Shrewsbury Chronicle*, 1911: weekly from October 6 to December 15.

92. Ring spinning was the drawing out of fibres to make cotton yarn, while the fibres were disentangled before spinning through carding.

93. LAC MG40 M10 (originals held by Bolton Archive Service, Greater Manchester).

94. LAC MG40 M62: Leeds City Council Treasurer's Department Distress Committee, 6–16.

95. WYAS LLD3/719 [197]: Records of all persons aided to emigrate, 1906–1912. They travelled in the *Dominion*.

96. Simon Fowler, "0950 to Toronto: The Emigration of the Unemployed from Norwich to Ontario in 1906," in *Families* 37, no. 3 (August 1998): 149.

97. *Ibid.*, 146–52.

98. HRO D/Ebn (Add) B148: Pendley estate. Correspondence with W. Brown of Tring, acting as agent for the estate.

99. *Ibid.*, Noyce's letter to W. Brown, March 3, 1913.

100. *Ibid.*

101. As Anglican minister, William Bilton had responsibility for the churches at Bunyan and Plympton.

102. BRO JN5: letter to Sir Herbert Charles Janes (their cousin), no date; letter to H.C. Janes, March 12, 1913. Herbert Janes, the son of a Hertfordshire farm labourer, worked as a delivery boy after leaving school. He met Mrs. Irons, a local Salvationist at the Luton Railway Mission, who inspired him to become a devout Christian and a lifelong Baptist. He later established a successful building firm.

103. LARO DDX 1302/2/2/4.

104. OA PAMH 1926#72: A boy farm learner's life in Ontario, Canada: letters to his mother in England, 1922. The scheme was one of many that were fostered under the Empire Settlement Act of 1922.

105. NTRO CATC 10/125/9: Empire migration. The committee was administered by City of Nottingham Council.

106. The Dakeyne name was taken from the Dakeyne Street Lad's Club in Sneinton (Nottinghamshire) just to the south of the city of Nottingham. Kohli, *The Golden Bridge*, 200–01.

107. NTRO DD2427/1–12: Heathcote letters.

108. *Ibid.*, /1, /2: January 19, April 16, 1931.

109. *Ibid.*, /4: December 4, 1933.

110. *Ibid.*, /5, /6, /10, /12: January 31, May 28, 1934, January 23, February 2, 1935.

111. LRO DDX 1357 2/1/10: Clitheroe.

CHAPTER 10: THE SEA CROSSING

1. William Lyon Mackenzie, *Sketches of Canada and the United States* (London: E. Wilson, 1833), 179–81.

2. LCA 920 MD 289: "All our Yesterdays: To Canada by Sailing Ship," by Edgar Andrew Collard, undated newspaper article (1854).

3. Having arrived in New York, Walker and his family would have gone up the Hudson River to Albany, where the Erie Canal commenced, and travelled along it to Buffalo on Lake Ontario. From there they would have travelled by land to Hamilton and then on to their final destination in Guelph Township.

4. DERO D1559Z/F1: transcript of John Walker's diary (n.d.), October 13, 1835.

5. ERO D/DVv/87: Robert Downes at Quebec, to his mother in Witham, Essex, 1817.

6. LAC MG24 I131 (m/f M-5567): Elizabeth Peters's diary, 7, 12, 16.

7. LAC MG24 H15: Journal of a voyage from London to Quebec, 1833, by Francis Thomas, 2–3.

8. *Ibid.*

9. Jackson's diary quoted in MacDonald, *Norfolk Folk*, 35.

10. *Ibid.*

11. LAC MG24 I131 (m/f M-5567): Elizabeth Peters's diary, 20.

12. The price of a passage from London and east coast ports was around £3 but around £2 if the vessel left from Liverpool and other principal ports on the west coast. If the shipper provided provisions, London and east coast crossings generally cost around £6, while Liverpool charges were lower, at between £4 and £5. Anon., *Information Published by His Majesty's Commissioners for Emigration Respecting the British Colonies in North America* (London: Charles Knight, publisher to the Society for the Diffusion of Useful Knowledge, 1832), 5. Anon., *Information for Emigrants to British North America* (London: C. Knight, 1842), 7–8.

13. LAC MG24 I131 (m/f M-5567): Elizabeth Peters's diary, 20.

14. Newspaper article, n.d., Padstow Museum.

15. Oliver Macdonagh, *A Pattern of Government Growth 1800–1860, The Passenger Acts and Their Enforcement* (London: Macgibbon & Kee, 1961), 150–51. Oliver MacDonagh, "Emigration and the State, 1833–55: An Essay in Administrative History," *Transactions of the Royal Historical Society*, Fifth Series, vol. 5 (London: The Royal Historical Society, 1955): 133–59. Edwin C. Guillet, *The Great Migration, The Atlantic Crossing by Sailing Ships Since 1770* (Toronto: University of Toronto Press, 1963), 13–19.

16. See for example *Hull Advertiser*, February 18, May 5, 1820.

17. See for example *Berwick Advertiser*, March 28, 1835, June 25, 1842.

18. Pedlar and Wethey, "From Cornwall to Canada in 1841," 245. The article is based on the later reminiscences of Samuel Pedlar who, when eight years of age, sailed in the *Clio* of Padstow with his family. Having written his story in the early 1890s, Pedlar offered it to his friend Charles Wethey, who rewrote it in a form that might interest newspapers and magazines, doing so in around 1903–04. Although it was never published, Wethey deposited his original hand-written manuscript in the Ontario Archives in 1905, thus making it available to later historians.

19. Jackson's diary quoted in MacDonald, *Norfolk Folk*, 38.

20. LCA 920 MD 289: "All Our Yesterdays: To Canada by Sailing Ship," by Edgar Andrew Collard, undated newspaper article (1854). The vessel had an A1 rating from Lloyd's, was 334 tons, and had been built in 1845.

21. Pedlar and Wethey, "From Cornwall to Canada in 1841," 246.

22. *Ibid.*, 247.

23. The *Hebe* passengers were taken in a sloop to Sydney Cape Breton, where they boarded a Liverpool vessel called the *Mercury*, which carried them to Quebec.

24. LAC MG24 H15: Journal of a voyage from London to Quebec, 1833, by Francis Thomas, 2, 5–7, 11.

25. BRO CRT 190/413; PP 1857–58(165)XLI.

26. *Quebec Gazette*, October 23, 1820.

27. NAB CO 384/4, f. 29: Special Meeting of the Quebec Emigration Society, October 11, 1819.

28. The proceeds of the immigrant tax were divided into fourths: between the Quebec Emigrant Hospital, the Montreal General Hospital, the Quebec Emigrant Society, and the Montreal Emigrant Society. Cowan, *British Emigration*, 56–57, 152–53.

29. Immigrant arrival numbers plummeted again in 1838–39 following the Upper and Lower Canada Rebellions of 1837–38.

30. Dickinson and Young, *Short History of Quebec*, 113–14. Ouellet, *Le Bas Canada*, 215.

31. Article in *La Minerve*, June 18, 1832, quoted in Ouellet, *Le Bas Canada*, 216.

32. LAC MG24 I99 (m/f M-128): diary kept by George Robinson during a voyage on an immigrant ship to Quebec (no page numbers).

33. *Ibid.*

34. *Ibid.*

35. Merna M. Forster, "Quarantine at Grosse Île," *Canadian Family Physician* 41 (May 1995): 841–48.

36. Around 18 percent of the 98,649 emigrants, mainly from Ireland, who boarded ship for Quebec in 1847 died before reaching their destination. Andre Charbonneau and Andre Sevigny, *1847 Grosse Île: A Record of Daily Events* (Ottawa: Canadian Heritage, 1997), 1–32.

37. Irish immigrants predominated from at least 1825, when official figures first became available (see Carrier and Jeffrey, *External Migration*, 95–96).

38. See PP 1841 session 1(298) XV for the 1831 to 1840 emigrant departures by port to Quebec. Emigrant departures from Yarmouth, King's Lynn, and Ipswich in East Anglia were only substantial for a brief period during the 1830s.

39. In 1842 alone, 1,207 immigrants sailed from Plymouth and another 1,173 went from Padstow; yet in that same year, only 1,035 left from London. PP 1843(109) XXIV.

40. Judging from the passengers carried in the *Edward Colston* from Bristol in June 1832, the catchment area of the port of Bristol was quite considerable. In addition to Bristol, a significant number of passengers came from Dursley (Gloucestershire), some from Somerset (Nailsea, Frome, Huntsill), and one person came from Chepstow in Wales (See *Montreal Gazette*, June 26, 1832).

41. For example, see PP 1847-48(964) XLVII for 1846–47 figures, PP 1851(348) XL for 1850 figures, 1854–55(464) XXXIX for 1854 figures, and PP 1859(218, Sess. 2)XXII for 1857–58 figures.

42. PP 1842(373) XXXI: immigration agent's report w/e August 7.

43. LAC MG24 J12: George Pashley fonds.

44. The Irish were especially vulnerable to Liverpool's unscrupulous shipping agents and lodging-house owners, who deceived them and charged extortionate prices. Such abuses led to the many protective measures that were introduced in the *Passenger Act of 1828*. MacDonagh, "Emigration and the State, 1833–55: An Essay in Administrative History," 134, 141–42.

45. The physical characteristics of a vessel greatly affected sailing performance as well as passenger comfort and safety. For an analysis of the different types of Aberdeen-registered vessels that were used to take emigrants to British North America, see Lucille H. Campey, *Fast Sailing and Copper-Bottomed: Aberdeen Sailing Ships and the Emigrants They Carried to Canada* (Toronto: Natural Heritage, 2002), 80–98.

46. The *Lloyd's Shipping Register* is available as a regular series from 1775, apart from the years 1785, 1788, and 1817.

47. A — first class condition, kept in the highest state of repair and efficiency and within a prescribed age limit at the time of sailing; AE —"the second description of the first class," fit, no defects but may be over a prescribed

age limit; E — second class, although unfit for carrying dry cargoes were suitable for long distance sea voyages; I — third class, only suitable for short voyages (i.e. not out of Europe). These letters were followed by the number 1 or 2, which signified the condition of the vessel's equipment (anchors, cables, and stores). Where satisfactory, the number 1 was used, and where not, 2 was used. George Blake, *Lloyd's Register of Shipping 1760–1960* (London: Lloyd's, 1960), 12–13, 26–27.

48. Still in use today and run by a Classification Society with a worldwide network of offices and administrative staff, the *Lloyd's Register* continues to provide standard classifications of quality for shipbuilding and maintenance.

49. The number of years that a ship could hold the highest code varied according to where it was built. In time, rivalries developed between ship owners and underwriters, and this led to the publication of two registers between 1800 and 1833 — the Ship owners Register (Red Book) and the Underwriters Register (Green Book). Their coverage was similar, but not identical. By 1834, with bankruptcies facing both sides, the two registers joined forces to become the *Lloyd's Register of British and Foreign Shipping.*

50. Cameron and Maude, *Assisting Emigration to Upper Canada*, 42–46

51. WHC 306/66: Purton Parish.

52. This contrasts sharply with the inferior quality of shipping offered to Irish immigrants, especially during the famine years of 1846–51, when unprecedented numbers came to North America.

53. LAC MG24 I131 (m/f M-5567): Elizabeth Peters's diary, 26.

54. LARO DDX 207/57: William Thompson to Cuthbert Relph, November 25, 1835.

55. LAC MG24 I131 (m/f M-5567): William Peters's diary, 15–16.

56. Francis Thomas, a passenger in the *Hebe*, travelled the Ottawa River/Rideau Canal route in 1834, describing it as "a dismal course, when nothing for miles could be seen but wood and water" (see LAC MG24 H15: Journal of a Voyage from London to Quebec, 11–12).

57. The Petworth immigrants mainly took the Ottawa River/Rideau Canal route. Although the barges they were on were towed by a succession of steamboats, they could remain in the same craft throughout the journey. See Cameron and Maude, *Assisting Emigration to Upper Canada*, 121–22.

58. Emigrants could halve their journey time to Hamilton by taking road transport from Montreal to Prescott, but this cost nearly six times the amount payable when the entire journey was made by river. Anon., *Information Published by His Majesty's Commissioners for Emigration*, 7–8.

59. Jackson's diary quoted in MacDonald, *Norfolk Folk*, 39–40.

60. Immigrants going to the Talbot settlements would have gone through the Welland Canal linking Lake Ontario with Lake Erie and disembarked at Port Stanley.

61. NTRO DD/H/151/202: Henry Rastall in Toronto to Edward Buck in Nottinghamshire, February 2, 1830.

62. Cowan, *British Emigration*, 57.

CHAPTER 11: THE ENGLISH IN ONTARIO AND QUEBEC

1. Henry Scadding, *The Address to the St. George's Society in the Cathedral of St. James, Toronto, April 23rd, 1860* (Toronto: Rowsell & Hutchison Printers, 1860), 5.

2. *Ibid.*, 10.

3. John Bull was invented in 1712 by John Arbuthnot, a Scot. He went through many modifications and by the twentieth century was usually depicted wearing a Union Jack waistcoat and having a bulldog by his side.

4. Patrick Cecil Telford White (ed.), *Lord Selkirk's Diary 1803–04: A Journal of His Travels Through British North America and the Northeastern United States* (Toronto: The Champlain Society, 1958), 217–18.

5. *Report of the Wesleyan Methodist Missionary Society* (1821), cviii.

6. Edwin Clarence Guillet, *The Pioneer Farmer and Backwoodsman*, vol. 1, 224–25.

7. Isabella Lucy Bird, *The Englishwoman in America* (Toronto: University of Toronto Press, 1966), 160. The book was first published in 1856.

8. An English farmer, *A Few Plain Directions to Persons Intending to Proceed as Settlers to His Majesty's Province of Upper Canada in North America* (London: Baldwin, Cradock & Joy, 1820), 61.

9. NTRO DD/H/151/202–3: Henry Rastall in Toronto to Edward Buck in Farndon Parish, Nottinghamshire, February 2, 1830.

10. Edward Thomas Coke, *A Subaltern's Furlough: Descriptive of Scenes in Various Parts of the United States, Upper and Lower Canada, New Brunswick and Nova Scotia During the Summer and Autumn of 1832*, vol. 1 (New York: J. & J. Harper, 1833).

11. LRO FANE/ 6/12/3: *Journal of Mary Chaplin, 1840*.

12. LRO MISC DEP 222/28: Harrison family papers. William Harrison to his son, George, April 6, 1844.

13. DRO CRO DD.HL(2) 349/1-4: Francis Howell to David Howell, July 28, 1844.

14. Cameron, *English Immigrant Voices*, 230–33. William Robinson to Thomas Sockett, October 14, 1836.

15. Cameron, *ibid.,* 149–51. James Parker to Harvey Whittington, September 1, 1833.

16. Horseracing was also introduced at the garrison cities of Halifax and Kingston by British Army officers. Howell, *Blood, Sweat and Cheers,* 17–18.

17. Colonel Fane raised funds from civilians and members of the 54th Regiment. LRO FANE 6/8/1/4 Francis Fane's diary (1851): October 22, November 2.

18. Guillet, *The Pioneer Farmer and Backwoodsman,* vol. 1, 225.

19. John E. Hall and R.O. McCulloch, *Sixty Years of Canadian Cricket* (Toronto: Bryant Printing & Publishing Co., 1895), 24, 128.

20. DRO CRO DD.HL(2) 331/1-4: Francis Howell to David Howell, August 11, 1843.

21. Tranter, *Sport, Economy and Society in Britain, 1750–1914,* 13–31.

22. Howell, *Blood, Sweat and Cheers,* 47–49.

23. The London Mechanics' Institute was founded by George Birkbeck in London in 1823. By the mid-nineteenth century, there were more than seven hundred institutes in towns and cities across Britain and overseas, some of which were the foundations of later colleges and universities.

24. LAC MG24 I48/16: John Lee fonds.

25. Bruce Elliott, "The English," in Paul Robert Magocsi (ed.), *The Encyclopaedia of Canada's Peoples* (Toronto: Published for the Multicultural History Society of Ontario by the University of Toronto Press, circa 1999), 483–84.

26. ETRC P129/002/001: Philip Harry Scowen fonds.

27. Ross McCormack, "Cloth Caps and Jobs: The Ethicity of English Immigrants in Canada," in *Ethnicity, Power and Politics in Canada,* edited by Jorgen Dahlie and Tissa Fernando (Toronto: Methuen, 1981), 38–55.

28. *Ibid.,* 47.

29. *Ibid.,* 43.

30. *Ibid.,* 41.

BIBLIOGRAPHY

PRIMARY SOURCES (MANUSCRIPTS)

Archives Nationales du Québec (ANQ)

P80, S1: Ruth Higginson collection.
P98: Moses Benedict fonds.
P11, S2: William H. Johnston and Reby Dodds.
P1000, D2, P278 (C141): An account of the first settlement of the township in Hull in 1820.
FC2949AYLM1939: "Aylmer Then and Now."

Bedfordshire Record Office (BRO)

CRT150/166: Newspaper article re: emigrants from Tingrith.
CRT190/413: Newspaper article re: James Tate.
HF89/5/1: Letter from Joseph Hooper.
JN5: Papers of Sir Herbert Charles James.
P6/24/1 to 5: Haynes Parish.
P22/11/2, 19/2: Willshamtead Parish.
P40/18: Oakley Parish.
P42/28/3/ 35, 36: Eversholt Parish.

P54/19: Ampthill Union.

PUBV 33/1 Vol. 3: Emigration Bedford Union.

R4/932: Russell collection.

Cambridgeshire Record Office (CARO)

G/C/AZ 35A, B: Cambridge, St. Mary the Great Parish.

P27/18/36: Cambridge, St. Clement Parish.

P31/8/2: Cambridge, St. Mary the Less Parish.

P32/12/6: Cambridge, St. Michael Parish.

P53/1/11: Account of the inhabitants of the parish of Croydon [Cambridge] by
      Francis Fulford, Rector (January 1, 1843).

P117/8/5: Melbourn Parish.

P126/28/5: Oakington Parish.

Bester, Charles F., Haddenham, *A Parish History* (typed m/s, 1981).

Centre for Kentish Studies (CKS)

P26/8/1: Biddenden Parish.

P45/8/2: Brenchley Parish.

P152/8/2: Frittenden Parish.

P181/18/27: Headcorn Parish.

P347/8; P347/12: Staplehurst Parish.

P348/8/1: Stockbury Parish.

P353/19/1: Stone-in-Oxney Parish.

P364/18/; P364 /19/4: Tenterden Parish.

U47/18: Walter H. Shadwell papers.

Cornwall Record Office (CRO)

XDDP 19/19/7: Meeting to discuss money for emigration, Saint Breock Parish.

DDX.407/47: Account of voyage from Plymouth to Quebec by William James, 1858.

FS.3/81: Diary 1849 by J. Grundy's grandfather of crossing to Quebec.

FS.3/1138: Diary of Thomas Nicholl of Redruth relating to emigrants from area
      (1834–51).

Cumbria Archive Service (CAS)

D/Hod/15/26/7: Will of Joseph Hodgson, farmer of West Gwillimbury.

D/WAL/3/8: Letter in 1858 from Joseph Bland in Cavan (Peterborough County).
D WAL/7/D: Emigration of Alston's poor.
DX 1065/60/1–6: Letters from Thomas Priestman in Upper Canada.

Derbyshire Record Office (DERO)

D1559Z/F1: Walker family of Borrowash. Typescript of a diary of John Walker.
D3155: Catton collection.
D3287/68/1/3: Girls' Friendly Society.
D3349/3: Metcalfe family of Killarch correspondence.
D3772/T31/16: Strutt estate papers.

Devon Record Office (DRO)

219/29/22a-c: Roper-Lethbridge letters, Devonshire families resident abroad. Letters addressed to Sir Roper-Lethbridge on the occasion of his presidential address to the Devonshire Association (3 Vols).
CRO DD.HL(2)/330–350: Letters from David Howell's son Francis while in Canada.

Eastern Townships Resource Centre (ETRC)

P006: Minnie Hallowell fonds.
P009: Thomas Johnson fonds.
P029: Arthur Virgin fonds.
P046: Reginald Conner fonds.
P059: Tom Martin fonds.
P074: Frank Grundy fonds.
P081: Lydia Sawyer fonds.
P092: William Hoste Webb fonds.
P110: Bernard Epps fonds.
P110/001.16/002b: "A History of the English-Speaking People of the Eastern Townships of Quebec (circa 1977)."
P129: Philip Harry Scowen fonds.
P134: Edward Short fonds.
P997/001.04/002: Recollections of James S. Ramage.
P997/001.04/007: Captain Joseph Perkins fonds.
P997/001.04/009: Edward William Brewster.
P997/001.06/005: Moses Elliott fonds.
P997/004.01/001a: Farmer's diary.

VC074: Richmond and Melbourne United Church fonds, 1888.

Essex Record Office (ERO)

D/Djg/F9: Jessopp family.
D/DU 161/394: Canada Company land.
D/DVv/87: Letters from Robert Downes.
D/P12/12: Widdington Parish.
D/P21/18/29: Steeple Bumpstead Parish.
T/G44 129: Bootys of Canada.

Hertfordshire Record Office (HRO)

D/Ebn (Add) B148: Pendley estate.
D/EHts/Q36: Ledger, Hertfordshire Certified Reformatory School.
D/EHts/Q39: Register, Hertfordshire Reformatory School.
D/P7 19/2: Ashwell Parish.
D/P/ 50 5/9: Hertingfordbury Parish.

Hull City Archives (HCA)

DMJ/415/37-40: Bravender letters.

Lancashire Record Office (Preston) (LARO)

FRL 1/126: Lancashire Society of Friends — Notes concerning emigration.
FRL 2/1/33/164: Letter concerning the Craggs family (Lancashire Society of Friends).
FRL 21/1/9/24: Emigrants' Library Association (Lancashire Society of Friends).
DDX 207/57, 58: Cuthbert Relph fonds.
DDX 374/8: Letter from Mrs. Jane Atkinson in Amherstburgh.
DDX 1134: Haslingden Operative Cotton Spinners Association.
DDX 1302/2/2/4: Letters from W.H. Barnes of Burnley.
DDX 1357 2/1/10: Clitheroe 800th anniversary celebrations.

Library and Archives Canada (LAC)

MG17-B1: United Society for the propagation of the Gospel fonds Series E (m/f A-221). Originals held at University of Oxford.

MG17-C2: Wesleyan Methodist Missionary Society 1791–1819 (copies on microfilm — originals at University of London).

MG8-G49: United Church (Wesleyan Methodist Circuit) fonds for Quyon (Pontiac County).

MG9 D7 21: Pembroke Wesleyan Methodist Circuit.

MG9 D7 22: West Mono Mission fonds.

MG21: Haldiman collection.

MG24 D27: Thomas J. Jones and family fonds.

MG24 H15: Journal of a voyage from London to Quebec, 1833, by Francis Thomas.

MG24 I19: Richard Hemsley and family fonds.

MG24 I99: George Robinson diary.

MG24 I20: Samuel Southby Bridge collection.

MG24 I131 (m/f M-5567): William Peters and family fonds.

MG24 I48: John Lee fonds.

MG24 I56: Norwich Emigration Records.

MG24 I59: John Langton and family fonds.

MG24 I181: John Walker collection.

MG24-I198: James Coleman fonds.

MG24 J12: George Pashley fonds.

MG24 J47: Charles Caleb Cotton and family fonds.

MG25 G271 Vol. 17: Parish histories of Onslow (Pontiac County) Eardley (Gatineau County) and Clarendon (Pontiac County).

MG25 G325: Wilson family collection.

MG25 G336 File 3: Wilkes — Lamb — Clarkson families collection.

MG25 G339: Jones family collection.

MG28 III41: Henry Elliott and son fonds.

MG29 C63: Peter Coleman and family fonds.

MG40 M10: Bolton and District Card and Ring Room Operatives Association.

MG40 M62: Leeds City Council Treasurer's Department Distress Committee.

M68-G46: Christ Church Parish fonds (Sorel).

RG17 Vol. 39 #3609: List of people sent by Working Men's Emigration Association, London, 1870.

RG313 C-718: Population return of the Township of Hull, 1825.

920 MD 154: Journal of James Moncrieff Wilson.

Lincolnshire Record Office (LRO)

FANE 6/8: Fane family papers.

FANE 6/12: Journal of Mary Chaplin.

MISC DEP 222/28: Harrison family papers.
MONO 30/4/68: Cartoons on emigration.
ANC: Manuscripts of the Earl of Ancaster.

Liverpool City Archives (LCA)

(LCA) 920 MD 289: Journal of a voyage from Quebec to Liverpool in 1848.

National Archives of Britain (NAB)

CO 384: Colonial Office Papers on emigration containing original correspondence concerning North American settlers.

National Archives of Scotland (NAS)

RHP 35156/1–2: Plans of Upper and Lower Canada, 1838–39.

Norfolk Record Office (NRO)

DN/BBD: Reverend H.G.B. Folland's papers.
MC 75/5: Letter Thomas Cook to his parents, 1869.
PD 111/82: Bressingham Parish.
PD 124/49: Carbrooke Parish.
PD 699/90: Heacham Parish.

Northamptonshire Record Office (NORO)

C(A) Box 85: Cartwright papers: emigration from Aynho Parish.
EY/82–88: Eydon Parish.
L(C) 1158: Raunds Parish.
PL /564: Syresham Parish.
ROP 963/10: "The Canadian Connection."
YZ 3305: Declaration of Richard Hall re: death certificate of Henry Long Hall.
YZ4008: Miss Moore's journal of her voyage from England to Quebec, 1763.
133p/14: Families emigrating from Geddington 1826–44.
197p/88: Long Buckby Parish.

Nottinghamshire Record Office (NTRO)

CATC10/125/9: Empire migration.
D744/1: Mrs. E. Jackson in Toronto.
DD592: Hannah Barclay letters.
DD2427: Heathcote letters.
DD4p/62/107/11: Portland papers.
DD/H/151/202: Henry Rastall in Toronto to Edward Buck in Nottinghamshire, February 2, 1830.
PR707: Papplewick Parish.
PR1900: East Drayton Parish.
PR6703: Gotham Parish.
PR7347: Carlton-on-Trent Parish.

Ontario Archives (OA)

F592 MU867, MU 868: Mary Sophia O'Brien fonds.
F634 MU113, MU114: Sarah Hill family fonds.
F1009 MU1724: George T. Denison fonds (letter book).
MU2928: Talbot Settlement Lease Book, 1825–1845.
PAMPH 1869#6c.1: A lecture on Canada as a field for emigration, with special reference to the inducements offered by the government of the province of Ontario: delivered in Hope Hall, Liverpool on June 30, 1869.
PAMPH 1926#72: A boy farm learner's life in Ontario, Canada: Letters to his mother in England.
RG 11-8-1: Department of Immigration numbered correspondence files (m/f MS 847).

Oxford University: Rhodes House Library (RHL)

United Society for the Propagation of the Gospel (USPG) Series E: Reports from Missionaries.

Royal Institution of Cornwall (RIC)

Cornish Memorial Scheme (W.I. survey).
Records of emigrant ships from Cornwall (based on newspaper extracts compiled by C.J. Davies).

Shropshire Record Office (SHRO)

448: Marrington Hall collection.
1536/5: Cholmondeley family papers.
1781/2: Shackerley estate papers.
M13042/1–6: Hill family of Sutton Heath.
N.W. Tildesley. "William Farmer's Emigration to Canada," *Shropshire Newsletter* 40 (June 1971). Published by the Shropshire Archaeological Society.

Somerset Record Office (SORO)

DD\LW/49: Frome vestry book.
DD/SF/4546: Sanford family.
T\PH\SAS/8/925/1: J.O. Lewis. *Letters from Poor Persons Who Emigrated to Canada from the Parish of Frome in the County of Somerset* (Frome: Frome Newspaper Co. Ltd., 1945).

Staffordshire County Record Office (STRO)

D240: Shrewsbury papers: estate memoranda and correspondence.
D260/M/E: Hatherton collection.
D593/v/10/474-475: Visit of the tenant-farmer delegates to Canada in 1890.
D615/P: Anson family papers.
D823/2/4b: Letters from Ontario, 1933–49.

Suffolk Record Office (Ipswich) (SROI)

Education File 26: Extract from "Gentleman's Magazine," May 1832: 457.
Education File 447: Letter in *Ipswich Journal* from an emigrant who went to Canada.
Education File 451: "Emigrant Ships of the 1830s" by H.W. Moffat in *Suffolk Review*, Bulletin of the Suffolk Local History Council, vol. 1 (1956–58), 46–47.
Education File 1617: "The Carlton Colville Emigrants," in *The East Anglian* 10 (1903–04): 278–81.
FC 105/G7: Plomesgate Union.
FC 105: Brandeston Parish.
FC 131: Benhall Parish.
HA 11: Rous family archives.
HA 30: Blois family archives.

Suffolk Record Office (Lowestoft) (SROL)

455: Woolnough family correspondence.
119/G5: Covehithe Parish.
124: Halesworth Parish.

University of Hull Archives (UHA)

DDX 60/50: Courtney family papers.

University of London, School of Oriental and African Studies (SOAS)

MMS: Methodist Missionary Society Papers.

Warwickshire Record Office (WRO)

DR (B) 19/108: Tamworth Parish.
DR (B) 100/95: Coleshill Parish.
DR 684/1: Bulkington Parish.

West Yorkshire Archive Service (WYAS)

LLD3/719 [197]: Records of all persons aided to emigrate 1906–12.
PL/3/7/1-4: Letters concerning boarding out and emigration 1887–90 (3 vols).
PL3/7/5: Leeds Board of Guardians, register of emigrant children 1888–95.

Wiltshire Record Office (WHC)

212B/5644: Purton Parish.
303/66: Purton emigration (typed notes).
1020: Longbridge Deverill Parish.
1306/105: Downton Parish.
1607: Brinkworth Parish.

PRINTED PRIMARY SOURCES AND
CONTEMPORARY PUBLICATIONS

An English Farmer. *A Few Plain Directions to Persons Intending to Proceed as Settlers to His Majesty's Province of Upper Canada in North America.* London: Baldwin, Cradock & Joy, 1820.

"An Immigrant Farmer" (pseudonym of Reverend Abbott). *Memoranda of a Settler in Lower Canada; or the Emigrant in North America, Being a Useful Compendium of Useful Practical Hints to Emigrants ... Together with an Account of Every Day Doings upon a Farm for a Year.* Montreal: 1842.

"An Important Letter of a Resident of Quebec as to the Disabilities of Protestants in the Province of Quebec: the Parish System." Toronto: Equal Rights Association for the province of Ontario, 1890.

Anon. *A Statement of the Satisfactory Results Which Have Attended Emigration to Upper Canada from the Establishment of the Canada Company Until the Present Period.* London: Smith, Elder & Co., 1841.

————. *Emigration: The British Farmers and Farm Labourer's Guide to Ontario.* Toronto: Blackett Robinson, 1880.

————. *Emigration: Extracts from Various Writers on Emigration, with Authentic Copies of Letters from Emigrants from Norfolk, Suffolk, and Sussex, Now Settled in Upper Canada, Containing Useful Information Respecting That Country.* Norfolk: Bacon and Kinnebrook, 1834.

————. *Emigration to Canada: The Province of Ontario, Its Soil, Resources, Institutions, Free Grant Lands ... for the Information of Intending Emigrants.* Toronto: Hunter, Rose, and Co., 1871.

————. *Handbook of Information Relating to the District of Algoma in the Province of Ontario: Letters from Settlers and Others, and Information as to Land Regulations.* Minister of the Interior, Government of Canada. London: McCorquodale & Co., circa 1894.

————. *Information for Emigrants to British North America.* London: C. Knight, 1842.

————. *Information Published by His Majesty's Commissioners for Emigration Respecting the British Colonies in North America.* London: Charles Knight, publisher to the Society for the Diffusion of Useful Knowledge, 1832.

Bouchette, Joseph. *A Topographical Dictionary of the Province of Lower Canada.* London: W. Faden, 1815.

————. *A Topographical Dictionary of the Province of Lower Canada.* London: Longman & Co, 1832.

————. *The British Dominions in North America: a Topographical and Statistical*

Description of the Provinces of Lower and Upper Canada, New Brunswick, Nova Scotia, the Islands of Newfoundland, Prince Edward Island and Cape Breton, vols I, II. London: Longman, Rees, Orme, Brown, Green and Longman, 1832.

Boulton, Henry John. *A Short Sketch of the Province of Upper Canada for the Information of the Labouring Poor Throughout England*. London: John Murray, 1826.

British American Land Company. *Information Respecting the Eastern Townships of Lower Canada*. London: W.J. Ruffy, 1833.

Canada. Government of Canada. *Sessional Papers* 34, Victoria (64) 1871, 24–25.

Cattermole, William. *Emigration: The Advantages of Emigration to Canada: Being the Substance of Two Lectures Delivered at the Town-Hall, Colchester, and the Mechanics' Institution, Ipswich*. London: Simpkin & Marshall; Woodbridge, ON: J. Loder, 1831.

Census of Ontario, 1881.

Champion, Thomas Edward. *The Anglican Church in Canada*. Toronto: Hunter, Rose, and Co., 1898.

Cobbett, William. *The Emigrant's Guide in 10 Letters Addressed to the Taxpayers of England; Containing Information of Every Kind, Necessary for Persons About to Emigrate; Including Several Authentic and Most Interesting Letters from English Emigrants, Now in America, to Their Relations in England*. London: author, 1829.

Coke, Edward Thomas. *A Subaltern's Furlough: Descriptive of Scenes in Various Parts of the United States, Upper and Lower Canada, New Brunswick and Nova Scotia During the Summer and Autumn of 1832*. Vol. 1. New York: J. & J. Harper, 1833.

Ermatinger, Edward. *Life of Col. Talbot and the Talbot Settlement*. St. Thomas, ON: A. McLachin's Home Journal Office, 1859.

Gourlay, Robert F. *Statistical Account of Upper Canada Compiled with a View to a Grand System of Emigration*. London: Simpkin & Marshall, 1822.

Hall, John E., and R.O. McCulloch. *Sixty Years of Canadian Cricket*. Toronto: Bryant Printing & Publishing Co., 1895.

Jameson, A.B. *Winter Studies and Summer Rambles in Canada*. London: Saunders & Otley, 1838.

Lizars, Robine, and Kathleen Macfarlane Lizars. *In the Days of the Canada Company: The Story of the Settlement of the Huron Tract and a View of the Social Life of the Period 1825–1850*. Toronto: W. Briggs, 1896.

Lloyd's Shipping Register 1775–1855.

Mackenzie, William Lyon. *Sketches of Canada and the United States*. London: E. Wilson, 1833.

MacTaggert, John. *Three Years in Canada: An Account of the Actual State of the Country in 1826–7–8, Comprehending Its Resources, Productions, Improvements and Capabilities and Including Sketches of the State of Society, Advice to Emigrants, etc.* Two volumes. London: 1829.

Martin, Robert Montgomery. *History, Statistics and Geography of Upper and Lower Canada.* London: Whittaker, 1838.

Oliver, Andrew [late of Montreal]. *A View of Lower Canada Interspersed with Canadian Tales and Anecdotes and Interesting Information to Intending Emigrants.* Edinburgh: Menzies, 1821.

Pickering, Joseph. *Enquiries of an Emigrant Being the Narrative of an English Farmer from the Year 1824 to 1830 During Which Period He Traversed the USA and the British Province of Canada with a View to Settle as an Emigrant.* London: Effingham Wilson, 1831.

Scadding, Reverend Henry. *The Address to the St. George's Society in the Cathedral of St. James, Toronto, April 23rd, 1860.* Toronto: Rowsell & Hutchison Printers, 1860.

Scrope, George Poulett. *Extracts of Letters from Poor Persons Who Emigrated Last Year to Canada and the United States for the Information of the Labouring Poor in This Country.* London: J. Ridgeway, 1831.

Sellar, Robert. *History of the County of Huntingdon and of the Seigneuries of Châteauguay and Beauharnois from Their First Settlement to the Year 1838.* Huntingdon, QC: *Canadian Gleaner*, 1888.

Society for the Propagation of the Gospel in Foreign Parts, *Annual Reports*.

Surtees, Scott Frederick. *Emigrant Letters from Settlers in Canada and South Australia Collected in the Parish of Banham, Norfolk.* London: Jarrold and Sons, 1852.

Thomas, C. *History of the Counties of Argenteuil, Quebec and Prescott, Ontario, from the Earliest Settlement to the Present.* Montreal: John Lovell, 1896.

Wesleyan Methodist Missionary Society, *Annual Reports*.

Wilson, William. *Letters from the Eastern Townships of Lower Canada Containing Information Respecting the Country Which Will Be Useful to Emigrants.* London: 1834.

OFFICIAL BRITISH GOVERNMENT PUBLICATIONS

Annual Reports of the Poor Law Commissioners for England and Wales. London: Charles Knight & Co., 1836–54.

British Parliamentary Papers: Annual Reports of the Immigration Agent at Quebec (1831–61).

British Parliamentary Papers: Colonial Land and Emigration Commissioners, Annual Reports (1841–72).

CONTEMPORARY NEWSPAPERS

Bath & Cheltenham Gazette
Bedfordshire Mercury
Bedfordshire Times and Independent
Berwick Advertiser
Brighton Patriot
Buckingham Post
Bury and Norwich Post
Clitheroe Advertiser
Courier of Upper Canada
Dumfries and Galloway Courier
Hull Advertiser
Hull Packet
Ipswich Journal
Kentish Independent
La Minerve
Liverpool Albion
Lloyd's List
Montreal Gazette
Norfolk Chronicle
North Devon Journal
Norwich Gazette
Norwich Mercury
Quebec Gazette
Quebec Mercury
Salisbury Journal
Sherbrooke Daily Record
Shrewsbury Chronicle
Suffolk Chronicle
West Devon and Cornish Advertiser

CONTEMPORARY MATERIAL OF LATER PRINTING

Bird, Isabella Lucy. *The Englishwoman in America*. Toronto: University of Toronto Press, 1966.

Channell, Leonard Stewart. *History of Compton County and Sketches of the Eastern Townships of St. Francis and Sherbrooke County*. Belleville, ON: Mika Publishing, 1975 [first published 1896].

Cobbett, William, and Ian Dyck, eds. *Rural Rides, Rural Rides in the Counties of Kent, Sussex, Hampshire, Wiltshire, Gloucestershire, Herefordshire, Worcestershire, Somerset, Oxfordshire, Berkshire, Essex, Suffolk, Norfolk, and Hertfordshire*. London: Penguin Books, 2001.

Reid, Richard, ed. *The Upper Ottawa Valley to 1855: A Collection of Documents Edited with an Introduction by Richard Reid*. Toronto: Champlain Society, 1990.

White, Patrick Cecil Telford, ed. *Lord Selkirk's Diary 1803–04: A Journal of His Travels Through British North America and the Northeastern United States*. Toronto: The Champlain Society, 1958.

Whitelaw, Marjorie, ed. *The Dalhousie Journals*, 3 vols. Ottawa: Oberon, 1978–82.

SECONDARY SOURCES

Agar, Nigel E. *The Bedfordshire Farm Worker in the 19th Century*. Bedford: Publications of the Bedfordshire Historical Record Society, vol. 60, 1981.

Aitken, Barbara B. "Searching Chelsea Pensioners in Upper Canada and Great Britain." *Families* 23, no. 3 (1984) [Part I]: 114–27; and no. 4 (1984) [Part II]: 178–97.

Albion, Robert Greenhalgh. *Forests and Seapower: The Timber Problems of the Royal Navy 1652–1862*. Cambridge, MA: Harvard Economic Studies, 1926.

Allen, Robert S. *The Loyal Americans: The Military Role of the Loyalist Provincial Corps and Their Settlement in British North America*. Ottawa: National Museum of Canada, circa 1983.

Allinson, Helen. *Farewell to Kent: Assisted Emigration in the Nineteenth Century*. Sittingbourne, Kent: Synjon Books, 2008.

Anon. "Nineteenth Century Emigration from Weardale." *Northumberland and Durham Family History Society* 21, no. 3 (Autumn 1996): 94.

Baehre, Rainer. "Pauper Emigration to Upper Canada in the 1830s." *Social History* 14, no. 28 (1981): 339–67.

Baigent, Peter, and Robert Ruegg. "Pauperism or Emigration? Case Studies of

Publicly-Backed Emigration Schemes in Woolwich, Kent, 1857 and 1869–70." *Family and Community History*, vol. 10/1 (May 2007), 19–33.

Bailey, Patrick. "Pioneer Settlers: East Anglia and Quebec." *The Amateur Historian* 4, no. 1 (1958): 9–11.

Barry, Gwen Rawlings. *History of Megantic County: Downhomers of Quebec's Eastern Townships.* Lower Sackville, NS: Evans Books, 1999.

Bean, P., and J. Melville. *Lost Children of the Empire.* London: Unwin Hyman, 1989.

Benn, Carl. *The War of 1812.* Oxford: Osprey, 2002.

Blake, George. *Lloyd's Register of Shipping 1760–1960.* London: Lloyd's, 1960.

Blanchard, Raoul. "Les Pays de l'Ottawa." *Étude Canadienne troisième série*, vol. 3. Grenoble, FR: Allier, 1949.

———. *L'Est du Canada Francais, "Province de Quebec."* Montreal: Publications de l'Institut Scientifique Franco-Canadien, 1935.

Bouquet, Michael. "Passengers from Torquay: Emigration from North America 1849–1859." In *Ports and Shipping in the South-West*, edited by H.E.S. Fisher. Exeter: University of Exeter, Exeter Papers in Economic History, 1971, no. 4, 131–47.

Brayshay, Mark. "The Emigration Trade in Nineteenth Century Devon." In *The New Maritime History of Devon*, Michael Duffy et al., London: Conway Maritime Press, 1994, vol. 2, 108–18.

———. "Government Assisted Emigration from Plymouth in the Nineteenth Century." *Report of the Transactions of the Devon Association for the Advancement of Science* 112 (1980), 185–213.

Brown, W.M. *The Queen's Bush: A Tale of the Early Days of Bruce County.* London: John Bale sons and Danielson Ltd., 1932.

Brunger, Alan G. "The Geographical Context of English Assisted Emigration to Upper Canada in the Early Nineteenth Century." *British Journal of Canadian Studies* 16, no. 1 (2003): 7–31.

Buckner, Phillip. "Introduction." *British Journal of Canadian Studies* 16, no.1 (2003), 1–5.

Bumsted, J.M., "The Consolidation of British North America, 1783–1860." In *Canada and the British Empire*, edited by Philip Buckner. Oxford: Oxford University Press, 2008, 43–47.

———. *The Peoples of Canada: A Pre-Confederation History*, vol. 1. Toronto: Oxford University Press, 1992.

Cameron, Wendy. "English Immigrants in 1830s Upper Canada: The Petworth Emigration Scheme." In Barbara J. Messamore, *Canadian Migration Patterns.* Toronto: University of Toronto Press, 2004, 91–100.

Cameron, Wendy, and Mary McDougall Maude. *Assisting Emigration to Upper*

Canada: The Petworth Project, 1832–37. Montreal: McGill-Queen's University Press, 2000.

Cameron, Wendy, Sheila Haines, and Mary McDougall Maude. *English Immigrant Voices: Labourers' Letters from Upper Canada in the 1830s.* Montreal: McGill-Queen's University Press, 2000.

Campey, Lucille H. *Fast Sailing and Copper-Bottomed: Aberdeen Sailing Ships and the Emigrant Scots They Carried to Canada.* Toronto: Natural Heritage, 2002.

———. *Les Écossais: the Pioneer Scots of Lower Canada, 1763–1855.* Toronto: Natural Heritage, 2006.

———. *Planters, Paupers and Pioneers: English Settlers in Atlantic Canada.* Toronto: Natural Heritage, 2010.

———. *Scottish Pioneers of Upper Canada, 1784–1855: Glengarry and Beyond.* Toronto: Natural Heritage, 2005.

Carrier, N.H., and J.R. Jeffrey. *External Migration: A Study of the Available Statistics 1815–1950.* London: HMSO, 1953.

Carrington, Philip. *The Anglican Church in Canada: A History.* Toronto: Collins, 1963.

Charbonneau, Andre, and Andre Sevigny. *1847 Grosse Île: A Record of Daily Events.* Ottawa: Canadian Heritage, 1997.

Charlesworth, Andrew. *An Atlas of Rural Protest in Britain, 1545–1900.* London: Croom Helm, 1983.

Clancy, Merrium et al. *Cornish Emigrants to Ontario.* Toronto: Toronto Cornish Association, 1998.

Clark, Samuel Delbert, *Church and Sect in Canada.* Toronto: University of Toronto Press, 1948.

Clarke, John. "A Geographical Analysis of Colonial Settlement in the Western District of Upper Canada, 1788–1850" (unpublished Ph.D. thesis, University of Western Ontario, 1970).

Conrad, Margaret, with Alvin Finkel and Cornelius Jaenen. *History of the Canadian Peoples. Vol. I. Beginnings to 1876.* Toronto: Copp Clark Pitman, 1993.

Constantine, S. "Empire Migration and Social Reform." *Migrants, Emigrants and Immigrants: A Social History of Migration,* edited by C.G. Pooley & I.D. Whyte. London: Routledge, 1991, 62–83.

Cooper, Nicholas. *Aynho: A Northamptonshire Village.* Banbury, Oxfordshire: Leopard's Head Press, 1984.

Courville, Serge [translated by Richard Howard]. *Quebec: A Historical Geography.* Vancouver: UBC Press, 2008.

Cowan, Helen. *British Emigration to British North America: The First Hundred Years.* Toronto: University of Toronto Press, 1961.

Craig, Gerald M. *Upper Canada: The Formative Years, 1784–1841.* Toronto: McClelland & Stewart, 1993.

Cross, Michael S. "The Age of Gentility: The Formation of the Aristocracy in the Ottawa Valley." Canadian Historical Association: *Historical Paper* 2, no. 1 (1967): 105–17.

———. "The Shiners' War: Social Violence in the Ottawa Valley in the 1830s." *Canadian Historical Review* 54, no. 1 (March 1973): 1–26.

Curtis, Fahey. "A Troubled Zion: The Anglican Experience in Upper Canada" (unpublished Ph.D. thesis, Carleton University, 1981).

Davis, Ralph. *The Industrial Revolution and British Overseas Trade.* Leicester: Leicester University Press, 1979.

Debenham, Mary H. *Men Who Blazed the Trail. Stories of the Church's Pioneers in Canada, Australia and New Zealand.* London: Society for the Propagation of the Gospel in Foreign Parts, 1926.

Dickinson, John A., and Brian Young, *A Short History of Quebec,* 2nd edition. Toronto: Longman, 1993.

Dictionary of Canadian Biography. Toronto: University of Toronto Press, 1979–85.

Elliott, Bruce. "Regional Patterns of English Immigration and Settlement in Upper Canada." In *Canadian Migration Patterns from Britain and North America,* edited by Barbara J. Messamore. Ottawa: University of Ottawa Press, 2004, 51–90.

———. "The English." *The Encyclopedia of Canada's Peoples.* Edited by Paul Robert Magocsi. Toronto: Published for the Multicultural History Society of Ontario by the University of Toronto Press, circa 1999, 462–88.

Elliott, Bruce S. *Irish Migrants in the Canadas: A New Approach.* Kingston, ON: McGill-Queen's University Press, 1988.

———. "'The famous township of Hull': Image and Aspirations of a Pioneer Quebec Community." *Social History* 12 (1969): 339–67.

Emerson, James. "Emerson Family History — From Durham Co., England to Durham Co., U.C." *Families* 29, no. 4 (1983): 229–39.

Erickson, Charlotte. *Leaving England: Essays on British Emigration in the Nineteenth Century.* Ithica, NY: Cornell University Press, 1994.

Ermatinger, Charles Oakes. *The Talbot Regime or the First Half Century of the Talbot Settlement.* St. Thomas, ON: The Municipal World Ltd., 1904.

Evans, Eric J. *The Forging of the Modern State: Early Industrial Britain, 1783–1870.* Harlow, Essex: Pearson Education, 2001.

Files, Angela E.M. "Loyalist Settlement Along the St. Lawrence in Upper Canada," *Grand River Branch (U. E. L. Association of Canada) Newsletter* 8, no. 1 (February 1996): 9–12.

Forster, Merna M. "Quarantine at Grosse Île." *Canadian Family Physician* 41 (May 1995): 841–48

Fowler, Simon. "0950 to Toronto: The Emigration of the Unemployed from Norwich to Ontario in 1906." *Families* 37, no. 3 (August 1998): 146–52.

Garrad, John Adrian. *The English and Immigration 1880–1910*. London; New York: Published for the Institute of Race Relations, by Oxford University Press, 1971.

Gates, Lillian Francis. *Land Policies in Upper Canada*. Toronto: University of Toronto Press, 1968.

Grainger, Jennifer. *Vanished Villages of Middlesex*. Toronto: Natural Heritage, 2002.

Gray, Charlotte. *Sisters in the Wilderness: The Lives of Susannah Moodie and Catherine Parr Traill*. Toronto: Penguin Books, 1999.

Guillet, Edwin. *Early Life in Upper Canada*. Toronto: University of Toronto, 1963. [reprint, original written in 1933]

Guillet, Edwin C. *The Great Migration: The Atlantic Crossing by Sailing Ships Since 1770*. Toronto: University of Toronto Press, 1963.

———. *The Pioneer Farmer and Backwoodsman*. Toronto: University of Toronto Press, 1963.

Hamil, Fred Coyne. *Lake Erie Baron: The Story of Colonel Thomas Talbot*. Toronto: Macmillan, 1955.

Hamilton, Phyllis. *With Heart and Hands and Voices: Histories of Protestant Churches of the Brome, Missisquoi, Shefford and Surrounding Area*. Montreal: Price-Patterson, 1996.

Hammond, J.L., and B. Hammond. *The Village Labourer, 1760–1832: A Study in the Government of England Before the Reform Bill*. London: Longmans, 1919.

Hanson, Carter F. *Emigration, Nation, Vocation: The Literature of English Emigration to Canada 1825–1900*. East Lansing, MI: Michigan State University Press, 2009.

Harris, Donald F. "Emigration from the Telford Area of Shropshire to the U.S.A. and Canada Before the First World War." A talk given to the Telford Historical and Archaeological Society, March 2, 2000.

———. "The Canadian Government's Use of Newspapers to Encourage Immigration in the Twenty Years Before the First World War, as Demonstrated in the Newspapers of Shropshire." The 5th annual lecture of the Friends of Shropshire Records and Research, Shrewsbury, November 3, 1999.

———. "The Church of England and Emigration to Canada: Rural Clergy in the County of Shropshire." *Journal of the Canadian Church Historical Society*, vol. XLI (1999): 5–26.

———. "The Promotion in Shropshire of Emigration to Canada in 1914 with Particular Reference to the Period from 1890." Unpublished Ph.D. thesis: University Of Birmingham, 1998.

———. "The Role of Shropshire Local Shipping Agents in Encouraging Emigration to Canada, 1890–1914." *Local Historian* 30, no. 4 (November 2000): 239–59.

Harrison, Phyllis, ed. *The Home Children — Their Personal Stories*. Winnipeg: Watson & Dwyer Publishing Ltd., 1979.

Hartley, Susan, and Pompi Parry. *Downton Lace: A History of Lace Making in Salisbury and the Surrounding Area*. Salisbury, Wiltshire: Salisbury and South Wiltshire Museum, 1991.

Heath-Stubbs, Mary. *Friendship's Highway: Being the History of the Girls' Friendly Society 1875–1935*. London: Girls' Friendly Society, 1935.

Hill, Judy. "The Dorking Emigration Scheme of 1832." *Family and Community History*, vol. 7/2 (November 2004): 115–28.

Hobsbawn, E.J., and George Rudé. *Captain Swing*. London: Lawrence & Wishart, 1969.

Horn, Pamela. "Agricultural Trade Unionism and Emigration." *The Historical Journal* 15, no. 1 (March 1972): 87–102.

Howell, Colin D. *Blood, Sweat and Cheers: Sport and the Making of Modern Canada: Themes in Canadian Social History*. Toronto: University of Toronto Press, 2001.

Howells, Gary. "Emigration and the New Poor Law: Norfolk Emigration Fever of 1836." *Rural History* 11, no. 2 (October 2000): 145–64.

———. "'On Account of Their Disreputable Characters': Parish-Assisted Emigration from Rural England, 1834–1860." *History* 88, no. 292 (October 2003). 587–605.

Hunter, Andrew F. *A History of Simcoe County*. Barrie, ON: Historical Committee of Simcoe County, 1948.

Hutchinson, Jean F. *The History of Wellington County*. Grand Valley, ON: Landsborough, 1997.

James-Korany, Margaret. "Blue Books as Sources for Cornish Emigration History." In *Cornish Studies One*, edited by Phillip Payton. Exeter, Devon: University of Exeter Press, 1993, 31–45.

Johnson, J.K. "The Chelsea Pensioners in Upper Canada." *Ontario History* 53, no. 4 (1961): 273–89.

Johnson, Stanley C. *A History of Emigration from the United Kingdom to North America, 1763–1912*. London: G. Routledge, 1913.

Johnston, H.J.M. *British Emigration Policy 1815–1830: Shovelling Out Paupers*. Oxford: Clarendon Press, 1972.

———. "Immigration to the Five Eastern Townships of the Huron Tract." *Ontario History* LIV (1962): 207–24.

Johnston, William. *History of the County of Perth from 1825 to 1902*. Stratford, ON: Beacon Herald Fine Printing Division, 1976.

Johnston, W.S., and H.J.M. Johnston. *History of Perth County to 1967*. Stratford, ON: Corporation of the County of Perth, 1967.

Joyce, Ellen, ed. *Girls' Friendly Society: Report of the Department for Members Emigrating 1883–1897*. Winchester, Hampshire: Girls' Friendly Society, 1897.

Kinsmen, Rev. Barry, *Fragments of Padstow's History*. Padstow, Cornwall: Padstow Parochial Church Council, 2003.

Kohli, Marjorie. *The Golden Bridge: Young Immigrants to Canada, 1838–1939*. Toronto: Natural Heritage, 2003.

Lansdown, M.J. *Formerly of ... Family Announcements in the Trowbridge Newspapers by Emigrants from West Wiltshire and Others Living Overseas, 1858–1915*. Devizes, Wiltshire: Wiltshire Family History Society, 1996.

Lee, Robert C. *The Canada Company and the Huron Tract, 1826–1853*. Toronto: Natural Heritage, 2004.

Little, John Irvine. *Nationalism, Capitalism and Colonization in Nineteenth Century Quebec: The Upper St. Francis District*. Kingston, ON: McGill-Queen's University Press, 1989.

Little, John Irving, ed. *Love Strong as Death: Lucy Peel's Canadian Journal, 1833–1836*. Waterloo, ON: Wilfred Laurier University Press, 2001.

Little, J.I. "The Methodistical Way: Revivalism and Popular Resistance to the Wesleyan Church Discipline in the Stanstead Circuit, 1821–52." *Studies in Religion* 31, no. 2 (2002): 171–94.

Lower, Arthur R.M. "Immigration and Settlement in Canada, 1812–1820." *Canadian Historical Review* vol. III (1922): 37–47.

MacDonagh, Oliver. *A Pattern of Government Growth 1800–1860: The Passenger Acts and Their Enforcement*. London: Macgibbon & Kee, 1961.

———. "Emigration and the State, 1833–55: An Essay in Administrative History." *Transactions of the Royal Historical Society,* Fifth Series, vol. 5 (London: The Royal Historical Society, 1955): 133–59.

MacDonald, Cheryl. *Norfolk Folk: Immigration and Migration in Norfolk County*. Delhi, ON: Norfolk Folk Book Committee, 2005.

MacDonald, Norman. *Canada, Immigration and Settlement 1763–1841*. London: Longmans & Co., 1939.

Machin, Frank. *The Yorkshire Miners: A History*, vol. 1. Barnsley, Yorkshire: National Union of Mineworkers, 1958.

Mack, Susan Muriel. *The History of Stephen Township*. Crediton, ON: Corporation of the Township of Stephen, 1992.

MacKay, Donald. *The Lumberjacks.* Toronto: Natural Heritage, 1998.

Magocsi, Paul Robert, ed. *The Encyclopedia of Canada's Peoples.* Toronto: Published for the Multicultural History Society of Ontario by the University of Toronto Press, circa 1999.

McAndless, J.E. "Telfer Cemetery (English Settlement) London Township." *Families* 14, no. 3 (1975): 71–78.

McCormack, Ross. "Cloth Caps and Jobs: The Ethnicity of English Immigrants in Canada." In *Ethnicity, Power and Politics in Canada,* edited by Jorgen Dahlie and Tissa Fernando. Toronto: Methuen, 1981, 38–55

McDonald, Terry. "A Door of Escape: Letters Home from Wiltshire and Somerset Emigrants to Upper Canada, 1830–1832." In Barbara J. Messamore, *Canadian Migration Patterns.* Toronto: University of Toronto Press, 2004, 101–19.

———. "Southern England and the Mania for Emigration." *British Journal of Canadian Studies* 16, no. 1 (2003): 32–43.

McGillivray, Allan. *Decades of Harvest: A History of the Township of Scott, 1807–1973.* Uxbridge, ON: Scott History Committee, 1986.

Merrium, Clancy, et al. *Cornish Emigrants to Ontario.* Toronto: Toronto Cornish Association, 1998.

Miller, Audrey Saunders, ed. *The Journals of Mary O'Brien.* Toronto: Macmillan of Canada, 1968.

Mills, David. *The Idea of Loyalty in Upper Canada, 1784–1850.* Kingston, ON: McGill-Queen's University Press, 1988.

Moodie, Susannah. *Roughing It in the Bush, or Life in Canada.* London: Virago Press, 1986.

Morley, Leslie M., C.E. Morley, and W.C. Murkar. *The Village of Pickering.* Pickering, ON: Corporation of the Village of Pickering, 1970.

Neatby, Hilda Marion. *Quebec: The Revolutionary Age, 1760–1791.* Toronto: McClelland & Stewart, 1966.

Neelin, James M., and Michael R. Neelin. *The Old Methodist Burying Ground in the Town of Perth, Lanark County, Ontario.* Ottawa: Ottawa Branch, Ontario Genealogical Society, 1978.

Noël, Françoise. *Competing for Souls: Missionary Activity and Settlement in the Eastern Townships, 1784–1851,* Sherbrooke, QC: University of Sherbrooke, 1988.

Nutbrown, Leslie Stuart. *The Descendants of Thomas Nutbrown.* Lennoxville, QC: The Author, 2001.

Ouellet, Fernand. *Le Bas Canada 1791–1840: Changements structuraux et crise* (Ottawa: Ottawa University, 1976) [Translated and adapted: Patricia Claxton, *Lower Canada, 1791–1840: Social Change and Nationalism* (Toronto: McClelland & Stewart, 1980)].

Parker, Roy. *The Shipment of Poor Children to Canada 1867–1917*. Bristol: University of Bristol, The Policy Press, 2008.

Parr, Joy. *Labouring Children*. London: Croom Helm, 1980.

Patterson, Gilbert. *Land Settlement in Upper Canada, 1783–1840*. Toronto: Ontario Archives, 1921.

Paxman, Jeremy. *The English: The Portrait of a People*. London: Michael Joseph, 1998.

Payton, Philip. "Cornish Emigration in Response to Changes in the International Copper Market in the 1860s." In *Cornish Studies Three*, edited by Philip Payton. Exeter, Devon: University of Exeter Press, 1995, 60–82.

———. "Cousin Jacks and Ancient Britons: Cornish Immigrants and Ethnic Identity." *Journal of Australian Studies*, vol. 68 (June 2001): 54–64.

———. "Reforming Thirties and Hungry Forties: The Genesis of Cornwall's Emigration Trade." In *Cornish Studies Four*, edited by Philip Payton. Exeter, Devon: University of Exeter Press, 1996, 107–27.

———. *The Cornish Overseas*. Fowey, Cornwall: Alexander Associates, 1999.

Pedlar, Samuel, and Charles Wethey. "From Cornwall to Canada in 1841." *Families* 22, no. 4 (1983): 244–53.

Pourbaix, Michel. *The History of a Christian Community: Eardley, Luskville, Pontiac*. Pontiac, QC: 1999.

Pursehouse, Eric. "The 1830 Wagon Train for Diss Emigrants," *Waveney Valley Studies: Gleanings from Local History*. Diss, Norfolk: Diss Publishing Co. (1966): 233–36.

Raistrick, Arthur, and Bernard Jenning. *A History of Lead Mining in the Pennines*. London: Longmans, Green & Co. Ltd., 1965.

Read, Colin. *The Rising in Western Upper Canada: The Duncombe Revolt and After*. Toronto: University of Toronto Press, 1982.

Richards, Alan E. "Devonians in Canada." *Devon Family Historian*, no. 40 (October 1986): 24–28.

Robertson, Norman. *History of the County of Bruce*. Toronto: William Briggs, 1906.

Rogers, G.A. "Pioneer Mill Sites in the Châteauguay Valley." *Connections* 15, no. 1 (September 1992): 7–15.

Rogers, G.A. "The Settlement of the Châteauguay Valley." *Connections* 14, no. 3 (1992): 2–6.

Rose, Michael E. *The English Poor Law 1780–1930*. Newton Abbot, Devon, UK: David & Charles, 1971.

Ross, Duncan. "Case Studies in Emigration: Cornwall, Gloucestershire and New South Wales, 1877–1886." *Economic History Review*, series 2, vol. 16 (1963–64): 272–89.

Rowe, John. "A Cornish Farmer in Ontario." *Agricultural History Review*, vol. 1 (1953): 44–47.

———. *Cornish Methodists and Emigrants*. Redruth, Cornwall: Cornish Methodist History, 1967.

Rowse, A.L. *The Cornish in America*. London: Macmillan, 1969.

Scott, James. *The Settlement of Huron County*. Toronto: Ryerson Press, 1966.

Sellar, Robert. *The Tragedy of Quebec: The Expulsion of Its Protestant Farmers*. Toronto: University of Toronto Press, 1907. [This title was reprinted by University of Toronto Press in 1974 with an introduction by Robert Hill].

Semple, Neil. *The Lord's Dominion: The History of Canadian Methodism*. Montreal, Buffalo: McGill-Queen's University Press, circa 1996.

Shepperson, W.S. *British Emigration to North America: Projects and Opinions in the Early Victorian Period*. Oxford: Blackwell, 1957.

Shipman, Scott D., ed. *English Bloods in the Backwoods of Muskoka, 1878*. Toronto: Natural Heritage, 2004.

Siebert, Wilbur Henry. "American Loyalists in the Eastern Seigneuries and Townships of the Province of Quebec." *Transactions of the Royal Society of Canada*, 3rd series (1913) vol. VII: 3–41.

———. "Loyalist Settlements in the Gaspé Peninsula." *Transactions of the Royal Society of Canada*, 3rd series, vol. VIII (1914): 399–405.

Snell, K.D. *Annals of the Labouring Poor: Social Change and Agrarian England, 1660–1900*. Cambridge: Cambridge University Press, 1985.

Stevenson, John. *Popular Disturbances in England, 1700–1832*. London: Longman, 1992.

Talbot, Allen G. "In Memory of the Tolpuddle Martyrs." *Ontario History* 62, no. 1 (1970): 63–69.

Thompson, John. *Hudson: The Early Years, Up to 1867*. Hudson, QC: Hudson Historical Society, 1999. Thompson's material was first published in 1967 as the author's thesis: "The Evolution of an English-Speaking Community in Rural French Canada, 1820–1867."

Traill, Catherine Parr. *The Backwoods of Canada*. Ottawa: Carlton University Press, 1997.

Tranter, Neil. *Sport, Economy and Society in Britain, 1750–1914*. Cambridge: Cambridge University Press, 1998.

Tyrell, S.J. *A Countryman's Tale*. London: Constable and Co. Ltd., 1973.

Wagner, Gillian. *Children of the Empire*. London: Weidenfeld and Nicolson, 1982.

Waymouth, David. *Downton, 7,000 Years of an English Village*. Downton, Wiltshire: Cromwell Press, 1999.

Whaley, Raymond. "The Bates and Lovekin Families: First Settlers of Clarke Township." *Families* 44, no. 1 (February 2005): 3–26.

Wheaton, Dean, *Letters from Bruce County Written by Pioneer Joseph Bacon, 1705–1882*. Indiana: Author House, 2006.

White, Paul. *Owen Sound: The Port City*. Toronto: Natural Heritage, 2000.

Williams, Barbara, ed. *A Gentlewoman in Upper Canada: The Journals, Letters and Art of Anne Langton*. Toronto: Clark, Irwin, 1950.

———— *Ann Langton, Pioneer Woman and Artist*. Peterborough, ON: Peterborough Historical Society, 1986.

Wilson, Everett. "John Wilkinson: Devout Methodist and Dereham Pioneer." *Families* 35, no. 3 (August 1996): 147–51.

Wright, Glen T. *The Caroline and Her Passengers, March–May 1832*. Guelph, ON: Wellington Branch, Ontario Genealogical Society, 2002.

INDEX

Abbott, John Joseph Caldwell, 426
Abbott, Reverend Joseph, 68–70, 100, 426, 432, 435
Abbott, Lemuel-Francis, 44
Acadians, 47, 421
Adam, William, 253
Adams, Charles, 456
Adams, Henry, 253
Adams, Samuel, 436
Adelaide, Township of (Middlesex County), 178–81, 356
Adolphustown, Township of (Lennox County), 175, 420, 443
Adsett, Thomas, 210
Ainley, William, 216
Ainsley, Henry Francis, 102
Alberta, Province of, 220
Aldborough, Township of (Elgin County), 163, 165
Algoma, District of, Ontario, 34, 231, 232, 244
Allen, Edmund and Jane, 151
Allen, Robert, 96
Allen, Thomas, 196
Alling, Dr. Robert, 204, 205, 450
Alston Parish (England), 11, 124, 153, 177, 437
Amabel, Township of (Bruce County), 220
American War of Independence, American Revolutionary War (1775–83), 36, 43, 44, 54
Amherstburg, Ontario, 233
Ancaster, Ontario, 110
Ancaster, Township of (Wentworth County), 182
Anglican mission/missionaries (see also Society for the Propagation of the Gospel), 22, 26, 31–33, 38, 40, 47, 64,

75, 82, 83, 113, 115, 212, 432
Anglicanism, Anglican ministers, 32, 33, 40, 63, 67, 68, 70, 77, 78, 80, 83, 90–92, 100, 113, 114, 117, 213, 217, 239, 250, 427, 459–60
Anglicans/congregation, 14, 32, 33, 39–41, 64, 65, 67, 71, 76, 91, 116, 117, 118, 163, 425, 435
Ansty, Charlotte, 450
Ansty, Francis, 450
Argenteuil, County of, Quebec, 9, 99, 100, 432
Argenteuil seigneury (Quebec), 68, 98
Arthur, Township of (Wellington County), 221
Arundel, Township of (Argenteuil County), 100–01
Ascot, Township of (Sherbrooke County), 431
Asphodel, Township of (Peterborough County), 149
Asquith, Arthur, 257
Asquith, Dora, 257
Atkinson, Jane and John, 233
Attfield, Ann (see Jones, Ann)
Augusta, Township of (Grenville County), 39, 419–20
Austin, Richard, 107, 119
Australia, 21, 170, 186, 187, 231, 236, 250, 416, 453–54
Aylen, Peter, 113, 434
Aylmer (Quebec), 107, 113, 115, 358
Aynho Parish (England), 207, 208, 450

Bacon, Joseph, 221
Baie Missisquoi, Quebec, 44
Bainbridge, Philip John, 211
Baker, William, 179

Balkwill, Ann, 213
Balkwill, John, 211–13
Ball, Mr. W., 245
Banham Parish (England), 86
Barclay, Hannah (see Parnham, Hannah)
Barford Township (Quebec), 75
Barker, Herbert, 248
Barlow, Ernest, 248
Barnardo, Thomas, 240, 241, 456–57
Barnes, John, 144
Barnes, W.H., 250
Barnett, Herbert, 233
Barnett, Joseph, 190
Barnston, Township of, Quebec, 77
Barrie, Ontario, 297, 357
Barter, Issac, 192
Bartlett, W.H., 89
Bath, Marquis of (John Alexander Thynne), 439
Bath (England), 159, 261, 325
Bay of Quinte, 32, 39–41, 47, 175, 176, 420
Bayham, Township of (Elgin County), 173, 443
Beauharnois seigneury (Quebec), 59, 64, 65, 425
Beaver Meadows, Quebec, 58, 60–61
Bedford, Duke of (Francis Russell), 234, 244
Bedford, Quebec, 76, 245
Bedfordshire County (England), 118, 187, 189, 190, 234, 245, 250, 270, 438
Bedfordshire Mercury, 189, 190
Bedfordshire Times and Independent, 245
Beecham, William, 155
Belleville, Ontario, 21, 145, 239, 248, 350–52, 355
Benedict, David, 107

Benedict, Moses, 107, 433
Benedict, Samuel, 105
Bennet, John, 233, 455
Benson, John, 70
Berkshire County (England), 81
Berwick Advertiser, 335, 338, 342, 462
Berwick-upon-Tweed (England), 154, 177, 267, 321, 327, 329–38, 341–43, 356, 381
Bible Christians (Methodist), 148, 213, 214, 216, 369
Biddenden Parish (England), 133–34
Biddlecomb, James, 193
Biddulph, Township of (Huron County), 211–13, 451
Bideford (England), 154, 273, 287, 320, 325, 337, 347, 359–65, 367, 368, 371, 373, 374, 379, 380, 382, 384, 386, 388, 390, 391, 393, 394, 398, 401
Bigelow, Levi, 114
Bilton, Alice, 250
Bilton, Reverend William, 250, 460
Binder, William, 242
Bird, George, 448
Bird, Isabella Lucy, 289, 465
Bird, Joseph, 69
Birkbeck, George, 466
Birks, Thomas Heath, 435
Birmingham (England), 239, 247
Birt, Louisa, 239, 240, 457–58
Bisbee, Rueben and Mary, 174
Bishop, Dinah, 21, 145
Black, Ellen, 240
Blake, John, 83
Blanchard, Township of (Perth County), 216–17
Bland, John, 123
Bland, Joseph, 436, 469
Blandford, Township of (Oxford County), 174, 181, 443
Bleckinship, Joseph, 69
Blenheim, Township of (Oxford County), 185, 354
Bogton, Quebec, 58, 61, 424

Bolton (England), 22, 23, 248, 254
Bolton, Township of, Quebec, 77–78
Bolton and District Card and Ring Room Operatives Provincial Association, 248, 254, 471
Booth, Reverend James, 61
Booty, William, 210, 451
Borton, Alfred, 450
Boscastle (England), 154, 340, 383
Boston, Massachusetts, 65, 104, 127
Bouchette, Joseph, 53, 65, 98, 420–22, 425
Boulton, Henry John, 31, 417
Bowden, Valerie (Ottewell), 453
Bowman, Baxter, 114
Bowmanville, Ontario, 34, 147, 148, 248, 442
Boyd, John, 67
Boyd, William, 67
Braithwaite, Edward, 61
Brant, County of (Ontario), 174, 183, 185, 445
Brant, Township of (Bruce County), 221
Brantford, Township of (Brant County), 174, 185, 345
Bravender, Isaac, 127, 128, 437
Brewster, Edward William, 247, 459
Brewster, Robert, 244–45
Bridge, Samuel Southby, 49
Bridgerman, John, 441
Bridgwater (England), 154, 156, 285, 286, 319, 322, 323, 329, 335, 338, 341, 345, 347, 348, 353, 367, 373, 376
Bridle, James, 198
Bridport (England), 227
Brighton Township (Northumberland County), 122
Brinkworth Parish (England), 138, 139, 157–59, 285–87, 358, 362, 375, 391, 440
Bristol (England), 93, 154, 261, 262, 273, 283, 285–87, 305, 306, 308–10, 312, 315,

317–26, 328, 329, 331, 332, 334–37, 339–41, 343, 345–48, 350, 352–54, 357–66, 368, 372–76, 378, 382, 383, 385, 386, 388, 389, 391, 392, 394, 395, 398–405, 411, 463
Bristol, Township of, Quebec, 117
Briston Parish (England), 183, 184
Bristow, Edward and Hannah, 25, 417
British American Land Company, 72–74, 77, 78, 83, 84, 86, 87, 92, 243, 429, 448
British Army, 20, 44, 55, 68, 139, 264, 291, 294, 421, 422, 459, 466
Broadhead, Charles H., 435
Broadhead, John, 435
Broadhead, Sabina, 435
Brock, Township of (Ontario County), 127
Brockton (England), 108
Brockville, Ontario, 39, 248, 354–57
Brome, County of (Quebec), 45, 54, 77, 93
Brome, Township of (Quebec), 77–80
Brompton Pulp and Paper Company (Richmond County), 93
Brown, Alfred Edward, 249
Brown, W.M., 219, 435
Bruce, County of, Ontario, 219–21
Bruce Mines, Ontario, 34, 231, 232, 458
Brunt, William, 456
Brussels, Ontario, 216
Buchanan, Alexander (the elder) (Quebec immigration agent), 24, 28, 83, 125, 416, 428
Buchanan, Alexander (Quebec immigration agent), 92, 107, 149, 150, 151, 185, 417, 428–29
Buckingham, Quebec, 114, 357
Buckingham, Township of, Quebec, 114, 116
Buckingham Post, 435

Buckinghamshire County
(England), 31, 113, 435
Budd James, 179
Bulkington Parish (England),
454
Burford Township (Brant
County), 164
Burr, James, 155
Burton:
Mary, 55
Napier Christie, 55, 60
Ralph, 55
Burtonville, Quebec, 58, 61
Burwash, Nathaniel, 101
Bury (England), 93
Bury, Township of, Quebec, 90,
91, 429, 431
Bury and Norwich Post, 86, 430
Burr, James, 155
Bye, George, 450
Bytown (*see also* Ottawa), 102,
108, 111, 113, 278, 295, 297,
350–58, 434

Caldwell Manor (*see* Foucault)
Callow, John, 214
Camborne, Ontario, 149
Cambridge, St. Mary the Great,
Parish (England), 240
Cambridgeshire County
(England), 141, 143, 146,
185, 228, 446
Canada Company, 83, 85, 86,
146, 190, 199, 200, 202–07,
209, 210, 212, 215, 218, 323,
324, 448, 450, 452
Cann, Robert, 213
Cape Breton, 327, 361, 389,
419, 462
Captain Swing, Swing riots, 23,
170, 182, 444
Caradoc, Township of
(Middlesex County), 443
Carleton, County of, Ontario,
111, 116
Carleton, Sir Guy, 42
Carleton Junction, Ontario, 248
Carling:
Isaac, 212, 213, 451
John, 212, 452
Thomas, 451
Carlingford, Ontario, 216, 452

Carlisle (England), 123, 125,
154, 176, 346, 384, 386, 390,
392, 395, 397, 458
Carlisle, Ontario, 176, 177
Carlton Colville Parish
(England), 185, 447
Carlton-on-Trent Parish
(England), 124, 437
Carter, George and Deziah, 445
Carter, Mary (*see* Jones, Mary)
Cartwright, William, 208, 450
Carver, George, 180, 446
Catholic Church, Roman
Catholic, 39, 94
Catholic Protection Society, 458
Cattermole, William, 86, 146,
203, 204, 322–24, 449
Cavagnal, Quebec (*see also*
Vaudreuil), 70
Cavan, Township of (Durham
County), 123, 125, 469
Census of 1837, 173
Census of 1881, 34, 35, 39, 45,
75, 110, 116, 118, 418, 420,
434
Centralia, Ontario, 212, 451
Chambly, Quebec, 37
Champ, Eliza, 193
Champ, James, 193
Chamberlain, David, 118
Chamberlin, Isaiah, 107, 120
Chamberlin, Nathaniel, 105
Channel Islands, 47
Channell, Leonard Stewart,
74, 427
Chaplin, Millicent Mary (Reeve),
30, 82, 89, 291, 417, 428
Chaplin, Colonel Thomas, 428
Chapman, Reverend Archibald,
212–13
Chapman, John, 186
Chapman, Reverend Thomas
Shaw, 91
Chapmanslade Parish
(England), 136
Charlottenburg, Township of
(Glengarry County), 419
Charlottetown, Prince Edward
Island, 59, 304, 322, 324,
329 , 337, 351, 363, 367, 425
Charlotteville, Township of
(Norfolk County), 177, 443

Chatham (England), 329, 332,
454
Chatham, Ontario, 170
Chatham, Township of
(Argenteuil County
Quebec), 98–100, 432
Châteauguay, Battle of, 49, 422
Châteauguay River/Valley
(Quebec), 63–65, 67
Chaudière River/Valley, 37, 421
Chelsea pensioners, 139–41,
160, 440–41
Cheshire County (England),
187, 219, 289
Chew, Abel, 456
Child, Thomas, 434
Children (*see* Home Children)
Children's Friend Society, 335,
337
Chinguacousy, Township of
(Peel County), 138
Cholera:
in Ontario, 209, 210
in Quebec, 270–72
on ships, 271–72
Cholmoneley, Thomas, 219, 453
Christie, Gabriel, 55, 423
Christie, Napier (*see* Burton,
Napier Christie)
Christie, William Penderlieth,
63
Church, Gardner and Girard,
107
Church of England (*see*
Anglican missions/ mission-
aries; Anglicanism)
Clarendon, Township of
(Pontiac County, Quebec),
117–18
Clarke, Josiah, 90
Clarke, Township of (Durham
County), 41, 152
Clemence, John and Mary, 151
Clinton, Ontario, 213, 215
Clitheroe (England), 35, 251,
252, 418
Clitheroe Advertiser, 252
Clough, Harry, 248
Coal miners/mining (*see*
Miners/mining)
Cobalt, Ontario, 233, 243, 244,
458

Cobbett, William, 134, 135, 438–39

Cobourg, Ontario, 126, 127, 147, 149, 151, 204, 232, 351, 358

Cockburn, James Pettison, 104

Coke, Edward Thomas, 291, 465

Colborne, Lieutenant Governor Sir John, 132, 133, 139–42

Colborne, Township of (Huron County), 215, 352

Colchester (England), 154, 203, 379

Colchester, Township of (Essex County), 443

Coleman, Francis, 442

Coleman, James, 217

Coleman, Peter, 147, 442

Collingwood, Township of (Grey County), 220

Compton, George, 195

Compton, Township of (Quebec), 32, 91, 93, 247, 431

Conant, Roger, 42

Congregational church/minister, 166–67

Conner, Reginald, 458

Cook, A.D., 325

Cook, Cornelius, 144

Cook, James, 208

Cookman, Francis, 424

Cookshire, Quebec, 243

Cooper, James and Harriet, 179

Cooper, Richard, 144

Cooper, William, 178–79

Copper Cliff, Ontario, 243, 458

Cork, Peter and Ann, 242

Cornwall, Ontario, 39, 248, 355

Cornwall, Township of (Stormont County), 419

Cornwall County (England), 26, 63, 83, 147–49, 151, 174, 185, 211, 213, 216, 220, 221, 231, 273, 287, 317, 370, 378, 442, 454–55

Corsley (Shedden), Ontario, 168

Corsley Parish (England), 135–37, 166, 167, 170, 319, 444

Côte St. Charles (see Vaudreuil)

Cottam, Ann, 83

Cotterell, Daniel, 325

Cotton, Reverend Charles Caleb, 75, 76, 427

Crabb, Anthony, 242

Cragg, Agnes and David, 418

Craig's Road (Quebec), 83, 71, 82

Cramahe Township (Northumberland County), 122

Cratfield Parish (England), 184

Crediton, Ontario, 212, 214, 451

Cricket, 237, 294–96, 456, 466

Cross, James, 234

Cross family, 87

Croydon Parish (England), 186, 447

Cumberland County (England), 22, 67–69, 123–25, 146, 151–53, 175–78, 423, 425, 445

Dakeyne Street Lads Band (Nottingham), 250

Dalhousie, Lord (George Ramsay, 9th Earl), 47, 98, 99, 101–04, 106

Dalhousie, Township of (Lanark County), 435

Dalziel, Reverend John, 91

Darlington, Township of (Durham County), 42, 147, 149, 152, 213, 353, 357, 358, 442

Darrington, Jonas, 448

Dartmouth (England), 154, 326, 329, 332, 335, 338, 342, 344, 381, 383, 388, 390, 391, 403

Davey, John, 442

Davey, Peter, 147

Davies, Ambrose, 160

Davies, Thomas, 448

De la Fosse, Frederick, 236–38, 456

Delaware, Township of (Middlesex County), 180, 181, 246, 292, 443

Denison, George T., 225–28, 453

Deptford (England), 308, 454

Derby (England), 245

Derbyshire County (England), 33, 208, 218, 263, 450, 453

Dereham, Township of (Oxford County), 174, 187

Devey, Eleanor Shelton, 108

Devey, Thomas, 108

Devizes (England), 174, 455

Devizes, Ontario, 174–75

Devon, Ontario, 212, 216

Devon County (England), 26, 48, 101, 107, 119, 120, 185, 211–16, 273, 287, 292, 295, 451, 452, 454

Dey, Joseph, 435

Disease (see Cholera)

Diss Parish (England), 430–31

Donaldson, John A., 234, 456

Donkin, Robert, 216

Dorchester (England), 227

Dorking (England), 141, 142, 182, 183, 325, 447

Dornorman, William, 142

Dorset County (England), 186, 188, 225–28, 286, 348

Douglastown, Quebec, 47

Douro, Township of (Peterborough County), 137

Downes, Robert, 20, 264, 416, 461

Downie, Township of (Perth County), 217–18

Downton Parish (England), 170–73, 191, 192, 285, 338, 430, 444–45

Drummond, Township of (Lanark County), 435

Drummondville, Quebec, 79, 80, 428

Dudswell, Township of (Quebec), 91

Dukes, William, 434

Dumfries, Township of (Upper Canada), 350

North Dumfries, Township of (Waterloo County), 187

South Dumfries, Township of (Brant County), 164

Dumfriesshire (Scotland), 425

Dummer, Township of (Peterborough County), 121, 137, 139, 152, 439

Dunany, Township of, Quebec, 100

Dundas, Ontario, 167, 357

Dundas County, Ontario, 39, 420

Dunderdale, John, 248

Dunderdale, William, 248

Dunham, Township of (Quebec), 76, 77

Dunn, John, 326

Dunn, William, 217

Dunnett, Reverend Mr., 452

Dunsmore, J.H., 452

Dunsmore, James, 452

Dunnville, Ontario, 249

Dunwich, Township of (Elgin County), 163, 165, 168, 443

Durham, County of, Ontario, 22, 41, 42, 122, 123, 125, 127, 140, 146, 147, 149, 152, 178, 213, 231, 317, 355, 438

Durham, Lord (John George Lambton), 31, 141, 418, 440

Durham, Ontario, 219

Durham, Township of (Quebec), 82

Durham boats, 278–79

Durham County (England), 22, 123, 177

Durham Road (Bruce and Grey Counties), 219, 221, 453

Durrington Parish (England), 13

Dursley (England), 325, 463

DuVernet, Henry, 106

Eacher, John Carrier, 244

East Anglia (England) (*see also* Norfolk and Suffolk), 74, 85, 92, 146, 154, 203, 323, 324, 432, 463

East Drayton Parish (England), 185, 198

East Flamborough, Township of (Wentworth County), 183

East Gwillimbury, Township of (York County), 122

East Hawkesbury, Quebec, 100

East Williams, Township of (Middlesex County), 176

Eastern Townships (Quebec), 24, 29, 32, 34, 35, 37, 44, 54, 71–97, 146, 230, 239, 242, 246, 247, 253, 291, 340, 341, 351, 355, 356, 427, 432, 448, 458

Easthope, Township of (Perth County), 209

Eaton, Township of, Quebec, 91, 431

Edgefield Parish (England), 183, 184

Edme, Henry, 60, 424

Edwards, Richard, 233, 455

Edwardsburgh, Township of (Grenville County), 419, 420

Edwardstown, Quebec, 59, 65, 66, 425

Egremont, Lord (George O'Brien Wyndham, 3rd Earl), 141, 276

Ekfrid Township (Middlesex County), 164

Eldon, Township of (Victoria County), 139

Elgin County, Ontario, 137, 162, 163, 166–68, 173, 174, 183, 443, 445, 452

Elizabethtown, Township of (Leeds County), 419, 420

Ellerton, Charles, 424

Ellice, Edward, 64, 65, 424

Elliot, Walton and Samuel, 446

Elliott, Henry, 147

Elliott, Moses, 81

Elliott, Zekiel, 81

Elma, Township of (Perth County), 218

Ely, Township of, Quebec, 427

Emerson, James and Ann (Gardiner), 123, 436

Emigration:
agents, 86, 140, 146, 202–04, 233, 247, 249, 271, 417, 424, 440, 456
causes, 16, 20, 21, 30, 33–35, 50, 55, 58, 67, 85, 93, 131, 149, 187, 220, 221, 225, 228, 229, 234, 242, 248–50, 252
financial assistance, 22–26, 33, 51, 62, 84–87, 92, 121, 124, 131–39, 141, 145, 146, 149, 153, 155, 166, 167, 173, 177, 178, 180–85, 189–91, 198, 203, 208, 221, 225, 229, 230, 234, 240, 244, 248–250, 276, 429–31,

437–42, 445, 446, 448, 450, 453, 454, 456, 460
hostility to, 25, 51, 52, 85, 134, 135, 145, 224, 227, 228
promotional literature, 19, 61, 62, 79, 87, 136, 202, 459

Emily, Township of (Victoria County), 139

Emmerison, Jonathan, 446

England:
agricultural changes, 20–23, 34, 132, 135, 149, 189, 234, 247, 249
cities, 22, 33, 34, 247, 229, 238, 240, 247–49
Industrial Revolution, 22, 30, 33, 85, 132, 229, 423, 455
social problems, 34, 229, 238–40, 247, 248

English ancestry/Englishness, 16, 35, 39, 40, 47, 54, 65, 67, 73–75, 77, 81, 83, 91, 99–101, 110–13, 116, 118, 151, 152, 162, 165, 168, 174, 177, 185, 205, 207, 210–13, 215, 216, 218, 220, 239, 244, 246, 288–90, 293–300, 420, 422, 427, 431, 432, 434, 465

Eramosa, Township of (Wellington County), 207

Erie Canal, 461

Ermatinger, Edward, 162, 165, 443, 444

Ernestown, Township of (Addington County), 41, 420

Essery, John, 451

Essex County (England), 21, 146, 162, 203, 210, 221, 416

Essex County, Ontario, 40, 168, 174, 233, 443

Etobicoke, Township of (York County), 184

Exeter (England), 101

Exeter, Ontario, 212–15, 452

Exmouth (England), 154, 316

Eydon Parish (England), 208, 450

Falloon, Reverend Daniel, 82

Falloon, Reverend Francis, 118, 436

Falmouth (England), 154, 185,

283, 315, 317, 319, 327–29, 331, 332, 335, 337, 344, 351, 354, 356, 359, 364, 369, 371–73, 375–82, 384, 389, 391, 392, 394, 395, 397, 400
Fane, Colonel Francis, 34, 246, 293, 294, 418, 459, 466
Farmer, Elizabeth (Yates), 110
Farmer, Mary Alice, 110, 434
Farmer, William, 107–10, 433–34
Farmer's Rapids, Farmer's Station, Ontario, 108, 113
Farnham, Township of, Quebec, 77–78
Featherston, John, 178, 446
Fenelon, Township of (Victoria County), 41, 128
Fenelon Falls, Ontario, 130
Field, Charles, 325
Findlay, Captain, 118, 436
First World War, 248, 249, 256, 456
Fisher, Robert, 199, 204, 448
Fitzroy, Township of (Carleton County), 111
Fitzwilliam, Earl (William Wentworth, 6th Earl), 273
Flamborough Township (Wentworth County), 183
Flanagan, Reverend John, 83
Flanders, John, 448
Fleamen, John, 178, 446
Fleetwood (England), 154, 381
Folland, Reverend H.G.B., 431
Ford, Mary, 21
Fort Niagara, 420
Foucault (Caldwell Manor), Quebec, 37, 45, 421
Fowey (England), 154, 274, 283, 287, 351, 353, 359, 363, 369, 379, 382, 384, 385, 388, 389, 391–93, 396–99, 402, 405, 408
Fowler, Mrs. L.L. (Althea Langtree), 251
Fox hunting, 294
France, 41, 422
Francis, Charles, 90
Francistown, Ontario, 213
Franklin, George, 435
Franklin, John, 442, 453

Franklin, Michael, 54
Franklin, Susannah, 221
Fraser, Nelson, 436
Fredericksburg, Township of (Lennox County), 420
Freeman, John, 215
French, Fanny, 450
French, James, 450
French Canadians, 42–44, 47, 49, 52, 63, 64, 71, 93, 94, 264, 289, 422, 427, 432–433
Friend, Thomas, 451
Friend, Wallace, 153
Frome, Ontario, 168, 170, 261
Frome Parish (England), 121, 134–37, 167, 168, 325, 439, 444, 458, 463
Fulford, Francis, 447
Fullarton, Township of (Perth County), 211, 216
Fullarton Corners, Ontario, 216
Fulmodeston Parish (England), 184

Galt, John, 202, 449
Galt, Ontario, 200, 210, 449
Garafraxa, Township of (Wellington County), 208
Garafraxa Road, 219, 221, 432
Gaspé Peninsula (Quebec), 45, 47, 309, 421–22
Gatineau Power Company, 109
Gatineau River (Quebec), 103, 105, 108–110
Georgina, Township of (Ontario County), 122
German immigrants, 37, 39, 75, 209, 210, 212, 218, 418–20, 436, 451
Gibb, John and George, 217
Gibson, J., 246
Giles, William, 450
Girls' Friendly Society, 240, 457–58
Gloucester (England), 282, 329, 332, 335, 338, 347, 350, 357, 360, 363, 364, 367, 381, 385, 390
Gloucester, Township of (Carleton County), 110, 112
Gloucestershire County (England), 154, 208, 218,

222, 227, 325, 438, 463
Goatcher, Stephen, 179, 446
Goderich, Ontario, 200, 203, 204, 215, 219, 350, 358
Goderich, Township of (Huron County), 215
Gold, Mr., 242
Golding, William, 158
Goodwin, Joseph, 450
Gore District (Ontario), 185, 357, 358, 438, 447
Gosfield, Township of (Essex County), 174, 443
Gosford Road (Eastern Townships), 351, 352, 356–57
Goulding, James, 194
Gourlay, Robert, 106, 433
Grafton, Ontario, 127
Graham, John, 178, 446
Graham, Joseph, 446
Graham, Thomas, 175–76
Granby, Township of, Quebec, 78
Gransden, Thomas, 155
Grant, I.A., 116, 435
Grant, William and Jane, 121, 436
Grantham, Township of (Quebec), 80, 82
Great Barford Parish (England), 190, 448
Great Ryburgh Parish (England), 87, 431
Great Yarmouth (England), 86, 430
Greenway, William, 451
Grenville, County of, Ontario, 39
Grenville, Township of (Quebec), 98, 99, 432
Grey, County of, Ontario, 219–20
Greystead, Ontario, 176, 177
Grosse Île (Quebec), 204, 270, 272, 449, 462, 463
Grundt, J., 468
Grundy, Frank, 93, 432
Guelph, Ontario, 34, 199, 200, 202–07, 219, 250, 258, 295, 350, 352
Guelph, Township of (Wellington County), 199,

203, 205, 207, 262, 461
Guillet, Dr. Edwin, 289, 294, 443–44
Gwillimbury, East Township of (York County), 122
Gwillimbury, West Township of (Simcoe County), 125, 468

Hagyard, Dr. Thomas, 215
Haldimand, Sir Frederick, 39, 44, 45, 419, 421
Haldimand, Township of (Northumberland County), 127
Halifax, Nova Scotia, 240, 258, 297, 409, 466
Halifax, Township of, Quebec, 82
Hallerton, Quebec, 58, 63, 64, 424
Hallowell, Millie, 36–37, 418
Hallowell family, 37, 447
Halton, County of, Ontario, 141, 142, 183, 447
Hamilton, George, 103, 104, 433
Hamilton, James, 175
Hamilton, Ontario, 34, 110, 134, 167, 175, 178, 182, 204, 209, 233, 251, 253, 257–59, 278, 346, 349, 350, 352–54, 356–58, 461, 464
Hamilton, Township of (Northumberland County), 438
Hamley, William, 83
Hampshire County (England), 93, 101, 249, 316, 454
Hampton, Ontario, 147
Harmony, Ontario, 218
Harpur, James, 183
Harris, James, 325
Harrison, Phyllis, 456
Harrison, Thomas, 97
Harrison, William, 292
Harrison family, 216
Harvey, Frank, 248
Harvey Hill Copper Mines (Quebec), 83
Harwich, Township of (Kent County), 443
Hatley, Township of, Quebec, 77

Hawkesbury, Quebec, 18, 100, 103
Hay, Township of (Huron County), 211–13
Hayle (England), 154, 370, 383
Haynes Parish emigration fund, 234, 456
Hayward, Thomas, 233
Hayworth, John, 119
Hazard, Reverend Henry, 64, 117
Heacham Parish (England), 87, 95, 286, 338, 431
Headcorn Parish (England), 133
Heals family, 216
Heasman, Henry, 181, 446
Heathcote, Annie and Jack, 251, 460
Helford (England), 154, 371
Helyer, James, 143
Heming, Edward Francis, 205, 206, 450
Hemmingford, Township of (Huntingdon County), 45, 54, 58, 59, 61, 64, 421, 424
Hempstall, Ann, 185, 198
Hempstall family, 185, 198
Hemsley, James, 146, 441
Hemsley, Richard, 145, 416, 441
Henrysburg, Quebec, 58, 61, 424
Henson, Richard, 245
Heriot, Frederick George, 428
Hertfordshire County (England), 249, 460
Hertfordshire Reformatory School for Boys, 242–44, 458
Hewitt, William, 218
Heytesbury, Earl of (Sir William à Court), 341
Heytesbury Parish (England), 136, 156, 157, 285, 319
Hibbert, Titus Ware, 126
Hibbert, Township of (Perth County), 213, 216
Higginson, Ruth, 435
Higgs, Henry, 171
Hill, John, 186
Hill, Thomas and Ann, 186
Hillier, Township of (Prince Edward County), 40
Hills, George, 182

Hilton, Alexander, 181, 446
Hinchinbrooke, Township of (Huntingdon County), 45, 67, 421, 425
Hoare, Henry, 249
Hodgson, John, 69, 100
Hodgson, Joseph, 125, 437, 468
Hodgson, Robert, 69
Holman, Lewis, 451
Holstead, Hiram, 248
Holt, Maria, 435
Holt Parish (England), 184
Home Children, 238–42, 456–57
   background, 238
   experiences, 239–42
   hostility to in Canada, 240
   placements, 239–40, 457
   supervision, 457
Homes, Andrew, 450
Hooper, Joseph, 187, 447
Hope, Township of (Durham County), 147, 317
Hope Town, Quebec, 47
Hore, William, 149
Horning, John, 207
Horningsham Parish (England), 136, 167, 444
Horseracing, 293, 294, 466
Houghton, Township of (Norfolk County), 164, 443
Howard, Henry, 101
Howard, J.M., 326
Howard, Dr. Thomas James, 101
Howard, Township of (Kent County), 169, 443
Howell, Francis, 292, 295, 465
Howes, Benjamin, 450
Howick, Township of (Huron County), 216
Howse, William, 87
Hoyle, Henry, 423
Hoyle, James, 242
Hoyle, Robert, 57, 423–24
Huckell, Benjamin, 435
Hudson, Quebec, 35, 68, 70, 252, 425
Hudson's Bay Company, 69
Hughes, John, 248
Hull (England), 51, 58, 59, 66, 79, 127, 154, 177, 185, 267, 272, 274, 275, 282, 283, 286,

287, 303–34, 33–49, 351, 352, 354, 355, 357, 358, 360–68, 370–80, 382, 383, 385–90, 392, 393, 395–401, 423

Hull, Quebec (*see also* Wrightstown), 104, 105–08, 110, 113, 115, 198, 435, 436

St. James Anglican Church, 113

Hull, Township of (Ottawa County), 98, 105, 107, 110, 116, 119, 433

Hull Advertiser, 303, 304–307

Hull Packet, 59, 275

Hullett, Township of (Huron County), 213, 215, 216

Huntingdon, Quebec, 67

Huntingdon County, Quebec, 45, 54, 57, 64, 67, 421, 422, 425

Huntly, James, 22

Huntly, Osmond Charles, 222

Huntsville, Ontario, 237, 238

Hurdon, John, 214

Huron County, Ontario, 210–16, 220, 231

Huron (Colonization) Road, 210, 213, 452

Huron Tract (Canada Company), 26, 164, 190, 201, 208, 210, 213, 215–18, 448–51

Hyde Park Corner, Ontario, 176

Ilfracombe (England), 154, 363

Immigrants:
taxes, 143, 166, 167
numbers, 23, 26, 86, 99, 100, 131, 174, 212, 216, 218, 262, 263, 270, 272, 281–83 319, 429, 430, 433, 434, 438, 447, 463
quarantine arrangements, 270–72, 348–50, 462
statistics, 26, 86, 185, 208, 246, 247, 417, 426, 430, 463

Ingoldesthorpe Parish (England), 87

Inverness, Township of, Quebec, 71, 82, 83, 429

Ipswich (England), 86, 93, 154, 203, 340, 430

Ipswich Journal, 449, 463

Ireland, 31, 50, 67, 100, 117, 118, 151, 165, 273, 281, 349, 463

Ireland, Township of (Quebec), 82, 83

Irish immigrants, 30, 33, 35, 51, 62, 64, 65, 67, 75, 83, 99, 100, 102, 110–14, 116–18, 124, 126, 137, 165, 199, 205, 209, 212, 216, 218, 220, 270, 272, 273, 288, 289, 297–300, 387, 420, 422, 425, 433–37, 463, 464

Île aux Noix, Québec, 57, 423–24

Île de Orléans (Québec), 20

Iles, John, 450

Isle of Wight (England), 141, 348

Jackson, Reverend Christopher, 77

Jackson, Mrs. E., 234–35, 456

Jackson, George, 177, 265, 267, 278, 332

Jackson, John, 248

Jackson, Marmaduke, 424

Jackson, Thomas, 96

Jackson family, 234

James, Mark, 93

Jameson, Anna B., 139, 440, 443

Janes, Herbert, 460

Jeanes, William, 168, 444

Jellyman, Joseph and Frances, 196

Jenkins, William, 243, 458

Jessopp, Henry, 21

Jessopp, Joseph, 416

Jewell, Alfred, 232–33

John Bull, 162, 289, 290, 465

Johnson, Sir John, 39

Johnson, Reverend M., 32

Johnson, Thomas, 326

Johnson, Reverend Thomas, 77, 78, 427

Johnston, Craster, 208

Johnston, Reverend John B.G., 113, 115

Johnston, Quebec, 39

Johnstone, Thomas, 248

Jones:
Ann (Attfield) (Mrs. Thomas), 175
Charles, 445
Mary (Carter), 445
Thomas J., 175, 445

Jones, George, 448

Jones, Joseph and Joan, 439

Jones, R., 127

Jones, William, 325

Julyan, Charles, 220

Keddy:
George, 61
John, 61
Joseph, 61

Kemp, Reverend John, 90

Kempton, Dr. J.W., 326

Kent, County of Ontario, 28, 41, 162, 168, 170, 174, 443

Kent County (England), 23, 24, 101, 113, 131, 133, 134, 146, 152, 155, 185, 203, 216, 222, 223, 285, 286, 324, 348, 349, 438, 454, 454

Kentish Independent, 454

Kettleburgh Parish (England), 184

Kettlestone Parish (England), 87, 96, 285, 340, 431

King, Charles, 193

King, James, 171

King Township (York County)

King's Lynn (England), 86–88, 95, 96, 285, 286, 337, 338, 340, 361, 364, 417, 430, 463

Kingsey, Township of, Quebec, 81, 242

Kingston, Ontario, 39, 40, 102, 122, 123, 278, 292, 295, 350–58, 466

Kingston, Township of (Frontenac County), 420

Kitchen, Thomas, 218

Knight, J., 183

Knook Parish (England), 136, 156, 157, 285, 319, 439

Knott, John, 233

Knott, William, 218

Knowlton, Quebec, 239

Knowlton Home, 239, 457

Lac Memphrémagog (Quebec), 44, 77, 79
Lachute, Quebec, 99–101, 432
Lacolle seigneury(Quebec), 22, 51–58, 60, 61, 63, 64, 422–24
Lake Champlain, 57, 423
Lake Erie, 26, 28, 32, 152, 162–64, 175, 178, 248, 359, 443, 465
Lake Huron, 201, 219, 358
Lake Ontario, 16, 22, 26, 32, 34, 35, 40–42, 47, 121, 122, 134, 138, 141, 142, 146, 147, 151, 152, 167, 175, 182, 183, 202, 220, 231, 248, 278, 420, 443, 461, 465
Lake Simcoe, 122, 125, 138, 141, 353
Lambton, County of, Ontario, 21, 250, 446
Lanark, County of, Ontario, 116, 352, 356
Lanark, Ontario, 435
Lancashire County (England), 22, 35, 41, 57, 93, 129, 131, 176, 209, 233, 248, 250, 251, 254, 277, 418
Lancashire Society of Friends
Lancaster (England), 154, 286, 324, 330, 352, 375
Lancaster, Ontario, 357
Lancaster, Shirley, 425
Land (*see also* Canada Company and British American Land Company)
  free land grants, 34, 40, 41, 44, 79, 81, 220, 231, 234, 236, 238, 437
  purchase of, 29, 37, 54, 55, 61, 64, 68, 77, 78, 100, 101, 107, 127, 128, 130, 181, 183, 200, 201, 205, 217, 426, 449
  rents and tenancies, 43, 45, 54, 64, 68, 87, 128, 148, 149, 165, 166, 177, 187, 232, 424, 425
Landlords, 54, 187, 207, 208, 276, 388
Langford, Samuel, 434
Langton, Anne, 129–31, 437

Langton, John, 41, 124, 128, 130, 137, 141, 420, 437
Langton family, 21, 131
Langtree, Althea (*see* Fowler, Mrs. L.L.)
Langtree, Thomas and Alice Ann, 252
Lawford, James, 448
Laxfield Parish (England), 199, 203, 204, 223
Lead miners (English), 22, 177–78
Leatherdale, Louisa, 210
Ledbury (England), 228
Leeds (England), 100
  assisted emigration from, 248–49
Leeds, Township of, Quebec, 71, 82, 83, 356
Lenham Parish (England), 203, 222, 223, 324, 438
Lennox, County of, Ontario, 175, 420
Lennoxville, Quebec, 230, 253–54
Lewis, George, 167
Lewis, J.O., 136, 436
Libby, William, 450
Lincoln, County of, Ontario, 41, 185
Lincolnshire County (England), 30, 34, 82, 113, 126, 219, 220, 228, 246, 291, 293, 424, 428, 435, 453
Lindsay, David, 78–79
Lister, William, 248
Litchfield, Earl of (Thomas Anson, 2nd Earl), 231
Litchfield, John, 245
Litchfield, Louise, 245
Littleton, Colonel E.G.F., 116, 435
Liverpool (England), 34, 60, 62, 93, 103, 104, 107, 112, 113, 118, 125, 146, 150, 154, 185, 208, 231, 238, 239, 263, 272, 273, 279, 280, 284, 463
  Catholic Protection Society, 458
  Irish who sailed from, 273
  Port, 303–37, 339–59, 362, 363, 365–415, 423, 451,

461–62
Liverpool Albion, 416
Lloyd's Shipping Register, 274–76, 463–64
Lobo, Township of (Middlesex County), 176–77
Logan, Township of (Perth County), 213, 216, 218
Londesborough (England), 215
Londesborough, Ontario, 215
London (England):
  City, 19, 24, 32, 33, 64, 111, 112, 133, 150, 175, 176, 186, 222, 223, 225, 229–31, 234, 238, 239, 245, 253, 274, 335, 337, 348, 435, 458
  Port, 154, 157–60, 173, 192, 222, 269, 271–73, 276, 283–87, 303–06, 308–59, 361–63, 366–92, 394–404, 409, 449, 461, 463
London, District of (Upper Canada), 353, 358, 448
London, Ontario, 28, 34, 139, 175, 177, 187, 188, 213, 215, 239, 297, 357, 358, 447, 451, 454
London, Township of (Middlesex County), 174–77, 186, 212, 246, 443, 445
London Road, 211–13
Longbridge Deverill Parish (England), 136, 138, 440
Loveless, Elizabeth, 187–88
Loveless, George, 186–88, 447
Lowe, Watson, 446
Lower Canada (*see also* Quebec)
  defence considerations, 42–45, 70, 422
  French/English relations, 42–45, 47, 48, 63, 70, 71, 74, 423
  timber trade, 22, 30, 55–57, 64, 93, 106
Lowestoft (England), 86, 154, 185, 339, 430
Loyalists, United Empire Loyalists, 16, 33, 36–42, 44, 45–47, 54, 73, 75, 81, 110, 114, 122, 152, 418–420

military, 38, 39, 419
Lucas, Luke, 218
Lunn, William, 448
Lutherans, 39

Mackenzie, William Lyon, 262, 461
MacLaren, James, 114
Macpherson, Annie, 239, 457
MacTaggert, John, 105, 433
Maiden Bradley (England), 121, 136, 261
Maidstone, Township of (Essex County), 443
Malahide, Township of (Elgin County), 173, 183, 443
Manitoba, Province of, 220, 221, 246, 453
Mann, Ann (Downer), 180, 446
Mann, Thomas, 218
Manning, John, 54
March, Township of (Carleton County), 116
Marchmont Home (Belleville), 239, 241
Markham, Township of (York County), 122, 127, 436
Martin, Henry Bryant, 279
Martin, Martin, 206–07, 450
Martin, William, 242
Maryport (England), 154, 313–15, 317, 319, 320, 323–26, 329, 330, 333, 334, 336, 340, 341, 342, 345, 346, 368, 370, 373, 384, 389, 390, 393, 423
Marysburgh, Township of (Prince Edward County), 39, 420
Massachusetts, State of, 105
Massey, Ontario, 244
Matilda, Township of (Dundas County), 39, 419
May, William, 211
Mayhew, Samuel, 321
McAndrew, Patrick, 248
McGillivray, Township of (Huron County), 213, 220, 451
Mechanics' Institutes, 297, 466
Medonte, Township of (Simcoe County), 125, 139, 140, 160

Melbourne, Township of, Quebec, 81, 82, 242
Mellish, Frank, 143, 441
Mersea, Township of (Essex County), 174, 443
Methodism/Methodists, missionaries (see also Bible Christians), 25, 31, 32, 61, 64–66, 70, 76, 77, 82, 83, 92, 118, 125, 127, 148, 186, 187, 208, 213, 215–17, 289, 319, 418, 426, 427, 436
Methodist churches, 61, 76, 188, 213, 216, 427, 442, 452
Methodist Missionary Society, 61, 62, 78, 424
Middlemore, Dr. John, 239, 457
Middlesex, County of, Ontario, 139, 162, 168, 174–78, 180, 183, 187, 214, 292, 293, 356, 443, 445, 451
Middleton, Township of (Norfolk County), 443
Midlands (England), 125, 132, 225, 247
Milburn, Thomas, 124, 177–78
Milford (England), 154, 316, 344
Military settlements, 37, 40, 79–81, 102, 116, 119, 120, 428, 435
Milne, Reverend George, 47
Milton Abbas (England), 225, 227
Miners/ mining:
  in England, 22, 34, 124, 177, 178, 231–33, 243, 442, 454, 455
  in Ontario, 34, 115, 231–33, 244, 458, 459
  in Quebec, 83, 116, 243
  in the United States, 231, 233, 243
Missisquoi, County of, Quebec, 45, 77, 93
Mitchell, John, 212
Mitchell, Ontario, 213
Moan, Edward, 325
Monkman, James, 128
Montreal, Quebec, 34, 35, 37, 49, 55, 60, 63, 67, 70, 71, 73, 101, 105, 114, 126, 134,

149, 151, 180, 242, 242, 252, 255–59, 271, 278, 380, 287, 289, 293, 295, 334, 350–53, 356–59, 419, 423, 462, 464
  Rugby Club, 296
  St. George's Society, 297
Montreal Gazette, 61, 62, 71, 131, 204, 325, 395, 424, 425, 438, 463
Moodie, Susanna, 130–31, 438
Moore, Andrew W., 41
Moore, Township of (Hastings County), 21
Moore family, 216
Morice, Reverend Charles, 63
Morris, Charles, 448
Morris, Reverend William, 67, 114
Morrisburg, Upper Canada, 49
Mosa, Township of (Middlesex County), 443
Mountain, Bishop George Jehoshophat, 63, 71
Murray, General James, 42–43
Muskoka, District of, Ontario, 236–38, 465

Napoleonic Wars (1803–15), 20, 41, 49, 54, 55, 57, 67, 103, 107, 110, 123, 163, 174, 422
Native peoples, 418, 420
Nelson, Township of (Halton County), 83, 142–43
Nepean, Township of (Carleton County), 110, 434
New Brunswick, Province of, 45, 51, 54, 59, 67, 282–87, 328, 350, 358, 419, 425
New Carlisle, Quebec, 45–47
New Edinburgh, Quebec, 111–12, 434
New England/New Englanders, 37, 41, 44, 45, 73, 74, 81, 100, 105, 110, 114, 117, 174
New Hampshire, State of, 81, 114, 14
New Ireland, Quebec, 355
New Liverpool, Quebec, 103, 104
New London, Quebec, 82

New Richmond, Quebec, 45, 47
New Whitby (*see* Whitby, Township of)
New York, State of, 37–39, 51, 53, 54, 57, 65, 123, 177, 263, 420, 423, 424, 461
New Zealand, 416, 453
Newark (England), 124
Newcastle, District of, Ontario, 62, 140, 438
Newcastle-upon-Tyne (England), 154, 284, 303, 304, 307, 313, 316–18, 321, 325, 327, 328, 332, 333, 336, 338, 343, 344, 345, 349, 359, 360–62, 364, 365, 375, 376, 387, 393, 395, 446,
Newfoundland, Colony of, 123, 269, 410
Newhaven (England), 154, 379
Newmarket, Ontario, 122, 144
Newport (England), 154, 364
Niagara, Township of (Lincoln County), 185, 354, 356
Niagara District, Ontario, 32, 40–42
Niagara Falls, Ontario, 291
Niagara-on-the-Lake, 50, 239
Nichol, Township of (Wellington County), 207–08
Nipissing, District of, Ontario, 244
Nissouri, Township of (Middlesex County), 174, 177
Norfolk, County of, Ontario, 40, 41, 164, 174, 177, 443, 445
Norfolk Chronicle and *Northern Gazette*, 85, 430
Norfolk County (England), 21, 23, 24, 74, 85–87, 89, 90, 92, 95, 96, 131, 146, 152, 183, 184, 203, 232, 285, 286, 338, 340, 417, 426, 430, 431, 438
North Bay, Ontario, 244
North Devon Journal, 398
North Dumfries, County of (Waterloo County), 187
Northamptonshire County (England), 67, 113, 207, 208, 435, 438
Northumberland, County of,

Ontario, 122, 126, 140, 147, 152, 231, 232, 438
Northumberland County (England), 28, 146, 176, 177, 208, 216–18
Norwich (England), 96, 249, 426
Norwich, Township of (Oxford County), 174
Norwich Gazette, 430
Norwich Mercury, 320, 337, 340
Nottawasaga, Township of (Simcoe County), 139, 233
Nottingham (England), 460
Nottingham and District Emigration Committee, 250
Nottinghamshire County (England), 124, 126, 185, 198, 205, 234, 251, 278, 292, 456, 460, 465
Nova Scotia, Province of, 51, 54, 239, 240, 282, 284, 409, 419, 421
Noyan seigneury, Quebec, 37, 45, 55, 57
Nutbrown, Leslie Stuart, 429
Nutbrown, Thomas, 83, 429

Oakland Township (Brant County), 164
O'Brien, Edward, 138
O'Brien, Mary Sophia (Gapper), 137, 138, 440
Odell, Joseph, 53, 54
Odell, William, 456
Odelltown, Quebec, 53–55, 61–63
Oliver, Andrew, 60, 423
Oliver, John, 451
Onslow, Township of, Quebec, 117–18
Ontario Immigration Agents, 224, 227, 233, 234
Ops, Township of (Victoria County), 139
Orford, Township of (Kent County), 443
Orford, Township of, Quebec, 28, 431
Orillia, Township of (Simcoe County), 126
Ormstown (Quebec), 66

St. James Anglican Church, 66
Oro, Township of (Simcoe County), 125, 137, 138, 152
Orr, Samuel, 100
Orrock, Mr., 335, 337
Oshawa, Ontario, 34, 42, 149, 251
Osnabruck Township (Stormont County), 39
Osprey, Township of (Grey County), 220
Otonabee, Township of (Peterborough County), 124
Ottawa, Ontario (*see also* Bytown), 34, 239, 254, 278, 295–97, 351–54, 356–58, 434
Ottawa County (Quebec)
Ottawa River/Valley, 63, 68, 94, 98–120, 278, 421, 436, 464
Timber trade, 103, 104, 111, 114
Ottewell:
Jane (Towle), 220
Philip, 220
Richard, 220
Owen Sound, Ontario, 219, 220, 453
Oxford County, Ontario, 174, 179, 181, 183–85, 187, 190, 443, 445
Oxford Township (Oxford County), 164
Oxfordshire County (England), 207, 227–28

Packham, William, 145, 441
Padstow (England), 149, 150, 154, 266–69, 273, 274, 282, 283, 318, 324, 325, 328, 331, 333, 335, 344–48, 350–53, 357, 360–64, 366, 368–70, 372, 375, 377, 378, 379, 381–85, 388, 390, 391, 442, 463
Palgrave Parish (England), 430
Palliser, Joseph, 100
Parker, Alice and Jim, 35, 252
Parker, James, 293, 466
Parkinson, Arthur, 259
Parnham, Hannah (Barclay), 124

Parnham, James, 125
Parr, Joy, 456–57
Parry Sound, District of,
    Ontario, 237
Pashley, Elizabeth (Frith),
    125–27
Pashley, George, 125–27, 273,
    331, 437
Passenger Act regulations
    (Atlantic crossings):
    1803, 264
    1817, 267
    1828, 267, 463
    1842, 267
    1855, 267
Passenger fares (Atlantic cross-
    ings), 88, 95, 150, 172, 189,
    263, 266, 276, 277, 280, 304,
    369, 431, 461
Passenger lists, 138, 192, 204,
    222, 302, 303, 323, 325, 329,
    338–41
Patterson, Meroyn, 325
Pattison, Walter, 248
Paupers/ the poor (see also
    Poor Laws):
    Assisted emigration of, 24,
        87, 131–38, 146, 155–60,
        166, 178, 182–85, 190, 192,
        208, 276, 338, 352, 354,
        358, 385–88, 430, 440, 453
    poverty in England, 24, 86,
        87, 88, 95, 96, 131–38,
        146, 152, 166, 173, 178,
        182–85, 208, 276, 438–39
Payne, James, 157
Payne, Levi, 137
Payne, Samuel, 171
Peachey, James, 39
Pearne, James, 319
Pearson, Hannah J., 435
Peckova, David, 450
Pedlar, George, 149
Pedlar, Henry, 149
Pedlar, Samuel, 267, 269, 442,
    462
Peel, County of, Ontario, 138,
    141, 143, 234, 455
Peel, Edmund, 29, 72–73
Peel, Lucy, 29, 72, 73, 89, 426
Pembroke, Township of
    (Renfrew County), 118

Penetanguishene, Ontario,
    141, 440
Penfold, William, 207
Pennsylvania, State of, 37, 123
Pennsylvania Germans, 209–10
Penrith (England), 67, 68,
    425–26
Penzance (England), 154, 322,
    357, 360, 364, 366, 368, 369,
    371–73, 376, 377, 380, 389,
    402
Perkins, Captain Joseph, 81, 428
Perry, James, 171
Perth, County of, Ontario,
    208–11, 213, 216–17
Perth, Ontario, 116, 248, 350,
    435–36
Peterborough, County of,
    Ontario, 121, 124, 125,
    137–40, 149, 151, 152, 167,
    177, 437, 438, 444
Peterborough, Ontario, 21, 124,
    129–31, 238, 240, 352, 437
Peters, Elizabeth, 264, 266, 277,
    278, 317, 461
Peters, William, 278, 317, 464
Petworth estate (England), 141,
    178, 207, 292, 284–86
    settlers in Ontario, 141–46,
        178, 181–83, 207, 209,
        210, 293, 447, 464
Petworth Emigration
    Committee, 141, 143, 182,
    276, 441, 446
Phillips, William, 179
Phillipson, Featherston, 178,
    446
Phillipsburg, Quebec, 76–77
Phosphate mines (Quebec),
    114, 116
Pickering, Joseph, 28, 31, 417
Pickering, Township of,
    Ontario County, 41, 122,
    124, 152, 349, 439
Pickett, Daniel, 436
Pilkington, Township of
    (Wellington County), 207
Pitt, William, 107, 120
Plymouth (England), 154, 214,
    265, 270, 273, 274, 282–84,
    304–07, 309, 310, 312–14,
    317, 318, 320–33, 335,

338–47, 349–54, 356–67,
    369–95, 397–404, 409, 411,
    413, 454, 463
Pontiac County (Quebec), 117,
    118, 436
Poole (England), 154, 227, 320,
    321, 324, 332, 336, 340, 343,
    355, 360, 370, 372, 374, 378,
    380, 399, 401
Poor Laws in England (see also
    Paupers), 85, 86, 430, 441,
    450
    Amendment Act of 1834,
        24, 429
    Poor Law Commissioners,
        24, 276, 429, 430, 442
    Poor Law Guardians, 24, 240
    Poor Law Unions, 86, 87,
        353, 430
Port Dover, Ontario, 359
Port Hope, Ontario, 123,
    127, 146, 147, 149, 351–53,
    357–59
Port Perry, Ontario, 151
Port St. Francis, Quebec, 87, 89,
    96, 97, 340–41
Port Stanley (Ontario), 167,
    183, 465
Port Talbot, Ontario, 139, 163,
    350
Portage du Fort (Quebec), 117
Portland, Duke of (William
    Cavendish-Bentinck, 6th
    Duke), 234, 250
Portland, Township of, Quebec,
    114
Portsmouth (England), 154, 171,
    191, 230, 284–86, 305–07,
    309, 310, 317, 322, 323, 325,
    326, 329, 330, 331, 333, 335,
    336, 338–40, 345, 361, 364,
    378 398, 399, 402, 403, 409,
    449, 454
Potton, Township of, Quebec,
    77
Prentice, Thomas, 448
Presbyterian(s), 39, 66, 216,
    217, 426, 445
Prescott, Ontario, 30, 126, 168,
    278, 352, 354, 464
Pressey, J., 171
Preston (England), 209, 233, 277

Price, William, 112, 434
Priestman, Thomas, 175, 176, 181, 445
Prince, James, 192
Prince Edward, County of, Ontario, 420
Prince Edward Island, 59, 67, 86, 356, 419, 430
Protestants (*see* Anglicans, Bible Christians, Congregationalists, Lutherans, and Methodists)
Prowse, Walter H., 435
Pullen, Frances, 181, 446
Purton Parish (England), 138, 276, 284, 342, 440
Putt, Henry, 242
Pyke, Reverend George, 71

Quakers (*see* Society of Friends)
Quarantine (*see* Immigration)
Quarantine Act, 271
Quebec City, 19, 33, 73, 79, 82, 83, 104, 112, 242, 264, 271, 272, 293, 294, 297
    port, 23, 30, 88, 154, 157–60, 192, 222, 261, 262, 263, 270, 273–75, 281–86, 302–04, 319–22, 324, 327, 329, 334, 336, 337, 351, 360, 367, 373, 380, 384, 385, 389, 401, 417, 423
Quebec Act of 1774, 43
Quebec Emigrant Society, 270
Quebec Gazette, 62, 86, 325, 326
Quebec Hotel (Portsmouth), 171, 172, 191–92
Quebec Immigration agent (*see* Buchanan)
Quebec Mercury, 204, 302, 426
Quebec Railway Company, 93
Quyon, Quebec, 117, 435–36

Railways, 93, 233, 244, 280
Raleigh, Township of (Kent County), 443
Rapley, William, 179
Rapson, James, 210, 451
Rastall, Henry, 278, 291, 465
Rawson, William, 265–66
Reach, Township of (Ontario County), 143, 151, 418

Reading, Ann, 435
Rebellions of 1837–38, 30, 31, 140, 262, 400, 441, 462
Reformatory schools (*see also* Hertfordshire Reformatory School), 33, 242–44, 458
Religion (*see also* Bible Christians, Church of England, Congregationalists, Lutherans, Methodists, Presbyterians), 31, 33, 42, 44, 125, 126, 176, 217
Regiments:
    Butler's Rangers, 38
    Jessup's Corps, 420
    King's Loyal Americans, 38
    King's Rangers, 38
    King's Royal Regiment of New York, 38, 39
    Middlesex Militia, 1st, 443
    Queen's Loyal Rangers, 38
    Royal Hampshire, 37th Regiment, 303
    Royal Highland Emigrants Regiment, 38
    Voltigeurs Canadiens, 422
Regular traders (ships), 274, 275, 282
Remittance men (*see also* De la Fosse, Frederick), 236–38
Renfrew, County of, Ontario, 118
Restigouche, Quebec, 45, 47, 287
Restronguet (England), 154, 378
Richards, Charles, 144
Richards, Robert, 248
Richelieu River/Valley, Quebec, 22, 37, 44, 45, 51, 53, 55–57, 421, 424
Richmond, County of, Quebec, 93, 242
Richmond, Ontario, 116–17
Rickard, John, 83
Rideau Canal, 101, 102, 111, 116, 278, 464
Rideau River/Valley, 79, 102, 103, 105, 112, 116, 428, 435
Riots and disturbances (England), 23, 85, 170, 182, 186, 444
Rivière du Lièvre (Quebec), 114

Rivière Rouge, Quebec, 100, 101
Roberts, George, 262, 268–69, 395
Robins, Paul, 266, 369
Robinson, George, 271, 272, 462
Robinson, John, 450
Robinson, Peter, 124, 137, 437
Robinson, William, 292, 293, 465
Robson, Elizabeth, 176
Rogers, Timothy, 41, 122
Roman Catholics (*see* Catholic Church)
Ross, Reverend George, 80
Routledge, Thomas, 176
Rowcliff, Thomas, 451
Rowland, Jesse, 218
Roxham, Quebec, 58, 61, 63
Rudkins, Jemina, 434
Rugby (football), 295–96
Russell County, Quebec, 109
Russeltown, Quebec, 59, 66, 67
Ruthly, George, 107, 119
Rye (England), 154, 285, 349
Rye, Maria, 239, 240, 457, 458

Saint John, New Brunswick, 59, 285, 303
Saint John the Baptist Anglican Church (Hallerton), 64
Saint Saviours Anglican Church (Lacolle), 63
Salisbury (England), 225–26
Sandwich, Ontario, 165
Sandwich, Township of (Essex County), 443
Sarnia, Township of (Lambton County), 250
Saugeen, Township of (Bruce County), 219
Sault Ste. Marie, Ontario, 34, 231, 232
Scadding, Reverend Henry, 288, 465
Scarborough (England), 154, 308, 312, 314, 315, 317, 319, 324, 340, 341, 360, 381
Scarborough Township (York County), 122
Scatcherd, John and Thomas, 177

Scotland, 31, 50, 100, 117, 126, 165, 212, 281
Scott, James, 133
Scott, Reverend Joseph, 79
Scott, William, 208
Scott, Township of (Ontario County), 41, 143, 420
Scottish immigrants, 37, 47, 51, 65, 83, 99, 100, 102, 112, 116, 137, 165, 205, 209, 210, 212, 217, 218, 220, 298, 299, 349, 418, 420–22, 425
Scowen, Philip Harry, 93, 432
Scriver, Frederick, 54
Scrope, G. Poulett, 136, 166, 439
Second World War, 251
Seigneuries, 37, 38, 43, 45, 52–59, 63–65, 67, 68, 94, 98
Selkirk, Lord (Thomas Douglas, 5th Earl of), 289
Sellar, Robert, 64, 65, 94, 422
Seven Years' War (1756–63), 44, 55, 423
Severs, John, 66
Shawville, Quebec, 117–18
Sheerness (England), 454
Shefford, Township of (Quebec), 77, 78, 350
Shelfanger Parish (England), 431
Shepherd, Andrew, 448
Shepherd, Thomas, 100
Shepherd, William, 100
Sherborne (England), 226
Sherbrooke, County of, Quebec, 29, 45, 84, 86, 90, 93, 431
Sherbrooke, Quebec, 72, 82, 89, 93, 239, 242, 243, 297, 429
Sherrington, Township of, Quebec, 64, 424
Shrewsbury (England), 247
Ship captains:
  Adams, J., 287, 312, 387
  Addison, 312
  Adey, 370, 378, 398
  Agar, 285, 391
  Agnew, 387
  Aichison, 403
  Aiton, 406–09, 411–14
  Akitt, 403
  Alcock, 339
  Allan, 366

Allen, 379, 386, 399
Anderson, 343, 379, 381, 383, 384, 390
Andrews, 366
Appleby, 399, 400
Appleton, J., 306, 308
Archibald, 320, 326, 336, 371
Armitage, 398
Armon, 369
Armstrong, 313, 320
Arnold, 320, 322, 324, 332, 336, 343, 365
Arthur, 310
Ashlea, 395
Askins, 370
Atkin, 397
Atkins, 397, 401
Atkinson, 284, 322, 334, 342, 365
Bagg, 323
Bainbridge, 388
Bains, 318
Balderson, 368
Baldison, 318
Bale, 401
Ball, W., 358
Ballantine, 400, 405, 407–15
Ballatine, 383
Balliston, 393
Balmans, 400
Bance, 371
Banks, 329
Barchard, William, 306
Barclay, 386, 387
Barker, 375
Barlow, 286, 323
Barnes, 311
Barnwell, 318,
Baron, 328
Barre, S., 307
Barrett, 309
Barrick, 333, 391
Barry, R., 308
Barry, Robert, 309, 311
Bartlett, 341, 345
Barton, 328
Batchelor, 303
Batten, 328
Baxter, 396
Bayle, 321
Beadle, 313
Bean, 305

Beart, 371
Beckett, 314, 318
Bee, 330
Bell, 287, 311, 341, 386, 388, 390, 391
Bennett, 314, 395
Benson, C., 356
Benson, Thomas, 304
Bentson, 322
Bernier, 316, 408
Berriman, 309
Berry, 312, 322, 331
Berryman, 314
Beswick, 378
Betty, 365
Beverley, 326
Bewes, 340
Bibbing, 337
Biggs, 341
Biglands, 313
Binnington, 303
Birkett, 311
Bishop, 325
Bisson, 274, 282, 377, 378, 381, 384, 385, 388, 391
Black, 331, 340, 389, 392, 394
Blain, 369
Blair, 286, 314, 326, 394
Blair, H., 318, 321, 327
Blair, Thomas, 341, 350
Blake, Robert, 316, 325, 340
Blandford, J., 355, 379
Blight, 402
Blyth, 339
Blythe, W., 274, 282, 352, 365
Boardman, 318
Bond, 395
Bonifant, 319
Bonneyman, 317, 324
Booth, 310, 409
Borland, 403–06, 408–13
Borrowdale, 389
Bouch, 312
Bowie, 317
Bowman, 330
Bowman, J., 306
Bowness, 400
Brady, Charles, 305
Bragg, 310
Braithwaite, 311, 328
Brewer, G., 274, 282, 351, 357, 360, 362–64, 366

Brisbane, 307
Broderick, 282, 329, 337, 345
Brough, 390
Brown, 269, 274, 283, 317,
    318, 324, 327, 330, 333,
    334, 337–39, 346, 364,
    365, 367, 370, 371, 383,
    388, 390, 392, 401, 402,
    412–15
Brown, D., 355, 376, 379, 383,
    386, 396, 398, 400
Brown, J., 357, 364
Brown, Joseph, 309
Brown, R., 355
Brown, T., 318, 324, 328,
    331, 333, 345–47, 350
Bruce, 317, 319
Brumage,375
Buchanan, 365
Buck, 304, 346
Bull, 284–86
Bullman, T., 282, 385, 389,
    392
Bunn, 367
Burden, 379
Burgess, 406–10
Burke, J., 379, 383
Burling, 319
Burnett, 325
Burns, 372, 383
Burton, 316, 320, 396
Butter, 266
Byers, 331, 339, 395
Cairn, 311
Calhoun, 394
Callendar, 329, 396
Callender, 316, 318, 320, 323
Calley, 404
Campbell, 332, 392
Campbell, John, 351, 381
Campion, 323
Cannon, William, 316
Cant, R., 358
Card, 407
Carey, 377
Carling, 319, 329
Carmish, 381
Carns, 310
Carr, 328
Carr, Andrew, 319
Carrick, 315, 318, 319
Carter, 385

Cartney, 377
Castling, 320
Catly, 326
Cawdrie, W., 282, 346, 347,
    354, 362, 365
Cawsey, H., 351
Chalker, 321
Chalmers, 283, 342, 345,
    369, 370, 372, 373, 376,
    378, 379
Chambers, 316, 324, 329,
    332, 334, 345, 351, 376
Chanceller, J., 308
Chancellor, 308
Chandler, 309, 400
Chapman, 398, 401, 404
Chapman, Thomas, 308
Chark, 328
Charles, 284, 381
Charlton, 310
Charter, 305
Child, 383
Christian, 309
Christiansen, 391
Christie, 327, 334, 339, 382,
    398
Clark, 308, 318, 320, 394
Clark, Thomas, 305
Clarke, George, 307
Clarkson, 323
Clay, 315
Cleeves, 322
Clementson, Thomas
Clucas, 327
Clunis, 331
Cockburn, 377, 391
Cockerell, 371
Cockerill, 400
Cockton, 314, 315, 317, 323,
    329
Codner, 282, 389, 392, 393,
    395
Collins, 320, 339, 342
Collinson, 311, 313, 316, 336,
    341, 343
Colman, 346
Coltman, 313
Coltman, T., 351
Coltsman, 321
Comer, 403
Comfort, 329
Connolly, 346, 379

Connot, P., 355
Constance, T. W.
Cook, 412
Cookman, 368
Cooper, 312
Corbett, 319
Cord, 310
Cordran, 339, 343
Corhill, 314
Corish, J., 305
Cork, 343
Cornforth, 339
Cosin, 320
Cossman, J.
Cothay, 375
Cotter, 387
Coulson, 339
Cower, 358
Cox, 282, 308, 312, 371
Craggs, 326
Craig, 326
Crampon, 384
Crawford, 248, 333, 345, 387,
    392, 395, 402
Creigh, 402
Croft, 311
Crosby, 310, 315, 399
Crossley, 370
Crossman, 386
Crouch, 316
Crowel, 388
Cruickshanks, 328, 393
Culliton, 399
Cummings, 366, 385, 400
Cunningham, 375
Curry, 343
Dady, 346
Dale, 328, 344, 345
Dale, H., 321, 324, 329, 331,
    333
Dale, Henry, 306
Daly, 369
Daniel, T., 331, 364
Danson, W., 303
Darley, 401
Dart, Richard, 398
Davenport, 321
Davidson, 303, 305, 310,
    315, 330, 332, 334, 359,
    371, 381, 390, 392
Davidson, Thomas, 312
Davie, 312

Davies, 283, 370, 389, 399, 404
Davies, Henry, 304, 306
Davis, 305, 340, 345, 372, 373, 376
Davis, Henry, 307
Davis, J.C., 309
Davison, 340
Dawson, 303, 310, 323, 396
Day, 341–42
Dearness, 325, 343
Deaton, 336
Dennis, 375
Dishrow, 368
Dixon, 314, 318, 319, 327
Dixon, James, 305
Dobson, 314, 353
Dobson, E., 353
Docker, 316
Dodd, 303
Dodd, John, 308
Dodds, 316, 325, 341
Dodge, 382
Donaldson, 322, 334
Donken, 402
Doran, 376
Dorval, A., 307
Dos, 396
Douglas, 283, 315, 332, 344, 359, 366, 367, 372, 376
Douglass, 308
Douglass, G., 317, 318, 328, 331
Douthwaite, 330, 333
Doyle, J., 304
Draper, W., 304
Drewery, 284, 370
Dring, 343
Driscoll, 321
Drummond, 319, 428
Drysdale, 390
Ducket, 371, 389
Duffett, 381
Duffill, J., 285, 369, 372, 275, 377, 388, 391, 394
Duffy, 351, 359
Dugald, 385
Duggan, 347
Dumble, 312
Duncan, 327, 368, 381, 383, 387, 389
Dunn, 371, 388

Dunstone, T., 374
Dutton, 410–15
East, 330
Easthope, R., 274, 282, 348, 352, 360, 362, 363, 368–70, 372, 375, 378, 381, 383
Ebbage, Thomas
Eddie, James, 338
Edkin, 312
Edwards, 347, 365, 395, 397
Eilwood, 397
Ekin, 328
Elder, 312
Elliott, 339, 341, 345, 347, 365
Elliott, James, 306
Ellis, 380, 396
Emerson, Robert, 309
England, Richard, 365, 368, 382, 392, 400, 403
Errington, 368
Eskdale, 343
Estelle, 304, 307
Evans, 322, 371–72
Evans, William, 304, 306
Everret, 366
Facey, 399
Faremouth, 379
Farley, 388
Farquharson, 387
Farrie, 379
Farthing, 379, 382, 384, 393
Fatherguay, 309
Fell, 309
Ferrie, J., 352
Fesbian, 377
Field, 282, 344, 376, 379, 381, 382, 384
Finlay, 368
Firt, 388
Fish, 342
Fisher, 345
Fisher, J., 307
Fitzgerald, 399
Flaherty, 401
Fleck, 368
Flegg, W., 356
Flemming, A., 357
Fletcher, 333
Fleure, 330
Flinn, 403, 405–06
Fly, 305

Forbes, 344
Ford, 327
Forest, 303
Forrest, 380
Forster, 318, 344, 365
Forster, J., 356
Foster, 285, 308, 331, 375, 386
Fowler, 344
Fox, 314, 331, 339, 386, 388, 399, 406
Frazer, J., 306
Freeman, 380
Freeman, James, 329
French, Henry, 305
Friend, 285, 286
Friend, D., 348, 352, 366
Frost, 331
Frost, B., 57
Froste, 320
Fulford, Robert, 306
Fullerton, 383
Fyall, 336
Gabbie, 310
Gain, 339
Gaitskill, W., 309
Gale, 359
Gales, 330
Gallilee, 392
Gamble, 321, 325
Gardner, 337
Garrick, 390
Gash, 323
Gaskin, Robert, 350
Gedds, 321
Gehl, 311
Gibb, 333
Gibson, 311
Gibson, Robert, 306
Giffney, 350
Gill, 318, 320, 324, 329, 337, 339, 397, 402
Gill, J., 389, 391, 396
Gillam, 321, 326, 336, 339
Gillard, 388
Gilmore, 395
Gilmour, 323
Gilpin, 380, 389, 397, 399, 403
Glaves, 311
Glover, 318, 321
Goldsworthy, 403
Gorman, 328

Gortley, 368
Gould, 392, 397
Goulder, 327
Gourlay, 313
Gowan, 342
Graffin, 404
Graham, 310, 313, 320, 330, 335, 388, 391, 397, 405–14
Grand, 397
Grandy, 343
Grange, 400–04, 406–09
Grant, A., 304
Grave, 393
Gray, 321, 370
Gray, A., 355
Grayson, H., 306, 307
Greig, 320, 323
Grieg, James, 204, 321, 322, 328, 329, 331, 332, 335
Grey, 382
Grieves, 381
Griffiths, 385
Gross, 319
Hagarty, 344, 366
Halbro, 376
Hale, C., 354
Hall, 303, 311, 313
Halliday, 318
Hallowell, 315
Halpin, 381
Hamilton, 312, 316, 317, 342, 344, 359, 369, 377
Hammond, 336
Hancock, 366
Hanna, 327
Hanson, 315
Hardcastle, 318
Hardy, 320, 325
Hare, 312
Harley, 403, 404, 407
Harper, 304, 320, 332, 368
Harrington, 327
Harris, 394
Harrison, 333, 343, 345, 346, 377, 385, 390, 397
Harvey, 335, 338
Harvey, A., 347
Hawes, 386, 389, 392, 395, 396, 404, 405
Hawkins, 368, 391
Haywood, 385
Headley, 340

Healy, 367
Heckler, 314, 335, 341
Hedwith, 365
Henderson, 334, 400
Henley, Edward, 303, 305, 307
Henly, Edward, 307
Henrys, 396
Hepburn, 320
Hepenstall, 341
Herron, 377, 388
Hescroft, 385
Heskit, 340
Hetherington, 313
Hewitt, 310, 313, 314, 326
Hewson, 316
Heyton, 313
Hick, 325, 333–35, 338, 346
Hicks, 355
Hill, 284, 325, 328, 331, 340, 356, 365, 368
Hill, David, 354
Hill, R., 358
Hillary, J., 304
Hillman, 368
Hindmarsh, 329
Hinson, 389
Hippell, J., 356
Hird, 318
Hitchins, 390
Hobbs, 393
Hockley, 412
Hodgson, 331, 334, 339
Hodson, 311, 367
Hoff, 320
Hogg, J., 367, 371
Honey, 402
Honston, 327
Hoodlap, 327
Hooper, 274, 282
Hooper, J., 274, 357, 366, 367
Hooter, 326
Hopper, 332, 338, 341
Hopper, Cuthbert, 325
Hopper, Robert, 323
Horn, J., 355
Howe, 371, 394
Hubert, 383
Hudson, 313, 319, 402
Hughes, 321, 397, 411
Hunt, 395

Hunter, 309, 321, 334, 366, 370, 390
Hurst, 321
Hutchins, 336, 381
Hutchinson, 370, 393
Huyens, 400
Hyland, 391, 394
Ibbs, 329
Innes, 311
Irons, 378, 381
Irvine, 307
Irwin, 323
Izatt, 399
Jack, 367
Jackson, 312, 318, 366, 379, 380
Jackson, Henry, 307, 308
Jago, W., 378
James, 330, 376, 404
James, William, 304
Jamieson, 318, 371, 396
Jefferson, Thomas, 304, 324
Jenkins, 390
Jenkinson, 307, 309, 311, 317, 319, 322, 380
Johns, 274, 282, 317, 321, 334, 335, 339, 376, 378, 381, 385, 391, 401, 403
Johnson, 303, 311, 312, 317, 409
Johnston, 396
Joll, 380
Jones, 315, 322, 323, 376, 383, 394, 400–04
Keating, 399
Keighley, 274, 283, 314, 315, 320, 324, 330, 333, 337, 342
Kelso, J., 355
Kemp, John, 337
Kendall, 342, 367, 376, 377, 389
Kenn, 316, 340
Kennedy, Robert, 307
Kenney, 393
Kent, 327
Kerr, 312, 414–15
Key, 377, 378
Kier, 382
Kinney, 399, 401
Kipsock, 328
Kirkhaugh, 316

Knarston, 285, 366, 379, 382, 385, 389
Knight, 285, 339
Knill, 313–16, 318, 320, 329, 338
Knox, 329, 339, 343
Krugie, 343
Labb, 405
Laing, 345
Laing, James, 350
Lamplough, 385
Landry, 346
Lane, 284
Lane, Edward, 341
Lang, 324, 335
Lang, W., 351
Langford, 385, 386, 388
Langford, Robert, 369, 382
Langlands, 405, 406
Langster, 371
Larby, 370, 376, 378
Larkin, 383
Last, 328
Laughton, 365
Laurie, 394
Lawson, 346, 386
Lawson, E., 356
Laxton, 397
Lear, 384
Leavitt, 391, 397
Lee, 398
Leggett, 328
Leitch, 328, 334, 387
Lenvitt, 387
Leslie, 345
Lester, 394
Leuty, T., 353, 359, 363
Lewens, 323
Lewis, 285, 325, 329, 365, 366, 370, 383
Lickis, 348
Liddle, 341
Lister, John, 305
Little, 327, 330
Little, Thomas, 351, 358, 365
Livingford, T., 354
Lobb, 408
Logan, 395
London, 315
Long, 382
Longford, 344
Lorby, 378

Lord, 401
Lorrens, 327
Lotherington, William, 313
Louttit, G., 349, 365
Lovering, 342
Low, 379
Loweryson, 265, 331, 332, 335, 338, 341
Lundy, 371
Luscombe, 332
Lyell, 312
Lyle, 323
Lyons, 404
Mabbey, 390, 393
MacDonnell, 400
Mackay, 346
Mackie, 365
Madge, 390
Magon, 322
Manning, 286, 387
Marianne, 324
Marklan, 351
Marshall, 282, 304, 305, 337, 340, 347, 357, 367
Marshead, 381
Martin, 274, 282, 322, 339, 359, 367, 370, 371, 375, 378, 382, 384, 385, 388, 389, 392, 395, 398
Martin, J., 378
Mason, George, 346, 350
Massey, 329
Matches, 319, 323, 325
Mathie, 321
Mathison, 368
Matthews, 367
Mattrass, 368
Mauleen, 313
Maxwell, Robert, 351
McAuley, 394
McBride, 369
McBride, R., 355
McBurnie, 401
McCappin, 350
McCormick, 308
McCoy, 341
McCutcheon, 382
McDonald, 321, 395
McDonough, 370
McDugal, 311
McEacham, 380
McFarlane, 327, 383

McGarry, 375, 377, 388
McGee, 318, 326
McGill, 308
McGraith, 393
McGrath, 356, 369
McKandy, 370
McKay, 388
McKechnie, 346, 357, 365, 368
McKenzie, 311, 313, 332, 341, 352, 397
McKie, 327
McLaren, 368
McLaughlin, 397
McLean, 340, 344, 358
McLeavy, 391
McLellan, 367, 390, 367, 390
McLeod, 321, 383
McMahon, 356, 383
McMaster, 366, 397, 400–10
McNeillage, 335
Meadus, 380
Mein, 398
Meldram, 303
Melvin, 303
Meritt, 404
Messenger, 318, 346
Metcalf, 284
Methley, 330
Michison, 315
Mickles, 368
Middleton, 320, 340, 343
Mildridge, 326
Miles, 395
Millar, 314, 318, 319
Miller, 310, 314, 316, 317
Mills, 327, 391, 397
Milne, 342,
Minnett, Thomas, 303, 305, 309, 310, 312
Mitchell, 313, 314, 320, 333, 336, 380
Molton, 393
Moncrieff, 335
Monday, 398, 401
Montgomery, 345, 394
Moon, 274, 282, 283, 325, 332, 333, 341, 382, 384, 386, 389, 390, 392, 393, 395, 401, 403
Moon, E., 353, 361, 363, 364, 366, 367, 369–71, 373,

376, 378–80, 382, 384,
387, 391, 392, 394
Moor, 314, 344
Moordaff, J. 309
Moore, 304, 325, 327, 331
Moore, W., 304
Moorhead, 393
Moorshead, W.H., 383, 384
Moorson, 343
Moran, 343, 393
Morgan, 287, 324, 331, 336
Morgan, D., 347
Morris, 345
Morrison, 304, 305, 309, 340,
371, 377
Morrison, James, 306
Morrough, 315
Mortley, W., 405
Morton, 341, 343
Mosey, 326
Muers, 329, 330, 335, 337
Muir, 345, 354, 365
Mullins, 322
Munro, 392
Murdock, 386
Murphy, 313, 367
Murray, 325
Myles, 393
Nance, 380, 381
Napier, 345
Nattrass, 383
Neagle, 344
Neil, 317
Nessfields, 304
Newell, 312
Newson, 332, 336, 339, 341
Newton, 370
Nicholas, 340, 367, 369,
377, 378, 381, 383, 384,
388, 392
Nichols, 282, 406
Nicholson, 304, 316, 317,
320, 329
Nickie, 384
Nixon, 372, 383, 390, 392,
409
Nockets, 342
Norman, W., 303–05
Norton, 384
Norway, 304
O'Flaherty, 401
Ocack, J., 356

Oldrive, 388
Olive, 402
Oliver, 363, 370, 396
Orchard, 383
Organ, W., 305
Ower, 397
Owston, 330
Park, 333
Parke, 345
Parkin, 390
Parkins, 316
Parnall, M., 367, 372, 377
Patching, 399
Pate, 341
Paton, 384, 392, 393, 397
Patten, David, 350
Patterson, 341, 397
Patterson, G., 305
Paul, 336
Paverley, 383
Payn, 368
Payus, 395
Peake, 322
Pearce, 334, 338, 391, 400
Pearce, H.G., 315
Pearson, 282, 339, 365, 367,
369, 380
Pearson, J., 352
Pecker, 313
Pecket, Joseph, 274, 283, 287,
343–46, 349
Penn, 384
Penny, 385
Penyack, R., 376
Perris, 376
Perry, 376, 381
Peters, 398
Petrie, 320
Pettingell, 391
Pewley, 327
Phelan, 346, 348, 365
Philips, 387–90, 392
Picket, J., 354
Pickiss, 386
Pilcher, 342
Pile, 380
Pinkersell, 394
Pitcairn, 344, 347
Pitt, 395
Plant, 395
Playter, 402
Plewes, 332

Plott, 380
Pollock, 281, 370
Pollock, J., 354
Pollyblank, 403
Poole, 333, 385
Pope, 308
Porder
Porteous, 314
Potts, 326
Pow, 401
Power, 344, 346, 351, 401
Pratt, 408
Preston, 366
Price, 304
Pringle, 371
Prouse, 336, 342
Purdy, 334
Purmon, 334
Quay, 368, 370
Quence, 399
Quick, 332
Quinn, 367
Rae, 346
Rainey, 377
Raisbeck, 317
Rattray, 314
Rawle, 409
Ray, 396, 397
Rayne, 319
Rea, 383
Reast, 318
Reay, T., 323
Redpath, 323
Reed, 400
Rees, 344
Reid, 306, 333, 346, 385
Reid, James, 350
Renardson, 371
Renney, 308
Rennison, 312
Reynolds, 316, 368, 395
Reynolds, R.K., 325
Rhiad, 396
Richards, 307, 319, 321,
322, 365, 368, 372, 389,
391–93, 398, 402
Richards, J., 317, 319, 341,
359, 378, 380
Richardson, 332, 342, 378,
380, 396
Riches, 328
Richie, 311

Rickard, 394

Ritchie, 376

Roach, 334

Roan, 328

Robertson, 379, 380

Robinson, 286, 215, 328, 334, 342, 353, 355, 378

Robson, 313, 332, 346, 389

Roca, 376

Roche, 340

Rodgers, 326, 343

Rods, 339

Rogers, 396, 400, 404

Rohann, 345

Roley, 396

Rorbut, 315

Ross, 383, 393

Rovely, 333

Rowell, 394, 397

Roxby, 339

Royal, 286, 306, 323, 326

Rudolf, 393

Russell, 312

Ryan, 329

Sacker, Robert, 303

Sadler, 283

Sadler, W.S., 372, 376, 378, 379, 382, 386, 388, 390, 392

Sampson, 285, 329, 343, 371

Sampson, Joseph, 322, 323, 338

Sanderson, 318, 339

Savage, 372, 375, 378

Scotland, 366

Scott, 305, 310, 320, 321, 367, 390, 395

Scurr, 340

Seaton, 333, 344, 346

Seaton, Thomas, 327

Sedman, 341

Sellers, 324

Sexton, 399

Shadwick, 385

Sharp, 341

Shaw, 330

Shearer, 311, 401

Sibbens, A., 349, 356

Signoti, 384

Sime, 313

Simmers, 348

Simmonds, 324, 334, 339, 342, 391, 402

Simpson, 274, 283, 287, 314, 316, 318, 321, 321, 330, 334, 341, 343, 344, 348, 352, 393, 394, 395

Simpson, Mosey, 351, 353

Simson, G., 308

Sinclair, 390

Sinnoti, 394

Skeach, R., 369, 371, 375, 378, 381, 384

Skinner, 339

Slack, 281

Slater, 365, 396

Sloeman, 340

Smallwood, 340

Smith, 383, 287, 303, 308, 309, 314, 315, 321, 322, 326, 328–30, 333, 336, 340, 366, 380, 382, 387, 390, 392, 395, 401

Smith, Hodgson, 320, 323, 331, 332

Smith, J., 358, 361

Smith, Justus, 114

Smith, Pater, 351

Smith, R., 369, 379, 381, 382, 384

Soles, 399

Sommerville, 323, 334

Spalding, 319

Sparks, John, 313, 315

Sparks, Joseph, 328, 331

Sparrow, 330

Spence, 303, 371

Spence, 303

Spencer, 371, 385, 398

Spring, John, 305

Spurgeon, 326

Stampwater, 326

Stanbury, 324

Steele, 309, 310, 319

Stephens, 324

Stephenson, 376, 387

Sterling, 384

Sterling, John, 308

Stevens, 387

Stevenson, 303

Stewart, 308, 339, 378, 384, 386, 390, 392, 395, 397

Stewart, H., 316

Stickney, 357

Stinson, 403

Stonehouer, Thomas, 307

Storey, 371

Stoup, 380

Stoveld, 322

Stanbury, 337

Straharn, 327

Strangham, 320

Straughan, 326

Strickland, 386

Stuart, John, 306

Stubbs, 395

Sullivan, 368

Summerson, 320

Summerson, William, 318

Summerville, 321

Sumpton, 314, 317, 336

Sumpton, Peter, 332

Sutton, 327

Swan, 309

Swinburh, 375

Swinburn, 336, 366, 367, 371, 377

Swinton, 318

Sybern, 391

Sykes, 389, 396

Symond, 384

Symonds, 363, 390, 409

Symons, J., 370

Tate, 390

Taylor, 311, 312, 319, 324, 326, 328, 336, 354, 367, 375, 377, 387, 390

Taylor, Joseph, 351

Taylor, Samuel, 306

Taylor, W., 329, 331, 337

Temperley, 333, 340

Terry, 312, 325, 338

Thom, 310, 321, 345, 401

Thomas, 285, 303, 319, 320, 338, 390, 397

Thompson, 310, 311, 319, 335, 339, 342, 359, 368, 371

Thompson, Thomas, 315, 317, 322, 384, 394

Thomson, 312, 313, 330, 347

Thornhill, 305

Thorpe, 324

Thrift, 286, 323, 333, 337, 345, 347, 376

Thule, 345
Thursby, 313
Thwaits, 393
Tickle, 340, 384
Tilley, 368
Todd, 308–10, 316, 333
Todd, John, 309
Tolson, 305
Tom, H., 283, 397, 398, 402, 411
Tomlinson, 399
Tonge, 366
Tonkin, H., 369
Toogood, 386
Tor, 313
Tottie, 393
Tozer, 274, 282, 370, 375, 377, 379, 381, 384, 385, 388, 389, 393
Trailer, 284, 341
Trait, 343
Treadwell, 366
Tripp, 286, 404
Tripp, J., 354
Tucker, 339
Turnbull, 340, 379
Turner, 317
Turney, 366
Tweedie, 324
Tyers, 324
Udale, 313
Udney, John, 311
Underwood, 400
Vandervold, 285, 358
Venill, 330
Vere, 347
Vinnis, 391, 394
Vivian, J., 283, 331, 332, 335, 344
Wade, 359, 372, 391
Wade, M.B., 340
Wadle, 403
Waite, 334
Wake, 307
Wakeham, 345
Wakeham, R.J., 357, 366, 371, 380
Walker, 305, 322, 387, 388
Wallace, 308, 310, 327
Walton, 284, 319
Warburton, J., 382, 384, 385, 388

Ward, 282, 310–15, 317, 319, 322, 342, 401
Wardle, 308
Ware, 286, 354
Warman, 346
Warnock, 312
Warren, 313, 342
Warwick, 395
Waters, 324
Watson, 310, 371, 383, 393
Wattes, 375
Watt, 303, 365
Watts, 286, 383, 415
Webb, 326
Webber, 353, 359–60
Webster, 343, 367, 369, 378, 381, 382, 384–85
Wedgewood, 310, 312
Welbank, 343
Welburn, John, 303
Welch, 387, 396
Weldridge, 313, 314, 316, 320
Wells, 369, 381
Welsh, 392
Weston, 329
Wharton, 382, 386
Wheatley, 331, 335, 338, 359
White, 304, 312, 339, 358, 368, 386, 403
Whiteway, 312
Whitfield, 339
Whitmore, John, 306
Whuite, 396
Wickholm, Samuel, 306
Wilburn, 380
Wilkie, 322
Wilkinson, 303, 310, 315, 390
Williams, 303, 318, 340, 366, 376, 380
Williamson, 357
Willie, 312
Willis, 304, 321, 342, 399, 401, 402
Willoughby, 367
Wills
Wilson, 304, 323, 336, 343, 345, 365, 367, 369, 380, 396, 399, 400, 404
Wilson, J., 303, 307
Winby, 332
Winn, 326
Winsted, 380

Wise, William, 306
Wokes, 282
Wokes, Thomas, 316, 317, 320, 325, 333, 335
Wood, 380, 394
Woodthorp, 318
Woodward, 327, 340
Worthingon, 345
Wrangler, 321
Wright, 327, 341, 343, 365, 370, 377
Wyle, 414
Wylie, 392, 399, 413, 415
Yonge, 369
Young, 337, 358
Younger, 318
Shipley, George, 176
Ships:
Abbey Lands, 374, 387
Abeona, 334
Abercromby, 349, 365
Aberdeen, 347, 351, 369, 373, 388
Abigail, 369, 381, 394
Acadia, 392
Accatia, 313
Achilles, 373, 383
Active, 311, 312, 317, 333
Actress, 345
Adario, 364
Addison, 317, 330, 333, 338
Adelaide, 274, 283, 359
Adept, 383
Admiral Boxer, 400
Admittance, 397
Adventure, 308
Affiance, 391
Agamemnon, 370, 374, 401
Agenoria, 312, 318, 350
Agnes, 321
Agnes Anderson, 399
Aid, 305
Ailsa, 385
Aimwell, 326
Airthy Castle, 261, 319, 329
Ajax, 310, 313, 373
Alarm, 321
Albatross, 309
Albinia, 349
Albion, 329, 339, 361, 380
Alchymist of Falmouth, 327, 356, 369, 378, 380

Alcyon, 330, 379
Alert, 322
Alexander, 315, 324, 393
Alexander Edwards, 401
Alfred, 383
Alice, 325
Alice and Anne, 400
Alicia, 315, 350
Allendale, 339, 430
Allies, 331
Almorah, 317, 319, 322
Alpha, 308
Amanthea, 321, 325
Amazon, 283, 329, 337, 345, 354, 360, 363, 365, 367, 369
America, 412
Amethyst, 313, 319, 331
Aminins, 331
Amity, 366
Amphitre, 303
Amyntas, 340
Andrew Marvel, 341, 345, 351, 360
Andrew White, 351
Andromache (Andromanche), 334, 366, 370, 390
Andromeda, 309, 322
Andus, 375
Anglesea, 284, 386, 402, 410
Anglo Saxon, 279, 394, 400–08, 410
Ann, 306, 308, 310, 312, 315, 316, 319, 325, 354, 360, 362, 366, 373
Ann Belle of Padstow, 357
Ann Crossman, 366
Ann Falcon, 400
Ann Jeffery, 347
Ann & Mary, 360, 375
Ann Mondel, 320
Ann Thompson, 398
Ann Wise, 327
Anna Liffey, 346
Annandale, 391
Anne, 326, 337, 375, 377, 388
Antarnos, 339
Aquamarine, 372, 379
Arab, 360, 363, 364, 371
Arabian, 319, 368, 391, 400
Araminta, 373
Archer, 321

Arcturus, 284, 354
Ardwell, 338
Arethusa, 306
Argo, 309, 373, 380
Argonaid, 403
Argus, 316, 317, 320, 330
Ariadne, 322
Army, 316
Arran, 393, 395, 400
Artemis, 328, 331
Arundel, 333
Ash, 393
Asia, 316, 322, 339, 385
Astrea, 333, 365, 366, 370, 373
Asturia, 329
Atalanta, 320, 341
Athelston, 336
Attaliah, 313
Auckland, 366
Aurelian, 344
Aurora, 311, 312, 314, 325, 329, 332, 339, 346, 381
Autumn, 303
Auxiler, 360
Auxiliary, 341
Ava, 284, 378, 381, 384, 385, 388, 393
Balfour of Whitehaven, 330, 413
Balmoral, 403
Baltic, 93, 282, 317, 320–22, 329, 332, 336, 339, 341, 343, 346, 347, 354, 362, 365, 430
Banffshire, 344
Bangalore, 402
Barbara, 325
Barlow, 387
Barnett, 310
Baron of Renfrew, 378
Bartley, 311
Bearborough Castle, 329
Belgian, 413–15
Belle of Padstow, 274, 282, 351, 352, 357, 360, 362, 363, 364, 366, 377, 378, 381, 384, 385, 388, 391
Belmont, 397, 399
Ben Johnson, 306
Ben Nevis, 388
Bengal, 383

Benjamin, 341
Berwick, 303
Berwick Castle, 267, 342, 356, 365
Berwick upon Tweed, 329–31, 333, 335, 337
Bess Grant, 377
Betty, 310, 312
Birman, 373
Birmingham, 403
Bisson, 383
Blanche, 393, 396
Blenheim, 366
Blessing, 305
Blonde, 373
Bloodhound, 410
Blucher, 310
Blythwood, 371
Bohemian, 279, 405–13
Bolina, 320, 325
Bolivar, 322, 341
Bolton, 313
Bowes, 397
Bows, 357
Bragila, 331, 337, 354
Brailsford, 305
Branches, 322
Brandon, 377
Branken, 344
Breeze, 328
Bride, 327
Bridget, 305
Bridgetown, 365
Brightman, 342
Brighton, 341
Britannia, 312, 335, 369, 377
British Empire, 386
British King, 335, 368
British Lady, 360
British Merchant, 343, 379
British Queen, 334, 360, 368
British Sovereign, 315, 317, 322
British Tar, 333
Briton, 308, 318, 319
Brixton, 330
Brockett, 387
Bromleys, 339
Broom, 390
Brothers, 304, 307, 309, 311, 317, 319, 322, 341, 379
Brunette, 359

Brunswick, 276, 284, 316, 325, 340, 342
Buenos Ayres Packet, 312
Burnhopeside, 370
Burrell, 284, 336, 362, 364
Cairo, 366
Calcutta, 366
Caldicut Castle, 310
Caledonia, 312, 319, 332, 342, 354
Caledonian, 318, 325
Callisto, 313
Calonia, 347
Calypso, 335, 381, 383
Cambrian, 343
Camden, 303
Cameron, 314
Camoens, 376
Canada, 108, 305, 333, 392
Canadian, 311, 316, 317, 331, 348, 397, 400, 405
Canning, 366
Canopus, 399
Canton, 366, 369, 390, 450
Cap Rouge, 402
Captain Ross, 333, 343
Carlton, 371
Carlton Packet, 346
Caroline, 203, 204, 222, 321, 322, 328, 329, 331, 332, 335, 338, 341, 386, 449
Caroline Alice, 362
Caroline of St. Ives, 331
Carouge, 319
Carricks, 316
Carron, 339, 341, 430, 447
Carshalton Park, 390
Cartha, 326, 327
Carthagenian, 367
Cate, 351
Catherine, 273, 305, 307, 333, 346, 350
Catherine McDonald, 321
Cato, 343, 356
Cauntless, 397
Caution, 366
Cawton, 323
Celia, 330, 334, 340
Centenary, 349
Centurion, 341
Ceres, 307
Champion, 316

Champlain, 321
Chapman, 327, 334, 339
Charity, 397
Charles, 393
Charles Chaloner, 394, 398, 399
Charles Jones, 375
Charles Saunders, 385
Charles Tennyson, 315
Charles Walton, 284, 387
Charlotte, 284, 311, 315, 341, 352, 370, 374, 375, 381, 383
Charlotte A. Stamler, 404
Chatham, 391, 394
Chester, 346
Cheviot, 330
Chieftain, 273, 318, 321, 327, 390
China, 394
Choice of Scarborough, 379
Cicero, 315
City of Derry, 374
City of Hamilton, 388, 391
City of Rochester, 328
City of Waterford, 356
Civility, 360, 367
Clara Symes, 381, 387, 389
Claremount, 305
Clarendon, 373, 373
Clarkson, 282, 308, 311–15, 321, 323
Clifton, 330
Clio, 303, 391, 325, 389, 391, 400
Clio of Padstow, 267–69, 274, 283, 345–47, 350, 352, 357, 360, 362–64, 369, 370, 372, 375, 378, 382, 383, 462
Clipper, 360
Clyde, 346, 362, 391
Coeur de Lion, 332, 367
Collina, 282, 347, 350, 357, 360, 363, 364, 385, 390
Collins, 333, 381
Colonial, 384
Columbine, 310, 375, 391
Columbus, 323, 368
Combatant, 344
Comet, 361
Commerce, 303, 309, 310

Commodore, 379
Concord, 304, 317, 321, 323, 325, 335
Congress, 321, 393, 397
Conquering Hero, 377
Conqueror, 387, 394
Consbrooke, 93, 354, 368
Conservator, 364, 367
Constance, 372, 375, 378
Consul, 395
Conying, 376
Copernicus, 409
Cordelia, 312
Coriolanus, 396
Cornubia, 342
Cornwall, 359, 381
Corsair, 323, 381
Cosmo, 360, 363, 364
Cosmopodite, 353, 359, 360
Cossack, 321
Countess Morley, 313
Countess of Durham, 367, 371
Countess of London, 394
Countess of Loudon, 402
Countess of Mulgrave, 381
Courier, 326
Crescent City, 393
Crowley, 365
Crown, 203, 325, 365, 399
Crusader, 359
Culdee, 351
Culloden, 403, 404, 407
Cumberland, 309, 344, 346, 351, 364
Curlew, 303
Cybele, 335, 341
Cynthia, 317
Cyprus, 383
Daedalus, 282, 385
Dahlia, 274, 282, 353, 357, 360, 364, 366, 367, 370, 375, 377, 379, 381, 384, 385, 388, 389, 393
Dalmarnock, 327
Damascus, 411–15
Danube, 319
Dart, 311
Davenport, 382, 397
David, 323
Dee, 350
Defence, 370

Delhi, 336
Delia, 352, 360, 370, 372, 378, 398
Dependent, 353, 367
Derwent, 318
Devereaux, 343
Deveron, 322
Dew Drop, 282, 316, 317
Dew Drop of Padstow, 320, 325, 335, 340, 379, 383
Diana, 284, 311, 341, 386
Dibdie, 382
Dido, 310
Dochfour, 335, 339
Dochtour, 334
Don, 303, 345, 354, 365, 376
Doncaster, 304
Donegal, 313, 319, 323, 325, 334
Dorcus Savage, 312
Doreen Prince, 404
Doric, 260
Dorothy Gales, 339
Dorothys, 336
Douglas, 359, 367, 372, 376
Dove, 332
Druid, 360
Dryad, 309
Duchess of Northumberland, 403
Duke of Clarence, 343
Duke of Manchester, 390
Duncan, 363
Durham, 374, 377, 383
Dykes of Maryport, 314, 315, 317, 323, 329, 341, 346, 398
E. Wilder [Farley], 406
Eagle, 303, 305, 307, 399, 402
Eagle of Padstow, 367, 372, 377, 390, 393
Earl Bathurst, 339
Earl Fitzwilliam, 307, 308
Earl Ketler, 329
Earl Moira, 327, 338
Earl of Aberdeen, 342
Earl of Dalhousie, 308, 317
Earl Stanhope, 318
Earus, 339
Economist, 325
Edinburgh, 356, 394
Edmund, 353

Edward, 325, 327, 332, 341, 352
Edward Colston, 463
Effort, 344, 388, 401
Eglington, 378
Elden, 342
Eldon, 335, 338
Eleanor, 310, 312, 329, 366
Electric, 393
Eleutheria, 338, 370
Eliza, 157, 285, 321, 334, 339, 358, 361, 389, 395, 400, 440
Eliza Ann, 385
Eliza Caroline, 373
Eliza Liddle, 87, 96, 285, 340
Eliza Morrison, 401
Elizabeth, 306, 313, 314, 328, 340, 371, 373, 376, 381, 386
Elizabeth Ann Bright, 402
Ellen, 379, 387
Ellen Oliver, 394
Ellentheria, 335
Ellergill, 313, 315, 319, 358, 361, 365
Ellison, 364
Elphinstone, 380
Elspeth, 384
Emerald, 356
Emma, 400
Emmanuel, 343, 352, 357, 360, 367, 372
Emperor, 361, 378
Emperor Alexander, 322
Emporium, 311
Empress of Britain, 254–56, 258
Empress of France, 257, 258
Empress of Ireland, 254–56
Emulous, 343
Endeavour, 311, 313, 316, 332
Endymion, 329, 332, 333
England, 285, 325, 329, 366, 368, 371
Englishman, 337
Envelope, 401
Equator, 385
Erato, 314
Erin's Queen, 374
Esk, 321, 325
Essex, 384

Esther, 323, 332, 336
Ethelred, 383
Euclid, 359, 388
Euphrasia, 329, 329
Euphrates, 308
Euphrosyne of Whitby, 285, 319, 322, 323, 338
Eurise, 393
Europe, 360
Eveline, 285, 323
Evening Star, 395
Evergreen, 343
Everthorpe, 397
Ewretta, 339
Exmouth, 320, 323, 329, 332
Experiment, 317, 319, 320
Fair Isle, 362
Fairfield, 342
Fairfields, 331
Falcon, 347
Falkenburg, 412
Fame, 303–05, 313
Fanny, 320
Favorite, 390
Favourite, 307
Fereda, 395
Fergus, 282, 352, 361, 365, 367, 370, 372, 375, 378, 382, 385, 389, 395, 397
Feronia, 397
Ferriland, 308
Fingal, 389, 392, 394
Fleetwood, 323
Florence, 362, 375, 401
Florida, 364
Forester, 329
Forfarshire, 380
Forster, 314, 318, 320, 232, 337, 362, 365
Friends, 265, 266, 278, 307, 308, 317, 319
Friendship, 310
Fullentire, 358
Gales, 310
Gartcraig, 386
General Gascoigne, 242
General Havelock, 403
General Wolfe, 323
Genova, 392
Gentoo, 383
George, 319, 339, 342, 346, 373

George Canning, 312
George Glen, 355
George Marsden, 285, 349
George Palmer, 330, 333
George Smith, 395, 395
George Wilkinson, 346
Gift, 382
Gipsy Queen, 401, 404, 407,
    409, 413
Gleadon, 311
Glemora, 317
Glenlyon, 396
Glenmannia, 396
Glenssilly, 385, 396
Glide, 390
Gloucester, 360
Golden Spring, 374
Goliath, 365, 374
Good Czar, 265, 267, 332
Good Intent, 382, 384, 385,
    388, 397
Good Intent (1), 363
Good Intent (2), 389, 391, 396
Governor Harvey, 364
Governor Jalkett, 368
Grace, 327, 330, 349
Graham, 371, 374
Graham Moore, 316
Gratitude, 394
Great Britain, 336, 366, 367,
    371, 375, 377, 391, 399,
    400
Greenock, 368, 374, 382
Grenada, 327
Guimare, 318
H C Kideton, 397
Halcyon, 314
Hampshire, 333, 340, 383
Hannah, 310
Hannibal, 340
Harding, 310
Harlequin, 395
Harmonia, 359
Harmony, 306, 337, 339,
    348, 396
Harriet, 304, 306
Harrington, 318
Harrison, 304, 306–07
Hartland, 360
Hartley, 340
Haughton le Spring, 365
Haverford, 258

Hawker, 304
Heath, 327, 333
Hebe, 265, 269, 312, 320,
    326, 462
Heber, 285, 339
Hector, 350
Helen, 285, 375, 379, 386
Helen Scott, 366
Henderson, 309, 310
Henrietta Mary, 365
Henry, 307
Henry Bliss, 366
Henry Cooke, 401, 454
Henry Tanner, 385
Hercules, 330
Hero, 285, 323, 340, 341 343
Heyden, 315
Hibernia, 344
Hibernian, 279, 402, 406–15
Highland Light, 404
Highland Mary, 370
Highlander, 336
Himalaya, 363
Hindoo, 333
Hirundo, 370
Home, 314
Hope, 306, 308, 320, 327, 328,
    334, 340, 343, 373, 394
Horatio, 313, 315, 348
Horsely Hill, 304
Hotspur, 397
Huddart, 306, 308
Hunter, 304
Hurlington, 330
Huron, 349, 356, 365
Huskisson, 340
Ida, 320, 327
Imogene, 346, 355
Indemnity, 86, 341, 430
Independence, 350
Independent, 345
Indian, 315, 365, 390, 400–04
Industry, 318, 341, 360
Infanta, 391, 396
Inspector, 401
Integrity, 307
Intrepid, 328, 390
Intrinsic, 371, 383
Ion, 402
Iona, 320, 323, 331, 332, 348
Iphigenia, 318
Ipswich, 331, 358

Ireland, 360, 367
Irton, 323, 330
Isabella, 267, 305, 308–10,
    312, 319, 322, 334, 362,
    379, 385, 389
Isis, 303
Itinerant, 316
Jabe, 392
Jackson, 318, 328
Jamaica, 359
James, 304, 319, 393
James & Ann, 338, 364
James & Thomas, 368
James and Mary Sinnott, 355
James Daughton, 323
James Hutchinson, 384
James Jardine, 403
James Moran, 371, 374
James Moran of St Ives, 393
Jane, 309, 312, 315, 320, 322,
    329, 342, 369, 383, 385,
    388–90
Jane & Barbara, 328, 346, 361
Jane Glassin, 393
Jane Lowden of Padstow, 382
Jane Vinet, 319
Janus, 317, 319
Java, 400
Jean, 311
Jean Rumney, 347
Jeanet Kidstone, 396
Jeronia, 400
Jessie, 355, 370
Jessie Boyle, 409
Jessie Stevens, 380
John, 303, 315, 332, 381, 384,
    394, 397
John & Jane, 345
John and Mary, 311, 347, 442
John and Robert, 357
John Barry, 315
John Bell, 367
John Bentley, 368
John Bolton, 371, 373
John Bull, 285, 375, 377, 381,
    388, 391, 394, 404, 406
John Bulmer, 321
John Clifton, 361
John Danford, 320
John Davies, 397
John Francis, 314, 316
John Hawkes, 363

John Howard, 308
John Howell, 396, 399, 400
John & James, 344, 347
John & Jane, 345
John Jardine, 374
John March, 327
John & Mary, 323, 330, 347,
  363
John Moore, 396
John Munn, 365
John Owens, 402
John & Robert, 346, 365, 368
John Stamp, 337
Jonothan Bromham, 361,
  363, 364
Jordanson, 330
Joseph Hume, 314
Joseph Storey, 339
Josepha, 382
Julius, 318
Julius Caesar, 318
Junior, 375
Juno, 384, 402
Jura, 405–09, 411, 412, 414
Justinian, 323
Kalmia, 380
Kamaskda, 314
Kate, 399
Kelsick Wood, 307, 318, 321,
  339
Kent, 308
Kilblain, 375
King William, 173, 192, 197,
  285, 338, 360
Kingston, 107, 306, 316, 323,
  340
Kirkella, 314
Kitson, 314
Lady, 327, 360, 403
Lady Ann, 318
Lady Cremorne, 321
Lady Eglington, 393
Lady Elgin, 376, 378, 381
Lady Falkland, 382
Lady Fitzherbert, 349, 383
Lady Francis, 309, 311
Lady Gordon, 311, 340
Lady Hobart, 391, 394–95
Lady Hood, 311
Lady Milton, 373, 388
Lady of the Lake, 363
Lady Peel, 274, 282, 376, 378,

381, 385, 389, 391, 395,
  401, 403
Lady Sale, 368
Lady Sale (1), 361
Lady Sale (2), 364
Lady Seaton, 369, 372
Lady Seymour, 392, 400
Lake Erie, 454
Lake Maniotoba, 255
Lake Manitoba, 256
Lake Superior, 454
Larne, 384
Latona, 311
Laura, 306
Laurel, 265, 366, 379, 382,
  385, 389
Laurentic, 255–56
Lavinia, 327, 339, 361, 369,
  370
Leander, 346, 348, 365, 371
Lee, 316, 398
Leo, 375
Leonard Dobbin, 285, 391,
  396, 440
Lian Romney, 343
Llan Rumney, 275, 361, 373
Lloyd, 159, 375, 440
Lloyds, 286
Lochiel, 340
Lockwoods, 368
London, 310
Lord Ashburton, 380
Lord Canterbury, 286, 354,
  361
Lord Collingwood, 371
Lord Elgin, 377
Lord Exmouth, 305, 307, 309
Lord George Bentinck, 388,
  389
Lord Melville, 286, 326
Lord Mulgrave, 401
Lord Ramsay, 365, 368, 373
Lord Seaton, 368
Lord Sidmouth, 330, 333
Lord Stanley, 318
Lord Suffield, 320
Lord Wellington, 380
Lord William Bentinck, 364
Lotus, 364, 373, 396, 411
Louisa, 286, 340, 387, 404
Louise, 394
Love, 311

Lowland Lass, 319
Lowther, 327
Loyalist, 330
Ludlow, 345
Lune, 366
Lyra, 327
M'Dannell, 403
Madison, 364
Magnet, 327
Maid of Erin, 377
Maida, 304, 307, 313, 314,
  316, 318, 342
Maister, 309
Majestic, 304
Manchester, 322, 327, 375
Mangerton, 387
Manique, 303, 428
Marchioness of Abercorn, 343,
  366, 378
Marchioness of Aberdeen, 344
Marchioness of Aberdeen of
  Padstow, 377
Margaret, 274, 282, 308, 314,
  317, 320, 329, 342, 345,
  367, 370, 376, 379, 381,
  382, 384, 388–90, 392,
  395, 403
Margaret Ann, 405
Margaret Miller, 316
Margaret Pollock, 393
Margertos, 387
Maria, 303, 310, 313, 326
Marie Eliza, 316, 373
Maria & Elizabeth, 373
Mariner, 318, 345
Marion, 408
Maris, 321
Marmion, 203, 323, 330, 332,
  338, 341, 345, 449
Marquis of Hastings of
  London, 384
Marquis of Wellesley, 350
Mars, 309, 313
Martha, 305, 309, 339
Martin, 322
Martin Luther, 270
Mary, 303, 321, 322, 326,
  339, 341, 342, 345, 355,
  368, 373
Mary Allen, 372
Mary Ann, 318, 359, 360,
  361

Mary Ann Halton, 347
Mary Bell, 338
Mary Bibby, 371
Mary Campbell, 362
Mary Carson, 397
Mary Cummings, 334
Mary Sharp, 384
Mary Stewart, 340
Matilda, 398
Mavrocordatos, 409
Mayflower, 340, 380
Mazeppa, 367
Medora, 365
Medusa, 323, 342
Melbourne, 402
Memnon, 321, 323
Mentor, 286, 390, 449
Merchant, 343, 359
Merchants Package, 328
Merlin, 334
Mersey, 359, 373
Messenger, 318
Meteor, 274, 283, 329, 355, 376, 379, 383, 386, 396, 398, 400
Milford, 367
Milicete, 383, 394
Milo, 339
Minerva, 306, 315, 320, 321, 326, 328, 329
Minnedorsa, 257
Minnesota, 403, 405, 406
Minstrel, 348, 361, 380
Mint, 321, 327
Miser, 326
Mist, 330
Modeley, 345
Mohawk, 360
Monarch, 305, 313
Monica, 334
Monique, 304
Montcalm, 259
Montclare, 259
Montezuma, 376, 377, 387, 391, 399
Montreal, 304, 312, 320, 328
Montrose, 260
Morning Star, 430
Mountaineer, 357, 374, 385, 404
Mundane, 370
Nancy, 303–05, 327

Naomi, 377
Napoleon, 345
Navarino, 326
Nelly, 328
Nelson, 326, 334, 349, 389, 393
Nelson Wood, 313, 334, 342, 358
Neptune, 336, 379
Nereid, 344
Nestor, 351, 373, 390
Nestorian, 454
New Brunswick, 328, 362
New Eagle, 332, 342
New Liverpool, 378, 378
New Prospect, 329
New York Packet, 374
New Zealand, 394
Newbiggin, 304
Newcastle, 315
Newham, 332
Newland, 348
Niagara, 390, 392, 438
Nicaragua, 367
Nicholson, 311, 326
Nightingale, 328
Nitherdale, 322
Norfolk, 343
Norna, 374
North American, 400–15
North Briton, 404, 406–07
Northern Light, 396
Northumberland, 320
Norwegian, 407–11
Nospareil, 340
Notham Castle, 330
Nova Scotian, 279, 284, 403–14
Oberon, 349
Ocean, 306, 312, 328, 362, 368, 370
Ocean Bride, 403
Ocean Pride, 401
Ocean Queen, 330, 347, 369
Ocean Queen of Bristol, 373, 376, 386, 389, 392, 395, 398, 405
Olive Branch, 382
Olympus, 369, 376
Ono of St. Ives, 380
Onondago, 324, 336
Ontario, 312

Onward, 396
Orbit, 286, 355, 383
Ord, 335
Oregon, 377, 388, 395, 401
Oriental, 283, 380, 388, 389, 392, 395, 397, 398, 401, 402, 411
Orlando, 286, 341, 350, 363, 371
Orontes, 256
Orwell, 371
Oscar, 329, 332, 344
Osiris, 395
Osprey, 399
Osward, 392
Oswego, 407
Othello, 328
Ottawa, 286, 317, 318, 328, 331, 336, 350, 371, 373, 376, 391, 395, 397
Oxenhop, 309, 310, 312
Pace, 329
Pactolus, 409
Pallas, 376
Panama, 395
Paragon of Truro, 370, 374
Paragos, 395
Parkins, 334
Parmella, 351
Pearl, 283, 359, 363, 366, 367, 369, 370, 372, 373, 376, 378, 379, 382, 385, 386, 388, 389, 392, 399, 404
Peel's-One, 370
Peggy, 305
Pembroke Castle, 324, 337
Penelope, 95, 286, 304, 338, 431
Percy, 311
Perseverence, 386
Persia, 404
Peruvian, 413–15
Peterborough, 322
Petuel, 401
Philip, 309
Phillis, 306, 307, 325
Philomela, 362
Phoenix, 374
Phya, 361, 364
Pied-Nez, 399
Pilgrim, 307, 396
Planter, 334, 389

Platina, 398
Pleiades, 310
Polly, 383
Pomona, 318, 331, 362
Pons Aelii, 313, 316
Port Glasgow, 355, 379
Portia, 319
Portly, 380
Portsea, 340
Posthorn, 341
Potomac, 365
Powerful, 409
Preston, 318, 324, 326, 339,
    342, 430
Priam, 320, 332
Prince Albert, 380
Prince Astutias, 307
Prince George, 286, 344, 348,
    352, 376
Prince Leopold, 342
Prince of Brazil, 328
Prince of Wales, 392
Prince Regent, 368, 382, 386,
    392, 395, 398
Prince Royal, 389
Princess Charlotte, 334, 368
Princess Royal, 374
Princess Victoria, 349
Priscilla, 313, 354, 362, 364,
    367, 377, 378, 380, 401
Procris, 320, 324, 332, 336,
    343
Providence, 345, 368
Pursuit, 371, 374
Pyrenees, 346
Quebec of Penzance, 380
Queen, 330, 347, 371, 411
Queen Adelaide, 263
Queen of the Lakes, 399
Queen Victoria, 372, 383,
    390, 392
Quinton, 334
R. Watson, 347
Rachel, 312
Rainbow, 352, 365
Rajah, 341
Rambler, 308, 390
Rankin, 374
Rapid, 324
Recovery, 309
Regalia, 326
Regatta, 336

Regent, 386
Regina, 259, 260, 324
Reith, 305
Reliance, 365
Renovation, 303
Resolution, 386, 388
Resolution of Penzance, 345,
    372–73
Resource, 286, 314, 361, 365
Restitution, 332, 341
Retrieve, 316
Retriever, 376
Reward, 273, 312, 331, 340,
    357, 362, 390, 437
Rhine, 376
Richard, 312
Richard & Harriet, 396
Richard Rimmer, 324
Richardson, 316
Rienza, 366
Robert Burns, 346, 384, 386,
    390, 392, 395, 397
Robert James Haynes, 313
Robert McWilliam, 382
Robert Watson, 345
Rockshire, 353, 371, 372
Rokeby, 332
Rolla, 313, 339, 360, 387,
    390
Romulus, 371
Rory O'More, 366
Rosa, 319
Rosalind, 331
Rose, 283, 375, 382, 384,
    386, 390, 392, 394, 397,
    399
Roseberry, 358
Rosehill, 304
Rosina, 303
Roslin Castle, 274, 283, 372,
    373, 376, 378, 379, 382,
    386, 388, 390, 392, 398,
    399, 401
Ross, 393
Royal Adelaide of Fowey,
    274, 283, 327, 329, 331,
    333, 335, 344, 353, 359,
    363, 369, 379, 381, 382,
    384, 392, 393, 398, 399,
    405, 408
Royal Albert, 368, 375
Royal William, 322, 335

Royal Yeoman, 305
Royalist, 374, 381
Ruby, 351
Ruckers, 326
Runa, 339
Ruthema, 256
Saham, 326
Saint Anne's, 361
Saint Mary, 320
Salem, 330, 393, 414
Salsian, 330
Samson, 386
Sampson, 285
Samuel, 318, 326
Santon, 309
Saphiras, 355
Sappho, 322
Sara Ann, 303
Sarah, 305, 324, 326, 336,
    358, 375, 380
Sarah & Eliza, 337
Sarah and Mary, 309
Sarah Bands, 394
Sarah Fleming, 384, 386
Sarah Louise, 399
Sarah Marianne, 320
Sarah Richardson, 365
Sarah Sands, 394, 396
Satellite, 397
Scarborough Castle, 326
Sceptre, 343
Scipio, 313, 330
Scotian, 257
Scotland, 391
Sea King, 371
Sea Queen, 364
Secret, 287, 379, 382, 384, 386,
    388, 390–91
Sedulous, 338
Senator, 406
Serepta, 346
Severn, 287, 336
Sheatlam Castle, 306
Shepherdess, 400
Sherbrooke, 355
Siam, 398
Silvanus, 356, 361
Sion Hill, 320
Sir Charles Napier, 391
Sir Edward Hamilton, 361,
    364, 371
Sir George Murray, 326

Sir George Prevost, 304, 305, 309, 312, 346
Sir Harry Smith, 392, 396
Sir Henry Pottinger, 262, 268, 388, 395
Sir Howard Douglas, 392
Sir James Anderson, 333
Sir Richard Jackson, 369, 376, 388
Sir Watkin, 318
Sir William Bensley, 324
Sir William Wallace, 327
Sisters, 287, 327, 361, 387, 390
Six Sisters, 324, 330, 333, 374
Skellton, 305
Sladacona, 399
Smales, 324
Snowden, 387
Sobraon, 374
Solway, 367, 385
Sophia, 345
Sophie, 317
Souter Johnny, 351, 358, 365, 380
Sovereign, 312, 351, 388
Speculation, 305, 307–08
Speed, 396
Spence, 315
Spermacetti, 374, 283, 353, 361, 363, 364, 366, 367, 369–71, 373, 376, 378, 379, 380, 382, 384, 387, 391, 392, 394
Spring Flower of Padstow, 283, 318, 324, 328, 329, 331, 333, 348, 353
St. Andrew, 376, 378, 384, 411, 413
St. Anne, 365, 368
St. David, 321, 324, 329, 331, 333, 414
St. George, 330, 333, 365
St. Helena, 306
St. James, 404
St. Lawrence, 308, 326, 399
St. Leonards, 454
St. Mary, 318, 324, 330, 334, 337, 339
St. Patrick, 399, 401, 411
Stadacona, 399, 401–02
Stately, 344

Steadfast, 398
Stentor, 365, 370
Storm King, 396
Strathblanc, 454
Strathisla, 317, 324
Streatlam Castle, 306
Strong, 377
Success, 331
Suffolk, 318
Sultana, 343
Sunbeam, 396
Sunflower, 368
Superior, 324
Susan, 317, 320, 358
Susannah, 311, 356
Sydney, 368, 383
Sylvan, 326
Sylvanus of Truro, 351, 361
Symmetry, 342
Symonds, 397
Syres, 326
Syria, 371, 373, 376
Syrian, 321
Tamarac, 375
Tamarlane, 345
Tane, 364
Tay, 287, 374, 387
Teesdale, 371
Temperance, 384
Teviotdale, 313, 316
Thailata, 403
The Duke, 387, 392
Themis, 310
Theresa, 364
Thistle, 375
Thomas, 345, 393, 394
Thomas Jackson, 311
Thomas James, 390
Thomas Ritchie, 333, 337, 343, 345, 348
Thomas Wallace, 315, 327, 347
Thompson, 396
Thorntons, 333
Three Bells, 392
Three Brothers, 305
Three Sisters, 310
Tobago, 312, 324
Tom, 315, 400
Tomagonaps, 401
Toronto, 287, 336, 341, 343, 344, 347, 362, 380, 383

Trader, 303
Trafalgar, 303, 308
Traveller, 312
Trial, 320, 330
Trident, 313
Triton, 367, 274, 283, 305, 307, 314, 315, 320, 324, 330, 333, 337, 342, 375, 395
Triton of Penzance, 357, 366, 371, 380
True Briton, 306, 318
Tulloch Castle, 339
Tynemouth Castle, 361
Ulster, 327
Union, 308
United Kingdom, 387
United Service, 402
Unity, 310, 312–14
Urania, 313, 318, 345, 346
Usk, 335, 336, 342
Valleyfield, 395
Velania, 347
Venerable, 399
Venture, 343
Venus, 324, 334, 39, 342, 344
Vesper, 368, 395, 446
Vestal, 324
Vibilia, 340
Victoria, 321, 331, 336, 347, 356, 364, 369, 373, 378, 380, 381, 383, 384, 391
Victoria of St. Ives, 370
Victorian, 255–58
Victory, 274, 275, 283, 387, 314, 316, 327, 330, 334, 340, 342–46, 349, 362, 368, 374
Videroy, 383
Vigilant, 324
Virginia, 371
Virginian, 254, 255
Vittoria, 277, 287, 303, 351, 353
Vivid, 377
Vixen, 397
Voluna of Padstow, 344, 346, 348, 363, 368, 369, 377, 379
Wallace, 308, 373
Warfinger, 328
Waterhen, 313
Waterloo, 319, 328, 331

Watermillock, 358

Wave, 381

Waverley, 411

Wellington, 336, 339, 344, 374, 386

Welsford, 337

Westminster, 360

Westmoreland, 315, 316, 318, 320, 329, 338

Whim, 306

Wilberforce, 318, 320

Wilding, 305

Wilkinson, 334

William, 312, 378

William Bromham, 380

William Dodd, 321

William Gibson, 368

William Glen Anderson, 331

William Hutt, 398

William & John, 340

William & Mary, 304, 324, 379, 379

William & Mary of Colchester, 324

William & Matthew, 304, 306

William Metcalfe, 364

William Peile, 362

William Perrie, 387, 394

William Pitt, 307, 313, 314, 316, 320, 326

William Rathbone, 408

William Ritchie, 340, 343, 430

William Shand, 321

William Tell, 311

William Wilberforce, 363

Wilson, 380

Windsor Forest, 404

Winscales, 318, 346, 353

Wolfe's Cove, 385

Woodbine, 327, 330, 369, 371, 375, 378, 381, 384

Woodbridge, 328

Woodman, 383

Woodstock, 394

Woodthorne, 321

Worthy of Devon, 390

Wyke Regis, 374, 380

Yorkshire Lass, 392, 394

Young, 304

Zealous, 372, 397

Zephyr, 388

Zetland, 394

Zodiac, 309

Zoma, 306

Shipton, Township of, Quebec, 81, 82

Short, Edward, 93

Shrewsbury (England), 247

Shropshire County (England), 107, 108, 110, 216, 218, 228, 233, 247, 433

Siddall, John and Diana, 176–77

Siddallville, Ontario, 177

Sidebottom, Charles S., 248

Silcox, Reverend Joseph, 166–68, 444

Simcoe, Lieutenant-Colonel John Graves, 47, 48, 163

Simcoe, County of, Ontario, 125, 126, 137, 139, 152, 160, 167, 218, 233, 357

Simcoe, Ontario, 177

Simmons, Henry, 246

Simons, Benjamin, 107, 119

Singer, William, 136

Skead, James, 111

Skipworth, Charles, 435

Smelt, Major William, 51–52

Smith, Arthur, 248

Smith, Captain Justus, 114

Smith, Samuel Edmund, 100

Smith, Township of (Peterborough County), 124, 125, 151

Smitham, Robert, 242

Smiths Falls, Ontario, 116, 117

Snape, Philip, 30, 417

Snell, George, 212

Snell, John, 212, 451

Society for the Propagation of the Gospel (SPG), 14, 32, 40, 63, 75, 78, 113, 212, 459

Society of Friends (Quakers), 32, 37, 40, 41, 47, 122, 175, 176, 418, 419, 42

Sockett, Reverend Thomas, 141, 145, 276, 292, 446

Somerset County (England), 121, 131, 134, 136, 137, 152, 166, 167, 222, 233, 243, 261, 325, 353, 438

Sons of England Societies, 297–98

Sorel, Quebec, 37, 38, 107, 108

South Shields (England), 154, 286, 305, 308, 310, 316, 382, 396, 398

Southampton (England), 154, 284, 286, 329, 366–68, 374, 379, 381, 383–88, 391, 393

Southwold, Township of (Elgin County), 166–68, 173, 443

Spencer, William, 142

Spilsbury, Francis, 124

St. Andrews (Quebec), 98–101, 426, 432, 435

St. Armand, Township of (Missisquoi County), 37, 45, 75–77

St. Catharines, Ontario, 355

St. Francis River (Quebec), 79, 81, 82, 84, 89, 428

St. Francis Tract (Quebec), 84, 90, 92, 429

St. Ives (England), 154

St. James Anglican Cathedral (Toronto), 288

St. James Anglican Church (Beckwith), 117

St. James' Anglican Church (Cavagnal), 70

St. James Anglican Church (Hull), 113

St. James Anglican Church (Ormstown), 66

St. John's (Newfoundland), 269

St. Lawrence River, 20, 37–39, 42, 44, 49, 51, 55, 57, 79, 101, 112, 123, 278, 279, 421

St. Marys, Ontario, 217

St. Michael's Mount (England), 154, 364

St. Thomas, Ontario, 162, 168, 173, 215, 452

St. Vincent, Township of (Grey County), 220, 357

Staffordshire County (England), 21, 113, 116, 231, 242, 243, 435

Stanbridge, Township of (Quebec), 76–77

Staniforth, George, 101

Stanlake, Richard, 451

Stanstead, County of, Quebec, 77

Stanstead, Township of, Quebec, 77

Stark, Adam, 325

Steamships, 189, 244, 262, 279, 280

Stedman, John, 183

Stephen, Township of (Huron County), 211–14, 216

Stockbury Parish (England), 134, 155, 327, 330, 332, 333, 336, 348, 355, 360, 361, 364, 365, 371, 376, 379, 382, 386

Stockton-on-Tees (England), 154

Storms (during sea crossings), 262, 267, 269–70

Stanfield, John, 447

Stanfield, Thomas, 447

Stanlake, Richard, 451

Strangford (England), 154, 307, 309

Stratford, Ontario, 209, 218

Stukely, Township of, Quebec, 79

Sturgeon Lake, Ontario, 124, 128–30

Sudbury, District of, Ontario, 243

Suffolk County (England), 24, 74, 85–90, 92, 93, 130, 131, 146, 152, 184–87, 199, 203, 204, 215, 222, 223, 228

Sunderland County (England), 154, 283–86, 303–13, 315, 317, 319, 320, 325, 326, 330, 339

Surrey County (England), 131, 141, 143, 182, 223, 246, 325

Surtees, Reverend Scott F., 87

Sussex County (England), 21, 23, 25, 26, 131, 141–45, 152, 178, 180–82, 205–09, 276, 384, 285, 286, 292, 323, 325, 326, 329, 336, 339, 341, 349

Sutton, John Ernest, 244

Sutton, Township of, Quebec, 77, 79

Swaffham Parish (England), 146

Symmes, Charles, 107

Talbot, Lord (Charles Chetwynd-Talbot), 21, 29, 30

Talbot, Colonel Thomas, 152, 162–66, 168, 173, 174, 443–44

Talbot Road, 165, 166

Talbot settlements (Elgin County), 137, 162, 166, 167, 443

Tate, James, 118–19

Tecumseth, Township of (Simcoe County), 125

Teeple, Edward, 187

Teepletown (Ontario), 187

Telfer settlement (Ontario), 177

Templeman, Reverend E.M.W., 33

Tenterden Parish (England), 133

Textile workers (*see also* Weavers), 22, 23, 67, 68, 248

Thames River/Valley (Ontario), 19, 28, 162–98, 454

Thames Road, 211

Thomas, Francis, 265

Thomas, Isaac, 448

Thompson, George, 248

Thompson, Joseph, 446

Thompson, William, 277

Three Rivers (Trois Rivières), Quebec, 37, 289

Tilbury, Township of (Kent County), 168

Timber trade, 22, 30, 50, 56, 57, 64, 93, 94, 106, 111–13, 119, 238, 262, 263, 272, 279

Timiskaming, District of, Ontario, 243

Tingrith Parish (England), 189–90

Tite, Dennis, 90

Tolpuddle Martyrs, 186–88, 447

Topley, James, 235

Torbay (England), 154, 385

Toronto, Ontario, 21, 30, 32, 34, 40, 127, 128, 143, 144, 147, 177, 184, 204, 240, 244, 245, 278, 297, 298, 337, 346, 349, 350–59

cricket clubs, 295

employment opportunities, 232–34, 242, 244, 250

immigration agents, 234

immigrant reception centre, 245

St. James Anglican Cathedral, 288

Toronto, Township of (Peel County), 143

Torquay (England), 154, 274, 282, 336, 373, 376, 379, 381, 382, 384, 386, 389, 392, 393, 395, 403

Towle, Jane (*see* Ottewell, Jane)

Townend, Joseph, 249

Trade Unions:

agricultural, 34, 225, 228

other, 225, 228–229

Traill, Catherine Parr, 130–31, 438

Traveller, Reuben, 435

Treasure, James, 167

Tring Parish (England), 249

Trivett, Thomas, 451

Truro (England), 154, 277, 319, 329, 347, 351, 361, 364, 367, 369, 370, 374, 381, 383, 386, 399

Tucker, John and Rex, 436

Tuckersmith, Township of (Huron County), 213

Turner, John, 450

Twopenny, Reverend, 134

Unemployed Workmen Act, 248

United Empire Loyalists (*see* Loyalists)

United States of America:

as a military threat, 42, 73, 116, 132, 152

as a preferred immigrant destination, 23, 31, 77, 94, 102, 103, 221, 228, 231, 233, 244–46, 292

Upper Canada (Ontario):

Americans in, 40–42, 44, 47

Courier of Upper Canada, 204, 449

defence considerations, 42, 49

English as percentage of population, 35, 152

Uren, John, 174

Usborne, Township of (Huron County), 211–16

Uxbridge Township (Ontario County), 122

Valentine, Thomas, 456
Vanstone, Mr., 200
Vaudreuil seigneury, Quebec, 22, 67, 68–71
Vaughan, Township of (York County), 122, 128, 137, 143
Verulam, Township of (Peterborough County), 128
Vespra, Township of (Simcoe County), 125, 152
Vickers, Arthur, 434
Victoria, County of, Ontario, 22, 41, 124, 139–41
Voice, Cornelius, 181

Wackford, James, 210
Waifs and Strays Society, 239
Wainfleet, Township of (Welland County), 175, 176, 181
Wainwright, John, 101
Wakefield, Township (Quebec), 113, 116
Walburton Parish (England), 143–45
Walker, John, 208, 262–64, 461
Walkerton, Ontario, 221
Wallace, Township of (Perth County), 218–19, 101
War of 1812–1814, 20, 44, 49–51, 55, 57, 79, 163, 423, 443
Warminster Parish (England), 136, 261
Warwick, Township of (Lambton County), 358, 446
Warwickshire County (England), 227, 228, 454
Waterloo, County of, Ontario, 26, 183, 187, 210, 218
Waterloo, Township of (Waterloo County), 201
Watson, Wallis, 248
Watts, John, 450
Weavers (see also Textile workers), 22, 67, 135, 425, 454
Weardale (England), 123, 178
Wearmouth, Joseph, 178
Webb, William Hoste, 93
Webber, George, 451

Webster, Peter, 100
Welland, County of, Ontario, 41, 175
Wellington, County of, Ontario, 207, 208, 221
Wellington, Duke of, 229
Wentworth, County of, Ontario, 41, 182, 183
Wentworth, Township of, Quebec, 100
Wesleyan Methodists (see Methodism)
West Country (England) (see also Cornwall, Devon, Dorset, Hampshire, and Somerset), 147, 149, 443
West Sussex (see Sussex County)
Westbury Parish (England), 136, 167, 444
Western, District of, Ontario, 185, 349–51, 353, 398
Westmeath, Township of (Renfrew County), 118
Westminster, Township of (Middlesex County), 168, 174
Westmorland County (England), 68, 78, 216
Wethey, Charles, 462
Weymouth (England), 154, 227, 305, 365, 366, 370, 373
Whale:
    James, 138, 440
    Jane, 139, 158
    Thomas, 139, 158
Whalley, James, 138–39
Whellams, Captain A.J., 224, 227, 453
Wherry, Samuel, 218
Whitby (England), 154, 283–85, 287, 311, 312, 317, 318, 320–24, 328, 333, 343, 349, 357–59, 379
Whitby, Ontario, 34, 126, 151, 220
Whitby, Township of (Ontario County), 134, 143, 149, 151
Whitchurch Township (York County), 325
White, George Harlow, 238
White, John and Elizabeth, 207

Whitehaven (England), 154, 304, 305, 306, 310–13, 318, 327
Whiteparish Parish (England), 138, 170, 173, 197, 285
Whitican, James, 325
Wickett, W.L., 215
Wickham, Township of, Quebec, 80, 82
Wilkinson, John, 187
Williams, James, 434
Williams, Township of (Middlesex County), 176, 187
Williamsburgh, Township of (Dundas County), 39
Willis, James, 451
Willoughby, Ann, 208
Wilmot, Township of (Waterloo County), 210
Wilson:
    Charles Broughton, 111
    Jane, 111
    William, 111
Wilson, James Moncrieff, 34, 112, 113, 418
Wilson, William, 84
Wiltshire County (England), 23, 26, 121, 131, 135–38, 152, 156–60, 166–74, 192, 197, 208, 225–28, 233, 261, 276, 284–86, 319, 323, 338, 341, 342, 358, 362, 375, 391, 429, 430, 444
Wimbourne (Dorset), 227
Windsor, Ontario, 165
Winfarthing Parish (England), 431
Wood, Percy, 456
Woodcroft, John, 456
Woodstock (England), 227
Woodstock, Ontario, 179, 181, 259, 294–95
Woolnough, Susan, 185
Woolwich (England), 229–30
Woolwich, Township of (Waterloo County), 26
Wootton Bassett (England), 159, 225, 227
Workhouses (English), 239, 245, 430, 441, 457
Working Men's Emigration Association, 230, 253–54

Workington (England), 154, 305–12, 315, 316, 318, 320, 321, 327, 396, 397, 423

Wormald, Albert, 248

Worsfield, John, 182

Wortham Parish (England), 430

Wright, George, 107

Wright, Philemon, 103–07, 109–10

Wright, Tiberius, 108

Wrightstown (*see also* Hull, Quebec), 105–07

Wyton, Ontario, 86, 177

Yarmouth (England), 86, 93, 154, 187, 282, 317–22, 324, 326, 327, 329, 334, 336, 339–44, 346, 358, 362, 365, 430

Yarmouth, Township of (Elgin County), 167, 173, 443

Yates, Elizabeth, 110

Yonge, Township of (Leeds County), 356

Yonge Street Monthly Meeting of Friends, 418

York (Upper Canada) (*see* Toronto)

York, County of, Ontario, 41, 122, 128, 137, 141, 143, 152, 183

York, Township of (York County), 122

Yorkshire County (England), 22, 26, 51, 52–63, 66, 82–84, 100, 101, 107, 124–28, 131, 137, 151, 152, 154, 177, 185, 205, 213, 215, 216, 273, 331, 424, 435
East Riding, 22, 51, 54, 56, 58, 83
North Riding, 51, 54, 60, 83
West Riding, 62, 125

Young, John, 156

Young, Sir John, 456

ABOUT THE AUTHOR

Ottawa-born Dr. Lucille Campey is a well-known writer and historian who began her career as a scientist and computer specialist, having previously obtained a degree in chemistry from Ottawa University. Following her marriage in 1967 to her English husband, Geoff, she moved to England. Lucille gained a masters degree at Leeds University based on a study of English medieval settlement patterns. Inspired by interest in her Nova Scotia–born father's Scottish roots and love of history, she studied Scottish emigration to Canada and was subsequently awarded a doctorate at Aberdeen University. Lucille went on to write eight books about Canada's Scottish pioneers. More recently, Lucille has turned her attention to English emigration to Canada with her ninth book, *Planters, Paupers and Pioneers: English Settlers in Atlantic Canada*, published in 2010. Lucille and Geoff live near Salisbury, England, and travel regularly in Canada.

Author photo by The Portrait Place, Priory Square, Salisbury, UK.

DUNDURN
www.dundurn.com

Visit us at
Dundurn.com
Definingcanada.ca
@dundurnpress
Facebook.com/dundurnpress